AF760910

Assessing Police and Other Public Safety Personnel Using the MMPI-2-RF

Assessing Police and Other Public Safety Personnel Using the MMPI-2-RF

A Practical Guide

David M. Corey
Yossef S. Ben-Porath

UNIVERSITY OF MINNESOTA PRESS
Minneapolis • London

Copyright 2018 by the Regents of the University of Minnesota

All rights reserved. No part of this publication may be reproduced, stored in a retrieval system, or transmitted, in any form or by any means, electronic, mechanical, photocopying, recording, or otherwise, without the prior written permission of the publisher.

Published by the University of Minnesota Press
111 Third Avenue South, Suite 290
Minneapolis, MN 55401-2520
http://www.upress.umn.edu

ISBN 978-0-8166-9884-4 (hc)

A Cataloging-in-Publication record for this book is available from the Library of Congress.

Printed in the United States of America on acid-free paper

The University of Minnesota is an equal-opportunity educator and employer.

24 23 22 21 20 19 18 10 9 8 7 6 5 4 3 2 1

CONTENTS

LIST OF TABLES

LIST OF FIGURES

PREFACE

We began investigating the Minnesota Multiphasic Personality Inventory-2 Restructured Form (MMPI-2-RF; Ben-Porath & Tellegen, 2008/2011) as a tool for assessing public safety employees—first with candidates and then with incumbents—more than a decade ago. This collaboration produced a series of peer-reviewed studies documenting the validity and utility of MMPI-2-RF scores as predictors of concurrent and future counterproductive behaviors of police officer candidates. These studies formed the foundation for the development and publication of an interpretive report (*MMPI-2-RF Police Candidate Interpretive Report* [PCIR]; Corey & Ben-Porath, 2014) for use in preemployment evaluations of police officers. We have since trained thousands of professionals in the use of the MMPI-2-RF and PCIR in police and public safety assessments.

MMPI-2-RF users who attended our trainings quickly learned to properly interpret test scores, owing in large part to the transparent and straightforward nature of the MMPI-2-RF general interpretive guidelines and the PCIR itself. But as with psychological assessments performed in all contexts, evaluations of police and public safety candidates and incumbent personnel rely on multiple methods, including findings from additional psychological tests, personal history information (collateral and self-report), and a clinical interview. Most often, when attendees struggle in our workshops or contact us for consultation, their concerns are not about test interpretation, but about how to integrate MMPI-2-RF results with other assessment findings. Their questions formed the impetus for this book.

Noting that well-developed guidelines for test construction, adaptation, and use are already available, Fernández-Ballesteros and colleagues called for the formulation of guidelines for the assessment process itself, "at least at the level of recommendations that could help the assessor to cope with the complexities and demands of assessment processes in various contexts of psychological assessment" (2001, p. 187). This book is a response to this call in the context of police and public safety assessments.

Its scope is broad: this single volume contains the information needed to effectively integrate MMPI-2-RF findings with other assessment data in preemployment and fitness-for-duty evaluations of candidates and incumbents, respectively, in the four primary public safety employment positions: police officers, correctional officers, firefighters/paramedics, and emergency dispatchers.

Although the guidelines and recommendations offered in this book are our own, we owe thanks to many who contributed to our work in this area. First among them is Anthony Tarescavage, who began collaborating with us on our empirical research as a Kent State graduate student and later as a postdoc; he is now on the Psychological Sciences faculty of John Carroll University. Anthony is first author of five of the empirical studies establishing the validity of the MMPI-2-RF in preemployment psychological evaluations of police officer candidates, and he provided data management and analysis support that went far beyond these seminal contributions. Anthony's productivity, keen intellect, clarity of writing, and strong moral compass are among his many distinctive qualities, for which we and many others are grateful.

Kent State undergraduate students Allison and Whitney Poston provided clerical support for this project. We are grateful for their efforts in putting together the tabular material included in this volume.

Many psychologist colleagues across the United States and Canada contributed valuable support in various ways, including by providing candidate test protocols and outcome data, often at great expense of time and effort. Others provided technical and scholarly support. In particular, we thank JoAnne Brewster, Bruce Cappo, Michael Cuttler, Catherine

Delsol, Paul Detrick, Gary Fischler, Herb Gupton, Matt Guller, David Hill, Diane Levitan, Catherine Martin-Doto, Monica Pilarc, Michael Roberts, Gary Rogers, Jocelyn Roland, Shelley Spilberg, Casey Stewart, Jay Supnick, Phil Trompetter, Ray Turner, Carol Vipari, Elizabeth White, Richard Wihera, and Richard Zonderman.

We are also grateful to Beverly Kaemmer and Tami Brown of the University of Minnesota Press editorial team, whose attention to detail, parsimony, and style is unmatched; we are particularly appreciative of Bev's leadership of the Press's Test Division, which sponsored our research and the development of the PCIR. The contributions of Auke Tellegen of the University of Minnesota are foundational to this book, both as co-author of the MMPI-2-RF and as a role model for applied psychological scholarship.

Finally, we thank our families, Denise and Alex (DMC), and Denise, Adam, Johnathan, and Ella (YBP), for their grace and forbearance during our frequent and sometimes long absences for travel and for being our lifelines both when home and away.

1

Introduction

Perhaps at no other time has the importance of selecting and employing psychologically competent police and other public safety personnel been more self-evident. News reports of inexplicable rudeness, indifference, and, most concerning, excessive uses of force—often including video images from dash-cams, body-cams, or bystanders—by the very persons sworn to "serve and protect" the public have become ubiquitous, leading to erosion in public trust of law enforcement officers, the vast majority of whom are dedicated public servants. The need to ensure that individuals in these positions are psychologically suited to carry out the "awesome power at their disposal" (*Duran v. City of Douglas*, 1990, at 1378) has been emphasized by a long line of special commissions and task forces, beginning with one created by President Lyndon Johnson (President's Commission on Law Enforcement and Administration of Justice, 1967) and most recently with that of President Obama (President's Task Force on 21st Century Policing, 2015). But calls for the universal screening of public safety personnel are insufficient without an earnest effort to ensure that these evaluations are evidence based and carried out in a manner consistent with best practices. Our purpose in writing this guide is to facilitate competent use of the MMPI-2-RF® (Minnesota Multiphasic Personality Inventory-2 Restructured Form®) when conducting assessments of police and other public safety candidates and personnel.

This guide is focused on two types of assessments, preemployment and fitness-for-duty evaluations, applied to four public safety job classes that have common requirements for emotional and psychological functioning:

law enforcement officers,[1] correctional officers,[2] firefighters/paramedics, and emergency communication (911) dispatchers. A substantial body of research documents associations between preemployment psychological evaluation findings and post-hire outcomes (e.g., performance problems, disciplinary actions, citizen complaints, involuntary termination of employment) in police candidates.[3] Research conducted with the MMPI instruments is reviewed in chapter 6 of this guide. In comparison, there is a dearth of literature on the prediction of post-hire outcomes for correctional officer, firefighter/paramedic, and dispatcher candidates. This is true for all personality and psychopathology measures. We rely on the extant literature for interpretive guidance and generalize findings from one job class to another only as justified. In broad terms, generalization of test findings is warranted when evidence demonstrates (a) consistency in job demands and psychological attributes across the four public safety positions, (b) construct validity of scale scores that can reasonably be expected to generalize across individuals assessed for various public safety positions, and (c) comparability in testing contexts and settings. Examples of how these generalizations are applied are included among the case studies reported in chapter 8.

Law enforcement officers, correctional officers, firefighters/paramedics, and emergency dispatchers comprise the first line of public safety defense in modern society. These workers are tasked with the responsibility to defend the homeland (e.g., border security, critical infrastructure protection, transportation security, domestic and international intelligence activities) and local communities from a wide range of threats to life and property. Their effectiveness in doing so depends not only on their emotional and psychological ability to perform the job but also on their ability to do so under conditions that are sometimes profoundly stressful and challenging. Failure to identify public safety candidates and personnel who, by virtue of personality and/or psychopathology, are unable to reliably perform these jobs safely and effectively can have devastating consequences for the community, other public safety officers, and public trust, as just discussed.

The California Commission on Peace Officer Standards and Training (POST) is widely considered the national and international leader in establishing evidence-based practice standards for assessment of law enforcement personnel (cf. Mitchell, 2017). Regulations and procedures established by the California POST Commission are routinely adopted by parallel commissions throughout the United States. For example, as discussed later, a Utah court ruled in *Brown v. Sandy City Appeal Board* that California POST regulations can reasonably be relied on by a psychologist in that state. The commission advocated successfully for legislation, California Government Code 1031(f)(2)(B), that obligates psychologists who conduct evaluations of candidates and incumbent peace officers (e.g., police officers, correctional officers, and probation and parole officers) to have and maintain competencies established by POST. The requisite competencies, enumerated in the POST manual (Spilberg & Corey, 2017), consist of the following eight areas of foundational knowledge:

Assessment Competence. Ability to properly gather, analyze, and integrate the full range of pertinent assessment data (personal health records, background investigation and other personal history information, psychological testing, clinical interview, and observations) to reach a determination of psychological suitability for exercising the powers of the position.

Clinical Competence. Ability to assess the impact of a candidate's emotional or mental condition, and normal and abnormal personality traits and adaptation, on psychological suitability for the position.

Communication Competence. Ability to communicate the necessary and appropriate findings, conclusions, and recommendations in a manner that is clear and useful to the hiring agency and others involved in the candidate screening process and conforms to regulatory requirements.

Jurisprudence Competence. Knowledge and application of federal and state statutes, regulations, and case law pertinent to psychological screening for the position, including but not limited to the federal Americans with Disabilities Act and Genetic Information Nondiscrimination Act, as well as related state laws.

Occupational Competence. Knowledge of the essential job functions, working conditions, chain of command, and the psychological demands and stressors inherent in the public safety position.

Procedural Competence. Knowledge and application of personnel screening procedures and criteria that comply with regulatory requirements and are responsive to the needs and considerations of the hiring authority.

Psychometric Competence. Understanding of psychological test properties, including test score validity, reliability, base rates, test norms, and group differences, and the ability to select appropriate tests for evaluating psychological suitability for a particular position and to make proper, accurate inferences from test scores.

Standards Competence. Knowledge and application of ethical principles, standards, and professional guidelines pertinent to personnel screening (privacy, confidentiality, informed consent, and disclosure).

Before being approved to conduct preemployment evaluations of police officer candidates, California psychologists must attest to possessing these competencies and provide documentation of having obtained relevant continuing education. They are also required to maintain their competence through documented biennial continuing education pertinent to these domains. We focus next on two of these competency domains, clinical and occupational competence, that are especially pertinent to using measures of personality and psychopathology to evaluate a candidate's suitability and an employee's fitness for duty.

Clinical competence has a dual focus: one centered on evaluating personality and psychopathology, and the other on assessing their impact on an individual's functional abilities related to public safety work. This dual focus requires the evaluator to have expertise both in clinical assessment and in understanding how personality and psychopathology interact ecologically in the real-world work environments of these positions. Consequently, occupational competence—knowledge of the essential job functions, working conditions, and psychological demands of the position—is also needed for the evaluator to be able to assess the impact of clinically relevant findings on an individual's ability to perform public safety functions. Although it is beyond the scope of this guide to explicate the full depth of occupational knowledge needed for each of the four positions, Table 1-1 lists the essential job functions that are typical for each.

The California POST Commission identified the psychologically relevant performance problems and job demands of police officers as a preliminary step toward isolating the traits and abilities necessary to safely

TABLE 1-1
Essential Job Functions of Public Safety Positions

Law Enforcement Officers:

- Enforce laws
- Respond to emergency and non-emergency calls
- Conduct interviews with suspects and witnesses
- Observe the activities of suspects
- Investigate crimes
- Obtain warrants and arrest suspects
- Write detailed reports and fill out forms
- Prepare cases and testify in court
- Collect and secure evidence from crime scenes
- Use force as authorized, justified, and necessary to protect themselves and others and to perform essential functions (e.g., carry out arrests)

Correctional Officers:

- Enforce rules and keep order within jails or prisons
- Supervise activities of inmates
- Aid in rehabilitation and counseling of offenders
- Inspect facilities to ensure that they meet standards
- Search inmates for contraband items
- Report on inmate conduct
- Use force as authorized, justified, and necessary to protect themselves and others and to perform essential functions (e.g., carry out searches)

Firefighters/Paramedics:

- Drive fire trucks and other emergency vehicles
- Put out fires using water hoses, fire extinguishers, and pumps
- Find and rescue victims in burning buildings or in other emergency situations
- Respond to 911 calls for emergency medical assistance, such as cardiopulmonary resuscitation (CPR) or bandaging a wound
- Assess a patient's condition and determine a course of treatment
- Follow guidelines learned in training or received from physicians who oversee their work
- Use backboards and restraints to keep patients still and safe in an ambulance during transport
- Help transfer patients to the emergency department of a health care facility and report their observations and treatment to the staff
- Create a patient care report, documenting the medical care given to the patient
- Replace used supplies and check or clean equipment after use
- Prepare written reports on emergency incidents
- Clean and maintain equipment
- Conduct drills and physical fitness training
- Provide public education on fire safety

Emergency Communications Dispatchers:

- Answer 911 telephone calls
- Determine the type of emergency and its location
- Decide the appropriate response based on agency procedures
- Relay information to the appropriate first-responder agency
- Assist people who are in life-threatening situations
- Coordinate the dispatch of emergency response personnel to accident scenes
- Give over-the-phone medical instructions before emergency personnel arrive
- Monitor and track the status of police, fire, and ambulance units
- Synchronize responses with other area communication centers
- Keep detailed records about calls

Source: U.S. Department of Labor, Bureau of Labor Statistics.

and effectively perform the essential functions of the position (Spilberg & Corey, 2017; tables 4.3 and 4.4, pp. 46–47). In Tables 1-2 and 1-3, we list the law enforcement officer job performance problems and job demands, respectively, and indicate which of them apply also to the other public safety positions. As Table 1-2 shows, all 32 problem behaviors apply both to law enforcement and correctional officers, and 30 of the problems (with the exception of those involving use of force and enforcement of laws) also apply to firefighter/paramedics and dispatchers. Similarly, Table 1-3 shows that both law enforcement and correctional officers are subject to all 17 of the psychological job demands. Firefighters/paramedics experience 14 of the 17 demands (all but those related to use of force and enforcement powers), and dispatchers are subject to all but the demands pertaining to use of force, enforcement powers, access to money and property,[4] and risk/threats of personal injury.

The Occupational Information Network (O*NET), functioning under the sponsorship of the U.S. Department of Labor/Employment and Training Administration, is the nation's primary source of occupational information. A central component of this resource is the O*NET database, containing information on hundreds of standardized and occupation-specific descriptors, which is continually updated by surveying a broad range of workers from each occupation. Table 1-4 lists a sample of the attributes rated in the O*NET database as important for each of the four public safety classifications: Police Patrol Officers; Correctional Officers and Jailers; Municipal Firefighters; and Police, Fire, and Ambulance Dispatchers. Although this list corresponds closely with the California POST Psychological Screening Dimensions, which we discuss next, it is important to keep in mind that there is not perfect synchrony in the weights assigned to all psychologically relevant competencies or traits. For example, "persuasion" (persuading others to change their minds or behavior) is a skill that the O*NET database weights as important for police (60 on a 100-point scale) and correctional officers (63/100), but is assigned considerably less weight (i.e., helpful but not important) for municipal firefighters (44/100) and emergency communications dispatchers (47/100). The reader should keep in mind that these are average weights, which may be allotted differently in different employment

TABLE 1-2
Public Safety Job Performance Problems

Problem	LEO	CORR	FF/PM	DISP
Excessive/inappropriate use of force	√	√	N/A	N/A
Misuse of authority	√	√	√	√
Partiality in enforcing the law (due to prejudice or dishonesty)	√	√	N/A	N/A
Bias/prejudice/intolerance (reflected in dealing with coworkers, citizens)	√	√	√	√
Substance abuse	√	√	√	√
Theft	√	√	√	√
Dishonesty	√	√	√	√
Law violation	√	√	√	√
Inappropriate reaction to crises/emergencies	√	√	√	√
Reaction to gradual stress buildup over time	√	√	√	√
Panic under stress	√	√	√	√
Disorderliness/sloppy—haphazard work	√	√	√	√
Inattention to detail	√	√	√	√
Failure to carry tasks to completion	√	√	√	√
Inability to work on several concurrent tasks	√	√	√	√
Poor prioritization skills	√	√	√	√
Hostility toward authority	√	√	√	√
Hot-temperedness	√	√	√	√
Failure to take work seriously	√	√	√	√
Impulsiveness	√	√	√	√
Inability to cope with job structure	√	√	√	√
Absenteeism	√	√	√	√
Turnover (due to cost of training)	√	√	√	√
Poor service attitude (officious, sarcastic, rude)	√	√	√	√
Disregard for rules and regulations	√	√	√	√
Recurrent somatic problems	√	√	√	√
Failure to keep up with paperwork	√	√	√	√
Tampering with evidence	√	√	√	√
Going through the motions without attention/vigilance	√	√	√	√
Low activity level	√	√	√	√
Inability to interpret rules	√	√	√	√
Inability to switch "roles" as required by the circumstances	√	√	√	√

LEO = Law Enforcement Officer; CORR = Correctional Officer; FF/PM = Firefighter/Paramedic; DISP = 911 Dispatcher
N/A = not applicable

TABLE 1-3
Public Safety Psychological Job Demands

Job Demand	LEO	CORR	FF/PM	DISP
Discretionary use of force	√	√	N/A	N/A
Verbal abuse from suspects, victims, bystanders, reporters, inmates, witnesses, etc.	√	√	√	√
Willingness to use force	√	√	N/A	N/A
Constant exposure to the worst elements of society; easy to become jaded/cynical	√	√	√	√
Discretionary use of enforcement powers	√	√	N/A	N/A
Access to money and property	√	√	√	N/A
Securing public trust	√	√	√	√
Decision making under extreme pressure/stress	√	√	√	√
Access to sensitive information	√	√	√	√
Periods of quiet/boredom interrupted by sudden emergency response	√	√	√	√
Responding to tragedies, emergencies, disasters, and highly stressful situations	√	√	√	√
Need to respond to a series of diverse calls and adapt responses ("shift gears" from routine to emergency calls)	√	√	√	√
Exposure to unpleasant/repugnant persons and situations	√	√	√	√
Public contact; communicating with the entire gamut of society; adapting effectively	√	√	√	√
Threats to personal safety, physical attacks	√	√	√	N/A
Serving a diverse community, regardless of culture or socioeconomic status	√	√	√	√
Risk of personal injury, including mortal injury	√	√	√	N/A

LEO = Law Enforcement Officer; CORR = Correctional Officer; FF/PM = Firefighter/Paramedic; DISP = 911 Dispatcher
N/A = not applicable

contexts and locations. Similarly, each of the selection criteria does not necessarily carry equal weight in a preemployment evaluation, and the hiring agency should be consulted to help ascertain what unique features of the job demands, working conditions, and setting may influence the relative importance of certain screening dimensions.

The California POST Psychological Screening Dimensions are generally recognized as the national standard for evaluating the psychological suitability of law enforcement officers, in large part due to the rigor applied to the job analysis and validation procedures that produced them. Mitchell (2017) referred to them as "the most sophisticated and ambitious effort yet to operationally define those psychological qualities" (p. 40). Hough (2016) independently examined the job activities and

TABLE 1-4
Attributes Rated as Important for All Four Public Safety Classifications

Domain	Attribute
Integrity	**Integrity**—Job requires being honest and ethical.
Stress Tolerance	**Stress Tolerance**—Job requires accepting criticism and dealing calmly and effectively with high-stress situations. **Self-Control**—Job requires maintaining composure, keeping emotions in check, controlling anger, and avoiding aggressive behavior, even in very difficult situations.
Decision Making and Judgment	**Critical Thinking**—Job requires using logic and reasoning to identify the strengths and weaknesses of alternative solutions, conclusions, or approaches to problems. **Independence**—Job requires developing one's own ways of doing things, guiding oneself with little or no supervision, and depending on oneself to get things done.
Conscientiousness	**Dependability**—Job requires being reliable, responsible, and dependable and fulfilling obligations. **Initiative**—Job requires a willingness to take on responsibilities and challenges. **Attention to Detail**—Job requires being careful about details and being thorough in completing work tasks. **Persistence**—Job requires persistence in the face of obstacles.
Interpersonal Skills	**Social Perceptiveness**—Job requires being aware of others' reactions and understanding why they react as they do. **Active Listening**—Job requires giving full attention to what other people are saying, taking time to understand the points being made, asking questions as appropriate, and not interrupting at inappropriate times. **Service Orientation**—Job requires actively looking for ways to help people.

*Source: O*NET OnLine Database, 2015.*

functions of police officers, as well as a large amount of literature identifying characteristics of effective police officers in community-oriented law enforcement settings. She identified a broad list of necessary personality attributes—conscientiousness, emotional maturity and stability, the ability to influence (persuasiveness), amicability, service orientation, and practical intelligence (judgment and decision making)—that she assessed as being "consistent with" the "more specific characteristics" contained in the California POST Psychological Screening Dimensions (p. 577).

TABLE 1-5
Psychological Screening Dimensions for Public Safety Positions

Psychological Screening Dimension	Description
Integrity	Maintaining high standards of personal conduct. Consists of attributes such as honesty, impartiality, trustworthiness, and abiding by laws, regulations, and procedures.
Impulse Control/ Attention to Safety	Taking proper precautions and avoiding impulsive and/or unnecessarily risky behavior to ensure the safety of both the public and public safety officers. Includes the ability and inclination to think before acting, to keep one's impulses in control, and to behave in conscious regard for the larger situation at hand.
Avoidance of Substance Abuse and Other Risk-Taking Behavior	Avoiding participation in behavior that is inappropriate, self-damaging, and can adversely affect organizational functioning, such as alcohol and drug abuse, domestic violence, sale of drugs, and problem gambling.
Emotional Regulation and Stress Tolerance	Maintaining composure and staying in control, particularly during life-threatening, time-critical events and other stressful situations. Includes taking the negative aspects of the job in stride and maintaining an even temperament, as well as accepting criticism rather than becoming overly defensive or allowing it to hamper job performance.
Conscientiousness/ Dependability	Exhibiting diligent, reliable, conscientious work patterns, performing in a timely manner in accordance with commitments, rules, regulations, and agency policies.
Decision-Making and Judgment	Making sound, common-sense decisions, demonstrated by the ability to size up situations quickly and take appropriate action. Involves the ability to sift through information to glean what's important and, once identified, to use that information effectively.
Social Competence	Communicating with others in a tactful and respectful manner and showing sensitivity and concern in one's interactions with others. Includes several facets, such as the ability to "read" people and be aware of the impact of words and behavior on others, showing sensitivity and concern toward the feelings of others, as well as tact and impartiality in treating all members of society.
Teamwork	Working effectively with others to accomplish goals, as well as subordinating personal interests for the good of the working unit and agency. Involves establishing and maintaining effective, cooperative working relationships with fellow workers, supervisors, and other stakeholders. Consists of sharing relevant information, providing assistance and support to coworkers, balancing personal ambitions with work goals, performing one's fair share in a group effort, and not allowing personal differences to affect working relationships. *Note: For Firefighters/Paramedics, this also includes the ability to tolerate close communal living in the course of a 24-hour shift.*

Psychological Screening Dimension	Description
Assertiveness/ Persuasiveness	Unhesitatingly taking control of situations in a calm and appropriately assertive manner, even under stressful or adverse conditions. Includes the ability to confront others, act assertively and without hesitation, not be easily intimidated, assert one's ideas and persuade others to adopt a necessary course of action, command respect, and emanate professionalism. *Note: For Law Enforcement and Correctional Officers, this also includes the ability to use force, confront suspects, and engage others physically, as necessary and appropriate. For Firefighters/Paramedics, the need for high levels of assertiveness may be substantially lower than for other public safety positions.*
Adaptability/ Flexibility	Adjusting to the sudden changes and competing demands inherent in public safety work. Consists of adjusting to planned and unplanned work changes, including different types of incidents that must be handled one right after another; prioritizing and working effectively on several very different tasks/projects at the same time; adjusting to differing supervisory styles; and adjusting physically and mentally to shift work. *Note: For Law Enforcement and Correctional Officers, this also includes the ability to make sudden adjustments in use of force, as appropriate.*

California POST Commission regulations require a comprehensive background investigation for all peace officer and dispatcher positions throughout the state of California, and this mandate specifies selection criteria that closely parallel those for law enforcement officers. The screening dimensions that apply to both law enforcement officers and dispatchers, which are linked to the traits listed in Table 1-4, are shown in Table 1-5. Facets of these dimensions that are unique to particular public safety positions are noted in italics. See Spilberg and Corey (2017, chapter 4) for a comprehensive discussion of these dimensions and the positive and counterproductive behaviors that correspond with each.

The relative weight that each of these dimensions will carry in evaluating a candidate or employee for a particular position and agency depends on many factors, including the population context in which the work is carried out (e.g., rural and demographically homogeneous vs. urban and demographically diverse), the volume and intensity of work performed in the agency, and the needs and preferences of the hiring authority.[5]

Using the Psychological Screening Dimensions in Both Preemployment and Fitness-for-Duty Evaluations of Public Safety Personnel

The original purpose of the California POST Psychological Screening Dimensions—to facilitate preemployment psychological evaluations of law enforcement officer candidates—may lead some to regard them, erroneously, as useful only for police candidate screening. As just discussed, they also have very strong linkage to the psychological position requirements for correctional officers, firefighters/paramedics, and emergency communication dispatchers. For this reason, they can be used to elucidate the psychological qualifications for those candidates as well. Less evident is the appropriateness of using the POST screening dimensions in fitness-for-duty evaluations for police and other public safety evaluations; however, there is a good rational and legal foundation for doing so, as we discuss next.

The California POST Psychological Screening Dimensions were intended originally to provide psychologists with "behaviorally based criteria . . . against which to evaluate the psychological suitability of candidates" (Spilberg & Corey, 2017, p. 143). The need for and practical significance of these criteria result from the fact that, when it is determined that a candidate has a mental health condition or problematic personality trait(s), the relevance of these findings to the candidate's suitability for employment can only be assessed by evaluating how the symptoms or traits affect these behavioral criteria. As criteria for assessing the job relevance of assessment findings, these dimensions are as important in fitness-for-duty evaluations as they are in preemployment screening. Two state appeal courts (*Sager v. Yuba County*; *Brown v. Sandy City Appeal Board*) have concluded the same.

In *Sager*, the California Court of Appeal ruled in support of a psychologist's reliance on the California POST Psychological Screening Dimensions in evaluating the impact of a deputy sheriff's diagnosed personality disorder on her ability to perform her duties in a safe and effective manner. In *Brown*, the Utah Court of Appeals faced the same question—whether the use of criteria developed for preemployment selection is warranted also in a fitness-for-duty evaluation—and decided similarly. But the

Brown court also addressed another question: whether it was appropriate for the psychologist evaluating a Utah police officer to rely on California standards. The court decided that it is, noting that the POST dimensions help "flesh out" the Utah standards. The *Brown* court concluded that the Utah psychologist's reliance on the POST standards was "analogous to the way that a court might use case law from sister jurisdictions: not as binding authority but as a reference to consider how other courts have analyzed and resolved a particular issue" (at ¶14).

Testing and Assessment

This guide focuses on the use of the MMPI-2-RF in both testing and assessment. Tests produce scores, which have inferential meaning for certain uses. The meaning of a test score comes partially from evidence of its validity: the collection of correlations and other statistics that tell us what the scale measures (convergent, construct, and predictive validity) and what it does not measure (discriminant validity). However, determining the meaning of a test score for a particular test taker requires integrating it with additional information from other sources, such as personal history questionnaires, employment records, background investigations, health care records, clinical interview, and other tests. It is this integrative assessment process with which this guide is primarily concerned.

When the validated inferences of a test score are in good agreement with information from all other assessment sources, conclusions about that test taker, at least with respect to the targeted construct, are easy to make and are usually correct. However, in the real world in which assessment occurs, the task is seldom so simple. Throughout this guide, we illustrate this integrative assessment process by using redacted material from actual cases.

Testing and assessment represent separate but related tasks. Meyer et al. (2001) observed that psychological testing "is a relatively straightforward process wherein a particular scale is administered to obtain a specific score. Subsequently, a descriptive meaning can be applied to the score on the basis of normative, nomothetic findings" (p. 143). In contrast, the task of psychological assessment is to combine test findings with historical data, direct observations, interview results, and information from third parties "to disentangle the competing possibilities" (Meyer et al., 2001, p. 144). This book is intended to provide practical guidance to assist in both tasks.

Concerning Standards of Practice

When describing the standards of practice for preemployment and fitness-for-duty assessments (chapters 5 and 9, respectively), we deliberately rely more heavily on certain sources than others, reflecting a hierarchy of authority that also exists in the professional literature. This hierarchy is reflected in a policy statement of the American Board of Police & Public Safety Psychology (ABPPSP, 2016), an affiliated specialty board of the American Board of Professional Psychology (ABPP). The ABPPSP provides a useful description of the sources of authority it relies on when comparing a specialist candidate's work product against the standard of practice. We cite it here in full because it also reflects the hierarchy of sources we considered when articulating the standard of practice in police and public safety assessment. This standard is defined as follows:

> [T]he ordinary diligence that a prudent or reasonable specialist in police and public safety psychology would exercise in light of the risks and benefits involved in a particular situation. As such, strict conformance to the standard of practice is most expected when an act or decision poses substantial risk of harm to an individual, organization, or community to which a professional duty is owed. . . . Several kinds of professional authority are relied upon when defining standards of practice (Heilbrun, DeMatteo, Marczyk, & Goldstein, 2008), in descending order of importance:
>
> 1. The APA Ethics Code and pertinent regulations, laws, and case law, which apply to all psychologists;
> 2. Professional practice guidelines and clinical practice guidelines published by the American Psychological Association linked to scientifically

derived evidence following a rigorous, formal review process with input from multiple stakeholders in professional psychology, and regulatory enforcement guidance (e.g., EEOC guidance for enforcement of ADA and GINA);

3. Publications that articulate broad principles and are developed using multiple sources of authority;
4. An overall description of research and practice as offered in the literature, through a national survey of views or practices, or a meta-analysis of empirical research;
5. Professional practice guidelines prepared through consensus among practitioners (e.g., IACP-PPSS guidelines);
6. Manuals for psychological tests or other assessment instruments that are carefully attentive to reliability and validity and help a reader assess the quality of the instrument and place it in the broader context of specialty practice;
7. The systematic review of what recognized scholars and practitioners in the field have written and taught regarding the elements that comprise competent practice;
8. A single study describing a survey, or offering an empirical description, of some particular aspect of specialty practice. (ABPPSP, 2016)

The recommendations and guidance in this book reflect the professional consensus represented in the American Psychological Association's Professional Practice Guidelines for Occupationally Mandated Psychological Evaluations (OMPE Guidelines; APA, 2017b), which were developed through deliberation among multiple groups representing several distinct specialties and interests in psychology and law, as well as a broad review of the professional literature and input from the public. They were written "for use by psychologists who conduct evaluations for purposes of addressing the needs of the referring party concerning the examinee's suitability, fitness, or eligibility for employment" (APA, 2017b) and, as such, apply to the conduct of both preemployment and fitness-for-duty evaluations. Table 1-6 lists the 13 aspirational statements contained in the OMPE professional practice guidelines.

TABLE 1-6
Professional Practice Guidelines for Occupationally Mandated Psychological Evaluations: Practice Guideline Statements

Preparing for an OMPE

1. Psychologists strive to understand the referring party's authority for mandating the evaluation and the legitimacy of a particular referral, prior to conducting the evaluation.
2. In addressing the referral question(s), psychologists endeavor to apply the criterion standard as defined by statutory, regulatory, administrative, and/or other authoritative sources.
3. Psychologists seek to understand the psychologically relevant demands and working conditions of the examinee's position.
4. Psychologists strive to support conclusions about the job-relevance of a psychological condition with established scientific and professional knowledge.
5. Psychologists endeavor to understand and meet their responsibilities to the referral source, the examinee, and other relevant parties to the evaluation.
6. Psychologists are mindful of the importance of maintaining competence when carrying out all phases of the evaluation.

Conducting an OMPE

7. Psychologists strive to ensure their impartiality when conducting occupationally mandated evaluations, as well as when forming their opinions.
8. Psychologists seek to select and rely on assessment tools validated for use with a population appropriate to the evaluation.
9. Psychologists endeavor to recognize individual and group differences, and the importance of practicing with cultural competence.
10. Psychologists strive to use multiple sources of relevant and reliable information collected according to established principles and methods.

Communicating OMPE Findings

11. Psychologists strive to provide opinions and make recommendations that are directly relevant to the referral question(s).
12. Psychologists seek to document the bases for their opinion(s) in language that is clear and appropriate to the targeted audience.
13. When the referral source or another party is responsible for determining the ultimate issue in a referral, psychologists strive to educate and inform rather than answer the ultimate issue.

Source: http://www.apa.org/practice/guidelines/index.aspx.

Organization of the Chapters

In Part I of this guide, we include a concise primer on the MMPI-2-RF. Chapter 2 provides a brief overview of the evolution of the MMPI instruments and a description of the MMPI-2-RF's 51 scales. Chapter 3 discusses inherent threats to the validity of scores on self-report measures generally, as well as how the MMPI-2-RF Validity Scales are used to assess these threats. Chapter 4 gives an overview of the hierarchical structure of the MMPI-2-RF substantive scales and a more detailed description of the constructs they assess, followed by a description of a recommended interpretive strategy for the inventory. Because our focus is on the nuts and bolts of conducting these evaluations, we occasionally refer the reader to the *MMPI-2-RF Manual for Administration, Scoring and Interpretation* (Ben-Porath & Tellegen, 2008/2011), the *MMPI-2-RF Technical Manual* (Tellegen & Ben-Porath, 2008/2011), *Interpreting the MMPI-2-RF* (Ben-Porath, 2012), and the *PCIR User's Guide* (Corey & Ben-Porath, 2014) for more technical details and in-depth treatment of certain topics.

Part II is devoted to preemployment psychological evaluations of candidates for the four public safety positions: police officer, correctional officer, firefighter/paramedic, and dispatcher. Chapter 5 focuses on the common procedural and legal requirements for these evaluations, as well as other foundational knowledge needed to conduct them. Chapter 6 begins with a brief overview of the history of using the MMPI instruments in preemployment evaluations of law enforcement personnel, followed by guidance on the adjustment of clinically oriented interpretive guidelines for the MMPI-2-RF; this adjustment is necessary to account for the impact of preselection and selection factors on personality test scores in preemployment screening contexts. Descriptive MMPI-2-RF findings are also provided for the four public safety positions in this chapter. Chapter 7 provides an overview of the MMPI-2-RF Police Candidate Interpretive Report (PCIR), including its rationale, structure, and features. In chapter 8, we describe an integrative strategy for combining MMPI-2-RF data with information from other elements of the assessment (e.g., background, clinical interview and direct observations, and other psychological tests), and we demonstrate this integrative strategy with case illustrations. Chapter 8 concludes with a discussion of how evidence-based findings from the MMPI-2-RF can be integrated into a legally defensible written report to the hiring agency.

Part III focuses on psychological fitness-for-duty evaluations of public safety employees. Chapter 9 discusses the foundational knowledge required for these assessments, including relevant federal statutes and regulations. In chapter 10, we discuss the implications of contextual factors—particularly the motivation to be seen as fit or unfit—on MMPI-2-RF scores in these evaluations, and we provide descriptive findings for MMPI-2-RF scores in fitness-for-duty evaluations. Finally, using a variety of case illustrations, we demonstrate in chapter 11 how MMPI-2-RF scores can be used to inform the two prongs of the fitness question; namely, whether the person has a mental impairment and, if so, how it interacts with the demands of the position.

2

An MMPI-2-RF Overview

The 338-item Minnesota Multiphasic Personality Inventory-2 Restructured Form (MMPI-2-RF; Ben-Porath & Tellegen, 2008/2011; Tellegen & Ben-Porath, 2008/2011) is the most up-to-date version of the most widely used omnibus measure of personality and psychopathology. In this chapter, we provide a brief description of the evolution of the MMPI instruments and of the 51 scales that make up the MMPI-2-RF.

Evolution of the MMPI Instruments

The Original MMPI

The original intent of the developers of the MMPI, Hathaway and McKinley (1943), was to construct a psychological test that could generate differential diagnoses. Their goal was to develop a measure that could be administered to any new patient presenting for services at the University of Minnesota Hospital and obtain a direct indication of whether that individual was likely to have one or more psychiatric disorders and, if so, which one(s). It is a mistake to attribute a nontheoretical approach to the construction of the original MMPI. Hathaway and McKinley's efforts, particularly the collection of items they used to develop the test, were informed by the then-prevailing descriptive Kraepelinian nosology, other existing surveys of psychiatric symptoms, and their own clinical experience. Thus, the item pool used to derive the MMPI was informed by, and reflected, the prevailing understanding of the symptoms, beliefs, and behaviors associated with commonly occurring forms of psychopathology. In contrast, the assignment of items to the eight original Clinical Scales was strictly empirical, with virtually no consideration given to item content.

The original MMPI Clinical Scales were developed using the method of contrasted groups. This involved administering a large pool of items to members of eight carefully assembled diagnostic groups and contrasting the responses of the members of each group with a sample of nonpatients. Items answered differently by the members of a given diagnostic group when endorsement frequencies were compared with the "normal" nonclinical sample were assigned to a scale designed to detect membership in that particular diagnostic group. The eight targeted diagnoses correspond to the labels of the eight original Clinical Scales: Hypochondriasis, Depression, Hysteria, Psychopathic Deviate, Paranoia, Psychasthenia, Schizophrenia, and Hypomania.

As detailed by Ben-Porath (2012), soon after the MMPI was put into clinical use it became evident that the instrument was not performing as intended. Rather than yielding distinctive indications of specific diagnoses to the exclusion of others, Clinical Scale profiles were frequently characterized by multiple and sometimes seemingly contradictory patterns of elevation. However, users of the test also noticed that certain patterns (i.e., combinations of scores) tended to recur and were associated with common features among the patients who produced them. This sparked empirical research designed to identify commonly occurring score patterns and the features associated with producing such results on the MMPI.

Because of the shift away from diagnosis, and to facilitate identification of score patterns on the test, the Clinical Scales were assigned numeric codes corresponding to their profile. By the late 1940s, the eight original Clinical Scales had been augmented by two additional measures: Masculinity-Femininity and Social Introversion. The numeric codes were used to describe patterns of scores on the MMPI Clinical Scale profile and were therefore called "code types." For example, a profile in which the first two scales (Hypochondriasis and Depression) had the highest scores would be designated a "12/21" code type. Code types played a pivotal role in MMPI interpretation. As just mentioned, Hathaway and McKinley's initial goal to develop scales that would lead directly to psycho-diagnoses was not realized. Early MMPI code-type research still focused on attempts to predict diagnoses, but was now based on patterns of scores across the MMPI profiles (e.g., Gough, 1946; Meehl, 1946; Schmidt, 1945). Soon thereafter, investigators began to expand their search to identify nondiagnostic correlates of MMPI code types, including various psychopathology symptoms, behavioral tendencies, and personality characteristics.

With the shift from single-scale scores to code types, the theoretical foundations and interpretation of the MMPI changed dramatically. The rather restricted goal of devising a differential diagnostic test was replaced by a broader, far more ambitious objective: to develop a scheme for classifying patients into meaningful types and detecting clinically meaningful empirical correlates of membership in these classes. Meehl (1954) articulated this goal and marshaled compelling evidence that actuarial interpretation of tests such as the MMPI—that is, interpreting test results on the basis of their known empirical correlates—consistently yielded more accurate information than clinical interpretation based on the user's own experiences with the instrument and impressions of the patient. He later issued his well-known call for a "good cookbook" (Meehl, 1956), designed to yield the information needed for actuarial, code-type-based MMPI interpretation.

Following Meehl's (1956) call, a number of large-scale investigations were conducted, yielding a broad empirical foundation for MMPI code-type interpretation (e.g., Gilberstadt & Duker, 1965; Marks & Seeman, 1963). However, at the same time that some MMPI authors were implementing Meehl's actuarial scheme, others were beginning to enter what had been largely forbidden territory, capitalizing on item content in MMPI scale construction and interpretation. As just reviewed, the early history of MMPI scale construction and interpretation was characterized by a strong emphasis on strictly empirical approaches. Some early exceptions to this trend involved the development of content-based subscales for the clinical scales first by Wiener and Harmon (1946) and later by Harris and Lingoes (1955). However, Wiggins (1966) was the first to launch a successful, full-fledged effort to develop content-based scales for the MMPI. In justifying this shift, Wiggins (1966) noted, "The viewpoint that a personality test protocol represents a communication between the subject and the tester (or institution which he represents) has much to commend it, not the least of which is the likelihood that this is the frame of reference adopted by the subject himself" (p. 2).

Wiggins (1966) began scale construction by examining the internal consistency of 26 content-based groupings of the MMPI item pool described originally by Hathaway and McKinley (1940). He then set about revising the content categories based on a rational analysis, followed by additional empirical analyses that yielded a set of 15 content dimensions that were promising enough to warrant further analyses. Eventually empirical analyses involving the entire item pool of the MMPI yielded a set of 13 internally consistent and relatively independent content scales. The significance of Wiggins's (1966) efforts cannot be overstated. His methods served as the prototype for all subsequent content-based scale development for the MMPI and, later, for other instruments. The psychometric success of his endeavor provided much needed empirical support for the still-fledgling content-based approach to MMPI scale construction and interpretation.

By the 1960s, the MMPI had become the most widely used (Sundberg, 1961) and studied (Welsh & Dahlstrom, 1956) measure of personality and psychopathology. Nonetheless, Hathaway (1960) expressed significant concern that, after nearly 20 years of research and clinical experience, the test had yet to be updated. He reiterated and more strongly expressed this concern 12 years later (Hathaway, 1972), and a research conference and book (Butcher, 1972) were dedicated to the topic of updating the MMPI. For various reasons, it was not until the early 1980s that the test publisher, the University of Minnesota Press, launched an effort to update the test, which produced the second edition of the inventory, the MMPI-2 (Butcher, Dahlstrom, Graham, Tellegen, & Kaemmer, 1989).

The MMPI-2

As implied by its name, the MMPI Restandardization Project had as its primary focus an update of the test's original norms, which were based on a sample of Minnesotans tested in the late 1930s. As the project evolved, several additional goals emerged: exploring the feasibility of developing a separate, adolescent-specific version of the test; replacing nonworking original MMPI items (i.e., ones that were not scored on the basic scales of the instrument) with new ones designed to assess then-contemporary issues not covered adequately by the original item pool (e.g., suicidal ideation); rewriting awkwardly phrased or otherwise problematic items; and developing a new method for deriving standard scores for the scales of the instrument. The project was launched in 1982 and culminated with the publication of a revised adult version of the test, the MMPI-2 (Butcher et al., 1989), and an adolescent-specific version, the MMPI-A (Butcher et al., 1992).

The MMPI-2 consists of 567 items. Its norms, collected throughout the United States during the mid-1980s, are based on a sample of 1,462 women and 1,138 men. Compared with the original normative sample of the test, the new sample was more representative of the U.S. population in terms of geographic residence and basic demographic features (e.g., race, age, and education). However, the new normative sample was considerably higher in socioeconomic status (SES) as indexed by education level in comparison with the U.S. population. This resulted in some early concerns that the new norms may be skewed as a result of the overrepresentation of individuals with higher education levels. Schinka and LaLone (1997) recalculated the MMPI-2 norms based on a reduced sample designed to match national SES distributions and concluded that the resulting norms were not meaningfully different from the MMPI-2 norms. Thus, the relatively high SES standing of the MMPI-2 normative sample did not affect the utility of the revised norms.

At the outset of the Restandardization Project, the committee overseeing its execution decided that the original Clinical Scales would be left essentially intact. This decision was made to ensure continuity between the original and restandardized versions of the test. Consequently, only a very small number of objectionable items (i.e., ones dealing with religious practices and beliefs, sexual orientation, and bowel and bladder movements) were deleted. Other items were slightly modified to correct grammatical errors, improve awkwardly phrased statements, or remove sexist language. Studies by Ben-Porath and Butcher (1989a, 1989b) established that scores on the slightly modified Clinical Scales were essentially interchangeable with the original versions of these scales.

An important innovation with the MMPI-2 was the introduction of Uniform T-scores (Tellegen & Ben-Porath, 1992). Briefly, these standard scores were developed to correct a long-recognized problem with MMPI T-scores. Because the raw score distributions for the Clinical Scales are differentially skewed, when linear T-scores are used (as had been done with the original inventory), the same standard score value does not correspond to the same percentile across different scales. The lack of percentile equivalence across scales makes direct comparisons of T-scores on different clinical scales potentially misleading. The solution adopted for the MMPI-2 was to compute the average distribution of non-K-corrected raw scores for men and women in the normative sample and correct each scale's distribution slightly to correspond to this composite. This is accomplished in the transformation of raw scores to T-scores. This approach yields percentile-equivalent T-scores while retaining the skewed nature of the scales' distributions.

As already mentioned, a secondary goal of the Restandardization Project was to replace nonworking MMPI items with new ones that would introduce new item content. These items were incorporated in a new set of scales introduced with the publication of the revised inventory, the MMPI-2 Content Scales (Butcher, Graham, Williams, & Ben-Porath, 1990). The MMPI-2 Content Scales were developed through a series of rational-conceptual and empirical analyses fashioned after the ones used by Wiggins (1966) in developing the original content scales for the MMPI. This process yielded a set of 15 content scales. As might be expected, some of these scales were similar in composition to the ones developed by Wiggins (1966). Nearly all the scales included new items; some (e.g., Type A Behaviors and Negative Treatment Indicators) were composed predominantly of new items.

During the decade following publication of the MMPI-2, research focused initially on comparing Clinical Scale scores based on the MMPI versus MMPI-2 norms. Surveys of practitioners (e.g., Webb, Levitt, & Rojdev, 1993) indicated that most were quick to adopt the revised instrument. Consequently, the focus of MMPI-2 research soon shifted to validating the new scales and exploring further scale development based (in part) on the new items added to the inventory. A revised edition of the MMPI-2 manual (Butcher, Graham, Ben-Porath, Tellegen, Dahlstrom, & Kaemmer, 2001) was published to incorporate the developments just mentioned. The 2001 manual was designed to update interpretive guidelines for some MMPI-2 scales included in the 1989 manual, formalize the discontinuation of others, and provide guidelines for interpreting several new scales developed during the decade following the revision. It did not introduce any changes in the norms or item composition of the MMPI-2 scales that were included in the 1989 manual.

Of the new scales included in the 2001 manual, the Personality Psychopathology Five (PSY-5) Scales, introduced first by Harkness, McNulty, and Ben-Porath (1995), have been the most influential. They are based on a personality model developed and described in detail by Harkness and McNulty (1994). The PSY-5 constructs originated from research conducted by Harkness (1992) using criteria for diagnosing personality disorders. They represent an early attempt to develop a dimensional model of personality-related psychopathology. Harkness et al. (1995) used the MMPI-2 item pool to construct scales corresponding to these five constructs, which are described later in the context of the MMPI-2-RF versions of these scales.

The MMPI-2 PSY-5 Scales were the product of the first effort to link the MMPI-2 to modern constructs that are the focus of personality and psychopathology research. However, the basic source of information on the test, the Clinical Scales, remained essentially unchanged 50 years after their introduction, in spite of Hathaway's (1960, 1972) earlier cited misgivings. Soon after the revision process was completed, one MMPI-2 Restandardization Committee member, Auke Tellegen, began work on a major research project designed to explore the feasibility of improving the

Clinical Scales. A decade later, this work culminated in the publication of the MMPI-2 Restructured Clinical (RC) Scales (Tellegen, Ben-Porath, McNulty, Arbisi, Graham, & Kaemmer, 2003), which represent the common denominator between the MMPI-2 and the MMPI-2-RF and are described next.

The MMPI-2 RC Scales

Tellegen et al. (2003) describe in detail the rationale, methods, and results of Tellegen's efforts to restructure the MMPI-2 Clinical Scales. In the following, we briefly summarize this work.

Why Restructure the Clinical Scales? The Clinical Scales' primary limitation is their weak discriminant validity. Because of unexpectedly (based on the constructs they assess) high correlations between them, amplified by considerable item overlap, the scores on the MMPI-2 Clinical Scales have limited discriminant abilities. This shortcoming is in part a product of how the empirical keying technique was applied in assigning items to them, which is based primarily on their ability to discriminate between a patient group and a common normal comparison sample. Because (essentially) the same normal reference group was used in constructing them, each of the eight scales included items that characterize either patient group or the difference between being a patient and not being one. Their heterogeneous makeup is another limitation, which diminishes their convergent validity. Finally, the near-total absence of theory to help guide their interpretation restricts the ability of MMPI users to rely on construct validity in Clinical Scale interpretation.

Goals and Method of Developing the RC Scales. Tellegen's goal in developing the RC Scales was to explore the feasibility of restructuring the Clinical Scales in a manner that would address directly the limitations just noted, yielding a parsimonious set of scales with improved discriminant and convergent validity that may be linked to contemporary theories and models of personality and psychopathology. Tellegen et al. (2003) describe in detail the methods used in developing the RC Scales; they are summarized briefly here. Scale development proceeded in four steps.

The first involved devising a marker of the MMPI common factor, which is overrepresented in the Clinical Scales because of how they were constructed. Tellegen et al. (2003) labeled this factor *Demoralization*. Step 2 was designed to identify the major distinctive core component of each Clinical Scale, which was hypothesized to consist of something other than Demoralization. Factor analyses were conducted separately with the items of each Clinical Scale combined with the Demoralization markers identified in Step 1. The first factor that emerged in each case included the Demoralization markers as well as Clinical Scale items that are primarily correlated with this construct. The second (and in some cases third) factor included items representing a core component of the Clinical Scale that was distinct from Demoralization. In Step 3, these core markers were refined further to yield a maximally distinct set of "Seed" (S) scales. This step included the removal of all item overlap and retention for the S scales of core items that correlated maximally with a given potential S scale and minimally with the remaining candidate S scales. Step 4 involved analyses of the entire MMPI-2 item pool. An item was added to a given S scale and included on the final Restructured Scale if it correlated more highly with that S scale than any other, the correlation exceeded a certain specified value, and it did not correlate beyond a specified level with any other Seed scale. The specific criteria varied across scales as detailed by Tellegen et al. (2003).

The result of this four-step process was a set of nine nonoverlapping scales representing Demoralization and a major distinctive core component of each of the eight original Clinical Scales. Restructured Scales were not developed for Clinical Scales 5 or 0 because the focus of the RC Scales was on measuring psychopathology. Further development efforts described later include the distinctive core components of these two scales. The 9 RC Scales are made up of 192 MMPI-2 items.

At the conclusion of the monograph introducing the RC Scales, Tellegen et al. (2003) noted,

> The introduction of the RC Scales may stimulate additional MMPI-2 scale development. It may prove worthwhile to search for and measure distinctive core features of important MMPI-2 scales other than the MMPI-2

> Clinical Scales, some of which may also be confounded with a strong Demoralization component. Investigations along these lines may lead to additional measures that are incrementally informative beyond the RC Scales. Through such efforts it may be possible eventually to capture the full range of attributes represented by the large body of MMPI-2 constructs with a set of new scales more transparent and effective than those currently available. (pp. 85–86)

Efforts along these lines led to the development and publication of the MMPI-2-RF, to which we turn next.

The MMPI-2-RF

The Minnesota Multiphasic Personality Inventory-2 Restructured Form (MMPI-2-RF; Ben-Porath & Tellegen, 2008/2011; Tellegen & Ben-Porath, 2008/2011) consists of 338 items that are scored on 51 scales. Ben-Porath (2012) notes that the authors' goal for the MMPI-2-RF was to represent the clinically significant substance of the MMPI-2 item pool with a comprehensive set of psychometrically adequate measures. As just described, the nine RC Scales were designed to assess major distinctive core components of the original MMPI Clinical Scales. These scales were carried over to the MMPI-2-RF in identical form. They are augmented by 33 substantive measures intended to canvass the full range of constructs that can be reliably and validly assessed with the MMPI-2 item pool, as well as 9 validity indicators. A central feature of the development of the MMPI-2-RF was the linkage of test scores to contemporary concepts and models of personality and psychopathology.

As listed and described briefly in Table 2-1, the MMPI-2-RF scales are divided into six sets. The *Validity Scales* include nine MMPI-2-RF measures designed to alert the interpreter to various threats to the validity of an individual test protocol. They include measures of inconsistent responding, overreporting, and underreporting. Use of these scales is discussed in detail in chapter 3. The remaining 42 substantive scales include 3 *Higher-Order Scales,* which indicate whether and to what extent a test

TABLE 2-1
MMPI-2-RF Scales

Validity Scales

VRIN-r *Variable Response Inconsistency*—Random responding
TRIN-r *True Response Inconsistency*—Fixed responding
F-r *Infrequent Responses*—Responses infrequent in the general population
Fp-r *Infrequent Psychopathology Responses*—Responses infrequent in psychiatric populations
Fs *Infrequent Somatic Responses*—Somatic complaints infrequent in medical patient populations
FBS-r *Symptom Validity*—Somatic and cognitive complaints associated at high levels with overreporting
RBS *Response Bias*—Exaggerated memory complaints
L-r *Uncommon Virtues*—Rarely claimed moral attributes or activities
K-r *Adjustment Validity*—Avowals of good psychological adjustment associated at high levels with underreporting

Higher-Order (H-O) Scales

EID *Emotional/Internalizing Dysfunction*—Problems associated with mood and affect
THD *Thought Dysfunction*—Problems associated with disordered thinking
BXD *Behavioral/Externalizing Dysfunction*—Problems associated with under-controlled behavior

Restructured Clinical (RC) Scales

RCd *Demoralization*—General unhappiness and dissatisfaction
RC1 *Somatic Complaints*—Diffuse physical health complaints
RC2 *Low Positive Emotions*—Lack of positive emotional responsiveness
RC3 *Cynicism*—Non-self-referential beliefs expressing distrust and a generally low opinion of others
RC4 *Antisocial Behavior*—Rule breaking and irresponsible behavior
RC6 *Ideas of Persecution*—Self-referential beliefs that others pose a threat
RC7 *Dysfunctional Negative Emotions*—Maladaptive anxiety, anger, irritability
RC8 *Aberrant Experiences*—Unusual perceptions or thoughts
RC9 *Hypomanic Activation*—Over-activation, aggression, impulsivity, and grandiosity

Specific Problems (SP) Scales
Somatic/Cognitive Scales

MLS *Malaise*—Overall sense of physical debilitation, poor health
GIC *Gastrointestinal Complaints*—Nausea, recurring upset stomach, and poor appetite
HPC *Head Pain Complaints*—Head and neck pain
NUC *Neurological Complaints*—Dizziness, weakness, paralysis, loss of balance, etc.
COG *Cognitive Complaints*—Memory problems, difficulties concentrating

Internalizing Scales

SUI *Suicidal/Death Ideation*—Direct reports of suicidal ideation and recent suicide attempts
HLP *Helplessness/Hopelessness*—Belief that goals cannot be reached or problems solved
SFD *Self-Doubt*—Lack of confidence, feelings of uselessness
NFC *Inefficacy*—Belief that one is indecisive and inefficacious
STW *Stress/Worry*—Preoccupation with disappointments, difficulty with time pressure
AXY *Anxiety*—Pervasive anxiety, frights, frequent nightmares
ANP *Anger Proneness*—Becoming easily angered, impatient with others
BRF *Behavior-Restricting Fears*—Fears that significantly inhibit normal activities
MSF *Multiple Specific Fears*—Fears of blood, fire, thunder, etc.

TABLE 2-1 (continued)

Externalizing Scales

JCP *Juvenile Conduct Problems*—Difficulties at school and at home, stealing
SUB *Substance Abuse*—Current and past misuse of alcohol and drugs
AGG *Aggression*—Physically aggressive, violent behavior
ACT *Activation*—Heightened excitation and energy level

Interpersonal Scales

FML *Family Problems*—Conflictual family relationships
IPP *Interpersonal Passivity*—Being unassertive and submissive
SAV *Social Avoidance*—Avoiding or not enjoying social events
SHY *Shyness*—Bashful, prone to feel inhibited and anxious around others
DSF *Disaffiliativeness*—Disliking people and being around them

Interest Scales

AES *Aesthetic-Literary Interests*—Literature, music, the theater
MEC *Mechanical-Physical Interests*—Fixing and building things, the outdoors, sports

Personality Psychopathology Five (PSY-5) Scales

AGGR-r *Aggressiveness-Revised*—Instrumental, goal-directed aggression
PSYC-r *Psychoticism-Revised*—Disconnection from reality
DISC-r *Disconstraint-Revised*—Under-controlled behavior
NEGE-r *Negative Emotionality/Neuroticism-Revised*—Anxiety, insecurity, worry, and fear
INTR-r *Introversion/Low Positive Emotionality-Revised*—Social disengagement and anhedonia

taker is likely experiencing problems in the domains of mood and affect, thought processes, and/or behavior; the nine *Restructured Clinical Scales* just discussed, which provide an indication of the individual's standing on the psychological constructs identified by Tellegen et al. (2003) as major distinctive core components of the original MMPI Clinical Scales; 23 *Specific Problems Scales*, the most narrowly focused MMPI-2-RF measures, which are subdivided into indicators of somatic and cognitive complaints, internalizing difficulties, externalizing behaviors, and interpersonal functioning; two *Interest Scales*, derived from the original MMPI Masculinity/Femininity scale; and five *Personality Psychopathology Five (PSY-5) Scales*, which are revised versions of similarly labeled MMPI-2 scales, designed, as noted previously, to provide a dimensional perspective on features of personality disorder–related psychopathology. The constructs assessed by the MMPI-2-RF substantive scales are described in detail by Ben-Porath (2012). Their use is discussed in chapter 4 of this guide.

Details about the MMPI-2-RF norms and procedures used to derive standard scores for the 51 scales are provided by Ben-Porath and Tellegen (2008/2011). Briefly, with the exception of a transition from gender-specific to nongendered norms, the MMPI-2-RF normative sample is essentially the same one used in standardizing the MMPI-2. The practice of reporting and interpreting gendered norms for MMPI scales began with the original test and was maintained with the MMPI-2. However, as detailed in chapter 6, the use of tests in certain areas, particularly in personnel screening, is governed by U.S. laws that prohibit reliance on group-specific norms. To address the resulting need for gender-neutral norms, a set of nongendered standard scores for all scales included in the MMPI-2 test manual (Butcher et al., 2001) was developed by Ben-Porath and Forbey (2003), who reported finding little to no interpretable differences between gender-normed and nongendered MMPI-2 scale scores. Consequently, the MMPI-2-RF standard scores were developed based on a nongendered MMPI-2 normative sample consisting of 1,138 men and 1,138 women. Uniform T-scores (described earlier) are used with all but the Validity and Interest Scales.

Two test manuals are available to guide MMPI-2-RF use. Chapter 1 of the *MMPI-2-RF Manual for Administration, Scoring and Interpretation* (Ben-Porath & Tellegen, 2008/2011) provides a description of the inventory and test materials. Chapter 2 discusses intended uses for the MMPI-2-RF, user qualifications, and the importance of protecting the materials to maintain test security. In chapter 3, the authors describe the MMPI-2-RF normative sample, which as just discussed includes most of the test takers used to develop the MMPI-2 norms, and the procedure used to develop Uniform T-scores (discussed earlier). Standard procedures for MMPI-2-RF administration and scoring are described in chapter 4 of the manual. These include assessing the testability of the test taker before its administration, adhering to standard administration and scoring procedures (delineated in the chapter), and the importance of supervised testing. Chapter 5 provides detailed interpretive guidelines for the 51 MMPI-2-RF scales, as well as a recommended approach to MMPI-2-RF interpretation. These guidelines are intended for use in clinical assessments with the MMPI-2-RF. As discussed in chapter 6 of this manual, special considerations require a different interpretive approach when using the test in police and public safety preemployment evaluations.

The *MMPI-2-RF Technical Manual* (Tellegen & Ben-Porath, 2008/2011) provides foundational information for test users. Chapter 1 discusses the background leading to the development of the MMPI-2-RF. Chapter 2 provides a description of the process used to develop the instrument. In chapter 3, the authors report and summarize the psychometric features of the inventory, including reliability estimates and standard errors of measurement for the 51 scales in the normative and clinical samples, intercorrelations between these scales in various samples, and a summary of the validity findings reported in Appendix A, which include correlations between MMPI-2-RF Substantive Scales and external criteria collected at mental health, medical, and forensic settings. A total of 53,970 validity coefficients are reported in Appendix A. The interpretive guidelines provided in chapter 5 of the *MMPI-2-RF Manual for Administration, Scoring and Interpretation* (Ben-Porath & Tellegen, 2008/2011) are based largely on these data. Appendix D of the *MMPI-2-RF Technical Manual* provides comparison group data—means and standard deviations on the 51 MMPI-2-RF scales for a wide range of samples representing settings and types of assessments in which the MMPI-2-RF is used. These data provide a method for the interpreter to compare a test taker's scores with those of a sample of individuals tested under similar circumstances. Appendix D includes a group labeled *Personnel Screening, Law Enforcement Candidate*; however, this sample has been superseded by the broader (in composition) 2,074-member Police Officer Candidate comparison group, discussed in chapter 6 of this guide and described in detail by Corey and Ben-Porath (2014).

A growing literature is available to guide use of the MMPI-2-RF in a variety of settings. As of this writing, this literature includes more than 300 peer-reviewed publications. A regularly updated reference list with links to the peer-reviewed articles is maintained by the MMPI publisher, the University of Minnesota Press (https://www.upress.umn.edu/test-division/mtdda/webdocs/references.pdf), and distributor Pearson (http://images.pearsonclinical.com/images/Assets/MMPI-2-RF/MMPI-2-RF_Bibliography.pdf). The list includes research on general topics, the MMPI-2-RF Validity Scales, studies conducted in forensic and correctional settings, research in mental health and medical settings, publications based on data collected in police and public safety settings, and research conducted in nonclinical settings (e.g., with college students).

The MMPI-2-RF can be scored by hand; however, this is a time-consuming and error-prone process (Allard & Faust, 2000; Simons, Goddard, & Patton, 2002). Computer scoring is available and can be used to produce the MMPI-2-RF Score Report, which provides scores on the 51 test scales as well as item-response information, and the MMPI-2-RF Interpretive Report for Clinical Settings, which includes all of the elements of the Score Report and, in addition, a computer-generated clinically focused interpretation of the results. A unique feature of this interpretive report is that all of the statements generated are annotated, indicating which scale scores they are based on and whether the statements are empirically or content based. For empirically based statements, the report includes references to the relevant literature, documenting the empirical support for the statement. A user's guide (Ben-Porath & Tellegen, 2011) is available to help guide use and customization of these reports. A third report option, the Police Candidate Interpretive Report (PCIR; Corey & Ben-Porath, 2014) is described in detail in chapter 7 of this guide.

Ben-Porath (2016) reports data indicating that, currently, MMPI-2 and MMPI-2-RF test use is fairly equal, although MMPI-2-RF use is growing and MMPI-2 use is diminishing. Gallo and Halgin (2011) recommend the MMPI-2-RF in their guide for establishing a police preemployment evaluation practice. Empirical studies of use of the MMPI-2-RF in preemployment evaluations of police officer candidates are described in chapter 6 of this guide, and data on use of the test in fitness-for-duty evaluations of public safety employees are reported in chapter 9.

In the following two chapters we provide some brief general guidelines for using the MMPI-2-RF validity (chapter 3) and substantive scales (chapter 4).

3

Assessing Protocol Validity with the MMPI-2-RF

Recognizing the inherent vulnerability of self-report measures to misleading responding, Hathaway and McKinley (1943) included Validity Scales, initially termed *validating scores,* in the original MMPI. The availability of these and subsequently introduced measures has enabled MMPI users to gauge, and consider in a comprehensive manner, the implications of potential impediments to the interpretability of individual test protocols. Ben-Porath (2012) describes a conceptual framework that has guided MMPI-2 (Butcher et al., 2001) and MMPI-2-RF (Ben-Porath & Tellegen, 2008/2011) Validity Scale interpretation for some time. This framework is briefly described in the first part of this chapter; however, the reader is encouraged to consult Ben-Porath's (2012) more detailed treatment of this subject. The current MMPI-2-RF validity indicators are described in the second part of this chapter. In the final section, we discuss use of the MMPI-2-RF Validity Scales to assess threats to protocol validity.

Threats to Protocol Validity

To provide useful information in response to the statements that make up a self-report measure of personality and psychopathology, a test taker must read, comprehend, and respond accurately to the test statements. Failure to do so, intentionally or unintentionally, can compromise the utility of the resulting test scores, in extreme cases rendering them uninterpretable. Therefore, before drawing any substantive inferences from self-report inventory scores, careful consideration must be given to the quality of the information provided by the test taker; that is, to the validity of the individual test protocol. Threats to protocol validity fall broadly into two categories that reflect the role of item content in invalid responding: non-content-based and content-based threats. Important distinctions can be made within each of these categories as well.

Non-content-Based Invalid Responding

Non-content-based invalid responding occurs when the test taker's responses are not based on an accurate reading and comprehension of the test items. To the extent that a test taker's responses do not reflect his or her reactions to the actual items, the responses obviously cannot gauge the individual's standing on the constructs of interest. This threat to validity can be divided further into three subtypes: nonresponding, random responding, and fixed responding.

Nonresponding occurs when the test taker fails to provide a scorable response to an item. This typically takes the form of the absence of a response, but if the test taker responds both "true" and "false" to a given item, this is also unscorable. Nonresponding may occur for a variety of reasons. Test takers who are uncooperative or defensive may fail to respond to some items, they may be unable to read or understand items, cognitive functioning deficits may result in confusion or obsessing over responses, or they may have limited introspection and insight. To the extent that nonresponding occurs in a given protocol, it has the effect of distorting the resulting test scores by lowering them artificially. If not identified and considered, nonresponding may lead to underestimation of the individual's standing on the constructs measured by the affected scales.

Random responding is characterized by an unsystematic response pattern that is not based on an accurate reading and comprehension of test items. It may be present to varying degrees in a given test protocol. Two types of random responding can be distinguished. *Intentional random responding* occurs when the individual has the capacity to respond relevantly to test items, but chooses to respond irrelevantly in an unsystematic manner. An uncooperative test taker may engage in intentional random responding to avoid a confrontation with the examiner over his or her refusal to participate. In this example, the test taker provides answers to items without reading or considering the content. He or she may do this throughout the test protocol or at various points along the way. *Unintentional random responding* occurs when the individual cannot respond relevantly to test items and responds without understanding their content. Test takers who respond in this way are often not aware that they are doing so. Unintentional random responding can result from reading or language comprehension difficulties, cognitive deficits or impairment, confusion or disorientation, or something as mundane as a test taker losing her or his place and mismarking the answer sheet. Regardless of whether it is intentional or unintentional, random responding has the effect of reducing the validity of the resulting scale scores by adding psychometric noise (unsystematic error variance).

Fixed responding is an invalidating test-taking approach characterized by a systematic response pattern that is not based on an accurate reading and comprehension of test items. If the test taker provides both true and false responses indiscriminately, then he or she is engaging in random responding. In contrast, when engaging in fixed responding, the test taker provides the same non-content-based responses (e.g., true) to various items without considering their content. In fixed responding, the indiscriminant responses are stereotypic, either true or false, or in the case of a Likert-scale response format, the test taker marks items indiscriminately at the same level without considering their content. Constructing scales with balanced keys or Likert-scale response formats does not make self-report measures less susceptible to this threat to protocol validity. An indiscriminant set of true responses is invalid regardless of whether the scoring key is balanced, and Likert scales provide even more possibilities for stereotypic responses.

Content-Based Invalid Responding

Content-based invalid responding occurs when the test taker skews her or his responses to items and, as a result, creates a misleading impression. This test-taking approach falls broadly into two classes, overreporting and underreporting.

Overreporting occurs when a test taker reports problems he or she does not actually have or exaggerates the significance of difficulties he or she does have. *Intentional overreporting* occurs when the individual knowingly slants his or her self-report to appear dysfunctional. Intentional overreporting is not synonymous with Malingering because, for example, in the absence of an external incentive, it may reflect a Factitious Disorder. However, intentional overreporting is not in itself an indication that psychopathology is absent. An individual with genuine psychological difficulties may amplify their extent or significance or may fabricate others, but nonetheless be experiencing significant dysfunction. *Unintentional overreporting* occurs when a test taker is unaware that she or he is describing her- or himself in an unrealistically negative manner. It is the test taker's self-concept rather than the self-report that is skewed. Individuals who engage in this test-taking approach mistakenly believe that their responses are accurate when, in fact, they are overreporting in comparison with how they are actually functioning.

Underreporting occurs when test takers describe themselves as having less serious or a smaller number of difficulties (or both) than they actually have. Here, too, a distinction may be drawn between intentional and unintentional underreporting. In *intentional underreporting,* the individual knowingly denies or minimizes the extent of his or her psychological difficulties or negative characteristics. This test-taking approach has been studied extensively in the field of industrial/organizational psychology under the label Impression Management (cf. Peck & Levashina, 2017). The resulting test scores underestimate the level of dysfunction. Differentiating denial from minimization is important but difficult. In the former, an individual blatantly denies problems that she or he knows exist; in the latter, the test taker may acknowledge some difficulties or negative characteristics, but minimizes their extent or impact. *Unintentional under-*

reporting occurs when the individual unknowingly denies or minimizes difficulties or negative characteristics. Here, too, objective and subjective indicators of psychological functioning would be at odds; however, in unintentional underreporting, this discrepancy results from the individual's distorted self-concept, rather than from an intentional effort to produce misleading test results.

The MMPI-2-RF Validity Scales

The MMPI-2-RF includes 10 measures of non-content-based and content-based invalid responding. The indicators are described briefly in this section, followed by a discussion of some important general considerations when using these scales.

MMPI-2-RF Measures of Non-content-Based Invalid Responding

Nonresponding is assessed globally with the *Cannot Say* (CNS) raw score, which reflects the number of unscorable responses to the 338 test items. The impact of nonresponding can vary dramatically as a function of the proportion of unscorable responses per scale. Computer scoring enables consideration of the scale-specific impact of nonresponding by providing the *Response%* statistic, which indicates the percentage of scorable responses to the items of each scale. As discussed in detail by Ben-Porath (2012), research findings indicate that if 90% of the responses to a given scale are scorable, it can be interpreted following standard guidelines. If the Response% statistic for a given scale falls below 90, nonelevated scores cannot be interpreted as indicating the absence of the problems the scale is being used to assess. Elevated scores can be interpreted with the understanding that they may provide an underestimate of the problems associated with a scale that has less than 90% scorable responses.

Random responding is assessed with the *Variable Response Inconsistency* (VRIN-r) scale. The VRIN-r score is based on the test taker's responses to 53 pairs of items that are similar in content. The raw VRIN-r score is the number of pairs answered inconsistently (i.e., true–false or false–true). The VRIN-r T-score is used to identify protocols marked by excessive random responding. It is not possible to distinguish between intentional versus unintentional responding based on the VRIN-r score. Doing so requires consideration of extra-test information, such as the test taker's reading and language comprehension ability and mental status. If potential causes of unintentional random responding can be ruled out, an intentional uncooperative test-taking approach is more likely the cause of a high VRIN-r score. Regardless of intentionality, excessive variable inconsistency compromises the interpretability of scores on the other validity scales and on the substantive scales of the MMPI-2-RF.

Fixed responding is assessed with the MMPI-2-RF *True Response Inconsistency* (TRIN-r) scale. The TRIN-r score is based on the test taker's responses to 26 pairs of items selected so that the members of each pair are quasi-reversals in content and keyed so that the raw TRIN-r score equals the number of pairs (inconsistently) answered true–true minus the number of pairs (inconsistently) answered false–false. Thus, higher raw TRIN-r scores indicate fixed (semantically inconsistent, indiscriminate) true responding, whereas lower scores indicate fixed false responding. The TRIN-r T-scores were derived by first transforming the raw scores into linear T-scores and then reflecting all T-score values below 50 (i.e., those deviating from the mean in the nonacquiescent direction). For example, an initial T-score of 80, indicative of acquiescence, is left unchanged, but a T-score of 20, indicating an equally large deviation in the nonacquiescent direction, is reflected and consequently also becomes 80. This was done to ensure that, like all the other validity indicators, only high TRIN-r T-scores indicate possible invalid responding. To distinguish acquiescent from nonacquiescent scores, the former are printed with the letter T (e.g., "80T") and the latter with the letter F ("80F"). Because there are fewer reasons why a test taker may unintentionally engage in such a response set (other than possible difficulties with double negatives), an excessive level of fixed inconsistent responding likely indicates an uncooperative test-taking approach.

There are five MMPI-2-RF *overreporting* scales. The *Infrequent Responses* (F-r) scale consists of 32 items rarely answered in the keyed direction by members of the MMPI-2-RF normative sample. Hathaway and McKinley's original criterion for selecting F scale items—that they be answered in the keyed direction by 10% of the normative sample—was applied to the MMPI-2-RF item pool using the current normative sample. Elevated scores on F-r are associated with overreporting of a broad range of psychological, cognitive, and somatic symptoms.

The *Infrequent Psychopathology Responses* scale (Fp-r) consists of 21 items rarely answered in the keyed direction by individuals with genuine, severe psychopathology. As a result, Fp-r scores are less likely to be confounded with severe disorder or distress than are F-r scores. The scale is therefore particularly helpful in assessing overreporting in settings and populations characterized by high base rates of significant psychological disorders, most notably those marked by psychotic symptoms.

The *Infrequent Somatic Responses* scale (Fs) consists of 16 items with somatic content that are uncommonly endorsed by medical patients receiving treatment for various physical diseases. Based on the same rare-symptoms rationale as the other two MMPI-2-RF infrequent response indicators (F-r and Fp-r), the Fs scale is designed to identify test takers who overreport somatic symptoms by endorsing a large number of somatic complaints rarely reported by medical patients. Research reviewed by Ben-Porath (2012) supports this interpretation of elevated Fs scores.

The *Symptom Validity* scale (FBS-r) consists of 30 items that are a subset of the 43 items that comprised the MMPI-2 version of this measure, which was originally developed to complement the MMPI-2 F scale by identifying individuals presenting with noncredible symptoms in the context of civil litigation. The FBS-r scale has been widely studied and is commonly used by neuropsychologists. As reflected in the respective interpretive recommendations, both Fs and FBS-r provide information about possible noncredible somatic symptom reporting. The two scales are only moderately correlated (.54 to .66 in the clinical samples reported by Tellegen and Ben-Porath, 2008/2011), indicating relatedness but not redundancy.

The *Response Bias* (RBS) scale is made up of 28 items designed to detect negative response bias in civil forensic evaluations. These items were selected on the basis of correlations with performance validity measures (e.g., the Word Memory Test; Green, Lees-Haley, & Allen, 2002) in a sample of disability claimants and personal injury litigants. Research reviewed by Ben-Porath (2012) indicates that the scale is particularly sensitive to noncredible memory complaints.

The MMPI-2-RF includes two underreporting measures. The *Uncommon Virtues* (L-r) scale consists of 14 items. Elevated L-r scores indicate that the test taker presented him- or herself in a favorable light by denying minor faults and shortcomings that most individuals acknowledge. When L-r scores indicate excessive underreporting the absence of elevation on the substantive scales is uninterpretable. However, elevated substantive scale scores can be interpreted with the understanding that they may underestimate the magnitude or severity of the problems they assess.

The other underreporting measure, the *Adjustment Validity* (K-r) scale, consists of 14 of the original MMPI K scale items. Elevated K-r scores indicate that the test taker presented him- or herself as well adjusted, with higher scores representing a higher level of adjustment. This type of self-presentation is associated with underreporting. However, as discussed next, the possibility that the test taker is in fact better adjusted than average also needs to be considered when interpreting an elevated K-r score. Extra-test indications that the individual is not well adjusted would support the conclusion that an elevated K-r score indicates underreporting, whereas evidence that he or she is well adjusted would temper this interpretation.

Among the protocol validity threats, underreporting is by far the most common in preemployment evaluations. Moreover, as discussed next, scores on the two MMPI-2-RF underreporting scales, L-r and K-r, are subject to confounds (traditional upbringing for L-r and good adjustment for K-r) that are likely more prevalent in public safety candidates than in the general population. This requires special considerations when using these scales in preemployment assessments. In chapter 6, we provide detailed guidance on using L-r and K-r scales when assessing public safety candidates.

Assessing Threats to Protocol Validity with the MMPI-2-RF Validity Scales: Consideration of Confounds

General interpretive guidelines and illustrations of use of the MMPI-2-RF Validity Scales are provided in chapter 6 of Ben-Porath (2012). Their use in police and public safety assessments is discussed and illustrated in chapters 8 and 11 of this guide. A critical consideration when interpreting MMPI-2-RF Validity Scale findings is that scores on these measures are confounded by factors other than the specific protocol validity threats they are used to assess. Table 3-1 (adapted from Table 6-11 in Ben-Porath, 2012) maps the MMPI-2-RF validity indicators onto the threats to protocol validity discussed earlier while identifying potential confounds that must be considered in their interpretation.

The "X"s in Table 3-1 link each of the MMPI-2-RF Validity Scales to the specific protocol threat they assess. Plus (+) and minus (−) signs identify confounds. Those denoted with a plus sign are likely to artificially increase scores on a designated scale. Confounds identified with a minus sign are likely to artificially reduce Validity Scale scores. Two types of confounds are identified in Table 3-1. Cells with a plus or minus sign that are shaded reflect "internal" confounds. These are protocol validity threats other than the one that a designated Validity Scale is intended to assess. For example, except for CNS, all of the MMPI-2-RF Validity Scales are marked by minus signs in the nonresponding row, reflecting that this threat can artificially lower scores on all of these measures. Cells with a plus or minus sign that are not shaded reflect "external" confounds. These are extra-test factors that can artificially elevate a Validity Scale score. For example, the plus sign in the "psychopathology" row under F-r indicates that genuine psychopathology can artificially elevate the F-r score.

Turning to the specific confounds identified in Table 3-1, as just noted, *nonresponding* can artificially lower scores on any of the MMPI-2-RF Validity Scales. Determining which scales may be affected is facilitated by computerized scoring, which provides the Response% statistic for each scale (as discussed earlier in this chapter). Because of the critical role of the Validity Scales in informing the interpreter about threats to the validity of an MMPI-2-RF protocol, special consideration needs to be given

TABLE 3-1
MMPI-2-RF Validity Scales: Threats to Protocol Validity, and Extra-Test Confounds

	Scales									
	CNS	VRIN-r	TRIN-r	F-r	Fp-r	Fs	FBS-r	RBS	L-r	K-r
Threats										
Non-content Based										
Nonresponding	X	–	–	–	–	–	–	–	–	–
Random responding		X		+	+	+	+	+	+	+
Fixed "true" responding			X	+	+	+	+	+	–	–
Fixed "false" responding			X	+	+	+	+	+	+	+
Content Based										
Overreporting				X	X	X	X	X		
Underreporting									X	X
Extra-Test Confounds										
Psychopathology				+	+	+	+	+		
Medical Conditions						+	+			
Traditional Upbringing									+	
Good Adjustment										+

X = Scale designed to assess this threat; + = Confound artifactually increases score; – = Confound artificially lowers score. Shaded area identifies confounds that can invalidate scores on the corresponding Validity Scales.

when more than 10% of responses to a given scale are unscorable (i.e., when Response% falls below 90). To draw the interpreter's attention, any Response% value below 90 is printed in bold in all MMPI-2-RF reports. Because scores on the VRIN-r, TRIN-r, F-r, and Fp-r scales can reach levels indicating that a protocol is invalid and uninterpretable, if the percentage of scorable items on these scales falls below 90 and responses in the keyed direction to items with unscorable responses would have raised the score up to or beyond the cutoff indicating an invalid protocol, the test results should be considered invalid.

A CNS score as low as 1 indicates that scores on some of the shorter MMPI-2-RF scales may be invalid. For example, the Suicidal/Death Ideation (SUI) scale is composed of five items. If just one is unanswered, the percentage of scorable responses to the SUI items falls to 80%, rendering a nonelevated score uninterpretable. Consequently, when CNS is greater than 0, the Response% statistic should be examined for all MMPI-2-RF scales. In such cases, the computer-generated reports will also include a list of the unscorable items with an indication of the scale(s) on which they are scored. This list can provide the interpreter a sense of the content of the items to which the test taker did not respond and facilitate identification of topics for follow-up with the examinee. For example, if a test taker does not provide scorable responses to a large number of items describing family conflict, this does not necessarily indicate that he or she experiences difficulties in this area, but it does identify an area for follow-up to determine why the examinee chose not to respond to those items.

As depicted in Table 3-1, random responding can artificially elevate scores on all of the MMPI-2-RF indicators of content-based invalid responding (i.e., overreporting and underreporting). If the VRIN-r T-score reaches 80, indicating an invalid MMPI-2-RF protocol owing to random responding, scores on the scales designated with plus signs in the Random Responding row of Table 3-1 are invalid and therefore uninterpretable. As the VRIN-r T-score approaches 80, caution should be exercised when drawing inferences from scores on the scales so designated in this row.

As seen in the next row in Table 3-1, fixed "true" responding can artificially increase scores on the overreporting indicators, whereas it may artificially lower scores on the MMPI-2-RF underreporting measures. This is because the vast majority of L-r and K-r items are keyed "false." If a test taker provides a large number of indiscriminant "true" responses or, in the extreme case, an all "true" protocol, low scores on the underreporting scales would not reflect the absence of underreporting. In contrast, fixed "false" responding can artificially elevate scores on both the overreporting and underreporting scales. Regardless of whether the indiscriminant fixed responding is in the "true" or "false" direction, if the TRIN-r T-score reaches or exceeds 80, the protocol is invalid and uninterpretable. This includes scores on both the overreporting and underreporting scales.

Turning to the extra-test confounds depicted in Table 3-1, the presence of genuine psychopathology can, to varying degrees, increase scores on the overreporting indicators. F-r is the most sensitive to the impact of genuine psychological difficulties and/or emotional distress. The greater the severity of the psychopathology or degree of emotional distress, the more likely it is to artificially elevate F-r scores. This is reflected in the interpretive guidelines for F-r listed in the *MMPI-2-RF Manual for Administration*

Scoring and Interpretation (Ben-Porath & Tellegen, 2008/2011), which indicate that individuals with genuine, severe psychopathology may score well above 100 on F-r and that the T-score must reach 120 for a protocol to be deemed invalid, even for individuals experiencing severe psychological dysfunction. As discussed earlier, the Fp-r scale was designed to be less sensitive to genuine psychopathology; however, scores on this overreporting scale can also, though to a lesser extent, be artificially elevated in individuals experiencing psychological dysfunction. The reduced susceptibility of Fp-r scores to this confound is reflected in the lower (than F-r) cutoff for invalidating a protocol based on the Fp-r scale, which the manual guidelines set at 100.

Scores on the remaining three overreporting indicators, Fs, FBS-r, and RBS, can also be elevated artificially by genuine psychopathology, though this effect is lowest for Fs. RBS scores in particular may be elevated because of internalizing dysfunction. However, T-scores in excess of 100 on these scales cannot be attributed solely to genuine psychopathology and likely reflect some degree of the overreporting assessed by these measures.

Medical conditions, particularly if they are severe and/or manifest in problems with multiple bodily systems, can, to some extent, increase scores on Fs and FBS-r, both of which include items that describe somatic problems. However, as noted in the manual guidelines, T-scores higher than 100 on these scales cannot be attributed solely to genuine medical problems and likely reflect some somatic symptom overreporting.

Table 3-1 identifies a traditional upbringing as a potential confound that can artificially elevate L-r scores. This reflects the content of the L-r items, which include virtues uncommon in the general population (e.g., never using foul language), to which individuals who grow up in traditional homes are raised to aspire. Research has shown that a traditional upbringing can elevate T-scores on the MMPI-2 L scale by about 5 points (Rosen, Baldwin, & Smith, 2016). This applies as well to the L-r scale, which is very similar in composition to L.

The final confound listed in Table 3-1, good adjustment, can artificially increase K-r scores. As noted earlier, the items on this scale are keyed to reflect the report of good psychological adjustment, which in clinical settings is unlikely to be valid and therefore reflects underreporting.

However, in nonclinical settings the report of better than average adjustment, which would be reflected in a higher than average K-r score, is not necessarily invalid. This is particularly true in settings where test takers are preselected for factors associated with better than average psychological adjustment, such as in preemployment evaluations.

Consideration of the confounds just discussed is embedded in the interpretive guidelines for the MMPI-2-RF Validity Scales listed in the test manual. However, these guidelines are generic and are most directly applicable to use of the test in clinical settings, where the base rate for psychopathology is higher than what would be expected in a preemployment context. Special considerations when interpreting the MMPI-2-RF Validity Scales in police and public safety contexts, including consideration of these potential confounds, are discussed in chapter 6 for preemployment evaluations and chapter 10 for fitness-for-duty evaluations.

4

Assessing Personality and Psychopathology with the MMPI-2-RF

The MMPI-2-RF includes 42 empirically validated measures of conceptually grounded constructs. Ben-Porath (2012) provides a detailed account of the development, conceptual foundations, and empirical support for these substantive scales. In this chapter, we provide an overview of the hierarchical structure of the MMPI-2-RF substantive scales along with a description and discussion of the constructs they assess, followed by an overview of the interpretive approach outlined in the test manual and detailed by Ben-Porath (2012).

The MMPI-2-RF Substantive Scales: Hierarchical Structure and Constructs

The MMPI-2-RF substantive scales are structured into three tiers—the Higher-Order (H-O) Scales, the Restructured Clinical (RC) Scales, and the Specific Problems (SP) Scales, the last representing the lowest, most narrowly focused level of measurement. Two exceptions to this scheme, the MMPI-2-RF Interest Scales and the MMPI-2-RF Personality Psychopathology Five (PSY-5) Scales, focus respectively on nonpsychopathology-related general interests and a model of personality-related psychopathology developed independently of the MMPI (Harkness & McNulty, 1994) for which MMPI-2 scales had been developed (Harkness, McNulty, & Ben-Porath, 1995) and widely studied.

In the following sections we describe the constructs assessed by the MMPI-2-RF substantive scales and the methods used to develop these measures.

The Higher-Order Scales

Investigators in the fields of personality and psychopathology have long sought to identify meaningful structural models that could provide an organizing descriptive framework for psychological assessment and psychodiagnosis. These efforts to delineate the structure of personality and psychopathology have proceeded along two primary lines of research. In one, nonclinical measures were used to study the structure of "normal" personality. The other focused on demarcating a higher-order structure of psychopathology. Both lines of research led to the development of hierarchical structural models, with broadly defined domains subsuming lower-level constructs. Factor-analytic studies of normal personality measures identified a common higher-order structure exemplified by Tellegen's (1995/2003) Multidimensional Personality Questionnaire (MPQ). The three higher-order factors of the MPQ are labeled *Positive Emotionality, Negative Emotionality,* and *Constraint.* Tellegen and Waller (2008) reported the results of a joint factor analysis of the MPQ, Gough's California Psychological Inventory, and the Eysenck Personality Questionnaire, showing that these three measures yield a highly congruent three-factor, higher-order structure.

In the psychopathology domain, investigators converged on two broad dimensions labeled (following Achenbach & Edelbrock, 1978) *internalizing* and *externalizing.* These broadband constructs have been identified as likely responsible for high rates of comorbidity within the two domains (Krueger, Chentsova-Dutton, Markon, Goldberg, & Ormel, 2003; Krueger, Markon, Patrick, & Iacono, 2005) and also as playing an etiological role in the development of internalizing and externalizing disorders (Dick, 2007; Hicks, DiRago, Iacono, & McGue, 2009; Krueger et al., 2002; Krueger & Markon, 2006; Vaidyanathan, Patrick, & Cuthbert, 2009). Across the two domains, combinations of internalizing and externalizing dysfunction have been implicated in the development of complex psychiatric disorders such as Posttraumatic Stress Disorder (PTSD; Miller, Fogler, Wolf, Kaloupek, & Keane, 2008), Psychopathy (Blonigen, Hicks, Krueger, Patrick, & Iacono, 2005), and Borderline Personality Disorder (James & Taylor, 2008), and gender differences on the internalizing and externalizing dimensions have been found to play a role in gender differences in the prevalence of common mental disorders (Kramer, Krueger, & Hicks, 2008).

A dimension associated with disordered thinking is conspicuously absent from the higher-order dimensions discussed thus far. Although understandable in the context of normal personality inventories, the consistent failure of factor-analytic studies of the MMPI/MMPI-2 and Personality Assessment Inventory (PAI) to identify a distinctive dimension related to thought dysfunction was puzzling, given the inclusion of relevant measures on both inventories. MMPI users and investigators have long been cognizant of the need to assess for thought dysfunction with the instrument. Meehl (1946), describing an early system for differential diagnosis based on profile patterns (i.e., code types), distinguished three broad domains of psychopathology assessable with the MMPI, labeled *Psychosis, Psychoneurosis,* and *Conduct Disorder.* His scheme for differentiating between the first two conditions primarily involved examination of the relative elevations of Clinical Scales 7 and 8. Thirty years later, H. A. Skinner and Jackson (1978) proposed an MMPI-based differential diagnostic model derived from existing code-type systems and concluded that the test is most useful in identifying three broad domains of psychopathology: neurotic, psychotic, and sociopathic. Along similar lines, an effort to develop a shorter version of the MMPI informed by "decades of research and clinical lore" (p. 362) prompted Swanson et al. (1995) to construct three scales: Subjective Distress, Acting-Out, and Psychosis.

Thus, throughout the test's history, clinicians either explicitly or implicitly used the MMPI to assess three broad types of psychopathology related to emotional, thought, and behavioral dysfunction (with the emotional domain at times bifurcating into emotional dysfunction and somatization), yet factor-analytic studies of the instrument consistently failed to identify a distinctive thought dysfunction dimension. Given the generalizability of this finding to other measures of abnormal and normal personality, the inadequacies of the MMPI Clinical Scales alone are insufficient to explain this failure. However, these shortcomings made an already complicated task of assessment even more difficult.

With this backdrop, Tellegen and Ben-Porath (2008/2011) described their development of the MMPI-2-RF substantive scales that, as discussed briefly in chapter 2 of this guide, began with construction of a set of Restructured Clinical (RC) Scales for the MMPI-2 (Tellegen et al., 2003). The availability of psychometrically improved measures of the nine major distinctive core dimensions embedded within the original Clinical Scales raised the possibility that improvements introduced with the RC Scales might yield a different higher-order structure. Indeed, in two factor-analytic studies of the RC Scales (Hoelzle & Meyer, 2009; Sellbom, Ben-Porath, & Bagby, 2008), the authors found a clearly differentiated thought dysfunction dimension marked by RC6 (Ideas of Persecution) and RC8 (Aberrant Experiences). Sellbom and colleagues also identified higher-order dimensions of internalizing (marked by RCd [Demoralization], RC2 [Low Positive Emotions], RC7 [Dysfunctional Negative Emotions]) and externalizing (marked by RC4 [Antisocial Behavior] and RC9 [Hypomanic Activation]). Hoelzle and Meyer (2009) identified the same dimensions, as well as two more narrowly focused factors marked by single RC Scales (RC1 [Somatic Complaints] and RC3 [Cynicism]).

Analyses, reported in detail by Tellegen and Ben-Porath (2008/2011), also indicated that the RC Scales conform to a higher-order structure reflective of the long-held code-type-based practice of differentiating between emotional, thought, and behavioral dysfunction. Specifically, these analyses pointed to a clear higher-order structure, with the Emotional/Internalizing domain marked by RCd, RC2, and RC7; Thought Dysfunction by RC6 and RC8; and the Behavioral/Externalizing dimension by RC4 and RC9. The combined items of the RC Scales found to be the primary markers of the three higher-order factors (i.e., RCd, RC2, RC4, RC6, RC7, RC8, and RC9) were factor analyzed in the samples used to derive the RC Scales. From each of these item-level analyses, a rotated three-factor solution and corresponding factor scores were obtained. Next, the three factor scores were correlated with each of the 567 MMPI-2 items in each of the derivation samples. Finally, a set of items was identified for each scale by selecting from the MMPI-2 item pool diverse and distinctive item markers associated statistically and conceptually with one, but not the other two, higher-order factors.

The three resulting scales were labeled *Emotional/Internalizing Dysfunction* (EID), a measure of difficulties in the domain of mood and affect; *Thought Dysfunction* (THD), a measure of disordered or unusual thinking; and *Behavioral/Externalizing Dysfunction* (BXD), which assesses problems associated with undercontrolled behavior. The three nonoverlapping Higher-Order (H-O) Scales provide dimensional measures related to the basic categorical distinctions provided by the MMPI 27/72, 68/86, and 49/94 code types, respectively. However, in contrast with the mutually exclusive nature of code-type-based interpretation, a dimensional measurement model allows for the identification of dysfunction in more than one of these broad domains (indicated by clinically elevated scores on more than one of the Higher-Order Scales) and can provide an indication of the relative prominence of problems, as reflected by the relative elevation of the H-O Scales. The scales also provide a link to a rich and expanding literature on internalizing and externalizing psychopathology.

The Restructured Clinical (RC) Scales

The rationale for and method used in developing the RC Scales were described in chapter 2 of this guide as the first step toward development of the MMPI-2-RF. Here, we describe briefly the constructs assessed by these measures. Detailed interpretive guidelines for the RC Scales are provided in chapter 5 of the *MMPI-2-RF Manual for Administration, Scoring and Interpretation* (Ben-Porath & Tellegen, 2008/2011).

RCd (Demoralization). Tellegen (1985) observed that an affect-laden phenomenon he labeled *Demoralization* was the source of problematic excessive intercorrelations between the Clinical Scales. He conceptualized it as the equivalent of the Pleasant/Unpleasant or Happy/Unhappy dimension of self-reported mood. Frank (1974, 1985) had identified amelioration of demoralization as the mechanism underlying the nonspecific effects of psychotherapy. Dohrenwend, Shrout, Egri, and Mendelsohn (1980) then linked Frank's demoralization construct to their finding of substantial intercorrelations between scores on psychiatric rating scales and equated its role in the assessment of psychopathology with that of taking a patient's temperature in medicine. Consistent with these views of demoralization, the RCd items reflect the presence of dysphoric affect, distress, self-attributed inefficacy, low self-esteem, and a sense of having given up.

RC1 (Somatic Complaints). Psychological disorders involving unexplained somatic complaints have been described and diagnosed since at least the civilization of ancient Egypt (Trimble, 2004). Lamberty (2008) provides a detailed historical review of the phenomenon of medically unexplained somatic symptom complaints, recounting that a "wandering uterus" was first implicated as causing unexplained physical symptoms in women in ancient Egypt, a theory later formalized in the label *Hysteria,* coined by the Greek physician Hippocrates. British physician Thomas Sydenham subsequently observed that symptoms of Hysteria could also be found in men and coined the term *Hypochondriasis* to designate Hysteria's male counterpart. The similarly labeled MMPI Clinical Scales 1 and 3 are the origin for the MMPI-2-RF RC1 scale, which is used to identify individuals who report a wide range of somatic concerns for which there is likely a psychological component.

RC2 (Low Positive Emotions). Tellegen (1985) posited that a lack of positive emotional responsiveness is a core personological risk factor for depression and is related to, but distinguishable from, demoralization (which is associated with dysphoric affect). Analyses designed to identify the distinctive core of Clinical Scale 2 corroborated this hypothesis when a subset of Scale 2 items with content reflecting low positive emotions emerged as markers of the major distinctive core component of this scale. Tellegen's conceptualization was consistent with a model proposed by Klein (1974), who distinguished acute dysphoria, an acute depressive reaction to situational factors, from Neurotic Depression; he characterized the latter as a chronic emotional or personality disorder related to low self-esteem, overly severe disappointment reactions, feelings of helplessness, and "Endogenomorphic Depression," which Klein postulated was associated with "a sharp, unreactive pervasive impairment of the capacity to experience pleasure or to respond affectively to the anticipation of pleasure" (p. 449). However, a lack or loss of positive emotional responsiveness characterizes other medical and mental health conditions and therefore cannot be considered pathognomonic of depression. Kring and Germans (2000) noted that the French physician T. H. Ribot coined the term "anhedonia" when describing a patient who experienced loss of pleasure secondary to liver damage, and following Rado (1956), Meehl (1962) characterized Anhedonia, which he defined as "a marked, widespread and refractory deficit in pleasure capacity" (p. 829), as "one of the most consistent and dramatic behavioral signs of [Schizophrenia]" (p. 829). The external correlates of RC2 (reviewed by Ben-Porath, 2012) are consistent with a lack of positive emotional responsiveness and corroborate its construct validity.

RC3 (Cynicism). Cynicism, as assessed by RC3, reflects the degree to which an individual holds misanthropic, negativistic, and mistrusting views of others. Cynicism is nonself-referential; it entails a generalized negative system of beliefs that humans are bad and not to be trusted, rather than a belief that one is being singled out by others for mistreatment. The cynicism construct has been the focus of two distinct bodies of literature in psychology: one, originating in behavioral medicine, focuses on cynicism as a risk factor for cardiovascular disease and other physical health problems; the other, emerging from police psychology, has centered on cynicism as a risk factor for police burnout and misconduct. Although cynicism typically has not been the focus of assessments conducted in mental health settings, the two lines of research just mentioned have documented significant health and public safety implications of individuals having higher levels of this construct. Empirical findings reviewed by Ben-Porath (2012) indicate that RC3 is the best MMPI-2-RF measure of cynicism and its correlates. Empirical correlates further indicate that individuals who produce elevated scores on RC3 are likely to have significantly impaired interpersonal relationships.

RC4 (Antisocial Behavior). Antisocial behavior is a core feature of Antisocial Personality Disorder (ASPD) and, depending on which model one follows, is either a core feature or a consequence of psychopathy. The items of RC4 cover a broad spectrum of conduct, including adult and/or juvenile criminal behavior, various other manifestations of juvenile misconduct, substance abuse, aggressive behavior, familial conflict, impulsive behavior, and deceit. The RC4 empirical correlates reviewed by Ben-Porath (2012) provide evidence in support of the construct validity of the scale as a measure of antisocial behavior. Across a wide range of settings, scores on RC4 are associated with rule breaking and irresponsible conduct linked empirically and conceptually to ASPD and psychopathy. With regard to ASPD, RC4 correlates include behaviors indicative of failure to conform to social norms, deceitfulness, impulsivity, aggressiveness, and consistent irresponsibility, as well as a history of juvenile misconduct. Strong associations between RC4 and substance abuse are consistent with the high comorbidity rates for the two conditions and the generally higher base rate of substance abuse than of criminal conduct. Higher RC4 scores have robust associations with the acting-out or social deviance facets of psychopathy, as well as the total psychopathy score on the two leading measures of this construct. Higher RC4 scores indicate a strong likelihood of acting-out behaviors that are likely to occur regardless of whether an individual meets diagnostic criteria for Antisocial Personality Disorder or psychopathy.

RC6 (Ideas of Persecution). The RC6 items describe self-referential beliefs that one is being singled out for mistreatment, ranging from being called names to being poisoned. As expected, scores on this scale are associated with paranoid delusional thought dysfunction; however, as implied by its label, the scale most directly assesses the extent to which a test taker reports experiencing persecutory thoughts. Current conceptualizations of persecutory delusional beliefs postulate that they are the product of unusual experiences that are anxiety inducing and are misinterpreted as signs of malevolent intent by others. Efforts to develop measures of persecutory beliefs have produced scales that are very similar in content to RC6. Studies of its empirical correlates support the construct validity of the scale and have identified paranoid delusions, less extreme persecutory beliefs, interpersonal suspiciousness and alienation, and mistrust as the strongest correlates of RC6. The possibility that the test taker is in fact experiencing some persecution needs always to be considered when interpreting scores on this scale.

RC7 (Dysfunctional Negative Emotions). Tellegen (1985) described Negative Emotionality (NEM) as a higher-order personality trait characterized by a tendency to worry, be anxious, feel victimized and resentful, and appraise situations generally in ways that foster negative emotions. He linked the construct to two well-known models: Gray's (1970) emotion-based psychobiological model, relating temperament to psychiatric disorder, and Freud's anxiety-signal system. Tellegen noted that both models included a second system (behavior activation in Gray's and a hope-signal system in Freud's) that closely resembled a construct he labeled *Positive Emotionality* (PEM), which is assessed on the MMPI-2-RF with RC2. The finding that the major distinctive (from the demoralization) component of MMPI Clinical Scale 7 (a measure of anxiety-related psychopathology) is in fact marked by a set of items describing dysfunctional negative emotions provides empirical support for Tellegen's model. Scores on the resulting scale, RC7, are indeed associated with a variety of dysfunctional negative emotions, most notably anxiety and anger, and in expected ways with features of PTSD and psychopathy. They are also associated with measures of Gray's (1970) Behavioral Inhibition System, which is consistent with Tellegen's (1985) conceptualization of Negative Emotionality. Some terminological confusion has been introduced by use of the label *Negative Affectivity* to describe a general mood-related disposition associated with a variety of personality variables related to psychological dysfunction (Watson & Clark, 1984) and responsible for phenotypic comorbidity reflected in measures of anxiety and depression. Used in this manner, the term "Negative Affectivity" is synonymous with demoralization, rather than with Negative Emotionality or Dysfunctional Negative Emotions.

RC8 (Aberrant Experiences). RC8 items describe a variety of sensory, perceptual, cognitive, and motor experiences that fall well outside the range of normal experiences. These phenomena have long been associated with thought disturbance, although they are neither unique to this form of psychopathology nor form an exhaustive list of its manifestations. The aberrant experiences assessed by RC8 have been linked with various psychotic disorders and, more broadly, with characteristics of individuals at increased risk for developing thought disorders. The empirical correlates of the scale include expected associations with personality characteristics related to unusual thinking and perceptual processes, well-established measures of psychosis proneness, and a host of clinical phenomena related to nonpersecutory symptoms of thought disorder. At the personality level, Tellegen and Ben-Porath (2008/2011) reported substantial correlations in college students between RC8 scores and the Absorption Scale on Tellegen's (1995/2003) MPQ. Of the two MPQ Absorption subscales, scores on RC8 were most strongly associated with the one measuring proneness to imaginative and altered states. It is important to consider, however, that there is no reason to assume that the aberrant experiences reported by an individual who scores high on this scale are associated specifically or exclusively with a primary thought disorder. They may, in some instances, be secondary to substance misuse and certain neurological conditions or, as indicated by the MPQ correlates just cited, associated with more benign but idiosyncratic perceptions and beliefs. In addition, Tarescavage, Brewster, et al. (2015) reported findings from a longitudinal study of hired police recruits, who were administered the MMPI-2-RF during their post-offer psychological evaluation, that higher scores on all thought dysfunction scales were related to post-hire supervisor ratings indicating a decreased ability to predict situational outcomes. Research reviewed by Ben-Porath (2012) provides good support for the construct validity of RC8 as a measure of psychosis proneness and, at higher levels, nonpersecutory psychotic symptoms.

RC9 (Hypomanic Activation). The construct targeted by RC9, hypomanic activation, represents a challenge for self-report measures because of the inherently transient nature of some of its core manifestations. Nevertheless, empirical correlates of RC9 reviewed by Ben-Porath (2012) include many of the features of manic and hypomanic states cataloged in Kraepelin's (1921) nosology and captured in subsequent empirical studies, as well as the two core temperamental traits identified by Kraepelin: aggression and overexcitation (i.e., activation). RC9 scores are not associated substantially with the expansive mood component of hypomania, which would instead be reflected in low scores on RC2; this highlights the need to consider scores on multiple MMPI-2-RF scales in the process of differential diagnosis. Most individuals with hypomanic personality traits do not go on to develop a full-fledged Bipolar Disorder, although these traits are associated with an increased risk for this diagnosis (cf. Kwapil et al., 2000). Thus, as is the case with all the RC Scales, an elevated score on RC9 indicates a need to consider a *possible* diagnosis of Bipolar Disorder (by referencing the actual diagnostic criteria). Personality correlates of RC9 include narcissism, manipulativeness, low harm avoidance, sensation seeking, and psychopathy features.

The Specific Problems (SP) and Interest Scales

Tellegen and Ben-Porath (2008/2011) indicate that their goal in developing the Specific Problems and Interest Scales was to augment the RC and H-O Scales with measures needed to derive a comprehensive instrument that assesses the broad range of constructs measurable with the MMPI-2 item pool. Several types of constructs were targeted in developing these scales. First, as mentioned in chapter 2, in the process of developing the RC Scales, Tellegen constructed Seed Scales for Clinical Scales 5 and 0, although final RC Scales were not derived for these measures because they do not focus on psychopathology. Development of measures of the distinctive constructs associated with these scales was intended to contribute toward canvassing the full range of domains assessed with the MMPI-2.

A second set of constructs targeted for further scale development emerged from Tellegen's factor analyses of the original Clinical Scales (described briefly in chapter 2). Several of these analyses identified more than one distinctive component in each scale. However, only one was judged the major distinctive component of a scale and was targeted for the restructuring effort. For example, analyses of Clinical Scale 3 identified distinctive demoralization, somatization, and cynicism components (assessed with RCd, RC1, and RC3, respectively) as well as a set of items related to social anxiety, a construct not represented by the RC Scales. These "excess" components of the heterogeneous Clinical Scales were also candidates for further scale development.

A third set of targeted constructs reflected the broader scope of some RC Scales. Although clearly less heterogeneous than the Clinical Scales, some of the restructured scales are multifaceted, suggesting the potential utility of developing more narrowly focused scales targeting subdomains of these measures. For example, RC4 contains items related to juvenile misconduct, substance abuse, and family difficulties, all of which are related conceptually and empirically to the targeted construct of antisocial behavior; however, it may also be helpful to assess each of these constructs separately with more focused scales. RC7 assesses a fairly broad range of dysfunctional negative emotions (related to anxiety, anger, and fear) that potentially are also worthy of separate assessment. Thus, RC Scale facets that may warrant separate, more narrowly focused assessments were also targeted for further scale development.

A fourth set of constructs considered for further scale development represented clinically significant attributes found in the MMPI-2 item pool but not represented (directly) by either the Clinical or RC Scales. For example, the MMPI-2 item pool includes a number of items that describe suicidal ideation or attempts. These items were added to the MMPI-2 as part of the Restandardization Project and therefore are not scored on any of the Clinical Scales. And although current suicidal ideation and recent suicide attempts are correlated with scores on RCd, these items are not scored on it. Tellegen and Ben-Porath (2008/2011) sought to include them on a possible restructured inventory and explored the development of a scale to do so. To identify similar possibilities, the authors examined the content of all the scales included in the MMPI-2 manual, as well as several prominent research scales. A number of the MMPI-2 Content Component Scales (e.g., Multiple Fears, Suicidal Ideation) were particularly helpful in this context.

Construction of the Specific Problems and Interest Scales followed an iterative process using methods similar to those employed in developing the RC Scales. As was the case with the latter, it was not possible to follow a simple recipe in these analyses. Judgment calls were made throughout the process, with an added final step designed to ensure that the resulting measures successfully assessed the targeted constructs. This step examined empirical correlates of the provisional SP Scales with a number of available data sets used later in the validation analyses reported in the *MMPI-2-RF Technical Manual* (Tellegen & Ben-Porath, 2008/2011). Only scales with meaningful empirical correlates were included in the final set of 23 Specific Problems and 2 Interest Scales.

The 23 Specific Problems Scales are organized into five domains identified through correlational analyses with the H-O and RC Scales. The domains and the scales included in each are described next, followed by a description of the Interest Scales.

Somatic/Cognitive Scales

As its label implies, scales in this set assess the extent to which a test taker presents with somatic and cognitive complaints. The latter were included in this group based on correlational analyses indicating that cognitive complaints are associated with the reporting of somatic symptoms.

The first scale in this set, *Malaise* (MLS), targets one of the multiple constructs embedded within the item pool of original Clinical Scale 3. The items scored on this scale, all of which were scored on the Harris–Lingoes Lassitude/Malaise (Hy3) scale, describe an overall sense of physical debilitation and poor health. Malaise has been hypothesized and found to play a role in various unexplained medical conditions associated with somatoform psychopathology. The next three somatic/cognitive scales, *Gastrointestinal Complaints* (GIC), *Head Pain Complaints* (HPC), and *Neurological Complaints* (NUC), assess specific types of somatic symptom reports. As discussed by Ben-Porath (2012), the MMPI was designed to be used in a medical setting with general medical patients, as well as with individuals with psychiatric disorders. Moreover, two of the original Clinical Scales targeted somatoform disorders marked by unexplainable physical symptoms. As a result, the MMPI and MMPI-2 included a relatively large number of items that describe specific somatic symptoms associated with somatoform conditions. A final scale in this set, *Cognitive*

Complaints (COG), was developed by analyzing items scored on two of the Harris–Lingoes subscales for Clinical Scale 8: Lack of Ego Mastery Cognitive and Lack of Ego Mastery Conative. These items describe various cognitive complaints related to memory, attention, and concentration.

Internalizing Scales

The nine Internalizing Specific Problems Scales can be divided into two subsets: four measures of constructs associated (both conceptually and statistically) with demoralization and five associated similarly with negative emotionality. The first of the demoralization-associated scales, *Suicidal/Death Ideation* (SUI), consists of items directly related to suicide and preoccupation with death. The importance of inquiring about suicide-related thoughts is highlighted by Wingate, Joiner, Walker, Rudd, and Jobes (2004), who, based on a review of the empirical literature, concluded that "patients' own self report of suicidal symptoms deserves considerable attention within the suicide assessment framework. Unless there are clear reasons to the contrary, self-report regarding suicide potential should be a major source of data" (p. 663). Reflecting this important point, Glassmire, Stolberg, Greene, and Bongar (2001) found that some individuals willing to endorse suicide-related MMPI-2 items do not acknowledge these experiences in face-to-face interviews, underscoring the importance of incorporating written self-report measures when obtaining information about possible suicidal thoughts.

The second demoralization-related Specific Problems Scale, *Helplessness/Hopelessness* (HLP), includes items keyed to convey pessimism about one's future prospects and the ability to improve them through self-change. The constructs of helplessness and hopelessness have figured prominently in the suicide risk assessment literature. More broadly, hopelessness, specifically negative expectations for the future, has been implicated as a risk factor for depressive and possibly also anxiety disorders (Miranda, Fontes, & Marroquin, 2008; Williams, Galanter, Dermatis, & Schwartz, 2008). Also within the mood disorder domain, hopelessness has been implicated in Bipolar Disorder in general and in different phases of the disorder (Valtonen et al., 2009). Finally, hopelessness and helplessness have also been identified as playing a role in various medical conditions, including hypertension (Stern, Dhanda, & Hazuda, 2009), other forms of cardiovascular disease (Pedersen, Denollet, Erdman, Serruys, & van Domburg, 2009), and metabolic syndrome (Valtonen et al., 2008).

The next measure of Internalizing dysfunction within the subset of demoralization-linked scales, *Self-Doubt* (SFD), is made up of items that describe low self-esteem and a sense of being inferior to others. The construct assessed by this scale is closely linked to the one measured by the final scale in this subset, *Inefficacy* (NFC), which consists of items keyed to convey an inability to make important decisions or achieve one's goals, particularly when facing crises or difficulties. Focusing specifically on self-doubt or low self-esteem, Orth, Robins, Trzesniewski, Maes, and Schmitt (2009) reported that strong cross-sectional correlations between low self-esteem and depression reflect a vulnerability to depression associated with premorbid self-doubt. Underscoring the importance of assessing self-doubt as part of a comprehensive psychological evaluation, Bhar, Ghahramanlou-Holloway, Brown, and Beck (2008) found that low self-esteem was a risk factor for suicidal ideation when controlling for depressed mood (i.e., demoralization) and hopelessness. Self-doubt has also been implicated as a risk factor for borderline and avoidant personality disorders (Lynum, Wilberg, & Karterud, 2008) and eating disorders (Dunkley & Grilo, 2007), and PTSD (Kashdan, Uswatte, Steger, & Julian, 2006).

Research in the area of self-efficacy distinguishes between general self-efficacy—defined by Bandura (1994) as "people's beliefs about their capabilities to produce designated levels of performance that exercise influence over events that affect their lives" (p. 71), which, according to Bandura (2001), is the foundation of human agency—and self-efficacy with respect to more narrowly defined areas of functioning. Wu (2009) evaluated the factorial stability of general self-efficacy in 25 countries and found that a single latent factor best accounted for the data in all. The NFC scale is a measure of general rather than domain-specific efficacy.

The next five Internalizing measures are all linked conceptually and empirically to the Negative Emotionality domain, assessed by RC7. The first, *Stress/Worry* (STW), includes items that describe experiencing stress and nervousness, time pressure, and being worry prone. Excessive worry (also termed "apprehensive expectation") is described as the essential feature of Generalized Anxiety Disorder (GAD) in the *DSM-5*.

The next Internalizing measure in the Negative Emotionality domain is *Anxiety* (AXY), a relatively brief scale made up of items that describe pervasive anxiety marked by near-daily experiences of fright and nightmares. Reiss and McNally (1985) differentiated between anxiety expectancy, an associative learning process in which the individual learns that a given stimulus arouses anxiety or fear, and anxiety sensitivity, an individual-differences variable involving the belief that anxiety experiences cause illness, embarrassment, or additional anxiety. The AXY items reflect a combination of both the expectation of frequent experiences of anxiety and anticipation that their impact will be pronounced. Anxiety sensitivity has been implicated in particular in PTSD (cf. Marshall, Miles, & Stewart, 2010).

The next Internalizing measure in the Negative Emotionality cluster, *Anger Proneness* (ANP), consists of items that describe becoming easily angered, irritable, and impatient when interacting with others and being overwhelmed with anger. Drawing from the work of Spielberger and colleagues (e.g., Spielberger, Jacobs, Russell, & Crane, 1983) and Novaco (1994), Eckhardt, Norlander, and Deffenbacher (2004) highlighted distinctions between hostility, an interpersonal attitude (measured on the MMPI-2-RF by RC3); anger, an affective experience; and aggression, a behavioral construct assessed on the MMPI-2-RF by a similarly named externalizing Specific Problems scale. Scarpa and Raine (1997) noted that the affective experience of anger does not always lead to aggressive behavior and that aggression and violence do not always occur within the context of angry affect.

The final two Negative Emotionality–related Internalizing scales are *Behavior Restricting Fears* (BRF), made up of items that describe various fears that inhibit and significantly restrict the individual's normal range of behaviors, and *Multiple Specific Fears* (MSF), which consists of items that describe various specific types of fears and phobias that tend to co-occur. The *DSM-5* similarly distinguishes between (a) anxiety and fears that result in avoidant behavior that impairs the individual's ability to work or carry out other responsibilities (i.e., agoraphobia) and (b) specific phobias involving the persistent fear of circumscribed objects or situations (simple phobia). The latter tend to co-occur and are classified into animal, natural environment, blood injection-injury, situational, and other subtypes, all of which are represented in the MSF item pool. The *DSM-5* includes a third fear-related disorder, Social Anxiety Disorder, features of which are assessed with the Interpersonal Scale *Shyness* on the MMPI-2-RF.

Externalizing Scales

The four Externalizing Specific Problems Scales are divided into two subsets of two scales each, associated, respectively, with the constructs assessed by RC4 (Antisocial Behavior) and RC9 (Hypomanic Activation). The first of the two RC4-related scales, *Juvenile Conduct Problems* (JCP), is made up of items that describe a history of juvenile misconduct involving stealing, negative peer group influence, and problematic behavior in school. Diagnostic criteria for adult Antisocial Personality Disorder require a history of juvenile Conduct Disorder, and numerous studies have demonstrated that such a history is predictive of various negative outcomes in adults.

The second of the two RC4-related scales, *Substance Abuse* (SUB), consists of items that describe problematic alcohol use, drug use, and misuse of prescription medication. Historically, efforts to identify individuals at risk for substance abuse with the MMPI avoided using transparent items for this purpose (e.g., MacAndrew, 1965). However, assessment of substance abuse with transparent items has been accomplished successfully with a number of psychometric devices such as the Addiction Severity Index (ASI; McLellan, Luborksy, O'Brien, & Woody, 1980), the Michigan Alcoholism Screening Test (MAST; Selzer, 1971), and the Drug Abuse Screening Test (DAST; B. F. Skinner, 1983). On the MMPI-2, the Addiction Acknowledgment Scale (AAS; Weed, Butcher, McKenna, & Ben-Porath, 1992) was used successfully in assessing substance abuse, with several studies (e.g., Stein, Graham, Ben-Porath, & McNulty, 1999;

Weed et al., 1992) indicating the superiority of the AAS over the nontransparent MMPI-2 MacAndrew Alcoholism Scale–Revised in identifying individuals with substance abuse problems.

The *Aggression* (AGG) scale is one of two Externalizing Specific Problems Scales associated with facets of RC9. It includes items that describe engaging in physically violent behavior toward others, acting violently in response to angry affect, and enjoying thoughts about, or actual infliction of, physical aggression toward others. Like the SUB scale, AGG is a transparent measure of a generally undesirable behavior. However, here too, commonly used measures of aggression have relied successfully on the use of transparent items (e.g., the Buss Perry Aggression Questionnaire; Buss & Perry, 1992).

The second Externalizing Specific Problems Scale associated with RC9, *Activation* (ACT), is made up of items that reflect racing thoughts, elated mood, a state of overexcitation, and cycling moods. This content resembles many of the items included in Eckblad and Chapman's (1986) Hypomanic Personality Scale (HYP), although the latter covers a somewhat broader domain than does ACT. Watson, Quilty, and Bagby (2010) examined the utility of MMPI-2-RF scales in differentiating patients diagnosed with Bipolar Disorder and Major Depression. ACT scores were the best MMPI-2-RF predictors of this differential diagnosis.

Interpersonal Scales

Scores on many of the MMPI-2-RF scales already discussed in this chapter are associated conceptually and empirically with interpersonal difficulties. What distinguishes the five scales included in this set is an exclusive focus on interpersonal functioning. The first scale, *Family Problems* (FML), for example, could reasonably have been included among the externalizing facets of RC4. It is made up of items that describe conflictual family relationships and alienation from members of one's family. Because items do not differentiate between current family and family of origin, FML elevations may indicate dysfunction in either set of relationships or both.

The second scale in this subset, *Interpersonal Passivity* (IPP), consists of items that, as keyed, describe submissiveness and unassertiveness in interpersonal functioning. Associations between assertiveness (or lack thereof) and various manifestations of psychological dysfunction have been demonstrated repeatedly. For example, Elliot and Gramling (1990) found that nonassertive individuals relied on different types of social support and were less likely to benefit from it than were those who were more assertive, and Lee and Swanson-Crockett (1994) found that assertiveness training improved the coping skills of a sample of nurses. Interpersonal passivity and submissiveness have also been linked with features of Dependent Personality Disorder. Bornstein (2005) reviewed the theoretical and empirical literature related to this association and concluded that an interaction between passive/submissive tendencies and situational factors best accounts for the long-observed link between this interpersonal style and the development of dependency.

The last three MMPI-2-RF measures of interpersonal functioning, *Social Avoidance* (SAV), *Shyness* (SHY), and *Disaffiliativeness* (DSF), assess various causes and effects of social isolation. The SAV items describe a lack of interest in, coupled with efforts to avoid, social situations, particularly those in which the individual is likely to be the center of attention. Items scored on SHY describe experiences of anxiety and discomfort associated with interacting with others. The DSF scale is made up of items that reflect a lack of interest in being around others and a preference for being on one's own. The three scales assess features of three *DSM-5* disorders marked by social withdrawal: Avoidant Personality Disorder, Social Anxiety Disorder, and Schizoid Personality Disorder, respectively. However, the constructs of social avoidance, shyness, and disaffiliativeness are not synonymous with these disorders.

Interest Scales

The MMPI-2-RF Interest Scales were derived from analyses of the original MMPI Clinical Scale 5, which Tellegen included in the development of the RC Scales, but because it is not a measure of psychopathology, was not used to derive a Restructured Clinical Scale. As described by Tellegen et al. (2003), in Step 2 of developing the RC Scales, which involved factor analyses of the items of each Clinical Scale along with a set of demoralization markers, he found that a four-factor solution for Scale 5 yielded a clear demoralization factor, another factor loading on items with aggressive/cynical content, and two factors marked by items describing aesthetic/literary and mechanical/physical interests, respectively. The latter two were designated as representing two major distinctive components of Scale 5. Two measures, labeled *Aesthetic–Literary Interests* (AES) and *Mechanical–Physical Interests* (MEC), were derived following analyses designed to identify items that attenuated the internal consistency of the resulting scales.

Tellegen's finding that the distinctive components of Scale 5 involved "interests" is consistent with Hathaway and McKinley's (1943) original label for the measure, the Interest Scale. Identification of two distinct sources of variance in Clinical Scale 5, reproducible in both genders, guided the development of the MMPI-2-RF Interest Scales. It is important to note that gender played no part in the selection of items for AES and MEC. Recognition that these scales measure primarily individual differences in occupational and leisurely activities reintroduces Hathaway and McKinley's (1943) original view of the Scale 5 item pool as representing items associated primarily with vocational interests.

The Personality Psychopathology Five (PSY-5) Scales

Attempts to develop dimensional models of normal personality and psychopathology were discussed earlier in this chapter. As discussed briefly in chapter 2, the Personality Psychopathology Five (PSY-5) Scales of the MMPI-2 were developed to assess a dimensional model of personality disorder proposed by Harkness and McNulty (1994). Harkness (1992) described his initial work in this area, noting that in assembling the item pool he used for this purpose, a list of *DSM-III-R* Axis II criteria was augmented with items reflecting psychopathy and normal personality constructs. Thus, in contrast with other five-factor models, which have been explored ex post facto as dimensional models of personality disorders (e.g., Widiger & Costa, 2002), the PSY-5 constructs originated directly from the clinical criteria for diagnosing these conditions.

Harkness (1992) administered to a number of samples a set of items written to canvass the *DSM-III-R* criteria, Cleckley's (1941) psychopathy descriptions, and Tellegen's (1995/2003) primary normal personality factors. Through application of a series of data-reduction techniques, Harkness and McNulty (1994) converged on a model composed of five underlying factors labeled Aggressiveness, Psychoticism, Constraint, Negative Emotionality/Neuroticism, and Positive Emotionality/Extraversion. Recognizing that MMPI-2 measures of the PSY-5 constructs could help provide a conceptually grounded assessment of personality disorders, Harkness, McNulty, and Ben-Porath (1995) developed the original set of PSY-5 Scales using a method they termed "replicated rational selection." Harkness and colleagues reasoned that because proper functioning of the scales was predicated on test takers' accurate comprehension of their content and its relation to the underlying construct, having laypersons participate in item selection would yield items that were most likely to be properly understood. Lay judges were provided detailed descriptions of the five constructs and were asked to select MMPI-2 items they deemed pertinent to each of the five dimensions. Items selected by the majority of the lay judges were assigned to provisional PSY-5 Scales. Harkness and McNulty then deleted some items that, based on their expert review, did not conform to the meaning of the PSY-5 construct for which they had been nominated by the majority of the lay judges. In a final step designed to enhance the discriminant validity of the resulting scales, item analyses were conducted, and items that were more highly correlated with a scale other than the one to which they had been assigned provisionally were dropped. In the process of developing the PSY-5 Scales, two constructs, constraint and low positive emotionality/extraversion, were reflected so that higher scores on all the scales would indicate likely dysfunction.

Following their initial publication, a sizable body of empirical research (reviewed by Ben-Porath, 2012) explored and established the psychometric properties of the PSY-5 Scales, providing substantial support for their construct validity. Availability of this literature, coupled with conceptual and empirical links to contemporary models of personality and psychopathology, led to the scales being carried over to the MMPI-2-RF. Harkness and McNulty revised the PSY-5 Scales using the reduced, 338-item booklet, a process described in detail by Harkness, Finn, McNulty, & Shields (2012). They began by identifying the "surviving" 96 of the 139 PSY-5 items and went through a series of steps designed to yield revised scales that would provide comparable and possibly improved measures of the PSY-5 constructs. On the basis of these analyses, 22 of the 96 surviving items were dropped from the revised scales, and 30 items not included on the original measures were added, yielding five nonoverlapping scales composed of 104 items.

The first of the PSY-5 Scales, *Aggressiveness* (AGGR-r), assesses a general disposition to engage in offensive, goal-directed behavior or instrumental aggression. Individuals who produce elevated scores on this scale use aggressive (physical or verbal) behavior to achieve a desired outcome, rather than in response to frustration or provocation. The second scale, *Psychoticism* (PSYC-r), assesses the verisimilitude or accuracy of the individual's inner perceptions of her or his outer social and object world. Individuals who score higher on this scale tend to misperceive others' intent and other important cues in their environment. The third dimension, *Disconstraint* (DISC-r), assesses a proclivity toward undercontrolled behavior and in particular poor impulse control. Test takers who score high on this scale have difficulties reining in their impulses. How this is manifest behaviorally depends on the impulses that the individual experiences. Low scores on this scale are associated with overly controlled behavior that is rigid and inflexible. The fourth scale in this set, *Negative Emotionality/Neuroticism* (NEGE-r), assesses a broad affective disposition to experience negative emotions, focusing on anxiety and nervousness. It is very similar to RC7, though more highly correlated with demoralization. The final PSY-5 scale, *Introversion/Low Positive Emotionality* (INTR-r), measures a broad disposition to experience low positive affect and avoid social experiences. It represents a combination of the constructs assessed with the interpersonal SAV scale and RC2.

Recently, a very similar five-factor model was proposed by the DSM-5 Personality Disorder workgroup as an alternative to the traditional categorical model for these disorders. Although the Alternative DSM-5 Model for Personality Disorders was ultimately not adopted for use in the diagnostic criteria for personality disorder, it is described in Section III of the *DSM-5*, "Emerging Measures and Models." The alternative model includes five broad trait domains labeled Negative Affectivity, Detachment, Antagonism, Disinhibition, and Psychoticism, which are described as developed from a review of existing trait models and later through research on samples of individuals who sought mental health services.

The actual diagnostic criteria for personality disorders remain essentially unchanged in the *DSM-5*. Although PSY-5 scale scores do not correspond directly to a specific personality disorder, it is possible to link each of the scales to one of the DSM-5 personality disorder clusters and to features of certain specific disorders as detailed by Ben-Porath (2012).

The MMPI-2-RF Substantive Scales: Interpretation

Detailed interpretive guidelines for the MMPI-2-RF, including a recommended structure for test interpretation and interpretive statements for each of the 51 scales, are provided in the test manual (Ben-Porath & Tellegen, 2008/2011). Ben-Porath (2012) elaborates on these guidelines and illustrates them with a series of case studies. As noted earlier, these guidelines are generally intended for clinical use of the MMPI-2-RF. Special considerations when using the test in preemployment assessments of police and public safety candidates are discussed in chapter 6 of this guide. Special considerations for fitness-for-duty evaluations are included in chapter 10. In this chapter, we provide a description of the general interpretive guidelines for the inventory.

Table 4-1 provides a recommended framework for organizing and reporting MMPI-2-RF findings and identifies the sources of information (the MMPI-2-RF scale scores) relevant to each of the domains assessed with the test. Because of the inherent limitations of self-report-based assessment, the first step in any interpretation is to appraise the validity of the test protocol. Therefore, the first part of the recommended framework for MMPI-2-RF interpretation presented in Table 4-1 is intended

TABLE 4-1
Recommended Framework and Sources of Information for MMPI-2-RF Interpretation

Domains	MMPI-2-RF Sources
I. Protocol Validity	
a. Content Nonresponsiveness	CNS, VRIN-r, TRIN-r
b. Overreporting	F-r, Fp-r, Fs, FBS-r, RBS
c. Underreporting	L-r, K-r
II. Substantive Scale Findings	
a. Somatic/Cognitive Dysfunction	RC1, MLS, GIC, HPC, NUC, COG
b. Emotional Dysfunction	EID, RCd, RC2, RC7, SUI, HLP, SFD, NFC, STW, AXY, ANP, BRF, MSF
c. Thought Dysfunction	THD, RC6, RC8, PSYC-r
d. Behavioral Dysfunction	BXD, RC4, RC9, JCP, SUB, AGG, ACT, AGGR-r, DISC-r
e. Interpersonal Functioning	FML, RC3, IPP, SAV, SHY, DSF, INTR-r
f. Interests	AES, MEC
g. Diagnostic Considerations	Most substantive scales
h. Treatment Considerations	All substantive scales

to facilitate consideration of scores on the Validity Scales. If the analysis of protocol validity indicates that interpretation of scores on the substantive scales is warranted, the substantive scales section of the framework presents the eight domains addressed: Somatic/Cognitive Dysfunction, Emotional Dysfunction, Thought Dysfunction, Behavioral Dysfunction, Interpersonal Functioning, Interests, Diagnostic Considerations, and Treatment Considerations. The placement of Somatic/Cognitive Dysfunction immediately following the protocol validity section reflects the need to consider the possible impact of somatoform psychopathology on MMPI-2-RF substantive scale scores, in effect providing a bridge between the validity and substantive scales.

When writing a narrative report of MMPI-2-RF findings, the first four domains can be addressed according to their relative prominence in the protocol. For example, when findings indicate that symptoms related to Emotional Dysfunction are likely to be the most prominent in a particular case, this topic would be addressed first, and scores on all the scales listed under this domain in Table 4-1 would be interpreted at this point. Typically, Interpersonal Functioning will be discussed in a report after the first four domains have been addressed. Interest scales are generally not pertinent in employment-related evaluations. The seventh and eighth domains in the substantive scale section of the framework deal with Diagnostic and Treatment Considerations. The interpretive framework just discussed applies broadly to clinical assessments using the MMPI-2-RF. In chapters 8 and 11, we describe and illustrate the use of integrative models specific to preemployment and fitness-for-duty evaluations, respectively.

5

Foundational Requirements of Preemployment Assessments

Before conducting any assessment for purposes of personnel selection, it is first necessary to determine the standards or criteria for qualifying (or, alternatively, disqualifying) a candidate.[1] When assessing public safety officer candidates, these criteria are generally a matter of jurisdictional law (statute and regulation), which most states have enacted for law enforcement officers and, to a lesser but still substantial degree, for firefighters/paramedics, dispatchers, and in particular, correctional officers. In an analysis of the state statutes and regulations related to preemployment psychological evaluations of law enforcement officer candidates, Corey and Borum (2013) reported that 38 states at that time mandated a psychological evaluation, with the majority specifying some variation of the minimum requirement that an acceptable candidate be "free from any physical, emotional, or mental conditions which might adversely affect his/her exercising the powers or duties of a peace officer" (Georgia Administrative Rules and Regulations 464-3-.02[1][e]). What constitutes a disqualifying "condition" in police and public safety screening is a question of singular importance. Answering it requires consideration of professional practice guidance, including statutory and regulatory law, and the sources of assessment data relevant to the selection criteria for a given position. These topics comprise the focus of this chapter.

The Standard of Practice in Personnel Screening

Statutory Requirements

Several U.S. laws and regulations have a controlling influence on preemployment psychological evaluation procedures. Principal among these are the Americans with Disabilities Act, Title I (ADA, 1990), as amended; the Civil Rights Act of 1964, Title VII; the Civil Rights Act of 1991; and the Genetic Information Nondiscrimination Act of 2008, Title II. Case law pertaining to these statutes as they apply to preemployment assessments of police and public safety candidates is discussed in detail in Corey and Borum (2013) and Spilberg and Corey (2017). Most states also have a version of these statutes with similar and sometimes more restrictive impact. A listing of all state-specific requirements is beyond the scope of this guide, but psychologists must consult them for the jurisdictions in which they practice. We next discuss the federal statutes and their effect on the standard of practice for preemployment psychological evaluations of police and public safety candidates.

Americans with Disabilities Act. Title I of the ADA (1990) is a federal statute that sets minimum protections for qualified persons with disabilities in the workplace. But beyond the ADA's broad purpose as an antidiscrimination act, it is also a procedural one. In relation to preemployment psychological evaluations that include an assessment of mental health (what the ADA terms a "medical" evaluation), the ADA addresses the following questions:

- ***What** kinds of tests and inquiries are considered medical?*

  The ADA's definition of a medical test or evaluation involves consideration of eight factors, including whether the procedure is "designed to reveal an impairment or physical or mental health" (EEOC, 1995). Although no one factor alone is determinative in defining what procedures or tests are medical under the ADA, established case law has decided that the MMPI-2 meets this definition (*Karraker v. Rent-A-Center, Inc.*, 2005). Consequently, for purposes of the ADA, the MMPI-2-RF is a medical test.

- ***Who** can be required to take a medical test?*

  If any candidate in a particular job category is mandated to submit to a medical test or evaluation as a condition of employment, the ADA requires the same for all candidates in that job category (29 C.F.R. §1630.14[b]). Therefore, for any position where an employer may desire to have a candidate submit to a medical/psychological evaluation, all candidates must be similarly tested.
- ***When** in the sequence of hiring can a medical test be given?*

  To ensure that job applicants are first evaluated on the basis of their abilities, not disabilities, the ADA requires a bright line between nonmedical and medical inquiries and evaluations. This demarcation is referred to as the "conditional offer of employment" (COE) because the job offer is conditioned on the candidate satisfactorily completing the medical evaluation. The phase of selection that precedes the COE is referred to as "pre-offer," and the phase that follows it is called the "post-offer" stage. Only after an employer has evaluated the candidate's suitability for employment on the basis of all relevant nonmedical information that could reasonably be gathered and analyzed is a COE considered a bona fide or "real" offer of employment (*Leonel v. American Airlines, Inc.*, 2005). At the post-offer stage, information from nonmedical background investigations should be expected to be routinely available to the screening professional to aid in conducting the most valid assessment (Spilberg & Corey, 2017).
- ***How** is confidential medical information to be protected?*

  The ADA contains strict provisions for protecting the confidentiality of medical information related to applicants and employees, with a short list of exceptions (29 C.F.R. §1630.14[b][1]). Not included in this list are other prospective employers, including other public safety agencies. As a consequence, preemployment psychological and other medical evaluations are employer specific and may not be used to qualify (or disqualify) a candidate for a single position with multiple employers.[2]
- ***Who** makes decisions about reasonable accommodation?*

  Under the ADA and the ADA Amendments Act of 2008, if a job candidate is deemed to be unqualified as a result of a disability, the employer must show that (a) the exclusionary criterion is "job related for the position in question and is consistent with business necessity"[3] (29 C.F.R.

§1630.10[a]) and (b) no reasonable accommodation could be made that would enable the candidate to perform the essential job functions (or to perform them without posing a direct threat), or that such reasonable accommodation would pose an undue hardship (29 C.F.R. §1630.9[a]). Fulfilling these obligations requires that the screening professional, as an agent of the employer, provide the information necessary for the employer to make that showing. Spilberg and Corey (2017) summarized these mutual duties this way:

> The responsibility for determining and implementing accommodation, when and for whom it is appropriate, rests with the employer; however, it is incumbent on the psychologist to communicate information necessary to make this determination, including the nature and degree of the impairment and what essential functions are impacted. (p. 156)

The *MMPI-2-RF Police Candidate Interpretive Report* (PCIR, discussed in chapter 7) is designed, in the case of police candidate screening, to facilitate these mutual duties by providing evidence-based linkages between scale scores and job-relevant functioning and performance as a police officer.

Civil Rights Act of 1964, Title VII. This federal statute prohibits discrimination in hiring and employment practices on the basis of race, color, religion, gender, or national origin,[4] whether as a result of disparate treatment (i.e., intentional discrimination) or disparate impact (unintended consequences). Disparate impact, also referred to as adverse impact, occurs when a hiring or employment practice has the effect of disproportionately excluding members of Title VII's protected classes, regardless of intent. The rule of thumb for assessing adverse impact in selection practices is the "four-fifths rule" (EEOC, 1979), which states that a hiring practice has adverse impact if it results in the protected class having a selection rate less than four-fifths (80%) of that of the majority group. For example, if the majority of applicants to a particular police agency are white and 82.4% of them pass the psychological evaluation, then a pass rate less than 65.92% (82.4×.80) for any minority group would be prima facie evidence of discrimination. This same method would be used to assess adverse impact on the basis of sex, religion, age, or any other protected group. Although this analysis is applied at the point of exclusion (e.g., the percentage of candidates in each class who are deemed to be psychologically unqualified), if adverse impact is detected, individual components of the assessment process would be subject to scrutiny to determine their contribution to the disparate result. Conversely, in the absence of a disparate selection ratio, the individual components of the assessment process are not subject to analysis, just as a medical examination does not need to be job relevant and consistent with business necessity unless it results in an adverse outcome on the basis of a disability. When adverse impact is proven, it falls to the employer to show that the test is nonetheless a valid predictor of performance in the position (i.e., "job-related and consistent with business necessity"), although it may still be found to be unlawful if it can be shown that an alternative test produces less adverse impact and is equally valid. We compared male and female, white and African American, and non-Hispanic white and Hispanic white candidates to determine whether the cutoffs recommended in this guide and used in the MMPI-2-RF Police Candidate Interpretive Report (PCIR) trigger differential proportions of negative findings in these candidate groups. In both the African American and Hispanic groups (the only racial/ethnic minority categories for which we have adequate sample sizes to conduct this analysis), the differential proportions fell above the .80 requirement on all scales, and the median ratio across all 51 scales is higher than .90. In a comparison of male and female candidates, we also found the ratio to exceed .80 on all scales, with a median ratio of 1.00. Thus, the interpretive guidelines in Appendix A of this guide, which are those used in the PCIR, show no evidence of adverse impact on women, African American, and Hispanic candidates.

Civil Rights Act of 1991. The Civil Rights Act of 1991 prohibits employers from adjusting the scores of, using different cutoff scores for, or otherwise altering the results of employment-related tests on the basis of race, color, religion, sex, or national origin. For this reason, when scoring the MMPI-2-RF or any other psychological test, test users should always use nongendered norms.[5] As discussed in chapter 2, this federal statute is the origin of using nongendered MMPI-2-RF norms and the availability of nongendered preemployment candidate comparison group data, such as in the PCIR or when using the personnel screening comparison groups available for the MMPI-2-RF (e.g., Personnel Screening, Law Enforcement Officer; Personnel Screening, Corrections Officer; Personnel Screening, Firefighters; Personnel Screening, Clergy; Personnel Screening, Dispatchers).

Genetic Information Nondiscrimination Act of 2008 (GINA), Title II. The implications of GINA, Title II, for preemployment psychological evaluations are not immediately evident when reviewing the statute, which is generally intended to prohibit an employer from acquiring or using genetic information in hiring and employment. However, genetic information includes information about an individual's genetic tests and the genetic tests of family members, as well as about the manifestation of a disease or disorder in an individual's family members (i.e., family medical history). Congress included family medical history in the prohibition because it can be used to determine whether someone has an increased risk of getting a disease, disorder, or condition in the future. "Family member" is defined broadly and includes dependents as the result of marriage, birth, adoption, or placement for adoption, as well as first-degree, second-degree, third-degree, and fourth-degree relatives of the person. First-degree relatives include an individual's parents, siblings, and children. Second-degree relatives include an individual's grandparents, grandchildren, uncles, aunts, nephews, nieces, and half-siblings. Third-degree relatives include an individual's great-grandparents, great-grandchildren, great-uncles/aunts, and first cousins. Fourth-degree relatives include an individual's great-great-grandparents, great-great-grandchildren, and first cousins once-removed (i.e., the children of the individual's first cousins). GINA, then, prohibits the acquisition of family medical history (i.e., information about the manifestation of disease or disorder in a candidate's family members) of any of these far-reaching dependents and relatives by any means (e.g., test, inventory, questionnaire, or interview). GINA allows for the inadvertent acquisition (but not use) of genetic information so long as the individual was first warned not to disclose it, using the following or similar language:

> The Genetic Information Nondiscrimination Act of 2008 (GINA) prohibits employers and other entities covered by GINA Title II from requesting or requiring genetic information of an individual or family member of the individual, except as specifically allowed by this law. To comply with this law, we are asking that you not provide any genetic information when responding to this request for medical information. "Genetic information," as defined by GINA, includes an individual's family medical history, the results of an individual's or family member's genetic tests, the fact that an individual or an individual's family member sought or received genetic services, and genetic information of a fetus carried by an individual or an individual's family member or an embryo lawfully held by an individual or family member receiving assistive reproductive services. (EEOC, 2008)

Professional Standards

Psychologists are expected to adhere to all 89 ethical standards in all 10 categories of the current APA *Ethical Principles for Psychologists and Code of Conduct* (EPPCC; APA, 2017a). Spilberg and Corey (2017), however, cite 7 categories and 44 standards, listed in Table 5-1, that have particular relevance for psychological screening. In states in which the EPPCC constitutes the accepted standard of care in licensing board enforcement policies and disciplinary case reviews, these ethical standards are also legal requirements.

Professionals performing preemployment psychological evaluations should also adhere to the *Standards for Educational and Psychological Testing* (AERA, APA, & NCME, 2014) unless there is a compelling professional reason why adherence to them is inappropriate. These standards, designed to promote sound testing practices and a shared basis for evaluating the quality of those practices, are intended for professionals who select tests as well as for those who interpret them. They address a wide range of issues in psychological testing, including foundations (validity, reliability/precision, errors of measurement, fairness); operations (test design and development; scores, scales, norms, and cutoff scores; test administration, scoring, reporting, and interpretation; supporting documentation for

TABLE 5-1
EPPCC Ethical Standards Especially Pertinent to Psychological Screening

Ethical Standard Category	APA Ethical Standards
Resolving Ethical Issues	1.01 Misuse of Psychologists' Work 1.02 Conflicts Between Ethics and Law, Regulations, or Other Governing Legal Authority 1.03 Conflicts Between Ethics and Organizational Demands 1.04 Informal Resolution of Ethical Violations
Competence	2.01 Boundaries of Competence 2.03 Maintaining Competence 2.04 Bases for Scientific and Professional Judgments 2.05 Delegation of Work to Others
Human Relations	3.01 Unfair Discrimination 3.02 Sexual Harassment 3.03 Other Harassment 3.04 Avoiding Harm 3.05 Multiple Relationships 3.06 Conflict of Interest 3.07 Third-Party Requests for Services 3.08 Exploitative Relationships 3.09 Cooperation with Other Professionals 3.10 Informed Consent 3.11 Psychological Services to or Through Organizations 3.12 Interruption of Psychological Services
Confidentiality	4.01 Maintaining Confidentiality 4.02 Discussing the Limits of Confidentiality 4.03 Recording 4.04 Minimizing Intrusions on Privacy 4.05 Disclosures 4.06 Consultations 4.07 Use of Confidential Information for Didactic or Other Purposes
Record Keeping	6.01 Documentation of Professional and Scientific Work and Maintenance of Records 6.02 Maintenance, Dissemination, and Disposal of Confidential Records of Professional and Scientific Work
Research and Publication	8.01 Institutional Approval 8.02 Informed Consent to Research 8.03 Informed Consent for Recording Voices and Images in Research 8.04 Client/Patient, Student, and Subordinate Research Participants 8.05 Dispensing with Informed Consent for Research
Assessment	9.01 Bases for Assessments 9.02 Use of Assessments 9.03 Informed Consent in Assessments 9.04 Release of Test Data

Ethical Standard Category	APA Ethical Standards
	9.05 Test Construction
	9.06 Interpreting Assessment Results
	9.07 Assessment by Unqualified Persons
	9.08 Obsolete Tests and Outdated Test Results
	9.09 Test Scoring and Interpretation Services
	9.10 Explaining Assessment Results
	9.11 Maintaining Test Security

APA (2007).

tests; and rights and responsibilities of test takers and test users); and testing applications (including psychological testing and assessment). The standards apply both to test users and publishers, and they contributed to many of the decisions we made when developing the PCIR. For example, when linking the interpretive statements in the "Job-Relevant Correlates" section of the PCIR to published, peer-reviewed research manuscripts, we were guided by Standard 10.14, which states, "Criterion-related evidence of validity should be available when recommendations or decisions are presented by the professional as having an actuarial basis."

Professional Practice Guidelines

The American Psychological Association (APA) approved a set of professional practice guidelines, *Occupationally Mandated Psychological Evaluations* (OMPE; APA, 2017b), which apply to "clinical evaluations[6] of individuals for occupational purposes, regardless of whether the evaluation is intended to obtain employment, to achieve licensure/certification, or to maintain either" (APA, 2017b, Introduction). The OMPE guidelines describe aspirational practices organized under three phases: (a) preparing for an OMPE, (b) conducting an OMPE, and (c) communicating OMPE findings.

The International Association of Chiefs of Police (IACP) publishes its own set of professional practice guidelines, *Preemployment Psychological Evaluation Guidelines* (IACP-PPSS, 2015). These guidelines reflect recommended psychological screening practices for police agencies and psychologists. They encompass evaluations not only of police officer candidates but also of other public safety candidates. For example, the guidelines define a preemployment psychological evaluation as "a specialized examination to determine whether *a public safety applicant* meets the minimum requirements for psychological suitability mandated by jurisdictional statutes and regulations, as well as any other criteria established by the hiring agency" (IACP-PPSS, 2015; Guideline 3.1; emphasis added).

Selection Criteria

A term commonly applied to preemployment psychological assessments of public safety candidates is "psychological *screening*." The traditional use of the term "screening" in medicine refers to efforts to identify an unrecognized condition in individuals without apparent signs or symptoms. In the context of preemployment psychological evaluations, the term connotes the fact that these assessments are primarily designed to "screen out" individuals who are at increased risk for engaging in counterproductive behavior, if hired, rather than to "select in" individuals with the most desirable qualities (Spilberg & Corey, 2017). That these evaluations are intended to screen out rather than select in is largely a consequence of the significant amount of preselection and selection efforts, discussed in chapter 6. The efforts produce a candidate pool that, for the most part, has the qualities sought by the hiring authority. At the point that a public safety candidate is referred for psychological screening, the employer typically seeks not to know if the candidate is an acceptable choice—that decision was made before the conditional offer of employment (discussed later in this chapter) that preceded it—but rather whether the candidate is unacceptable because of an "unrecognized condition" that will give rise to future counterproductive behavior. Under most state statutes and regulations, only conditions that "might adversely affect performance" in the position are disqualifying.[7] In the federal arena, when public safety employees have access to classified national security information, an individual's initial or continuous eligibility for employment is evaluated in part against the *Adjudicative Guidelines* (SEAD, 2017). Until 2005, these guidelines—which date back nearly seven decades and concern behaviors and personal history linked to loyalty, suitability for employment, and the maintenance of security of classified information—included "emotional, mental, and personality *disorders*" as a category giving rise to heightened security concerns. But in the 2005 revision of the guidelines, this category was renamed "psychological *conditions*." By making this revision, the criterion was

> broadened and made more neutral, and deleting the term "disorders" avoided having to fit an applicant's behavior into a category defined by the medical or psychiatric communities as a "disorder." It allowed consideration of behavior that raises questions about a person's reliability, trustworthiness, and judgment whether or not it is officially defined as a "disorder." (Herbig, 2011, p. 29)

This revision corresponds with a broader recognition in the professional literature and practice guidelines that the boundaries between normality and abnormality are often unclear and contribute to unreliability in the use of diagnostic criteria for purposes of categorical decisions (cf. Frances, Widiger, & Sabshin, 1991).

The movement away from the use of diagnostic categories as criteria for disqualification, and toward reliance on more dimensional constructs, is also supported by psychometric evidence (discussed in detail in chapter 6) showing that personality test scores substantially lower than the traditional cutoff used for determining clinical significance (e.g., 65T on the MMPI-2 and MMPI-2-RF) are predictive of important counterproductive behaviors (Lowmaster & Morey, 2012; Sellbom, Fischler, & Ben-Porath, 2007). For example, Tarescavage, Corey, and Ben-Porath (2015) demonstrated in a longitudinal study of 136 male police officers in the Portland (Oregon) Police Bureau that candidates with a score as low as 45T on RC7 were at more than six times the risk of exhibiting "restraint and control problems" under stress conditions compared to those with lower RC7 scores. Similar findings have been reported by Tarescavage, Brewster,

Corey, and Ben-Porath (2015); Tarescavage, Corey, and Ben-Porath (2016); Tarescavage, Corey, Gupton, and Ben-Porath (2015); and Tarescavage, Fischler, et al. (2015).

Professional practice guidelines also emphasize the importance of relying on nondiagnostic indicators of job-relevant personality constructs when making selection decisions. The Preemployment Psychological Evaluation Guidelines (IACP-PPSS, 2015) just discussed include the admonishment that, rather than focusing on "clinical diagnoses or psychiatric labeling of applicants," screening psychologists "should be focused on the individual applicant's ability to safely and effectively perform the essential functions of the position under consideration" (Guideline 11.3). Guidance from the California POST *Peace Officer Psychological Screening Manual* (Spilberg & Corey, 2017) is similar:

> The test of whether the candidate's condition is disqualifying is determined by an individualized assessment of its impact on the candidate's emotional regulation/stress tolerance, assertiveness/persuasiveness, and/or other POST Dimensions, rather than based on stereotypical symptoms or course of the condition. (p. 144)

It is incumbent on the screening professional to determine what, if any, statutes, regulations, administrative rules, or institutional policy may govern the public safety candidate evaluation in a particular jurisdiction and for a specific public safety position. As discussed in chapter 1, in the absence of an established standard or as a minimum standard, the 10 California POST Psychological Screening Dimensions listed in Table 1-5 are appropriate for use with any of the four public safety positions, with adjustments made to the weight given to one dimension or another in light of factors unique to a particular position and/or agency. Detrick and Chibnall (2013) noted that these selection criteria resulted from a large-scale research project that was "arguably the most sophisticated undertaking of its kind to date" (p. 373). In an as yet unpublished study based on a national survey of mostly experienced police psychologists (more than 85% of the 56 respondents had conducted more than 1,000 evaluations), Corey (2016) reported that 78.6% of the experts relied on the California POST Psychological Screening Dimensions as a principal component of their selection criteria.

Assessment Methodology

The tests and other components to be used in a preemployment evaluation of a public safety candidate may also be determined by law, regulation, administrative rule, or agency policy. In the absence of local requirements, the "basic model" (Mitchell, 2017; Serafino, 2010) of assessment methodology in these evaluations consists of no fewer than two psychological tests (one a broadband measure of abnormal personality functioning, the other a measure of normal-range personality), a clinical interview, and a review of background information, when available. This basic model is also reflected in the IACP-PPSS (2015) preemployment psychological evaluation guidelines. Next, we briefly review several important considerations concerning each of these assessment components.

Psychological Testing

The choice to use the MMPI-2-RF as an omnibus measure of personality and psychopathology is consistent with the general admonition to select tests for which (a) access is restricted by the publisher to qualified professionals, (b) a comprehensive test manual is available, (c) adequate reliability and validity for its intended use are demonstrated through peer-reviewed research, (d) constructs are measured that are conceptually linked to the selection criteria (e.g., those listed in Table 1-5), and (e) measures of test-taking orientation or protocol validity are included (Ackerman, 2010; Melton, Petrila, Poythress, & Slobogin, 2007; Otto, Edens, & Barcus, 2000; Spilberg & Corey, 2017). Corey (2016), based on the national survey just discussed, reported that the MMPI-2-RF was the most frequently used (44.6%) measure of abnormal psychological functioning in preemployment psychological evaluations of police candidates, in contrast to 37.5% each for the MMPI-2 and PAI (some respondents reported using more than one test of psychopathology). It is important to note that 100% of the respondents reported using at least one omnibus written measure of psychopathology.

The choice of which test of normal-range personality to use in conjunction with the MMPI-2-RF should rest on these same criteria. Preferably, there would also exist evidence demonstrating a relationship between the chosen test's scale scores and post-hire behavior in one or more of the four public safety positions, pertinent to the problem behaviors listed in Table 1-2. Selection of a normal-range personality test should also be based on its potential to augment interpretation of the MMPI-2-RF by means of complementary and divergent findings. In other words, refined interpretations of both tests are optimized when there is some overlap in the constructs they measure (e.g., the Behavioral/Externalizing Dysfunction [BXD] Scale on the MMPI-2-RF and the Socialization [So] scale on the California Psychological Inventory-434); however, users should be mindful that variations in item content can result in meaningfully different facets of a construct being measured, even among similarly named scales (e.g., Low Positive Emotions [RC2] and the Positive Emotions subscale from the NEO PI-R).

Collateral Background Information

The IACP-PPSS (2015) Preemployment Psychological Evaluation Guidelines state, "Information regarding the applicant's relevant history (e.g., school, work, interpersonal, family, legal, financial, substance use, mental health) should be collected and integrated with psychological test and interview data in a standardized manner" (Guideline 10.1). Corey (2016) reported from the unpublished national survey previously cited that 57.1% of screening psychologists obtain this history from the formal background investigation report provided by the prospective hiring agency, 66.1% obtain it from a written personal history questionnaire, and 83.9% acquire it during the clinical interview of the candidate (the majority of psychologists reported using two or all three of these methods). Mitchell (2017) noted the general principle "that the more thorough and comprehensive the background investigation, the lower the psychological disqualification rate" (p. 34).[8]

A psychological assessment that does not integrate background information provided from collateral sources (e.g., current and former coworkers, supervisors, neighbors, romantic partners, polygraph examination) inescapably relies heavily, if not primarily, on self-report data. When the candidate responds honestly, and there is no gap between his or her self-report and how others report the candidate's history and reputation, the absence of collateral information likely is of little or no consequence. However, not all candidates report accurately, sometimes as a result of a lack of awareness or naïveté and other times because of intentional deception. Without collateral data, one can validly assess neither the reliability of a candidate's self-report nor the degree to which the candidate's self-assessment and reputation are at odds. The assessment of psychosocial functioning is best accomplished through the integration of multiple sources of information, including collateral data. Graham's (2012) cautionary statement about interpreting MMPI-2 scores without the benefit of collateral information applies equally well to the MMPI-2-RF and all other personality tests:

> The interpretive data will not apply completely and unfailingly to each person with specified MMPI-2 scores. In interpreting MMPI-2 scores, one is dealing in probabilities. A particular extratest characteristic is more likely than another to apply to a person with a higher score on a scale than a person with a lower [score] on that scale, but there can never be complete certainty that it will. The inferences generated from an individual's MMPI-2 scores should thus be validated against other test and non-test information available about that individual. (p. 283)

Often public safety agencies do not make background information available to the screening professional because of the mistaken belief that this allows for an unbiased evaluation. However, when an assessment depends exclusively on the candidate's self-report and on observations from the narrow slice of behavior displayed in the interview, critical pieces of information may be missing. Rather than biasing the evaluation, background findings, when properly integrated with testing and interview data, can complement these equally important sources of self-report data. In chapter 8, we illustrate the essential utility of background information to the assessment of public safety candidates and how to integrate personal history with test and interview information. The importance of collateral background data to conducting reliable and valid assessments has been recognized in the newest California Commission on Peace Officer Standards and Training (POST) regulations, which require that law enforcement agencies provide their screening psychologists and psychiatrists with pertinent information collected from the background investigation (POST Commission Regulation 1955[e][3]). The IACP Preemployment Psychological Evaluation Guidelines (IACP-PPSS, 2015; Guideline 10.2) also include this expectation. Indeed, so vital are the collection and clarification of collateral background information to psychological screening that California POST Regulation 1955(d)(2) requires that background investigators, examining physicians, examining psychologists, and others involved in the hiring decision "shall work cooperatively to ensure that each has the information necessary to conduct their respective investigations and/or assessments of the candidate."

Clinical Interview

Two aspects of the clinical interview deserve particular comment: its place in the sequence of the assessment components and its function. With regard to sequencing, we recommend that it always *follow* the administration and review of psychological testing. A candidate's responses to test items frequently raise questions, and the interview offers an opportunity to clarify them. Although we do not recommend reading item content to the candidate verbatim, item-level information contained in the MMPI-2-RF and other test reports may alert the psychologist to potential problems that warrant follow-up. For example, if candidates were to respond "true" to this statement on a hypothetical test, "At times I feel commanded to do things I know are wrong," asking them to explain their response is likely to yield little helpful information since, once made aware of the psychologist's concern, candidates typically reply that they misunderstood the item content or incorrectly recorded their answers (Spilberg & Corey, 2017). Instead, it is generally more useful to construct probing interview questions designed to assess a particular concern. In the example just given, the psychologist is advised, of course, to assess not only for the possibility of delusional thinking and command hallucinations but also for other obsessional preoccupations that may account for the item response, neither of which assessment requires an inquiry concerning the specific item response. For example, without referencing the test item, the interviewer may ask, "Have you ever felt directed to do things you knew were wrong?" In the relatively rare instance when a candidate may be experiencing command hallucinations, this is more likely to be acknowledged in answer to a general question than in clarification of a response to a specific item that the candidate is likely to understand was the "wrong" answer. Unless testing precedes the interview, such clarifications are precluded.

Although some practitioners read item content to a candidate verbatim, we believe this is contrary to best practice. As just noted, reading selected items verbatim to candidates risks informing them that they have given the "wrong" response. Rarely will a test taker acknowledge an actual problem in this context, and the resulting discussion is unlikely to be illuminating. More troubling, it can affect how the test taker responds to future administrations of the test, leaving them compromised. When it is necessary to discuss a specific item with a candidate, we recommend that the screening professional take care to do so in a way that does not inform the examinee that the inquiry pertains to his or her response to a particular test item. This can be done by paraphrasing the item and asking about it in the broader context of the clinical interview.

The purpose of the assessment interview is to obtain information necessary for an understanding of the candidate's emotional, interpersonal, and behavioral functioning (relevant to the psychological screening dimensions in Table 1-5 or other qualification criteria) that cannot be ascertained by other means. In general, if the information can be obtained another way (such as in a written questionnaire), it is usually more efficient and economical to do so. What interviews do uniquely well is provide opportunities to observe job-relevant behavior (e.g., emotional and behavioral regulation, social competence, adaptability, judgment) and test rival hypotheses generated from a review of both psychological testing and background information gathered from collateral and self-report questionnaires.

Psychological testing in post-offer assessments is focused primarily on identifying problems, not assets or strengths.[9] Yet the challenge in psychological assessment is to evaluate not only the maladaptive aspects of an individual but also the adaptive, compensatory features. When assessing for psychopathology, for example, relevant indicators include distress, functional impairment, and behaviors characteristic of the condition. But the presence of these indicators is not proof of pathology without first ruling out indicators of their opposite; namely, indicators of psychological health, including flexibility, self-confidence, productivity, self-esteem, autonomy, efficiency, and stable relationships (Frances et al., 1991). Interviews, like background information, provide an occasion to evaluate the merits of hypotheses that rival those generated by psychological testing.

6

Special Considerations and Interpretive Guidelines for Using the MMPI-2-RF in Preemployment Assessments of Public Safety Candidates

The MMPI was developed for use in mental health and medical settings. The interpretive guidelines included in the MMPI-2-RF manual (Ben-Porath & Tellegen, 2008/2011), with elaborations and case illustrations provided by Ben-Porath (2012), apply primarily to assessments conducted in these settings—although clinically elevated scores (T-score 65 and higher) on MMPI-2-RF substantive scales indicate likely significant impairment regardless of setting. For reasons discussed later in this chapter, such elevations are uncommon in police and public safety candidates. However, a substantial body of research indicates that, for many of the substantive scales, scores deviating substantially from the mean for police candidates (i.e., T-scores in the 55–64 range) are associated with significantly increased risk for negative outcomes, as are more uncommonly occurring clinically elevated scores.

As discussed briefly in chapter 1, there is a dearth of research on the prediction of post-hire outcomes for correctional officer, firefighter/paramedic, and dispatcher candidates. This is true for all personality and psychopathology measures. Consequently, the public safety–specific research reviewed in this chapter focuses on candidates for law enforcement positions, and based on this literature, we are able to provide comprehensive interpretive guidelines for this population in Appendix A. Descriptive MMPI-2-RF findings (scale-score means and standard deviations, elevation rates) are available for all four public safety positions that are the focus of this guide and are provided in the final section of this chapter. Use of descriptive data when interpreting MMPI-2-RF findings for police, firefighter, correctional officer, and dispatcher candidates is presented in the case studies in chapter 8.

We begin this chapter with a review of the literature on using the MMPI, the MMPI-2, and now the MMPI-2-RF in assessing police candidates. This review is followed by a discussion of how to incorporate information from the 2,074-member MMPI-2-RF Police Officer Candidate comparison group when interpreting the MMPI-2-RF results of a candidate, followed by an examination of interpretive guidelines that incorporate these research findings and the comparison group data for using the MMPI-2-RF in police candidate assessments. The chapter concludes with a discussion of the descriptive data available to guide MMPI-2-RF use with firefighter, correctional officer, and dispatcher candidates.

Research on the Original MMPI and MMPI-2 in Police Candidate Evaluations

A substantial body of empirical research on preemployment police candidate evaluations was conducted with the MMPI and later the MMPI-2. This section offers a selective review of the main findings of this research and identifies some issues that remain pertinent to contemporary use of the MMPI-2-RF.

The Original MMPI

Early empirical studies conducted with the original MMPI found that several scales were effective in identifying police candidates at risk for counterproductive behaviors post-hire. Marsh (1962) reported the results of a 10-year longitudinal study conducted with the Los Angeles County Sheriff's Department. The subjects were 619 male deputy sheriffs hired between 1947 and 1950. The author reported that scores on MMPI Clinical Scales 9 (positively) and 2 (negatively) correlated with preventable auto accidents during an officer's first and second years on the force. Ten years later, Azen, Snibbe, and Montgomery (1973) conducted a follow-up study of 95 deputies from this cohort. These authors replicated and extended Marsh's (1962) findings, in particular that officers' pre-hire MMPI Scale 9 score was associated with an increased risk for being involved in any type of traffic accident over the course of 20 years of service.

In one of the most comprehensive early MMPI studies, Blum (1964) conducted a longitudinal investigation of 87 male police applicants who were hired subsequently by a major metropolitan police agency. Seven years after testing, each officer's personnel records were reviewed for evidence of negative outcomes (charges of misconduct, motor vehicle accidents, sick leave use, and termination) and positive outcomes (career progression and commendations). Blum reported significant correlations (.20 or higher) between MMPI scale scores and various outcomes, with Validity Scale F and Clinical Scale 8 having the largest number of significant correlations (three each) with negative outcomes. Blum concluded that "personality problems loom largest in determining the chances for later misconduct as a policeman; they also play a role in risk for accidents and illness. They seem to play no role in whether or not a man is commended" (p. 131).

Saxe and Reiser (1976) compared MMPI scores of three police candidate groups: 100 who were rejected, 100 who were hired but separated from service within 3 years, and 100 who were hired and served successfully for at least 3 years. They reported significant group differences between rejected and successful candidates, and between separated and successful officers, on most MMPI scales. However, they noted that most candidates scored within normal limits, even on scales that differentiated successful from unsuccessful candidates. The authors viewed the absence of clinically elevated preemployment scores among officers who went on to engage in counterproductive behavior as limiting the ability of the MMPI to identify potentially problematic candidates. They recommended that use of "successful officer norms" be explored, and they demonstrated that the separated officers scored approximately one-half of a standard deviation above the mean of successful officers on Clinical Scale 7. The absence of clinically significant elevations among police candidates has figured prominently in criticisms of the utility of the

MMPI in screening law enforcement candidates. We return to this topic later in this section.

Beutler, Storm, Kirkish, Scogin, and Gaines (1985) examined the prediction of negative outcomes in officers sampled from a variety of departments, finding that scores on Clinical Scales 1, 2, 4, 6, and 7 were associated significantly with subsequent police supervisor ratings and various measures of post-hire counterproductive behavior. The most notable correlations were between Clinical Scale 6 and technical proficiency, Clinical Scales 4 and 7 and at-fault motor vehicle accidents, Clinical Scale 1 and use-of-force reprimands, and Clinical Scale 2 and letters of complaint. Like Saxe and Reiser (1976), Beutler and colleagues commented on the absence of clinically significant elevations among officers who exhibited counterproductive behaviors, but they noted that this was the result of the automatic disqualification of candidates who produced elevated scores on MMPI scales associated with emotional and thought dysfunction. Anticipating future developments, the authors observed that they were able to detect substantial associations between MMPI scale scores and outcomes in spite of the absence of clinically elevated scores.

The MMPI-2

Following publication of the MMPI-2 (Butcher et al., 1989), initial questions were raised about the comparability of scores generated with the original and revised versions of the inventory and whether original MMPI findings such as the ones just reviewed could be assumed to carry over to the MMPI-2. Hargrave, Hiatt, Ogard, and Carr (1994) administered both versions of the test to a sample of incumbent police officers. When MMPI-2 raw scores were converted to original MMPI T-scores, Clinical Scale scores were essentially interchangeable across the two versions, indicating that minor rewording and loss of a small number of items had no appreciable effect on officers' Clinical Scale scores. When scored using the MMPI-2 norms, Clinical Scale scores were appreciably (at least 5 T-score points) lower on Scales 2, 3, 4, 6, and 9 for both genders, and on Scales 5 and 7 for men. This was consistent with findings obtained from other samples in various settings. These differences were addressed by lowering the cutoff for clinically significant elevation from a T-score of 70 on the original MMPI to 65 on the MMPI-2. Hargrave and colleagues concluded that the two versions of the inventory would yield comparable results when used as a component of the preemployment assessment process, but noted the need for new MMPI-2 validation studies.

Boes, Chandler, and Timm (1997) studied MMPI and MMPI-2 scores of police officers who had been administered the test as part of their preemployment psychological evaluations. Their sample included 439 known-offender (adjudicated as having committed corrupt acts) officers from 69 police departments and a sample of matched controls (who had not committed these acts) from the same departments. The authors reported finding few MMPI score differences between the groups, but they did report higher scores on Clinical Scale 4 and on the L scale for integrity violators than the nonviolator control subjects. However, they commented on the relatively modest effect sizes for these differences. This data set and some of the problems with the analyses just mentioned were revisited and addressed in a subsequent MMPI-2-RF study (Tarescavage et al., 2016), discussed in the next section.

Detrick, Chibnall, and Rosso (2001) provided descriptive data and reported correlations between MMPI-2 scores and scores on the Inwald Personality Inventory (IPI; Inwald, 1992), an instrument designed specifically for the assessment of police officer candidates, for a sample of 461 Midwestern law enforcement candidates who were administered these tests as part of a preemployment evaluation. This was one of the first MMPI-2 studies published following the Civil Rights Act legislation discussed in chapter 5, which prohibited the use of gender- and race-based norms in preemployment evaluations. The authors provided the first descriptive findings for police candidates using the MMPI-2 non-gendered norms. Consistent with prior studies with the original MMPI, and highlighted by the overall lowering of T-scores on the MMPI-2, mean Clinical Scale T-scores were substantially lower than the general population mean (50). The standard deviations associated with these lower means were also substantially smaller than the general population standard T-score deviations (10). Finally, Detrick and colleagues noted that, whereas correlations between MMPI-2 Clinical Scales and IPI scale scores were generally moderate and in the expected direction, this was true only for non-K-corrected Clinical Scale scores. Applying the standard K correction to the five Clinical Scales with which it was used (1, 4, 7, 8, and 9) substantially attenuated their correlations with relevant IPI scales, in some cases reducing sizable correlations to zero. This study led MMPI-2 experts (e.g., Graham, 2012, and Greene, 2011) to recommend that non-K-corrected scores be relied on when the test is used in preemployment evaluations. These data were also revisited in the context of the MMPI-2-RF in a study by Detrick, Ben-Porath, and Sellbom (2016), discussed later in this chapter.

A Paradigm Shift

Sellbom et al. (2007) conducted the most comprehensive, prospective police candidate study carried out with the MMPI-2. It was the first to include the Restructured Clinical (RC) Scales (Tellegen et al., 2003), which, as discussed in chapter 4, are also part of the MMPI-2-RF. The authors examined the ability of pre-hire MMPI-2 scores of 426 candidates to predict future misconduct of police officers who, at the time of the study, had been employed from 7 to 9 years. In addition to reporting associations between pre-hire MMPI-2 scores and a host of outcome variables, these authors sought to address two challenges raised by the findings of prior research. As noted earlier, descriptive statistics reported for both MMPI and MMPI-2 scores of police officer candidates indicated that, as a group, they score considerably lower than the general population and they evidence substantially reduced scale score variability.

Sellbom and colleagues (2007) reasoned that the lower scores with reduced variability observed in police officer candidates were likely the product of preselection and selection effects. *Preselection effects* are ones that limit the range of scores of individuals referred by law enforcement agencies for a preemployment psychological evaluation. These include any self-selection that may occur among those who choose to seek employment in law enforcement as well as any exclusions that might apply (e.g., a significant criminal record). The impact of preselection factors likely increased substantially following enactment of the Americans with Disabilities Act (ADA; discussed in chapter 5) and, in particular, the requirement that candidates be evaluated only on the basis of nonmedical factors (e.g., past conduct, reliability, employment, and criminal history) before receiving a conditional offer of employment and being referred for a preemployment psychological evaluation. Whereas prior to the ADA police agencies could refer potential candidates for a psychological evaluation before determining that they were prepared to hire them, post-ADA candidates, as discussed earlier, must be given a bona fide conditional offer of employment before being referred for an evaluation.

Selection factors stem from the use of MMPI scores as part of the prehire decision-making process, where it stands to reason that candidates whose MMPI scores raise suitability concerns are less likely to be hired. For example, in the study by Beutler and colleagues (1985) discussed earlier, candidates with clinically elevated scores on any of a number of Clinical Scales were automatically disqualified and, therefore, unavailable for the follow-up part of the study. Similarly, when reporting their results, Boes et al. (1997) noted that candidates with the most problematic MMPI protocols were likely not hired.

Sellbom and colleagues (2007) estimated preselection effects in their sample by comparing the means and associated standard deviations of MMPI-2 T-scores of the full sample of 426 candidates with the known means and standard deviations of the general population (T-scores of 50 and 10, respectively). Mean scores on the Clinical Scales (particularly the more informative non-K-corrected scores) and the RC Scales were generally 5–15 T-score points lower than those of the general population, and standard deviations were generally 2 to 5 T-score units lower (e.g., a 20% to 50% reduction in scale-score variability). Selection effects were estimated by comparing mean scores and standard deviations of the 426 candidates with the 291 individuals among them who "passed" the psychological evaluation and were hired. Selection effects were considerably smaller than those produced by preselection, but they still resulted in a further lowering of mean scores and their associated standard deviations.

These preselection (in particular) and selection effects have significant research and practice implications. The reduced variability of pre-hire scale scores attenuates correlations between these scores and the criteria used in studying their validity as predictors of subsequent counterproductive behaviors. Correlations essentially reflect the extent to which variance in a predictor variable (MMPI score) is associated with variance in a criterion (counterproductive behavior). Reduced variance in the predictor variables (stemming from preselection and selection factors) artificially attenuates their correlations with outcome variables. Sellbom and colleagues (2007) applied a formula derived from the work of Hunter and Schmidt (1990) to estimate the true correlation between MMPI-2 scores and outcome variables in their study:

$$r_c = \frac{r_u \cdot (SD_u \div SD_r)}{\sqrt{(1+r_u^2)+(r_u^2)\cdot(SD_u \div SD_r)^2}}$$

where r_c is the estimated correct correlation between the predictor and criterion variable, r_u is the uncorrected or observed correlation, SD_r is the restricted or observed standard deviation, and SD_u is the unrestricted standard deviation. To correct for preselection factors, Sellbom and colleagues (2007) set SD_r to equal 10 (the standard deviation of T-scores in the general population) and inserted the r_u and SD_u values obtained in their analyses to calculate the corrected validity coefficient, r_c.

Boes and colleagues (1997), in the MMPI-2 study just reviewed, assumed incorrectly that by including an equal number of violators and nonviolators in their analyses they were countering the impact of range restriction on their results and alleviating the need to correct for it. They were correct in noting that equal cell sizes could correct for the impact of range restriction stemming from the low base rate of integrity violations among police officers; however, it did not correct for range restriction in the candidates' MMPI scores.

From a practice standpoint, the absence of clinically elevated scores stemming from preselection and selection factors creates a need to identify nonclinically elevated cutoffs associated with an estimated increased risk for subsequent adverse outcomes. To address this need, Sellbom and colleagues (2007) reported relative risk ratios associated with T-score cutoffs of 60 and 55. Relative risk ratios (RRRs) quantify the increased risk for a given outcome associated with scoring at or above the designated cutoff versus scoring below the cutoff. For example, a relative risk ratio equal to 2.0 for a cutoff 55T on a given scale indicates that those who score at or above 55T on that scale are at twice the risk of the associated negative outcome as are those who score below 55T on that scale.

Applying the Hunter and Schmidt (1990) correction for range restriction just mentioned, Sellbom and colleagues (2007) reported for a sample of 291 male police officers uncorrected and range-restriction-corrected correlations between pre-hire scores on the MMPI-2 Clinical, RC, and Substance Abuse scales and post-hire internal affairs and civilian review authority complaints, termination of employment for cause, and supervisory ratings. The authors found that the RC Scales—particularly RC3 (Cynicism), RC4 (Antisocial Behavior), RC6 (Ideas of Persecution), and RC8 (Aberrant Experiences)—had the best predictive utility among the MMPI-2 scales they examined. For example, higher scores on RC6 were significantly associated with termination for cause, complaints from members of the public, use of excessive force, rude behavior, displaying a bad attitude toward members of the public, being uncooperative toward supervisors, being a defendant in civil litigation, deceptiveness, abuse of authority, failure to take responsibility for mistakes, using one's position for personal advantage, showing biased attitudes toward others, poor response to constructive feedback, and an indication that, given an opportunity to reconsider the initial hire decision, the officer's supervisor would not rehire him or her. The uncorrected correlations between prehire RC6 scores and the outcomes just listed ranged from .15 to .29. The range-restriction-corrected correlations were from .35 to .60.

Sellbom and colleagues' (2007) results indicate that even utilizing an interpretive cutoff of 60T yielded low elevation rates for the RC Scales. For example, 1.7% and 0.4% of employed officers scored $\geq$60T on RC3 and RC4, respectively. Furthermore, Sellbom and colleagues (2007) noted that, as a result of various preselection and selection factors, none of the officers included in their study scored above 60T on RC6. Thus, the empirical correlates just mentioned reflect associations between non-clinically elevated RC6 scores and the outcome variables. This, in turn, indicates that substantial deviations from the mean RC6 score of police candidates are associated with substantially increased risk for negative outcomes at T-score levels well below 65. To quantify this risk, Sellbom and colleagues calculated RRRs for statistically significant correlations. They reported, for example, that 26.3% of officers who, during the pre-hire evaluation, scored at or above 55T on RC6 were identified by their supervisors several years later as having engaged in rude behavior toward members of the public. Only 6.5% of those who scored below 55T on RC6 in the pre-hire testing were similarly identified, producing an RRR of roughly 4 (26.3/6.5), indicating that candidates who score at or above this cutoff on RC6 are four times more likely to engage in rude behavior toward civilians compared with those who score below 55 on this scale.

Sellbom and colleagues' (2007) results demonstrated several important considerations pertaining to use of the MMPI in pre-hire assessments of police candidates. First, these authors found that, when corrected for range restriction, correlations between pre-hire scores and subsequent counterproductive behaviors were of a meaningful magnitude, reflecting medium to large effect sizes. Second, they demonstrated the need for and appropriateness of using lower (than the traditional 65T) cutoffs to properly interpret police candidates' MMPI-2 scale scores. Their results also replicated those of Detrick and colleagues (2001) in finding generally stronger validity for non-K-corrected versus K-corrected Clinical Scale scores. Finally, their findings indicated that the MMPI-2-RF RC Scales, developed by Tellegen et al. (2003), provided substantial improvements above the non-K-corrected Clinical Scale scores in prospective prediction of police candidates' problematic behavior.

In summary, 50 years of empirical research have demonstrated the validity of MMPI and MMPI-2 scale scores as predictors of negative outcomes in police candidates, although studies using different outcome criteria did not necessarily produce consistent findings (i.e., different scales were found to work best across these studies). The substantial improvement resulting from restructuring the Clinical Scales reported by

Sellbom and colleagues (2007) was a positive indicator of the prospects for using the MMPI-2-RF, which includes the RC Scales complemented by additional measures constructed with similar methods, in preemployment assessments of police candidates. Their findings also introduced important methodological considerations for future research in this area, including use of range restriction corrections and identification of risk for adverse outcomes associated with subclinical cutoffs.

Research on the MMPI-2-RF in Police Candidate Evaluations

After the MMPI-2-RF was published in 2008, Weiss and Weiss (2010) identified the updated inventory as having "considerable promise in the area of pre-employment screening" (p. 68). They listed as particular benefits the availability of law enforcement applicant norms in the *MMPI-2-RF Technical Manual* (Tellegen & Ben-Porath, 2008/2011), inclusion of the Restructured Clinical (RC) Scales with their evidence of predictive validity for police officer performance (Sellbom et al., 2007), and the smaller number of items (338 versus 567 in the MMPI-2), which makes the test easier to administer as part of the additional testing that is required typically in a preemployment evaluation (see chapter 5). Weiss and Weiss (2010) also commented on the need for research to support use of the MMPI-2-RF in preemployment assessments of police candidates.

Since Weiss and Weiss (2010) issued their call, an extensive body of empirical research has been published and is available to guide use of the MMPI-2-RF in the assessment of police candidates. Some of this research was conducted with archival MMPI-2 data sets, from which the MMPI-2-RF scales were scored. Use of archival data for this purpose is possible because the 338 MMPI-2-RF items are embedded in the 567-item MMPI-2 booklet and is supported by findings that MMPI-2-RF scores derived from the MMPI-2 and MMPI-2-RF booklets are essentially interchangeable (Tarescavage, Alosco, Ben-Porath, Wood, & Luna-Jones, 2015; Tellegen & Ben-Porath, 2008/2011; van der Heijden, Egger, & Derksen, 2010).

We begin our review of this literature by examining the results of an innovative study of the assessment of underreporting in police candidates, followed by six investigations that provide empirical correlates (including longitudinal outcomes) of MMPI-2-RF scores produced by men and women undergoing preemployment evaluations for law enforcement positions. Altogether, the studies described in this chapter include data obtained from 1,892 police candidates tested throughout the United States. The vast majority (93%) of these candidates were men, reflecting the relatively small proportion of female law enforcement officers (10%–20% nationally, depending on agency size); for several of these studies the small number of female candidates did not allow for meaningful analyses by gender. This underscores the need to follow up with additional research using larger samples of female candidates.

Underreporting Scales

Detrick and Chibnall (2014) examined the impact of the demand characteristics associated with preemployment evaluations of police officer candidates, which incentivize test takers to present in a favorable manner by underreporting problems, a ubiquitous challenge in this type of assessment. They also investigated the sensitivity of the MMPI-2-RF Validity Scales, Uncommon Virtues (L-r) and Adjustment Validity (K-r), to underreporting by police candidates. Employing a differential prevalence research design, the authors compared scores generated by a sample of 62 police candidates (53 men and 9 women) tested twice, first under high-demand conditions and a second time in a low-demand context. The *high-demand* condition involved completion of the MMPI-2-RF as part of the routine preemployment evaluation. For the *low-demand* condition the subjects of the study were administered the MMPI-2-RF a second time after completing 6 months of training in the academy. Participants were informed that the post-academy assessment results would be used strictly for research purposes, there would be no consequences to them resulting from this testing, and the results would not be shared with any police personnel.

Consistent with the authors' hypothesis that the low-demand condition would result in a greater willingness to acknowledge psychological problems, participants scored higher in the low-demand condition on several MMPI-2-RF substantive scales, with some of the highest effect sizes found on measures of externalizing dysfunction. Participants also had higher scores in the low-demand condition on measures of emotional dysfunction and the interpersonal scales. As expected, participants scored higher on L-r and K-r in the high-demand condition, demonstrating that scores on these scales are sensitive to underreporting. With an innovative set of regression analyses, Detrick and Chibnall (2014) found that higher preemployment L-r scores were associated with a proclivity to underreport behavioral dysfunction and cynicism, whereas higher K-r scores were associated with underreporting of emotional dysfunction and cynicism.

Detrick and Chibnall's (2014) study underscores several important considerations related to using the MMPI-2-RF in police candidate assessments. As just noted, participants in their study scored higher on L-r and K-r in the high-demand (preemployment evaluation) when compared with the low-demand (no stake in the evaluation) condition, providing evidence of the sensitivity of the MMPI-2-RF underreporting indicators to this type of threat to protocol validity. However, even in the low-demand condition, officers' mean (and associated standard deviation) scores on L-r and K-r were 57.7 (14.4) and 60.6 (7.8), respectively, likely reflecting the potential confounds that complicate interpreting scores on these scales (discussed in chapter 3). That is, law enforcement candidates are more likely than would be a random sample of the general adult population to have been raised in a traditional home, and as discussed earlier, they are more likely to be better adjusted. Due to the preselection and selection factors discussed earlier in this chapter, these candidates also are more likely than members of the normative sample to exhibit a higher number of moral virtues. Proper consideration of these confounds requires taking into account the base rate of MMPI-2-RF scores in police candidate assessments, which can be accomplished by using the Police Officer Candidate comparison group discussed later in this chapter.

In chapter 10, we discuss the practice of retesting, with altered instructions, candidates whose underreporting scores indicate the possibility of defensive or deceptive responding, and we review the literature pertaining to that practice. We recommend against the use of altered instructions when administering any standardized test, and we explain our rationale for this recommendation in that chapter.

Substantive Scales

Detrick et al. (2016) reported correlations between MMPI-2-RF substantive scale scores and results on the Inwald Personality Inventory (Inwald, Knatz, & Schusman, 1982), which, as discussed earlier, is a psychological test specifically designed and validated to screen police candidates. Their sample consisted of 277 male police officer candidates from four Midwestern police agencies varying in size. The authors tested a series of conceptually based hypotheses about correlations between scores on these two measures, which were administered to the sample as part of a post-offer preemployment psychological evaluation.

Findings were largely consistent with the authors' conceptually formed hypotheses, supporting the construct validity of MMPI-2-RF scales in a police candidate sample. For example, as expected, Emotional/Internalizing Dysfunction (EID) scores were primarily associated with IPI measures of internalizing difficulties such as depression and obsessional thoughts, as well as with some IPI measures of interpersonal conflict. Also as expected, BXD scores were most strongly correlated with a range of IPI measures of acting-out and externalizing behavior, such as admission of alcohol and drug use, having been in trouble with the law, and an admitted history of job absenteeism. Thought Dysfunction (THD) had a broader than anticipated range of correlates. As expected, scores on this scale were strongly correlated with results on the IPI Unusual Experiences/Thoughts and Undue Suspiciousness scales. Other correlates included IPI measures of nontraditional, antisocial attitudes and of temperamental acting-out proclivities. Although not linked conceptually with THD, these correlates are consistent with the findings of Sellbom and colleagues (2007) discussed earlier, who reported that pre-hire RC6 and RC8 scores predicted a host of on-the-job conduct problems in police officer candidates who were hired.

As was the case in the Sellbom et al. (2007) study just mentioned, mean scores and associated standard deviations in the Detrick et al. (2016) study were substantially deflated and restricted when compared with the MMPI-2-RF normative sample. For example, the mean EID score for the 277 police candidates included in this study was 34, with a standard deviation of 4 (in contrast with the mean and standard deviation on this and all other MMPI-2-RF scales in the normative sample, which, by definition, are 50 and 10, respectively). Almost none of the individuals included in the study produced a clinically elevated EID score (≥65T), indicating that scores below 65 but substantially above average for the sample are associated with a range of risk factors assessed by the IPI. Similar findings were reported for most of the MMPI-2-RF substantive scales.

Tarescavage, Brewster, Corey, and Ben-Porath (2015) examined associations between pre-hire MMPI-2-RF scores and post-hire performance ratings for a sample of 131 male police officers employed in the northeastern United States. After consulting with several police chiefs and supervisory personnel, the second author of the study created a supervisor survey of police officer performance. Supervisors completed the survey after they had observed officers' behavior for a time period ranging from 1 month to 2.5 years ($M=1.1$, $SD=0.5$ years). The authors selected 39 survey items that addressed constructs related to the California POST screening dimensions (Spilberg & Corey, 2017), as well as one global rating, as the criteria in their investigation.

Uncorrected and range restriction–corrected correlations (see the earlier discussion of Sellbom et al., 2007) between MMPI-2-RF scores and the selected criteria indicated that scales from the emotional dysfunction domain were substantially associated with emotional control and stress problems (problems with anger interfering with job performance), routine task performance problems (difficulties drawing crime or accident scenes), decision-making and judgment problems (overlooking violations), and problem-solving difficulties. Scores on MMPI-2-RF scales from the thought dysfunction domain were associated with marksmanship problems and difficulty predicting situational outcomes. Scores from measures included in the behavioral dysfunction domain were correlated with various outcomes related to acting out, such as integrity problems and alcohol and drug use. Scores on MMPI-2-RF measures of interpersonal functioning were associated with problems such as failing to utilize training under stressful conditions, difficulties with assertiveness and social skills, and shortcomings in oral communication skills. Overall, the corrected correlations were mainly of a medium effect size.

A comparison of the MMPI-2-RF means and standard deviations for the study sample with those found for the Police Officer Candidate comparison group (discussed later) showed that the two samples produced comparably suppressed and range-restricted scores, indicating that in this investigation, as with Sellbom et al. (2007) and Detrick et al. (2016), correlations between pre-hire MMPI-2-RF scores and problematic job-relevant behaviors reflect individual differences that, for the most part, are associated with T-scores that fall below 65.

Tarescavage, Corey, and Ben-Porath (2015) investigated the predictive validity of the MMPI-2-RF in a sample of 136 male police officers hired by the Portland (Oregon) Police Bureau. Supervisor ratings of performance and problem behaviors were obtained during the officers' initial probationary period, when they were closely monitored by a field training officer. Each of the officers had been administered the MMPI-2 (converted for the purpose of this study to the MMPI-2-RF) or MMPI-2-RF as part of his preemployment evaluation and subsequently completed a training academy and a 16-week field training program. The officers were evaluated daily during the field training program, and these daily evaluations were subsequently used by training division personnel to complete the Selection Validation Survey (SVS), a measure developed by this guide's first author to assess police officers' performance during their initial probationary period. The SVS is organized into three sections: Problem Behaviors, Field Performance Dimensions, and General Performance Dimensions. Problem Behaviors include items such as academic learning problems, failure to engage subjects as necessary, and rude behavior. Field Performance Dimensions include items such as decision making, assertiveness/control, and multitasking. General Performance Dimensions include items such as initiative and drive, commitment, integrity, and teamwork. Problem Behaviors were coded as absent, problem during probation, or problem leading to separation. Field Performance Dimensions items were rated under normal and stress conditions. General Performance Dimensions problems were rated as either absent or present. The SVS also includes two Likert scale ratings for overall performance and potential for hiring similar employees. Except for the latter Likert scale ratings, data for all the other variables were derived from archival records that included observation ratings of recruits made daily by their field training officers.

Descriptive analyses indicated that this sample produced deflated means and restricted ranges of scores on MMPI-2-RF substantive scales comparable to those found in the other study samples described in this section and to the Police Officer Candidate comparison group discussed in the following section. Next, the authors reported uncorrected and range restriction–corrected correlations between pre-hire MMPI-2-RF scores and SVS ratings of officers' performance during their probationary period. Scores on scales in the emotional domain of the MMPI-2-RF were moderately correlated with various emotional control and stress problems, including decision making under stress and restraint and control problems under stress, as well as with routine task performance problems, such as learning problems under normal conditions and radio operation problems. Scales in this domain were also associated with subsequent problems in the areas of conscientiousness and commitment, as well as with an overall negative performance evaluation. Scales in the thought dysfunction domain were not correlated substantially with most of the SVS criteria. By contrast, scores on the MMPI-2-RF behavioral dysfunction measures were correlated with problems such as failure to accept feedback and interpersonal difficulties. Scores on the BXD, RC9, and DISC-r scales were negatively correlated with failure to engage subjects, indicating that particularly low scores on these measures were associated with problematic performance. Scales in the somatic domain did not have many meaningful associations with SVS ratings. In contrast, scores on the MMPI-2-RF measures of interpersonal functioning were associated with assertiveness and control problems, interpersonal difficulties, and problems with teamwork.

As is the case in the other studies discussed in this section, the correlations between pre-hire MMPI-2-RF scores and probationary-period performance ratings reflect scale-score variance that occurs for the most part below T-score 65. Using the methodology applied in the earlier described study by Sellbom et al. (2007), Tarescavage, Corey, and Ben-Porath (2015) reported relative risk ratios associated with various subclinical MMPI-2-RF scores. Substantially increased risk for various negative outcomes was found using cutoffs of 45T and 50T. For example, officers scoring at or above 50T on the Cognitive Complaints (COG) scale were at twice the risk for experiencing multitasking problems under stress when compared with those who scored below 50T on this scale.

Tarescavage, Corey, Gupton, and Ben-Porath (2015) used essentially the same methodology as the one just described in the Tarescavage, Corey, and Ben-Porath (2015) study to examine the predictive validity of MMPI-2-RF scores of 145 male police officers employed by the Honolulu Police Department. Here, too, the sample of hired police officers produced mean scores and standard deviations that were substantially lower than those found in the general population. After correcting for range restriction, scores on scales from all the domains assessed by the MMPI-2-RF were correlated with various negative outcomes with medium to large effect sizes. In the emotional domain, some of the strongest correlations were found between scores on RC2 and problems in the areas of emotional control and stress, routine task performance, decision making and judgment, and social competence and teamwork. Higher scores on scales in the thought dysfunction domain were correlated with learning problems, navigation problems, radio operation difficulties, and problems with multitasking. As was the case in the study by Tarescavage, Corey, and Ben-Porath (2015), scores in the externalizing domain were negatively correlated with a number of variables (assertiveness, social competence and teamwork, and interpersonal problems), indicating that particularly low scores on these scales are associated with negative outcomes. Scores on the MMPI-2-RF measures of interpersonal functioning were also correlated with a number of negative outcomes.

Relative risk ratio analyses were conducted to identify the increase in risk for negative outcomes associated with various MMPI-2-RF scale cutoffs. Overall, these analyses pointed to significantly increased risk for a host of negative outcomes associated with cutoffs ranging from 45T to 65T. For example, compared with individuals who scored below this cutoff, those who scored 45T or higher on RC1 were at 8.67 times higher risk for being rated by their supervisors as having difficulties restraining and controlling subjects under stressful conditions.

Tarescavage, Corey, and Ben-Porath (2016) used the archival data set collected by Boes and colleagues (1997), described earlier in the context of a study of the ability of pre-hire MMPI scores to predict police officers' future serious integrity violations. These authors surveyed more than 2,000 police departments throughout the United States, seeking to locate officers with one of 10 prespecified integrity violations that resulted in termination. They identified 439 officers with at least one of the 10 designated violations and matched them with 439 officers of the same gender, age, and length of employment who did not have any of the designated violations. These officers were employed by 69 agencies in 29 states spread throughout the country, including departments in the Northeast, South, Midwest, Southwest, and West (Boes et al., 1997).

A potential confound in the Boes et al. (1997) study design was that approximately one-third of the nonviolator group had a history of disciplinary infractions that were less serious than the integrity violations that were the focus of the study. The infractions included misconduct such as alcohol abuse, firearms misuse, use of excessive force, falsification of time worked, failure to appear for court testimony, and supervisory problems. In fact, the authors reported that for the entire sample, such subthreshold violations were the best predictors of the more serious subsequent integrity violations. Consequently, this subsample was not optimal as a nonviolating contrast group.

Tarescavage, Corey, and Ben-Porath (2016) analyzed this data set, which included information about all violations as well as responses to the 550 original MMPI items, to examine whether the psychometric refinements introduced with the MMPI-2-RF scales and elimination of the confound just discussed would result in improved prediction of integrity violations. After removal of invalid protocols and data for 40 female police officers, the sample studied by Tarescavage et al. (2016) included 417 male officers. The first task was to determine whether it is possible to score the MMPI-2-RF from the original MMPI, which contains 274 of the 338 items of the restructured instrument (the remaining items were added to the MMPI-2). The authors estimated MMPI-2-RF raw scores for scales that were missing items by prorating based on the remaining items. To examine the fidelity of the prorated scores, a similar procedure was applied to three MMPI-2 samples, and the resulting estimated and actual T-scores were compared, yielding correlations of .90 or higher for 44 of the 51 MMPI-2-RF scales. The remaining seven scales were excluded from further analyses. The prorated raw scores for the 44 scales were then converted to MMPI-2-RF T-scores. In the three samples used to test the fidelity of the estimation procedure, prorated T-scores for the scales included in the investigation were all within 2 T-score points of the actual scale scores.

The first analysis reported by Tarescavage and colleagues (2016) involved a comparison of the MMPI-2-RF mean T-scores and associated standard deviations for the Boes et al. (1997) sample and those of the 1,037 men included in the Police Officer Candidate comparison group (discussed in the next section). Mean T-scores for the two samples were quite similar, with the vast majority falling within 1 or 2 points of each other and only one comparison (for TRIN-r) exceeding 5 T-score points, the benchmark used typically to identify an interpretable difference (Graham, 2012). The remarkable similarity between the Boes et al. sample and the MMPI-2-RF Police Officer Candidate comparison group bolsters substantially the likelihood that the predictive analyses discussed next generalize to the MMPI-2-RF.

To examine the predictive validity of MMPI-2-RF scores, Tarescavage et al. (2016) identified a subsample of 161 officers who had not committed any of the integrity violations or other disciplinary infractions just discussed and contrasted their scores with those of individuals who committed each violation and infraction. Following the procedures of Sellbom and colleagues (2007) described earlier in this chapter, the authors calculated uncorrected and range restriction–corrected correlations between the pre-hire MMPI-2-RF scores and post-hire violations and infractions.

Scores on several MMPI-2-RF substantive scales were meaningfully correlated (with corrected correlations typically of a small to medium effect size) with future integrity violations and disciplinary infractions. Scales from the emotional, thought, and behavioral domains were positively associated with use of excessive force, supervisory problems, substandard work performance, conduct unbecoming, procedural violations, private use of equipment, failure to attend court, embezzlement/fraud, accidents, dropping cases inappropriately, and off-duty violations.

As is the case with all of the samples used in the studies described in this section, the correlations just mentioned reflect, by and large, variance that occurs below 65T. To examine the potential utility of lower cutoffs, Tarescavage and colleagues (2016) conducted relative risk ratio analyses and reported finding a substantially increased risk for integrity violations and disciplinary infractions associated with cutoffs ranging from 45T to 60T. For example, of the officers who had a T-score at or above 55T on RC4, 28.6% were subsequently disciplined for conduct unbecoming, compared with only 8.8% of those who scored below 55T on this scale, which produces a relative risk ratio of 3.3, indicating a threefold increase in the risk for misconduct in candidates who scored at or above 55T on RC4.

Tarescavage, Fischler, et al. (2015) reported descriptive findings and correlations between pre-hire MMPI-2-RF scores and selected scales from the California Psychological Inventory (CPI; Gough, 1956) and the IPI (described earlier in the study by Detrick et al., 2016) for a sample of 588 male and 124 female police candidates from two Midwestern states, as well as correlations with outcome data for 426 of the male candidates who were subsequently hired. The men in this sample were a subset of those included in the MMPI-2 study reported by Sellbom et al. (2007) discussed earlier. Tarescavage, Fischler, and colleagues augmented the sample used in the earlier study with one obtained in a different state using the same methodology (supervisor ratings obtained after the officer had been employed for several years), and they reported findings for the full range of MMPI-2-RF substantive scales, whereas Sellbom and colleagues reported only limited findings for the RC Scales.

Descriptive analyses indicated that the male and female candidates produced very similar means and standard deviations on the MMPI-2-RF scales, with the exception that men who were hired scored approximately 5 T-score points higher on the DISC-r scale than women who were hired. Both genders produced generally lower means and standard deviations on the substantive scales when compared with the men and women in the MMPI-2-RF normative samples.

Correlations between pre-hire MMPI-2-RF and CPI scores were reported for the female candidates. The CPI scales examined in this investigation included special measures developed by Roberts and Johnson (2001) for police candidate evaluations. Several sizable associations were found between females' MMPI-2-RF scores and the special CPI scale indexes. For example, RC7 scores were substantially correlated with a CPI composite predicting a self-reported history of job performance problems; RC1, RC7, MLS, and HPC scores were associated with an index predicting increased risk of being rated poorly by the evaluating psychologist; and RCd, RC3, RC6, and BRF scores were correlated with an indicator of increased risk for being fired for cause. Scores on several externalizing scales also were correlated with a wide range of CPI risk indicators. Of note is that the vast majority of women included in this study scored below 65T on most MMPI-2-RF scales, indicating that, as is the case with male candidates, subclinical deviations from the Police Officer Candidate comparison group mean are associated with a wide range of risk factors in female candidates.

Male candidates produced similar (to the females) patterns of correlations with the CPI risk indicators. Correlations between MMPI-2-RF scales and scores on the IPI were generally consistent with those reported by Detrick et al. (2016) for a different sample. Scores on the MMPI-2-RF measures of emotional dysfunction were substantially correlated with IPI measures of anxiety, phobic personality, and depression. Externalizing dysfunction scores were correlated with IPI measures of substance abuse, antisocial attitudes, hyperactivity, and lack of assertiveness. Measures of interpersonal functioning were associated with antisocial attitudes, lack of assertiveness, and sexual concerns.

In the subset of men for whom outcome data were available, higher scores on the substantive scales were associated substantially with a broad range of negative outcomes. For example, higher pre-hire MMPI-2-RF scores on emotional dysfunction measures were correlated with subsequent complaints from members of the public, use of excessive force and inappropriate language, and poor ethics. Scores on the thought dysfunction measures were associated with outcomes such as deceptive behavior, rude behavior, being uncooperative toward peers, missing court appearances, and being fired for cause. Behavioral dysfunction measures were correlated with sustained internal affairs complaints, missing court appearances, and poor response to feedback. Interpersonal functioning measures were correlated with outcomes such as inappropriate sexual attitudes, conduct unbecoming, and poor integrity ratings.

As in several of the previously discussed studies, relative risk ratios were calculated to assist in quantifying the increased risk associated with various subclinical MMPI-2-RF scale-score cutoffs. These analyses demonstrated substantially increased risk for various outcomes associated with cutoffs ranging from 45T to 65T, as well as for low scores on some scales and clinically elevated scores on most substantive scales.

Summary of MMPI-2-RF Findings

The studies just described provide a sound empirical foundation for using the MMPI-2-RF in assessments of police officer candidates. The job-relevant correlates included in the interpretive guidelines provided later in this chapter and in Appendix A are based on a distillation of the findings just reviewed, incorporating ones that were replicated across samples, criteria, and settings. This research also demonstrates the relevance and utility of using the MMPI-2-RF in preemployment evaluations of police candidates, establishing that the inventory meets federal and state legal and regulatory requirements for use of psychological tests that can predict relevant outcomes in such assessments. Several general conclusions can be drawn about assessing police candidates with the MMPI-2-RF.

Each of the studies just reviewed provided descriptive findings for the MMPI-2-RF substantive scales. The reported means and standard deviations were remarkably consistent across studies, including the investigation conducted by Tarescavage et al. (2016) that used a data set compiled mainly in the 1980s with the original MMPI. This consistency points to the stability of police candidate psychological characteristics over time and across geographic regions. Moreover, descriptive findings reported by the various authors were also quite similar to the means and standard deviations on the 51 MMPI-2-RF scales in the 2,074-member Police Officer Candidate comparison group discussed in the next section.

Of particular note, in light of the relative paucity of data available for female police candidates and officers, similarities between male and female mean scores and standard deviations on the MMPI-2-RF scales reported by Tarescavage, Fischler, et al. (2015) and in the comparison group just mentioned indicate that outcome findings with the male samples can reasonably be generalized to female candidates. This is further supported by the comparability of correlations between MMPI-2-RF scores and specialized CPI scales designed to predict various risks associated with hiring police candidates.

The six samples used in the MMPI-2-RF substantive scales validation studies varied in terms of their ethnic and racial group composition, which was generally consistent with demographic characteristics of the populations in the geographic regions where the data were collected. The most diverse samples were available in the studies by Detrick et al. (2016); Tarescavage et al. (2016); and Tarescavage, Corey, Gupton, and Ben-Porath (2015). As just noted, all of the study samples had very similar MMPI-2-RF scores. In addition, there was considerable convergence in the empirical correlates found in these investigations. Along with a long line of research documenting the cross-cultural generalizability of MMPI findings (summarized by Graham, 2012), these results support use of the MMPI-2-RF with members of diverse racial and ethnic groups.

The MMPI-2-RF Police Candidate Comparison Group

MMPI-2-RF results for a sample of 2,074 police officer candidates (the Police Officer Candidate comparison group) are described and discussed in this section. This sample replaced the 674-member Law Enforcement Candidate comparison group, which was among the comparison groups included in the MMPI-2-RF manual (Tellegen & Ben-Porath, 2008/2011; Appendix D) and the MMPI-2-RF *User's Guide for Reports*, second edition (Ben-Porath & Tellegen, 2011). The original comparison group consisted entirely of a sample of California Highway Patrol candidates assessed throughout the state. For the expanded comparison group we included MMPI-2-RF and MMPI-2 (converted to the MMPI-2-RF) protocols of police candidates from various regions throughout North America.

Group Composition

The Police Officer Candidate comparison group is made up of 1,037 females and 1,037 males. Inclusion of an equal number of men and women, which, as discussed earlier, does not accurately represent the gender distribution of entry-level police officers, was designed to allow for use of a single, nongendered comparison group to conform to the prohibition against using gender-based norms in employment-related testing mandated in the Civil Rights Act of 1991, as discussed in chapter 5.

The geographic origins of the 2,074 members of the Police Officer Candidate comparison group are listed in Table 6-1. The sample consists of police candidates from four regions and includes individuals assessed for entry-level police officer positions in ethnically heterogeneous urban areas as well as more rural communities throughout various geographic regions of the United States and one in Canada. Agreements with some of the agencies that provided these expanded comparison group data preclude listing them by name. Because in some agencies race/ethnicity data were not recorded for individual protocols, we are unable to provide a specific breakdown of this variable. Nevertheless, based on available information about the race/ethnicity makeup of the agencies for which these individuals were assessed, we can conclude that the Police Officer Candidate comparison group adequately represents the population of individuals assessed for a broad range of entry-level law enforcement positions in North America.

TABLE 6-1
Geographic Distribution of the Police Officer, Firefighter/Paramedic, Correctional Officer, and Dispatcher Candidate Comparison Groups

Region	Men	Women	Total
Police Officer Candidate Comparison Group			
Midwest	131	131	262
Northeast and Canada Pacific	165	165	330
Pacific	136	136	272
South	224	224	448
West and Northwest	381	381	762
TOTAL	1,037	1,037	2,074
Firefighter/Paramedic Candidate Comparison Group			
Midwest	61	61	122
Northeast and Canada Pacific	29	29	58
South	—	—	—
West and Northwest	95	95	190
TOTAL	185	185	370
Correctional Officer Candidate Comparison Group			
Midwest	—	—	—
Northeast and Canada Pacific	—	—	—
South	—	—	—
West and Northwest	1,518	1,518	3,036
TOTAL	1,518	1,518	3,036
Dispatcher Candidate Comparison Group			
Midwest	31	31	62
Northeast and Canada Pacific	—	—	—
South	12	12	24
West and Northwest	147	147	294
TOTAL	190	190	380

Table 6-2 provides descriptive statistics for age and years of education of members of the Police Officer Candidate comparison group. The mean age for members of both genders was roughly 27 years, and both had completed an average of just over 14 years of education. Consistent with our just-noted inference that the Police Officer Candidate sample matches the population of recruits demographically, these statistics match reported averages in 44 police agencies randomly selected from the 91 largest municipal law enforcement agencies in the United States, in which the mean age for new police officers is 27.4 years, with a mean of 14.3 years of education (Castaneda & Ridgeway, 2010).

TABLE 6-2
Available Demographics for the Police Officer, Firefighter/Paramedic, Correctional Officer, and Dispatcher Candidate Comparison Groups

	N	Age Mean (SD)	Years of Education Mean (SD)
Police Officer Candidate Comparison Group			
Men	1,037	27.2 (5.8)	14.4 (2.6)
Women	1,037	27.2 (6.3)	14.5 (2.9)
Total	2,074	27.2 (6.1)	14.4 (2.7)
Firefighter/Paramedic Candidate Comparison Group			
Men	185	28.7 (6.8)	n/a
Women	185	29.9 (6.6)	n/a
Total	370	29.3 (6.9)	n/a
Correctional Officer Candidate Comparison Group			
Men	1,518	30.8 (8.8)	13.5 (2.4)
Women	1,518	31.4 (8.4)	14.2 (2.6)
Total	3,036	31.0 (8.6)	13.8 (2.5)
Dispatcher Candidate Comparison Group			
Men	190	30.2 (8.2)	14.1 (3.3)
Women	190	31.4 (8.5)	14.1 (4.2)
Total	380	30.8 (8.3)	14.1 (3.8)

Comparison Group Findings

Means and standard deviations of the 51 MMPI-2-RF scales for the Police Officer Candidate comparison group are reported in Table 6-3. As discussed earlier, these data reflect substantially below-average means (compared with general population norms) on nearly all of the substantive scales and most of the validity scales of the inventory. Standard deviations associated with these means show markedly reduced variability compared with the general population norms, which is also discussed earlier in this chapter. These findings, coupled with the MMPI-2-RF research results reviewed earlier, indicate the need for, and utility of, using lower than the traditional T-score 65 cutoff when assessing police candidates with the inventory.

Table 6-4 reports the percent of Police Officer Candidate comparison group members who score at or below various T-score cutoffs. As depicted in this table, T-scores greater than 65 on the inconsistent

TABLE 6-3
Means and Standard Deviations for the Police Officer, Firefighter/Paramedic, Correctional Officer, and Dispatcher Candidate Comparison Groups

	Police Officer (N=2,074)		Firefighter/ Paramedic (N=370)		Correctional Officer (N=3,036)		Dispatcher (N=380)	
	M	SD	M	SD	M	SD	M	SD
VRIN-r	41	7	40	6	43	8	42	7
TRIN-r	52F	6	52F	5	52F	7	53F	6
F-r	44	4	43	2	45	4	44	4
Fp-r	45	5	44	4	46	6	45	5
Fs	45	6	44	5	46	6	46	7
FBS-r	46	6	48	6	46	6	49	7
RBS	46	7	46	6	46	7	48	7
L-r	59	13	58	14	60	13	61	13
K-r	63	8	66	7	61	8	63	8
EID	36	6	35	5	38	7	37	7
THD	44	7	42	6	45	7	43	7
BXD	46	7	44	7	46	8	43	7
RCd	40	5	39	4	41	6	41	6
RC1	42	7	41	6	44	7	44	7
RC2	41	6	40	6	42	7	42	8
RC3	44	10	40	7	47	10	42	8
RC4	45	7	42	7	45	7	43	7
RC6	47	7	45	6	47	8	46	6
RC7	38	6	37	5	39	6	39	6
RC8	44	7	43	6	44	7	44	8
RC9	43	8	41	7	43	8	41	7
MLS	42	6	41	5	44	7	44	7
GIC	46	4	46	3	47	5	47	6
HPC	44	6	43	4	45	6	45	6
NUC	46	7	45	6	46	8	47	8
COG	43	5	42	5	44	6	43	6
SUI	46	2	45	1	46	2	46	2
HLP	42	4	41	3	43	5	42	5
SFD	43	4	43	3	44	5	44	5
NFC	41	6	40	5	43	7	41	6
STW	41	6	41	6	43	7	43	7
AXY	45	4	44	2	45	5	45	4
ANP	41	5	40	4	41	6	41	4
BRF	44	5	44	4	45	6	45	6
MSF	45	8	43	6	47	8	46	8
JCP	48	9	45	7	49	9	45	7
SUB	45	6	44	5	44	5	44	5

	Police Officer (N=2,074)		Firefighter/ Paramedic (N=370)		Correctional Officer (N=3,036)		Dispatcher (N=380)	
	M	SD	M	SD	M	SD	M	SD
AGG	42	6	40	6	43	7	41	5
ACT	44	9	44	9	44	9	44	10
FML	43	7	42	7	44	7	43	7
IPP	46	6	48	6	47	7	48	8
SAV	46	8	45	7	47	8	48	9
SHY	41	6	40	5	43	7	42	7
DSF	46	5	45	4	46	6	46	6
AES	42	8	41	8	41	8	46	9
MEC	56	11	60	10	54	11	53	11
AGGR-r	51	7	49	6	51	7	49	7
PSYC-r	44	7	42	6	45	8	43	7
DISC-r	50	8	49	6	48	8	46	7
NEGE-r	39	6	38	6	41	7	40	7
INTR-r	47	7	46	7	48	8	48	9

response (VRIN-r and TRIN-r) and overreporting (F-r, Fp-r, Fs, FBS-r, and RBS) Validity Scales are extremely rare in police candidates. This is not the case with the MMPI-2-RF underreporting indicators, as would be expected in light of the demand characteristics of these assessments. L-r T-scores that exceed 80 are relatively uncommon; however, a K-r T-score above 70 occurs in 17.6% of law enforcement candidates. Elevation rates for substantive scale cutoffs are provided beginning at T-score 55. As reported in Table 6-3, scores at this level often fall more than two standard deviations above the comparison group mean. This is particularly true for MMPI-2-RF measures of emotional dysfunction. For example, T-scores of 55 or higher on Emotional/Internalizing Dysfunction (EID) occur in less than 1% of police candidates. Clinically elevated T-scores (at or above 65) are extremely rare for all substantive scales. By and large, less than 10% of Police Officer Candidate comparison group members score at or above 60T on the MMPI-2-RF substantive scales.

As just noted, the percent of comparison group members scoring at or above cutoffs typically used with the underreporting scales is relatively high. This reflects the high base rate for underreporting in preemployment

TABLE 6-4

Elevation Rates for the Police Officer (LEO; N = 2,074), Firefighter/Paramedic (FF/PM; N = 370), Correctional Officer (CO; N = 3,036), and Dispatcher (DISP; N = 380) Candidate Comparison Groups

Scale	Cutoff	LEO	FF/PM	CO	DISP
VRIN-r	75T	0.0	0.0	0.2	0.0
VRIN-r	70T	0.1	0.0	0.5	0.0
VRIN-r	65T	0.4	0.3	1.1	0.3
VRIN-r	60T	1.4	0.5	2.8	0.8
VRIN-r	55T	3.4	2.7	7.2	5.5
TRIN-r	70T	0.8	0.5	1.7	1.1
TRIN-r	65T	5.2	6.8	10.1	8.7
TRIN-r	60T	5.2	6.8	10.1	8.7
TRIN-r	55T	28.5	38.1	45.4	46.6
F-r	85T	0.0	0.0	0.1	0.0
F-r	80T	0.0	0.0	0.1	0.0
F-r	75T	0.1	0.0	0.3	0.0
F-r	70T	0.4	0.0	0.4	0.0
F-r	65T	0.7	0.0	0.9	0.5
F-r	60T	1.1	0.0	1.7	1.1
F-r	55T	2.2	0.5	4.3	3.7
Fp-r	85T	0.0	0.0	0.1	0.0
Fp-r	80T	0.0	0.0	0.1	0.0
Fp-r	75T	0.1	0.0	0.5	0.0
Fp-r	70T	0.1	0.0	0.5	0.0
Fp-r	65T	1.1	0.3	1.4	0.8
Fp-r	60T	1.1	0.3	1.4	0.8
Fp-r	55T	3.8	1.1	6.8	6.6
Fs	90T	0.1	0.0	0.0	0.3
Fs	85T	0.1	0.0	0.0	0.3
Fs	80T	0.2	0.0	0.1	0.5
Fs	75T	0.2	0.0	0.1	0.5
Fs	70T	1.0	0.0	0.6	1.3
Fs	65T	2.7	0.8	2.5	3.4
Fs	60T	2.7	0.8	2.5	3.4
Fs	55T	7.7	4.9	9.9	9.7
FBS-r	80T	0.0	0.0	0.1	0.0
FBS-r	75T	0.1	0.0	0.1	0.0
FBS-r	70T	0.1	0.0	0.1	0.5
FBS-r	65T	0.2	0.0	0.3	1.3
FBS-r	60T	1.4	2.2	1.6	3.7
FBS-r	55T	3.8	5.1	5.0	8.9
RBS	75T	0.1	0.0	0.0	0.0
RBS	70T	0.5	0.0	0.2	0.3
RBS	65T	0.7	0.0	0.6	0.8
RBS	60T	2.7	0.5	2.4	3.4
RBS	55T	7.4	5.9	7.5	8.9

Scale	Cutoff	LEO	FF/PM	CO	DISP
L-r	90T	2.6	2.7	2.8	3.7
L-r	85T	5.8	5.1	6.2	7.1
L-r	80T	10.1	9.2	10.3	10.5
L-r	75T	15.9	14.6	16.6	18.2
L-r	70T	22.8	20.8	24.0	27.1
L-r	65T	32.6	29.5	34.2	36.8
L-r	60T	45.0	42.2	46.9	49.5
L-r	55T	59.5	52.7	62.4	63.7
K-r	70T	17.6	27.8	13.7	18.4
K-r	65T	53.5	65.4	43.7	55.3
K-r	60T	67.3	77.8	57.8	66.1
K-r	55T	87.6	94.6	81.9	87.4
EID	70T	0.0	0.0	0.1	0.0
EID	65T	0.1	0.0	0.3	0.3
EID	60T	0.3	0.0	0.9	0.3
EID	55T	0.9	0.3	2.3	1.3
THD	70T	0.5	0.0	0.6	0.5
THD	65T	0.7	0.3	1.4	1.1
THD	60T	3.8	1.4	4.6	3.7
THD	55T	8.7	4.3	10.5	9.5
BXD	70T	0.4	0.0	0.3	0.0
BXD	65T	1.1	0.3	1.5	0.5
BXD	60T	4.4	2.4	4.7	1.3
BXD	55T	12.2	7.3	13.7	4.7
RCd	70T	0.0	0.0	0.2	0.0
RCd	65T	0.1	0.0	0.5	0.0
RCd	60T	0.5	0.3	1.0	0.8
RCd	55T	1.3	0.5	2.7	1.1
RC1	70T	0.3	0.0	0.1	0.3
RC1	65T	0.6	0.0	0.7	1.1
RC1	60T	1.7	0.5	2.5	3.7
RC1	55T	4.9	1.6	8.0	8.2
RC2	70T	0.0	0.3	0.2	0.5
RC2	65T	0.2	0.3	1.1	1.1
RC2	60T	0.9	1.1	2.2	2.6
RC2	55T	2.7	1.1	4.8	4.5
RC3	70T	3.2	0.5	4.5	1.6
RC3	65T	4.4	0.5	7.6	3.2
RC3	60T	8.0	1.6	11.9	4.5
RC3	55T	12.2	3.0	17.9	6.3
RC4	70T	0.5	0.0	0.3	0.0
RC4	65T	1.6	0.3	1.4	1.3
RC4	60T	2.5	1.4	2.5	1.3
RC4	55T	6.8	3.5	8.7	5.0
RC6	70T	1.5	0.3	1.4	0.8
RC6	65T	3.1	1.4	3.3	1.8

TABLE 6-4 (continued)

Scale	Cutoff	LEO	FF/PM	CO	DISP
RC6	60T	6.9	5.7	8.7	5.0
RC6	55T	24.6	16.5	28.2	18.7
RC7	70T	0.0	0.0	0.3	0.0
RC7	65T	0.3	0.0	0.6	0.5
RC7	60T	0.9	0.0	1.4	0.8
RC7	55T	1.9	0.8	2.7	1.6
RC8	70T	0.9	0.0	0.6	1.3
RC8	65T	1.8	0.3	1.1	2.9
RC8	60T	3.0	1.4	2.4	3.4
RC8	55T	10.6	8.1	11.3	9.5
RC9	70T	0.4	0.0	0.6	0.0
RC9	65T	1.4	0.3	1.5	0.0
RC9	60T	3.1	3.0	3.8	2.1
RC9	55T	7.4	4.1	7.9	4.5
MLS	70T	0.1	0.0	0.0	0.3
MLS	65T	0.3	0.0	0.8	0.8
MLS	60T	0.9	0.5	2.0	2.6
MLS	55T	3.7	1.6	7.6	7.1
GIC	70T	0.8	0.0	1.5	1.6
GIC	65T	0.8	0.0	1.5	1.6
GIC	60T	4.5	2.4	6.1	6.8
GIC	55T	4.5	2.4	6.1	6.8
HPC	70T	0.4	0.0	0.4	0.5
HPC	65T	1.3	0.5	1.9	1.8
HPC	60T	1.3	0.5	1.9	1.8
HPC	55T	4.9	2.2	6.5	7.6
NUC	70T	0.6	0.5	1.2	2.6
NUC	65T	2.1	1.1	3.6	5.3
NUC	60T	2.1	1.1	3.6	5.3
NUC	55T	9.6	7.0	11.7	12.4
COG	70T	0.1	0.0	0.2	0.3
COG	65T	0.2	0.3	0.4	0.5
COG	60T	1.2	0.3	1.2	1.3
COG	55T	3.0	2.4	3.7	3.9
SUI	70T	0.0	0.0	0.1	0.0
SUI	65T	0.7	0.3	1.2	1.1
SUI	60T	0.7	0.3	1.2	1.1
SUI	55T	0.7	0.3	1.2	1.1
HLP	70T	0.0	0.0	0.0	0.0
HLP	65T	0.1	0.0	0.3	0.0
HLP	60T	1.2	0.0	3.0	2.4

Scale	Cutoff	LEO	FF/PM	CO	DISP
HLP	55T	1.2	0.0	3.0	2.4
SFD	70T	0.0	0.0	0.6	0.5
SFD	65T	0.9	0.3	1.7	0.8
SFD	60T	0.9	0.3	1.7	0.8
SFD	55T	2.8	3.0	4.8	5.3
NFC	70T	0.0	0.0	0.3	0.0
NFC	65T	0.2	0.0	0.9	0.3
NFC	60T	1.1	0.0	1.7	1.6
NFC	55T	2.3	0.5	3.7	3.2
STW	70T	0.2	0.3	0.4	0.8
STW	65T	0.8	0.8	2.0	2.1
STW	60T	0.8	0.8	2.0	2.1
STW	55T	3.2	3.0	5.8	6.6
AXY	70T	1.0	0.0	1.4	1.1
AXY	65T	1.0	0.0	1.4	1.1
AXY	60T	1.0	0.0	1.4	1.1
AXY	55T	6.4	2.7	8.3	6.3
ANP	70T	0.3	0.0	0.6	0.0
ANP	65T	0.7	0.8	1.3	0.3
ANP	60T	0.7	0.8	1.3	0.3
ANP	55T	1.2	0.8	2.5	0.8
BRF	70T	0.3	0.3	1.0	0.5
BRF	65T	0.3	0.3	1.0	0.5
BRF	60T	2.1	1.1	3.4	2.9
BRF	55T	11.8	7.3	17.9	17.1
MSF	70T	1.5	0.0	1.4	2.1
MSF	65T	3.0	0.0	5.4	4.5
MSF	60T	3.0	0.0	5.4	4.5
MSF	55T	7.5	1.9	11.1	8.7
JCP	70T	3.8	1.1	3.7	1.6
JCP	65T	3.8	1.1	3.7	1.6
JCP	60T	10.4	3.0	11.6	3.4
JCP	55T	24.4	14.1	25.6	14.7
SUB	70T	0.0	0.0	0.1	0.0
SUB	65T	0.3	0.0	0.4	0.0
SUB	60T	1.9	1.6	1.8	1.8
SUB	55T	9.9	9.7	6.9	8.9
AGG	70T	0.1	0.0	0.1	0.0
AGG	65T	0.6	0.3	0.8	0.0
AGG	60T	1.8	1.6	2.8	0.5
AGG	55T	5.1	3.2	7.1	1.8
ACT	70T	0.9	0.5	1.1	1.1
ACT	65T	4.1	3.8	3.3	6.3

TABLE 6-4 (continued)

Scale	Cutoff	LEO	FF/PM	CO	DISP
ACT	60T	4.1	3.8	3.3	6.3
ACT	55T	10.9	9.2	9.5	11.3
FML	70T	0.1	0.3	0.2	0.5
FML	65T	0.5	0.8	0.9	1.1
FML	60T	1.3	1.6	2.8	2.6
FML	55T	4.4	3.5	6.2	5.5
IPP	70T	0.3	0.3	0.6	0.3
IPP	65T	1.2	1.6	2.0	2.9
IPP	60T	3.7	5.4	5.1	9.2
IPP	55T	8.0	12.4	11.4	18.7
SAV	70T	1.6	0.8	2.6	3.9
SAV	65T	4.0	1.9	5.2	6.8
SAV	60T	4.0	1.9	5.2	6.8
SAV	55T	12.3	8.6	14.3	18.2
SHY	70T	0.3	0.0	1.0	1.1
SHY	65T	1.2	0.5	2.9	2.4
SHY	60T	1.2	0.5	2.9	2.4
SHY	55T	2.8	1.9	5.6	4.7
DSF	70T	0.3	0.0	0.5	1.3
DSF	65T	1.7	0.5	2.5	2.6
DSF	60T	1.7	0.5	2.5	2.6
DSF	55T	9.9	7.3	14.1	12.9
AGGR-r	70T	0.5	0.0	0.8	0.5
AGGR-r	65T	6.7	3.5	7.4	3.4
AGGR-r	60T	13.9	8.9	15.1	10.0
AGGR-r	55T	26.8	14.1	27.5	19.2
PSYC-r	70T	0.2	0.0	0.5	0.0
PSYC-r	65T	1.2	0.3	1.4	1.1
PSYC-r	60T	2.6	1.1	3.0	2.9
PSYC-r	55T	9.5	5.9	12.0	9.7
DISC-r	70T	1.2	0.0	1.0	0.3
DISC-r	65T	3.6	2.2	4.2	2.1
DISC-r	60T	7.1	3.5	6.9	3.4
DISC-r	55T	21.2	14.9	17.5	9.2
NEGE-r	70T	0.0	0.0	0.3	0.0
NEGE-r	65T	0.5	0.0	0.7	0.5
NEGE-r	60T	1.0	0.0	1.5	1.3
NEGE-r	55T	2.2	1.4	3.8	3.7
INTR-r	70T	0.6	0.5	1.6	2.4
INTR-r	65T	2.0	0.8	3.1	4.5
INTR-r	60T	7.4	4.3	9.1	12.1
INTR-r	55T	11.3	7.6	14.6	18.4

candidates, as well as the impact of confounds discussed in chapter 3 and earlier in this chapter (i.e., a traditional upbringing for L-r and good adjustment for K-r) in the context of the Detrick and Chibnall (2014) study. In light of these findings we do not recommend applying the standard guidelines to these scales when interpreting police candidates' MMPI-2-RF scores. Concern about the possible deleterious effects of underreporting is indicated if a police candidate's L-r score reaches or exceeds 81T, but particularly in cases where it reaches or exceeds 86T, which occurs in only 5.8% of the Police Officer Candidate comparison group. As reflected in Table 6-4, more than half of police candidates score at or above 65T on K-r, reflecting both the highly preselected (and therefore well-adjusted) nature of this population and the impact of attempting to appear psychologically healthy. As a consequence, only T-scores that reach the highest possible value on this scale (72) can be viewed as indicating a *possibility* of significant underreporting.

Interpretive Guidelines for Police Candidates

Interpretive guidelines for use with police candidates, incorporating the research and comparison group findings reviewed in this chapter, are presented in Tables A-1 through A-50 of Appendix A. Tables A-1 through A-10 provide guidelines for interpreting scores on Cannot Say and the nine MMPI-2-RF Validity Scales, and Tables A-11 through A-50 include guidelines for interpreting candidates' scores on the substantive scales. It is important to note that these guidelines are intended to supplement the ones included in the *MMPI-2-RF Manual for Administration, Scoring and Interpretation* (Ben-Porath & Tellegen, 2008/2011). However, if a different cutoff for the same interpretation is listed in an Appendix A table, it should be used rather than the one listed in the test manual. For example, for reasons discussed next, Table A-9 provides substantially different cutoffs for interpreting L-r than does Table 5-10 of the test manual. When using the MMPI-2-RF as part of a preemployment assessment, the guidelines included in Table A-9 should be applied. In this section, we highlight and discuss some of the unique features of the guidelines provided in Tables A-1 through A-50. Use of the guidelines is illustrated with case studies in chapter 8.

Validity Scales

Table A-1 recommends a much lower cutoff for identifying problematic unscorable responding based on the Cannot Say count (a raw score of 5) than is found in the parallel MMPI-2 manual table (5-2). This is because unscorable responses are extremely rare among police candidates. As indicated in Table A-1, less than 1% of the MMPI-2-RF Police Officer Candidate comparison group provides five or more unscorable responses. Tables A-2 and A-3 indicate that, although not necessarily invalidating the protocol, T-scores in the 70–79 range on VRIN-r and TRIN-r are similarly rare among police candidates, and they raise concerns about a careless test-taking approach, which is quite unexpected in this setting. T-scores of 80 or above on these scales, which do invalidate the protocol, do not occur in the Police Officer Candidate comparison group. Interpretive guidelines for the five overreporting scales (Tables A-4 through A-8) indicate the rarity of this test-taking approach among police candidates.

Reflecting the demand characteristics of preemployment evaluations, underreporting is the most common threat to protocol validity. Consequently the interpretive guidelines for the MMPI-2-RF underreporting scales are more elaborate than the ones included in the test manual. For L-r, the highest cutoff included in the test manual (Table 5-10) is T-score 80, which is very uncommon in the general population. However, as indicated in Table A-9, just over 10% of the MMPI-2-RF Police Officer Candidate comparison group members score 81T or above on this scale. Information about the rate at which comparison group members produce T-scores of 86 (5.8%), 91 (2.6%), 95 (1.1%), 100 (0.1%), and 105 (none) on L-r is included in the guidelines for these cutoffs, along with interpretive implications that include consideration of potential confounds discussed in chapter 3, which for L-r involves a traditional upbringing. Of note in this context is that in clinical settings consideration should be given to the possibility that a protocol is invalid when L-r ≥ 80T. However, in preemployment evaluations of highly selected candidates, users should consider the asymmetrical impact of underreporting (i.e., that nonelevated scores on the substantive scales cannot be interpreted as indicating the absence of problems assessed by those scales, whereas elevated scores can be interpreted as indicating the presence of problems, but possibly underestimating their magnitude), rather than deeming a protocol invalid on the basis of an elevated L-r score. Finally, although a small number of studies has reported associations between L or L-r scores and adverse outcomes in law enforcement candidates, for both conceptual and empirical reasons we do not recommend using validity scales for purposes other than assessing protocol validity threats. Conceptually, validity scales are designed and optimized to measure test-taking approaches, not psychological constructs. Empirically, no adverse outcomes are better predicted by L-r than by MMPI-2-RF substantive scales.

Interpretive guidelines for K-r (Table A-10) reflect how uncommon it is for police candidates to score low on this scale (e.g., 0.1% score 31 or lower on K-r and less than 4% score 45 or below on this scale). Conversely, owing to the confound of good adjustment discussed in chapter 3 and the preselection processes discussed earlier in this chapter, elevated K-r T-scores that in other settings would very likely reflect underreporting (e.g., 69) are common in this population. Indeed 17.6% of the comparison group produced the highest possible K-r T-score, 72.

Substantive Scales

Interpretive guidelines for the MMPI-2-RF substantive scales are provided in Tables A-11 through A-50, with the exception of the Interest Scales, which we do not recommend interpreting in this or other public safety settings. The guidelines listed in these tables supplement the ones included in the parallel test manual tables, which need to be consulted in any case where a substantive scale score reaches clinically significant elevation (i.e., T-score 65 or higher) in order to obtain the relevant clinically focused findings that apply in any setting. The appendix tables list police candidate–specific implications of clinically elevated scores in addition to providing interpretive guidelines for lower cutoffs associated with adverse outcomes in police candidates.

The guidelines listed in Tables A-11 through A-50 include recommendations for interpreting substantive scale scores that fall below, sometimes well below, 65T. This represents a significant change from past MMPI practice in the assessment of public safety candidates or for test users accustomed to clinical assessments. This change can be somewhat "disorienting," particularly for experienced clinicians. The empirical findings that support and have guided our development of these recommendations were reviewed in detail earlier in this chapter. They include both comparison group findings and job-relevant correlates. Use of these guidelines is illustrated in chapter 8, and they have also been incorporated in the MMPI-2-RF Police Candidate Interpretive Report, described in chapter 7.

The substantive scale interpretive guidelines include two general types of statements that can be found, as an example, in Table A-11 for the Emotional/Internalizing Dysfunction (EID) scale. Statements under the heading "Comparison Group Findings" are construct-based in the sense that they describe potential problems on the basis of the construct assessed by a given substantive scale. In most cases, two types of statements are included under this heading, one for scores that are not clinically elevated but nevertheless are uncommon among police candidates (occurring in 5% of comparison group members or less), and another for clinically elevated scores. In Table A-11, the nonclinically elevated statement listed for T-scores 54–64 reads,

> *The test taker reports a comparatively large number of emotional problems for a police officer candidate.*

As seen in Table 6-4, only .9% of the Police Officer Candidate comparison group members score 55 or higher on EID; although not depicted in Table 6–4, another .2% score at 54T.

The statement associated with a clinically significant elevation on this scale reflects the greater concern associated with producing a clinically significant elevation on EID:

> *The test taker's responses indicate a level of emotional distress that may be incompatible with public safety requirements for good emotional adjustment. This level of emotional distress is very uncommon among police officer candidates.*

As seen in Table 6-4, only 0.1% of comparison group members produces a clinically significant EID score.

The second type of substantive scale statements included in the appendix tables appears under the heading "Job-Relevant Correlates." These statements and the recommended cutoffs for applying them are based on a synthesis of the empirical correlates and relative risk ratios reported in the studies described earlier in this chapter. Statements under the subheading "Compared with other police officer candidates the test taker is more likely to:" are based on correlations with other self-report measures obtained in police officer candidate samples that included both individuals who were subsequently hired and those who were not. Statements under the subheading "The test taker is more likely than most police officers or trainees to exhibit difficulties:" are based on correlations with outcome data obtained in samples of hired candidates during academy or field training, probation, and/or the postprobation period. In other words, the set of statements in the first subheading is based on findings concurrent to the preemployment evaluation, whereas those in the second subheading are founded on prospective predictive results. Both types of job-relevant correlates statements can be applied beginning at the T-scores designated in each appendix table. In the case of EID, the designated cutoff for job-relevant correlates is a 56 T-score.

It is not surprising that the most broadly focused MMPI-2-RF substantive scales have the largest and broadest range of job-relevant correlates, whereas the more narrowly focused measures typically have a smaller number and narrower range of correlates. For some scales (e.g., RC1 in Table A-15), no job-relevant correlates are reported because we did not find ones that generalized across studies. For some scales that do have job-relevant correlates (e.g., RC6 in Table A-19), only concurrent correlates are listed because we did not find prospective ones that generalized across studies. For a small number of scales (e.g., RC9 in Table A-22), comparison group findings and job-relevant correlates are listed for low scores found to be associated with adverse outcomes in our empirical studies. Finally, for some scales for which we did not find any empirical correlates (e.g., GIC in Table A-24), comparison group findings are listed only for clinically elevated T-scores.

In the next chapter we discuss and illustrate a process for integrating the interpretive statements listed in Tables A-1 through A-50 in an MMPI-2-RF interpretation and how this may also be accomplished by using the MMPI-2-RF Police Candidate Interpretive Report (PCIR; Corey & Ben-Porath, 2014).

Comparison Group Data for Firefighter/Paramedic, Correctional Officer, and Dispatcher Candidates

Tables 6-3 and 6-4 include comparison group data for the three other public safety candidate groups (firefighters/paramedics, correctional officers, and dispatchers) that are the focus of this guide. As reported in Table 6-1, these samples are smaller (firefighters/paramedics, dispatchers) or less geographically diverse (all three groups) than the Police Officer Candidate comparison group, and so obtaining data on them is more challenging. However, it should be noted that all the samples meet the minimum size (200) required of an MMPI-2-RF comparison group (Ben-Porath & Tellegen, 2011), and we do not find substantial score differences as a function of geographic location in the police candidate sample. Demographically (Table 6-2) the police candidates are somewhat younger than the correctional officer and dispatcher candidates (with the firefighters/paramedics falling in between). Years of education are comparable across groups (though these data are not available for the firefighter/paramedic candidates). The racial/ethnic makeup of the groups is not reported because this information was not systematically recorded in the MMPI data sets made available to us. Based on our familiarity with the catchment areas from which these groups were obtained, the racial/ethnic makeup of each group is fairly comparable, with the exception of the correctional officer sample that likely overrepresents candidates of Hispanic origin.

Table 6-3 includes means and standard deviations on the 51 MMPI-2-RF scales for the four comparison groups. Figures 6-1 through 6-5 provide a visual comparison of the four groups. By convention, group mean differences must reach or exceed 5 T-score points to be considered meaningful. With the exception of the Mechanical Physical Interests (MEC)

FIGURE 6-1 Police Officer, Firefighter/Paramedic, Correctional Officer, and Dispatcher Candidates: MMPI-2-RF Validity Scales

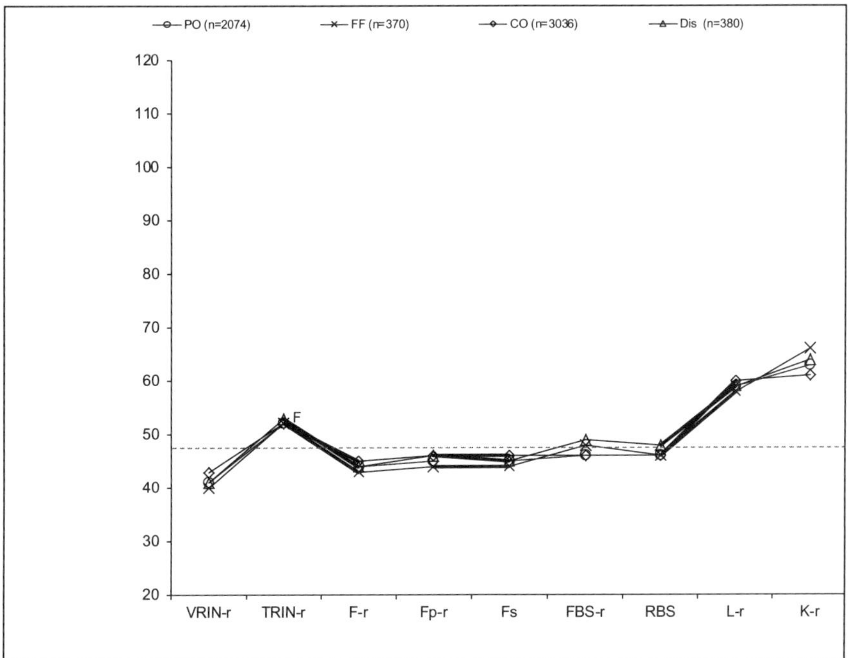

	VRIN-r	TRIN-r	F-r	Fp-r	Fs	FBS-r	RBS	L-r	K-r
Mean - PO	41	52 F	44	45	45	46	46	59	63
Standard Dev	7	6	4	5	6	6	7	13	8
Mean - FF	40	52 F	43	44	44	48	46	58	66
Standard Dev	6	5	2	4	5	6	6	14	7
Mean - CO	43	52 F	45	46	46	46	46	60	61
Standard Dev	8	7	4	6	6	6	7	13	8
Mean - Dis	42	53 F	44	45	46	49	48	61	63
Standard Dev	7	6	4	5	7	7	7	13	8

scale, which, as discussed earlier, along with the Aesthetic Literary Interests (AES) scale, is not recommended for use with public safety candidates, none of the group differences reaches 5 T-score points, and most means fall within 2 to 3 points of each other, with comparable standard deviations. This remarkable similarity across the four comparison groups reflects commonalities in the selection process leading to a conditional offer of employment for all four positions (e.g., passing a background investigation), as well as common demand characteristics to appear well adjusted.

Table 6-4 provides a comparison of elevation rates for the four groups at different MMPI-2-RF scale-score cutoffs. Here, too, the findings are generally quite comparable across groups, although a comparison of elevation rates on K-r indicates that firefighters/paramedics are particularly

FIGURE 6-2 Police Officer, Firefighter/Paramedic, Correctional Officer, and Dispatcher Candidates: MMPI-2-RF Higher-Order (H-O) and Restructured Clinical (RC) Scales

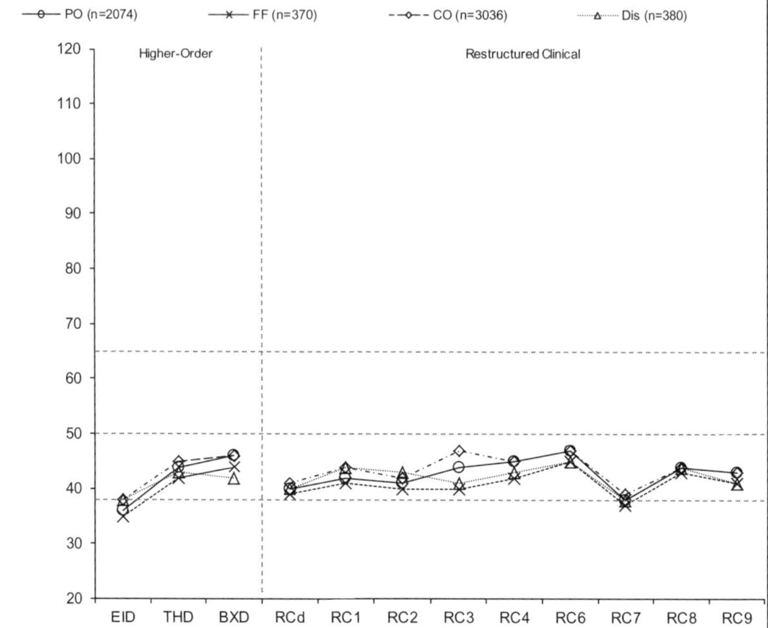

	EID	THD	BXD	RCd	RC1	RC2	RC3	RC4	RC6	RC7	RC8	RC9
Mean - PO	36	44	46	40	42	41	44	45	47	38	44	43
Standard Dev	6	7	7	5	7	6	10	7	7	6	7	8
Mean - FF	35	42	44	39	41	40	40	42	45	37	43	41
Standard Dev	5	6	7	4	6	6	7	7	6	5	6	7
Mean - CO	38	45	46	41	44	42	47	45	47	39	44	43
Standard Dev	7	7	8	6	7	7	10	7	8	6	7	8
Mean - Dis	37	43	43	41	44	42	42	43	46	39	44	41
Standard Dev	7	7	7	6	7	8	8	7	6	6	8	7

likely to present as extremely well adjusted. Whether this reflects a genuinely higher level of adjustment or a stronger incentive to appear well adjusted among firefighter/paramedic candidates cannot be determined on the basis of these descriptive data.

In summary, these groups' largely comparable composition and remarkably similar MMPI-2-RF descriptive findings are consistent with our observations in chapter 1 that the essential job functions of police officers, firefighters/paramedics, correctional officers, and dispatchers (Table 1-1), and the psychological demands for these positions

FIGURE 6-3 Police Officer, Firefighter/Paramedic, Correctional Officer, and Dispatcher Candidates: MMPI-2-RF Somatic/Cognitive and Internalizing Scales

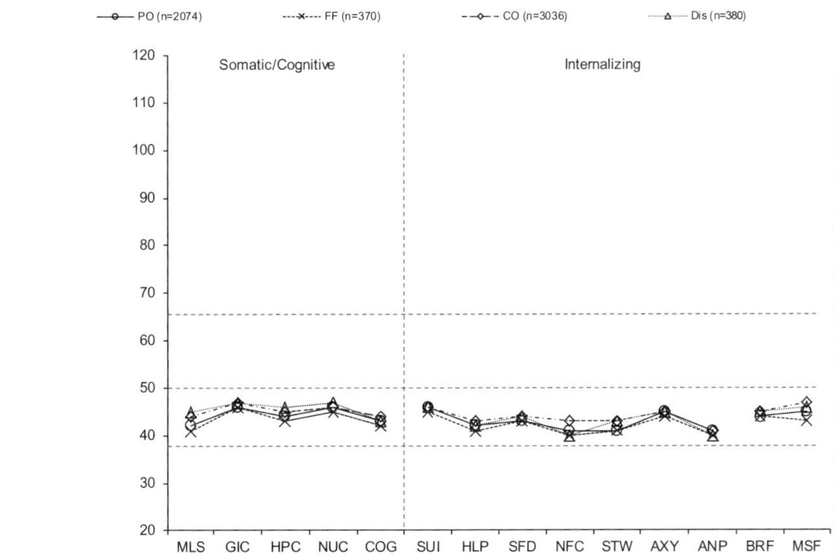

	MLS	GIC	HPC	NUC	COG	SUI	HLP	SFD	NFC	STW	AXY	ANP	BRF	MSF
Mean - PO	42	46	44	46	43	46	42	43	41	41	45	41	44	45
Standard Dev	6	4	6	7	5	2	4	4	6	6	4	5	5	8
Mean - FF	41	46	43	45	42	45	41	43	40	41	44	40	44	43
Standard Dev	5	3	4	6	5	1	3	3	5	6	2	4	4	6
Mean - CO	44	47	45	46	44	46	43	44	43	43	45	41	45	47
Standard Dev	7	5	6	8	6	2	5	5	7	7	5	6	6	8
Mean - Dis	44	47	45	47	43	46	42	44	41	43	45	41	45	46
Standard Dev	7	6	6	8	6	2	5	5	6	7	4	4	6	8

(Table 1-3) are largely similar. Because the potential problems that public safety employers seek to avoid (Table 1-2) are also similar, and a common set of attributes rated as important for all four positions can be identified (Table 1-4), these similarities are also consistent with our discussion in chapter 1 of the likely applicability of findings from police candidate research to preemployment assessments for all four public safety positions. Use of the descriptive findings reported here and available in the MMPI-2-RF Score Report is illustrated with case studies in chapter 8.

FIGURE 6-4 Police Officer, Firefighter/Paramedic, Correctional Officer, and Dispatcher Candidates: MMPI-2-RF Externalizing, Interpersonal, and Interest Scales

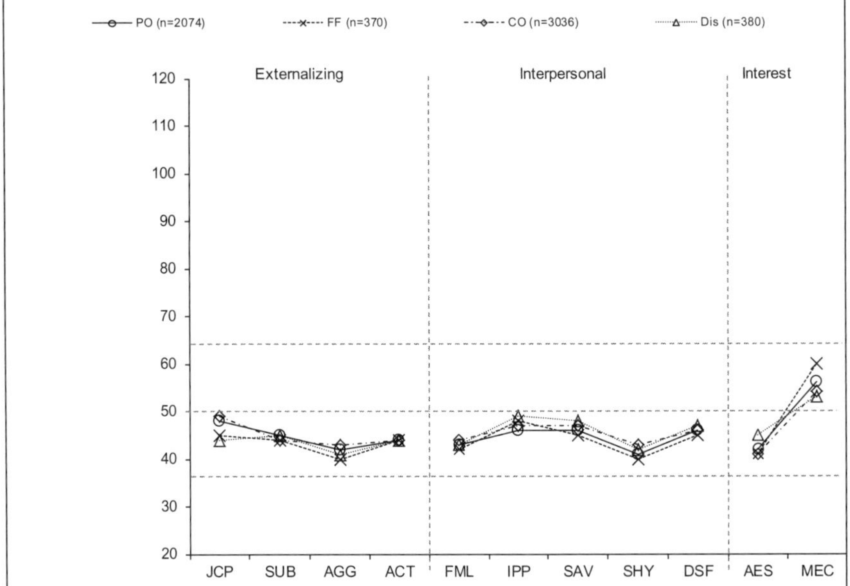

	JCP	SUB	AGG	ACT	FML	IPP	SAV	SHY	DSF	AES	MEC
Mean - PO	48	45	42	44	43	46	46	41	46	42	56
Standard Dev	9	6	6	9	7	6	8	6	5	8	11
Mean - FF	45	44	40	44	42	48	45	40	45	41	60
Standard Dev	7	5	6	9	7	6	7	5	4	8	10
Mean - CO	49	44	43	44	44	47	47	43	46	41	54
Standard Dev	9	5	7	9	7	7	8	7	6	8	11
Mean - Dis	45	44	41	44	43	48	48	42	46	46	53
Standard Dev	7	5	5	10	7	8	9	7	6	9	11

Important Considerations When Using the MMPI-2-RF in Preemployment Evaluations of Public Safety Candidates

The empirically grounded interpretive guidelines presented in this chapter should be followed with due consideration given to some inherent and specific limitations of their research base. First, as with any body of empirical correlates, associations between MMPI-2-RF scores and criteria, even after correcting for range restriction, are insufficient to justify definitive conclusions based on test scores alone. This critical caveat is underscored in the Integrative Model for Psychological Screening (Spilberg & Corey,

FIGURE 6-5 Police Officer, Firefighter/Paramedic, Correctional Officer, and Dispatcher Candidates: MMPI-2-RF PSY-5 Scales

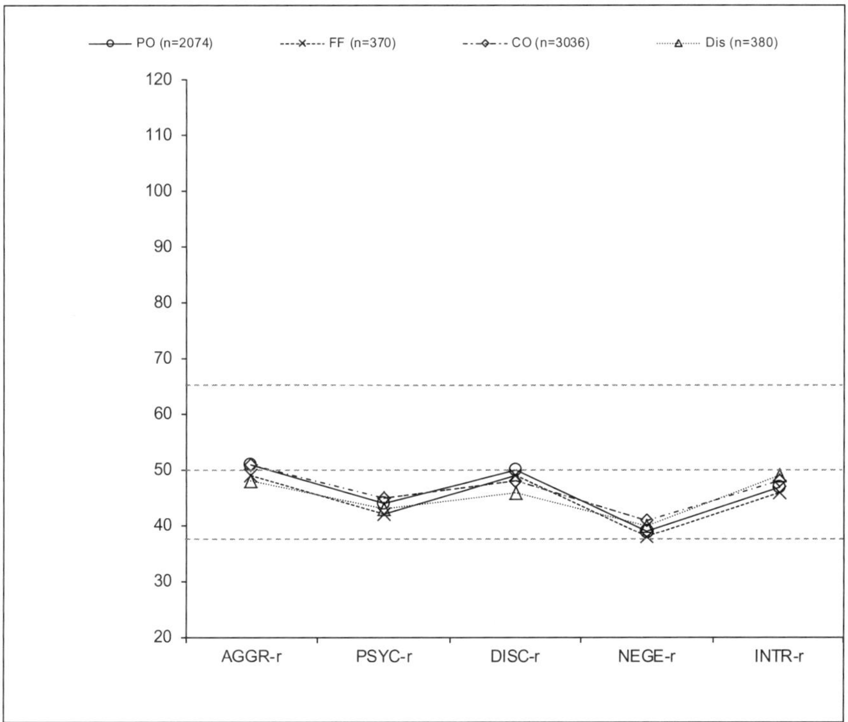

	AGGR-r	PSYC-r	DISC-r	NEGE-r	INTR-r
Mean - PO	51	44	50	39	47
Standard Dev	7	7	8	6	7
Mean - FF	49	42	49	38	46
Standard Dev	6	6	6	6	7
Mean - CO	51	45	48	41	48
Standard Dev	7	8	8	7	8
Mean - Dis	49	43	46	40	48
Standard Dev	7	7	7	7	9

2017) described and illustrated in detail in chapter 8. A key tenet of this model is that, when integrating assessment findings, they should be weighted according to their psychometric strength. Data with stronger known reliability and validity (psychological test findings) are afforded greater weight. However, no single data source can be absolutely determinative. That is, no single test score or set of scores provides sufficient grounds alone to disqualify a candidate. Indeed, in some cases, other data sources may mitigate test score findings, as illustrated in the case of Mr. G, reported in chapter 8.

Specific limitations of the research reviewed in this chapter are methodological in nature. As discussed earlier, the vast majority of the candidates studied in MMPI investigations with public safety candidates have been men, reflecting the gender imbalance in these occupations. The data for female candidates are promising, but less conclusive owing to their relative dearth. No data are available to directly compare MMPI-2-RF psychometrics with minority and majority candidates, leaving it possible only to rely on findings with other populations, which have generally demonstrated comparable operation of MMPI-2-RF scores as a function of gender, minority status, and age (Marek, Ben-Porath, Sellbom, McNulty, & Heinberg, 2015). Nevertheless, when weighting assessment findings as a function of their known psychometric strength, assessors should, to some extent, allow greater leeway for mitigating negative test findings based on other sources when assessing female and minority candidates. This is not to say, however, that test findings should be ignored in these cases, because the psychometric strength of other sources considered in the integrative model is also relatively unknown for these populations.

7

The MMPI-2-RF Police Candidate Interpretive Report (PCIR)

The MMPI-2-RF Police Candidate Interpretive Report (PCIR) is intended for use by professionals qualified to interpret the MMPI-2-RF in the context of preemployment psychological evaluations of police and other law enforcement officer candidates. Its computer-generated narrative focuses on identifying problems; it does not convey potential strengths. The information it contains should be considered in the context of the test taker's background, the demands of the position under consideration, the clinical interview, findings from supplemental tests, and other relevant information.

In this chapter we provide an overview of the structure and content of the report and illustrate it with the case of Mr. C, a 34-year-old male police officer candidate (Figure 7-1). Item content that would normally be included in the report is redacted here for the purpose of maintaining test security. The PCIR includes all of the information provided in the MMPI-2-RF Score Report (see Ben-Porath & Tellegen, 2011, for a complete description of this report) augmented by a detailed, automated interpretation of the test scores focusing on their implications for the test taker's suitability for employment as a police officer, as well as item-level responses.

The PCIR is designed to efficiently and consistently integrate the available literature to guide use of the inventory in preemployment assessments of law enforcement candidates. This includes the nearly 54,000 empirical correlates listed in the *MMPI-2-RF Technical Manual* (Tellegen & Ben-Porath, 2008/2011) and more than 300 peer-reviewed publications, among them the seven studies described in chapter 6 that focus on assessment of police candidates and are incorporated in the interpretive guidelines included in Appendix A of this practical guide. Full consideration and integration of this vast quantity of information are possible without the PCIR; however, when properly done, that process could take considerably more than an hour per case and could lead to interpretations that can be inconsistent, both across and within examiners. Inconsistency in interpreting MMPI-2-RF results can occur in two forms: by failing to identify interpretable scores (frequently at levels below 65T) and their evidence-based correlates, and/or by erroneously interpreting scores at levels that are not warranted by the empirical literature. The PCIR provides this information and consistency for a nominal cost beyond that of a standard Score Report.

Structure and Content of the Police Candidate Interpretive Report

The first seven pages of the PCIR are identical to those of the standard MMPI-2-RF Score Report, with the exception that any score interpreted in the PCIR is bolded on page 7 of the report, which provides scores on the 51 MMPI-2-RF scales organized by the relevant interpretive domains. In Mr. C's case, scores on L-r, K-r, SFD, THD, RC8, BXD, RC9, AGG, FML, and SAV are printed in bold. The automated interpretation begins on page 8 of the PCIR and consists of seven major sections: Synopsis, Protocol Validity, Clinical Findings, Diagnostic Considerations, Comparison Group Findings, Job-Relevant Correlates, and Item-Level Information. All interpretive statements in the report are annotated with Endnotes, which in Mr. C's case begin on page 16 of the report, indicating for each statement whether it is based on empirical correlates or test item content or is an inference of the report authors. Any statement identified as being based on empirical correlates includes reference numbers associated with the Research Reference List, which appears immediately following the Endnotes section.

Synopsis

The Synopsis section provides a brief overview of the major findings pertaining to the interpretability of the results, any substantive scale scores in the clinically interpretable range (T-score 65 or higher), comparison group findings, and job-relevant correlates.

Protocol Validity

The Protocol Validity section provides information about three types of threats to the validity of the test results: content nonresponsiveness (unscorable and/or inconsistent responses), overreporting, and underreporting. For cases in which possible validity threats are indicated, the prevalence of these scores in the Police Officer Candidate comparison group is reported.

For cases in which no protocol validity concerns are indicated by scores on the Validity Scales, a brief statement to that effect will appear in this section. Underreporting, the most common threat to protocol validity in police candidate evaluations (Detrick & Chibnall, 2014), is addressed with special PCIR features designed to assist examiners in the inferential task of differentiating candidates who, consistent with their self-presentation, are, in fact, morally virtuous and well adjusted from those who are actively engaged in deceptive efforts.

In cases where L-r is substantially elevated, the report prints MMPI-2-RF items with potentially verifiable historical content to aid the examiner in detecting discrepancies from other self-report and/or background information. The report authors selected these items from the entire booklet that included potentially verifiable content. When evaluating what inferences to draw from elevated underreporting scores, these items, in addition to the consideration of other collateral information, can aid test users in differentiating naïve responses (often occurring in individuals with a background stressing traditional values) from intentionally deceptive ones. An illustration using these item responses is provided in the following chapter with the case of Mr. B.

Clinical Findings

The interpretation provided in this section of the report is divided into five areas, each described in a separate paragraph (but without a subheading): Somatic/Cognitive Dysfunction, Emotional/Internalizing Dysfunction, Thought Dysfunction, Behavioral/Externalizing Dysfunction, and Interpersonal Functioning. Findings on the substantive scales are interpreted in these paragraphs if clinically elevated cutoffs (T-score 65 or higher) are reached. In Mr. C's case, on page 9 of the report, this involves interpretation of clinically elevated AGG, FML, and SAV scores.

Diagnostic Considerations

This section can be suppressed at the user's option before generating the report (see the PCIR *User's Guide* for details). Diagnostic possibilities are listed under four possible subheadings: Emotional/Internalizing Disorders, Thought Disorders, Behavioral/Externalizing Disorders, and Interpersonal Disorders. If none of the possibilities listed under any of these subheadings is indicated by the test scores, that subheading is not printed in the report. In Mr. C's case, at the top of page 10 of the report, diagnostic considerations are listed for Behavioral/Externalizing and Interpersonal Disorders.

Comparison Group Findings

Construct-based statements that describe implications of clinically elevated substantive scale scores, as well as statements about possible implications of uncommonly high (but not clinically elevated) scores for police officer candidates, are included in this section of the PCIR. The composition of the PCIR comparison group and its use in this manner were discussed in detail in chapter 6. Base-rate information (derived from the Police Officer Candidate comparison group) is provided for both clinically elevated and nonelevated scores that generate interpretive statements.[1] If scores on the Validity Scales indicate the need for caution in interpreting the results of the substantive scales, a cautionary statement is printed.

Interpretation is divided into the same five areas described in the Clinical Findings section. These statements are included only if the candidate's score falls above the cutoffs listed in Appendix A of this practical guide—although, as reflected in Appendix A, scores on four substantive scales (RC9, IPP, AGGR-r, and DISC-r) are interpreted also when they fall at or below the designated cutoffs. The cutoffs were selected to identify scores that are at least two standard deviations above (or below) the Police Officer Candidate comparison group mean and that occur in less than 10% of comparison group members. Statements based on clinically elevated scores (T-score 65 or higher) emphasize more substantial implications for compatibility with requirements for public safety.

If none of the scale scores for a given subsection meets the cutoffs listed in Appendix A, the associated section heading is not printed. For cases in which scale scores for all five subsections fail to meet or exceed the designated cutoffs, a statement is printed indicating that the candidate scored within normal limits for the general population and police candidates. An illustration of the comparison group findings included in the PCIR can be found on pages 10–11 of Mr. C's report (Figure 7-1).

Job-Relevant Correlates

This section consists of interpretive statements supported by the empirical studies referenced in chapter 6. Periodic updates of the PCIR will include additional statements warranted by future research. As noted in the report's introduction to this section, these statements are organized by both problem domain and correlate source.

The 10 problem domains addressed in this section of the report correspond closely to the California POST Psychological Screening Dimensions discussed in chapter 1. When a candidate's test scores are not associated with problems in a particular domain, a statement is printed at the end of this section indicating the domain(s) for which no risk of problems was indicated.

Correlate-based interpretive statements (listed by scale in Appendix A of this guide) are derived from two sources: (a) those in which scores on other self-report measures (CPI, IPI) obtained in various police candidate samples served as the criteria and (b) others involving correlations with performance outcome criteria in studies of hired candidates. Statements derived from correlations with self-report measures begin with "Compared with other police officer candidates," and statements originating from outcome studies with police recruits and police officers begin with "He [or she] is more likely than most police officers or trainees." As previously discussed, the studies on which each statement is based are denoted with endnote annotation. Annotations indicate the scale(s) and score(s) associated with each statement and provide reference numbers linked to citations for the supporting research. The selection ratio (that is, the proportion of candidates in the comparison group who meet or exceed the cutoff score) for each scale is 8% or less, with most falling under 5%. Mr. C's job-relevant correlates are included in pages 11–12 of his PCIR (Figure 7-1).

Item-Level Information

The final main section of the PCIR provides four types of item-level information under the headings: Unscorable Responses, Critical Responses, User-Designated Item-Level Information (which is optional), and Critical Follow-Up Items.

UNSCORABLE RESPONSES

A list of items to which the candidate did not provide scorable answers appears under the heading Unscorable Responses. Unscorable responses occur when the test taker either fails to mark an answer or responds both True and False to an item. Unscorable items are listed in the order in which they appear in the MMPI-2-RF protocol. The scale or scales on which each item is scored appear in parentheses following the item number and content. This makes it possible to examine the content of the unscorable items to detect possible themes to explore during the clinical interview. As seen at the bottom of page 12 of his PCIR, Mr. C produced scorable responses to all of the MMPI-2-RF items.

CRITICAL RESPONSES

A second type of item-level information appears under the heading Critical Responses. It relies on scale-level data to identify a candidate who is probably experiencing critical difficulties that may warrant immediate attention. If he or she generates an elevated score on one or more of the scales designated as having critical content, then item-level data can be used to identify the specific difficulties being reported by the test taker. Ben-Porath and Tellegen (2011) designated seven MMPI-2-RF substantive scales as having critical item content that might require immediate attention and follow-up: Suicidal/Death Ideation (SUI), Helplessness/Hopelessness (HLP), Anxiety (AXY), Ideas of Persecution (RC6), Aberrant Experiences (RC8), Substance Abuse (SUB), and Aggression (AGG). Items answered by the candidate in the keyed direction on a critical scale are listed if her or his T-score on that scale is 65 or higher. The percentage of the MMPI-2-RF normative sample (NS) and Police Officer Candidate comparison group (CG) who answered each item listed in the keyed direction is provided in parentheses following the item content. In Mr. C's PCIR (p. 13 of Figure 7-1), five critical responses are listed for the Aggression scale on which he produced a clinically elevated score. As noted earlier, the content of these five items, which would be printed in an actual PCIR, is redacted here to protect test security.

USER-DESIGNATED ITEM-LEVEL INFORMATION

Pearson software (see *PCIR User's Guide* for specific details) provides an option for the user to designate additional scales and/or alternative cutoff levels for generating a third type of item-level information. Users can select any MMPI-2-RF scale for inclusion in this part of the report. By default, item-level information for a selected scale will be printed if a candidate's score reaches a level for which interpretive recommendations are provided in the *MMPI-2-RF Manual for Administration, Scoring and Interpretation* (excluding interpretive recommendations for low scores). For the substantive scales, the initial default T-score cutoff is 65. The initial default values for the validity indicators vary depending on the interpretive recommendations provided in chapter 5 of the *Manual for Administration, Scoring and Interpretation* (Ben-Porath & Tellegen, 2008/2011). Once a user has designated a cutoff for a given scale, it is possible to save it as the new default value for that scale. For example, if 60T is selected as the cutoff for RC6, this value can be retained as the new default for generating item-level responses for RC6.

The ability to customize cutoffs can be particularly helpful in assessments such as preemployment screening of police officer candidates in which interpretable deviations from reference group means occur at lower levels. For example, as just described, nonclinically elevated scores are interpreted in both the Comparison Group Findings and Job-Relevant Correlates sections of the PCIR. The option to select additional scales to generate User-Designated Item-Level Information, in addition to those included in the Critical Responses section, can be used when an initial review of the results identifies areas requiring further attention.

An MMPI-2-RF PCIR can be reprinted with different options selected (for example, adding scales to the User-Designated Item-Level Information list) without incurring additional cost. One way to use this option is to begin with a preliminary examination of the report with no scales selected for this section. If the user then identifies additional scales or alternative cutoffs that might provide useful information, these options can be selected and the report reprinted. This is illustrated in Mr. C's case on pages 13–15, which includes items answered in the keyed direction on all of the substantive scales interpreted in his PCIR. A detailed illustration of how to use the Pearson software to select additional scales and alternative cutoffs for inclusion in this section can be found in the PCIR *User's Guide*.

CRITICAL FOLLOW-UP ITEMS

This section contains a list of items identified by police officer screening experts as having critical content and warranting follow-up. Clinicians are encouraged to follow up on these statements with the candidate by making related inquiries, rather than reciting the item(s) verbatim. Each item is followed by the candidate's response, the percentage of Police Officer Candidate comparison group members who gave this response, and the scale(s) on which the item appears. As seen on page 15 of Figure 7-1, Mr. C responded in the keyed direction to seven of these items. As noted, the percentage of the MMPI-2-RF normative sample (NS) and Police Officer Candidate comparison group (CG) who answered each item listed in the keyed direction is provided in parentheses following the item content, along with the scales on which the item is scored.

These data, as well as all the item-level information included in the PCIR, is intended to support the interview portion of a police candidate evaluation. However, as we discussed in chapter 5, **we do not recommend reading item content to the candidate verbatim**. A more useful strategy, and one likely to produce more reliable information while maintaining test security, is to use the item content to construct probing interview questions designed to assess the underlying issue.

Annotation

Standard 6.11 of the *Standards for Educational and Psychological Testing* (AERA, APA, & NCME, 2014) states that the sources, rationale, and empirical basis for interpretation should be available. To meet this standard, the annotation feature of the PCIR identifies the origin of the interpretive statements (that is, attributes the statements to the individual's score[s] on a specific scale or scales); indicates whether the statements are based on the test taker's responses, direct empirical correlates, or construct-based inferences; and provides citations to empirical studies that support the correlate-based statements. Annotation is provided in the Endnotes (see page 16 of Mr. C's PCIR) and Research Reference List sections (p. 17).

Endnotes

As a general rule, the construct-based statements appearing in the Comparison Group Findings section will be identified as originating from test responses (that is, scale item content). Statements in the Job-Relevant Correlates section are based on setting-specific empirical correlates of the MMPI-2-RF substantive scales. Additional statements will be added to the PCIR periodically as the research base for use of the MMPI-2-RF in police candidate assessments continues to develop. Statements in the Clinical Findings section will, for the most part, be identified as based on test content or empirical correlates. Any PCIR statement identified as correlate-based includes a list of research references that appear in the next and final section of the report.

Research Reference List

This section includes a list of the empirical studies cited in the report in support of correlate-based statements. With the exception of the *MMPI-2-RF Technical Manual* (Tellegen & Ben-Porath, 2008/2011), all of these publications appear in peer-reviewed journal articles. The reference for each article includes a highlighted Digital Object Identifier (doi) number. When viewed on an Internet-connected device, the doi numbers provide hyperlinked access to the publisher's website for each article.

The Case of Mr. C

A PCIR based on the MMPI-2-RF scores of Mr. C, a 34-year-old police candidate, is reproduced in Figure 7-1. As mentioned, the first six pages of the report are identical to what would appear in an MMPI-2-RF Score Report based on the same set of responses. The first PCIR-specific element appears on page 7 of Mr. C's report, where any score interpreted in the report is printed in bold along with the scale abbreviation. In Mr. C's case, this includes his uncommonly low scores on the underreporting indicators, L-r and K-r. On page 8, the synopsis succinctly summarizes the implications of clinically elevated MMPI-2-RF scores as well as any comparison group findings or job-relevant correlates associated with

MMPI 2 RF®

Minnesota Multiphasic
Personality Inventory-2
Restructured Form®
Yossef S. Ben-Porath, PhD, & Auke Tellegen, PhD

MMPI-2-RF®
Police Candidate Interpretive Report
David M. Corey, PhD, & Yossef S. Ben-Porath, PhD

Name:	Mr. C
Age:	34
Gender:	Male
Marital Status:	Married
Years of Education:	14
Date Assessed:	11/11/2013

Copyright © 2014 by the Regents of the University of Minnesota. All rights reserved.
Distributed exclusively under license from the University of Minnesota by NCS Pearson, Inc. Portions reproduced from the MMPI-2-RF test booklet. Copyright © 2008 by the Regents of the University of Minnesota. All rights reserved. Portions excerpted from the *MMPI-2-RF Manual for Administration, Scoring, and Interpretation.* Copyright © 2008, 2011 by the Regents of the University of Minnesota. All rights reserved. Used by permission of the University of Minnesota Press.

Minnesota Multiphasic Personality Inventory-2-Restructured Form and **MMPI-2-RF** are registered trademarks of the University of Minnesota. **Pearson** is a trademark in the U.S. and/or other countries of Pearson Education, Inc., or its affiliate(s).

This report contains copyrighted material and trade secrets. The qualified licensee may excerpt portions of this output report, limited to the minimum text necessary to accurately describe their significant core conclusions, for incorporation into a written evaluation of the examinee, in accordance with their profession's citation standards, if any. No adaptations, translations, modifications, or special versions may be made of this report without prior written permission from the University of Minnesota Press.

[4.0 / 57 / __VERSION__]

ALWAYS LEARNING PEARSON

FIGURE 7-1 Mr. C's MMPI-2-RF Police Candidate Interpretive Report

MMPI-2-RF Validity Scales

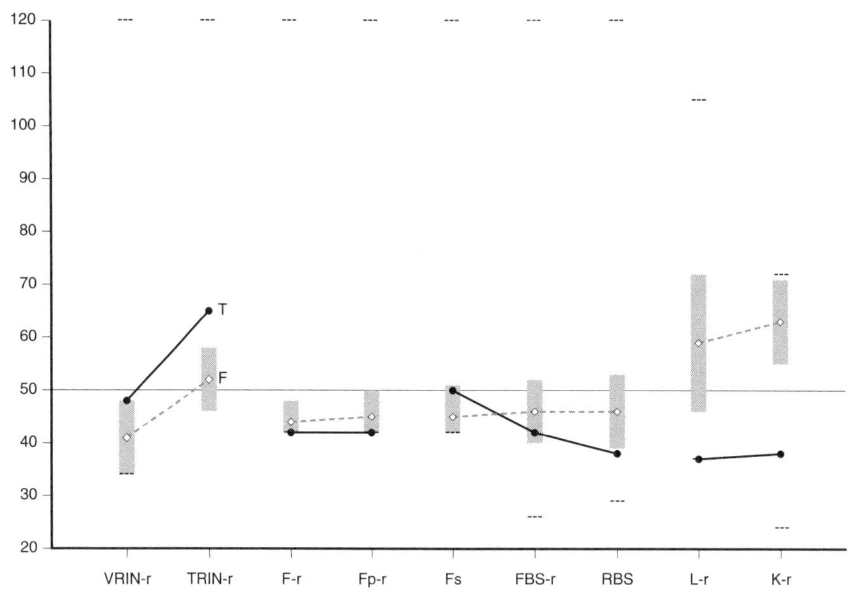

	VRIN-r	TRIN-r	F-r	Fp-r	Fs	FBS-r	RBS	L-r	K-r
Raw Score:	3	13	0	0	1	5	2	0	4
T Score:	48	65 T	42	42	50	42	38	37	38
Response %:	100	100	100	100	100	100	100	100	100

Cannot Say (Raw): 0 Percent True (of items answered): 42%

Comparison Group Data: Personnel Screening, Police Officer Candidate (Men and Women), N = 2074

	VRIN-r	TRIN-r	F-r	Fp-r	Fs	FBS-r	RBS	L-r	K-r
Mean Score (◇- - -◇):	41	52 F	44	45	45	46	46	59	63
Standard Dev (±1 SD):	7	6	4	5	6	6	7	13	8
Percent scoring at or below test taker:	92	99	75	78	92	32	20	4	0.7

The highest and lowest T scores possible on each scale are indicated by a "---"; MMPI-2-RF T scores are non-gendered.

VRIN-r Variable Response Inconsistency
TRIN-r True Response Inconsistency
F-r Infrequent Responses
Fp-r Infrequent Psychopathology Responses
Fs Infrequent Somatic Responses
FBS-r Symptom Validity
RBS Response Bias Scale
L-r Uncommon Virtues
K-r Adjustment Validity

FIGURE 7-1 Mr. C's MMPI-2-RF Police Candidate Interpretive Report, continued

MMPI-2-RF Higher-Order (H-O) and Restructured Clinical (RC) Scales

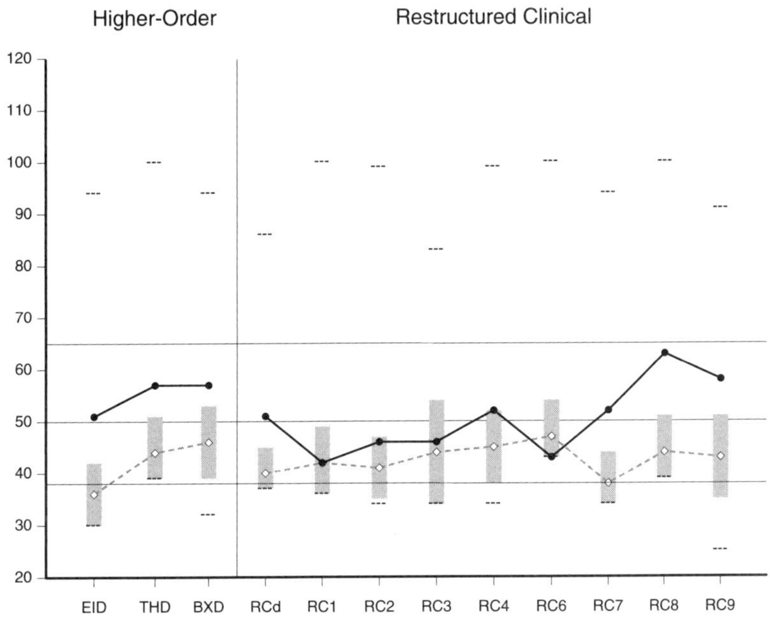

	EID	THD	BXD	RCd	RC1	RC2	RC3	RC4	RC6	RC7	RC8	RC9
Raw Score:	10	3	9	4	1	3	4	5	0	7	5	16
T Score:	51	57	57	51	42	46	46	52	43	52	63	58
Response %:	100	100	100	100	100	100	100	100	100	100	100	100

Comparison Group Data: Personnel Screening, Police Officer Candidate (Men and Women), N = 2074

	EID	THD	BXD	RCd	RC1	RC2	RC3	RC4	RC6	RC7	RC8	RC9
Mean Score (◇- - -◇):	36	44	46	40	42	41	44	45	47	38	44	43
Standard Dev (±1 SD):	6	7	7	5	7	6	10	7	7	6	7	8
Percent scoring at or below test taker:	98	96	96	97	68	88	65	87	75	97	98	97

The highest and lowest T scores possible on each scale are indicated by a "---"; MMPI-2-RF T scores are non-gendered.

EID Emotional/Internalizing Dysfunction
THD Thought Dysfunction
BXD Behavioral/Externalizing Dysfunction

RCd Demoralization
RC1 Somatic Complaints
RC2 Low Positive Emotions
RC3 Cynicism
RC4 Antisocial Behavior

RC6 Ideas of Persecution
RC7 Dysfunctional Negative Emotions
RC8 Aberrant Experiences
RC9 Hypomanic Activation

FIGURE 7-1 Mr. C's MMPI-2-RF Police Candidate Interpretive Report, continued

MMPI-2-RF Somatic/Cognitive and Internalizing Scales

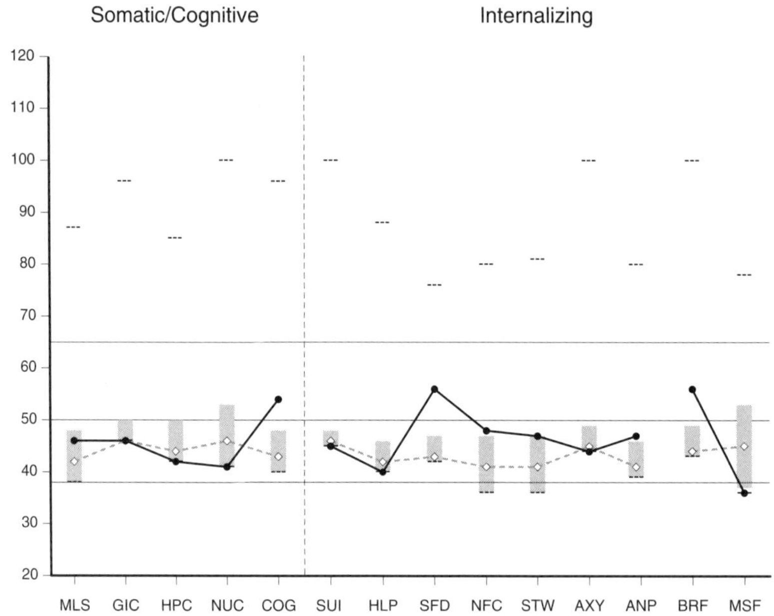

	MLS	GIC	HPC	NUC	COG	SUI	HLP	SFD	NFC	STW	AXY	ANP	BRF	MSF
Raw Score:	1	0	0	0	2	0	0	2	2	2	0	1	1	0
T Score:	46	46	42	41	54	45	40	56	48	47	44	47	56	36
Response %:	100	100	100	100	100	100	100	100	100	100	100	100	100	100

Comparison Group Data: Personnel Screening, Police Officer Candidate (Men and Women), N = 2074

	MLS	GIC	HPC	NUC	COG	SUI	HLP	SFD	NFC	STW	AXY	ANP	BRF	MSF
Mean Score (◇- - -◇):	42	46	44	46	43	46	42	43	41	41	45	41	44	45
Standard Dev (±1 SD):	6	4	6	7	5	2	4	4	6	6	4	5	5	8
Percent scoring at or below test taker:	87	95	83	65	97	99.3	88	99.1	91	91	94	94	98	25

The highest and lowest T scores possible on each scale are indicated by a "---"; MMPI-2-RF T scores are non-gendered.

MLS Malaise
GIC Gastrointestinal Complaints
HPC Head Pain Complaints
NUC Neurological Complaints
COG Cognitive Complaints
SUI Suicidal/Death Ideation
HLP Helplessness/Hopelessness
SFD Self-Doubt
NFC Inefficacy
STW Stress/Worry
AXY Anxiety
ANP Anger Proneness
BRF Behavior-Restricting Fears
MSF Multiple Specific Fears

FIGURE 7-1 Mr. C's MMPI-2-RF Police Candidate Interpretive Report, continued

MMPI-2-RF® Police Candidate Interpretive Report
11/11/2013, Page 5 Mr. C

MMPI-2-RF Externalizing, Interpersonal, and Interest Scales

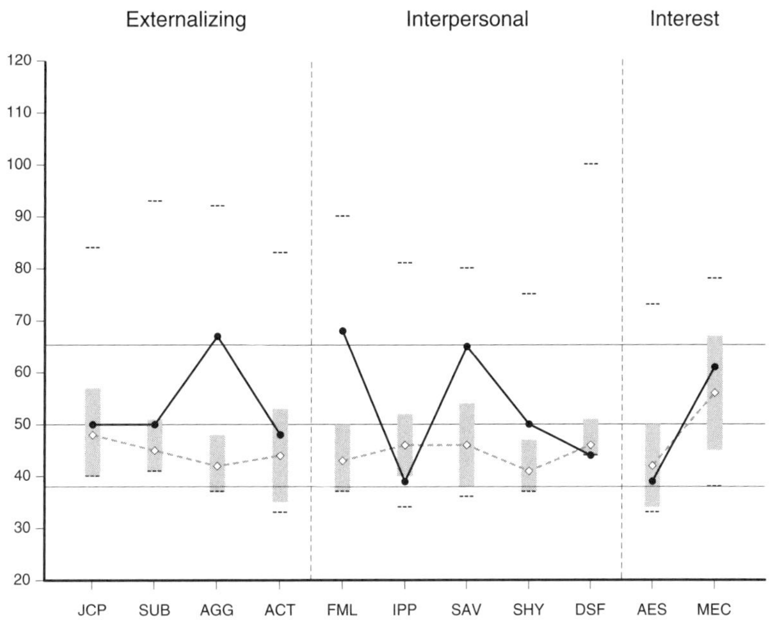

	JCP	SUB	AGG	ACT	FML	IPP	SAV	SHY	DSF	AES	MEC
Raw Score:	1	1	5	3	6	1	7	3	0	1	5
T Score:	50	50	67	48	68	39	65	50	44	39	61
Response %:	100	100	100	100	100	100	100	100	100	100	100

Comparison Group Data: Personnel Screening, Police Officer Candidate (Men and Women), N = 2074

	JCP	SUB	AGG	ACT	FML	IPP	SAV	SHY	DSF	AES	MEC
Mean Score (◇---◇):	48	45	42	44	43	46	46	41	46	42	56
Standard Dev (±1 SD):	9	6	6	9	7	6	8	6	5	8	11
Percent scoring at or below test taker:	76	90	99.9	79	99.9	20	98	95	90	57	73

The highest and lowest T scores possible on each scale are indicated by a "---"; MMPI-2-RF T scores are non-gendered.

JCP Juvenile Conduct Problems
SUB Substance Abuse
AGG Aggression
ACT Activation

FML Family Problems
IPP Interpersonal Passivity
SAV Social Avoidance
SHY Shyness
DSF Disaffiliativeness

AES Aesthetic-Literary Interests
MEC Mechanical-Physical Interests

FIGURE 7-1 Mr. C's MMPI-2-RF Police Candidate Interpretive Report, continued

MMPI-2-RF PSY-5 Scales

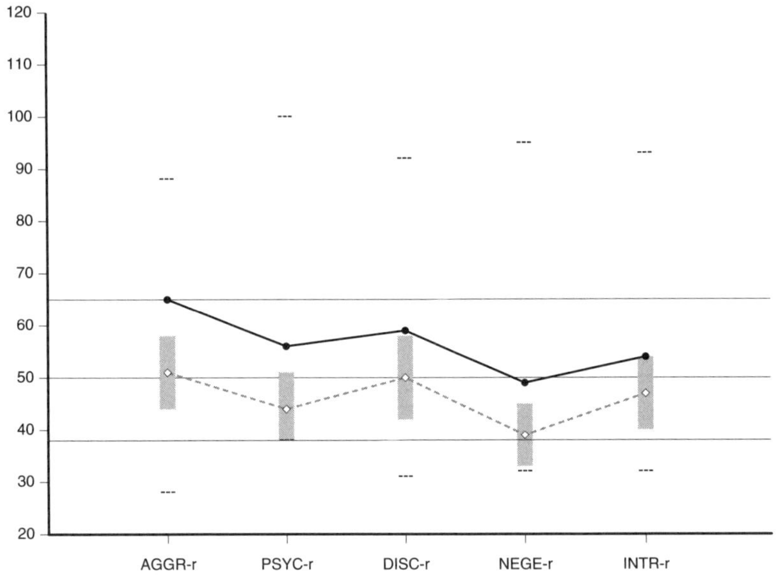

	AGGR-r	PSYC-r	DISC-r	NEGE-r	INTR-r
Raw Score:	13	3	10	6	8
T Score:	65	56	59	49	54
Response %:	100	100	100	100	100

Comparison Group Data: Personnel Screening, Police Officer Candidate (Men and Women), N = 2074

Mean Score (◇--◇):	51	44	50	39	47
Standard Dev (±1 SD):	7	7	8	6	7
Percent scoring at or below test taker:	98	95	93	95	89

The highest and lowest T scores possible on each scale are indicated by a "---"; MMPI-2-RF T scores are non-gendered.

AGGR-r Aggressiveness-Revised
PSYC-r Psychoticism-Revised
DISC-r Disconstraint-Revised
NEGE-r Negative Emotionality/Neuroticism-Revised
INTR-r Introversion/Low Positive Emotionality-Revised

FIGURE 7-1 Mr. C's MMPI-2-RF Police Candidate Interpretive Report, continued

MMPI-2-RF T SCORES (BY DOMAIN)

PROTOCOL VALIDITY

Content Non-Responsiveness

0	48	65 T
CNS	VRIN-r	TRIN-r

Over-Reporting

42	42	50	42	38
F-r	Fp-r	Fs	FBS-r	RBS

Under-Reporting

37	**38**
L-r	**K-r**

SUBSTANTIVE SCALES

Somatic/Cognitive Dysfunction

42	46	46	42	41	54
RC1	MLS	GIC	HPC	NUC	COG

Emotional Dysfunction — 51 EID

51	45	40	**56**	48		
RCd	SUI	HLP	**SFD**	NFC		
46	54					
RC2	INTR-r					
52	47	44	47	56	36	49
RC7	STW	AXY	ANP	BRF	MSF	NEGE-r

Thought Dysfunction — **57 THD**

43
RC6
63
RC8
56
PSYC-r

Behavioral Dysfunction — **57 BXD**

52	50	50		
RC4	JCP	SUB		
58	**67**	48	65	59
RC9	**AGG**	ACT	AGGR-r	DISC-r

Interpersonal Functioning

68	46	39	**65**	50	44
FML	RC3	IPP	**SAV**	SHY	DSF

Interests

39	61
AES	MEC

Scale scores shown in bold font are interpreted in the report.

Note. This information is provided to facilitate interpretation following the recommended structure for MMPI-2-RF interpretation in Chapter 5 of the *MMPI-2-RF Manual for Administration, Scoring, and Interpretation*, which provides details in the text and an outline in Table 5-1.

FIGURE 7-1 Mr. C's MMPI-2-RF Police Candidate Interpretive Report, continued

This interpretive report is intended for use by a professional qualified to interpret the MMPI-2-RF in the context of preemployment psychological evaluations of police and other law enforcement officer candidates. ***It focuses on identifying problems; it does not convey potential strengths.*** *The information it contains should be considered in the context of the test taker's background, the demands of the position under consideration, the clinical interview, findings from supplemental tests, and other relevant information.*

The interpretive statements in the Protocol Validity section of the report are based on T scores derived from the general MMPI-2-RF normative sample, as well as scores obtained by the multisite sample of 2,074 individuals that make up the Police Officer Candidate comparison group.

The interpretive statements in the Clinical Findings and Diagnostic Considerations sections of the report are based on T scores derived from the general MMPI-2-RF normative sample. Following recommended practice, only T scores of 65 and higher are considered clinically significant. Scores at this clinical level are generally rare among police officer candidates.

Statements in the Comparison Group Findings and Job-Relevant Correlates sections are based on comparisons with scores obtained by the Police Officer Candidate comparison group. Statements in these sections may be based on T scores that, although less than 65, are nevertheless uncommon in reference to the comparison group.

Sources for interpretive statements in all sections are listed in the Endnotes section of this report. See User's Guide for the MMPI-2-RF Police Candidate Interpretive Report *for detailed information on report features.*

SYNOPSIS

This is a valid MMPI-2-RF protocol. Scores on the substantive scales indicate clinically significant behavioral and interpersonal dysfunction. Behavioral-externalizing problems relate to aggression. Interpersonal difficulties include family problems and social avoidance.

Comparison group findings point to additional possible concerns about self-doubt, odd perceptions and beliefs, and excitation.

Possible job-relevant problems are identified in the following domains: Emotional Control and Stress Tolerance, Routine Task Performance, Decision-Making and Judgment, Feedback Acceptance, Assertiveness, Social Competence and Teamwork, Integrity, Conscientiousness and Dependability, Substance Use, and Impulse Control.

FIGURE 7-1 Mr. C's MMPI-2-RF Police Candidate Interpretive Report, continued

PROTOCOL VALIDITY

Content Non-Responsiveness

There are no problems with unscorable items in this protocol. The test taker responded relevantly to the items on the basis of their content.

Over-Reporting

There are no indications of over-reporting in this protocol.

Under-Reporting

The candidate's scores show no evidence of under-reporting, indicating a cooperative test-taking approach.

The test taker claimed no uncommon virtues[1]. This very rare pattern of responding is found in only 4.0% of the Police Officer Candidate comparison group members.

In addition, he reported being much less well-adjusted than members of the general population[2]. Less than 1% of the Police Officer Candidate comparison group reported this low level of psychological adjustment. As detailed later in this report, his scores on the substantive scales do indeed raise significant concerns about the candidate's psychological adjustment.

CLINICAL FINDINGS

Clinical-level symptoms, personality characteristics, and behavioral tendencies of the test taker are described in this section and organized according to an empirically guided framework. (Please see Chapter 8, Yossef S. Ben-Porath, Interpreting the MMPI-2-RF, *for details.) Statements containing the word "reports" are based on the item content of MMPI-2-RF scales, whereas statements that include the word "likely" are based on empirical correlates of scale scores. Specific sources for each statement can be accessed with the annotation features of this report.*

The test taker reports engaging in physically aggressive, violent behavior and losing control[3], and is indeed likely to have a history of violent behavior toward others[4].

The test taker reports conflictual family relationships and lack of support from family members[5]. He is indeed likely to have family conflicts and to experience poor family functioning[6], to have strong negative feelings about family members[7], and to blame family members for his difficulties[7]. He reports not enjoying social events and avoiding social situations[8]. He is likely to be introverted[9], to have difficulty forming close relationships[10], and to be emotionally restricted[11].

There are no indications of clinically significant somatic, cognitive, emotional, or thought dysfunction in this protocol.

FIGURE 7-1 Mr. C's MMPI-2-RF Police Candidate Interpretive Report, continued

DIAGNOSTIC CONSIDERATIONS

This section provides recommendations for psychodiagnostic assessment based on the test taker's MMPI-2-RF results. It is recommended that he be evaluated for the following:

Behavioral-Externalizing Disorders

- Disorders associated with interpersonally aggressive behavior such as intermittent explosive disorder[12]

Interpersonal Disorders

- Disorders associated with social avoidance such as avoidant personality disorder[13]

COMPARISON GROUP FINDINGS

This section describes the MMPI-2-RF substantive scale findings in the context of the Police Officer Candidate comparison group. Specific sources for each statement can be accessed with the annotation features of this report. ***Job-related correlates of these results, if any, are provided in the subsequent Job-Relevant Correlates section.***

Emotional/Internalizing Problems

The test taker reports a comparatively high level of self-doubt for a police officer candidate[14]. Only 2.8% of comparison group members convey this or a greater lack of confidence.

Unusual Thoughts, Perceptions, and Beliefs

The test taker reports a comparatively high level of unusual thinking for a police officer candidate[15]. Only 8.7% of comparison group members convey such thoughts at this or a higher level. More specifically, he reports a relatively high level of odd perceptions and thoughts for a police officer candidate[16]. Only 3.0% of comparison group members convey this or a greater level of unusual experiences.

Behavioral/Externalizing Problems

The test taker reports a comparatively large number of behavioral problems for a police officer candidate[17]. Only 7.3% of comparison group members convey this or a greater level of behavioral difficulties. More specifically, he reports a relatively high level of excitability for a police officer candidate[18]. Only 4.8% of comparison group members convey this or a greater level of stimulation and irritable temperament or disinhibition. In particular, his responses indicate a level of physically violent behavior that may be incompatible with public safety requirements for behavioral control[12]. This level of aggression is very uncommon among police officer candidates. Only 0.6% of comparison group members give evidence of this or a greater level of physically violent behavior.

Interpersonal Problems

The test taker's responses indicate a level of family problems that may be incompatible with public safety requirements for good interpersonal functioning[19]. This level of family conflict is very uncommon among police officer candidates. Only 0.5% of comparison group members give evidence of this or a

FIGURE 7-1 Mr. C's MMPI-2-RF Police Candidate Interpretive Report, continued

greater level of family problems. His responses also indicate a level of social avoidance that may impede conformance with public safety requirements for good interpersonal functioning[20]. This level of socially avoidant behavior is very uncommon among police officer candidates. Only 4.0% of comparison group members demonstrate this or a greater level of social avoidance.

JOB-RELEVANT CORRELATES

Job-relevant personality characteristics and behavioral tendencies of the test taker are described in this section and organized according to ten problem domains commonly identified in the professional literature as relevant to police officer candidate suitability. (Please see User's Guide for MMPI-2-RF Police Candidate Interpretive Report *for details.) Statements that begin with "Compared with other police officer candidates" are based on correlations with other self-report measures obtained in police officer candidate samples that included individuals who were subsequently hired as well as those who were not. Statements that begin with "He is more likely than most police officers or trainees" are based on correlations with outcome data obtained in samples of hired candidates during academy or field training, probation, and/or the post-probation period. Specific sources for each statement can be accessed with the annotation features of this report.*

Emotional Control and Stress Tolerance Problems

Compared with other police officer candidates, the test taker is more likely to worry about problems and be uncertain about how to deal with them[21] and to become impatient with others over minor infractions[22].

He is more likely than most police officers or trainees to exhibit difficulties performing under stressful conditions[23].

Routine Task Performance Problems

The test taker is more likely than most police officers or trainees to exhibit difficulties carrying out tasks under non-stressful conditions[24].

Decision-Making and Judgment Problems

Compared with other police officer candidates, the test taker is more likely to have thoughts, perceptions, and/or experiences that are rarely reported[25].

Feedback Acceptance Problems

The test taker is more likely than most police officers or trainees to exhibit difficulties accepting and responding to constructive performance feedback[26].

Assertiveness Problems

Compared with other police officer candidates, the test taker is more likely to avoid situations that others generally view as benign and non-intimidating[27] and to be ill at ease in dealing with others[28].

He is more likely than most police officers or trainees to exhibit difficulties in demonstrating a command presence and controlling situations requiring order or resolution[29].

FIGURE 7-1 Mr. C's MMPI-2-RF Police Candidate Interpretive Report, continued

Social Competence and Teamwork Problems

Compared with other police officer candidates, the test taker is more likely to have a history of problems getting along with others[22]; to be opinionated and outspoken[22]; and to be demanding[22]. He is also more likely to have a limited social support network[28] and to have difficulty trusting others[22].

He is more likely than most police officers or trainees to exhibit difficulties reading people, listening to others, and adapting his language and approach to the requirements of the situation[23]. He is also more likely to exhibit difficulties stemming from rude and/or overbearing behavior that results in complaints from the public[30] and cooperating with peers and/or supervisors[31].

Integrity Problems

Compared with other police officer candidates, the test taker is more likely to have skeptical and/or antisocial views of the world[22] and to believe that life is unfair and that exploiting opportunities for personal gain is justified[22].

He is more likely than most police officers or trainees to exhibit difficulties leading to integrity violations[32] and sustained internal affairs investigations[32].

Conscientiousness and Dependability Problems

The test taker is more likely than most police officers or trainees to exhibit difficulties reliably attending court[33]; with punctuality and attendance[23]; and with reliable work behavior and dependable follow-through[34].

Substance Use Problems

Compared with other police officer candidates, the test taker is more likely to have a history of substance use problems[35].

Impulse Control Problems

Compared with other police officer candidates, the test taker is more likely to behave impulsively or without adequate consideration of the consequences or implications of his actions[22].

He is more likely than most police officers or trainees to exhibit difficulties reacting to situations with the proper degree of emotional and behavioral restraint and control, and avoiding impulsive and/or unnecessarily risky behavior[36].

ITEM-LEVEL INFORMATION

Unscorable Responses

The test taker produced scorable responses to all the MMPI-2-RF items.

FIGURE 7-1 Mr. C's MMPI-2-RF Police Candidate Interpretive Report, continued

Critical Responses

Seven MMPI-2-RF scales--Suicidal/Death Ideation (SUI), Helplessness/Hopelessness (HLP), Anxiety (AXY), Ideas of Persecution (RC6), Aberrant Experiences (RC8), Substance Abuse (SUB), and Aggression (AGG)--have been designated by the test authors as having critical item content that may require immediate attention and follow-up. Items answered by the individual in the keyed direction (True or False) on a critical scale are listed below if his T score on that scale is 65 or higher. The percentage of the MMPI-2-RF normative sample (NS) and of the Police Officer Candidate (Men and Women) comparison group (CG) that answered each item in the keyed direction are provided in parentheses following the item content.

Aggression (AGG, T Score = 67)

23. Item Content Omitted. (True; NS 39.0%, CG 7.8%)
26. Item Content Omitted. (True; NS 19.9%, CG 3.3%)
84. Item Content Omitted. (True; NS 12.1%, CG 1.8%)
316. Item Content Omitted. (True; NS 45.1%, CG 30.7%)
337. Item Content Omitted. (True; NS 50.2%, CG 17.4%)

User-Designated Item-Level Information

The following item-level information is based on the report user's selection of additional scales, and/or of lower cutoffs for the critical scales from the previous section. Items answered by the test taker in the keyed direction (True or False) on a selected scale are listed below if his T score on that scale is at the user-designated cutoff score or higher. The percentage of the MMPI-2-RF normative sample (NS) and of the Police Officer Candidate (Men and Women) comparison group (CG) that answered each item in the keyed direction are provided in parentheses following the item content.

Thought Dysfunction (THD, T Score = 57)

12. Item Content Omitted. (True; NS 22.2%, CG 5.8%)
199. Item Content Omitted. (True; NS 12.1%, CG 6.7%)
330. Item Content Omitted. (True; NS 15.2%, CG 3.5%)

Behavioral/Externalizing Dysfunction (BXD, T Score = 57)

61. Item Content Omitted. (False; NS 61.6%, CG 58.7%)
84. Item Content Omitted. (True; NS 12.1%, CG 1.8%)
107. Item Content Omitted. (True; NS 47.3%, CG 35.5%)
131. Item Content Omitted. (True; NS 43.3%, CG 32.9%)
156. Item Content Omitted. (True; NS 59.8%, CG 45.9%)
205. Item Content Omitted. (True; NS 13.0%, CG 8.6%)
226. Item Content Omitted. (True; NS 21.5%, CG 38.1%)
237. Item Content Omitted. (False; NS 27.4%, CG 17.2%)
316. Item Content Omitted. (True; NS 45.1%, CG 30.7%)

FIGURE 7-1 Mr. C's MMPI-2-RF Police Candidate Interpretive Report, continued

Aberrant Experiences (RC8, T Score = 63)

12. Item Content Omitted. (True; NS 22.2%, CG 5.8%)
32. Item Content Omitted. (True; NS 21.1%, CG 15.0%)
199. Item Content Omitted. (True; NS 12.1%, CG 6.7%)
257. Item Content Omitted. (True; NS 12.4%, CG 4.3%)
330. Item Content Omitted. (True; NS 15.2%, CG 3.5%)

Hypomanic Activation (RC9, T Score = 58)

26. Item Content Omitted. (True; NS 19.9%, CG 3.3%)
39. Item Content Omitted. (True; NS 51.0%, CG 42.1%)
61. Item Content Omitted. (False; NS 61.6%, CG 58.7%)
72. Item Content Omitted. (True; NS 81.5%, CG 52.6%)
84. Item Content Omitted. (True; NS 12.1%, CG 1.8%)
97. Item Content Omitted. (True; NS 50.5%, CG 24.4%)
107. Item Content Omitted. (True; NS 47.3%, CG 35.5%)
118. Item Content Omitted. (True; NS 57.4%, CG 55.1%)
131. Item Content Omitted. (True; NS 43.3%, CG 32.9%)
143. Item Content Omitted. (True; NS 27.5%, CG 20.5%)
207. Item Content Omitted. (True; NS 66.9%, CG 43.2%)
219. Item Content Omitted. (True; NS 51.5%, CG 35.1%)
244. Item Content Omitted. (True; NS 56.9%, CG 84.9%)
305. Item Content Omitted. (True; NS 37.6%, CG 59.4%)
316. Item Content Omitted. (True; NS 45.1%, CG 30.7%)
337. Item Content Omitted. (True; NS 50.2%, CG 17.4%)

Self-Doubt (SFD, T Score = 56)

89. Item Content Omitted. (True; NS 35.9%, CG 6.1%)
232. Item Content Omitted. (True; NS 21.9%, CG 2.6%)

Family Problems (FML, T Score = 68)

19. Item Content Omitted. (False; NS 17.0%, CG 7.8%)
58. Item Content Omitted. (True; NS 57.3%, CG 37.4%)
103. Item Content Omitted. (True; NS 38.6%, CG 7.6%)

FIGURE 7-1 Mr. C's MMPI-2-RF Police Candidate Interpretive Report, continued

180. Item Content Omitted. (True; NS 30.4%, CG 17.4%)
215. Item Content Omitted. (True; NS 23.8%, CG 5.2%)
307. Item Content Omitted. (True; NS 19.1%, CG 3.6%)

Social Avoidance (SAV, T Score = 65)

47. Item Content Omitted. (False; NS 57.1%, CG 49.5%)
57. Item Content Omitted. (False; NS 22.1%, CG 15.1%)
109. Item Content Omitted. (False; NS 40.0%, CG 24.6%)
153. Item Content Omitted. (False; NS 25.9%, CG 29.6%)
201. Item Content Omitted. (False; NS 24.8%, CG 12.0%)
222. Item Content Omitted. (False; NS 19.6%, CG 6.2%)
278. Item Content Omitted. (True; NS 28.3%, CG 13.8%)

Critical Follow-up Items

This section contains a list of items to which the test taker responded in a manner warranting follow-up. The items were identified by police officer screening experts as having critical content. Clinicians are encouraged to follow up on these statements with the candidate by making related inquiries, rather than reciting the item(s) verbatim. Each item is followed by the candidate's response, the percentage of Police Officer Candidate comparison group members who gave this response, and the scale(s) on which the item appears.

26. Item Content Omitted. (True; 3.3%; RBS, RC9, AGG, AGGR-r)
84. Item Content Omitted. (True; 1.8%; BXD, RC9, AGG, AGGR-r)
257. Item Content Omitted. (True; 4.3%; VRIN-r, RC8, COG)
318. Item Content Omitted. (True; 2.8%; VRIN-r, RC7, ANP)
322. Item Content Omitted. (True; 4.0%; TRIN-r, EID, RC7)
330. Item Content Omitted. (True; 3.5%; THD, RC8, PSYC-r)
337. Item Content Omitted. (True; 17.4%; VRIN-r, RC9, AGG)

FIGURE 7-1 Mr. C's MMPI-2-RF Police Candidate Interpretive Report, continued

ENDNOTES

This section lists for each statement in the report the MMPI-2-RF score(s) that triggered it. In addition, each statement is identified as a Test Response, if based on item content, a Correlate, if based on empirical correlates, or an Inference, if based on the report authors' judgment. (This information can also be accessed on-screen by placing the cursor on a given statement.) For correlate-based statements, research references (Ref. No.) are provided, keyed to the consecutively numbered reference list following the endnotes.

[1] Test Response: L-r=37
[2] Test Response: K-r=38
[3] Test Response: AGG=67
[4] Correlate: AGG=67, Ref. 10, 16, 17
[5] Test Response: FML=68
[6] Correlate: FML=68, Ref. 4, 17
[7] Correlate: FML=68, Ref. 17
[8] Test Response: SAV=65
[9] Correlate: SAV=65, Ref. 1, 2, 3, 7, 9, 17
[10] Correlate: SAV=65, Ref. 1, 5, 8, 9, 17
[11] Correlate: SAV=65, Ref. 17
[12] Inference: AGG=67
[13] Correlate: SAV=65, Ref. 18
[14] Test Response: SFD=56
[15] Test Response: THD=57
[16] Test Response: RC8=63
[17] Test Response: BXD=57
[18] Test Response: RC9=58
[19] Inference: FML=68
[20] Inference: SAV=65
[21] Correlate: FML=68, Ref. 15
[22] Correlate: RC9=58, Ref. 6, 15
[23] Correlate: SAV=65, Ref. 11, 14
[24] Correlate: RC8=63, Ref. 11, 13; FML=68, Ref. 11, 14
[25] Correlate: RC8=63, Ref. 6, 15
[26] Correlate: AGG=67, Ref. 12
[27] Correlate: SAV=65, Ref. 15
[28] Correlate: SAV=65, Ref. 6, 15
[29] Correlate: SAV=65, Ref. 11
[30] Correlate: RC9=58, Ref. 15; AGG=67, Ref. 14
[31] Correlate: AGG=67, Ref. 12, 13, 14
[32] Correlate: RC8=63, Ref. 15
[33] Correlate: RC8=63, Ref. 13
[34] Correlate: SAV=65, Ref. 11, 12
[35] Correlate: RC9=58, Ref. 6, 11, 15
[36] Correlate: RC9=58, Ref. 15

FIGURE 7-1 Mr. C's MMPI-2-RF Police Candidate Interpretive Report, continued

MMPI-2-RF® Police Candidate Interpretive Report
11/11/2013, Page 17 Mr. C

RESEARCH REFERENCE LIST

The following studies are sources for empirical correlates identified in the Endnotes section of this report.

1. Anderson, J. L., Sellbom, M., Ayearst, L., Quilty, L. C., Chmielewski, M., & Bagby, R. M. (2015). Associations between DSM-5 Section III personality traits and the Minnesota Multiphasic Personality Inventory 2-Restructured Form (MMPI-2-RF) scales in a psychiatric patient sample. *Psychological Assessment, 27,* 801-815. doi: 10.1037/pas0000096

2. Anderson, J. L., Sellbom, M., Pymont, C., Smid, W., De Saeger, H. & Kamphuis, J. H. (2015). Measurement of DSM-5 Section II personality disorder constructs using the MMPI-2-RF in clinical and forensic samples. *Psychological Assessment, 27,* 786-800. doi: 10.1037/pas0000103

3. Ayearst, L. E., Sellbom, M., Trobst, K. K., & Bagby, R. M. (2013). Evaluating the interpersonal content of the MMPI-2-RF Interpersonal Scales. *Journal of Personality Assessment, 95,* 187-196. doi: 10.1080/00223891.2012.730085

4. Block, A. R., Ben-Porath, Y. S., & Marek, R. J. (2013). Psychological risk factors for poor outcome of spine surgery and spinal cord stimulator implant: A review of the literature and their assessment with the MMPI-2-RF. *The Clinical Neuropsychologist, 27,* 81-107. doi: 10.1080/13854046.2012.721007

5. Cox, A., Courrege, S. C., Felder, A. H., & Weed, N. C. (2017). Effects of augmenting response options of the MMPI-2-RF: An extension of previous findings. *Cogent Psychology, 4,* 1323988. doi: 10.1080/23311908.2017.1323988

6. Detrick, P., Ben-Porath, Y. S., & Sellbom, M. (2015). Associations between MMPI-2-RF (Restructured Form) and Inwald Personality Inventory (IPI) scale scores in a law enforcement preemployment screening sample. *Journal of Police and Criminal Psychology.* Advance online publication. doi: 10.1007/s11896-015-9172-7

7. Finn, J. A., Ben-Porath, Y. S., & Tellegen, A. (2015). Dichotomous versus polytomous response options in psychopathology assessment: Method or meaningful variance? *Psychological Assessment, 27,* 184-193. doi: 10.1037/pas0000044

8. Forbey, J. D., Lee, T. T. C., & Handel, R. W. (2010). Correlates of the MMPI-2-RF in a college setting. *Psychological Assessment, 22,* 737-744. doi: 10.1037/a0020645

9. Franz, A. O., Harrop, T. M., & McCord, D. M. (2017). Examining the construct validity of the MMPI-2-RF Interpersonal Functioning Scales using the Computerized Adaptive Test of Personality Disorder as a comparative framework. *Journal of Personality Assessment, 99,* 416-423. doi: 10.1080/00223891.2016.1222394

10. Sellbom, M. (2016). Elucidating the validity of the externalizing spectrum of psychopathology in correctional, forensic, and community Samples. *Journal of Abnormal Psychology, 125,* 1027-1038. doi: 10.1037/abn0000171

FIGURE 7-1 Mr. C's MMPI-2-RF Police Candidate Interpretive Report, continued

11. Tarescavage, A. M., Brewster, J., Corey, D. M., & Ben-Porath, Y. S. (2015). Use of pre-hire MMPI-2-RF police candidate scores to predict supervisor ratings of post-hire performance. *Assessment, 22,* 411-428. doi: 10.1177/1073191114548445

12. Tarescavage, A. M., Corey, D. M., & Ben-Porath, Y. S. (2015). Minnesota Multiphasic Personality Inventory-2-Restructured Form (MMPI-2-RF) predictors of police officer problem behavior. *Assessment, 22,* 116-132. doi: 10.1177/1073191114534885

13. Tarescavage, A. M., Corey, D. M., & Ben-Porath, Y. S. (2016). A prorating method for estimating MMPI-2-RF scores from MMPI responses: Examination of score fidelity and illustration of empirical utility in the PERSEREC police integrity study sample. *Assessment, 23,* 173-190. doi: 10.1177/1073191115575070

14. Tarescavage, A. M., Corey, D. M., Gupton, H. M., & Ben-Porath Y. S. (2015). Criterion validity and practical utility of the Minnesota Multiphasic Personality Inventory-2-Restructured Form (MMPI-2-RF) in assessments of police officer candidates. *Journal of Personality Assessment, 97,* 382-394. doi: 10.1080/00223891.2014.995800

15. Tarescavage, A. M., Fischler, G. L., Cappo, B., Hill, D. O., Corey, D. M., & Ben-Porath, Y. S. (2015). Minnesota Multiphasic Personality Inventory-2-Restructured Form (MMPI-2-RF) predictors of police officer problem behavior and collateral self-report test scores. *Psychological Assessment, 27,* 125-137. doi: 10.1037/pas0000041

16. Tarescavage, A. M., Glassmire, D. M., & Burchett, D. (2016). Introduction of a conceptual model for integrating the MMPI-2-RF into HCR-20V3 violence risk assessments and associations between the MMPI-2-RF and institutional violence. *Law and Human Behavior, 40,* 626-637. doi: 10.1037/lhb0000207

17. Tellegen, A., & Ben-Porath, Y. S. (2008/2011). *The Minnesota Multiphasic Personality Inventory-2-Restructured Form (MMPI-2-RF): Technical manual.* Minneapolis: University of Minnesota Press.

18. Van der Heijden, P. T., Egger, J. I. M., Rossi, G., Grundel, G., & Derksen, J. J. L. (2013). The MMPI-2 Restructured Form and the standard MMPI-2 Clinical Scales in relation to DSM-IV. *European Journal of Psychological Assessment, 29,* 182-188. doi: 10.1027/1015-5759/a000140

End of Report

FIGURE 7-1 Mr. C's MMPI-2-RF Police Candidate Interpretive Report, continued

Mr. C's substantial deviations from the comparison group mean. A detailed assessment of the validity of Mr. C's protocol follows on page 9. As illustrated in Mr. C's case, low scores on L-r or K-r can trigger interpretive statements here. Low scores can also produce interpretive statements for some of the substantive scales. Clinical findings and diagnostic considerations appear next. The small number of statements in this section reflects the low number of clinically elevated scores in Mr. C's protocol. Comparison group findings, including statements about the relatively low base rate of these findings in police candidates, appear beginning on page 10 of Mr. C's PCIR. Job-relevant correlates associated with Mr. C's MMPI-2-RF results are described beginning on page 11, and item-level data are reported on pages 12–15. As mentioned earlier, the content of items that Mr. C answered in the keyed direction is redacted in Figure 7-1 to maintain test security. Annotation, including the scale scores associated with each of the statements included in Mr. C's PCIR, appears on page 16 of his report. The annotation includes reference numbers for every correlate-based statement, with the citation and hyperlinks to the actual articles appearing on page 17 of Mr. C's PCIR.

Important Considerations When Using the MMPI-2-RF Police Candidate Interpretive Report in Preemployment Evaluations of Public Safety Candidates

At the conclusion of chapter 6, we identified some important limitations of the research base available to guide use of the MMPI-2-RF in preemployment evaluations of public safety candidates. Two such limitations are the insufficiency of test scores alone to predict adverse outcomes and the composition of available candidate and officer samples, which reflects the very high proportion of men in public safety positions, with limited availability of female data or comparative validity studies with minorities. We noted that the integrative model, which is described in detail in chapter 8, addresses the insufficiency issue by indicating that no single source is sufficiently strong to be solely dispositive and that test findings can, and in some instances should, be mitigated by other findings (from interview, background, or collateral information). We also commented that in the case of female and minority candidates, the relative dearth of empirical research should lead examiners to allow greater leeway for the other sources just mentioned to mitigate test findings. Because the PCIR is based on the same empirical research base, the same caveats and considerations should be applied when it is used in preemployment evaluations.

In the following chapter we describe and illustrate how to integrate MMPI-2-RF results, including ones obtained with the PCIR, with other sources of information in preemployment assessments of public safety candidates.

8

Using the MMPI-2-RF in Preemployment Assessments of Police and Public Safety Candidates

Case Illustrations and Guidance for Evidence-Based Report Writing

We demonstrate in this chapter how MMPI-2-RF score information can be integrated with personal history and background information, interview findings, and other test data to evaluate the psychological suitability of candidates in all four public safety job categories (police, corrections, firefighter/paramedic, and dispatcher). We also show how, when conducting evaluations of police officer candidates, information from the Police Candidate Interpretive Report (PCIR; discussed in chapter 7) can be integrated with other assessment data to arrive at suitability determinations with enhanced relevance, consistency, and defensibility. We begin by describing a model for integrating information from various sources used in psychological assessments of police and other public safety candidates.

An Integrative Model for Psychological Screening

Spilberg and Corey (2017) proposed a model for systematically integrating information from a psychological assessment of a police officer candidate to arrive at a suitability determination and "to minimize reliance on impressionistic judgments and maximize use of evidence-based methods and strategies" (p. 143). This five-step model, adapted here for use with all public safety candidates, is shown in Table 8-1.

The importance of beginning the integrative process with the consideration of test scores cannot be overemphasized. Indeed, the first two steps in the process involve a review of test data (protocol validity and

TABLE 8-1
Five-Step Model for Integrating Psychological Screening Data

Step	Description
1	**Assess Protocol Validity** Evaluate test scores for evidence of content nonresponsiveness, inconsistency, overreporting, and underreporting. MMPI-2-RF interpretation always begins with an inspection of the Validity Scales to determine whether the substantive test results are interpretable and, if so, whether any interpretive caveats are called for.
2	**Assess Findings from Substantive Scale Scores** Identify and interpret relevant findings from the substantive scale scores, first using standard norms and then, if available, position-specific comparison group norms.
3	**Assess Background Findings** Evaluate relevant personal history information from all available sources.
4	**Assess Interview Findings** Evaluate interview findings to determine how they are convergent with, divergent from, and/or complementary to relevant test findings and background information.
5	**Identify Relevant Risk Findings** Determine whether the weight of the findings (convergent, complementary, and divergent) supports the conclusion that the candidate meets the selection standards: a. Considering all risk-related findings from all sources, what evidence-based inferences can be drawn from them? Eliminate those that do not map onto the psychological screening dimensions or other selection criteria. b. What divergent findings mitigate these inferences? Eliminate those inferences that are outweighed by divergent findings of sufficient relevance, reliability, and validity. c. Are any surviving risk-related inferences of sufficient relevance and quality to warrant the candidate's disqualification?

Adapted with permission from Spilberg and Corey (2017).

substantive scales, respectively). This is because the accuracy of assessment judgments is optimized when data from within and across various assessment sources are weighted according to their relevance and reliability (Heilbrun, Grisso, & Goldstein, 2009), and the source with the greatest *known* relevance and reliability in police candidate assessments is psychological testing. The model then proceeds to a consideration of background information, for which relevance and reliability are less well established than for testing, but that nonetheless has greater empirical support than data obtained from the interview, which comprises the fourth step. The integrative process takes place at Step 5, when the examiner considers and weighs testing, background, and interview data to reach a suitability determination. We next illustrate these steps in a series of case studies based on actual, redacted screening assessments.

About the Case Studies

The cases we have selected for demonstration are not easy ones. Each falls in that gray zone in which screening professionals struggle over the interpretation and integration of mixed data—some indicating that the candidate possesses very positive traits and behavioral characteristics and at least one other data source indicating a substantial risk of future counterproductive behavior relevant to the screening dimensions (see chapter 1, Table 1-5). It is in this gray zone where the challenge of psychological assessment occurs. By using the integrative model just described, the task is made simpler, the process more systematic and reliable, and the outcome, therefore, made more valid, defensible, and intelligible.

The cases involve candidates for all four job categories: police officer, correctional officer, firefighter/paramedic, and emergency communications dispatcher. Although the facts in each case study reflect the actual material in the assessment record, details that might reveal each individual's identity have been altered. None of these alterations meaningfully changes the record.

Owing to space limitations, we have not reproduced the full set of assessment data in each case study (e.g., full results from the test of normal personality, the entire background investigation report, the candidate's complete responses to the personal history questionnaire, the screening psychologist's comprehensive interview notes, and complete medical records). Instead, we have selected the data from these various sources as appropriate to illustrate a particular case and to show how that information is integrated with findings from the MMPI-2-RF to reach a determination of suitability for a particular position. Individual readers may disagree with the suitability determinations provided in our case illustrations, just as screening professionals may come to different conclusions about candidates in actual practice. Our objective is not to suggest that there is only one possible or "right" determination in any case, but rather to guide readers' understanding of how the professional in each case applied the integration model to arrive at a determination—and to use the cases as launch points for other related guidance.

Each of the cases in this chapter illustrates the integration of MMPI-2-RF findings with collateral background information, self-reported history, clinical interview findings, and findings from normal personality testing. As discussed in chapter 5, this comprises the "basic model" of psychological screening of police and other public safety candidates. The cases we selected all used the California Psychological Inventory (CPI, version 434; Gough & Bradley, 1996), although any valid measure of normal personality could be substituted so long as it meets the criteria we cited in chapter 5. Local jurisdiction law may impose additional criteria on the selection of tests.

For readers wanting to delve more thoroughly into the process of data integration in public safety candidate assessments, we recommend reading all the cases, not just those from particular job categories. The material in each case is germane to all public safety evaluations, and they all have the same assessment components and psychological screening dimensions against which the assessment data are analyzed. In our first case, that of Mr. B, we also orient the reader to the integrative model. Finally, we have included two kinds of case studies: brief reviews, in which we focus on particular findings from the MMPI-2-RF while summarizing findings from other assessment components to illustrate key points, and comprehensive reviews, in which we provide lengthier, detailed analyses and discussion of the assessment data to illustrate the use of the MMPI-2-RF in the integrative model.

Comprehensive Review: Mr. B, Correctional Officer Candidate

Assessment Issues Presented

- Orientation to the integrative model
- Interpreting underreporting scores and the inference of deception

- Use of MMPI-2-RF items with historically verifiable content in conjunction with extra-test data (interview and background information) to assess for intentional deception

Referral Summary

Mr. B is a 31-year-old, never married, male correctional officer candidate. During the 2 years prior to his assessment, he worked in the construction field, and over the previous 4 years he worked in a warehouse loading trucks. He had no public safety experience. Mr. B earned a high school diploma and bachelor's degree. The background investigation found a number of "omissions and inconsistencies" in his self-reported history (discussed later under "Background Findings"). Regarding his references, the background investigator summarized, "Applicant is consistently described as someone who would be eligible for rehire by employers and who had no serious concerns, issues, or disciplinary actions."

Assessing Protocol Validity

A review of Mr. B's MMPI-2-RF scores (Figure 8-1) shows that he provided scorable responses to all 338 test items (CNS=0) and was consistent in his responding (VRIN-r=34T; TRIN-r=57). There also is no evidence of overreporting (F-r, Fp-r, Fs, FBS-r, and RBS are all below their respective score thresholds for interpreting the possibility of overreporting). Underreporting, however, is indicated by marked elevations on L-r (91T) and K-r (72T).

As we discussed in chapter 3, evidence of underreporting does not invalidate an MMPI-2-RF protocol in a personnel screening context. Owing to the impact of preselection and selection factors, demand characteristics, and other considerations, indications of possible underreporting are commonly found in police and public safety candidate protocols. This underscores the importance of scrutinizing the reliability of a candidate's self-report whenever L-r reaches or exceeds 81T and/or there is collateral

MMPI 2 RF®

Minnesota Multiphasic
Personality Inventory-2
Restructured Form®

Score Report

MMPI-2-RF®

Minnesota Multiphasic Personality Inventory-2-Restructured Form®

Yossef S. Ben-Porath, PhD, & Auke Tellegen, PhD

Name:	Mr. B
Age:	31
Gender:	Male
Marital Status:	Never Married
Years of Education:	17
Date Assessed:	02/22/2015

PsychCorp

Copyright © 2008, 2011, 2012 by the Regents of the University of Minnesota. All rights reserved.
Distributed exclusively under license from the University of Minnesota by NCS Pearson, Inc. Portions reproduced from the MMPI-2-RF test booklet. Copyright © 2008 by the Regents of the University of Minnesota. All rights reserved. Portions excerpted from the *MMPI-2-RF Manual for Administration, Scoring, and Interpretation*. Copyright © 2008, 2011 by the Regents of the University of Minnesota. All rights reserved. Used by permission of the University of Minnesota Press.

MMPI-2-RF, the **MMPI-2-RF logo,** and **Minnesota Multiphasic Personality Inventory-2-Restructured Form** are registered trademarks of the University of Minnesota. **Pearson,** the **PSI logo,** and **PsychCorp** are trademarks in the U.S. and/or other countries of Pearson Education, Inc., or its affiliate(s).

TRADE SECRET INFORMATION
Not for release under HIPAA or other data disclosure laws that exempt trade secrets from disclosure.

[3.0 / 2 / QG]

ALWAYS LEARNING PEARSON

FIGURE 8-1 Mr. B's MMPI-2-RF Score Report

MMPI-2-RF® Score Report
02/22/2015, Page 2 Mr. B

MMPI-2-RF Validity Scales

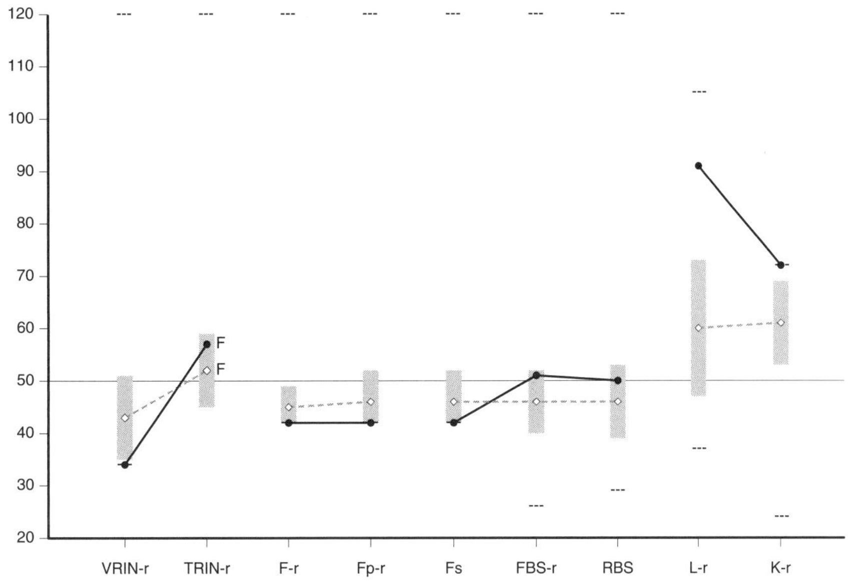

	VRIN-r	TRIN-r	F-r	Fp-r	Fs	FBS-r	RBS	L-r	K-r
Raw Score:	0	10	0	0	0	8	5	11	14
T Score:	34	57 F	42	42	42	51	50	91	72
Response %:	100	100	100	100	100	100	100	100	100

Cannot Say (Raw): 0 Percent True (of items answered): 25%

Comparison Group Data: Personnel Screening, Corrections Officer (Men and Women), N = 3036

	VRIN-r	TRIN-r	F-r	Fp-r	Fs	FBS-r	RBS	L-r	K-r
Mean Score (◇- - -◇):	43	52 F	45	46	46	46	46	60	61
Standard Dev (±1 SD):	8	7	4	6	6	6	7	13	8
Percent scoring at or below test taker:	17	90	69	69	65	87	81	99.1	100

The highest and lowest T scores possible on each scale are indicated by a "---"; MMPI-2-RF T scores are non-gendered.

VRIN-r Variable Response Inconsistency
TRIN-r True Response Inconsistency
F-r Infrequent Responses
Fp-r Infrequent Psychopathology Responses
Fs Infrequent Somatic Responses
FBS-r Symptom Validity
RBS Response Bias Scale
L-r Uncommon Virtues
K-r Adjustment Validity

FIGURE 8-1 Mr. B's MMPI-2-RF Score Report, continued

MMPI-2-RF® Score Report
02/22/2015, Page 3 Mr. B

MMPI-2-RF Higher-Order (H-O) and Restructured Clinical (RC) Scales

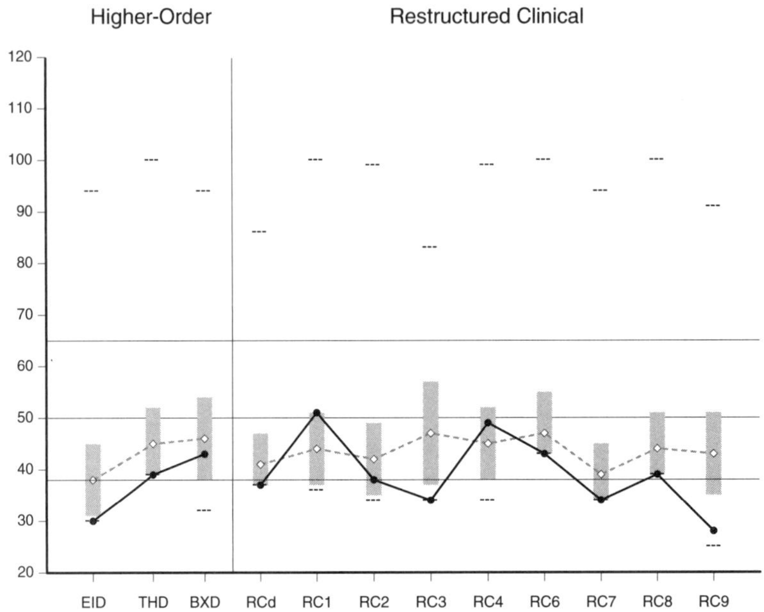

	EID	THD	BXD	RCd	RC1	RC2	RC3	RC4	RC6	RC7	RC8	RC9
Raw Score:	0	0	3	0	3	1	0	4	0	0	0	1
T Score:	30	39	43	37	51	38	34	49	43	34	39	28
Response %:	100	100	100	100	100	100	100	100	100	100	100	100
Comparison Group Data: Personnel Screening, Corrections Officer (Men and Women), N = 3036												
Mean Score (◇--◇):	38	45	46	41	44	42	47	45	47	39	44	43
Standard Dev (±1 SD):	7	7	8	6	7	7	10	7	8	6	7	8
Percent scoring at or below test taker:	16	54	45	50	86	46	13	78	72	37	53	3

The highest and lowest T scores possible on each scale are indicated by a "---"; MMPI-2-RF T scores are non-gendered.

EID Emotional/Internalizing Dysfunction
THD Thought Dysfunction
BXD Behavioral/Externalizing Dysfunction
RCd Demoralization
RC1 Somatic Complaints
RC2 Low Positive Emotions
RC3 Cynicism
RC4 Antisocial Behavior
RC6 Ideas of Persecution
RC7 Dysfunctional Negative Emotions
RC8 Aberrant Experiences
RC9 Hypomanic Activation

FIGURE 8-1 Mr. B's MMPI-2-RF Score Report, continued

MMPI-2-RF® Score Report
02/22/2015, Page 4

Mr. B

MMPI-2-RF Somatic/Cognitive and Internalizing Scales

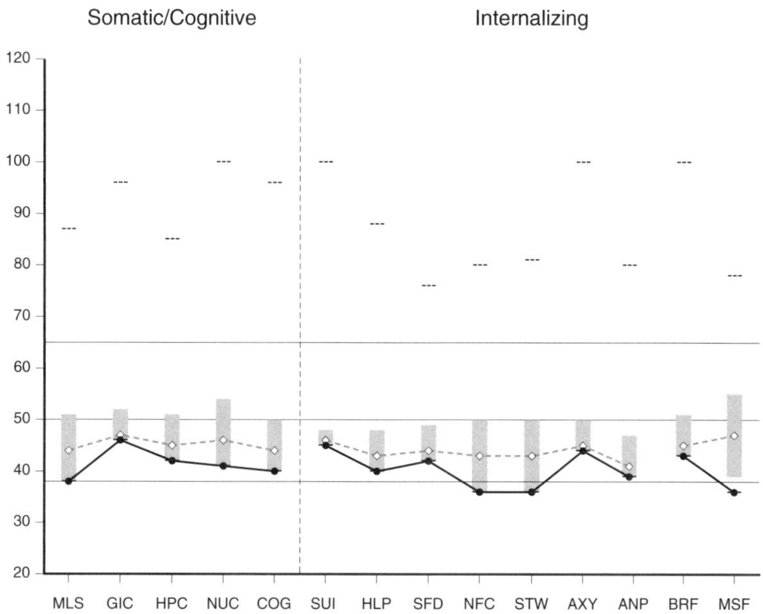

	MLS	GIC	HPC	NUC	COG	SUI	HLP	SFD	NFC	STW	AXY	ANP	BRF	MSF
Raw Score:	0	0	0	0	0	0	0	0	0	0	0	0	0	0
T Score:	38	46	42	41	40	45	40	42	36	36	44	39	43	36
Response %:	100	100	100	100	100	100	100	100	100	100	100	100	100	100

Comparison Group Data: Personnel Screening, Corrections Officer (Men and Women), N = 3036

Mean Score (◇- - -◇):	44	47	45	46	44	46	43	44	43	43	45	41	45	47
Standard Dev (±1 SD):	7	5	6	8	6	2	5	5	7	7	5	6	6	8
Percent scoring at or below test taker:	52	94	76	62	70	99	80	85	41	40	92	75	82	18

The highest and lowest T scores possible on each scale are indicated by a "---"; MMPI-2-RF T scores are non-gendered.

MLS	Malaise	SUI	Suicidal/Death Ideation	AXY	Anxiety
GIC	Gastrointestinal Complaints	HLP	Helplessness/Hopelessness	ANP	Anger Proneness
HPC	Head Pain Complaints	SFD	Self-Doubt	BRF	Behavior-Restricting Fears
NUC	Neurological Complaints	NFC	Inefficacy	MSF	Multiple Specific Fears
COG	Cognitive Complaints	STW	Stress/Worry		

FIGURE 8-1 Mr. B's MMPI-2-RF Score Report, continued

MMPI-2-RF Externalizing, Interpersonal, and Interest Scales

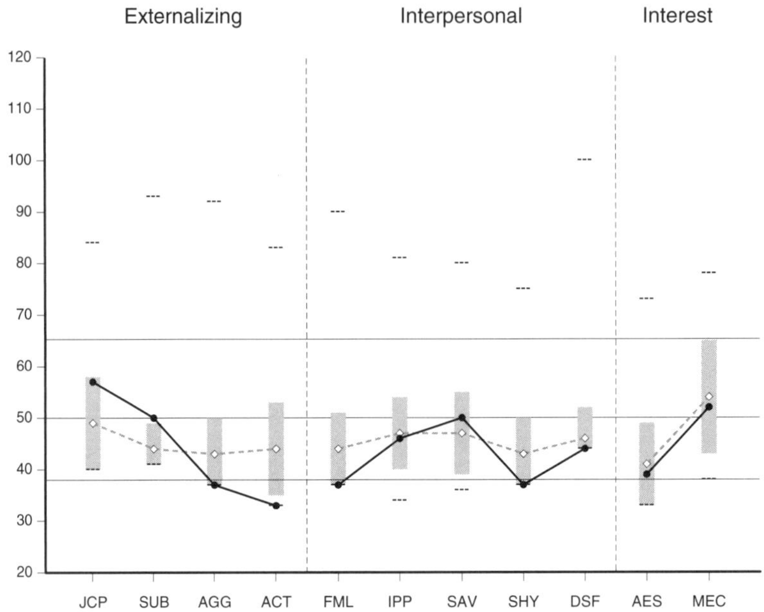

	JCP	SUB	AGG	ACT	FML	IPP	SAV	SHY	DSF	AES	MEC
Raw Score:	2	1	0	0	0	3	3	0	0	1	3
T Score:	57	50	37	33	37	46	50	37	44	39	52
Response %:	100	100	100	100	100	100	100	100	100	100	100

Comparison Group Data: Personnel Screening, Corrections Officer (Men and Women), N = 3036

	JCP	SUB	AGG	ACT	FML	IPP	SAV	SHY	DSF	AES	MEC
Mean Score (◇- - -◇):	49	44	43	44	44	47	47	43	46	41	54
Standard Dev (±1 SD):	9	5	7	9	7	7	8	7	6	8	11
Percent scoring at or below test taker:	88	93	51	23	42	61	76	42	86	61	51

The highest and lowest T scores possible on each scale are indicated by a "---"; MMPI-2-RF T scores are non-gendered.

JCP Juvenile Conduct Problems
SUB Substance Abuse
AGG Aggression
ACT Activation

FML Family Problems
IPP Interpersonal Passivity
SAV Social Avoidance
SHY Shyness
DSF Disaffiliativeness

AES Aesthetic-Literary Interests
MEC Mechanical-Physical Interests

FIGURE 8-1 Mr. B's MMPI-2-RF Score Report, continued

MMPI-2-RF PSY-5 Scales

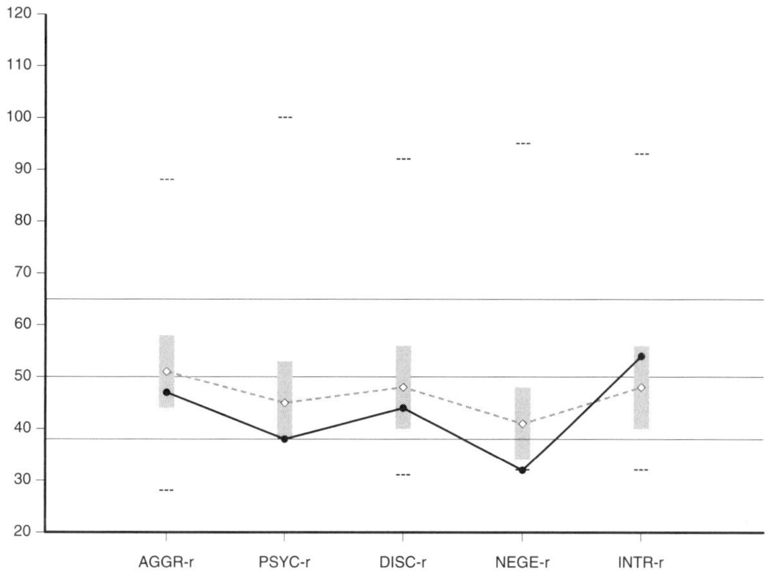

	AGGR-r	PSYC-r	DISC-r	NEGE-r	INTR-r
Raw Score:	8	0	4	0	8
T Score:	47	38	44	32	54
Response %:	100	100	100	100	100

Comparison Group Data: Personnel Screening, Corrections Officer (Men and Women), N = 3036

Mean Score (◇- - -◇):	51	45	48	41	48
Standard Dev (±1 SD):	7	8	8	7	8
Percent scoring at or below test taker:	40	51	37	20	85

The highest and lowest T scores possible on each scale are indicated by a "---"; MMPI-2-RF T scores are non-gendered.

AGGR-r Aggressiveness-Revised
PSYC-r Psychoticism-Revised
DISC-r Disconstraint-Revised
NEGE-r Negative Emotionality/Neuroticism-Revised
INTR-r Introversion/Low Positive Emotionality-Revised

FIGURE 8-1 Mr. B's MMPI-2-RF Score Report, continued

MMPI-2-RF T SCORES (BY DOMAIN)

PROTOCOL VALIDITY

Domain								
Content Non-Responsiveness		0 CNS	34 VRIN-r	57 F TRIN-r				
Over-Reporting		42 F-r	42 Fp-r		42 Fs	51 FBS-r	50 RBS	
Under-Reporting		91 L-r	72 K-r					

SUBSTANTIVE SCALES

Somatic/Cognitive Dysfunction		51 RC1	38 MLS	46 GIC	42 HPC	41 NUC	40 COG	
Emotional Dysfunction	30 EID	37 RCd	45 SUI	40 HLP	42 SFD	36 NFC		
		38 RC2	54 INTR-r					
		34 RC7	36 STW	44 AXY	39 ANP	43 BRF	36 MSF	32 NEGE-r
Thought Dysfunction	39 THD	43 RC6						
		39 RC8						
		38 PSYC-r						
Behavioral Dysfunction	43 BXD	49 RC4	57 JCP	50 SUB				
		28 RC9	37 AGG	33 ACT	47 AGGR-r	44 DISC-r		
Interpersonal Functioning		37 FML	34 RC3	46 IPP	50 SAV	37 SHY	44 DSF	
Interests		39 AES	52 MEC					

Note. This information is provided to facilitate interpretation following the recommended structure for MMPI-2-RF interpretation in Chapter 5 of the *MMPI-2-RF Manual for Administration, Scoring, and Interpretation*, which provides details in the text and an outline in Table 5-1.

FIGURE 8-1 Mr. B's MMPI-2-RF Score Report, continued

ITEM-LEVEL INFORMATION

Unscorable Responses

The test taker produced scorable responses to all the MMPI-2-RF items.

Critical Responses

Seven MMPI-2-RF scales--Suicidal/Death Ideation (SUI), Helplessness/Hopelessness (HLP), Anxiety (AXY), Ideas of Persecution (RC6), Aberrant Experiences (RC8), Substance Abuse (SUB), and Aggression (AGG)--have been designated by the test authors as having critical item content that may require immediate attention and follow-up. Items answered by the individual in the keyed direction (True or False) on a critical scale are listed below if his T score on that scale is 65 or higher.

The test taker has not produced an elevated T score (≥ 65) on any of these scales.

End of Report

This and previous pages of this report contain trade secrets and are not to be released in response to requests under HIPAA (or any other data disclosure law that exempts trade secret information from release). Further, release in response to litigation discovery demands should be made only in accordance with your profession's ethical guidelines and under an appropriate protective order.

FIGURE 8-1 Mr. B's MMPI-2-RF Score Report, continued

evidence of inconsistent or deceptive reporting in other components of the assessment process. Mr. B's L-r score of 91T meets this threshold and highlights the importance of interpreting the substantive scores with caution. This caveat is a function of the asymmetrical impact of underreporting on the substantive scales (Ben-Porath, 2012; see chapter 3 for discussion); namely, that nonelevated scores cannot be interpreted as indicating the absence of problems assessed by those scales (because the denial of problems may be an artifact of deception or distortion), and any score elevations that do exist (Mr. B's protocol has none), although interpretable at designated levels, may underestimate the problems measured by those scales (cf. Forbey, Lee, Ben-Porath, Arbisi, & Gartland, 2013).

Mr. B's L-r score (91T) indicates that he reports a very high level of moral virtuousness (fewer than 1% of Correctional Officer comparison group members claim more uncommon virtues; see Figure 8-1, p. 2, identifying the "Percent scoring at or below test taker" on L-r as 99.1% of the comparison group members), and his K-r score (72T, which is the ceiling on this scale) indicates a comparatively high level of psychological adjustment even among correctional officer candidates. As discussed in-depth in the PCIR *User's Guide*, high underreporting scores present three rival hypotheses that require confirmation from other collateral sources:

1. The candidate is well adjusted and endowed with positive virtues and presents these qualities accurately.
2. The candidate is well adjusted and endowed with positive virtues, but exaggerates or otherwise distorts these qualities.
3. The candidate presents, but does not actually possess, these qualities.

Collateral evidence to consider when choosing among these three possibilities includes information from the background investigation concerning the candidate's integrity and psychosocial functioning; evidence of consequential or material discrepancies in the self-reported history or between the self-reported history and confirmed background; and evidence from other tests or test items. With respect to this last source, we listed in Table 4-10 of the PCIR *User's Guide* 11 MMPI-2-RF items that contain potentially verifiable historical information. These items can aid test users in differentiating naïve responses (i.e., lacking in self-reflection or having a rigidly moralistic self-perception, often seen in individuals with a background stressing traditional values) from intentionally deceptive ones. Although these items are printed automatically in the PCIR if a test taker produces elevated scores on L-r, users of the MMPI-2-RF Score Report will need to manually check for the candidate's responses to them. Mr. B answered seven of the historically verifiable items listed in Table 4-10 of the PCIR *User's Guide*. Although for reasons of test security these items are not reprinted in this guide, they pertain to his past experiences and behavior. As we proceed through the remaining steps of our integrative model, we will want to be especially alert for information that might contradict these responses and, more generally, his self-report of being highly virtuous and well adjusted.

Because the "basic model" of psychological screening involves at least one broadband test of personality and psychopathology, and another measuring normal-range personality traits, screening examiners whose batteries include a test of normal personality with underreporting measures (e.g., positive impression management, good impression, defensiveness) have another source for evaluating these hypotheses, especially since candidates who are being deceptive are unlikely to be deceptive on just a single test or even a single component of the assessment process. In other words, candidates who are deceptive respond in this manner on testing, on personal history questionnaires, and in interviews, and they are often inconsistent in their deceptive reporting.

In the case of Mr. B, the assessment battery included the MMPI-2-RF and the CPI-434 (Gough & Bradley, 1996). Underreporting on the CPI is measured in three ways: the test taker's T-score on the Good Impression (Gi) scale; the difference between T-scores on Gi and Communality (Cm), with a difference ≥ 30T indicating positive impression management; and a protocol validity algorithm ("Fake Good") score > 60 (Gough & Bradley, 1996, p. 70). In Mr. B's case, all three methods indicate underreporting on the CPI (Gi = 81T, Gi-Cm = 33T, and Fake Good = 61.59).

When underreporting scores are high, screening professionals are sometimes tempted to readminister a test, with instructions to respond honestly (i.e., recentering instructions). We advise against this practice for two reasons: it alerts the candidate to respond differently but not necessarily more accurately, and altering standard instructions by inserting a caveat to answer honestly violates test standardization, thereby rendering the results uninterpretable against standardized norms. A preferred procedure when an evaluator concludes that retesting is warranted is to administer an alternate test measuring similar constructs, but still using the test's standard instructions. See chapter 10 for an in-depth discussion of recentering instructions.

Substantive Scale Findings

The review of substantive scale scores on the MMPI-2-RF, as discussed in chapter 4, always begins with an analysis of clinically significant findings (≥65T), followed by an analysis of moderately elevated or subclinical scores that are uncommon relative to the appropriate personnel comparison group, if available. Mr. B's scores on the MMPI-2-RF substantive scales are all well below 65T and indicate no clinically significant somatic, cognitive, emotional, thought, or behavioral dysfunction. However, in light of the evidence of possible underreporting just discussed, the absence of scale elevations cannot be interpreted as indicating the absence of problems measured by these scales. Mr. B's substantive scale scores also show no moderate-level elevations relative to the Correctional Officer comparison group, although the interpretive caveat just mentioned applies here too: the absence of comparison group findings cannot be interpreted as indicating the absence of problems they are used to assess.

One of the features of the MMPI-2-RF is the interpretability of a number of substantive scale scores at both upper and lower cutoffs (Ben-Porath, 2012; Ben-Porath & Tellegen, 2008/2011). Among these scales is the Hypomanic Activation (RC9) scale. Ben-Porath and Tellegen (2008/2011) note that the interpretive caution warranted by underreporting, whether intentional or unintentional, applies specifically to nonelevated (i.e., subclinical) scores and *particularly* to low scores (i.e., 38T or lower). Thus, Mr. B's score on RC9 (28T) *should not* be interpreted to mean, as it would in a non-underreported protocol, that he reports "a below-average level of activation and engagement with his environment" (Ben-Porath & Tellegen, 2008/2011, p. 44); rather, it should not be interpreted at all.

A review of Mr. B's scores on normal personality testing (CPI, where higher scores indicate better adjustment) reveals a similar pattern of denial of problems and claims of positive virtues. Using general adult norms, his scores (other than on Gi and Cm) ranged from 65T on Fx to 43T on Sa; using correctional officer norms (Roberts & Johnson, 2001), his scores ranged from 75T on Sc to 50T on Sa. The "fake good" indicators from that protocol, which we previously discussed, also preclude interpreting these scores to reflect the absence of problems.

Our review reveals so far that Mr. B presents implausibly as highly morally virtuous, well adjusted, and free of problems. We now review the remaining sources of assessment information in this case to see how their findings converge with or diverge from these test findings.

Background Findings

On the Statement of Personal History (SPH) that Mr. B completed for the hiring agency, a county sheriff's office, he failed to list a job he held for 4 years (2008–2012), although there is no indication that there was negative information from that job that he was trying to conceal. When asked about the omission by the background investigator, he "expressed surprise" and said he was sorry that he "really slipped up." He disclosed two traffic citations from 2005 and 2007, but he did not list five traffic citations occurring in 1999, 2002, and 2004. During the background interview, which took place after completing the SPH, Mr. B was asked whether there were any additional citations that he did not list, and he replied that there "may have been one other," but he did not specify the year or the infraction. He mischaracterized one traffic conviction as a "fix-it ticket" that was later dropped, but DMV records showed that it was not dropped and that he also received a concurrent conviction for failure to carry proof of insurance, which he also failed to list on the SPH or mention in the background interview. Parenthetically, it is not uncommon for public safety employers to make conditional offers of employment to candidates when such discrepancies exist, in part because memory is fallible and deceptive intent is not always clear.

Individuals associated with three former employers, including both supervisors and coworkers, provided very positive references for Mr. B. He was described as "stellar," well liked, easy to get along with, and accepting of direction. Personal references described him as "very smart," responsible, goal oriented, dependable, and "solid." None of the references were negative.

Mr. B disclosed in the background interview that he had been served a restraining order 7 years earlier and that it remained in effect for 1 year. The restraining order resulted from an incident in which he was charged and convicted of unlawful possession of a firearm, but this conviction was later expunged. The petitioner of the restraining order was Mr. B's former domestic partner. As he explained to the background investigator, Mr. B and several of his friends encountered the petitioner at a pool hall shortly after they had broken up. She called the police, alleging that he had been following her. When the police arrived and questioned Mr. B, he consented to a search of his vehicle, resulting in his arrest for the unlawful possession of a firearm.

In her petition for the restraining order, Mr. B's former domestic partner alleged that he had been "severely verbally abusive," sent her numerous harassing messages and voicemail, and drank heavily. She stated that she was "afraid that he'll break into my home and hurt me."

An isolated negative report such as this is also not uncommon in background investigations of candidates who go on to receive a conditional offer of employment. Background investigators, who are often current or retired law enforcement officers, cannot ascertain the truth in these "he said, she said" controversies, and when the allegations contained in them are in opposition to all of the other references, they are sometimes either dismissed as noncredible or considered too anomalous to warrant being given much, if any, weight. To some extent, the investigators also may reason that if the candidate is what the negative reference alleges, the psychological evaluation will bring it to light.

Candidates with credibility problems in the background are also more likely to be given conditional offers of employment when the hiring agency does not use detection-of-deception procedures (e.g., polygraph, voice stress analysis) or, as in the case of Mr. B, is in a jurisdiction that prohibits their use. When the hiring agency does use detection-of-deception procedures, the psychologist's access to the findings from them may facilitate more valid assessments.

Mr. B disclosed on his SPH that he had been in one physical altercation when he was 24 years old (7 years earlier). He explained that he had been drinking in a bar when a friend he was with "got mouthy" with another male patron, who then pushed his friend; Mr. B then stepped in, at which point a physical altercation ensued. The police were called, no arrests were made, but all of the individuals involved in the fight, including Mr. B, were ordered to leave. A police report confirmed Mr. B's version of the events.

In short, the background investigation revealed several discrepancies and omissions in his self-report involving information that would not have been disqualifying. In addition, all of his references were positive with the exception of one from a former domestic partner, whose successful petition for a restraining order 7 years earlier alleged harassment, verbal abuse, and alcohol abuse. The background investigation revealed nothing that would contradict Mr. B's assertion that he was, at least at the time of the evaluation, psychologically well adjusted.

Interview Findings

Although Mr. B completed a personal history questionnaire during the written testing phase of the evaluation and before the interview, we treat the information he provided in that questionnaire as a component of the interview. This is because his responses consist of self-reported history given in anticipation of the interview, and because the interview itself is largely structured around that history (e.g., as a review and clarification of certain historical and behavioral admissions related to the candidate's developmental, educational, occupational/military, substance use, avocational, legal, medical, and psychological history). As we noted in chapter 5, one of the purposes of the interview is to clarify personal history, and another is to test hypotheses that derive from the psychological testing and background investigation.

All of the material from the testing and background investigation presented so far in this case study was reviewed by the evaluator before conducting the interview. This is an essential procedural practice. In Mr. B's case, the evaluator had identified the candidate's responses to items in the history questionnaire that were consistent with, and discrepant from, information contained in the background investigation. This review produced the list of discrepancies shown in Table 8-2. Thus, the evaluator knew before the interview started that Mr. B had been deceptive, but the candidate's explanation for this was unknown. The evaluator also did not yet know whether there were any aspects of Mr. B's psychosocial functioning that would contradict his denial of problems and claims of good psychological adjustment. The screening professional constructed an interview strategy to elicit information needed to resolve these questions.

There are often discrepancies between facts contained in the background investigation and a candidate's self-report, sometimes owing to deception but more often a result of legitimate differences in perspectives or recollection about what occurred. However, discrepancies across self-reports are a characteristic marker of integrity problems and are associated with future counterproductive behavior (Cuttler & Muchinsky, 2006). It is also true that police and public safety candidates, like all persons, may lie on occasion, both by omission and commission. But not all lies are equally significant. Intentional and consequential lies (i.e., materially false statements and omissions of significant negative history) are of far greater importance to a screening professional than discrepancies resulting from the candidate's misunderstanding, confusion, or erroneous beliefs about what was being asked (Spilberg & Corey, 2017). In Mr. B's case, the discrepancies listed in Table 8-2 are consequential.

As an interview strategy, the evaluator chose to inquire initially about all aspects of the candidate's history without confronting him with these discrepancies. In this way, the evaluator was able to more reliably assess

TABLE 8-2
Discrepancies between Mr. B's Self-Reports and Background

Self-Reported in Personal History Questionnaire	Self-Reported to the Background Investigator	Discovered or Reported through Collateral Means
Two traffic citations in lifetime	Two traffic citations in lifetime and maybe one other	Seven traffic citations in lifetime
Not asked	Said that a "fix-it" ticket for an equipment violation on his car was "dropped" after he showed proof of repair	Was convicted of the equipment violation; it was not dropped
Had never been in a physical altercation and had never been involved in fighting after drinking	Had been in one fight 7 years before in a bar after drinking	Police report confirmed Mr. B's version of the event
Had never committed, or been accused of committing, threats of physical harm or stalking directed at a spouse or romantic partner, and had never been named in a legal restraining order for behavior that threatened others	Had been named in a physical restraining order petition filed by a former romantic partner; court ordered it for a duration of 1 year, because his ex-girlfriend mistakenly thought he was stalking her	Petition showed that Mr. B's former romantic partner filed it because she alleged he was stalking her and had repeatedly harassed and verbally abused her

Mr. B's positive adjustment, since, if the interview had begun by confronting him with his omissions and false statements, the remainder of the interview might have been overly influenced by it.

In the interview, Mr. B initially presented as engaging, self-confident (but not cocky), and affable. As the interview progressed through the various domains of his personal history, the screening professional was careful to probe for information that would aid in confirming the candidate's responses to the seven historically verifiable MMPI-2-RF items he had answered in the keyed direction (discussed earlier). Both the background information and the responses he gave in the interview were consistent with six of the seven items (his response to one item could not be verified). The evaluator also probed for evidence of good psychological adjustment, and Mr. B did, in fact, appear to function very effectively in all domains of his life—work, family, social relationships (notwithstanding the allegations from the incident with his girlfriend 7 years earlier). In addition, he showed good evidence of all of the psychological screening dimensions listed in Table 1-5 except for integrity.

Once the evaluator completed his standard interview, he informed Mr. B that there were several discrepancies in his statements in the interview and personal history questionnaire compared to information from the background investigation. The examiner went through the discrepancies listed in Table 8-2 and asked Mr. B to explain each one. With regard to the traffic citations, he implausibly said he simply forgot about the other five citations. He explained that he characterized the fix-it ticket as having been dropped because he "honestly thought it had." Concerning his false denials on the personal history questionnaire of fighting, fighting after drinking, being accused of stalking, and being served with a restraining order, in each case his explanation was that he "must've misread the question." At this point in the interview, Mr. B's demeanor changed dramatically from a fluid and engaging style to a defensive, curt, and arrogant one.

Identifying Relevant Risk Findings

As listed in Table 8-1, this fifth step in the integrative model requires that the psychologist examine the findings from all three sources (testing, background, and interview) to answer three questions, which we now apply to the findings in Mr. B's case.

a. Considering all risk-related findings from all sources, what evidence-based inferences can be drawn?

Test Findings. The one risk-related finding from Mr. B's test results involves the inference of intentional deception, which derives from his underreporting scores on the MMPI-2-RF and the CPI. Although these scores also raised two rival hypotheses (i.e., no deception vs. unintentional/naïve deception), the integrative model requires that we list at this stage only the risk-related inferences and, moreover, only those that "map onto" or conceptually link to the selection standards (see Table 1-5). The inference of intentional deception links directly to the Integrity dimension and, therefore, is relevant to our analysis. Because there are no other risk-related findings in the psychological test results, we now turn to the other assessment sources.

Background Findings. There are several risk-related findings contained in the background investigation. First, Mr. B falsely reported the number of traffic citations he received, omitting five citations in his SPH and four in his background interview, which is relevant to the Integrity/Ethics dimension. (He also failed to list a 4-year period of employment on the SPH, but this does not involve an omission of negative history and so is not counted as a risk-related finding relevant to Integrity/Ethics.) Second, an ex-girlfriend 7 years earlier made serious allegations of harassment, stalking, verbal abuse, and alcohol abuse; the court granted her petition for a 1-year restraining order against Mr. B owing to these allegations and a credible fear that he would break into her home and hurt her. This history constitutes a static risk factor for future partner abuse (Kropp, Hart, Webster, & Eaves, 1995) and represents conduct with particularly troubling implications for public safety officers (cf. Corey & Stewart, 2014). Mr. B's history of an alcohol-related bar fight is another risk-related finding, as is his arrest for unlawful possession of a firearm. Collectively, this history is relevant to the Impulse Control/Attention to Safety, Integrity/Ethics, Emotional Regulation/Stress Tolerance, Decision-Making and Judgment, and Avoiding Substance Abuse and Other Risk-Taking Behavior dimensions.

Interview Findings. The risk findings in the interview all relate to deception (i.e., Integrity/Ethics): four instances of false denial of significant negative personal history (fighting, fighting after drinking, being accused of stalking, and being served with a restraining order) and the omission of five traffic citations from his self-reported driving history (even after having been informed by the background investigator that his driving record revealed seven citations). It is arguable that Mr. B's defensive, curt, and arrogant response to being confronted in the interview with his various self-report discrepancies is another risk factor, although it, too, is ultimately implicated in his pattern of deception.

b. What divergent findings might mitigate these inferences?

The integrative model requires that we eliminate any identified risk-related inference that is mitigated by divergent findings of sufficient relevance, reliability, and validity. If credible, Mr. B's explanations for his omissions and false denials would constitute divergent findings mitigating the inference that his deception was intentional. However, it should be noted that Mr. B's scores on the VRIN-r and TRIN-r scales reflect assiduously careful attention to response consistency, and he completed both the history questionnaire and the MMPI-2-RF in the same session. Also, no other reading errors were found in his responses to the personal history questionnaire. Thus, it is not credible that Mr. B misread only the four questions about which his personal history was the most negative.

Mr. B's very positive references from all sources and a current background that is wholly positive are findings that diverge from the inference of intentional deception. However, even if these divergent findings are reliable, they are irrelevant to the particular findings of deception in this evaluation. If we accept that Mr. B is nearly always honest in his dealings with employers and others, this does not negate the relevance of lying (consequentially) in this evaluation. Indeed, even if these positive findings are valid, they are valid only for purposes of characterizing his past behavior. Mr. B's behavior in this assessment stands on its own and cannot be mitigated by behavior before or outside it. Thus, we conclude that the inference of intentional deception is not mitigated by any divergent data in the assessment record of sufficient relevance, reliability, and validity, and that it therefore survives the analysis.

c. Are any surviving risk-related inferences of sufficient relevance and quality to warrant the candidate's disqualification?

In some jurisdictions, this is an "ultimate question" that belongs to the employer. In others, it is the screening professional who has the responsibility for making this determination. In either case, the decision maker will necessarily rely on the relevance and quality of the inferences when making it. In Mr. B's case, the inference of deception is relevant both because of its job relatedness and because of its impact on the evaluator's ability to accurately assess the candidate's standing on the other screening dimensions. For a correctional officer, integrity is a requirement for reliable performance in a sworn position involving the enforcement of laws and regulations in a secure facility, conducting searches for contraband, writing official reports and providing sworn testimony, and promoting prosocial behavior in inmates. Consequently, Mr. B does not meet the selection criteria and is unqualified to be a correctional officer.

Comprehensive Review: Mr. M, Police Officer Candidate

Assessment Issues Presented

- Interpreting moderate underreporting scale scores
- Interpreting low and moderate substantive scale scores
- Use of the PCIR
- Integrating information from medical records with other assessment data

Referral Summary

Mr. M is a 29-year-old, recently divorced, male police officer candidate with a high school education. At the time of the evaluation, he was living with his romantic partner, their newborn baby, and three young children from his prior relationship. Mr. M's references were mostly positive. He worked part-time as an unarmed security officer. He recently graduated from a local police academy as a self-sponsored cadet and was described by one instructor as "talking too much."

Assessing Protocol Validity

Mr. M's PCIR (Figure 8-2) includes (on page 9 of the report) a narrative interpretation of protocol validity. As noted, the protocol contained no unscorable items, no indications of response inconsistency, and "no clear

MMPI 2 RF®

Minnesota Multiphasic
Personality Inventory-2
Restructured Form®

Yossef S. Ben-Porath, PhD, & Auke Tellegen, PhD

MMPI-2-RF®

Police Candidate Interpretive Report

David M. Corey, PhD, & Yossef S. Ben-Porath, PhD

Name:	Mr. M
Age:	29
Gender:	Male
Marital Status:	Divorced
Years of Education:	15
Date Assessed:	05/10/2015

Copyright © 2014 by the Regents of the University of Minnesota. All rights reserved.
Distributed exclusively under license from the University of Minnesota by NCS Pearson, Inc. Portions reproduced from the MMPI-2-RF test booklet. Copyright © 2008 by the Regents of the University of Minnesota. All rights reserved. Portions excerpted from the *MMPI-2-RF Manual for Administration, Scoring, and Interpretation.* Copyright © 2008, 2011 by the Regents of the University of Minnesota. All rights reserved. Used by permission of the University of Minnesota Press.

Minnesota Multiphasic Personality Inventory-2-Restructured Form and **MMPI-2-RF** are registered trademarks of the University of Minnesota. **Pearson** is a trademark in the U.S. and/or other countries of Pearson Education, Inc., or its affiliate(s).

This report contains copyrighted material and trade secrets. The qualified licensee may excerpt portions of this output report, limited to the minimum text necessary to accurately describe their significant core conclusions, for incorporation into a written evaluation of the examinee, in accordance with their profession's citation standards, if any. No adaptations, translations, modifications, or special versions may be made of this report without prior written permission from the University of Minnesota Press.

[4.0 / 57 / __VERSION__]

ALWAYS LEARNING PEARSON

FIGURE 8-2 Mr. M's MMPI-2-RF Police Candidate Interpretive Report

MMPI-2-RF Validity Scales

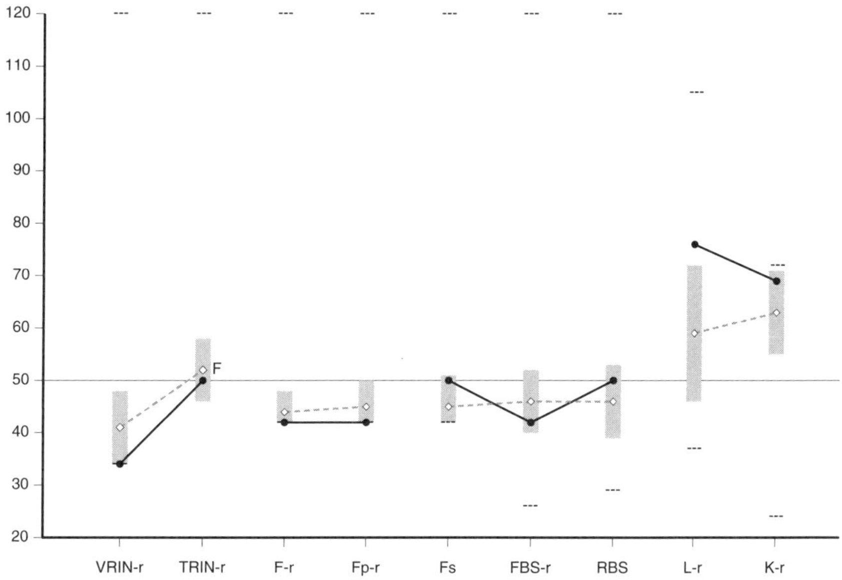

	VRIN-r	TRIN-r	F-r	Fp-r	Fs	FBS-r	RBS	L-r	K-r
Raw Score:	0	11	0	0	1	5	5	8	13
T Score:	34	50	42	42	50	42	50	76	69
Response %:	100	100	100	100	100	100	100	100	100

Cannot Say (Raw): 0 Percent True (of items answered): 34%

Comparison Group Data: Personnel Screening, Police Officer Candidate (Men and Women), N = 2074

	VRIN-r	TRIN-r	F-r	Fp-r	Fs	FBS-r	RBS	L-r	K-r
Mean Score (◇- - -◇):	41	52 F	44	45	45	46	46	59	63
Standard Dev (±1 SD):	7	6	4	5	6	6	7	13	8
Percent scoring at or below test taker:	28	62	75	78	92	32	81	90	82

The highest and lowest T scores possible on each scale are indicated by a "---"; MMPI-2-RF T scores are non-gendered.

VRIN-r	Variable Response Inconsistency
TRIN-r	True Response Inconsistency
F-r	Infrequent Responses
Fp-r	Infrequent Psychopathology Responses
Fs	Infrequent Somatic Responses
FBS-r	Symptom Validity
RBS	Response Bias Scale
L-r	Uncommon Virtues
K-r	Adjustment Validity

FIGURE 8-2 Mr. M's MMPI-2-RF Police Candidate Interpretive Report, continued

MMPI-2-RF® Police Candidate Interpretive Report
05/10/2015, Page 3 Mr. M

MMPI-2-RF Higher-Order (H-O) and Restructured Clinical (RC) Scales

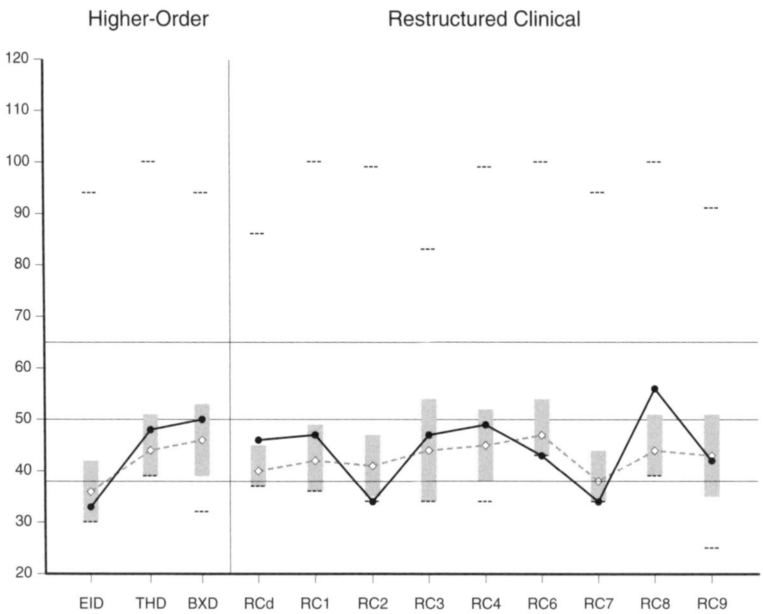

	EID	THD	BXD	RCd	RC1	RC2	RC3	RC4	RC6	RC7	RC8	RC9
Raw Score:	1	1	6	2	2	0	5	4	0	0	3	7
T Score:	33	48	50	46	47	34	47	49	43	34	56	42
Response %:	100	100	100	100	100	100	100	100	100	100	100	100

Comparison Group Data: Personnel Screening, Police Officer Candidate (Men and Women), N = 2074

Mean Score (◇--◇):	36	44	46	40	42	41	44	45	47	38	44	43
Standard Dev (±1 SD):	6	7	7	5	7	6	10	7	7	6	7	8
Percent scoring at or below test taker:	47	82	81	92	82	29	72	77	75	45	95	47

The highest and lowest T scores possible on each scale are indicated by a "---"; MMPI-2-RF T scores are non-gendered.

EID	Emotional/Internalizing Dysfunction	RCd	Demoralization	RC6	Ideas of Persecution
THD	Thought Dysfunction	RC1	Somatic Complaints	RC7	Dysfunctional Negative Emotions
BXD	Behavioral/Externalizing Dysfunction	RC2	Low Positive Emotions	RC8	Aberrant Experiences
		RC3	Cynicism	RC9	Hypomanic Activation
		RC4	Antisocial Behavior		

FIGURE 8-2 Mr. M's MMPI-2-RF Police Candidate Interpretive Report, continued

MMPI-2-RF® Police Candidate Interpretive Report
05/10/2015, Page 4 Mr. M

MMPI-2-RF Somatic/Cognitive and Internalizing Scales

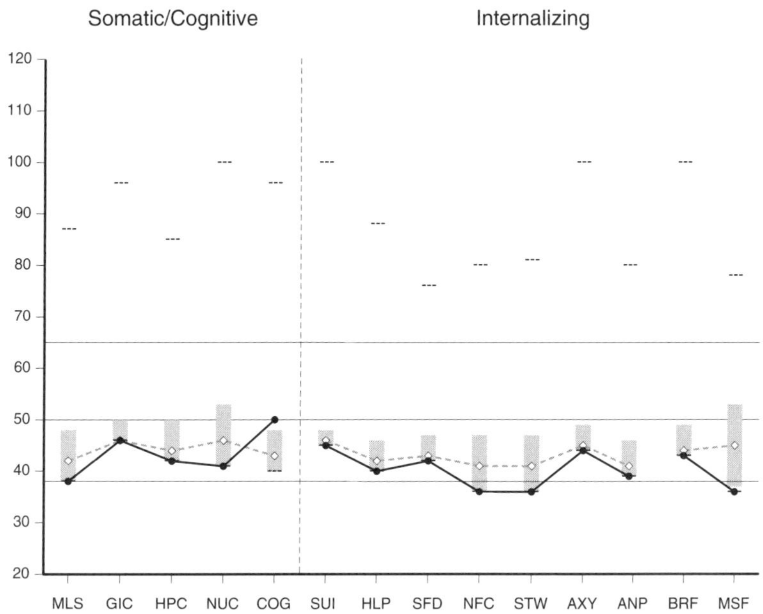

	MLS	GIC	HPC	NUC	COG	SUI	HLP	SFD	NFC	STW	AXY	ANP	BRF	MSF
Raw Score:	0	0	0	0	1	0	0	0	0	0	0	0	0	0
T Score:	38	46	42	41	50	45	40	42	36	36	44	39	43	36
Response %:	100	100	100	100	100	100	100	100	100	100	100	100	100	100

Comparison Group Data: Personnel Screening, Police Officer Candidate (Men and Women), N = 2074

	MLS	GIC	HPC	NUC	COG	SUI	HLP	SFD	NFC	STW	AXY	ANP	BRF	MSF
Mean Score (◇- - ◇):	42	46	44	46	43	46	42	43	41	41	45	41	44	45
Standard Dev (±1 SD):	6	4	6	7	5	2	4	4	6	6	4	5	5	8
Percent scoring at or below test taker:	63	95	83	65	93	99.3	88	90	50	48	94	81	88	25

The highest and lowest T scores possible on each scale are indicated by a "---"; MMPI-2-RF T scores are non-gendered.

MLS	Malaise	SUI	Suicidal/Death Ideation	AXY	Anxiety
GIC	Gastrointestinal Complaints	HLP	Helplessness/Hopelessness	ANP	Anger Proneness
HPC	Head Pain Complaints	SFD	Self-Doubt	BRF	Behavior-Restricting Fears
NUC	Neurological Complaints	NFC	Inefficacy	MSF	Multiple Specific Fears
COG	Cognitive Complaints	STW	Stress/Worry		

FIGURE 8-2 Mr. M's MMPI-2-RF Police Candidate Interpretive Report, continued

MMPI-2-RF Externalizing, Interpersonal, and Interest Scales

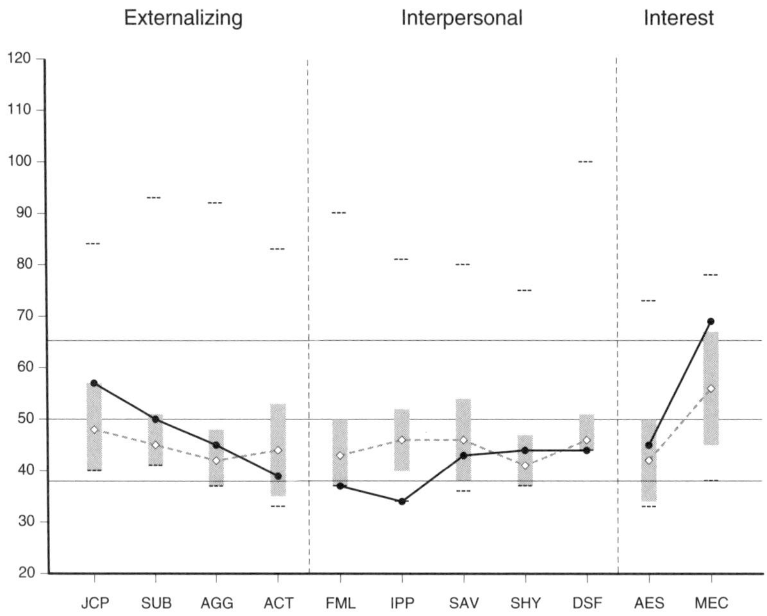

	JCP	SUB	AGG	ACT	FML	IPP	SAV	SHY	DSF	AES	MEC
Raw Score:	2	1	1	1	0	0	1	1	0	2	7
T Score:	57	50	45	39	37	34	43	44	44	45	69
Response %:	100	100	100	100	100	100	100	100	100	100	100

Comparison Group Data: Personnel Screening, Police Officer Candidate (Men and Women), N = 2074

	JCP	SUB	AGG	ACT	FML	IPP	SAV	SHY	DSF	AES	MEC
Mean Score (◇---◇):	48	45	42	44	43	46	46	41	46	42	56
Standard Dev (+1 SD):	9	6	6	9	7	6	8	6	5	8	11
Percent scoring at or below test taker:	90	90	84	42	47	5	45	80	90	79	91

The highest and lowest T scores possible on each scale are indicated by a "---"; MMPI-2-RF T scores are non-gendered.

JCP	Juvenile Conduct Problems	FML	Family Problems	AES	Aesthetic-Literary Interests
SUB	Substance Abuse	IPP	Interpersonal Passivity	MEC	Mechanical-Physical Interests
AGG	Aggression	SAV	Social Avoidance		
ACT	Activation	SHY	Shyness		
		DSF	Disaffiliativeness		

FIGURE 8-2 Mr. M's MMPI-2-RF Police Candidate Interpretive Report, continued

MMPI-2-RF PSY-5 Scales

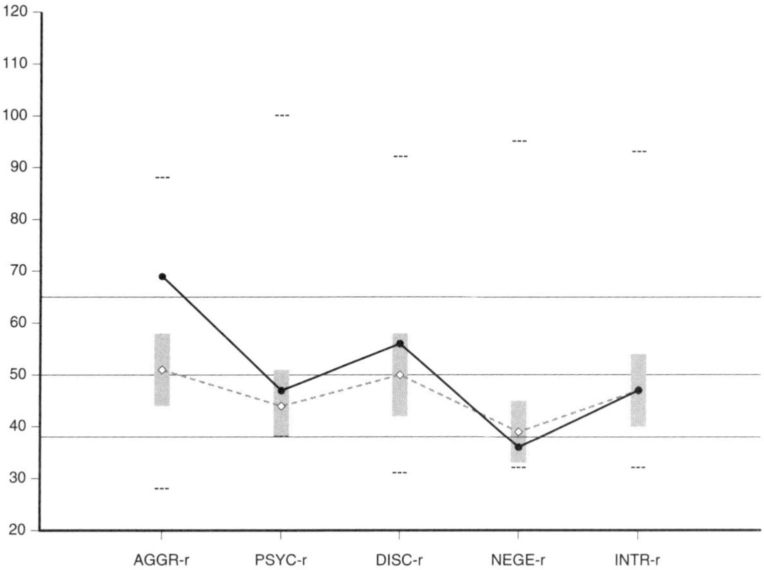

	AGGR-r	PSYC-r	DISC-r	NEGE-r	INTR-r
Raw Score:	14	1	9	1	5
T Score:	69	47	56	36	47
Response %:	100	100	100	100	100

Comparison Group Data: Personnel Screening, Police Officer Candidate (Men and Women), N = 2074

Mean Score (◇---◇):	51	44	50	39	47
Standard Dev (±1 SD):	7	7	8	6	7
Percent scoring at or below test taker:	99.5	80	87	50	62

The highest and lowest T scores possible on each scale are indicated by a "---"; MMPI-2-RF T scores are non-gendered.

AGGR-r Aggressiveness-Revised
PSYC-r Psychoticism-Revised
DISC-r Disconstraint-Revised
NEGE-r Negative Emotionality/Neuroticism-Revised
INTR-r Introversion/Low Positive Emotionality-Revised

FIGURE 8-2 Mr. M's MMPI-2-RF Police Candidate Interpretive Report, continued

MMPI-2-RF® Police Candidate Interpretive Report
05/10/2015, Page 7 Mr. M

MMPI-2-RF T SCORES (BY DOMAIN)

PROTOCOL VALIDITY

Content Non-Responsiveness		0 CNS	34 VRIN-r	50 TRIN-r				
Over-Reporting		42 F-r	42 Fp-r		50 Fs	42 FBS-r	50 RBS	
Under-Reporting		**76 L-r**	**69 K-r**					

SUBSTANTIVE SCALES

Somatic/Cognitive Dysfunction		47 RC1	38 MLS	46 GIC	42 HPC	41 NUC	50 COG	
Emotional Dysfunction	33 EID	46 RCd	45 SUI	40 HLP	42 SFD	36 NFC		
		34 RC2	47 INTR-r					
		34 RC7	36 STW	44 AXY	39 ANP	43 BRF	36 MSF	36 NEGE-r
Thought Dysfunction	48 THD	43 RC6						
		56 RC8						
		47 PSYC-r						
Behavioral Dysfunction	50 BXD	49 RC4	57 JCP	50 SUB				
		42 RC9	45 AGG	39 ACT	**69 AGGR-r**	56 DISC-r		
Interpersonal Functioning		37 FML	47 RC3	**34 IPP**	43 SAV	44 SHY	44 DSF	
Interests		45 AES	69 MEC					

Scale scores shown in bold font are interpreted in the report.

Note. This information is provided to facilitate interpretation following the recommended structure for MMPI-2-RF interpretation in Chapter 5 of the *MMPI-2-RF Manual for Administration, Scoring, and Interpretation*, which provides details in the text and an outline in Table 5-1.

FIGURE 8-2 Mr. M's MMPI-2-RF Police Candidate Interpretive Report, continued

MMPI-2-RF® Police Candidate Interpretive Report
05/10/2015, Page 8 Mr. M

This interpretive report is intended for use by a professional qualified to interpret the MMPI-2-RF in the context of preemployment psychological evaluations of police and other law enforcement officer candidates. ***It focuses on identifying problems; it does not convey potential strengths.*** *The information it contains should be considered in the context of the test taker's background, the demands of the position under consideration, the clinical interview, findings from supplemental tests, and other relevant information.*

The interpretive statements in the Protocol Validity section of the report are based on T scores derived from the general MMPI-2-RF normative sample, as well as scores obtained by the multisite sample of 2,074 individuals that make up the Police Officer Candidate comparison group.

The interpretive statements in the Clinical Findings and Diagnostic Considerations sections of the report are based on T scores derived from the general MMPI-2-RF normative sample. Following recommended practice, only T scores of 65 and higher are considered clinically significant. Scores at this clinical level are generally rare among police officer candidates.

Statements in the Comparison Group Findings and Job-Relevant Correlates sections are based on comparisons with scores obtained by the Police Officer Candidate comparison group. Statements in these sections may be based on T scores that, although less than 65, are nevertheless uncommon in reference to the comparison group.

Sources for interpretive statements in all sections are listed in the Endnotes section of this report. See User's Guide for the MMPI-2-RF Police Candidate Interpretive Report *for detailed information on report features.*

SYNOPSIS

This is a valid MMPI-2-RF protocol. There are no indications of clinically significant problems in the areas of somatic or cognitive complaints, or of clinically significant emotional, thought, behavioral, or interpersonal dysfunction.

Comparison group findings point to possible concerns about overly assertive behavior.

Possible job-relevant problems are identified in the following domains: Emotional Control and Stress Tolerance and Social Competence and Teamwork.

FIGURE 8-2 Mr. M's MMPI-2-RF Police Candidate Interpretive Report, continued

PROTOCOL VALIDITY

This is a valid MMPI-2-RF protocol. There are no problems with unscorable items. The test taker responded to the MMPI-2-RF in a remarkably consistent manner. He was deliberate in his approach to the assessment. There are no clear indications of over- or under-reporting.

However, the test taker presented himself in a positive light by denying minor faults and shortcomings that most people acknowledge[1]. This level of virtuous self-presentation may reflect a background stressing traditional values. It is also common among police officer candidates. Elevated scores on the substantive scales may to some extent underestimate the problems assessed by those scales[2].

In addition, the test taker presented himself as very well-adjusted[3]. This reported level of psychological adjustment is relatively rare in the general population but more common among police officer candidates. If there is collateral evidence that this individual is not well adjusted, any absence of elevation on the substantive scales should be interpreted with caution[4].

CLINICAL FINDINGS

There are no indications of clinically significant somatic, cognitive, emotional, thought, or behavioral dysfunction in this protocol.

DIAGNOSTIC CONSIDERATIONS

No specific psychodiagnostic recommendations are indicated by this MMPI-2-RF protocol.

COMPARISON GROUP FINDINGS

This section describes the MMPI-2-RF substantive scale findings in the context of the Police Officer Candidate comparison group. Specific sources for each statement can be accessed with the annotation features of this report. ***Job-related correlates of these results, if any, are provided in the subsequent Job-Relevant Correlates section.***

Interpersonal Problems

The test taker's responses indicate a level of overly assertive behavior that may be incompatible with public safety requirements for behavioral control[5]. This level of domineering behavior is very uncommon among police officer candidates. Only 5.1% of comparison group members give evidence of this level over-assertive behavior.

FIGURE 8-2 Mr. M's MMPI-2-RF Police Candidate Interpretive Report, continued

JOB-RELEVANT CORRELATES

Job-relevant personality characteristics and behavioral tendencies of the test taker are described in this section and organized according to ten problem domains commonly identified in the professional literature as relevant to police officer candidate suitability. (Please see User's Guide for MMPI-2-RF Police Candidate Interpretive Report *for details.) Statements that begin with "Compared with other police officer candidates" are based on correlations with other self-report measures obtained in police officer candidate samples that included individuals who were subsequently hired as well as those who were not. Statements that begin with "He is more likely than most police officers or trainees" are based on correlations with outcome data obtained in samples of hired candidates during academy or field training, probation, and/or the post-probation period. Specific sources for each statement can be accessed with the annotation features of this report.*

Emotional Control and Stress Tolerance Problems

Compared with other police officer candidates, the test taker is more likely to become impatient with others over minor infractions[6].

Social Competence and Teamwork Problems

The test taker is more likely than most police officers or trainees to exhibit difficulties cooperating with peers and/or supervisors[7].

The candidate's test scores are not associated with problems in the following domains:

- Routine Task Performance
- Decision-Making and Judgment
- Feedback Acceptance
- Assertiveness
- Integrity
- Conscientiousness and Dependability
- Substance Use
- Impulse Control

ITEM-LEVEL INFORMATION

Unscorable Responses

The test taker produced scorable responses to all the MMPI-2-RF items.

Critical Responses

Seven MMPI-2-RF scales--Suicidal/Death Ideation (SUI), Helplessness/Hopelessness (HLP), Anxiety (AXY), Ideas of Persecution (RC6), Aberrant Experiences (RC8), Substance Abuse (SUB), and Aggression (AGG)--have been designated by the test authors as having critical item content that may require immediate attention and follow-up. Items answered by the individual in the keyed direction (True or False) on a critical scale are listed below if his T score on that scale is 65 or higher.

FIGURE 8-2 Mr. M's MMPI-2-RF Police Candidate Interpretive Report, continued

The test taker has not produced an elevated T score (≥ 65) on any of these scales.

User-Designated Item-Level Information

The following item-level information is based on the report user's selection of additional scales, and/or of lower cutoffs for the critical scales from the previous section. Items answered by the test taker in the keyed direction (True or False) on a selected scale are listed below if his T score on that scale is at the user-designated cutoff score or higher. The percentage of the MMPI-2-RF normative sample (NS) and of the Personnel Screening, Police Officer Candidate (Men and Women) comparison group (CG) that answered each item in the keyed direction are provided in parentheses following the item content.

Aberrant Experiences (RC8, T Score = 56)

32. Item Content Omitted. (True; NS 21.1%, CG 15.0%)
199. Item Content Omitted. (True; NS 12.1%, CG 6.7%)
257. Item Content Omitted. (True; NS 12.4%, CG 4.3%)

Aggressiveness-Revised (AGGR-r, T Score = 69)

24. Item Content Omitted. (False; NS 74.6%, CG 96.5%)
39. Item Content Omitted. (True; NS 51.0%, CG 42.1%)
104. Item Content Omitted. (True; NS 67.1%, CG 53.0%)
147. Item Content Omitted. (True; NS 75.2%, CG 88.8%)
182. Item Content Omitted. (True; NS 33.6%, CG 72.4%)
197. Item Content Omitted. (True; NS 62.5%, CG 80.8%)
239. Item Content Omitted. (True; NS 60.7%, CG 91.9%)
256. Item Content Omitted. (True; NS 65.7%, CG 33.2%)
276. Item Content Omitted. (True; NS 50.0%, CG 77.6%)
302. Item Content Omitted. (True; NS 67.9%, CG 87.8%)
316. Item Content Omitted. (True; NS 45.1%, CG 30.7%)
319. Item Content Omitted. (False; NS 64.7%, CG 95.1%)
321. Item Content Omitted. (True; NS 31.3%, CG 27.2%)
327. Item Content Omitted. (True; NS 41.7%, CG 22.0%)

Critical Follow-up Items

This section contains a list of items to which the test taker responded in a manner warranting follow-up. The items were identified by police officer screening experts as having critical content. Clinicians are encouraged to follow up on these statements with the candidate by making related inquiries, rather than reciting the item(s) verbatim. Each item is followed by the candidate's response, the percentage of Police Officer Candidate comparison group members who gave this response, and the scale(s) on which the item appears.

FIGURE 8-2 Mr. M's MMPI-2-RF Police Candidate Interpretive Report, continued

257. Item Content Omitted. (True; 4.3%; VRIN-r, RC8, COG)

FIGURE 8-2 Mr. M's MMPI-2-RF Police Candidate Interpretive Report, continued

MMPI-2-RF® Police Candidate Interpretive Report
05/10/2015, Page 13 Mr. M

ENDNOTES

This section lists for each statement in the report the MMPI-2-RF score(s) that triggered it. In addition, each statement is identified as a Test Response, if based on item content, a Correlate, if based on empirical correlates, or an Inference, if based on the report authors' judgment. (This information can also be accessed on-screen by placing the cursor on a given statement.) For correlate-based statements, research references (Ref. No.) are provided, keyed to the consecutively numbered reference list following the endnotes.

[1] Test Response: L-r=76
[2] Correlate: L-r=76, Ref. 2, 3, 6
[3] Test Response: K-r=69
[4] Correlate: K-r=69, Ref. 2, 3, 6
[5] Inference: IPP=34
[6] Correlate: AGGR-r=69, Ref. 1, 5
[7] Correlate: AGGR-r=69, Ref. 4

FIGURE 8-2 Mr. M's MMPI-2-RF Police Candidate Interpretive Report, continued

RESEARCH REFERENCE LIST

The following studies are sources for empirical correlates identified in the Endnotes section of this report.

1. Detrick, P., Ben-Porath, Y.S., & Sellbom, M. (2015). Associations between MMPI-2-RF (Restructured Form) and Inwald Personality Inventory (IPI) scale scores in a law enforcement preemployment screening sample. *Journal of Police and Criminal Psychology.* Advance online publication. doi: 10.1007/s11896-015-9172-7

2. Forbey, J. D., Lee, T. T. C., Ben-Porath, Y. S., Arbisi, P. A., & Gartland, D. (2013). Associations between MMPI-2-RF validity scale scores and extra-test measures of personality and psychopathology. *Assessment, 20,* 448-461. doi: 10.1177/1073191113478154

3. Sellbom, M., & Bagby, R. M. (2008). The validity of the MMPI-2-RF (Restructured Form) L-r and K-r scales in detecting under-reporting in clinical and non-clinical samples. *Psychological Assessment, 20,* 370-376. doi: 10.1037/a0012952

4. Tarescavage, A. M., Corey, D. M., & Ben-Porath, Y. S. (2016). A prorating method for estimating MMPI-2-RF scores from MMPI responses: Examination of score fidelity and illustration of empirical utility in the PERSEREC police integrity study sample. *Assessment, 23,* 173-190. doi: 10.1177/1073191115575070

5. Tarescavage, A. M., Fischler, G. L., Cappo, B., Hill, D. O., Corey, D. M., & Ben-Porath, Y. S. (2015). Minnesota Multiphasic Personality Inventory-2-Restructured Form (MMPI-2-RF) predictors of police officer problem behavior and collateral self-report test scores. *Psychological Assessment, 27,* 125-137. doi: 10.1037/pas0000041

6. Tellegen, A., & Ben-Porath, Y. S. (2008/2011). *The Minnesota Multiphasic Personality Inventory-2-Restructured Form (MMPI-2-RF): Technical manual.* Minneapolis: University of Minnesota Press.

End of Report

FIGURE 8-2 Mr. M's MMPI-2-RF Police Candidate Interpretive Report, continued

indications of over- or underreporting." Although the report notes that Mr. M presented himself in a positive light by denying minor faults and shortcomings that most people acknowledge, it also points out that this level of virtuous self-presentation is common among police officer candidates. Indeed, 15.9% of the members of the Police Officer Candidate comparison group (N=2,074) scored at or above Mr. M's score on L-r (76T). Nevertheless, the report reminds the user that elevated scores on the substantive scales "may to some extent underestimate the problems assessed by those scales" (p. 9). Mr. M also presented himself as very well adjusted (K-r=69T), but this, too, is commonly found among police officer candidates, with 37.9% of Police Officer Candidate comparison group members scoring at or above this level. In light of the possibility of underreporting, the PCIR advises the user, "If there is collateral evidence that this individual is not well adjusted, any absence of elevation on the substantive scales should be interpreted with caution" (p. 9).

Mr. M's scores on the three underreporting measures of the CPI present a similar pattern. He scored at 73T on the Gi scale, 45T on the Cm scale, and 60.1T on the Fake Good algorithm, providing mixed evidence of underreporting and warranting caution when interpreting the absence of negative findings as meaning the absence of problems.

Substantive Scale Findings

A review of Mr. M's scores on the MMPI-2-RF substantive scales reveals a moderate elevation on RC8 (Aberrant Experiences; 56T), a very low score on IPP (Interpersonal Passivity; 34T, which is at the floor on this scale), and a clinically elevated score on AGGR-r (Aggressiveness-Revised; 69T). Users of the PCIR can see at a glance which MMPI-2-RF scores are interpreted in the report (Figure 8-2, p. 7) by noting those scales and scores that are printed in **bold font**. Although RC8 is elevated relative to other police officer candidates, it is not interpreted at this score level in the PCIR. This is because 10.6% of the members of the Police Officer Candidate comparison group score at or above this level, and scores in the PCIR are generally interpreted at cutoffs that occur in less than

10% of comparison group members. This leaves IPP and AGGR-r as the two substantive scales interpreted in Mr. M's protocol, which we discuss later under "Identifying Relevant Risk Findings."

The PCIR also includes Critical Follow-Up Items that police officer screening experts identified as having critical content warranting follow-up. In Mr. M's case, he responded in the keyed direction to item 257 (Figure 8-2, p. 12). The parenthetical information that follows the item (the item is printed out in the actual report but is omitted here for test security) indicates that Mr. M responded true to that item; only 4.3% of members of the Police Officer Candidate comparison group responded true; and the item appears on VRIN-r, RC8, and COG. The screening professional would want to probe in the interview for information relevant to the content of the item (having to do with unusual thoughts), but without reading the item verbatim or otherwise alerting the candidate to the fact that the inquiry relates to a response he gave on the test.

A review of Mr. M's scores on normal-range testing (CPI) reveals no significant findings using either general adult or police applicant norms. Against general adult norms, his scores (not including Gi and Cm, reviewed earlier) ranged from 70T on Do, to 51T on To. Using police applicant norms (Roberts & Johnson, 2001), his two highest scores were on In (62T) and Sy (61T), and his two lowest scores were on So (38T) and To (30T). In light of possible underreporting, and consistent with the protocol validity admonishment in the PCIR, caution should be used when interpreting these scores to indicate the absence of problems and (on the CPI) the presence of positive traits.

Background Findings

Mr. M's current and former employers and coworkers gave entirely positive references and described him as dependable, honest, having integrity, "and devoted to his children and family." However, his next-door neighbor, who is the brother of Mr. M's domestic partner, reported "hearing them argue in the past." The background investigation included no other details concerning this report. When, as here, a background investigator fails to provide enough elaboration to enable the screening professional to weigh the reliability and significance of the information, the evaluator should contact the investigator to obtain it. It would be helpful to know, for example, if the reporter was motivated to hurt Mr. M's employment prospects, when the alleged argument(s) occurred, and whether Mr. M was also overheard to be shouting, throwing or breaking objects, or verbally abusing his partner. It is notable that sharing this kind of information between the screening professional and the background investigator is specifically authorized under California POST regulations (POST Commission Regulation 1953[g][3]) and constitutes a best practice.

The background investigation also revealed that Mr. M served in the U.S. Marine Corps (USMC) for 5 years until receiving a general discharge 4 years ago for use of a synthetic drug as a substitute for marijuana. At the time that the background investigation was completed, Mr. M's DD 214—the Certificate of Release or Discharge from Active Duty, which characterizes the service member's formal discharge conditions—had not been received.

He also was delinquent on multiple debts to creditors, several of which were seriously past due, which he attributed to his recent divorce, and he and his ex-wife had filed for bankruptcy 5 years earlier. The background investigation stated that "any illegal drug use was done at an early age," but this appears to contradict the facts pertaining to his military discharge. It also concluded that "he is not known to drink or abuse alcohol."

Interview Findings

Mr. M described a tumultuous upbringing by a twice-divorced mother and a violent stepfather in a home in which marijuana was used regularly. He said he also regularly smoked marijuana throughout high school. He reported being expelled twice in high school for fighting and vandalism, and being suspended repeatedly for fighting. He stated, "I was the bully that picked on the bullies."

Mr. M disclosed in the interview that he was diagnosed with ADHD as a child and took prescribed stimulants during his freshman year only, after which, he said, he outgrew it. He said he filed for a service-connected disability 6 years earlier and, in the course of his Compensation and Pension (C&P) evaluation by the Department of Veterans Affairs (VA), he was diagnosed with PTSD, anxiety, and depression, in addition to several physical conditions resulting from injuries sustained in Afghanistan. He reported that he was awarded a 40% disability rating for his psychiatric conditions and continues to receive monthly disability benefits. He said he experiences night terrors at least once a week and only sleeps 3 or 4 hours per night because of difficulty falling and staying asleep. On his personal history questionnaire, Mr. M reported that he had never been in counseling; however, in the interview he said that he attended a 30-day rehabilitation center for alcohol abuse while enlisted in the USMC. He said he continued to drink, without abuse, until last year, when he entered the police academy.

Mr. M said he received a prescription for medications from a VA psychiatrist to treat symptoms related to his conditions, but he could not recall what they were and said he had not taken or been prescribed any for more than a year. In light of Mr. M's relatively recent treatment history, his psychiatric disability rating, and his disclosure of significant insomnia and night terrors, the screening professional told the candidate and hiring agency that she would need to review the candidate's psychiatric treatment records from the VA, as well as his C&P evaluation and determination letter, before deciding about his psychological suitability. This is an important practice and should be done routinely in such instances. On receiving the records, the psychologist discovered that the candidate was prescribed two antidepressants for depression and a sympatholytic drug for treatment of anxiety symptoms, which included night terrors. The psychiatric records revealed that Mr. M had been given a 90-day supply of these medications 5 months prior to the evaluation.

In the interview, the candidate described an incident in which he had been offended by a comment made by a fellow marine about the collateral deaths of some Afghan women and children. With apparent pride, Mr. M said that he hit the marine in the face and broke his jaw. He said there were no disciplinary consequences resulting from this assault. Mr. M also reported that, when his commanding officer questioned him about his use of the synthetic drug—which Mr. M claimed he did not know was illegal—the officer grabbed his shirt and, in turn, Mr. M assaulted him. He implausibly insisted that there were no disciplinary consequences for this assault, although it is notable that his general discharge occurred shortly after that incident. Without the candidate's DD 214, it is not possible to determine the classification of his discharge and the reasons for it.

The screening professional characterized her impression of Mr. M in the interview as being arrogant, inappropriately familiar, and flippant. She noted that he often expressed annoyance and irritation in response to her questions.

Identifying Relevant Risk Findings

a. Considering all risk-related findings from all sources, what evidence-based inferences can be drawn?

Test Findings. The Clinical Findings section of Mr. M's PCIR states that there are "no indications of clinically significant somatic, cognitive, emotional, thought, or behavioral dysfunction in this protocol" (Figure 8-2, p. 9), despite AGGR-r being at 69T. This is because of an interpretive convention that Personality Psychopathology Five (PSY-5) scale scores are not interpreted in the Clinical Findings section unless either a Higher-Order (H-O) scale or Restructured Clinical (RC) scale within its associated domain is also clinically elevated (see *Interpreting the MMPI-2-RF*; Ben-Porath, 2012, p. 320). AGGR-r falls in the Behavioral Dysfunction domain with H-O Scale BXD (Behavioral/Externalizing Dysfunction) and RC Scale RC4 and RC9. Therefore, unless BXD, RC4, or RC9 is at or above 65T, AGGR-r is not to be interpreted independently in the Clinical Findings section.

In the Comparison Group Findings section of the PCIR, the implications of Mr. M's score on the IPP scale, part of the Interpersonal Problems domain, are described as follows:

> The test taker's responses indicate a level of overly assertive behavior that may be incompatible with public safety requirements for behavioral control.

> This level of domineering behavior is very uncommon among police officer candidates. Only 5.1% of comparison group members give evidence of this level of over-assertive behavior. (Figure 8-2, p. 9)

Note that only the IPP score is interpreted in the Comparison Group Findings (CGF) section, and not AGGR-r. This is because the CGF interpretation is identical for both low IPP and high AGGR-r, and in that instance the interpretation of AGGR-r is suppressed to avoid redundancy.

The Job-Relevant Correlates (JRC) section of the PCIR contains statements referring to two types of correlates: other self-report measures obtained in police officer candidate samples that included individuals who were subsequently hired as well as those who were not, and outcome data obtained in samples of hired candidates during academy or field training, probation, and/or the postprobation period. As explained in the italicized boilerplate language at the top of page 10 of Mr. M's PCIR, the self-report correlates can be recognized in the report by the statement stem, "Compared with other police officer candidates," and the outcome correlates will always begin with, "The test taker is more likely than most police officers or trainees."

Mr. M's scores on AGGR-r produced one of each type of correlate. The self-report correlate is associated with Emotional Control and Stress Tolerance Problems: "Compared with other police officer candidates, the test taker is more likely to become impatient with others over minor infractions." The outcome correlate is associated with Social Competence and Teamwork Problems: "The test taker is more likely than most police officers or trainees to exhibit difficulties cooperating with peers and/or supervisors."

Mr. M's score on the CPI produced no clear findings associated with evidence-based inferences other than his low score on the Tolerance scale (To=30T) when compared to police applicant norms. Possible inferences to be considered in connection with other collateral evidence include intolerance, distrust, prejudice, self-centeredness, and having little concern about the feelings of others (Gough & Bradley, 1996). Job-relevant correlates of low scores on To found in the police literature include disciplinary actions and negative supervisor ratings (Aamodt, 2004).

Background Findings. Mr. M's background investigation is a good example of an inadequate effort to clarify negative information. But even a background investigation that leaves as many unanswered questions as Mr. M's is a valuable contributor to the assessment and underscores the importance of having access to collateral background information. Mr. M's history reveals a general discharge from the military for illegal drug use, which infers the potential for excessive risk-taking behavior, low conscientiousness, and integrity problems. His long-standing debt delinquencies also infer low conscientiousness.

Interview Findings. Principal among the interview findings is evidence of a current, serious, and presently untreated mental health condition with substantial impairment in one or more major life activities (sleep), with strong confirmatory evidence provided by collateral medical records. This, of course, is relevant to the Emotional Control/Stress Resilience dimension. The interview also yielded findings related to Mr. M's interpersonal behavior and traits that are consistent with findings on the MMPI-2-RF IPP/AGGR-r scales showing overly assertive and highly domineering behavior, which are pertinent to the Social Competence and Teamwork dimensions. In addition to the job-relevant correlates of the AGGR-r scale listed in the PCIR, elevated AGGR-r scores are associated with DSM-5 Cluster B disorders, in particular with narcissistic and antisocial personality disorders, and are negatively correlated with the Agreeability dimension of the Five-Factor Model of personality (Ben-Porath, 2012).

b. What divergent findings might mitigate these inferences?

Mr. M's scores on the MMPI-2-RF substantive scales do not reflect the range of clinical problems suggested by his mental health history. However, as noted in the protocol validity section of the PCIR, collateral evidence that he is not well adjusted should lead us to interpret cautiously any absence of elevation on the substantive scales. There is strong evidence of divergent findings suggesting poor psychological adjustment, as indicated by Mr. M's mental health records and his disclosure of current sleep impairment (i.e., night terrors and insomnia), marital arguments overheard by his next-door neighbor, and chronic, long-standing financial problems. Therefore, the absence of substantive scale score elevations on the MMPI-2-RF is not sufficiently reliable to mitigate inferences from the collateral findings. Rather, Mr. M's responses to the relevant MMPI-2-RF items are contradicted by the records just mentioned, and this provides evidence of serious and consequential deception.

Mr. M's work and personal references indicate positive and cooperative relationships with supervisors and coworkers. These findings are divergent from test and interview findings, including those related to Mr. M's military history, which indicate poor interpersonal functioning. However, the reliability of these background findings is undermined by the poor quality of the background investigation and the comparatively strong reliability and validity of the test and interview findings (including subsequently obtained collateral information); therefore, the negative inferences derived from the testing and interview survive this analysis.

c. Are any surviving risk-related inferences of sufficient relevance and quality to warrant the candidate's disqualification?

The quality of the risk-related inferences pertaining to Mr. M's mental health problems is high, and it is amplified by his denial of problems in written testing. The screening professional took the prudent step of acquiring mental health records showing recent treatment that Mr. M prematurely terminated against medical advice, and he reported in the interview ongoing night terrors and insomnia, giving further support to his need for treatment. In addition, his self-reported military history, behavior in the interview, and substantive scale scores on both the MMPI-2-RF and CPI indicate significantly problematic interpersonal traits and behaviors.

As we have discussed previously, evidence of a mental health condition or impairment should be considered in light of its job relevance. This is determined by the impact of the condition on the candidate's functioning as measured against the screening dimensions. In Mr. M's case, his untreated sleep disorder, depression, anxiety, and PTSD would be reasonably expected to impair emotional regulation and stress resilience, impulse control/attention to safety, decision-making/judgment, and avoidance of substance abuse and other risk-taking behavior. In addition, his domineering and excessively assertive behavior would be reasonably expected to impair social competence, teamwork, adaptability/flexibility, and assertiveness/persuasiveness. The various false statements Mr. M made in the interview (e.g., initially stating that he had never been in treatment and then disclosing his residential treatment for alcohol abuse) also raise concerns about his integrity and decision-making/judgment.

There are certainly other findings in this assessment that one could arguably cite as further indications of the risks Mr. M would pose as a police officer, but doing so would only "gild the lily" and, in our opinion, undermine the defensibility of the determination made by the evaluating psychologist that Mr. M fails to meet the suitability criteria for the position. Although it may be tempting to cite, for example, his significant history of juvenile conduct problems, his purportedly resolved ADHD, or a potentially relapsed alcohol use disorder, the quality of the evidence related to each of these findings is weak, and anchoring an otherwise strongly supported determination of unsuitability to these findings would only undermine the defensibility of the decision.

Brief Review: Mr. K, Corrections Deputy Candidate

Assessment Issues Presented

- Use of the PCIR in evaluating a correctional officer candidate in a rural county whose job functions substantially overlap with those of a patrol deputy
- An MMPI-2-RF protocol with moderate (<65T) substantive scale elevations interpreted only in the Comparison Group Findings section of the PCIR and with no interpretive statements generated in the Job-Relevant Correlates section

Referral Summary

Mr. K is a 38-year-old married male seeking a first-time appointment as a corrections deputy with a rural county sheriff's office, in which corrections deputies also perform patrol and enforcement functions and carry firearms (except when performing corrections duties inside the jail). In addition, appointment to a full-time patrol deputy is made at the sheriff's discretion from the pool of incumbent corrections deputies without an updated psychological evaluation. At the time of the evaluation, Mr. K was unemployed, having been laid off from his decade-long position with a farm equipment company owing to an economic reduction in force. He spent his entire childhood and adulthood in the same small, rural community.

Use of the PCIR for Non–Police Officer Positions

The empirical support for the interpretive statements in the PCIR derives from three sources. In the Clinical Findings section, in which statements are generated only for scales with a T-score of 65 or higher, the empirical support comes from the broad literature pertaining to the general adult population and is not specific to any personnel category. In the Comparison Group Findings section, the construct-based statements describe implications of clinically elevated substantive scale scores, as well as statements about possible implications of uncommonly high (but not clinically elevated) scores for police officer candidates. Base-rate information (derived from the Police Officer Candidate comparison group) is provided for both clinically elevated and nonelevated scores that generate interpretive statements. Finally, in the Job-Relevant Correlates section of the PCIR, empirical support rests on a series of studies, summarized in chapter 6, that pertain exclusively to police candidates and officers. Consequently, the use of the PCIR should be limited to evaluations of candidates for positions with job functions having substantial similarity to those in the Police Officer Candidate comparison group.

As noted in the background summary for Mr. K, the hiring agency is essentially creating a pool of eligible patrol deputies by hiring corrections deputies who meet the same qualification standards, assigning them limited patrol functions in addition to their corrections duties, and observing their relative competencies in these dual roles. In this case, the functional overlap between the corrections deputy and patrol deputy positions is quite high, justifying the use of the PCIR for screening corrections deputy candidates. This conclusion is also validated by a comparison of the counterproductive behaviors to those contained in the 10 problem domains used as the organizing structure for the Job-Related Correlates section of the PCIR (*User's Guide,* Table 4-7). Each of the 10 domains contains job-relevant problems that are counterproductive for both corrections deputies and patrol deputies.

Assessing Protocol Validity

As noted in the PCIR (Figure 8-3, p. 8), "This is a valid MMPI-2-RF protocol. There are no problems with unscorable items. The test taker responded to the items relevantly on the basis of their content, and there are no indications of over- or underreporting."

Substantive Scale Findings

A review of the scores printed in bold font on the "MMPI-2-RF T-Scores (By Domain)" (Figure 8-3, p. 7) shows that two scales in Mr. K's protocol are interpreted in the report: RC2 (54T) and SAV (59T). However, at these moderate levels, they are interpreted only in the Comparison Group Findings (CGF) section; they are not associated with any job-relevant correlates.

The comparison group finding associated with Mr. K's RC2 score is listed under the "Emotional/Internalizing Problems" domain heading. (Note that p. 7 of the PCIR lists each of the substantive scales by their associated construct domain, with the Higher-Order scale appearing to the left of the bracket, followed by the associated RC scale to the right of the bracket, and the remaining substantive scales [Specific Problems and PSY-5 scales] associated with that RC scale. Any scale interpreted in the PCIR's CGF section will always be listed under the same domain label that appears on this page.) The CGF statement indicates, "The test taker reports a comparatively low level of positive emotional experiences for a police officer candidate. Only 5.4% of comparison group members convey this or a lower level of positive emotions" (Figure 8-3, p. 9). At this

MMPI 2 RF®

Minnesota Multiphasic
Personality Inventory-2
Restructured Form®
Yossef S. Ben-Porath, PhD, & Auke Tellegen, PhD

MMPI-2-RF®
Police Candidate Interpretive Report
David M. Corey, PhD, & Yossef S. Ben-Porath, PhD

Name:	Mr. K
Age:	38
Gender:	Male
Marital Status:	Married
Years of Education:	17
Date Assessed:	04/19/2015

Copyright © 2014 by the Regents of the University of Minnesota. All rights reserved.
Distributed exclusively under license from the University of Minnesota by NCS Pearson, Inc. Portions reproduced from the MMPI-2-RF test booklet. Copyright © 2008 by the Regents of the University of Minnesota. All rights reserved. Portions excerpted from the *MMPI-2-RF Manual for Administration, Scoring, and Interpretation*. Copyright © 2008, 2011 by the Regents of the University of Minnesota. All rights reserved. Used by permission of the University of Minnesota Press.

Minnesota Multiphasic Personality Inventory-2-Restructured Form and **MMPI-2-RF** are registered trademarks of the University of Minnesota. **Pearson** is a trademark in the U.S. and/or other countries of Pearson Education, Inc., or its affiliate(s).

This report contains copyrighted material and trade secrets. The qualified licensee may excerpt portions of this output report, limited to the minimum text necessary to accurately describe their significant core conclusions, for incorporation into a written evaluation of the examinee, in accordance with their profession's citation standards, if any. No adaptations, translations, modifications, or special versions may be made of this report without prior written permission from the University of Minnesota Press.

[4.0 / 57 / __VERSION__]

ALWAYS LEARNING PEARSON

FIGURE 8-3 Mr. K's MMPI-2-RF Police Candidate Interpretive Report

MMPI-2-RF® Police Candidate Interpretive Report
04/19/2015, Page 2 Mr. K

MMPI-2-RF Validity Scales

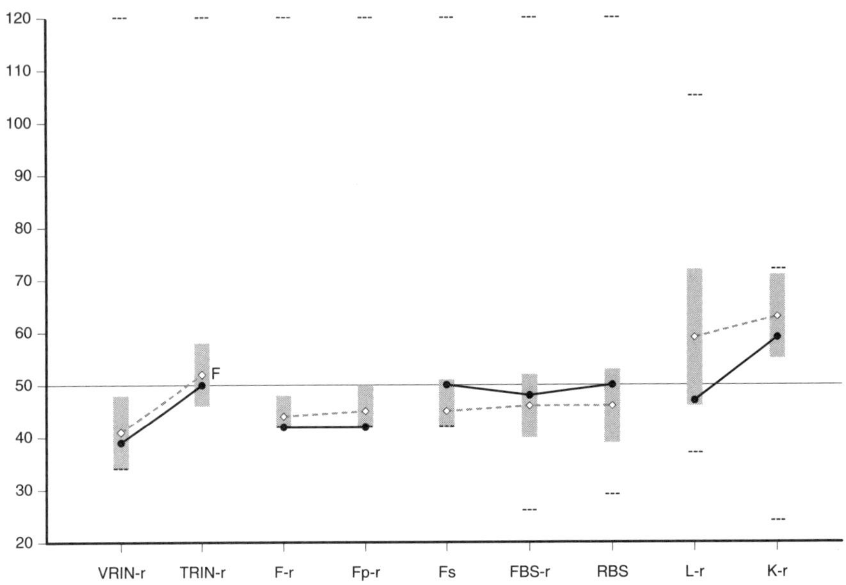

	VRIN-r	TRIN-r	F-r	Fp-r	Fs	FBS-r	RBS	L-r	K-r
Raw Score:	1	11	0	0	1	7	5	2	10
T Score:	39	50	42	42	50	48	50	47	59
Response %:	100	100	100	100	100	100	100	100	100

Cannot Say (Raw): 0   Percent True (of items answered): 31 %

Comparison Group Data: Personnel Screening, Police Officer Candidate (Men and Women), N = 2074

	VRIN-r	TRIN-r	F-r	Fp-r	Fs	FBS-r	RBS	L-r	K-r
Mean Score (◇- - -◇):	41	52 F	44	45	45	46	46	59	63
Standard Dev (±1 SD):	7	6	4	5	6	6	7	13	8
Percent scoring at or below test taker:	59	62	75	78	92	69	81	26	33

The highest and lowest T scores possible on each scale are indicated by a "---"; MMPI-2-RF T scores are non-gendered.

VRIN-r Variable Response Inconsistency
TRIN-r True Response Inconsistency
F-r Infrequent Responses
Fp-r Infrequent Psychopathology Responses
Fs Infrequent Somatic Responses
FBS-r Symptom Validity
RBS Response Bias Scale
L-r Uncommon Virtues
K-r Adjustment Validity

FIGURE 8-3 Mr. K's MMPI-2-RF Police Candidate Interpretive Report, continued

MMPI-2-RF Higher-Order (H-O) and Restructured Clinical (RC) Scales

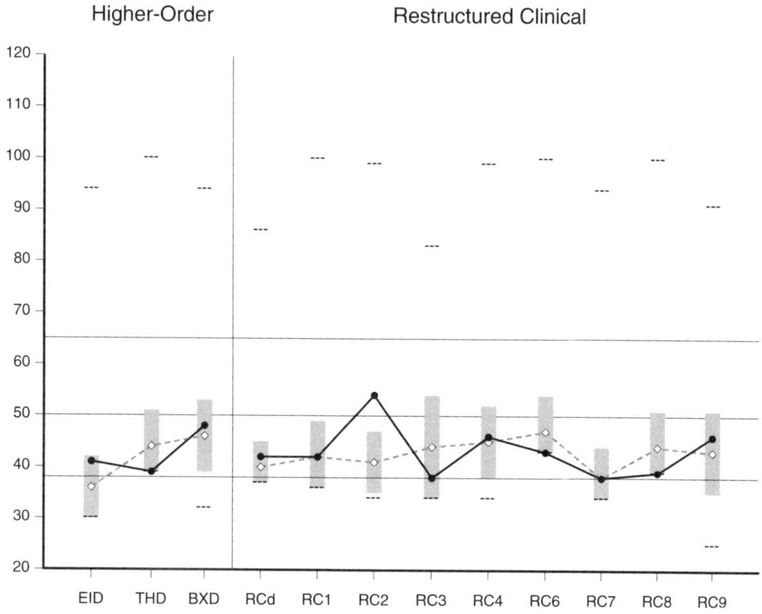

	EID	THD	BXD	RCd	RC1	RC2	RC3	RC4	RC6	RC7	RC8	RC9
Raw Score:	4	0	5	1	1	5	1	3	0	1	0	10
T Score:	41	39	48	42	42	54	38	46	43	38	39	46
Response %:	100	100	100	100	100	100	100	100	100	100	100	100

Comparison Group Data: Personnel Screening, Police Officer Candidate (Men and Women), N = 2074

	EID	THD	BXD	RCd	RC1	RC2	RC3	RC4	RC6	RC7	RC8	RC9
Mean Score (◇--◇):	36	44	46	40	42	41	44	45	47	38	44	43
Standard Dev (±1 SD):	6	7	7	5	7	6	10	7	7	6	7	8
Percent scoring at or below test taker:	83	57	70	84	68	97	35	66	75	68	53	73

The highest and lowest T scores possible on each scale are indicated by a "---"; MMPI-2-RF T scores are non-gendered.

EID Emotional/Internalizing Dysfunction
THD Thought Dysfunction
BXD Behavioral/Externalizing Dysfunction

RCd Demoralization
RC1 Somatic Complaints
RC2 Low Positive Emotions
RC3 Cynicism
RC4 Antisocial Behavior

RC6 Ideas of Persecution
RC7 Dysfunctional Negative Emotions
RC8 Aberrant Experiences
RC9 Hypomanic Activation

FIGURE 8-3 Mr. K's MMPI-2-RF Police Candidate Interpretive Report, continued

MMPI-2-RF® Police Candidate Interpretive Report
04/19/2015, Page 4 Mr. K

MMPI-2-RF Somatic/Cognitive and Internalizing Scales

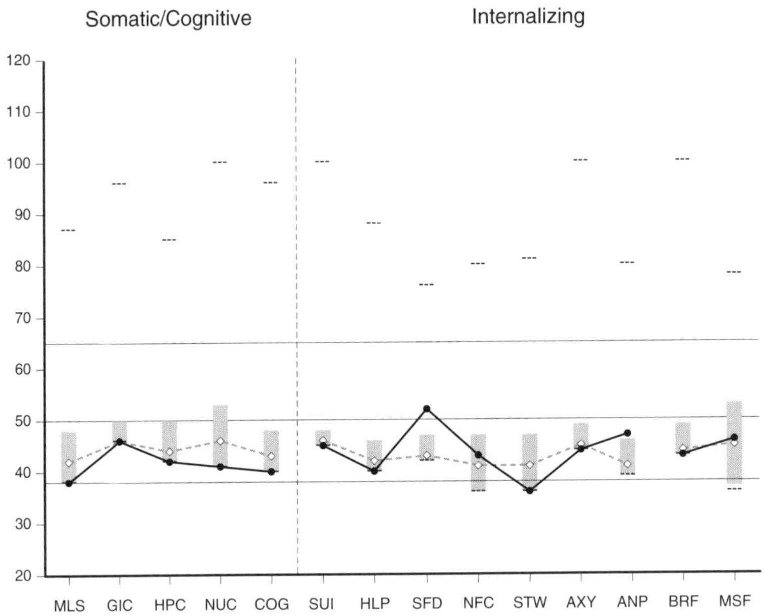

	MLS	GIC	HPC	NUC	COG	SUI	HLP	SFD	NFC	STW	AXY	ANP	BRF	MSF
Raw Score:	0	0	0	0	0	0	0	1	1	0	0	1	0	2
T Score:	38	46	42	41	40	45	40	52	43	36	44	47	43	46
Response %:	100	100	100	100	100	100	100	100	100	100	100	100	100	100

Comparison Group Data: Personnel Screening, Police Officer Candidate (Men and Women), N = 2074

Mean Score (◇--◇):	42	46	44	46	43	46	42	43	41	41	45	41	44	45
Standard Dev (±1 SD):	6	4	6	7	5	2	4	4	6	6	4	5	5	8
Percent scoring at or below test taker:	63	95	83	65	77	99.3	88	97	79	48	94	94	88	64

The highest and lowest T scores possible on each scale are indicated by a "---"; MMPI-2-RF T scores are non-gendered.

MLS Malaise
GIC Gastrointestinal Complaints
HPC Head Pain Complaints
NUC Neurological Complaints
COG Cognitive Complaints
SUI Suicidal/Death Ideation
HLP Helplessness/Hopelessness
SFD Self-Doubt
NFC Inefficacy
STW Stress/Worry
AXY Anxiety
ANP Anger Proneness
BRF Behavior-Restricting Fears
MSF Multiple Specific Fears

FIGURE 8-3 Mr. K's MMPI-2-RF Police Candidate Interpretive Report, continued

MMPI-2-RF Externalizing, Interpersonal, and Interest Scales

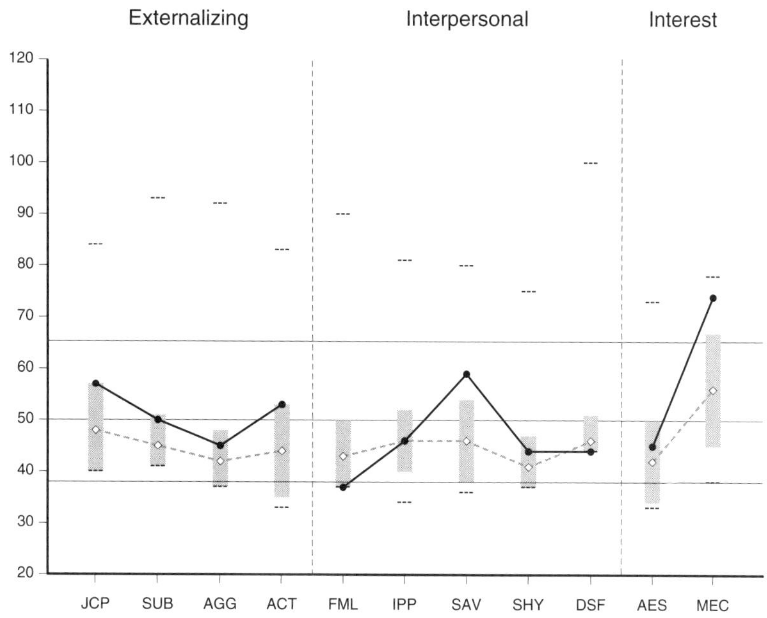

	JCP	SUB	AGG	ACT	FML	IPP	SAV	SHY	DSF	AES	MEC
Raw Score:	2	1	1	4	0	3	6	1	0	2	8
T Score:	57	50	45	53	37	46	59	44	44	45	74
Response %:	100	100	100	100	100	100	100	100	100	100	100

Comparison Group Data: Personnel Screening, Police Officer Candidate (Men and Women), N = 2074

	JCP	SUB	AGG	ACT	FML	IPP	SAV	SHY	DSF	AES	MEC
Mean Score (◇---◇):	48	45	42	44	43	46	46	41	46	42	56
Standard Dev (±1 SD):	9	6	6	9	7	6	8	6	5	8	11
Percent scoring at or below test taker:	90	90	84	89	47	65	96	80	90	79	97

The highest and lowest T scores possible on each scale are indicated by a "---"; MMPI-2-RF T scores are non-gendered.

JCP Juvenile Conduct Problems
SUB Substance Abuse
AGG Aggression
ACT Activation
FML Family Problems
IPP Interpersonal Passivity
SAV Social Avoidance
SHY Shyness
DSF Disaffiliativeness
AES Aesthetic-Literary Interests
MEC Mechanical-Physical Interests

FIGURE 8-3 Mr. K's MMPI-2-RF Police Candidate Interpretive Report, continued

MMPI-2-RF PSY-5 Scales

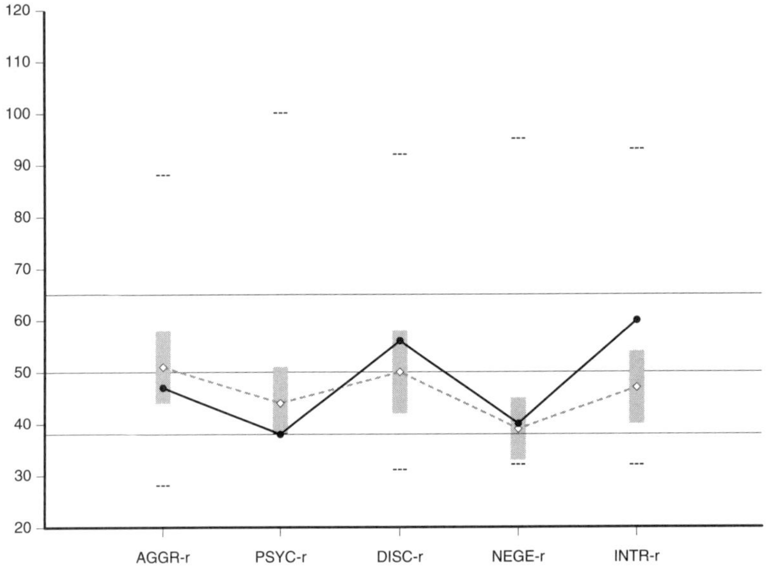

	AGGR-r	PSYC-r	DISC-r	NEGE-r	INTR-r
Raw Score:	8	0	9	2	10
T Score:	47	38	56	40	60
Response %:	100	100	100	100	100

Comparison Group Data: Personnel Screening, Police Officer Candidate (Men and Women), N = 2074

	AGGR-r	PSYC-r	DISC-r	NEGE-r	INTR-r
Mean Score (◇- - ◇):	51	44	50	39	47
Standard Dev (±1 SD):	7	7	8	6	7
Percent scoring at or below test taker:	39	55	87	67	97

The highest and lowest T scores possible on each scale are indicated by a "---"; MMPI-2-RF T scores are non-gendered.

AGGR-r Aggressiveness-Revised
PSYC-r Psychoticism-Revised
DISC-r Disconstraint-Revised
NEGE-r Negative Emotionality/Neuroticism-Revised
INTR-r Introversion/Low Positive Emotionality-Revised

FIGURE 8-3 Mr. K's MMPI-2-RF Police Candidate Interpretive Report, continued

MMPI-2-RF® Police Candidate Interpretive Report
04/19/2015, Page 7

Mr. K

MMPI-2-RF T SCORES (BY DOMAIN)

PROTOCOL VALIDITY

Content Non-Responsiveness

0	39	50
CNS	VRIN-r	TRIN-r

Over-Reporting

42	42	50	48	50
F-r	Fp-r	Fs	FBS-r	RBS

Under-Reporting

47	59
L-r	K-r

SUBSTANTIVE SCALES

Somatic/Cognitive Dysfunction

42	38	46	42	41	40
RC1	MLS	GIC	HPC	NUC	COG

Emotional Dysfunction

41	42	45	40	52	43		
EID	RCd	SUI	HLP	SFD	NFC		
	54	60					
	RC2	INTR-r					
	38	36	44	47	43	46	40
	RC7	STW	AXY	ANP	BRF	MSF	NEGE-r

Thought Dysfunction

39	43
THD	RC6
	39
	RC8
	38
	PSYC-r

Behavioral Dysfunction

48	46	57	50		
BXD	RC4	JCP	SUB		
	46	45	53	47	56
	RC9	AGG	ACT	AGGR-r	DISC-r

Interpersonal Functioning

37	38	46	**59**	44	44
FML	RC3	IPP	**SAV**	SHY	DSF

Interests

45	74
AES	MEC

Scale scores shown in bold font are interpreted in the report.

Note. This information is provided to facilitate interpretation following the recommended structure for MMPI-2-RF interpretation in Chapter 5 of the *MMPI-2-RF Manual for Administration, Scoring, and Interpretation*, which provides details in the text and an outline in Table 5-1.

FIGURE 8-3 Mr. K's MMPI-2-RF Police Candidate Interpretive Report, continued

This interpretive report is intended for use by a professional qualified to interpret the MMPI-2-RF in the context of preemployment psychological evaluations of police and other law enforcement officer candidates. ***It focuses on identifying problems; it does not convey potential strengths.*** *The information it contains should be considered in the context of the test taker's background, the demands of the position under consideration, the clinical interview, findings from supplemental tests, and other relevant information.*

The interpretive statements in the Protocol Validity section of the report are based on T scores derived from the general MMPI-2-RF normative sample, as well as scores obtained by the multisite sample of 2,074 individuals that make up the Police Officer Candidate comparison group.

The interpretive statements in the Clinical Findings and Diagnostic Considerations sections of the report are based on T scores derived from the general MMPI-2-RF normative sample. Following recommended practice, only T scores of 65 and higher are considered clinically significant. Scores at this clinical level are generally rare among police officer candidates.

Statements in the Comparison Group Findings and Job-Relevant Correlates sections are based on comparisons with scores obtained by the Police Officer Candidate comparison group. Statements in these sections may be based on T scores that, although less than 65, are nevertheless uncommon in reference to the comparison group.

Sources for interpretive statements in all sections are listed in the Endnotes section of this report. See User's Guide for the MMPI-2-RF Police Candidate Interpretive Report *for detailed information on report features.*

SYNOPSIS

This is a valid MMPI-2-RF protocol. There are no indications of clinically significant problems in the areas of somatic or cognitive complaints, or of clinically significant emotional, thought, behavioral, or interpersonal dysfunction.

Comparison group findings point to possible concerns about a low level of positive emotions and social avoidance.

PROTOCOL VALIDITY

This is a valid MMPI-2-RF protocol. There are no problems with unscorable items. The test taker responded to the items relevantly on the basis of their content, and there are no indications of over- or under-reporting.

FIGURE 8-3 Mr. K's MMPI-2-RF Police Candidate Interpretive Report, continued

MMPI-2-RF® Police Candidate Interpretive Report
04/19/2015, Page 9 Mr. K

CLINICAL FINDINGS

There are no indications of clinically significant somatic, cognitive, emotional, thought, or behavioral dysfunction in this protocol.

DIAGNOSTIC CONSIDERATIONS

No specific psychodiagnostic recommendations are indicated by this MMPI-2-RF protocol.

COMPARISON GROUP FINDINGS

This section describes the MMPI-2-RF substantive scale findings in the context of the Police Officer Candidate comparison group. Specific sources for each statement can be accessed with the annotation features of this report. ***Job-related correlates of these results, if any, are provided in the subsequent Job-Relevant Correlates section.***

Emotional/Internalizing Problems

The test taker reports a comparatively low level of positive emotional experiences for a police officer candidate[1]. Only 5.4% of comparison group members convey this or a lower level of positive emotions.

Interpersonal Problems

The test taker reports a comparatively high level of social avoidance for a police officer candidate[2]. Only 7.0% of comparison group members convey this or a greater preference for avoiding social interaction.

JOB-RELEVANT CORRELATES

Job-relevant personality characteristics and behavioral tendencies of the test taker are described in this section and organized according to ten problem domains commonly identified in the professional literature as relevant to police officer candidate suitability. (Please see User's Guide for MMPI-2-RF Police Candidate Interpretive Report *for details.) Statements that begin with "Compared with other police officer candidates" are based on correlations with other self-report measures obtained in police officer candidate samples that included individuals who were subsequently hired as well as those who were not. Statements that begin with "He is more likely than most police officers or trainees" are based on correlations with outcome data obtained in samples of hired candidates during academy or field training, probation, and/or the post-probation period. Specific sources for each statement can be accessed with the annotation features of this report.*

The candidate's test scores are not associated with any correlates.

FIGURE 8-3 Mr. K's MMPI-2-RF Police Candidate Interpretive Report, continued

MMPI-2-RF® Police Candidate Interpretive Report
04/19/2015, Page 10 Mr. K

ITEM-LEVEL INFORMATION

Unscorable Responses

The test taker produced scorable responses to all the MMPI-2-RF items.

Critical Responses

Seven MMPI-2-RF scales--Suicidal/Death Ideation (SUI), Helplessness/Hopelessness (HLP), Anxiety (AXY), Ideas of Persecution (RC6), Aberrant Experiences (RC8), Substance Abuse (SUB), and Aggression (AGG)--have been designated by the test authors as having critical item content that may require immediate attention and follow-up. Items answered by the individual in the keyed direction (True or False) on a critical scale are listed below if his T score on that scale is 65 or higher.

The test taker has not produced an elevated T score (≥ 65) on any of these scales.

Critical Follow-up Items

This section contains a list of items to which the test taker responded in a manner warranting follow-up. The items were identified by police officer screening experts as having critical content. Clinicians are encouraged to follow up on these statements with the candidate by making related inquiries, rather than reciting the item(s) verbatim. Each item is followed by the candidate's response, the percentage of Police Officer Candidate comparison group members who gave this response, and the scale(s) on which the item appears.

The test taker did not respond to any critical follow-up items in the keyed direction.

FIGURE 8-3 Mr. K's MMPI-2-RF Police Candidate Interpretive Report, continued

MMPI-2-RF® Police Candidate Interpretive Report
04/19/2015, Page 11 Mr. K

ENDNOTES

This section lists for each statement in the report the MMPI-2-RF score(s) that triggered it. In addition, each statement is identified as a Test Response, if based on item content, a Correlate, if based on empirical correlates, or an Inference, if based on the report authors' judgment. (This information can also be accessed on-screen by placing the cursor on a given statement.) For correlate-based statements, research references (Ref. No.) are provided, keyed to the consecutively numbered reference list following the endnotes.

[1] Test Response: RC2=54
[2] Test Response: SAV=59

End of Report

FIGURE 8-3 Mr. K's MMPI-2-RF Police Candidate Interpretive Report, continued

moderate level of elevation, RC2 would not be interpreted as indicating problems associated with depression or anhedonia.

The CGF finding associated with SAV is listed under the Interpersonal Problems domain and states, "The test taker reports a comparatively high level of social avoidance for a police officer candidate. Only 7.0% of comparison group members convey this or a greater preference for avoiding social interaction" (Figure 8-3, p. 9).

Of note is that there are no adverse correlates associated with either of these deviations from the comparison group mean, as indicated by the statement under Job-Relevant Correlates on the bottom of page 9 of the report: "The candidate's test scores are not associated with any correlates."

Background Findings

Mr. K's background is entirely "clean"—that is, free of negative references, legal problems, negative juvenile history, substance use problems, and so on. The background investigation concluded that he was "universally regarded by his associates, supervisors, and his peers, both personally and professionally."

Interview Findings

Mr. K presented in the interview as professional, engaged, responsive to questions, and self-reflective. This last observation was apparent when the interviewer asked Mr. K to elaborate on two traits that psychological testing suggests are prominent features of his personality: a tendency to not experience strong positive emotions (without implying that he is depressed) and a tendency to avoid social situations. Mr. K explained that he hears from his wife "all the time" that he tends to be "flat-line, I don't get excited about plans, but then I don't ever get low either." He added, "But at the same time she appreciates that when things are going sideways around me, I don't ever get flustered." Mr. K also explained that he has never enjoyed parties, and although he would not "sign up for one," he would also not decline to attend a dinner party if his wife wanted to go.

Identifying Relevant Risk Findings

a. Considering all risk-related findings from all sources, what evidence-based inferences can be drawn from them?

Test Findings. Mr. K's scores on RC2 and SAV are unusually elevated relative to other police officer candidates, although they are not associated with any counterproductive behavior as a police trainee or officer. The nonclinical interpretations warranted by these scores support the following risk-related inferences: he displays a comparatively low level of positive emotions and a comparatively high level of social avoidance for a police officer candidate.

Background Findings. No risk-related inferences can be drawn from Mr. K's nonproblematic background.

Interview Findings. No risk-related inferences can be drawn from Mr. K's positive interview findings, which were generally confirmatory of the testing and background findings showing him to be psychologically well adjusted.

b. What divergent findings might mitigate these inferences?

Although the findings from psychological testing raise the hypothesis that Mr. K may be somewhat socially avoidant and comparatively less inclined to experience positive emotions, the absence of adverse job-relevant correlates mitigates the job relevance of these findings. Moreover, research shows that RC2 scores are largely associated with deficits in anticipatory rather than consummatory pleasure (Ben-Porath, 2012). Recall Mr. K's statement in the interview that his wife complains that he is often "flat line." He explained this by stating, "I don't get excited about plans, but then I don't ever get low either." Mr. K's references also reported nothing suggestive of mood instability, pessimism, low energy, or social disengagement, all of which we would expect to see if RC2 reached the level of clinical significance. Thus, the interview also offers a divergent finding that reasonably mitigates potential risk-related inferences from RC2. Inferences from moderate-range scores should not be mitigated solely because of the score magnitude or because the candidate offers an alternative explanation. But when, as in the case of Mr. K, the scale magnitude is low, *and* there is no behavioral *or* collateral evidence to support the risk-related inferences, *and* research findings support an alternative interpretation that is aligned with findings across data sources, mitigation is warranted. In this case, these considerations give greater weight to the conclusion that Mr. K has a mild deficit in *anticipatory pleasure* rather than depressive tendencies, and the absence of any job-relevant correlates associated with an RC2 score at 54T further supports mitigation of any risk-related inferences from this scale.

Similarly, Mr. K's score on SAV (59T) does not rise to a level of clinical significance and, therefore, would not justify an inference suggestive of psychopathology (e.g., avoidant personality disorder). It is important to keep in mind the threshold levels at which job-relevant correlates are triggered for each scale on the PCIR, which are included in the Appendix of this practical guide. In the case of SAV, only clinically significant scores (≥65T) generate statements in the Job-Relevant Correlates section of the PCIR. A score on SAV of 65T or greater would warrant risk-related inferences such as a tendency to avoid situations that others generally view as benign or nonintimidating, to be ill at ease in many social situations, and to have difficulties displaying diligent and reliable work behavior; however, with his score at 59T, the only supported inference is the comparison group finding that Mr. K "reports a comparatively high level of social avoidance for a police officer candidate" and that "[o]nly 7.0% of comparison group members convey this or a greater preference for avoiding social interaction" (Figure 8-3, p. 9). Indeed, Mr. K conceded as much in the interview when he stated that has never enjoyed parties, and although he would not "sign-up for one," he would also not decline to attend a dinner party if his wife wanted to go. Consequently, it is appropriate to retain the risk-related findings associated with Mr. K's moderately elevated SAV scale score, noting that, in comparison to other police officer candidates, he may have a more limited social support network. However, this is mitigated by the absence of adverse job-relevant correlates.

c. Are any surviving risk-related inferences of sufficient relevance and quality to warrant the candidate's disqualification?

Even if we retain the risk-related inferences associated with both scale RC2 and SAV, they are of insufficient relevance and quality to warrant Mr. K's disqualification. This is because of the anticipated interaction between Mr. K's personality traits and the demands/working conditions of the job in a rural setting. In the context of the full range of assessment data available in Mr. K's case, the supported risk-related inferences of the moderately elevated RC2 (54T) and SAV (59T) scales, respectively, are that he tends to experience low anticipatory pleasure and prefers intimate interactions to parties and group interactions. For a rural patrol deputy and correctional officer, these traits may actually serve more as protective factors than risk factors. Rural patrol deputies necessarily spend long periods of time alone and have very little interaction with others. The ability to tolerate solitude and to not experience high anticipatory pleasure may actually enable Mr. K to function more effectively in this position. Therefore, the examiner concluded that Mr. K met the psychological suitability criteria for a correctional officer.

Comprehensive Review: Mr. G, Reserve Police Officer Candidate

Assessment Issues Presented

- Mitigating significantly negative test findings with significantly positive background and interview information
- Use of the PCIR

Referral Summary

Mr. G, age 32, is a married male applying for the position of reserve police officer in an urban police agency. At the time of this evaluation, he was working as a security officer, which he had done for the past 2 years while attending college. He completed a bachelor's degree in criminal justice and criminology just months before submitting his application. He never served in the military. He has a significantly problematic late adolescent and young adult history, but a positive adult history.

Assessing Protocol Validity

Mr. G's MMPI-2-RF scores (Figure 8-4) on measures of response consistency (VRIN-r and TRIN-r) and overreporting (F-r, Fp-r, Fs, FBS-r, and RBS) are within normal limits (i.e., within one standard deviation of their respective Police Officer Candidate comparison group means). Mr. G's score on L-r (42T) is an unusual finding among law enforcement officer candidates (only 8.7% of members of the comparison group have a raw score of 1, and only 4.0% claim no uncommon virtues at all) that raises questions about why he would not attempt to portray himself in a more positive light as do most individuals under similar circumstances.

As reviewed in chapter 6, Detrick and Chibnall (2014) studied test-retest responses to the MMPI-2-RF by police candidates, first in a preemployment evaluation (high-demand) context and later after they completed the academy and were retested only for anonymous research purposes (low-demand context). They reported that, whereas mean L-r and K-r scores were lower in the low-demand context, and the substantive scale scores were higher, they were not consistently so. The authors found that a lowering of L-r was the sole predictor of increases in the behavioral-externalizing domain (BXD, RC4, JCP, and DISC-r), whereas a change in K-r predicted inverse changes in EID, RC7, HLP, BRF, and NEGE-r. Applying Detrick and Chibnall's research to Mr. G's underreporting configuration of low L-r and moderately high K-r would lead us to anticipate that any elevations found in the substantive scales would likely be on the externalizing behavior scales BXD, RC4, JCP, and DISC-r.

Substantive Scale Findings

Mr. G's substantive scale scores, with primary elevations being on scales BXD (60T), RC4 (68), JCP (70T), and DISC-r (69T), are consistent with Detrick and Chibnall's (2014) findings. Elevations on SUB (55T) and AGG (56) scales, both facets of the Externalizing Problems domain, also are notable, although more muted.

The PCIR Clinical Findings section (Figure 8-4, p. 9) includes interpretive statements corresponding to clinically elevated scales (≥65T) only, as well as diagnostic considerations associated with RC4. The statements in the Comparison Group Findings section (pp. 9–10) also pertain to Behavioral Dysfunction scales BXD, DISC-r, RC4, JCP, SUB, and AGG, respectively.

Mr. G's protocol is associated with numerous Job-Relevant Correlates (Figure 8-4, pp. 10–11) within all problem domains except for Decision-Making and Judgment, and Assertiveness. Also unusual is the low score on Cynicism (RC3; 34T), indicating that Mr. G describes others as well intentioned and trustworthy and disavows cynical beliefs about them. A lack of social reticence is also seen in his comparatively low scores on other Specific Problems (SP) scales in the Interpersonal Functioning domain (IPP, SAV, SHY, and DSF), which are generally correlated with RC3 (Ben-Porath, 2012).

A review of scores from normal-range personality testing in this assessment protocol reveals Mr. G's two highest CPI scores, using general adult norms, to be Dominance (Do; 70T) and Empathy (Em; 69T) and his two lowest scores to be Socialization (So; 49T) and Achievement via Compliance (Ac; 54T). Using police applicant norms (Roberts & Johnson, 2001), the two highest scores are on the Self-Acceptance (Sa; 68T) and Empathy (63T) scales, and the two lowest are on the Socialization (28T) and Achievement via Compliance (29T) scales.

MMPI 2 RF®

Minnesota Multiphasic
Personality Inventory-2
Restructured Form®
Yossef S. Ben-Porath, PhD, & Auke Tellegen, PhD

MMPI-2-RF®
Police Candidate Interpretive Report
David M. Corey, PhD, & Yossef S. Ben-Porath, PhD

Name:	Mr. G
Age:	32
Gender:	Male
Marital Status:	Married
Years of Education:	16
Date Assessed:	10/14/2014

Copyright © 2014 by the Regents of the University of Minnesota. All rights reserved.
Distributed exclusively under license from the University of Minnesota by NCS Pearson, Inc. Portions reproduced from the MMPI-2-RF test booklet. Copyright © 2000 by the Regents of the University of Minnesota. All rights reserved. Portions excerpted from the *MMPI-2-RF Manual for Administration, Scoring, and Interpretation.* Copyright © 2008, 2011 by the Regents of the University of Minnesota. All rights reserved. Used by permission of the University of Minnesota Press.

Minnesota Multiphasic Personality Inventory-2-Restructured Form and **MMPI-2-RF** are registered trademarks of the University of Minnesota. **Pearson** is a trademark in the U.S. and/or other countries of Pearson Education, Inc., or its affiliate(s).

This report contains copyrighted material and trade secrets. The qualified licensee may excerpt portions of this output report, limited to the minimum text necessary to accurately describe their significant core conclusions, for incorporation into a written evaluation of the examinee, in accordance with their profession's citation standards, if any. No adaptations, translations, modifications, or special versions may be made of this report without prior written permission from the University of Minnesota Press.

[4.0 / 57 / __VERSION__]

ALWAYS LEARNING PEARSON

FIGURE 8-4 Mr. G's MMPI-2-RF Police Candidate Interpretive Report

MMPI-2-RF® Police Candidate Interpretive Report
10/14/2014, Page 2 Mr. G

MMPI-2-RF Validity Scales

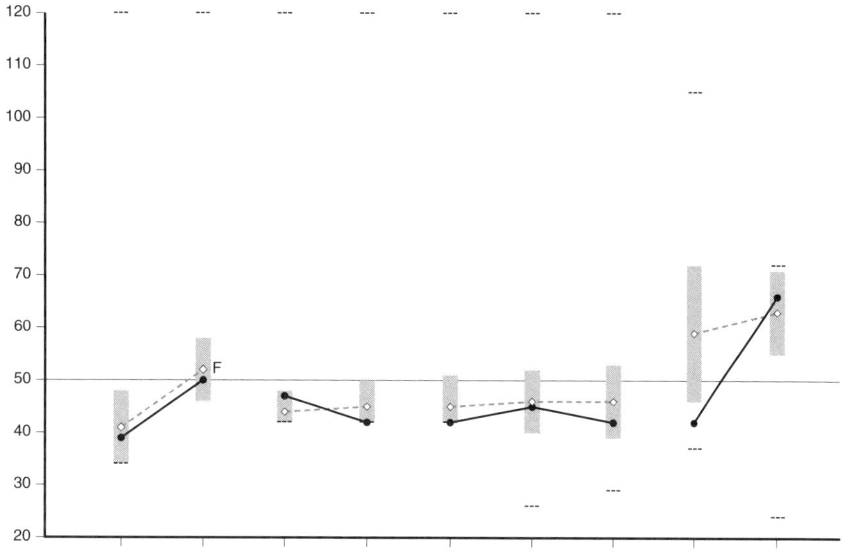

	VRIN-r	TRIN-r	F-r	Fp-r	Fs	FBS-r	RBS	L-r	K-r
Raw Score:	1	11	1	0	0	6	3	1	12
T Score:	39	50	47	42	42	45	42	42	66
Response %:	100	100	100	100	100	100	100	100	100

Cannot Say (Raw): 0 Percent True (of items answered): 34%

Comparison Group Data: Personnel Screening, Police Officer Candidate (Men and Women), N = 2074

	VRIN-r	TRIN-r	F-r	Fp-r	Fs	FBS-r	RBS	L-r	K-r
Mean Score (◇---◇):	41	52 F	44	45	45	46	46	59	63
Standard Dev (±1 SD):	7	6	4	5	6	6	7	13	8
Percent scoring at or below test taker:	59	62	94	78	70	49	41	13	62

The highest and lowest T scores possible on each scale are indicated by a "---"; MMPI-2-RF T scores are non-gendered.

VRIN-r	Variable Response Inconsistency	Fs	Infrequent Somatic Responses	L-r	Uncommon Virtues
TRIN-r	True Response Inconsistency	FBS-r	Symptom Validity	K-r	Adjustment Validity
F-r	Infrequent Responses	RBS	Response Bias Scale		
Fp-r	Infrequent Psychopathology Responses				

FIGURE 8-4 Mr. G's MMPI-2-RF Police Candidate Interpretive Report, continued

MMPI-2-RF® Police Candidate Interpretive Report
10/14/2014, Page 3 Mr. G

MMPI-2-RF Higher-Order (H-O) and Restructured Clinical (RC) Scales

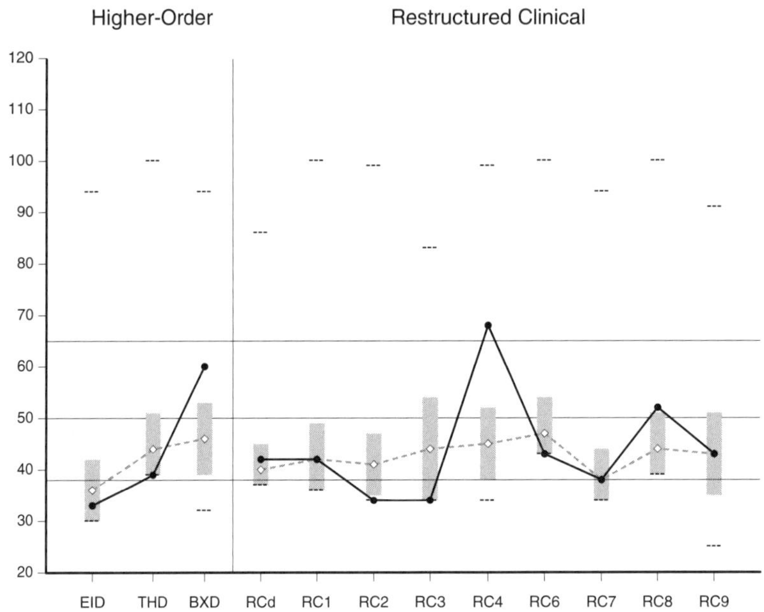

	EID	THD	BXD	RCd	RC1	RC2	RC3	RC4	RC6	RC7	RC8	RC9
Raw Score:	1	0	10	1	1	0	0	11	0	1	2	8
T Score:	33	39	60	42	42	34	34	68	43	38	52	43
Response %:	100	100	100	100	100	100	100	100	100	100	100	100

Comparison Group Data: Personnel Screening, Police Officer Candidate (Men and Women), N = 2074

Mean Score (◇- - ◇):	36	44	46	40	42	41	44	45	47	38	44	43
Standard Dev (±1 SD):	6	7	7	5	7	6	10	7	7	6	7	8
Percent scoring at or below test taker:	47	57	98	84	68	29	21	99.5	75	68	89	57

The highest and lowest T scores possible on each scale are indicated by a "---"; MMPI-2-RF T scores are non-gendered.

EID Emotional/Internalizing Dysfunction
THD Thought Dysfunction
BXD Behavioral/Externalizing Dysfunction

RCd Demoralization
RC1 Somatic Complaints
RC2 Low Positive Emotions
RC3 Cynicism
RC4 Antisocial Behavior

RC6 Ideas of Persecution
RC7 Dysfunctional Negative Emotions
RC8 Aberrant Experiences
RC9 Hypomanic Activation

FIGURE 8-4 Mr. G's MMPI-2-RF Police Candidate Interpretive Report, continued

MMPI-2-RF Somatic/Cognitive and Internalizing Scales

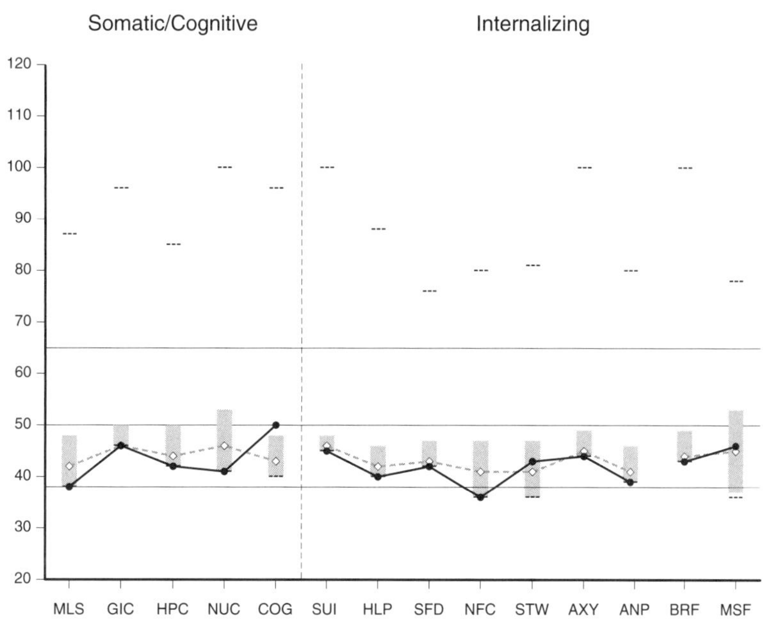

	MLS	GIC	HPC	NUC	COG	SUI	HLP	SFD	NFC	STW	AXY	ANP	BRF	MSF
Raw Score:	0	0	0	0	1	0	0	0	0	1	0	0	0	2
T Score:	38	46	42	41	50	45	40	42	36	43	44	39	43	46
Response %:	100	100	100	100	100	100	100	100	100	100	100	100	100	100

Comparison Group Data: Personnel Screening, Police Officer Candidate (Men and Women), N = 2074

Mean Score (◇---◇):	42	46	44	46	43	46	42	43	41	41	45	41	44	45
Standard Dev (±1 SD):	6	4	6	7	5	2	4	4	6	6	4	5	5	8
Percent scoring at or below test taker:	63	95	83	65	93	99.3	88	90	50	78	94	81	88	64

The highest and lowest T scores possible on each scale are indicated by a "---"; MMPI-2-RF T scores are non-gendered.

MLS	Malaise	SUI	Suicidal/Death Ideation	AXY	Anxiety
GIC	Gastrointestinal Complaints	HLP	Helplessness/Hopelessness	ANP	Anger Proneness
HPC	Head Pain Complaints	SFD	Self-Doubt	BRF	Behavior-Restricting Fears
NUC	Neurological Complaints	NFC	Inefficacy	MSF	Multiple Specific Fears
COG	Cognitive Complaints	STW	Stress/Worry		

FIGURE 8-4 Mr. G's MMPI-2-RF Police Candidate Interpretive Report, continued

MMPI-2-RF Externalizing, Interpersonal, and Interest Scales

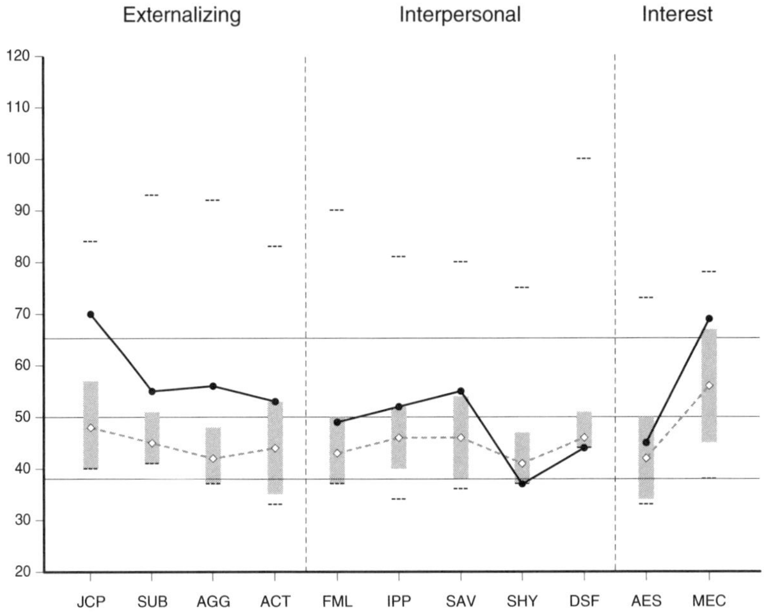

	JCP	SUB	AGG	ACT	FML	IPP	SAV	SHY	DSF	AES	MEC
Raw Score:	4	2	3	4	2	5	5	0	0	2	7
T Score:	70	55	56	53	49	52	55	37	44	45	69
Response %:	100	100	100	100	100	100	100	100	100	100	100

Comparison Group Data: Personnel Screening, Police Officer Candidate (Men and Women), N = 2074

	JCP	SUB	AGG	ACT	FML	IPP	SAV	SHY	DSF	AES	MEC
Mean Score (◇--◇):	48	45	42	44	43	46	46	41	46	42	56
Standard Dev (±1 SD):	9	6	6	9	7	6	8	6	5	8	11
Percent scoring at or below test taker:	99	98	98	89	90	92	93	57	90	79	91

The highest and lowest T scores possible on each scale are indicated by a "---"; MMPI-2-RF T scores are non-gendered.

JCP	Juvenile Conduct Problems	FML	Family Problems	AES	Aesthetic-Literary Interests
SUB	Substance Abuse	IPP	Interpersonal Passivity	MEC	Mechanical-Physical Interests
AGG	Aggression	SAV	Social Avoidance		
ACT	Activation	SHY	Shyness		
		DSF	Disaffiliativeness		

FIGURE 8-4 Mr. G's MMPI-2-RF Police Candidate Interpretive Report, continued

MMPI-2-RF® Police Candidate Interpretive Report
10/14/2014, Page 6 Mr. G

MMPI-2-RF PSY-5 Scales

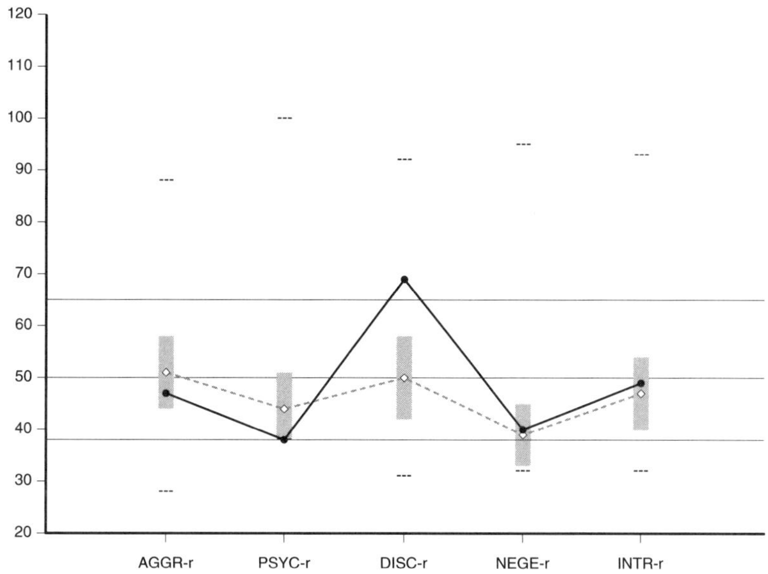

	AGGR-r	PSYC-r	DISC-r	NEGE-r	INTR-r
Raw Score:	8	0	13	2	6
T Score:	47	38	69	40	49
Response %:	100	100	100	100	100

Comparison Group Data: Personnel Screening, Police Officer Candidate (Men and Women), N = 2074

Mean Score (◇---◇):	51	44	50	39	47
Standard Dev (±1 SD):	7	7	8	6	7
Percent scoring at or below test taker:	39	55	99	67	72

The highest and lowest T scores possible on each scale are indicated by a "---"; MMPI-2-RF T scores are non-gendered.

AGGR-r Aggressiveness-Revised
PSYC-r Psychoticism-Revised
DISC-r Disconstraint-Revised
NEGE-r Negative Emotionality/Neuroticism-Revised
INTR-r Introversion/Low Positive Emotionality-Revised

FIGURE 8-4 Mr. G's MMPI-2-RF Police Candidate Interpretive Report, continued

MMPI-2-RF® Police Candidate Interpretive Report
10/14/2014, Page 7

Mr. G

MMPI-2-RF T SCORES (BY DOMAIN)

PROTOCOL VALIDITY

Domain	Higher-Order							
Content Non-Responsiveness		0	39	50				
		CNS	VRIN-r	TRIN-r				
Over-Reporting		47	42		42	45	42	
		F-r	Fp-r		Fs	FBS-r	RBS	
Under-Reporting		42	66					
		L-r	K-r					

SUBSTANTIVE SCALES

Domain	Higher-Order							
Somatic/Cognitive Dysfunction		42	38	46	42	41	50	
		RC1	MLS	GIC	HPC	NUC	COG	
Emotional Dysfunction	33	42	45	40	42	36		
	EID	RCd	SUI	HLP	SFD	NFC		
		34	49					
		RC2	INTR-r					
		38	43	44	39	43	46	40
		RC7	STW	AXY	ANP	BRF	MSF	NEGE-r
Thought Dysfunction	39	43						
	THD	RC6						
		52						
		RC8						
		38						
		PSYC-r						
Behavioral Dysfunction	**60**	**68**	**70**	**55**				
	BXD	**RC4**	**JCP**	**SUB**				
		43	**56**	53	47	**69**		
		RC9	**AGG**	ACT	AGGR-r	**DISC-r**		
Interpersonal Functioning		49	34	52	55	37	44	
		FML	RC3	IPP	SAV	SHY	DSF	
Interests		45	69					
		AES	MEC					

Scale scores shown in bold font are interpreted in the report.

Note. This information is provided to facilitate interpretation following the recommended structure for MMPI-2-RF interpretation in Chapter 5 of the *MMPI-2-RF Manual for Administration, Scoring, and Interpretation*, which provides details in the text and an outline in Table 5-1.

FIGURE 8-4 Mr. G's MMPI-2-RF Police Candidate Interpretive Report, continued

This interpretive report is intended for use by a professional qualified to interpret the MMPI-2-RF in the context of preemployment psychological evaluations of police and other law enforcement officer candidates. ***It focuses on identifying problems; it does not convey potential strengths.*** *The information it contains should be considered in the context of the test taker's background, the demands of the position under consideration, the clinical interview, findings from supplemental tests, and other relevant information.*

The interpretive statements in the Protocol Validity section of the report are based on T scores derived from the general MMPI-2-RF normative sample, as well as scores obtained by the multisite sample of 2,074 individuals that make up the Police Officer Candidate comparison group.

The interpretive statements in the Clinical Findings and Diagnostic Considerations sections of the report are based on T scores derived from the general MMPI-2-RF normative sample. Following recommended practice, only T scores of 65 and higher are considered clinically significant. Scores at this clinical level are generally rare among police officer candidates.

Statements in the Comparison Group Findings and Job-Relevant Correlates sections are based on comparisons with scores obtained by the Police Officer Candidate comparison group. Statements in these sections may be based on T scores that, although less than 65, are nevertheless uncommon in reference to the comparison group.

Sources for interpretive statements in all sections are listed in the Endnotes section of this report. See User's Guide for the MMPI-2-RF Police Candidate Interpretive Report *for detailed information on report features.*

SYNOPSIS

This is a valid MMPI-2-RF protocol. Scores on the substantive scales indicate clinically significant behavioral dysfunction. Behavioral-externalizing problems include antisocial behavior and juvenile conduct problems.

Comparison group findings point to additional possible concerns about past or current substance use, physically aggressive behavior, and poor impulse control.

Possible job-relevant problems are identified in the following domains: Emotional Control and Stress Tolerance, Routine Task Performance, Feedback Acceptance, Social Competence and Teamwork, Integrity, Conscientiousness and Dependability, Substance Use, and Impulse Control.

FIGURE 8-4 Mr. G's MMPI-2-RF Police Candidate Interpretive Report, continued

PROTOCOL VALIDITY

This is a valid MMPI-2-RF protocol. There are no problems with unscorable items. The test taker responded to the items relevantly on the basis of their content, and there are no indications of over- or under-reporting.

CLINICAL FINDINGS

Clinical-level symptoms, personality characteristics, and behavioral tendencies of the test taker are described in this section and organized according to an empirically guided framework. (Please see Chapter 8, Yossef S. Ben-Porath, Interpreting the MMPI-2-RF, *for details.) Statements containing the word "reports" are based on the item content of MMPI-2-RF scales, whereas statements that include the word "likely" are based on empirical correlates of scale scores. Specific sources for each statement can be accessed with the annotation features of this report.*

The test taker reports a significant history of acting-out, antisocial behavior[1] and is likely to have poor impulse control[2], to have been involved with the criminal justice system[3], and to have difficulties with individuals in positions of authority[4]. He is also likely to act out when bored[6] and to have antisocial characteristics[7]. He reports a history of problematic behavior at school[8]. He is likely to have a history of juvenile delinquency and criminal and antisocial behavior[9] and to experience conflictual interpersonal relationships[10].

There are no indications of clinically significant somatic, cognitive, emotional, or thought dysfunction in this protocol.

DIAGNOSTIC CONSIDERATIONS

This section provides recommendations for psychodiagnostic assessment based on the test taker's MMPI-2-RF results. It is recommended that he be evaluated for the following:

Behavioral-Externalizing Disorders

- Antisocial personality disorder, substance use disorders, and other externalizing disorders[11]

COMPARISON GROUP FINDINGS

This section describes the MMPI-2-RF substantive scale findings in the context of the Police Officer Candidate comparison group. Specific sources for each statement can be accessed with the annotation features of this report. ***Job-related correlates of these results, if any, are provided in the subsequent Job-Relevant Correlates section.***

FIGURE 8-4 Mr. G's MMPI-2-RF Police Candidate Interpretive Report, continued

Behavioral/Externalizing Problems

The test taker reports a comparatively large number of behavioral problems for a police officer candidate[12]. Only 4.4% of comparison group members convey this or a greater level of behavioral difficulties. More specifically, his responses indicate a level of disconstraint that may be incompatible with public safety requirements for good behavioral control[13]. This level of poor impulse control is very uncommon among police officer candidates. Only 2.1% of comparison group members give evidence of this or a greater level of disconstraint.

His responses indicate a level of antisocial behavior that may be incompatible with public safety requirements for behavioral control[14]. This level of rule-breaking behavior is very uncommon among police officer candidates. Only 0.9% of comparison group members demonstrate this or a greater level of antisocial behavior. In particular, his responses indicate a history of juvenile conduct problems that may impede conformance with public safety requirements for behavioral control and adherence to rules[15]. This level of juvenile misconduct is very uncommon among police officer candidates. Only 3.8% of comparison group members give evidence of this or a larger number of juvenile conduct problems. He reports a comparatively large number of problems with substance use for a police officer candidate[16]. Only 9.9% of comparison group members convey this or a greater level of misusing substances.

The test taker reports a comparatively high level of physically aggressive behavior for a police officer candidate[17]. Only 5.1% of comparison group members convey this or a greater level of inappropriately aggressive behavior.

JOB-RELEVANT CORRELATES

Job-relevant personality characteristics and behavioral tendencies of the test taker are described in this section and organized according to ten problem domains commonly identified in the professional literature as relevant to police officer candidate suitability. (Please see User's Guide for MMPI-2-RF Police Candidate Interpretive Report *for details.) Statements that begin with "Compared with other police officer candidates" are based on correlations with other self-report measures obtained in police officer candidate samples that included individuals who were subsequently hired as well as those who were not. Statements that begin with "He is more likely than most police officers or trainees" are based on correlations with outcome data obtained in samples of hired candidates during academy or field training, probation, and/or the post-probation period. Specific sources for each statement can be accessed with the annotation features of this report.*

Emotional Control and Stress Tolerance Problems

Compared with other police officer candidates, the test taker is more likely to become easily discouraged[18]; to have difficulty coping with stress[19]; and to easily become irritated and annoyed by others[20]. He is also more likely to become impatient with others over minor infractions[20].

Routine Task Performance Problems

Compared with other police officer candidates, the test taker is more likely to have a history of motor vehicle violations or difficulties[21] and to have a history of job performance problems[22].

FIGURE 8-4 Mr. G's MMPI-2-RF Police Candidate Interpretive Report, continued

Feedback Acceptance Problems

Compared with other police officer candidates, the test taker is less likely to reflect on his behavior[23] and more likely to brush off criticism and other negative feedback[23].

He is more likely than most police officers or trainees to exhibit difficulties accepting and responding to constructive performance feedback[24].

Social Competence and Teamwork Problems

Compared with other police officer candidates, the test taker is more likely to be self-centered[20]; to engage in conflicts with authority[25]; and to have a history of problems getting along with others[26]. He is also more likely to be opinionated and outspoken[26]; to fail to consider others' needs and feelings[26]; and to have difficulty creating and sustaining mutually satisfying relationships[26].

He is more likely than most police officers or trainees to exhibit difficulties stemming from rude and/or overbearing behavior that results in complaints from the public[27] and cooperating with peers and/or supervisors[28].

Integrity Problems

Compared with other police officer candidates, the test taker is more likely to fail to integrate ethical considerations into his decision-making[29]; to have a history of conflicts with the law and other violations of social norms[25]; and to have skeptical and/or antisocial views of the world[26]. He is also more likely to lack a commitment to societal rules[25] and to be self-indulgent[25].

He is more likely than most police officers or trainees to exhibit difficulties leading to integrity violations[30]; sustained internal affairs investigations[31]; and investigations about conduct unbecoming a police officer[32].

Conscientiousness and Dependability Problems

Compared with other police officer candidates, the test taker is more likely to have a history of absenteeism or tardiness[25].

He is more likely than most police officers or trainees to exhibit difficulties with punctuality and attendance[33].

Substance Use Problems

Compared with other police officer candidates, the test taker is more likely to have a history of substance use problems[34].

Impulse Control Problems

Compared with other police officer candidates, the test taker is more likely to behave impulsively or without adequate consideration of the consequences or implications of his actions[35].

He is more likely than most police officers or trainees to exhibit difficulties reacting to situations with the proper degree of emotional and behavioral restraint and control, and avoiding impulsive and/or unnecessarily risky behavior[36]. He is also more likely to exhibit difficulties with anger management[20].

FIGURE 8-4 Mr. G's MMPI-2-RF Police Candidate Interpretive Report, continued

The candidate's test scores are not associated with problems in the following domains:
- Decision-Making and Judgment
- Assertiveness

ITEM-LEVEL INFORMATION

Unscorable Responses

The test taker produced scorable responses to all the MMPI-2-RF items.

Critical Responses

Seven MMPI-2-RF scales--Suicidal/Death Ideation (SUI), Helplessness/Hopelessness (HLP), Anxiety (AXY), Ideas of Persecution (RC6), Aberrant Experiences (RC8), Substance Abuse (SUB), and Aggression (AGG)--have been designated by the test authors as having critical item content that may require immediate attention and follow-up. Items answered by the individual in the keyed direction (True or False) on a critical scale are listed below if his T score on that scale is 65 or higher.

The test taker has not produced an elevated T score ($\geq$ 65) on any of these scales.

Critical Follow-up Items

This section contains a list of items to which the test taker responded in a manner warranting follow-up. The items were identified by police officer screening experts as having critical content. Clinicians are encouraged to follow up on these statements with the candidate by making related inquiries, rather than reciting the item(s) verbatim. Each item is followed by the candidate's response, the percentage of Police Officer Candidate comparison group members who gave this response, and the scale(s) on which the item appears.

257. Item Content Omitted. (True; 4.3%; VRIN-r, RC8, COG)
329. Item Content Omitted. (True; 4.2%; VRIN-r, BXD, RC4, AGG, AGGR-r)
337. Item Content Omitted. (True; 17.4%; VRIN-r, RC9, AGG)

FIGURE 8-4 Mr. G's MMPI-2-RF Police Candidate Interpretive Report, continued

MMPI-2-RF® Police Candidate Interpretive Report
10/14/2014, Page 13 Mr. G

ENDNOTES

This section lists for each statement in the report the MMPI-2-RF score(s) that triggered it. In addition, each statement is identified as a Test Response, if based on item content, a Correlate, if based on empirical correlates, or an Inference, if based on the report authors' judgment. (This information can also be accessed on-screen by placing the cursor on a given statement.) For correlate-based statements, research references (Ref. No.) are provided, keyed to the consecutively numbered reference list following the endnotes.

[1] Test Response: RC4=68
[2] Correlate: RC4=68, Ref. 1, 8, 9, 10, 11, 17, 19, 20, 21, 22, 24, 29, 36, 40; DISC-r=69, Ref. 36
[3] Correlate: RC4=68, Ref. 3, 12, 16, 22, 26, 36
[4] Correlate: RC4=68, Ref. 36; JCP=70, Ref. 36
[5] Correlate: RC4=68, Ref. 36
[6] Correlate: RC4=68, Ref. 8, 36
[7] Correlate: RC4=68, Ref. 1, 2, 5, 6, 8, 12, 13, 14, 15, 16, 17, 19, 23, 24, 25, 26, 27, 28, 29, 30, 36, 37, 39
[8] Test Response: JCP=70
[9] Correlate: RC4=68, Ref. 4, 22, 26, 36; JCP=70, Ref. 18, 36
[10] Correlate: RC4=68, Ref. 1, 36; JCP=70, Ref. 36
[11] Correlate: RC4=68, Ref. 2, 13, 24, 29, 36, 38, 39, 41; JCP=70, Ref. 38
[12] Test Response: BXD=60
[13] Inference: DISC-r=69
[14] Inference: RC4=68
[15] Inference: JCP=70
[16] Test Response: SUB=55
[17] Test Response: AGG=56
[18] Correlate: RC4=68, Ref. 35
[19] Correlate: RC4=68, Ref. 7, 35
[20] Correlate: BXD=60, Ref. 35
[21] Correlate: BXD=60, Ref. 7, 35; RC4=68, Ref. 7
[22] Correlate: BXD=60, Ref. 7, 35; RC4=68, Ref. 35
[23] Correlate: DISC-r=69, Ref. 35
[24] Correlate: AGG=56, Ref. 32
[25] Correlate: BXD=60, Ref. 7, 35; RC4=68, Ref. 7, 35
[26] Correlate: BXD=60, Ref. 7, 35
[27] Correlate: AGG=56, Ref. 34
[28] Correlate: AGG=56, Ref. 32, 33, 34
[29] Correlate: BXD=60, Ref. 33, 35; RC4=68, Ref. 35
[30] Correlate: BXD=60, Ref. 33, 35; RC4=68, Ref. 33, 35; JCP=70, Ref. 33; DISC-r=69, Ref. 35
[31] Correlate: BXD=60, Ref. 33, 35; RC4=68, Ref. 33, 35; DISC-r=69, Ref. 35
[32] Correlate: BXD=60, Ref. 35; JCP=70, Ref. 33
[33] Correlate: JCP=70, Ref. 35
[34] Correlate: BXD=60, Ref. 7, 31, 35; RC4=68, Ref. 7, 31, 35; DISC-r=69, Ref. 7, 35
[35] Correlate: BXD=60, Ref. 7, 35; DISC-r=69, Ref. 7, 35
[36] Correlate: JCP=70, Ref. 31, 33; DISC-r=69, Ref. 35

FIGURE 8-4 Mr. G's MMPI-2-RF Police Candidate Interpretive Report, continued

RESEARCH REFERENCE LIST

The following studies are sources for empirical correlates identified in the Endnotes section of this report.

1. Anderson, J. L., Sellbom, M., Ayearst, L., Quilty, L. C., Chmielewski, M., & Bagby, R. M. (2015). Associations between DSM-5 Section III personality traits and the Minnesota Multiphasic Personality Inventory 2-Restructured Form (MMPI-2-RF) scales in a psychiatric patient sample. *Psychological Assessment, 27,* 801-815. doi: 10.1037/pas0000096

2. Anderson, J. L., Sellbom, M., Pymont, C., Smid, W., De Saeger, H. & Kamphuis, J. H. (2015). Measurement of DSM-5 Section II personality disorder constructs using the MMPI-2-RF in clinical and forensic samples. *Psychological Assessment, 27,* 786-800. doi: 10.1037/pas0000103

3. Arbisi, P. A., Sellbom, M., & Ben-Porath, Y. S. (2008). Empirical correlates of the MMPI-2 Restructured Clinical (RC) Scales in psychiatric inpatients. *Journal of Personality Assessment, 90,* 122-128. doi: 10.1080/00223890701845146

4. Binford, A., & Liljequist, L. (2008). Behavioral correlates of selected MMPI-2 Clinical, Content, and Restructured Clinical scales. *Journal of Personality Assessment, 90,* 608-614. doi: 10.1080/00223890802388657

5. Bolinskey, P. K., Trumbetta, S. L., Hanson, D. R., & Gottesman, I. I. (2010). Predicting adult psychopathology from adolescent MMPIs: Some victories. *Personality and Individual Differences, 49,* 324-330. doi: 10.1016/j.paid.2010.01.026

6. Burchett, D. L., & Ben-Porath, Y. S. (2010). The impact of over-reporting on MMPI-2-RF substantive scale score validity. *Assessment, 17,* 497-516. doi: 10.1177/1073191110378972

7. Detrick, P., Ben-Porath, Y. S., & Sellbom, M. (2015). Associations between MMPI-2-RF (Restructured Form) and Inwald Personality Inventory (IPI) scale scores in a law enforcement preemployment screening sample. *Journal of Police and Criminal Psychology.* Advance online publication. doi: 10.1007/s11896-015-9172-7

8. Finn, J. A., Ben-Porath, Y. S., & Tellegen, A. (2015). Dichotomous versus polytomous response options in psychopathology assessment: Method or meaningful variance? *Psychological Assessment, 27,* 184-193. doi: 10.1037/pas0000044

9. Forbey, J. D., & Ben-Porath, Y. S. (2007). A comparison of the MMPI-2 Restructured Clinical (RC) and Clinical Scales in a substance abuse treatment sample. *Psychological Services, 4,* 46-58. doi: 10.1037/1541-1559.4.1.46

10. Forbey, J. D., & Ben-Porath, Y. S. (2008). Empirical correlates of the MMPI-2 Restructured Clinical (RC) Scales in a non-clinical setting. *Journal of Personality Assessment, 90,* 136-141. doi: 10.1080/00223890701845161

FIGURE 8-4 Mr. G's MMPI-2-RF Police Candidate Interpretive Report, continued

11. Forbey, J. D., Ben-Porath, Y. S., & Gartland, D. (2009). Validation of the MMPI-2 Computerized Adaptive Version (MMPI-2-CA) in a correctional intake facility. *Psychological Services, 6,* 279-292. doi: 10.1037/a0016195

12. Handel, R. W., & Archer, R. P. (2008). An investigation of the psychometric properties of the MMPI-2 Restructured Clinical (RC) Scales with mental health inpatients. *Journal of Personality Assessment, 90,* 239-249. doi: 10.1080/00223890701884954

13. Kamphuis, J. H., Arbisi, P. A., Ben-Porath, Y. S., & McNulty, J. L. (2008). Detecting comorbid Axis-II status among inpatients using the MMPI-2 Restructured Clinical Scales. *European Journal of Psychological Assessment, 24,* 157-164. doi: 10.1027/1015-5759.24.3.157

14. Kastner, R. M., Sellbom, M., & Lilienfeld, S. O. (2012). A comparison of the psychometric properties of the Psychopathic Personality Inventory full-length and short-form versions. *Psychological Assessment, 24,* 261-267. doi: 10.1037/a0025832

15. Klein Haneveld, E., Kamphuis, J. H., Smid, W., & Forbey, J. D. (2017). Using MMPI-2-RF correlates to elucidate the PCL-R and its four facets in a sample of male forensic psychiatric patients. *Journal of Personality Assessment, 99,* 398-407. doi: 10.1080/00223891.2016.1228655

16. Menton, W. H., Crighton, A. H., Tarescavage, A. M., Marek, R. J., Hicks, A. D., & Ben-Porath, Y. S. (2017). Equivalence of laptop and tablet administrations of the Minnesota Multiphasic Personality Inventory-2 Restructured Form. *Assessment.* doi: 0.1177/1073191117714558

17. Phillips, T. R., Sellbom, M., Ben-Porath, Y. S., & Patrick, C. J. (2014). Further development and construct validation of MMPI-2-RF indices of global psychopathy, fearless-dominance, and impulsive-antisociality in a sample of incarcerated women. *Law and Human Behavior, 38(1),* 34-46. doi: 10.1037/lhb0000040

18. Sellbom, M. (2016). Elucidating the validity of the externalizing spectrum of psychopathology in correctional, forensic, and community Samples. *Journal of Abnormal Psychology, 125,* 1027-1038. doi: 10.1037/abn0000171

19. Sellbom, M., Anderson, J. L., & Bagby, R. M. (2013). Assessing DSM-5 Section III Personality Traits and Disorders with the MMPI-2-RF. *Assessment, 20,* 709-722. doi: 10.1177/1073191113508808

20. Sellbom, M., & Ben-Porath, Y. S. (2005). Mapping the MMPI-2 Restructured Clinical (RC) Scales onto normal personality traits: Evidence of construct validity. *Journal of Personality Assessment, 85,* 179-187. doi: 10.1207/s15327752jpa8502_10

21. Sellbom, M., Ben-Porath, Y. S., & Bagby, R. M. (2008). Personality and psychopathology: Mapping the MMPI-2 Restructured Clinical (RC) Scales onto the five factor model of personality. *Journal of Personality Disorders, 22,* 291-312. doi: 10.1521/pedi.2008.22.3.291

22. Sellbom, M., Ben-Porath, Y. S., Baum, L. J., Erez, E., & Gregory, C. (2008). Predictive validity of the MMPI-2 Restructured Clinical (RC) Scales in a batterers' intervention program. *Journal of Personality Assessment, 90,* 129-135. doi: 10.1080/00223890701845153

FIGURE 8-4 Mr. G's MMPI-2-RF Police Candidate Interpretive Report, continued

23. Sellbom, M., Ben-Porath, Y. S., & Graham, J. R. (2006). Correlates of the MMPI-2 Restructured Clinical (RC) Scales in a college counseling setting. *Journal of Personality Assessment, 86,* 89-99. doi: 10.1207/s15327752jpa8601_10

24. Sellbom, M., Ben-Porath, Y. S., Lilienfeld, S. O., Patrick, C. J., & Graham, J. R. (2005). Assessing psychopathic personality traits with the MMPI-2. *Journal of Personality Assessment, 85,* 334-343. doi: 10.1207/s15327752jpa8503_10

25. Sellbom, M., Ben-Porath, Y. S., Patrick, C. J., Wygant, D. B., Gartland, D. M., & Stafford, K. P. (2012). Development and Construct Validation of MMPI-2-RF Indices of Global Psychopathy, Fearless-Dominance, and Impulsive-Antisociality. *Personality Disorders: Theory, Research, and Treatment, 3(1),* 17-38. doi: 10.1037/a0023888

26. Sellbom, M., Ben-Porath, Y. S., & Stafford, K. P. (2007). A comparison of measures of psychopathic deviance in a forensic setting. *Psychological Assessment, 19,* 430-436. doi: 10.1037/1040-3590.19.4.430

27. Sellbom, M., Graham, J. R., & Schenk, P. (2006). Incremental validity of the MMPI-2 Restructured Clinical (RC) Scales in a private practice sample. *Journal of Personality Assessment, 86,* 196-205. doi: 10.1207/s15327752jpa8602_09

28. Shkalim, E. (2015). Psychometric evaluation of the MMPI-2/MMPI-2-RF Restructured Clinical Scales in an Israeli sample. *Assessment, 22,* 607-618. doi: 10.1177/1073191114555884

29. Simms, L. J., Casillas, A., Clark, L. A., Watson, D., & Doebbeling, B. I. (2005). Psychometric evaluation of the Restructured Clinical Scales of the MMPI-2. *Psychological Assessment, 17,* 345-358. doi: 10.1037/1040-3590.17.3.345

30. Sullivan, K. A., Elliott, C. D., Lange, R. T., & Anderson, D. S. (2013). A known groups evaluation of the Response Bias Scale in a neuropsychological setting. *Applied Neuropsychology: Adult, 20,* 20-32. doi: 10.1080/09084282.2012.670149

31. Tarescavage, A. M., Brewster, J., Corey, D. M., & Ben-Porath, Y. S. (2015). Use of pre-hire MMPI-2-RF police candidate scores to predict supervisor ratings of post-hire performance. *Assessment, 22,* 411-428. doi: 10.1177/1073191114548445

32. Tarescavage, A. M., Corey, D. M., & Ben-Porath, Y. S. (2015). Minnesota Multiphasic Personality Inventory-2-Restructured Form (MMPI-2-RF) predictors of police officer problem behavior. *Assessment, 22,* 116-132. doi: 10.1177/1073191114534885

33. Tarescavage, A. M., Corey, D. M., & Ben-Porath, Y. S. (2016). A prorating method for estimating MMPI-2-RF scores from MMPI responses: Examination of score fidelity and illustration of empirical utility in the PERSEREC police integrity study sample. *Assessment, 23,* 173-190. doi: 10.1177/1073191115575070

34. Tarescavage, A. M., Corey, D. M., Gupton, H. M., & Ben-Porath Y. S. (2015). Criterion validity and practical utility of the Minnesota Multiphasic Personality Inventory-2-Restructured Form (MMPI-2-RF) in assessments of police officer candidates. *Journal of Personality Assessment, 97,* 382-394. doi: 10.1080/00223891.2014.995800

FIGURE 8-4 Mr. G's MMPI-2-RF Police Candidate Interpretive Report, continued

MMPI-2-RF® Police Candidate Interpretive Report
10/14/2014, Page 18 Mr. G

35. Tarescavage, A. M., Fischler, G. L., Cappo, B., Hill, D. O., Corey, D. M., & Ben-Porath, Y. S. (2015). Minnesota Multiphasic Personality Inventory-2-Restructured Form (MMPI-2-RF) predictors of police officer problem behavior and collateral self-report test scores. *Psychological Assessment, 27,* 125-137. doi: 10.1037/pas0000041

36. Tellegen, A., & Ben-Porath, Y. S. (2008/2011). *The Minnesota Multiphasic Personality Inventory-2-Restructured Form (MMPI-2-RF): Technical manual.* Minneapolis: University of Minnesota Press.

37. Van der Heijden, P. T., Egger, J. I. M., Rossi, G., & Derksen, J. J. L. (2012). Integrating psychopathology and personality disorders conceptualized by the MMPI-2-RF and the MCMI-III: A structural validity study. *Journal of Personality Assessment, 4,* 345-357. doi: 10.1080/00223891.2012.656861

38. Van der Heijden, P. T., Egger, J. I. M., Rossi, G., Grundel, G., & Derksen, J. J. L. (2013). The MMPI-2 Restructured Form and the standard MMPI-2 Clinical Scales in relation to DSM-IV. *European Journal of Psychological Assessment, 29,* 182-188. doi: 10.1027/1015-5759/a000140

39. Wolf, E. J., Miller, M. W., Orazem, R. J., Weierich, M. R., Castillo, D. T., Milford, J., Kaloupek, D. G., & Keane, T. M. (2008). The MMPI-2 Restructured Clinical Scales in the assessment of posttraumatic stress disorder and comorbid disorders. *Psychological Assessment, 20,* 327-340. doi: 10.1037/a0012948

40. Wygant, D. B., Boutacoff, L. A., Arbisi, P. A., Ben-Porath, Y. S., Kelly, P. H., & Rupp, W. M. (2007). Examination of the MMPI-2 Restructured Clinical (RC) Scales in a sample of bariatric surgery candidates. *Journal of Clinical Psychology in Medical Settings, 14,* 197-205. doi: 10.1007/s10880-007-9073-8

41. Zahn, N., Sellbom, M., Pymont, C., & Schenk, P. W. (2017). Associations between MMPI-2-RF scale scores and self-reported personality disorder criteria in a private practice sample. *Journal of Psychopathology and Behavioral Assessment.*doi: 10.1007/s10862-017-9616-8

End of Report

FIGURE 8-4 Mr. G's MMPI-2-RF Police Candidate Interpretive Report, continued

Background Findings

Mr. G's background reveals three chronologically distinct behavior patterns. In the period up to age 19, he was compliant with school and societal rules, and he behaved in a prosocial fashion. Beginning his freshman year in college, while away from home for the first time, he was arrested for underage DUI while driving on the college campus. A year later, he was arrested on a charge of interfering with police officers during a political protest event at the college. (The record associated with this arrest was subsequently expunged.) He worked as a sales associate for two retail clothing stores to help pay for college, but he was fired from both positions for "no-call" and "no-show" absences that, according to Mr. G's statement to the background investigator, were a result of hangovers from late-night drinking and partying. At the age of 23, he dropped out of college without completing his degree.

At 25 years of age Mr. G stopped drinking alcohol. He wrote in his Statement of Personal History, "My drinking in years past has historically been a contributing factor in many of the poor decisions I made. Unfortunately, it took me more time than it should have to realize that. Once I understood what alcohol was doing to me, I never took another sip." Collateral references affirmed this self-report and found no evidence to the contrary. Mr. G returned to college at the age of 29 and completed his studies about a year before he applied to be a police officer. In addition to attending college and working as a security officer, Mr. G volunteered at two police agencies, providing mentorship to at-risk teens in juvenile diversion programs. After an extensive background investigation involving dozens of references, both listed and developed, the background investigator concluded,

> [Mr. G] appears to be an overall responsible, honest, reliable, hardworking and trustworthy person. He was responsive and cooperative during the background investigation. He made lots of mistakes and was irresponsible when he was young, but he appears to have learned from his mistakes and has worked hard to improve his life by volunteering to help other young people avoid the same mistakes he made.

Interview Findings

Mr. G avowed a strong commitment to sobriety. He claimed participation in weekly AA meetings since he quit drinking 6 years ago. He evidenced strong personal insight, self-reflection, and acceptance of personal accountability. No discrepancies between self-reported and collaterally obtained background information were identified. He described his motivation for becoming a reserve police officer as stemming from his commitment to sobriety ("Being of service to others helps me combat my narcissism, and narcissism will lead me to think I can drink again. I'm happiest when I'm thinking of others"). No indications of naïveté were found in the interview. Mr. G persuasively expressed remorse for his past irresponsibility and displayed a strong understanding of the ways that his past misconduct posed harm and risk not only to himself but also to others.

Identifying Relevant Risk Findings

a. ***Considering all risk-related findings from all sources, what evidence-based inferences can be drawn?***

Test Findings. Mr. G's PCIR identifies multiple Comparison Group Findings that reveal a comparatively high number of reported difficulties that are reported by only 5.1% or less of the Police Officer Candidate comparison group. These include behavioral problems, poor impulse control, antisocial conduct, juvenile conduct problems, substance use problems, and physically aggressive behavior. The report also indicates a wide range of Job-Relevant Correlates, in comparison both to police officer candidates and police officers/trainees, in 8 of the 10 problem domains: Emotional Control & Stress Tolerance Problems, Routine Task Performance Problems, Feedback Acceptance Problems, Social Competence & Teamwork Problems, Integrity Problems, Conscientiousness & Dependability Problems, Substance Use Problems, and Impulse Control Problems. A central feature of the PCIR is its source-annotated identification of risk-related findings associated with MMPI-2-RF scores and the listing of these annotations in the Endnotes section (Figure 8-4, p. 13). A review of these Endnotes shows that the 34 risk-related statements in Mr. G's PCIR derive from six scales, each associated with the Behavioral Dysfunction domain: RC4 (68T), JCP (70T), BXD (60T), SUB (55T), AGG (56T), and DISC-r (69T).

Mr. G's score on the So scale of the CPI indicates social immaturity, poor impulse control, and a propensity toward substance abuse, crime, and violence. His score on the Ac scale is associated with organizational nonconformity, giving up easily, and tending to be unsure of his own ability and to value personal pleasure and short-term gains.

Background Findings. Mr. G's behavioral problems identified from the background investigation occurred between the ages of 19 and 25 and involve many of the problems associated with his psychological test results. These include being arrested for drunk driving and interfering with the duties of a police officer, academic failure in college, two job terminations for failing to show up on time or at all, and substance use problems. (Note that at this step we are focused solely on risk-related findings; positive findings from psychological testing, background investigation, and the interview will be addressed at the next step, which deals with divergent findings that might mitigate these inferences.)

Interview Findings. There are no risk-related findings from Mr. G's interview other than those that are associated with his background. His self-reported history during the interview was entirely consistent with the collateral evidence, and no new risk-related findings were identified from the interview.

b. What divergent findings might mitigate these inferences?

Test Findings. One of the user-designated features of the various MMPI-2-RF reports, including the PCIR, is the option to set the T-score level at which the report prints for a given scale the items that the candidate answered in the keyed direction. The vast majority of the items that Mr. G answered in the keyed direction on each of the Behavioral Dysfunction scales pertains to his behavior between ages 19 and 25. This alone does not mitigate the risks associated with these scale scores, but it does illustrate that a candidate like Mr. G, whose juvenile and/or young adult history is replete with rule-breaking and norm-violating behavior and who honestly responds to these items, will inevitably produce similar scores that reflect that history even when, as here, that history is followed by a substantial and sustained period of prosocial behavior and rehabilitation. To be clear, the mere fact that the items giving rise to a scale's elevation pertain to past conduct, as opposed to current symptoms and behavior, does not itself mitigate the risk-related findings supported by empirical research. Indeed, a significant body of evidence demonstrates the strong predictive relationship between past and future behavior (Golder, Hall, Engstrom, Higgins, & Logan, 2014; Jager, Keyes, & Schulenberg, 2015; Tackett, Herzhoff, Kushner, & Rule, 2015; Woodhams & Toye, 2007). However, when past behavior has been followed by a stable, substantial, and verified period of behavior that is opposite of it and by persuasive evidence of changes in personal attributes (e.g., cognitive, clinical, personality, moral) presumed necessary to sustain the contemporary behavior, that predictive relationship is weakened, as discussed next.

Background Findings. It is not just past behavior that predicts future behavior. Risk factors are generally sorted as either *static risk markers* or *dynamic risk factors* (Kraemer et al., 1997). Static risk markers refer to past factors correlated with a future adverse behavior, event, or condition that cannot change and are not subject to intervention. Examples of static risk markers include a history of arrest, dropping out of college, having been fired from a job, and having been divorced. In contrast, dynamic or variable risk factors refer to behaviors, conditions, or traits associated with future problems that can be altered or ameliorated by treatment or intervention. Examples of dynamic risk factors include the amount and frequency of substance use, severity of mental health symptoms, attitudes, certain personality constructs, and the degree of conflict experienced in a romantic relationship. Dynamic risk factors often account for the greatest variance in the prediction of future problems even after controlling for static markers (cf. Wilson, Desmarais, Nicholls, Hart, & Brink, 2013).

Mr. G's background reveals multiple static risk markers (e.g., being fired from two jobs, academic failure in college, two arrests, substance use problems) that are reflected in his MMPI-2-RF scores and background findings, but no evidence of dynamic risk factors (e.g., current or contemporary problems associated with substance use, antisocial conduct or attitudes, affiliation with problematic peers, marital problems, occupational problems). Furthermore, there is good evidence to indicate that Mr. G's behavior and adaptation over the 7 years preceding the evaluation were consistently prosocial, norm-conforming, and consonant with his self-reported rehabilitation.

Blumstein and Nakamura (2009) introduced the concept of a "redemption period" following a criminal offender's last offense. They observed that many ex-offenders seeking employment "could be haunted by a stale record" (p. 327). Using data from a state criminal history repository, they estimated for various crime types and ages the declining hazard of rearrest with time "clean." Blumstein and Nakamura concluded that for many crimes there exists a redemption period after which a person with a criminal record, who remained free of further contact with the criminal justice system, is of no greater risk than a nonoffender of the same age—"an indication of redemption from the mark of crime" (p. 327). Similarly, some police candidates with problematic juvenile or early adult histories demonstrate a sufficiently reliable and well-documented redemption period to justify reducing the weight ordinarily assigned to these static risk markers.

Interview Findings. When determining whether static risk markers from a candidate's relatively distant past, and Behavioral Dysfunction scale scores based primarily on those static markers, warrant mitigation, attention should be paid not simply to the presence or absence of dynamic risk factors but also to evidence of *protective factors* that serve to reduce future risk. Gaspar, Seabright, Reynolds, and Yam (2015) concluded from a series of innovative experiments that the predictive power of a static marker involving a prior immoral act (e.g., stealing, lying, driving intoxicated) is mediated by how the individual thinks about his or her immoral behavior. They found that persons who reflected counterfactually on their prior moral lapses (i.e., they falsely minimized their own culpability, opportunities to have made more responsible choices, and accountability) were much more likely to engage in future counterproductive behavior (e.g., lying on unrelated tasks with real monetary stakes) than those who reflected factually.

With this in mind, it is important to note that Mr. G's reflection on his past behavior during the interview was entirely factual and demonstrated clear evidence of acceptance of his culpability, identification of available alternative choices that he failed to take, and acceptance of personal accountability. He made no effort to engage in moral rationalization of his past misconduct. He established a clear line of demarcation between his past antisocial behavior and his commitment to prosocial conduct, which was confirmed by his collateral references in the background investigation. Thus, there was substantial evidence of a sustained change in Mr. G's behavior over the prior 7 years that, in combination with the protective factor observed in the interview (factual reflection), supported mitigation of the risk-related findings.

c. ***Are any surviving risk-related inferences of sufficient relevance and quality to warrant the candidate's disqualification?***

Risk mitigation does not equal risk elimination. The many job-relevant correlates observed in the empirical literature between scales in the Behavioral Dysfunction domain and later counterproductive behavior as a police officer were documented without regard to other mitigating factors. In the final analysis, screening professionals are not expected to be flawless in their decisions; rather, they are expected to apply the level of care at which an ordinary, prudent professional with the same training and experience in good standing in the same or a similar community would practice under the same or similar circumstances. Spilberg and Corey (2017) present the case that screening psychologists are the "risk assessors," but the employer is the "risk manager." As such, they argue that in cases where a psychologist believes that evidence-based risk is appropriately mitigated by other evidence, it is generally prudent to confer with the hiring agency concerning the employer's tolerance for taking on the risk. When doing so, providing a clear and rational argument for why and how risk mitigation is warranted by other relevant findings—in a conversation with the employer and/or in the body of the written report—both aids the employer's decision making and helps document the psychologist's rationale in the event the evaluation comes under review at a later time.

In the case of Mr. G, the examining psychologist determined, in consultation with the hiring agency, that the well-documented redemption period, strong evidence of protective factors, and the nature of the reserve police officer position[1] warranted mitigation of the risks associated with his test results. Therefore, Mr. G was judged to be psychologically qualified for the position.

Brief Review: Mr. L, Police Officer Candidate

Assessment Issues Presented

- An MMPI-2-RF protocol with all but one substantive scale score (Activation; ACT) within normal limits of the Police Officer Candidate comparison group and with no interpretive statements generated in the Job-Relevant Correlates section
- Use of the integration model to demonstrate how clinically significant elevation on a single scale, when convergent with other reliable, independent, and relevant assessment data, may support disqualification

Referral Summary

Mr. L is a 22-year-old divorced male seeking a first-time appointment as a police officer with a small police department. At the time of the evaluation, Mr. L worked as a full-time retail loss prevention officer, where he had been employed for about a year and a half. This was the only job he had held; he previously attended a community college, but did not earn a degree.

The two work references interviewed during the background investigation included his immediate supervisor and one coworker. Both recommended against Mr. L being hired as a police officer. The supervisor reported that Mr. L's emotions and reactions tend to be heightened with the level of stress that surrounds him. It gets in the way of his decision-making process, and he becomes visibly frustrated. In the heat of the moment, Mr. L defaults to going against training and is easily overwhelmed with accumulated work.

Mr. L's coworker reported that he would act "weird at work and would get too amped up over certain situations." The hiring agency considered rejecting Mr. L on the basis of these negative work references, but decided to make a conditional offer of employment and refer him to the psychological evaluation since all of the other nonwork references were entirely positive. (Small police agencies often have significantly fewer applicants owing to a remote location; typically lower pay; limited opportunities for special assignments, training, and promotion; and fewer exciting calls. This can lead to candidates being advanced and considered further along in the assessment process in comparison to large agencies where the higher volume of candidates often results in earlier disqualification when negative personal history information is discovered. This is not to say that small agencies apply a lower standard to their ultimate hiring decisions compared to large agencies.)

Assessing Protocol Validity

As shown in Figure 8-5, Mr. L's score on the Adjustment Validity (K-r) scale is at 72T (which is the ceiling on the scale), indicating that he presented himself as remarkably well adjusted. As noted in the PCIR, 17.6% of the Police Officer Candidate comparison group scored at this level. In light of Mr. L's generally positive background investigation, at least with respect to his general adjustment, and considering his score on the Uncommon Virtues scale (L-r; 52T), this self-presentation does not undermine the validity of this protocol, although elevated scores on the substantive scales may underestimate the problems they assess.

Substantive Scale Findings

Only one of the substantive scale scores is clinically elevated (≥65T), with Activation at 67T. As noted in the Comparison Group Findings of the PCIR (Figure 8-5, p. 10),

MMPI-2-RF®

Minnesota Multiphasic
Personality Inventory-2
Restructured Form®
Yossef S. Ben-Porath, PhD, & Auke Tellegen, PhD

MMPI-2-RF®
Police Candidate Interpretive Report
David M. Corey, PhD, & Yossef S. Ben-Porath, PhD

Name:	Mr. L
Age:	22
Gender:	Male
Marital Status:	Divorced
Years of Education:	13
Date Assessed:	06/06/2015

Copyright © 2014 by the Regents of the University of Minnesota. All rights reserved.
Distributed exclusively under license from the University of Minnesota by NCS Pearson, Inc. Portions reproduced from the MMPI-2-RF test booklet. Copyright © 2008 by the Regents of the University of Minnesota. All rights reserved. Portions excerpted from the *MMPI-2-RF Manual for Administration, Scoring, and Interpretation.* Copyright © 2008, 2011 by the Regents of the University of Minnesota. All rights reserved. Used by permission of the University of Minnesota Press.

Minnesota Multiphasic Personality Inventory-2-Restructured Form and **MMPI-2-RF** are registered trademarks of the University of Minnesota. **Pearson** is a trademark in the U.S. and/or other countries of Pearson Education, Inc., or its affiliate(s).

This report contains copyrighted material and trade secrets. The qualified licensee may excerpt portions of this output report, limited to the minimum text necessary to accurately describe their significant core conclusions, for incorporation into a written evaluation of the examinee, in accordance with their profession's citation standards, if any. No adaptations, translations, modifications, or special versions may be made of this report without prior written permission from the University of Minnesota Press.

[4.0 / 57 / __VERSION__]

ALWAYS LEARNING PEARSON

FIGURE 8-5 Mr. L's MMPI-2-RF Police Candidate Interpretive Report

MMPI-2-RF Validity Scales

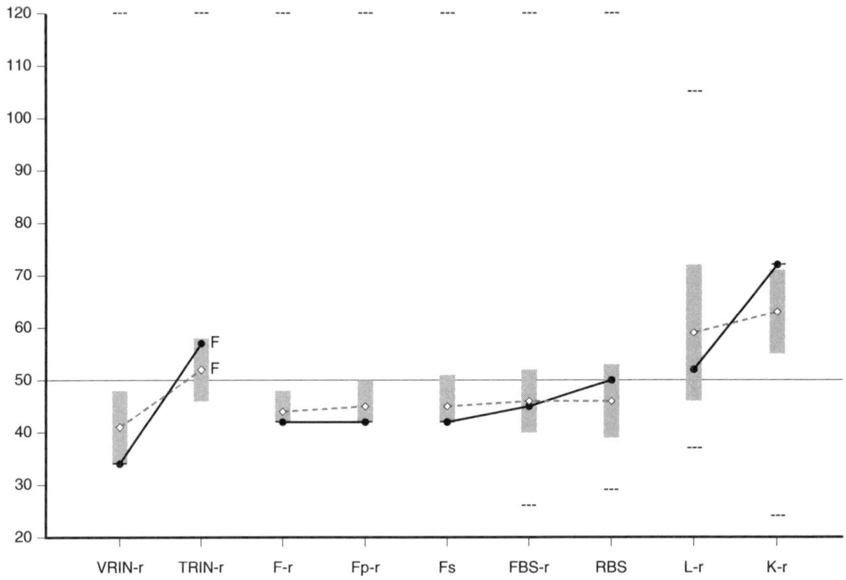

	VRIN-r	TRIN-r	F-r	Fp-r	Fs	FBS-r	RBS	L-r	K-r
Raw Score:	0	10	0	0	0	6	5	3	14
T Score:	34	57 F	42	42	42	45	50	52	72
Response %:	100	100	100	100	100	100	100	100	100

Cannot Say (Raw): 0 Percent True (of items answered): 33%

Comparison Group Data: Personnel Screening, Police Officer Candidate (Men and Women), N = 2074

	VRIN-r	TRIN-r	F-r	Fp-r	Fs	FBS-r	RBS	L-r	K-r
Mean Score (◇---◇):	41	52 F	44	45	45	46	46	59	63
Standard Dev (±1 SD):	7	6	4	5	6	6	7	13	8
Percent scoring at or below test taker:	28	92	75	78	70	49	81	41	100

The highest and lowest T scores possible on each scale are indicated by a "---"; MMPI-2-RF T scores are non-gendered.

VRIN-r	Variable Response Inconsistency	Fs	Infrequent Somatic Responses	L-r	Uncommon Virtues
TRIN-r	True Response Inconsistency	FBS-r	Symptom Validity	K-r	Adjustment Validity
F-r	Infrequent Responses	RBS	Response Bias Scale		
Fp-r	Infrequent Psychopathology Responses				

FIGURE 8-5 Mr. L's MMPI-2-RF Police Candidate Interpretive Report, continued

MMPI-2-RF Higher-Order (H-O) and Restructured Clinical (RC) Scales

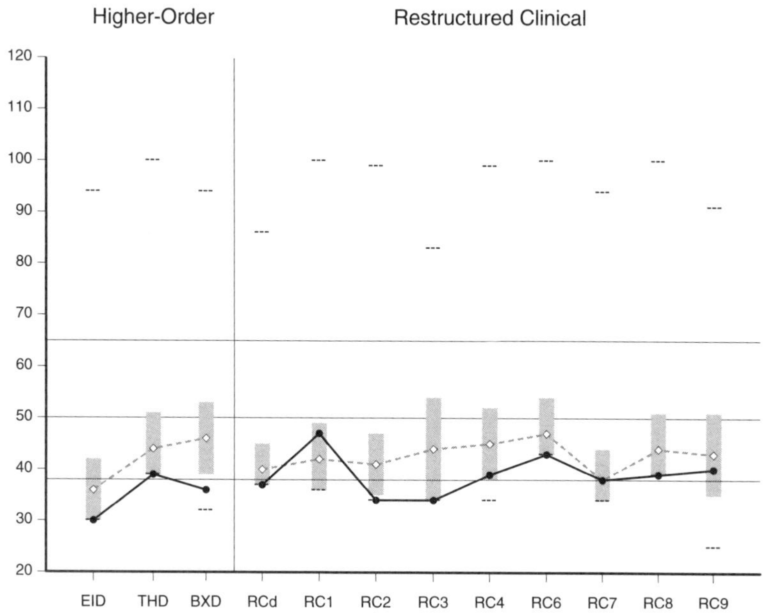

	EID	THD	BXD	RCd	RC1	RC2	RC3	RC4	RC6	RC7	RC8	RC9
Raw Score:	0	0	1	0	2	0	0	1	0	1	0	6
T Score:	30	39	36	37	47	34	34	39	43	38	39	40
Response %:	100	100	100	100	100	100	100	100	100	100	100	100

Comparison Group Data: Personnel Screening, Police Officer Candidate (Men and Women), N = 2074

	EID	THD	BXD	RCd	RC1	RC2	RC3	RC4	RC6	RC7	RC8	RC9
Mean Score (◇--◇):	36	44	46	40	42	41	44	45	47	38	44	43
Standard Dev (±1 SD):	6	7	7	5	7	6	10	7	7	6	7	8
Percent scoring at or below test taker:	24	57	17	62	82	29	21	33	75	68	53	38

The highest and lowest T scores possible on each scale are indicated by a "---"; MMPI-2-RF T scores are non-gendered.

EID Emotional/Internalizing Dysfunction
THD Thought Dysfunction
BXD Behavioral/Externalizing Dysfunction

RCd Demoralization
RC1 Somatic Complaints
RC2 Low Positive Emotions
RC3 Cynicism
RC4 Antisocial Behavior

RC6 Ideas of Persecution
RC7 Dysfunctional Negative Emotions
RC8 Aberrant Experiences
RC9 Hypomanic Activation

FIGURE 8-5 Mr. L's MMPI-2-RF Police Candidate Interpretive Report, continued

MMPI-2-RF® Police Candidate Interpretive Report
06/06/2015, Page 4 Mr. L

MMPI-2-RF Somatic/Cognitive and Internalizing Scales

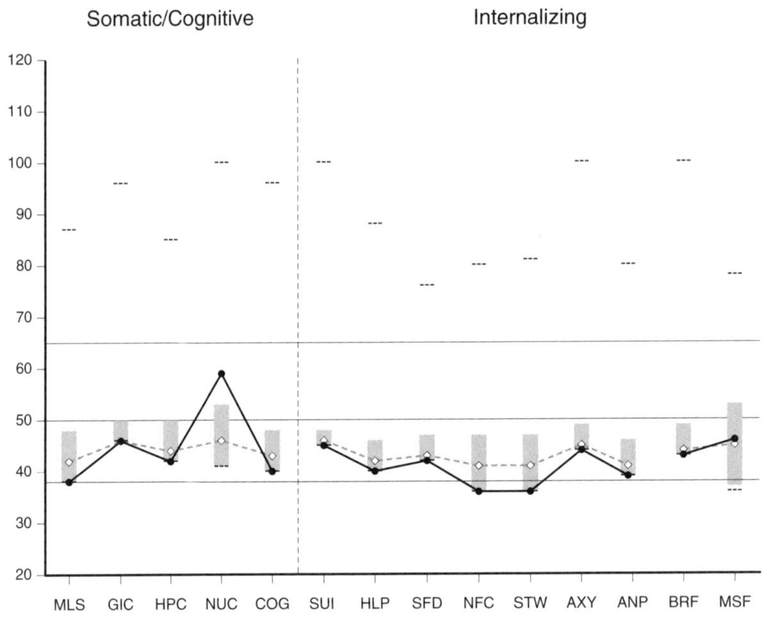

	MLS	GIC	HPC	NUC	COG	SUI	HLP	SFD	NFC	STW	AXY	ANP	BRF	MSF
Raw Score:	0	0	0	2	0	0	0	0	0	0	0	0	0	2
T Score:	38	46	42	59	40	45	40	42	36	36	44	39	43	46
Response %:	100	100	100	100	100	100	100	100	100	100	100	100	100	100

Comparison Group Data: Personnel Screening, Police Officer Candidate (Men and Women), N = 2074

	MLS	GIC	HPC	NUC	COG	SUI	HLP	SFD	NFC	STW	AXY	ANP	BRF	MSF
Mean Score (◇- - ◇):	42	46	44	46	43	46	42	43	41	41	45	41	44	45
Standard Dev (±1 SD):	6	4	6	7	5	2	4	4	6	6	4	5	5	8
Percent scoring at or below test taker:	63	95	83	98	77	99.3	88	90	50	48	94	81	88	64

The highest and lowest T scores possible on each scale are indicated by a "---"; MMPI-2-RF T scores are non-gendered.

MLS Malaise
GIC Gastrointestinal Complaints
HPC Head Pain Complaints
NUC Neurological Complaints
COG Cognitive Complaints
SUI Suicidal/Death Ideation
HLP Helplessness/Hopelessness
SFD Self-Doubt
NFC Inefficacy
STW Stress/Worry
AXY Anxiety
ANP Anger Proneness
BRF Behavior-Restricting Fears
MSF Multiple Specific Fears

FIGURE 8-5 Mr. L's MMPI-2-RF Police Candidate Interpretive Report, continued

MMPI-2-RF® Police Candidate Interpretive Report
06/06/2015, Page 5 Mr. L

MMPI-2-RF Externalizing, Interpersonal, and Interest Scales

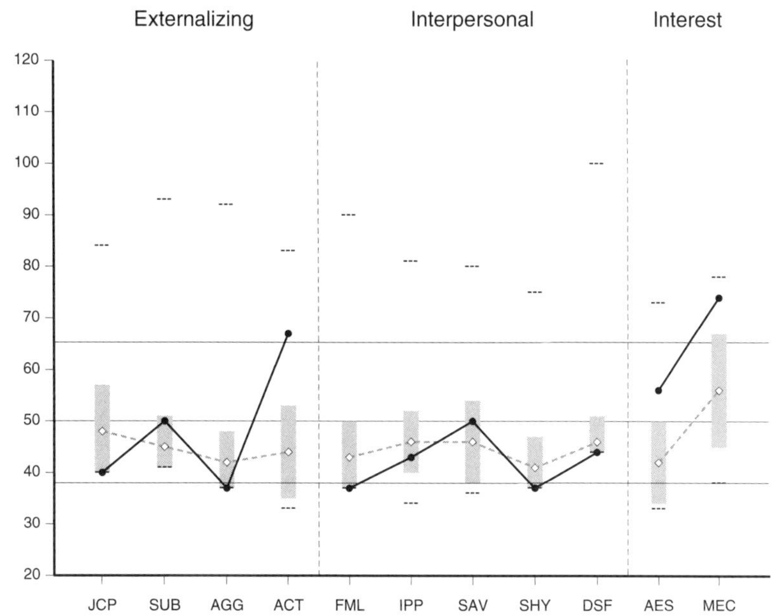

	JCP	SUB	AGG	ACT	FML	IPP	SAV	SHY	DSF	AES	MEC
Raw Score:	0	1	0	6	0	2	3	0	0	4	8
T Score:	40	50	37	67	37	43	50	37	44	56	74
Response %:	100	100	100	100	100	100	100	100	100	100	100

Comparison Group Data: Personnel Screening, Police Officer Candidate (Men and Women), N = 2074

	JCP	SUB	AGG	ACT	FML	IPP	SAV	SHY	DSF	AES	MEC
Mean Score (◇---◇):	48	45	42	44	43	46	46	41	46	42	56
Standard Dev (±1 SD):	9	6	6	9	7	6	8	6	5	8	11
Percent scoring at or below test taker:	46	90	56	99.1	47	44	78	57	90	96	97

The highest and lowest T scores possible on each scale are indicated by a "---"; MMPI-2-RF T scores are non-gendered.

JCP Juvenile Conduct Problems
SUB Substance Abuse
AGG Aggression
ACT Activation

FML Family Problems
IPP Interpersonal Passivity
SAV Social Avoidance
SHY Shyness
DSF Disaffiliativeness

AES Aesthetic-Literary Interests
MEC Mechanical-Physical Interests

FIGURE 8-5 Mr. L's MMPI-2-RF Police Candidate Interpretive Report, continued

MMPI-2-RF PSY-5 Scales

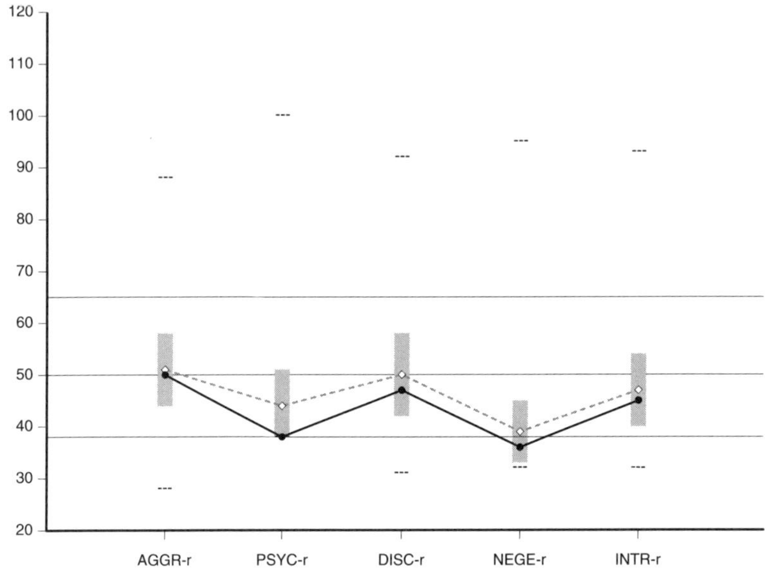

	AGGR-r	PSYC-r	DISC-r	NEGE-r	INTR-r
Raw Score:	9	0	5	1	4
T Score:	50	38	47	36	45
Response %:	100	100	100	100	100

Comparison Group Data: Personnel Screening, Police Officer Candidate (Men and Women), N = 2074

Mean Score (◇- - -◇):	51	44	50	39	47
Standard Dev (±1 SD):	7	7	8	6	7
Percent scoring at or below test taker:	57	55	42	50	48

The highest and lowest T scores possible on each scale are indicated by a "---"; MMPI-2-RF T scores are non-gendered.

AGGR-r Aggressiveness-Revised
PSYC-r Psychoticism-Revised
DISC-r Disconstraint-Revised
NEGE-r Negative Emotionality/Neuroticism-Revised
INTR-r Introversion/Low Positive Emotionality-Revised

FIGURE 8-5 Mr. L's MMPI-2-RF Police Candidate Interpretive Report, continued

MMPI-2-RF® Police Candidate Interpretive Report
06/06/2015, Page 7 Mr. L

MMPI-2-RF T SCORES (BY DOMAIN)

PROTOCOL VALIDITY

Content Non-Responsiveness

0	34	57 F
CNS	VRIN-r	TRIN-r

Over-Reporting

42	42		42	45	50
F-r	Fp-r		Fs	FBS-r	RBS

Under-Reporting

52	**72**
L-r	**K-r**

SUBSTANTIVE SCALES

Somatic/Cognitive Dysfunction

47	38	46	42	59	40
RC1	MLS	GIC	HPC	NUC	COG

Emotional Dysfunction

30
EID

37	45	40	42	36		
RCd	SUI	HLP	SFD	NFC		
34	45					
RC2	INTR-r					
38	36	44	39	43	46	36
RC7	STW	AXY	ANP	BRF	MSF	NEGE-r

Thought Dysfunction

39
THD

43
RC6
39
RC8
38
PSYC-r

Behavioral Dysfunction

36
BXD

39	40	50		
RC4	JCP	SUB		
40	37	**67**	50	47
RC9	AGG	**ACT**	AGGR-r	DISC-r

Interpersonal Functioning

37	34	43	50	37	44
FML	RC3	IPP	SAV	SHY	DSF

Interests

56	74
AES	MEC

Scale scores shown in bold font are interpreted in the report.

Note. This information is provided to facilitate interpretation following the recommended structure for MMPI-2-RF interpretation in Chapter 5 of the *MMPI-2-RF Manual for Administration, Scoring, and Interpretation*, which provides details in the text and an outline in Table 5-1.

FIGURE 8-5 Mr. L's MMPI-2-RF Police Candidate Interpretive Report, continued

MMPI-2-RF® Police Candidate Interpretive Report
06/06/2015, Page 8 Mr. L

This interpretive report is intended for use by a professional qualified to interpret the MMPI-2-RF in the context of preemployment psychological evaluations of police and other law enforcement officer candidates. ***It focuses on identifying problems; it does not convey potential strengths.*** *The information it contains should be considered in the context of the test taker's background, the demands of the position under consideration, the clinical interview, findings from supplemental tests, and other relevant information.*

The interpretive statements in the Protocol Validity section of the report are based on T scores derived from the general MMPI-2-RF normative sample, as well as scores obtained by the multisite sample of 2,074 individuals that make up the Police Officer Candidate comparison group.

The interpretive statements in the Clinical Findings and Diagnostic Considerations sections of the report are based on T scores derived from the general MMPI-2-RF normative sample. Following recommended practice, only T scores of 65 and higher are considered clinically significant. Scores at this clinical level are generally rare among police officer candidates.

Statements in the Comparison Group Findings and Job-Relevant Correlates sections are based on comparisons with scores obtained by the Police Officer Candidate comparison group. Statements in these sections may be based on T scores that, although less than 65, are nevertheless uncommon in reference to the comparison group.

Sources for interpretive statements in all sections are listed in the Endnotes section of this report. See User's Guide for the MMPI-2-RF Police Candidate Interpretive Report *for detailed information on report features.*

SYNOPSIS

Scores on the MMPI-2-RF validity scales raise concerns about the possible impact of under-reporting on the validity of this protocol. With that caution noted, scores on the substantive scales indicate clinically significant behavioral dysfunction. Behavioral-externalizing problems relate to excessive activation.

PROTOCOL VALIDITY

Content Non-Responsiveness

There are no problems with unscorable items in this protocol. The test taker responded to the MMPI-2-RF in a remarkably consistent manner. He was deliberate in his approach to the assessment.

FIGURE 8-5 Mr. L's MMPI-2-RF Police Candidate Interpretive Report, continued

Over-Reporting

There are no indications of over-reporting in this protocol.

Under-Reporting

The test taker presented himself as remarkably well-adjusted[1]. This reported level of psychological adjustment is rare in the general population and relatively uncommon among police officer candidates. Only 17.6% of comparison group members reported this level of good psychological adjustment. Any absence of elevation on the substantive scales should be interpreted with caution. Elevated scores on the substantive scales may underestimate the problems assessed by those scales[2].

CLINICAL FINDINGS

Clinical-level symptoms, personality characteristics, and behavioral tendencies of the test taker are described in this section and organized according to an empirically guided framework. (Please see Chapter 8, Yossef S. Ben-Porath, Interpreting the MMPI-2-RF, *for details.) Statements containing the word "reports" are based on the item content of MMPI-2-RF scales, whereas statements that include the word "likely" are based on empirical correlates of scale scores. Specific sources for each statement can be accessed with the annotation features of this report.*

The following interpretation needs to be considered in light of cautions noted about the possible impact of under-reporting on the validity of this protocol.

The test taker reports episodes of over-activation such as heightened excitation and energy level[3] and may have a history of symptoms associated with manic or hypomanic episodes[4].

There are no indications of clinically significant somatic, cognitive, emotional, or thought dysfunction in this protocol. However, because of indications of possible under-reporting described earlier, such problems cannot be ruled out.

DIAGNOSTIC CONSIDERATIONS

This section provides recommendations for psychodiagnostic assessment based on the test taker's MMPI-2-RF results. It is recommended that he be evaluated for the following:

Emotional-Internalizing Disorders

- Cycling mood disorder[5]

Behavioral-Externalizing Disorders

- Manic or hypomanic episode or other conditions associated with excessive energy and activation[6]

FIGURE 8-5 Mr. L's MMPI-2-RF Police Candidate Interpretive Report, continued

COMPARISON GROUP FINDINGS

This section describes the MMPI-2-RF substantive scale findings in the context of the Police Officer Candidate comparison group. Specific sources for each statement can be accessed with the annotation features of this report. ***Job-related correlates of these results, if any, are provided in the subsequent Job-Relevant Correlates section.***

The following interpretation needs to be considered in light of cautions noted about the possible impact of under-reporting on the validity of this protocol.

Behavioral/Externalizing Problems

The test taker's responses indicate a level of over-activation that may be incompatible with public safety requirements for behavioral control and sound judgment[7]. This level of excitability is very uncommon among police officer candidates. Only 4.1% of comparison group members give evidence of this or a greater level of activation.

JOB-RELEVANT CORRELATES

Job-relevant personality characteristics and behavioral tendencies of the test taker are described in this section and organized according to ten problem domains commonly identified in the professional literature as relevant to police officer candidate suitability. (Please see User's Guide for MMPI-2-RF Police Candidate Interpretive Report *for details.) Statements that begin with "Compared with other police officer candidates" are based on correlations with other self-report measures obtained in police officer candidate samples that included individuals who were subsequently hired as well as those who were not. Statements that begin with "He is more likely than most police officers or trainees" are based on correlations with outcome data obtained in samples of hired candidates during academy or field training, probation, and/or the post-probation period. Specific sources for each statement can be accessed with the annotation features of this report.*

The following interpretation needs to be considered in light of cautions noted about the possible impact of under-reporting on the validity of this protocol.

The candidate's test scores are not associated with any correlates.

ITEM-LEVEL INFORMATION

Unscorable Responses

The test taker produced scorable responses to all the MMPI-2-RF items.

Critical Responses

Seven MMPI-2-RF scales--Suicidal/Death Ideation (SUI), Helplessness/Hopelessness (HLP), Anxiety (AXY), Ideas of Persecution (RC6), Aberrant Experiences (RC8), Substance Abuse (SUB), and

FIGURE 8-5 Mr. L's MMPI-2-RF Police Candidate Interpretive Report, continued

Aggression (AGG)--have been designated by the test authors as having critical item content that may require immediate attention and follow-up. Items answered by the individual in the keyed direction (True or False) on a critical scale are listed below if his T score on that scale is 65 or higher.

The test taker has not produced an elevated T score (≥ 65) on any of these scales.

Critical Follow-up Items

This section contains a list of items to which the test taker responded in a manner warranting follow-up. The items were identified by police officer screening experts as having critical content. Clinicians are encouraged to follow up on these statements with the candidate by making related inquiries, rather than reciting the item(s) verbatim. Each item is followed by the candidate's response, the percentage of Police Officer Candidate comparison group members who gave this response, and the scale(s) on which the item appears.

The test taker did not respond to any critical follow-up items in the keyed direction.

FIGURE 8-5 Mr. L's MMPI-2-RF Police Candidate Interpretive Report, continued

ENDNOTES

This section lists for each statement in the report the MMPI-2-RF score(s) that triggered it. In addition, each statement is identified as a Test Response, if based on item content, a Correlate, if based on empirical correlates, or an Inference, if based on the report authors' judgment. (This information can also be accessed on-screen by placing the cursor on a given statement.) For correlate-based statements, research references (Ref. No.) are provided, keyed to the consecutively numbered reference list following the endnotes.

[1] Test Response: K-r=72
[2] Correlate: K-r=72, Ref. 1, 3, 5
[3] Test Response: ACT=67
[4] Correlate: ACT=67, Ref. 2, 5, 6
[5] Correlate: ACT=67, Ref. 6
[6] Correlate: ACT=67, Ref. 4, 6
[7] Inference: ACT=67

FIGURE 8-5 Mr. L's MMPI-2-RF Police Candidate Interpretive Report, continued

RESEARCH REFERENCE LIST

The following studies are sources for empirical correlates identified in the Endnotes section of this report.

1. Forbey, J. D., Lee, T. T. C., Ben-Porath, Y. S., Arbisi, P. A., & Gartland, D. (2013). Associations between MMPI-2-RF validity scale scores and extra-test measures of personality and psychopathology. *Assessment, 20,* 448-461. doi: 10.1177/1073191113478154

2. Menton, W. H., Crighton, A. H., Tarescavage, A. M., Marek, R. J., Hicks, A. D., & Ben-Porath, Y. S. (2017). Equivalence of laptop and tablet administrations of the Minnesota Multiphasic Personality Inventory-2 Restructured Form. *Assessment.* doi: 0.1177/1073191117714558

3. Sellbom, M., & Bagby, R. M. (2008). The validity of the MMPI-2-RF (Restructured Form) L-r and K-r scales in detecting under-reporting in clinical and non-clinical samples. *Psychological Assessment, 20,* 370-376. doi: 10.1037/a0012952

4. Sellbom, M., Bagby, R. M., Kushner, S., Quilty, L. C., & Ayearst, L. E. (2011). Diagnostic construct validity of the MMPI-2 Restructured Form (MMPI-2-RF) scale scores. *Assessment, 19,* 176-186. doi: 10.1177/1073191111428763

5. Tellegen, A., & Ben-Porath, Y. S. (2008/2011). *The Minnesota Multiphasic Personality Inventory-2-Restructured Form (MMPI-2-RF): Technical manual.* Minneapolis: University of Minnesota Press.

6. Watson, C., Quilty, L. C., & Bagby, R. M. (2011). Differentiating bipolar disorder from major depressive disorder using the MMPI-2-RF: A receiver operating characteristics (ROC) analysis. *Journal of Psychopathology and Behavioral Assessment, 33,* 368-374. doi: 10.1007/s10862-010-9212-7

End of Report

FIGURE 8-5 Mr. L's MMPI-2-RF Police Candidate Interpretive Report, continued

> The test taker's responses indicate a level of over-activation that may be incompatible with public safety requirements for behavioral control and sound judgment. This level of excitability is very uncommon among police officer candidates. Only 4.1% of comparison group members give evidence of this or a greater level of activation.

Thus, Mr. L's ACT score is anomalous both in comparison to the normative sample and police officer candidates. External correlates of ACT include a history of manic or hypomanic episodes and a current high level of activation.

Data Integration

Screening evaluators are cautioned against making suitability determinations on the basis of a single test score or of any other single data source unless justified (IACP-PPSS, 2015, Guideline 11.4). Spilberg and Corey (2017) emphasize that "no single test score or risk rating should be considered dispositive in the absence of corroborating evidence" (p. 96). However, as these authors also note,

> Psychologists may appropriately give weight to consistent predictive patterns found in validated measures of job relevant constructs; however, it is the psychologist's responsibility to weigh findings from all data sources—written tests, clinical interview, and personal history (including self-reported history, background investigation, detection-of-deception methods, and psychologically relevant health records)—before reaching a suitability determination. (p. 96)

The MMPI-2-RF Activation scale measures a construct that is reflected in the direct, on-the-job observations of Mr. L's supervisor and coworker in a position (retail loss prevention) that has contextual similarities to the work of a police officer, thereby providing a compelling source of corroborating and convergent evidence. No divergent findings undermine that evidence. Therefore, unless the hiring agency chooses to accept the risk of counterproductive behavior related to Emotional Regulation & Stress Tolerance, Impulse Control/Attention to Safety, and Decision-Making and Judgment posed by these data, these convergent findings would disqualify Mr. L as a police officer candidate.

Brief Review: Ms. Y, Dispatcher Candidate

Assessment Issues Presented

- Use of the MMPI-2-RF Score Report (with use of the Dispatcher Candidate comparison group) in evaluating a dispatcher candidate with substantial prior experience in the position
- An MMPI-2-RF protocol with no clinically elevated H-O or RC Scales, but with clinically elevated Anxiety (ANX) and Multiple Specific Fears (MSF) scales and collateral source data consistent with these findings

Referral Summary

Ms. Y is a 48-year-old divorced female seeking a position as a 911 dispatcher in a large urban emergency communications center responsible for police, fire, and emergency medical dispatching. Ms. Y previously worked for 6 years as a 911 call taker at a smaller facility, but left that position 10 years ago to be home with her young children.

Assessing Protocol Validity

As shown in the Score Report (Figure 8-6, p. 2), Ms. Y produced a valid and interpretable protocol. However, her score on VRIN-r (73T) measuring variable response inconsistency is anomalous in personnel settings in which test takers are normally quite attentive to item content. Although her score is not high enough to indicate an invalid protocol, it falls nearly two and a half standard deviations above the normative sample mean

(50T) and more than four standard deviations above the Dispatcher Candidate comparison group (CG) mean (42T, SD=7; see Table 6-3), which should alert the examiner to look for other evidence indicating inattention or carelessness.

Substantive Scale Findings

Ms. Y's scores on the H-O and RC Scales are not clinically elevated, but her scores on EID (54T) and BXD (57T) are more than two standard deviations above the respective CG means, which, as listed in Table 6-3, are 37T for EID (SD=7) and 43T for BXD (SD=7). These moderately elevated but deviant (in contrast to the CG means) scores should lead the examiner to be vigilant for evidence in the interview, background investigation, and other testing of behavior consistent with these constructs; yet, in the absence of outcome and other empirical data that would support inferences for moderately elevated scores, no specific predictions of counterproductive work behavior can be supported. However, Ms. Y's MMPI-2-RF protocol reveals three clinically elevated Specific Problems Scale scores in the Internalizing domain: Stress & Worry (STW; 65T), Anxiety (AXY; 80T), and Multiple Specific Fears (MSF; 65T)—all facets of EID, which, as just discussed, is markedly elevated relative to other dispatcher candidates in the CG. The scores on the three facet scales indicate, respectively, an above-average level of stress and worry, her self-report of feeling pervasively anxious, and her self-report of multiple specific fears of certain animals and acts of nature. The *MMPI-2-RF Manual for Administration, Scoring and Interpretation* (Ben-Porath & Tellegen, 2008/2011) indicates that these scores are associated with being stress reactive and worry prone, engaging in obsessive rumination, experiencing significant anxiety and anxiety-related problems, intrusive ideation, sleep difficulties including nightmares, and posttraumatic distress. They are also correlated with being risk averse and harm avoidant. Finally, these scores indicate the need to evaluate for disorders involving stress and worry, anxiety, and specific phobias.

MMPI 2 RF®

Minnesota Multiphasic
Personality Inventory-2
Restructured Form®

Score Report

MMPI-2-RF®
Minnesota Multiphasic Personality Inventory-2-Restructured Form®
Yossef S. Ben-Porath, PhD, & Auke Tellegen, PhD

Name:	Ms. Y
Age:	47
Gender:	Female
Marital Status:	Separated
Years of Education:	13
Date Assessed:	03/02/2016

PsychCorp

Copyright © 2008, 2011, 2012 by the Regents of the University of Minnesota. All rights reserved.
Distributed exclusively under license from the University of Minnesota by NCS Pearson, Inc. Portions reproduced from the MMPI-2-RF test booklet. Copyright © 2008 by the Regents of the University of Minnesota. All rights reserved. Portions excerpted from the *MMPI-2-RF Manual for Administration, Scoring, and Interpretation.* Copyright © 2008, 2011 by the Regents of the University of Minnesota. All rights reserved. Used by permission of the University of Minnesota Press.

MMPI-2-RF, the **MMPI-2-RF logo,** and **Minnesota Multiphasic Personality Inventory-2-Restructured Form** are registered trademarks of the University of Minnesota. **Pearson,** the **PSI logo,** and **PsychCorp** are trademarks in the U.S. and/or other countries of Pearson Education, Inc., or its affiliate(s).

This report contains copyrighted material and trade secrets. The qualified licensee may excerpt portions of this output report, limited to the minimum text necessary to accurately describe their significant core conclusions, for incorporation into a written evaluation of the examinee, in accordance with their profession's citation standards, if any. No adaptations, translations, modifications, or special versions may be made of this report without prior written permission from the University of Minnesota Press.

[4.0 / 57 / __VERSION__]

ALWAYS LEARNING PEARSON

FIGURE 8-6 Ms. Y's MMPI-2-RF Score Report

MMPI-2-RF Validity Scales

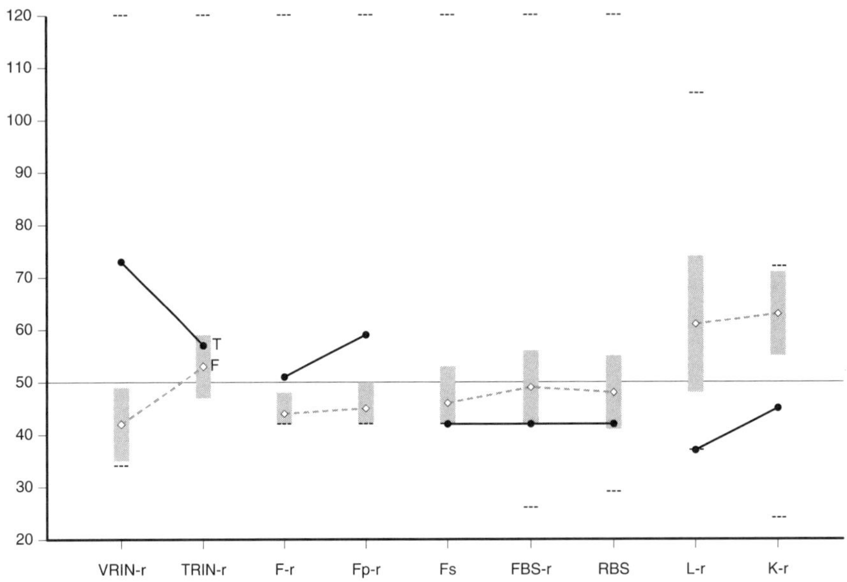

	VRIN-r	TRIN-r	F-r	Fp-r	Fs	FBS-r	RBS	L-r	K-r
Raw Score:	8	12	2	2	0	5	3	0	6
T Score:	73	57 T	51	59	42	42	42	37	45
Response %:	100	100	100	100	100	100	100	100	100

Cannot Say (Raw): 0 Percent True (of items answered): 45%

Comparison Group Data: Dispatcher Candidate (Men and Women), N = 380

	VRIN-r	TRIN-r	F-r	Fp-r	Fs	FBS-r	RBS	L-r	K-r
Mean Score (◇--◇):	42	53 F	44	45	46	49	48	61	63
Standard Dev (±1 SD):	7	6	4	5	7	7	7	13	8
Percent scoring at or below test taker:	100	91	96	99.2	68	19	24	2	4

The highest and lowest T scores possible on each scale are indicated by a "---"; MMPI-2-RF T scores are non-gendered.

VRIN-r	Variable Response Inconsistency	Fs	Infrequent Somatic Responses	L-r	Uncommon Virtues
TRIN-r	True Response Inconsistency	FBS-r	Symptom Validity	K-r	Adjustment Validity
F-r	Infrequent Responses	RBS	Response Bias Scale		
Fp-r	Infrequent Psychopathology Responses				

FIGURE 8-6 Ms. Y's MMPI-2-RF Score Report, continued

MMPI-2-RF® Score Report
03/02/2016, Page 3

Ms. Y

MMPI-2-RF Higher-Order (H-O) and Restructured Clinical (RC) Scales

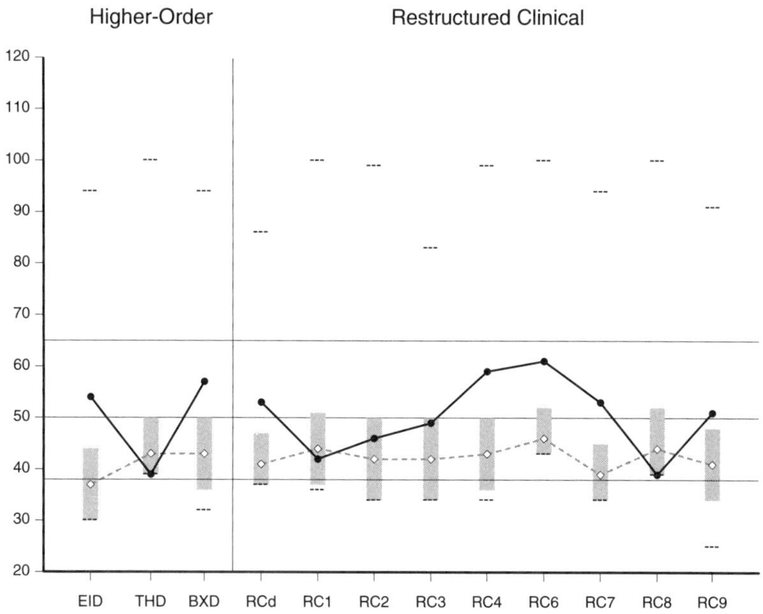

	EID	THD	BXD	RCd	RC1	RC2	RC3	RC4	RC6	RC7	RC8	RC9
Raw Score:	13	0	9	5	1	3	6	8	2	8	0	13
T Score:	54	39	57	53	42	46	49	59	61	53	39	51
Response %:	100	100	100	100	100	100	100	100	100	100	100	100

Comparison Group Data: Dispatcher Candidate (Men and Women), N = 380

	EID	THD	BXD	RCd	RC1	RC2	RC3	RC4	RC6	RC7	RC8	RC9
Mean Score (◇---◇):	37	43	43	41	44	42	42	43	46	39	44	41
Standard Dev (±1 SD):	7	7	7	6	7	8	8	7	6	6	8	7
Percent scoring at or below test taker:	99	63	99	97	57	82	85	99	98	98	57	94

The highest and lowest T scores possible on each scale are indicated by a "---"; MMPI-2-RF T scores are non-gendered.

EID Emotional/Internalizing Dysfunction
THD Thought Dysfunction
BXD Behavioral/Externalizing Dysfunction
RCd Demoralization
RC1 Somatic Complaints
RC2 Low Positive Emotions
RC3 Cynicism
RC4 Antisocial Behavior
RC6 Ideas of Persecution
RC7 Dysfunctional Negative Emotions
RC8 Aberrant Experiences
RC9 Hypomanic Activation

FIGURE 8-6 Ms. Y's MMPI-2-RF Score Report, continued

MMPI-2-RF® Score Report
03/02/2016, Page 4

Ms. Y

MMPI-2-RF Somatic/Cognitive and Internalizing Scales

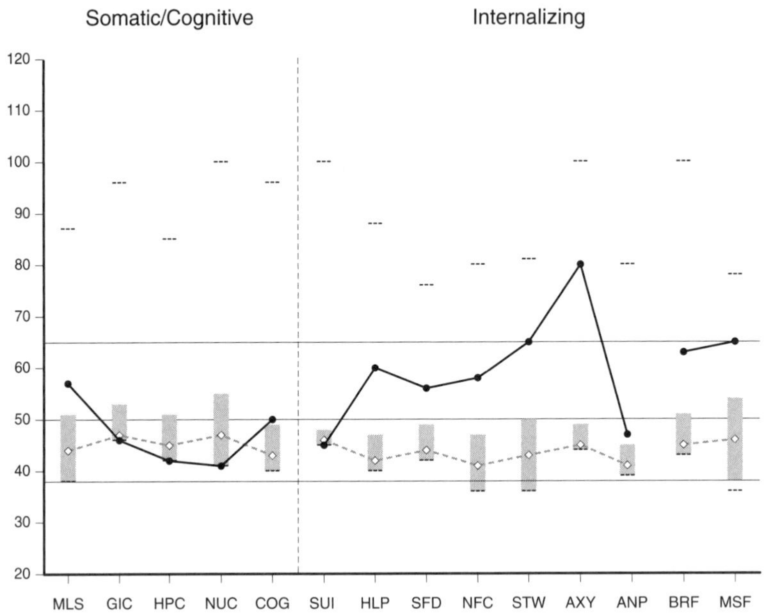

	MLS	GIC	HPC	NUC	COG	SUI	HLP	SFD	NFC	STW	AXY	ANP	BRF	MSF
Raw Score:	3	0	0	0	1	0	2	2	5	5	3	1	2	7
T Score:	57	46	42	41	50	45	60	56	58	65	80	47	63	65
Response %:	100	100	100	100	100	100	100	100	100	100	100	100	100	100

Comparison Group Data: Dispatcher Candidate (Men and Women), N = 380

	MLS	GIC	HPC	NUC	COG	SUI	HLP	SFD	NFC	STW	AXY	ANP	BRF	MSF
Mean Score (◇--◇):	44	47	45	47	43	46	42	44	41	43	45	41	45	46
Standard Dev (±1 SD):	7	6	6	8	6	2	5	5	6	7	4	4	6	8
Percent scoring at or below test taker:	97	93	74	59	92	99	100	99.2	98	99.2	100	93	99.5	98

The highest and lowest T scores possible on each scale are indicated by a "---"; MMPI-2-RF T scores are non-gendered.

MLS	Malaise	SUI	Suicidal/Death Ideation	AXY	Anxiety
GIC	Gastrointestinal Complaints	HLP	Helplessness/Hopelessness	ANP	Anger Proneness
HPC	Head Pain Complaints	SFD	Self-Doubt	BRF	Behavior-Restricting Fears
NUC	Neurological Complaints	NFC	Inefficacy	MSF	Multiple Specific Fears
COG	Cognitive Complaints	STW	Stress/Worry		

FIGURE 8-6 Ms. Y's MMPI-2-RF Score Report, continued

MMPI-2-RF® Score Report
03/02/2016, Page 5 Ms. Y

MMPI-2-RF Externalizing, Interpersonal, and Interest Scales

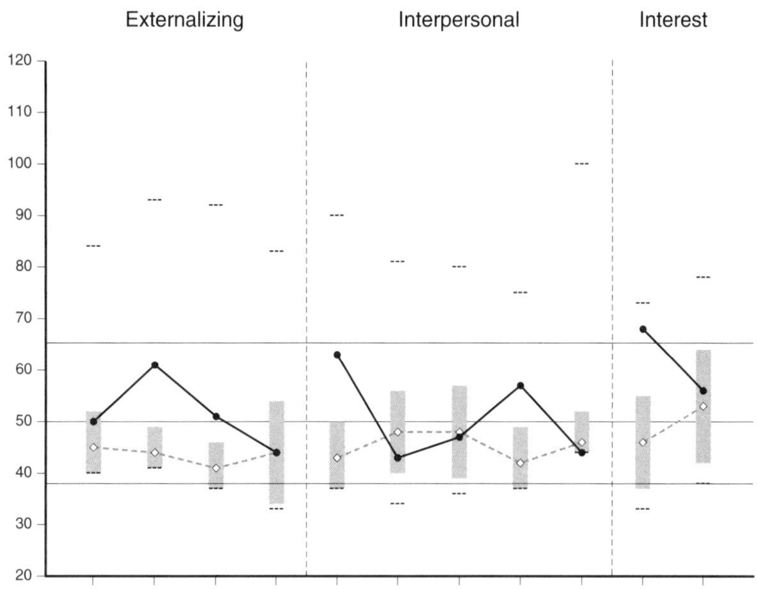

	JCP	SUB	AGG	ACT	FML	IPP	SAV	SHY	DSF	AES	MEC
Raw Score:	1	3	2	2	5	2	2	5	0	6	4
T Score:	50	61	51	44	63	43	47	57	44	68	56
Response %:	100	100	100	100	100	100	100	100	100	100	100

Comparison Group Data: Dispatcher Candidate (Men and Women), N = 380

	JCP	SUB	AGG	ACT	FML	IPP	SAV	SHY	DSF	AES	MEC
Mean Score (◇--◇):	45	44	41	44	43	48	48	42	46	46	53
Standard Dev (±1 SD):	7	5	5	10	7	8	9	7	6	9	11
Percent scoring at or below test taker:	85	100	98	61	99	36	59	98	87	99.2	71

The highest and lowest T scores possible on each scale are indicated by a "---"; MMPI-2-RF T scores are non-gendered.

JCP Juvenile Conduct Problems
SUB Substance Abuse
AGG Aggression
ACT Activation
FML Family Problems
IPP Interpersonal Passivity
SAV Social Avoidance
SHY Shyness
DSF Disaffiliativeness
AES Aesthetic-Literary Interests
MEC Mechanical-Physical Interests

FIGURE 8-6 Ms. Y's MMPI-2-RF Score Report, continued

MMPI-2-RF PSY-5 Scales

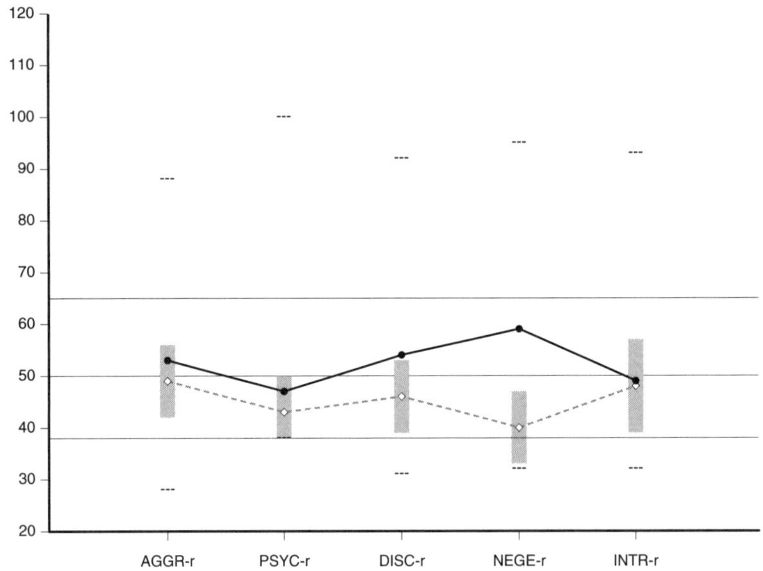

	AGGR-r	PSYC-r	DISC-r	NEGE-r	INTR-r
Raw Score:	10	1	8	10	6
T Score:	53	47	54	59	49
Response %:	100	100	100	100	100

Comparison Group Data: Dispatcher Candidate (Men and Women), N = 380

	AGGR-r	PSYC-r	DISC-r	NEGE-r	INTR-r
Mean Score (◇- - -◇):	49	43	46	40	48
Standard Dev (±1 SD):	7	7	7	7	9
Percent scoring at or below test taker:	81	82	91	99	66

The highest and lowest T scores possible on each scale are indicated by a "---"; MMPI-2-RF T scores are non-gendered.

AGGR-r Aggressiveness-Revised
PSYC-r Psychoticism-Revised
DISC-r Disconstraint-Revised
NEGE-r Negative Emotionality/Neuroticism-Revised
INTR-r Introversion/Low Positive Emotionality-Revised

FIGURE 8-6 Ms. Y's MMPI-2-RF Score Report, continued

MMPI-2-RF® Score Report
03/02/2016, Page 7 Ms. Y

MMPI-2-RF T SCORES (BY DOMAIN)

PROTOCOL VALIDITY

Domain	Higher-Order							
Content Non-Responsiveness		0 CNS	73 VRIN-r	57 T TRIN-r				
Over-Reporting		51 F-r	59 Fp-r		42 Fs	42 FBS-r	42 RBS	
Under-Reporting		37 L-r	45 K-r					

SUBSTANTIVE SCALES

Domain	Higher-Order							
Somatic/Cognitive Dysfunction		42 RC1	57 MLS	46 GIC	42 HPC	41 NUC	50 COG	
Emotional Dysfunction	54 EID	53 RCd	45 SUI	60 HLP	56 SFD	58 NFC		
		46 RC2	49 INTR-r					
		53 RC7	65 STW	80 AXY	47 ANP	63 BRF	65 MSF	59 NEGE-r
Thought Dysfunction	39 THD	61 RC6						
		39 RC8						
		47 PSYC-r						
Behavioral Dysfunction	57 BXD	59 RC4	50 JCP	61 SUB				
		51 RC9	51 AGG	44 ACT	53 AGGR-r	54 DISC-r		
Interpersonal Functioning		63 FML	49 RC3	43 IPP	47 SAV	57 SHY	44 DSF	
Interests		68 AES	56 MEC					

Note. This information is provided to facilitate interpretation following the recommended structure for MMPI-2-RF interpretation in Chapter 5 of the *MMPI-2-RF Manual for Administration, Scoring, and Interpretation*, which provides details in the text and an outline in Table 5-1.

FIGURE 8-6 Ms. Y's MMPI-2-RF Score Report, continued

ITEM-LEVEL INFORMATION

Unscorable Responses

The test taker produced scorable responses to all the MMPI-2-RF items.

Critical Responses

Seven MMPI-2-RF scales--Suicidal/Death Ideation (SUI), Helplessness/Hopelessness (HLP), Anxiety (AXY), Ideas of Persecution (RC6), Aberrant Experiences (RC8), Substance Abuse (SUB), and Aggression (AGG)--have been designated by the test authors as having critical item content that may require immediate attention and follow-up. Items answered by the individual in the keyed direction (True or False) on a critical scale are listed below if her T score on that scale is 65 or higher. The percentage of the MMPI-2-RF normative sample (NS) and of the Dispatcher Candidate (Men and Women) comparison group (CG) that answered each item in the keyed direction are provided in parentheses following the item content.

Anxiety (AXY, T Score = 80)

146. Item Content Omitted. (True; NS 1.8%, CG 0.5%)
228. Item Content Omitted. (True; NS 17.3%, CG 1.1%)
275. Item Content Omitted. (True; NS 5.0%, CG 0.3%)

End of Report

FIGURE 8-6 Ms. Y's MMPI-2-RF Score Report, continued

ITEM RESPONSES

1: 1	2: 1	3: 1	4: 2	5: 1	6: 2	7: 1	8: 1	9: 1	10: 2
11: 1	12: 2	13: 2	14: 2	15: 2	16: 1	17: 1	18: 2	19: 1	20: 2
21: 1	22: 1	23: 2	24: 2	25: 1	26: 2	27: 2	28: 1	29: 1	30: 2
31: 2	32: 2	33: 2	34: 2	35: 2	36: 1	37: 2	38: 1	39: 1	40: 1
41: 2	42: 1	43: 2	44: 2	45: 1	46: 2	47: 2	48: 2	49: 2	50: 1
51: 2	52: 2	53: 1	54: 1	55: 2	56: 2	57: 1	58: 1	59: 1	60: 1
61: 2	62: 2	63: 2	64: 1	65: 1	66: 2	67: 2	68: 1	69: 1	70: 1
71: 2	72: 1	73: 1	74: 2	75: 2	76: 2	77: 1	78: 1	79: 2	80: 2
81: 2	82: 2	83: 1	84: 2	85: 1	86: 2	87: 1	88: 1	89: 1	90: 1
91: 1	92: 2	93: 2	94: 1	95: 1	96: 2	97: 1	98: 1	99: 1	100: 1
101: 2	102: 1	103: 1	104: 1	105: 1	106: 2	107: 2	108: 1	109: 1	110: 2
111: 1	112: 2	113: 1	114: 1	115: 2	116: 1	117: 2	118: 1	119: 2	120: 2
121: 2	122: 2	123: 1	124: 2	125: 1	126: 1	127: 1	128: 1	129: 2	130: 2
131: 1	132: 1	133: 2	134: 1	135: 1	136: 1	137: 2	138: 2	139: 2	140: 1
141: 1	142: 1	143: 1	144: 2	145: 1	146: 1	147: 1	148: 2	149: 2	150: 2
151: 1	152: 2	153: 1	154: 1	155: 2	156: 1	157: 1	158: 2	159: 2	160: 1
161: 2	162: 1	163: 2	164: 2	165: 2	166: 2	167: 1	168: 2	169: 2	170: 2
171: 1	172: 2	173: 2	174: 1	175: 2	176: 2	177: 1	178: 2	179: 2	180: 1
181: 2	182: 2	183: 1	184: 2	185: 2	186: 1	187: 1	188: 2	189: 1	190: 2
191: 1	192: 2	193: 2	194: 1	195: 1	196: 2	197: 1	198: 1	199: 2	200: 2
201: 1	202: 1	203: 2	204: 2	205: 2	206: 2	207: 2	208: 2	209: 2	210: 2
211: 1	212: 1	213: 1	214: 2	215: 2	216: 2	217: 2	218: 2	219: 1	220: 1
221: 1	222: 2	223: 2	224: 2	225: 2	226: 1	227: 1	228: 1	229: 2	230: 2
231: 2	232: 2	233: 1	234: 2	235: 2	236: 2	237: 2	238: 2	239: 1	240: 2
241: 1	242: 2	243: 2	244: 1	245: 1	246: 1	247: 2	248: 2	249: 1	250: 2
251: 2	252: 2	253: 2	254: 1	255: 2	256: 1	257: 2	258: 1	259: 2	260: 2
261: 2	262: 2	263: 2	264: 2	265: 1	266: 1	267: 2	268: 2	269: 1	270: 2
271: 1	272: 1	273: 2	274: 2	275: 1	276: 1	277: 2	278: 2	279: 2	280: 2
281: 2	282: 1	283: 1	284: 1	285: 2	286: 1	287: 2	288: 1	289: 2	290: 1
291: 2	292: 2	293: 1	294: 2	295: 2	296: 1	297: 2	298: 1	299: 2	300: 2
301: 2	302: 1	303: 1	304: 2	305: 1	306: 2	307: 1	308: 2	309: 1	310: 2
311: 2	312: 2	313: 1	314: 2	315: 2	316: 1	317: 2	318: 2	319: 1	320: 1
321: 2	322: 2	323: 1	324: 1	325: 1	326: 2	327: 2	328: 2	329: 2	330: 2
331: 2	332: 2	333: 1	334: 2	335: 2	336: 1	337: 1	338: 1		

FIGURE 8-6 Ms. Y's MMPI-2-RF Score Report, continued

Background Findings

The background investigation revealed that Ms. Y had been disciplined twice (i.e., counseling memo and written reprimand) in her previous call taker position for refusing to accept compulsory overtime. For the past 10 years she stayed at home with her two school-age children and consequently had few collateral references available for the background investigator to interview other than family and friends. These sources provided generally positive references, although one friend questioned whether "it's a good time for her to be doing this since she's in the middle of a nasty divorce."

Interview Findings

Ms. Y presented in the interview as stressed and anxious, which conforms to expectations based on her three clinically elevated MMPI-2-RF scores just discussed. When the examiner commented on this, she became tearful and explained that she "really needs this job" because she is in the process of finalizing a contentious divorce and has to have a means of supporting herself. Ms. Y asserted that she has "done this job before," although when challenged by the examiner she conceded that a call taker (who receives information from a 911 caller and routes the call to a police, fire, or emergency medical dispatcher) is not the same job as an emergency dispatcher who communicates with both the caller and emergency response personnel.

Ms. Y explained her anxiety as stemming from her uncertain future. But she insisted that it would not interfere with her performance as a dispatcher because she is "able to leave it all behind" when she goes to work. However, when discussing her work history and, in particular, the two disciplinary events for refusing to accept mandated overtime, she said she turned them down because she was "stressed out" from having already performed a large amount of overtime and because of chronic marital problems, which she thought would be resolved when she stopped working.

Discussion

Ms. Y's high level of internalizing problems manifested in substantial stress, worry, and anxiety—a finding consistent with her moderately elevated (and, in comparison to members of the Dispatcher Candidate comparison group, quite deviant) score on EID. This carries a high risk of undermining the requisite emotional control, stress resilience, and adaptability/flexibility required for successful performance in the position of dispatcher. In addition, the agency to which she applied is an extremely busy public safety answering point with a very high number of calls for service—more than four times the volume she experienced in her prior position. The position of police/fire dispatcher would require that she learn a large number of codes and procedures that she did not learn in her previous position as a call taker, and her training performance would also likely be challenged by the high level of stress and anxiety she was experiencing at the time. Ms. Y was not receiving any mental health care—neither medication nor counseling—and the stresses of the upcoming mediation and court proceedings related to her divorce, alimony, and child custody would reasonably be anticipated to add to her current adaptation challenges. In consideration of these facts, the examiner concluded that Ms. Y did not meet the agency's qualification standards, and she was determined to be psychologically unqualified for the position.

Brief Review: Mr. Q, Firefighter/Paramedic Candidate

Assessment Issues Presented

- Use of the MMPI-2-RF Score Report (with use of the Firefighter Candidate comparison group)[2] in evaluating an entry-level firefighter/paramedic candidate with no clinically elevated H-O or RC Scales, but with a single anomalous score (Interpersonal Passivity; IPP = 68T) in the Interpersonal domain

Referral Summary

Mr. Q is a 29-year-old, never married male seeking an entry-level position as a firefighter/paramedic in a small rural fire protection district where he has served for 4 years as a volunteer firefighter/EMT.

Assessing Protocol Validity

As shown in the Score Report (Figure 8-7, p. 2), Mr. Q's Validity Scale scores indicate that he attended carefully to item content. The protocol reveals no indications of overreporting. His scores on the two underreporting scales, L-r (62T) and K-r (72T), indicate a comparatively high level of self-reported adjustment relative to the normative sample (for which the mean is always 50T), but within normal limits for a firefighter (mean L-r for the Firefighter CG is 58T, SD=14; mean K-r=66T, SD=7). Taken as a whole, this protocol is valid and interpretable, although his scores on the substantive scales may underestimate the problems they assess.

Substantive Scale Findings

Mr. Q's scores on the H-O and RC Scales are not clinically elevated. In comparison to the Firefighter Candidate CG, two of these scales, RC2 (50T) and RC6 (56T), fall more than one standard deviation above the mean, as shown in Figure 8-7 (p. 3). However, in the absence of outcome and other empirical data that would support inferences for moderately elevated scores, no specific predictions of counterproductive work behavior should be made on the basis of these scores. Only one of the substantive scale scores, Interpersonal Passivity (IPP; 68T) is clinically elevated, and it is three and a half standard deviations above the mean for the Firefighter Candidate CG (48T, SD=6), which is approximately equivalent to the 99.7th percentile.

MMPI 2 RF®

Minnesota Multiphasic
Personality Inventory-2
Restructured Form®

Score Report

MMPI-2-RF®
Minnesota Multiphasic Personality Inventory-2-Restructured Form®
Yossef S. Ben-Porath, PhD, & Auke Tellegen, PhD

Name:	Mr. Q
Age:	29
Gender:	Male
Marital Status:	Never Married
Years of Education:	16
Date Assessed:	10/27/2016

PsychCorp

Copyright © 2008, 2011, 2012 by the Regents of the University of Minnesota. All rights reserved.
Distributed exclusively under license from the University of Minnesota by NCS Pearson, Inc. Portions reproduced from the MMPI-2-RF test booklet. Copyright © 2008 by the Regents of the University of Minnesota. All rights reserved. Portions excerpted from the *MMPI-2-RF Manual for Administration, Scoring, and Interpretation.* Copyright © 2008, 2011 by the Regents of the University of Minnesota. All rights reserved. Used by permission of the University of Minnesota Press.

MMPI-2-RF, the **MMPI-2-RF logo,** and **Minnesota Multiphasic Personality Inventory-2-Restructured Form** are registered trademarks of the University of Minnesota. **Pearson,** the **PSI logo,** and **PsychCorp** are trademarks in the U.S. and/or other countries of Pearson Education, Inc., or its affiliate(s).

TRADE SECRET INFORMATION
Not for release under HIPAA or other data disclosure laws that exempt trade secrets from disclosure.

[3.1 / 57 / QG]

ALWAYS LEARNING PEARSON

FIGURE 8-7 Mr. Q's MMPI-2-RF Score Report

MMPI-2-RF® Score Report
10/27/2016, Page 2 Mr. Q

MMPI-2-RF Validity Scales

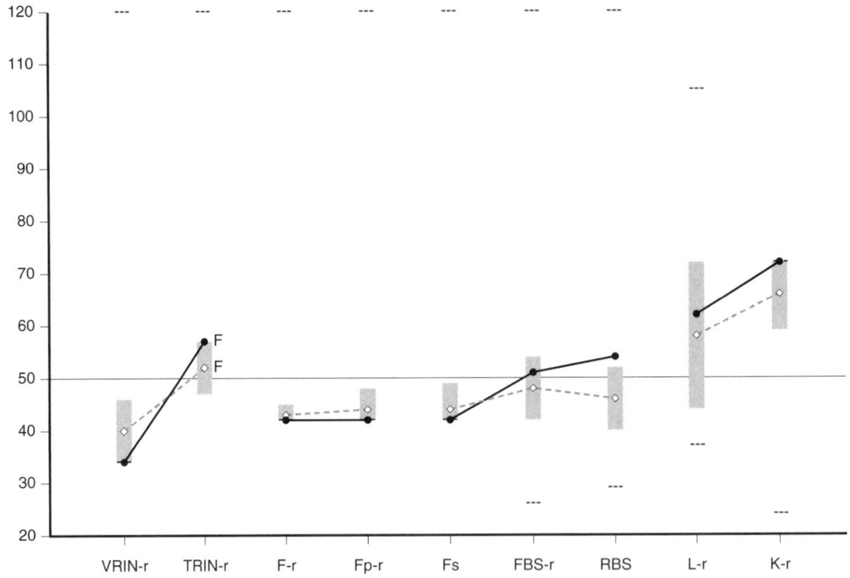

	VRIN-r	TRIN-r	F-r	Fp-r	Fs	FBS-r	RBS	L-r	K-r
Raw Score:	0	10	0	0	0	8	6	5	14
T Score:	34	57 F	42	42	42	51	54	62	72
Response %:	100	100	100	100	100	100	100	100	100

Cannot Say (Raw): 0 Percent True (of items answered): 24%

Comparison Group Data: Personnel Screening, Firefighter (Men and Women), N = 370

Mean Score (◇--◇):	40	52 F	43	44	44	48	46	58	66
Standard Dev (±1 SD):	6	5	2	4	5	6	6	14	7
Percent scoring at or below test taker:	31	93	82	85	76	85	94	71	100

The highest and lowest T scores possible on each scale are indicated by a "---"; MMPI-2-RF T scores are non-gendered.

VRIN-r Variable Response Inconsistency
TRIN-r True Response Inconsistency
F-r Infrequent Responses
Fp-r Infrequent Psychopathology Responses
Fs Infrequent Somatic Responses
FBS-r Symptom Validity
RBS Response Bias Scale
L-r Uncommon Virtues
K-r Adjustment Validity

FIGURE 8-7 Mr. Q's MMPI-2-RF Score Report, continued

MMPI-2-RF Higher-Order (H-O) and Restructured Clinical (RC) Scales

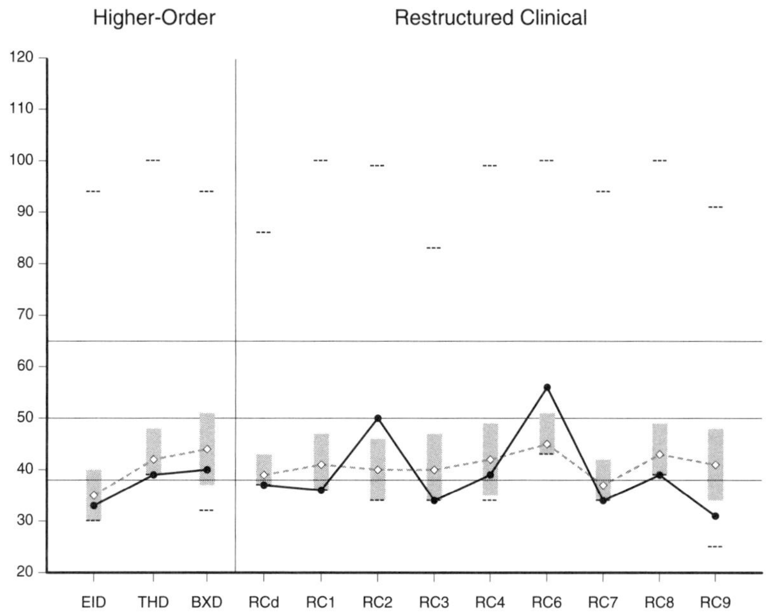

	EID	THD	BXD	RCd	RC1	RC2	RC3	RC4	RC6	RC7	RC8	RC9
Raw Score:	1	0	2	0	0	4	0	1	1	0	0	2
T Score:	33	39	40	37	36	50	34	39	56	34	39	31
Response %:	100	100	100	100	100	100	100	100	100	100	100	100

Comparison Group Data: Personnel Screening, Firefighter (Men and Women), N = 370

	EID	THD	BXD	RCd	RC1	RC2	RC3	RC4	RC6	RC7	RC8	RC9
Mean Score (◇--◇):	35	42	44	39	41	40	40	42	45	37	43	41
Standard Dev (±1 SD):	5	6	7	4	6	6	7	7	6	5	6	7
Percent scoring at or below test taker:	51	70	38	62	51	96	35	48	94	49	65	6

The highest and lowest T scores possible on each scale are indicated by a "---"; MMPI-2-RF T scores are non-gendered.

EID Emotional/Internalizing Dysfunction
THD Thought Dysfunction
BXD Behavioral/Externalizing Dysfunction

RCd Demoralization
RC1 Somatic Complaints
RC2 Low Positive Emotions
RC3 Cynicism
RC4 Antisocial Behavior

RC6 Ideas of Persecution
RC7 Dysfunctional Negative Emotions
RC8 Aberrant Experiences
RC9 Hypomanic Activation

FIGURE 8-7 Mr. Q's MMPI-2-RF Score Report, continued

MMPI-2-RF® Score Report
10/27/2016, Page 4

Mr. Q

MMPI-2-RF Somatic/Cognitive and Internalizing Scales

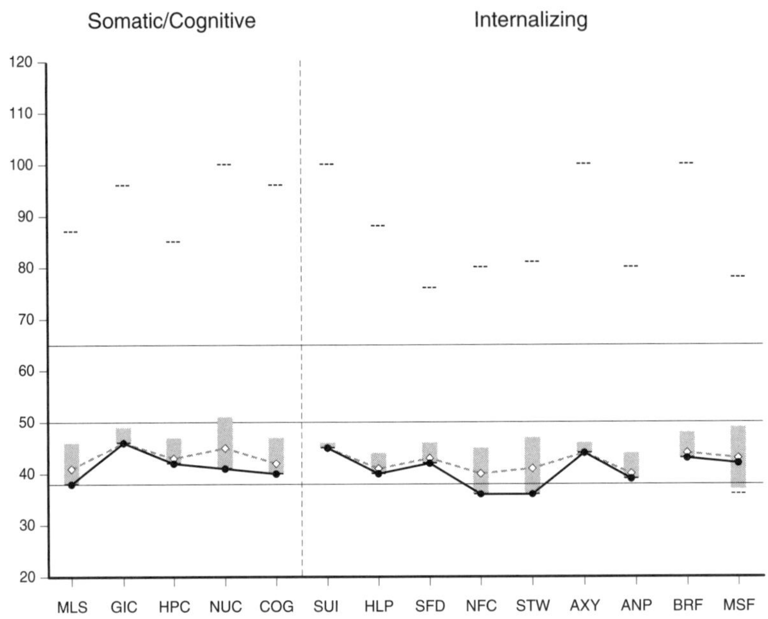

	MLS	GIC	HPC	NUC	COG	SUI	HLP	SFD	NFC	STW	AXY	ANP	BRF	MSF
Raw Score:	0	0	0	0	0	0	0	0	0	0	0	0	0	1
T Score:	38	46	42	41	40	45	40	42	36	36	44	39	43	42
Response %:	100	100	100	100	100	100	100	100	100	100	100	100	100	100

Comparison Group Data: Personnel Screening, Firefighter (Men and Women), N = 370

	MLS	GIC	HPC	NUC	COG	SUI	HLP	SFD	NFC	STW	AXY	ANP	BRF	MSF
Mean Score (◇--◇):	41	46	43	45	42	45	41	43	40	41	44	40	44	43
Standard Dev (±1 SD):	5	3	4	6	5	1	3	3	5	6	2	4	4	6
Percent scoring at or below test taker:	69	98	86	72	80	99.7	93	90	59	46	97	89	93	56

The highest and lowest T scores possible on each scale are indicated by a "---"; MMPI-2-RF T scores are non-gendered.

MLS Malaise
GIC Gastrointestinal Complaints
HPC Head Pain Complaints
NUC Neurological Complaints
COG Cognitive Complaints
SUI Suicidal/Death Ideation
HLP Helplessness/Hopelessness
SFD Self-Doubt
NFC Inefficacy
STW Stress/Worry
AXY Anxiety
ANP Anger Proneness
BRF Behavior-Restricting Fears
MSF Multiple Specific Fears

FIGURE 8-7 Mr. Q's MMPI-2-RF Score Report, continued

MMPI-2-RF Externalizing, Interpersonal, and Interest Scales

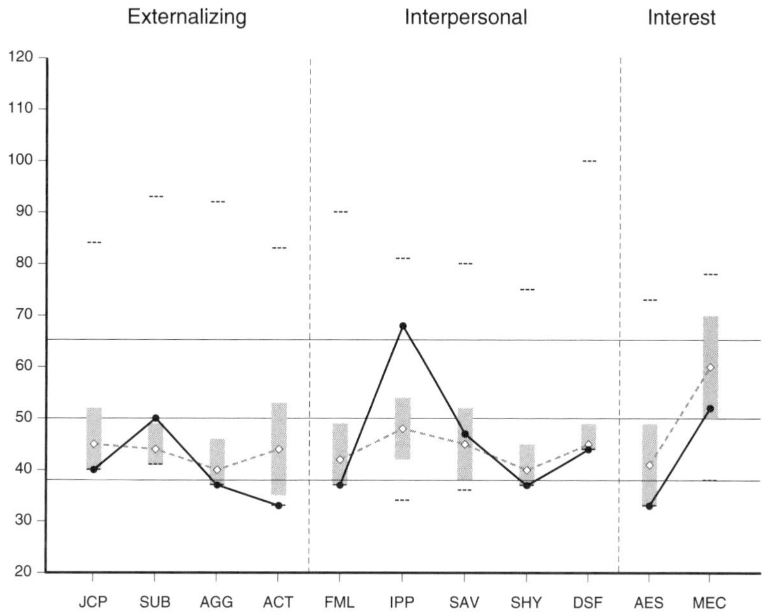

	JCP	SUB	AGG	ACT	FML	IPP	SAV	SHY	DSF	AES	MEC
Raw Score:	0	1	0	0	0	8	2	0	0	0	3
T Score:	40	50	37	33	37	68	47	37	44	33	52
Response %:	100	100	100	100	100	100	100	100	100	100	100

Comparison Group Data: Personnel Screening, Firefighter (Men and Women), N = 370

	JCP	SUB	AGG	ACT	FML	IPP	SAV	SHY	DSF	AES	MEC
Mean Score (◇---◇):	45	44	40	44	42	48	45	40	45	41	60
Standard Dev (±1 SD):	7	5	6	9	7	6	7	5	4	8	10
Percent scoring at or below test taker:	64	90	71	20	50	99.7	74	63	93	35	29

The highest and lowest T scores possible on each scale are indicated by a "---"; MMPI-2-RF T scores are non-gendered.

JCP Juvenile Conduct Problems
SUB Substance Abuse
AGG Aggression
ACT Activation

FML Family Problems
IPP Interpersonal Passivity
SAV Social Avoidance
SHY Shyness
DSF Disaffiliativeness

AES Aesthetic-Literary Interests
MEC Mechanical-Physical Interests

FIGURE 8-7 Mr. Q's MMPI-2-RF Score Report, continued

MMPI-2-RF PSY-5 Scales

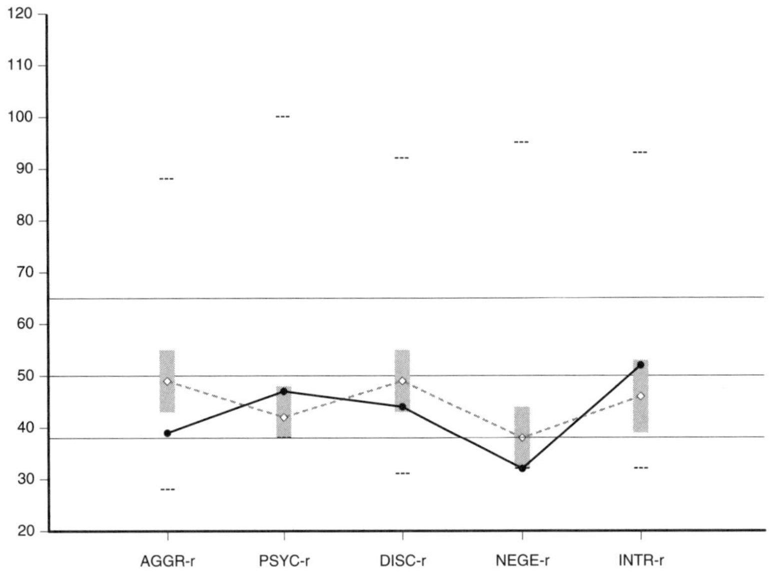

	AGGR-r	PSYC-r	DISC-r	NEGE-r	INTR-r
Raw Score:	4	1	4	0	7
T Score:	39	47	44	32	52
Response %:	100	100	100	100	100

Comparison Group Data: Personnel Screening, Firefighter (Men and Women), N = 370

	AGGR-r	PSYC-r	DISC-r	NEGE-r	INTR-r
Mean Score (◇- - -◇):	49	42	49	38	46
Standard Dev (±1 SD):	6	6	6	6	7
Percent scoring at or below test taker:	4	86	28	29	88

The highest and lowest T scores possible on each scale are indicated by a "---"; MMPI-2-RF T scores are non-gendered.

AGGR-r Aggressiveness-Revised
PSYC-r Psychoticism-Revised
DISC-r Disconstraint-Revised
NEGE-r Negative Emotionality/Neuroticism-Revised
INTR-r Introversion/Low Positive Emotionality-Revised

FIGURE 8-7 Mr. Q's MMPI-2-RF Score Report, continued

MMPI-2-RF T SCORES (BY DOMAIN)

PROTOCOL VALIDITY

Content Non-Responsiveness

CNS	VRIN-r	TRIN-r
0	34	57 F

Over-Reporting

F-r	Fp-r	Fs	FBS-r	RBS
42	42	42	51	54

Under-Reporting

L-r	K-r
62	72

SUBSTANTIVE SCALES

Somatic/Cognitive Dysfunction

RC1	MLS	GIC	HPC	NUC	COG
36	38	46	42	41	40

Emotional Dysfunction — EID: 33

RCd	SUI	HLP	SFD	NFC
37	45	40	42	36

RC2	INTR-r
50	52

RC7	STW	AXY	ANP	BRF	MSF	NEGE-r
34	36	44	39	43	42	32

Thought Dysfunction — THD: 39

RC6
56

RC8
39

PSYC-r
47

Behavioral Dysfunction — BXD: 40

RC4	JCP	SUB
39	40	50

RC9	AGG	ACT	AGGR-r	DISC-r
31	37	33	39	44

Interpersonal Functioning

FML	RC3	IPP	SAV	SHY	DSF
37	34	68	47	37	44

Interests

AES	MEC
33	52

Note. This information is provided to facilitate interpretation following the recommended structure for MMPI-2-RF interpretation in Chapter 5 of the *MMPI-2-RF Manual for Administration, Scoring, and Interpretation*, which provides details in the text and an outline in Table 5-1.

FIGURE 8-7 Mr. Q's MMPI-2-RF Score Report, continued

MMPI-2-RF® Score Report
10/27/2016, Page 8 Mr. Q

ITEM-LEVEL INFORMATION

Unscorable Responses

The test taker produced scorable responses to all the MMPI-2-RF items.

Critical Responses

Seven MMPI-2-RF scales--Suicidal/Death Ideation (SUI), Helplessness/Hopelessness (HLP), Anxiety (AXY), Ideas of Persecution (RC6), Aberrant Experiences (RC8), Substance Abuse (SUB), and Aggression (AGG)--have been designated by the test authors as having critical item content that may require immediate attention and follow-up. Items answered by the individual in the keyed direction (True or False) on a critical scale are listed below if his T score on that scale is 65 or higher.

The test taker has not produced an elevated T score ($\geq$ 65) on any of these scales.

End of Report

This and previous pages of this report contain trade secrets and are not to be released in response to requests under HIPAA (or any other data disclosure law that exempts trade secret information from release). Further, release in response to litigation discovery demands should be made only in accordance with your profession's ethical guidelines and under an appropriate protective order.

FIGURE 8-7 Mr. Q's MMPI-2-RF Score Report, continued

ITEM RESPONSES

1: 1	2: 1	3: 2	4: 1	5: 2	6: 2	7: 1	8: 1	9: 2	10: 2
11: 2	12: 2	13: 2	14: 2	15: 2	16: 2	17: 1	18: 2	19: 1	20: 2
21: 2	22: 2	23: 2	24: 2	25: 1	26: 2	27: 2	28: 1	29: 2	30: 2
31: 2	32: 2	33: 2	34: 1	35: 2	36: 2	37: 1	38: 1	39: 2	40: 2
41: 2	42: 2	43: 2	44: 2	45: 2	46: 2	47: 2	48: 2	49: 2	50: 2
51: 2	52: 1	53: 2	54: 2	55: 2	56: 2	57: 1	58: 2	59: 1	60: 2
61: 2	62: 2	63: 2	64: 2	65: 1	66: 2	67: 2	68: 2	69: 1	70: 1
71: 2	72: 2	73: 1	74: 2	75: 1	76: 2	77: 2	78: 1	79: 2	80: 1
81: 2	82: 1	83: 1	84: 2	85: 1	86: 2	87: 2	88: 1	89: 2	90: 2
91: 2	92: 2	93: 2	94: 1	95: 1	96: 2	97: 2	98: 1	99: 2	100: 2
101: 2	102: 1	103: 2	104: 2	105: 1	106: 2	107: 2	108: 2	109: 1	110: 2
111: 1	112: 2	113: 1	114: 2	115: 1	116: 2	117: 2	118: 1	119: 2	120: 2
121: 2	122: 2	123: 2	124: 2	125: 1	126: 1	127: 1	128: 1	129: 2	130: 2
131: 2	132: 2	133: 2	134: 1	135: 2	136: 2	137: 2	138: 2	139: 2	140: 1
141: 2	142: 2	143: 2	144: 2	145: 2	146: 2	147: 2	148: 2	149: 2	150: 2
151: 2	152: 2	153: 1	154: 2	155: 2	156: 2	157: 1	158: 2	159: 2	160: 2
161: 2	162: 1	163: 1	164: 2	165: 2	166: 2	167: 2	168: 2	169: 2	170: 2
171: 2	172: 2	173: 2	174: 1	175: 2	176: 2	177: 2	178: 2	179: 2	180: 2
181: 2	182: 1	183: 1	184: 2	185: 2	186: 1	187: 2	188: 2	189: 1	190: 1
191: 2	192: 2	193: 2	194: 2	195: 1	196: 2	197: 2	198: 2	199: 2	200: 2
201: 1	202: 1	203: 2	204: 2	205: 2	206: 2	207: 2	208: 2	209: 2	210: 2
211: 1	212: 1	213: 2	214: 2	215: 2	216: 2	217: 1	218: 2	219: 2	220: 1
221: 1	222: 1	223: 2	224: 2	225: 2	226: 2	227: 1	228: 2	229: 2	230: 2
231: 2	232: 2	233: 2	234: 1	235: 2	236: 2	237: 2	238: 2	239: 1	240: 2
241: 1	242: 2	243: 2	244: 2	245: 2	246: 1	247: 2	248: 2	249: 2	250: 2
251: 2	252: 2	253: 2	254: 1	255: 2	256: 2	257: 2	258: 2	259: 2	260: 2
261: 2	262: 1	263: 2	264: 2	265: 1	266: 2	267: 2	268: 2	269: 1	270: 2
271: 2	272: 1	273: 2	274: 2	275: 2	276: 2	277: 2	278: 2	279: 2	280: 2
281: 2	282: 1	283: 1	284: 2	285: 2	286: 1	287: 2	288: 2	289: 2	290: 1
291: 2	292: 2	293: 1	294: 2	295: 1	296: 2	297: 2	298: 2	299: 2	300: 2
301: 2	302: 2	303: 2	304: 2	305: 2	306: 2	307: 2	308: 2	309: 2	310: 2
311: 2	312: 2	313: 1	314: 2	315: 2	316: 2	317: 2	318: 2	319: 2	320: 2
321: 2	322: 2	323: 1	324: 2	325: 1	326: 2	327: 2	328: 2	329: 2	330: 2
331: 2	332: 2	333: 1	334: 2	335: 2	336: 2	337: 2	338: 2		

FIGURE 8-7 Mr. Q's MMPI-2-RF Score Report, continued

Background Findings

The background investigation revealed that Mr. Q is very well regarded by the hiring agency on the basis of his performance over the course of 4 years as a volunteer firefighter. During this time, he has performed also as a "sleeper" (working 24-hour shifts alongside paid professional firefighters/paramedics) while completing his studies and practicum for his paramedic certificate, which he finished last month. Notably, several references who worked beside Mr. Q at the fire district cited his ability to engage people, confront them when necessary, and gain their compliance. He has no history of disciplinary action or counterproductive behavior on or off the job, and there were no other adverse findings reported from the background investigation.

Interview Findings

Mr. Q presented as reserved and quiet, but not shy. He maintained good eye contact throughout the interview and engaged the examiner appropriately. Consistent with the advice provided in this guide to not ask the candidate to explain particular item responses associated with an elevated scale (at least not by reciting an item verbatim), the examiner explained to Mr. Q that his test results suggest that he sees himself as being rather unassertive and asked the candidate to talk about how that is manifested both at and away from work. Mr. Q explained that he is "low-key" and is comfortable deferring to the wants and interests of others in his personal life because most things "just don't matter as much to me as they seem to matter to others." As an example, he said that he defers to his girlfriend to choose restaurants, movies, weekend activities, and so on, because she has strong opinions about what she likes and he does not care as much. On the other hand, he said that when it comes to issues about which he either feels strongly or over which he has responsibility, he is not passive, although he is not authoritarian or abrasive in presenting his position. He appeared in the interview to be self-reflective and nondefensive.

Discussion

In our previous discussion involving Mr. L, we cautioned against making suitability determinations on the basis of a single test score or any other single data source unless justified, and we emphasized the importance of weighing findings from all data sources before reaching a suitability determination. In our current case involving Mr. Q, Interpersonal Passivity (IPP) is clinically elevated. Although there is convincing empirical evidence demonstrating that even moderately elevated MMPI-2-RF scores in the Interpersonal domain correlate with a broad range of counterproductive behaviors in police officers (see chapter 6; see also Ben-Porath, Corey, & Tarescavage, 2017), these correlations are found with elevations on SAV, SHY, DSF, and INTR-r and with *low scores* on IPP. Moreover, to the extent that Mr. Q's IPP score may be more a reflection of his low persuasion skills rather than assertiveness skills, it is worth noting that persuasion is not a highly weighted skill with firefighters, in contrast to police and correctional officers (see chapter 1). Finally, Mr. Q's background informants reported no problems with assertiveness as a volunteer (and part-time paid) firefighter position over a period of 4 years in the same agency to which he is now applying. Thus, applying Step 5b of our integrative model (Table 8-1)—consideration of divergent data that might mitigate the risk-related findings—the background information carries significant weight as a result of its relevance and reliability. In consideration of these facts, the examiner concluded that Mr. Q meets the agency's qualification standards, and he was determined to be psychologically qualified for the position.

Evidence-Based Report Writing Using the PCIR

The prospective audiences of a written report documenting the findings and suitability determination from a preemployment psychological evaluation are many and varied. In addition to the hiring agency, future readers of the report may include the candidate, a second-opinion psychologist or other expert reviewer, legal counsel for the employer and/or plaintiff, a civil service commission or appeal board, the court of ultimate jurisdiction, and the psychologist's licensing board and professional ethics committee. In the unfortunate event of a serious future adverse event after a candidate is hired, the report may be read by a host of other individuals responding to or adjudicating the event. To some degree, each of these potential audiences influences the content of the report to the extent that the report writer considers their interests. Collectively, these audiences coalesce to underscore three important functions of a written preemployment psychological evaluation report.

Functions of a Written Report

REACHING AND DOCUMENTING THE SUITABILITY DETERMINATION

When writing a report using the data integration model we applied earlier in this chapter as a framework, the screening psychologist describes the job-relevant, risk-related findings from the psychological testing, personal history, and clinical interview; describes any mitigating facts supported by the evidence and how they weigh against some or all of these risks; and then explains his or her rationale for the opinion that the aggregate findings warrant qualification or disqualification. This written analytic process is essentially one of "thinking out loud" and serves both to facilitate the formation of the suitability determination and to document it for the hiring agency and other prospective readers.

EXPLAINING THE EVIDENTIARY SUPPORT AND RATIONALE FOR THE SUITABILITY DETERMINATION

"Explanations, not opinions, are the reason one is an expert" (Grisso, 2008, p. 33). Even if the screening psychologist were able to work through the data integration process and reach a suitability judgment without a written report, it is still necessary to explain the evidence relied on for that judgment, as well as how the assessor arrived at that determination. Otto, DeMier, and Boccaccini (2014) observe, "The only time the expert is in complete control of the information that is and is not presented is when writing the report" (p. 12). The attentive screening psychologist will include in the report those risk-related findings and inferences that are consequential and relevant to the selection criteria. A well-written report "connects the dots," shows what the evaluator thinks and why he or she thinks it, and explains the evaluator's rejection of other possible opinions and conclusions. Grisso (2008) regards the act of writing one's conclusions in a psychological assessment report as a form of hypothesis testing. Having formed a general idea of the conclusion, Grisso contends that writing the explanation for that conclusion "forces us to lay the foundation for how we got there; having to describe that foundation in detail inevitably identifies challenges to our conclusion; and usually this will (or should) modify our thinking" (p. 67).

DISSUADING CHALLENGES AND REPELLING CRITICISM

In addition to helping reach and document the suitability determination and explaining the evidentiary support and rationale for that determination, a third function of the written report is to provide prospective challengers and critics (e.g., civil service commissioners, plaintiff's attorney, second-opinion evaluator, licensing board, ethics panel) of the evaluation with a testimonial record that is clear and compelling. The quality of a preemployment psychological screening report is judged ultimately not by whether only one suitability determination could have been reached from the data, but rather whether the suitability determination reached by the screening psychologist was justified by valid, reliable, and job-relevant data. In other words, the important consideration is not whether the report writer "got it right," but rather whether other reasonable experts could have reached the same conclusion. The evaluator is best positioned to articulate how and why the suitability judgment was made, and the best opportunity to make the case is when the facts and rationale are fresh in the mind of the assessor. As Appelbaum (2010) observed, "The quality of our reports is often the most tangible and visible measure of our professionalism" (p. 43), and is the single best—indeed, perhaps even the only—opportunity to produce an extemporaneous record of the examiner's rationale for his or her opinion. The report serves to dissuade potential challenges and repel criticism, and it also creates a testimonial record of how the psychologist integrated the assessment data to form his or her suitability determination and why he or she rejected alternative interpretations and inferences.

Minimum Elements of a Written Report

In a preemployment psychological evaluation of a police or public safety candidate, no single format is required except when mandated by law, regulation, or the hiring authority. The IACP Police Psychological Services Section's Preemployment Psychological Evaluation Guidelines (IACP-PPSS, 2015) recommend that, at a minimum, written reports (a) include a "clear determination of the applicant's psychological suitability for employment based upon an analysis of all psychological assessment materials, including background information, test data, and interview results" (Guideline 11.1); (b) include ratings and/or recommendations expressly linked to the "skills, behaviors, attributes and other personal characteristics associated with effective and counterproductive job performance" in the position (11.2); and (c) focus "on the individual applicant's ability to safely and effectively perform the essential functions of the position under consideration" (11.3). The evidence-based findings from the PCIR can contribute to each of these three elements.

PROVIDES GENERAL GUIDANCE

Because the written report has both an immediate audience (the hiring agency) and the prospective audiences mentioned earlier, care must be taken to ensure that the testimonial record is written in a way that clearly states and adequately explains the examiner's determination and contains nothing to undermine confidence in that decision. These objectives are best met by a narrative that clearly states the examiner's opinions and is well written, error free, jargon free, precise, internally consistent (i.e., contains no contradictions), and objective. Otto et al. (2014) provide valuable advice for writing forensic psychological reports (including fitness-for-duty evaluation reports) that meet each of these objectives.

Using Findings from the PCIR

We developed the PCIR so that the evidence-based, risk-related statements could be incorporated easily into a written report. Although the report is protected by copyright law, the fair use doctrine allows its users to extract text from the PCIR and insert it into the examiner's written report as he or she deems appropriate. When doing so, it is necessary that the examiner decide first that the evidence-based inference is supported by the MMPI-2-RF score, when considered in the context of the other assessment data, as illustrated earlier in this chapter.

In the following example involving Mr. N, a 28-year-old male police officer candidate, the evaluation was based on findings from the MMPI-2-RF PCIR (Figure 8-8), normal personality testing, self-reported personal history, the hiring agency's background information, and clinical interview. Using the data integration model applied throughout this chapter, the screening psychologist wrote the following report narrative:

> The findings from this assessment reveal no evidence of a psychological disorder that would preclude safe and effective performance as a police officer. However, Mr. N's responses to personality testing produced findings characterized by significant deviations from police candidate norms. He reported a number of specific fears that are unusual for police officer candidates; indeed, only 1.5% of police candidates on average give evidence of this or a greater level of fearfulness. In addition, he reported a comparatively high level of self-doubt and shyness for a police officer candidate, with only 2.8% of police candidates on average conveying this level or greater of low self-confidence and interpersonal inhibition. He reported a comparatively high level of irresponsible behavior for a police officer candidate; only 4.0% of police candidates report this or a greater level of acting out. These test scores correspond with empirical research findings that place him at elevated risk for a wide range of counterproductive behaviors as a police officer, including: difficulty coping with stress, difficulties carrying out tasks under non-stressful conditions, avoiding making decisions, failing to take action, acting hesitantly, and giving up easily and not persevering in the face of challenges.

When judging the validity of test-based predictions, a source of data normally relied upon—although not dispositive—is contemporary evidence of performance in other situations, particularly in situations similar to those in a job candidate's targeted position. In that regard, it is compelling to note that both of Mr. N's current supervisors report negative information concerning his performance. One supervisor reported that Mr. N's work productivity was dramatically below par for a worker with his level of experience, and that he had difficulty performing without direct supervision. This supervisor attributed Mr. N's performance problems to difficulty making decisions on his own. Another supervisor reported that Mr. N "has had trouble focusing on his work, making mistakes more frequently," and "does not seem to care as much about working hard or the quality of his work as he used to." This same supervisor said that Mr. N "takes criticism personally" and "sometimes gets defensive about it," including being "in a bad mood the rest of the day." Finally, he noted that Mr. N "gets easily flustered or frustrated when either he has a large amount of work to be done or something comes up unexpectedly." He said this has been "true of [Mr. N] the entire time he has been employed" at Acme Consulting. Neither supervisor recommended Mr. N for a law enforcement officer position.

These collateral reports of employment-related problems are consistent with the findings from personality testing that show a tendency to be lacking in self-confidence, socially inhibited, and irresponsible. In addition, Mr. N's test results that indicate a comparatively high level of antisocial behavior for a police candidate are particularly problematic in light of the background investigation report of a domestic assault in 2010 in which he slapped his previous girlfriend in the face when he learned she was involved romantically with another person.

Although there are attributes of Mr. N that render him an attractive candidate for a law enforcement position (e.g., he presented as polite, considerate and well-mannered in the interview; he was professional and thoughtful in his answers; and he communicated effectively), the synchrony between the test results and his background (both recent and remote) produce a compelling basis for concluding that he is at high risk for similar kinds of counterproductive behavior in a law enforcement position, particularly with respect to problems in emotional control and stress tolerance, impulse control and attention to safety, and decision-making and judgment. In addition, this assessment contains no persuasive evidence that mitigates or outweighs the risk-related findings. Therefore, in consideration of the full range of assessment and supplemental data available to me, I conclude that Mr. N fails to meet the standards for psychological qualification as a police officer with the Acme Police Department.

In this example, the examiner used the base-rate information contained in the Comparison Group Findings section of the PCIR (Figure 8-8, pp. 9–10) both to describe the problematic personality findings and to show how unusual they are for police candidates. The examiner then used the findings from the Job-Relevant Correlates section (Figure 8-8, pp. 10–11) to describe how these problematic traits are likely to manifest as a police officer or trainee and in what problem domains they are likely to occur. The examiner's use of the content in the Comparison Group Findings and Job-Relevant Correlates sections of the PCIR contributed to an explanatory report narrative that anchored the determination (unqualified) to the candidate's personality traits and to risk-related findings—both retrospectively by linking the test results with past problems identified in the background investigation and prospectively by linking them to likely future counterproductive behavior as a police officer or trainee. Finally, the examiner explained the rejection of alternative interpretations of the evidence.

MMPI 2 RF®

Minnesota Multiphasic
Personality Inventory-2
Restructured Form®

Yossef S. Ben-Porath, PhD, & Auke Tellegen, PhD

MMPI-2-RF®

Police Candidate Interpretive Report

David M. Corey, PhD, & Yossef S. Ben-Porath, PhD

Name:	Mr. N
Age:	28
Gender:	Male
Marital Status:	Married
Years of Education:	16
Date Assessed:	06/06/2016

Copyright © 2014 by the Regents of the University of Minnesota. All rights reserved.
Distributed exclusively under license from the University of Minnesota by NCS Pearson, Inc. Portions reproduced from the MMPI-2-RF test booklet. Copyright © 2008 by the Regents of the University of Minnesota. All rights reserved. Portions excerpted from the *MMPI-2-RF Manual for Administration, Scoring, and Interpretation.* Copyright © 2008, 2011 by the Regents of the University of Minnesota. All rights reserved. Used by permission of the University of Minnesota Press.

Minnesota Multiphasic Personality Inventory-2-Restructured Form and **MMPI-2-RF** are registered trademarks of the University of Minnesota. **Pearson** is a trademark in the U.S. and/or other countries of Pearson Education, Inc., or its affiliate(s).

This report contains copyrighted material and trade secrets. The qualified licensee may excerpt portions of this output report, limited to the minimum text necessary to accurately describe their significant core conclusions, for incorporation into a written evaluation of the examinee, in accordance with their profession's citation standards, if any. No adaptations, translations, modifications, or special versions may be made of this report without prior written permission from the University of Minnesota Press.

[4.0 / 57 / __VERSION__]

ALWAYS LEARNING PEARSON

FIGURE 8-8 Mr. N's MMPI-2-RF Police Candidate Interpretive Report

MMPI-2-RF Validity Scales

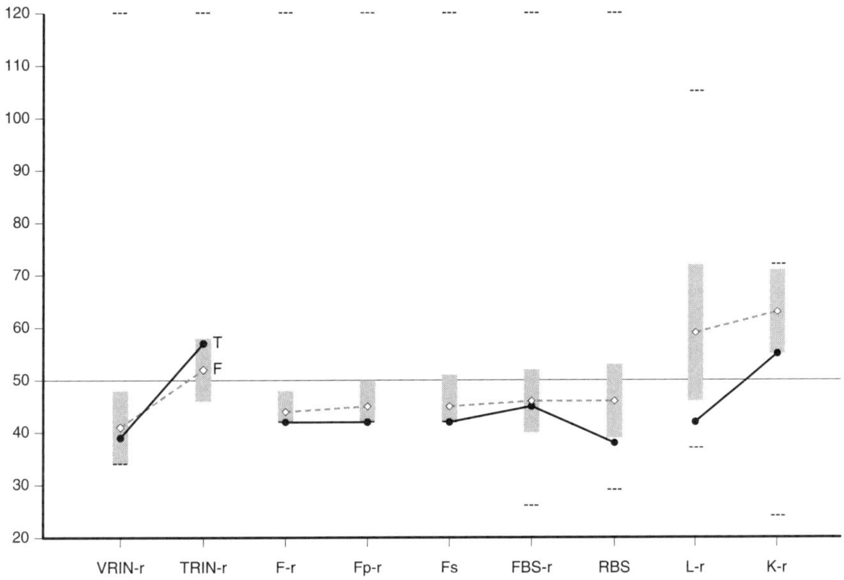

	VRIN-r	TRIN-r	F-r	Fp-r	Fs	FBS-r	RBS	L-r	K-r
Raw Score:	1	12	0	0	0	6	2	1	9
T Score:	39	57 T	42	42	42	45	38	42	55
Response %:	100	100	100	100	100	100	100	100	100

Cannot Say (Raw): 0 Percent True (of items answered): 36%

Comparison Group Data: Personnel Screening, Police Officer Candidate (Men and Women), N = 2074

	VRIN-r	TRIN-r	F-r	Fp-r	Fs	FBS-r	RBS	L-r	K-r
Mean Score (◇- - -◇):	41	52 F	44	45	45	46	46	59	63
Standard Dev (±1 SD):	7	6	4	5	6	6	7	13	8
Percent scoring at or below test taker:	59	92	75	78	70	49	20	13	20

The highest and lowest T scores possible on each scale are indicated by a "---"; MMPI-2-RF T scores are non-gendered.

VRIN-r	Variable Response Inconsistency	Fs	Infrequent Somatic Responses	L-r	Uncommon Virtues
TRIN-r	True Response Inconsistency	FBS-r	Symptom Validity	K-r	Adjustment Validity
F-r	Infrequent Responses	RBS	Response Bias Scale		
Fp-r	Infrequent Psychopathology Responses				

FIGURE 8-8 Mr. N's MMPI-2-RF Police Candidate Interpretive Report, continued

MMPI-2-RF Higher-Order (H-O) and Restructured Clinical (RC) Scales

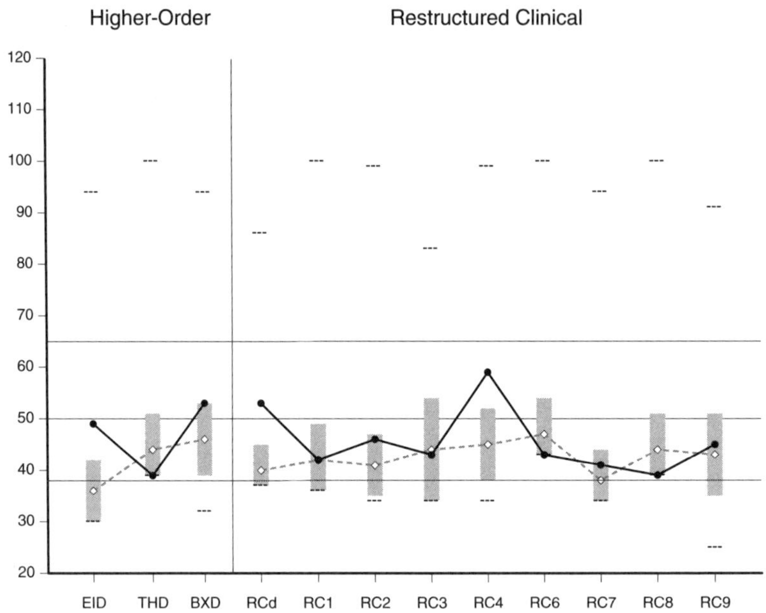

	EID	THD	BXD	RCd	RC1	RC2	RC3	RC4	RC6	RC7	RC8	RC9
Raw Score:	9	0	7	5	1	3	3	8	0	2	0	9
T Score:	49	39	53	53	42	46	43	59	43	41	39	45
Response %:	100	100	100	100	100	100	100	100	100	100	100	100

Comparison Group Data: Personnel Screening, Police Officer Candidate (Men and Women), N = 2074

	EID	THD	BXD	RCd	RC1	RC2	RC3	RC4	RC6	RC7	RC8	RC9
Mean Score (◇--◇):	36	44	46	40	42	41	44	45	47	38	44	43
Standard Dev (±1 SD):	6	7	7	5	7	6	10	7	7	6	7	8
Percent scoring at or below test taker:	97	57	88	98	68	88	57	98	75	81	53	66

The highest and lowest T scores possible on each scale are indicated by a "---"; MMPI-2-RF T scores are non-gendered.

EID Emotional/Internalizing Dysfunction
THD Thought Dysfunction
BXD Behavioral/Externalizing Dysfunction

RCd Demoralization
RC1 Somatic Complaints
RC2 Low Positive Emotions
RC3 Cynicism
RC4 Antisocial Behavior

RC6 Ideas of Persecution
RC7 Dysfunctional Negative Emotions
RC8 Aberrant Experiences
RC9 Hypomanic Activation

FIGURE 8-8 Mr. N's MMPI-2-RF Police Candidate Interpretive Report, continued

MMPI-2-RF Somatic/Cognitive and Internalizing Scales

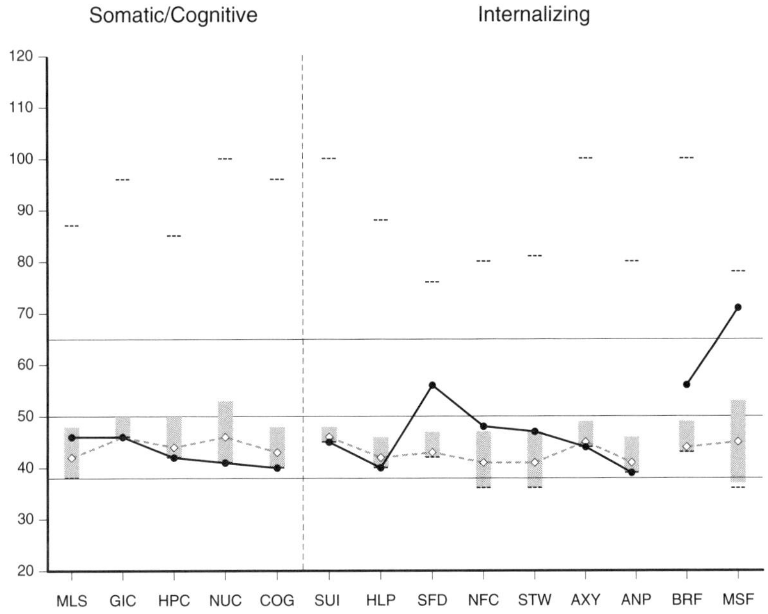

	MLS	GIC	HPC	NUC	COG	SUI	HLP	SFD	NFC	STW	AXY	ANP	BRF	MSF
Raw Score:	1	0	0	0	0	0	0	2	2	2	0	0	1	8
T Score:	46	46	42	41	40	45	40	56	48	47	44	39	56	71
Response %:	100	100	100	100	100	100	100	100	100	100	100	100	100	100

Comparison Group Data: Personnel Screening, Police Officer Candidate (Men and Women), N = 2074

Mean Score (◇--◇):	42	46	44	46	43	46	42	43	41	41	45	41	44	45
Standard Dev (±1 SD):	6	4	6	7	5	2	4	4	6	6	4	5	5	8
Percent scoring at or below test taker:	87	95	83	65	77	99.3	88	99.1	91	91	94	81	98	99.3

The highest and lowest T scores possible on each scale are indicated by a "---"; MMPI-2-RF T scores are non-gendered.

MLS	Malaise	SUI	Suicidal/Death Ideation	AXY	Anxiety
GIC	Gastrointestinal Complaints	HLP	Helplessness/Hopelessness	ANP	Anger Proneness
HPC	Head Pain Complaints	SFD	Self-Doubt	BRF	Behavior-Restricting Fears
NUC	Neurological Complaints	NFC	Inefficacy	MSF	Multiple Specific Fears
COG	Cognitive Complaints	STW	Stress/Worry		

FIGURE 8-8 Mr. N's MMPI-2-RF Police Candidate Interpretive Report, continued

MMPI-2-RF® Police Candidate Interpretive Report
06/06/2016, Page 5 Mr. N

MMPI-2-RF Externalizing, Interpersonal, and Interest Scales

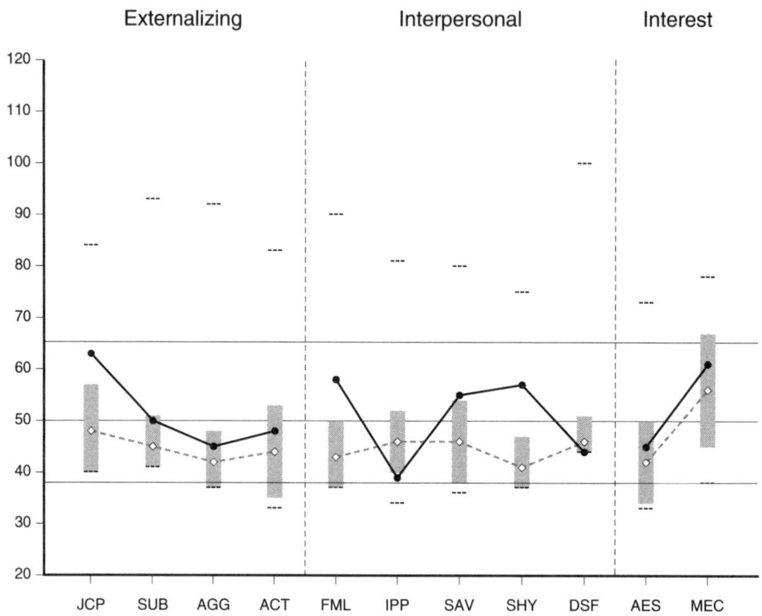

	JCP	SUB	AGG	ACT	FML	IPP	SAV	SHY	DSF	AES	MEC
Raw Score:	3	1	1	3	4	1	5	5	0	2	5
T Score:	63	50	45	48	58	39	55	57	44	45	61
Response %:	100	100	100	100	100	100	100	100	100	100	100

Comparison Group Data: Personnel Screening, Police Officer Candidate (Men and Women), N = 2074

Mean Score (◇---◇):	48	45	42	44	43	46	46	41	46	42	56
Standard Dev (±1 SD):	9	6	6	9	7	6	8	6	5	8	11
Percent scoring at or below test taker:	96	90	84	79	99	20	93	99	90	79	73

The highest and lowest T scores possible on each scale are indicated by a "---"; MMPI-2-RF T scores are non-gendered.

JCP Juvenile Conduct Problems
SUB Substance Abuse
AGG Aggression
ACT Activation
FML Family Problems
IPP Interpersonal Passivity
SAV Social Avoidance
SHY Shyness
DSF Disaffiliativeness
AES Aesthetic-Literary Interests
MEC Mechanical-Physical Interests

FIGURE 8-8 Mr. N's MMPI-2-RF Police Candidate Interpretive Report, continued

MMPI-2-RF® Police Candidate Interpretive Report
06/06/2016, Page 6 Mr. N

MMPI-2-RF PSY-5 Scales

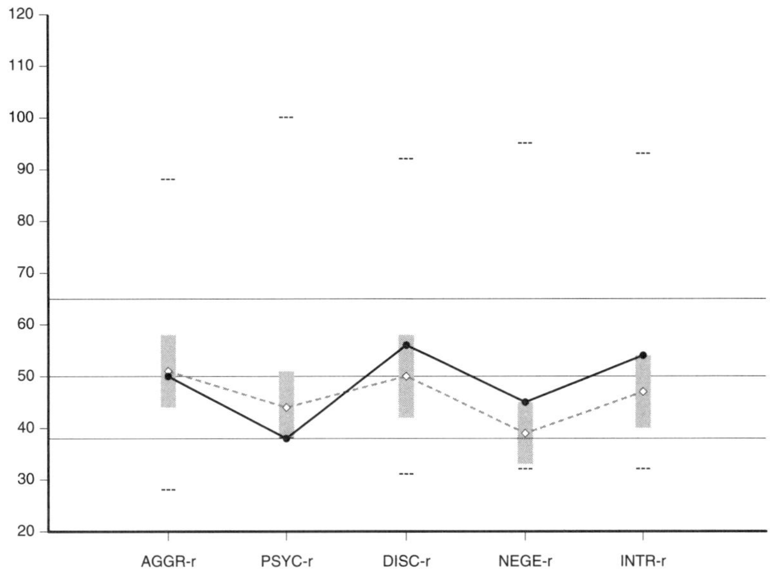

	AGGR-r	PSYC-r	DISC-r	NEGE-r	INTR-r
Raw Score:	9	0	9	4	8
T Score:	50	38	56	45	54
Response %:	100	100	100	100	100

Comparison Group Data: Personnel Screening, Police Officer Candidate (Men and Women), N = 2074

Mean Score (◇--◇):	51	44	50	39	47
Standard Dev (±1 SD):	7	7	8	6	7
Percent scoring at or below test taker:	57	55	87	87	89

The highest and lowest T scores possible on each scale are indicated by a "---"; MMPI-2-RF T scores are non-gendered.

AGGR-r Aggressiveness-Revised
PSYC-r Psychoticism-Revised
DISC-r Disconstraint-Revised
NEGE-r Negative Emotionality/Neuroticism-Revised
INTR-r Introversion/Low Positive Emotionality-Revised

FIGURE 8-8 Mr. N's MMPI-2-RF Police Candidate Interpretive Report, continued

MMPI-2-RF® Police Candidate Interpretive Report
06/06/2016, Page 7 Mr. N

MMPI-2-RF T SCORES (BY DOMAIN)

PROTOCOL VALIDITY

Content Non-Responsiveness

CNS	VRIN-r	TRIN-r
0	39	57 T

Over-Reporting

F-r	Fp-r	Fs	FBS-r	RBS
42	42	42	45	38

Under-Reporting

L-r	K-r
42	55

SUBSTANTIVE SCALES

Somatic/Cognitive Dysfunction

RC1	MLS	GIC	HPC	NUC	COG
42	46	46	42	41	40

Emotional Dysfunction

EID
49

RCd	SUI	HLP	**SFD**	NFC
53	45	40	**56**	48

RC2	INTR-r
46	54

RC7	STW	AXY	ANP	BRF	**MSF**	NEGE-r
41	47	44	39	56	**71**	45

Thought Dysfunction

THD
39

RC6	RC8	PSYC-r
43	39	38

Behavioral Dysfunction

BXD
53

RC4	JCP	SUB
59	63	50

RC9	AGG	ACT	AGGR-r	DISC-r
45	45	48	50	56

Interpersonal Functioning

FML	RC3	IPP	SAV	**SHY**	DSF
58	43	39	55	**57**	44

Interests

AES	MEC
45	61

Scale scores shown in bold font are interpreted in the report.

Note. This information is provided to facilitate interpretation following the recommended structure for MMPI-2-RF interpretation in Chapter 5 of the *MMPI-2-RF Manual for Administration, Scoring, and Interpretation*, which provides details in the text and an outline in Table 5-1.

FIGURE 8-8 Mr. N's MMPI-2-RF Police Candidate Interpretive Report, continued

This interpretive report is intended for use by a professional qualified to interpret the MMPI-2-RF in the context of preemployment psychological evaluations of police and other law enforcement officer candidates. ***It focuses on identifying problems; it does not convey potential strengths.*** *The information it contains should be considered in the context of the test taker's background, the demands of the position under consideration, the clinical interview, findings from supplemental tests, and other relevant information.*

The interpretive statements in the Protocol Validity section of the report are based on T scores derived from the general MMPI-2-RF normative sample, as well as scores obtained by the multisite sample of 2,074 individuals that make up the Police Officer Candidate comparison group.

The interpretive statements in the Clinical Findings and Diagnostic Considerations sections of the report are based on T scores derived from the general MMPI-2-RF normative sample. Following recommended practice, only T scores of 65 and higher are considered clinically significant. Scores at this clinical level are generally rare among police officer candidates.

Statements in the Comparison Group Findings and Job-Relevant Correlates sections are based on comparisons with scores obtained by the Police Officer Candidate comparison group. Statements in these sections may be based on T scores that, although less than 65, are nevertheless uncommon in reference to the comparison group.

Sources for interpretive statements in all sections are listed in the Endnotes section of this report. See User's Guide for the MMPI-2-RF Police Candidate Interpretive Report *for detailed information on report features.*

SYNOPSIS

This is a valid MMPI-2-RF protocol. Scores on the substantive scales indicate clinically significant emotional dysfunction. Emotional-internalizing findings relate to fears.

Comparison group findings point to additional possible concerns about self-doubt, irresponsible behavior, family conflict, and shyness.

Possible job-relevant problems are identified in the following domains: Emotional Control and Stress Tolerance, Routine Task Performance, Decision-Making and Judgment, Assertiveness, Social Competence and Teamwork, Integrity, Conscientiousness and Dependability, and Substance Use.

FIGURE 8-8 Mr. N's MMPI-2-RF Police Candidate Interpretive Report, continued

PROTOCOL VALIDITY

This is a valid MMPI-2-RF protocol. There are no problems with unscorable items. The test taker responded to the items relevantly on the basis of their content, and there are no indications of over- or under-reporting.

CLINICAL FINDINGS

Clinical-level symptoms, personality characteristics, and behavioral tendencies of the test taker are described in this section and organized according to an empirically guided framework. (Please see Chapter 8, Yossef S. Ben-Porath, Interpreting the MMPI-2-RF, *for details.) Statements containing the word "reports" are based on the item content of MMPI-2-RF scales, whereas statements that include the word "likely" are based on empirical correlates of scale scores. Specific sources for each statement can be accessed with the annotation features of this report.*

The test taker reports multiple specific fears of certain animals and acts of nature[1].

There are no indications of clinically significant somatic, cognitive, thought, or behavioral dysfunction in this protocol.

DIAGNOSTIC CONSIDERATIONS

This section provides recommendations for psychodiagnostic assessment based on the test taker's MMPI-2-RF results. It is recommended that he be evaluated for the following:

Emotional-Internalizing Disorders

- Specific phobias[2]

COMPARISON GROUP FINDINGS

This section describes the MMPI-2-RF substantive scale findings in the context of the Police Officer Candidate comparison group. Specific sources for each statement can be accessed with the annotation features of this report. ***Job-related correlates of these results, if any, are provided in the subsequent Job-Relevant Correlates section.***

Emotional/Internalizing Problems

The test taker's responses indicate a level of multiple specific fears that may be incompatible with public safety requirements for good emotional adjustment[2]. This level of fearfulness is very uncommon among police officer candidates. Only 1.5% of comparison group members give evidence of this or a greater level of fearfulness.

FIGURE 8-8 Mr. N's MMPI-2-RF Police Candidate Interpretive Report, continued

MMPI-2-RF® Police Candidate Interpretive Report
06/06/2016, Page 10 Mr. N

He reports a comparatively high level of self-doubt for a police officer candidate[3]. Only 2.8% of comparison group members convey this or a greater lack of confidence.

Behavioral/Externalizing Problems

The test taker reports a comparatively high level of irresponsible behavior for a police officer candidate[4]. Only 4.0% of comparison group members convey this or a greater level of acting out.

Interpersonal Problems

The test taker reports a comparatively high level of family conflict for a police officer candidate[5]. Only 4.4% of comparison group members convey this or a greater level of family problems. He also reports a relatively high level of social anxiety for a police officer candidate[6]. Only 2.8% of comparison group members convey this or a greater level of shyness and inhibition.

JOB-RELEVANT CORRELATES

Job-relevant personality characteristics and behavioral tendencies of the test taker are described in this section and organized according to ten problem domains commonly identified in the professional literature as relevant to police officer candidate suitability. (Please see User's Guide for MMPI-2-RF Police Candidate Interpretive Report *for details.) Statements that begin with "Compared with other police officer candidates" are based on correlations with other self-report measures obtained in police officer candidate samples that included individuals who were subsequently hired as well as those who were not. Statements that begin with "He is more likely than most police officers or trainees" are based on correlations with outcome data obtained in samples of hired candidates during academy or field training, probation, and/or the post-probation period. Specific sources for each statement can be accessed with the annotation features of this report.*

Emotional Control and Stress Tolerance Problems

Compared with other police officer candidates, the test taker is more likely to become easily discouraged[7]; to have difficulty coping with stress[8]; and to worry about problems and be uncertain about how to deal with them[9].

Routine Task Performance Problems

Compared with other police officer candidates, the test taker is more likely to have a history of motor vehicle violations or difficulties[10] and to have a history of job performance problems[7].

He is more likely than most police officers or trainees to exhibit difficulties carrying out tasks under non-stressful conditions[11].

Decision-Making and Judgment Problems

Compared with other police officer candidates, the test taker is more likely to avoid making decisions, fail to take action, or do anything that may prompt scrutiny from others[12].

FIGURE 8-8 Mr. N's MMPI-2-RF Police Candidate Interpretive Report, continued

Assertiveness Problems

Compared with other police officer candidates, the test taker is more likely to be ill at ease in dealing with others[13]; to feel inadequate[13]; and to be unsure and act hesitantly[13].

Social Competence and Teamwork Problems

Compared with other police officer candidates, the test taker is more likely to engage in conflicts with authority[8].

Integrity Problems

Compared with other police officer candidates, the test taker is more likely to fail to integrate ethical considerations into his decision-making[7]; to have a history of conflicts with the law and other violations of social norms[8]; and to lack a commitment to societal rules[8]. He is also more likely to be self-indulgent[8].

He is more likely than most police officers or trainees to exhibit difficulties leading to integrity violations[14] and sustained internal affairs investigations[14].

Conscientiousness and Dependability Problems

Compared with other police officer candidates, the test taker is more likely to give up easily and not persevere in the face of challenges[12] and to have a history of absenteeism or tardiness[8].

He is more likely than most police officers or trainees to exhibit difficulties with punctuality and attendance[12].

Substance Use Problems

Compared with other police officer candidates, the test taker is more likely to have a history of substance use problems[15].

The candidate's test scores are not associated with problems in the following domains:
- Feedback Acceptance
- Impulse Control

ITEM-LEVEL INFORMATION

Unscorable Responses

The test taker produced scorable responses to all the MMPI-2-RF items.

Critical Responses

Seven MMPI-2-RF scales--Suicidal/Death Ideation (SUI), Helplessness/Hopelessness (HLP), Anxiety (AXY), Ideas of Persecution (RC6), Aberrant Experiences (RC8), Substance Abuse (SUB), and Aggression (AGG)--have been designated by the test authors as having critical item content that may require immediate attention and follow-up. Items answered by the individual in the keyed direction (True or False) on a critical scale are listed below if his T score on that scale is 65 or higher.

FIGURE 8-8 Mr. N's MMPI-2-RF Police Candidate Interpretive Report, continued

The test taker has not produced an elevated T score (≥ 65) on any of these scales.

User-Designated Item-Level Information

The following item-level information is based on the report user's selection of additional scales, and/or of lower cutoffs for the critical scales from the previous section. Items answered by the test taker in the keyed direction (True or False) on a selected scale are listed below if his T score on that scale is at the user-designated cutoff score or higher. The percentage of the MMPI-2-RF normative sample (NS) and of the Personnel Screening, Police Officer Candidate (Men and Women) comparison group (CG) that answered each item in the keyed direction are provided in parentheses following the item content.

Behavioral/Externalizing Dysfunction (BXD, T Score = 53)

21. Item Content Omitted. (True; NS 47.1%, CG 37.0%)
61. Item Content Omitted. (False; NS 61.6%, CG 58.7%)
66. Item Content Omitted. (True; NS 20.3%, CG 20.4%)
107. Item Content Omitted. (True; NS 47.3%, CG 35.5%)
156. Item Content Omitted. (True; NS 59.8%, CG 45.9%)
223. Item Content Omitted. (True; NS 12.3%, CG 20.3%)
226. Item Content Omitted. (True; NS 21.5%, CG 38.1%)

Antisocial Behavior (RC4, T Score = 59)

5. Item Content Omitted. (True; NS 36.7%, CG 20.8%)
19. Item Content Omitted. (False; NS 17.0%, CG 7.8%)
21. Item Content Omitted. (True; NS 47.1%, CG 37.0%)
66. Item Content Omitted. (True; NS 20.3%, CG 20.4%)
126. Item Content Omitted. (False; NS 17.3%, CG 11.4%)
141. Item Content Omitted. (True; NS 34.2%, CG 20.3%)
156. Item Content Omitted. (True; NS 59.8%, CG 45.9%)
223. Item Content Omitted. (True; NS 12.3%, CG 20.3%)

Neurological Complaints (NUC, T Score = 41)

No items that are scored on this scale were answered in the keyed direction.

Juvenile Conduct Problems (JCP, T Score = 63)

21. Item Content Omitted. (True; NS 47.1%, CG 37.0%)
66. Item Content Omitted. (True; NS 20.3%, CG 20.4%)
223. Item Content Omitted. (True; NS 12.3%, CG 20.3%)

Disconstraint-Revised (DISC-r, T Score = 56)

21. Item Content Omitted. (True; NS 47.1%, CG 37.0%)
42. Item Content Omitted. (True; NS 10.3%, CG 45.9%)
61. Item Content Omitted. (False; NS 61.6%, CG 58.7%)
66. Item Content Omitted. (True; NS 20.3%, CG 20.4%)
75. Item Content Omitted. (True; NS 50.3%, CG 55.4%)
107. Item Content Omitted. (True; NS 47.3%, CG 35.5%)

FIGURE 8-8 Mr. N's MMPI-2-RF Police Candidate Interpretive Report, continued

156. Item Content Omitted. (True; NS 59.8%, CG 45.9%)
223. Item Content Omitted. (True; NS 12.3%, CG 20.3%)
226. Item Content Omitted. (True; NS 21.5%, CG 38.1%)

Critical Follow-up Items

This section contains a list of items to which the test taker responded in a manner warranting follow-up. The items were identified by police officer screening experts as having critical content. Clinicians are encouraged to follow up on these statements with the candidate by making related inquiries, rather than reciting the item(s) verbatim. Each item is followed by the candidate's response, the percentage of Police Officer Candidate comparison group members who gave this response, and the scale(s) on which the item appears.

261. Item Content Omitted. (True; 3.2%; VRIN-r, TRIN-r, FBS-r, EID, RCd)
337. Item Content Omitted. (True; 17.4%; VRIN-r, RC9, AGG)

FIGURE 8-8 Mr. N's MMPI-2-RF Police Candidate Interpretive Report, continued

ENDNOTES

This section lists for each statement in the report the MMPI-2-RF score(s) that triggered it. In addition, each statement is identified as a Test Response, if based on item content, a Correlate, if based on empirical correlates, or an Inference, if based on the report authors' judgment. (This information can also be accessed on-screen by placing the cursor on a given statement.) For correlate-based statements, research references (Ref. No.) are provided, keyed to the consecutively numbered reference list following the endnotes.

[1] Test Response: MSF=71
[2] Inference: MSF=71
[3] Test Response: SFD=56
[4] Test Response: RC4=59
[5] Test Response: FML=58
[6] Test Response: SHY=57
[7] Correlate: RC4=59, Ref. 5
[8] Correlate: RC4=59, Ref. 1, 5
[9] Correlate: FML=58, Ref. 5
[10] Correlate: RC4=59, Ref. 1
[11] Correlate: FML=58, Ref. 2, 4
[12] Correlate: SHY=57, Ref. 5
[13] Correlate: SHY=57, Ref. 1, 5
[14] Correlate: RC4=59, Ref. 3, 5
[15] Correlate: RC4=59, Ref. 1, 2, 5

FIGURE 8-8 Mr. N's MMPI-2-RF Police Candidate Interpretive Report, continued

RESEARCH REFERENCE LIST

The following studies are sources for empirical correlates identified in the Endnotes section of this report.

1. Detrick, P., Ben-Porath, Y. S., & Sellbom, M. (2015). Associations between MMPI-2-RF (Restructured Form) and Inwald Personality Inventory (IPI) scale scores in a law enforcement preemployment screening sample. *Journal of Police and Criminal Psychology.* Advance online publication. doi: 10.1007/s11896-015-9172-7

2. Tarescavage, A. M., Brewster, J., Corey, D. M., & Ben-Porath, Y. S. (2015). Use of pre-hire MMPI-2-RF police candidate scores to predict supervisor ratings of post-hire performance. *Assessment, 22,* 411-428. doi: 10.1177/1073191114548445

3. Tarescavage, A. M., Corey, D. M., & Ben-Porath, Y. S. (2016). A prorating method for estimating MMPI-2-RF scores from MMPI responses: Examination of score fidelity and illustration of empirical utility in the PERSEREC police integrity study sample. *Assessment, 23,* 173-190. doi: 10.1177/1073191115575070

4. Tarescavage, A. M., Corey, D. M., Gupton, H. M., & Ben-Porath Y. S. (2015). Criterion validity and practical utility of the Minnesota Multiphasic Personality Inventory-2-Restructured Form (MMPI-2-RF) in assessments of police officer candidates. *Journal of Personality Assessment, 97,* 382-394. doi: 10.1080/00223891.2014.995800

5. Tarescavage, A. M., Fischler, G. L., Cappo, B., Hill, D. O., Corey, D. M., & Ben-Porath, Y. S. (2015). Minnesota Multiphasic Personality Inventory-2-Restructured Form (MMPI-2-RF) predictors of police officer problem behavior and collateral self-report test scores. *Psychological Assessment, 27,* 125-137. doi: 10.1037/pas0000041

End of Report

FIGURE 8-8 Mr. N's MMPI-2-RF Police Candidate Interpretive Report, continued

ITEM RESPONSES

1: 2	2: 1	3: 2	4: 1	5: 1	6: 2	7: 1	8: 1	9: 2	10: 2
11: 2	12: 2	13: 1	14: 2	15: 2	16: 1	17: 2	18: 1	19: 2	20: 2
21: 1	22: 2	23: 2	24: 2	25: 1	26: 2	27: 2	28: 1	29: 2	30: 2
31: 2	32: 2	33: 2	34: 2	35: 2	36: 2	37: 2	38: 1	39: 2	40: 2
41: 2	42: 1	43: 2	44: 1	45: 1	46: 2	47: 2	48: 1	49: 2	50: 1
51: 2	52: 1	53: 1	54: 1	55: 1	56: 2	57: 1	58: 1	59: 1	60: 1
61: 2	62: 2	63: 2	64: 1	65: 1	66: 1	67: 2	68: 2	69: 1	70: 2
71: 2	72: 1	73: 1	74: 2	75: 1	76: 2	77: 2	78: 1	79: 2	80: 1
81: 2	82: 2	83: 1	84: 2	85: 1	86: 2	87: 2	88: 1	89: 1	90: 1
91: 1	92: 2	93: 2	94: 1	95: 1	96: 2	97: 2	98: 1	99: 1	100: 2
101: 2	102: 1	103: 1	104: 1	105: 1	106: 2	107: 1	108: 2	109: 2	110: 2
111: 2	112: 2	113: 1	114: 1	115: 2	116: 2	117: 2	118: 2	119: 2	120: 2
121: 2	122: 2	123: 2	124: 2	125: 1	126: 2	127: 1	128: 1	129: 2	130: 2
131: 2	132: 2	133: 2	134: 1	135: 2	136: 2	137: 2	138: 2	139: 2	140: 1
141: 1	142: 2	143: 1	144: 2	145: 2	146: 2	147: 1	148: 1	149: 2	150: 2
151: 2	152: 2	153: 2	154: 1	155: 2	156: 1	157: 1	158: 2	159: 2	160: 2
161: 2	162: 1	163: 1	164: 2	165: 2	166: 2	167: 1	168: 2	169: 2	170: 2
171: 2	172: 2	173: 2	174: 1	175: 2	176: 2	177: 2	178: 2	179: 2	180: 1
181: 2	182: 2	183: 1	184: 2	185: 2	186: 1	187: 1	188: 2	189: 1	190: 1
191: 2	192: 2	193: 2	194: 2	195: 1	196: 1	197: 1	198: 2	199: 2	200: 2
201: 1	202: 1	203: 2	204: 2	205: 2	206: 2	207: 1	208: 2	209: 2	210: 2
211: 1	212: 1	213: 1	214: 2	215: 2	216: 2	217: 1	218: 2	219: 1	220: 2
221: 1	222: 1	223: 1	224: 2	225: 2	226: 1	227: 1	228: 2	229: 1	230: 2
231: 2	232: 2	233: 2	234: 1	235: 2	236: 2	237: 1	238: 2	239: 1	240: 2
241: 1	242: 2	243: 2	244: 1	245: 2	246: 1	247: 2	248: 2	249: 1	250: 2
251: 2	252: 2	253: 2	254: 1	255: 2	256: 2	257: 2	258: 1	259: 1	260: 2
261: 1	262: 1	263: 1	264: 2	265: 1	266: 2	267: 2	268: 2	269: 1	270: 2
271: 2	272: 1	273: 2	274: 2	275: 2	276: 1	277: 2	278: 2	279: 2	280: 2
281: 2	282: 1	283: 1	284: 2	285: 2	286: 2	287: 2	288: 2	289: 2	290: 2
291: 2	292: 2	293: 1	294: 2	295: 2	296: 2	297: 2	298: 1	299: 1	300: 2
301: 2	302: 1	303: 2	304: 2	305: 2	306: 2	307: 2	308: 2	309: 1	310: 2
311: 2	312: 2	313: 1	314: 2	315: 2	316: 2	317: 2	318: 2	319: 2	320: 1
321: 1	322: 2	323: 1	324: 1	325: 1	326: 2	327: 2	328: 2	329: 2	330: 2
331: 2	332: 2	333: 1	334: 2	335: 2	336: 2	337: 1	338: 2		

FIGURE 8-8 Mr. N's MMPI-2-RF Police Candidate Interpretive Report, continued

9

Foundational Requirements of Fitness-for-Duty Evaluations

Inherent to all public safety positions is the potential of serious harm to others when an incumbent is unable to safely and effectively perform the job's essential functions—a status commonly referred to as being "unfit for duty" (Corey & Borum, 2013; Rostow & Davis, 2004; Stone, 2000). When on the basis of objective evidence it is reasonably suspected that a public safety employee is unfit for duty as a result of a mental health condition, an employer is both permitted and, in fact, obligated to require the employee to submit to a psychological fitness-for-duty evaluation (FFDE; Mayer & Corey, 2017).

Case law across the United States is replete with examples of courts having decided that an FFDE is permissible when public safety, including the safety of coworkers, is at risk. This applies equally to police officers (*Brownfield v. City of Yakima*, 2010; *Conte v. Horcher*, 1977; *Krocka v. City of Chicago*, 2000; *Watson v. City of Miami Beach*, 1999), correctional officers (*Colon v. City of Newark*, 2006; *Flynn v. Sandahl*, 1995; *Rice v. City of Oakland*, 1999), firefighters (*Aldrup v. Caldera*, 2001; *Coffman v. Indianapolis Fire Department*, 2009; *Jenkins v. City of Sandusky*, 2008), and dispatchers (*Wisbey v. City of Lincoln*, 2009).

Professional Practice Guidelines

Two sources of professional practice guidance are available to psychologists who conduct FFDEs of police officers and other public safety personnel.

These are the American Psychological Association's Professional Practice Guidelines for Occupationally Mandated Psychological Evaluations (APA, 2017b; OMPE Guidelines), which are discussed in chapter 1 (see Table 1-6 for a listing of the guideline statements), and the IACP-PPSS Fitness-for-Duty Evaluation Guidelines (IACP-PPSS, 2014; FFDE Guidelines). In addition to underscoring the broad principles of ethical practice applied to these evaluations, both sets of guidelines emphasize the following: the importance of ensuring that the criterion for assessing fitness is identified and that an FFDE is justified by law and institutional policy; that multiple sources of relevant and valid data are used; and that findings, opinions, and conclusions from the evaluation are properly and narrowly communicated. We next turn to a discussion of each of these topics.

Identifying the Fitness Criterion

As in any forensic mental health assessment, an FFDE begins with an understanding of the psycholegal question(s) underlying the referral (Heilbrun et al., 2009; APA, 2017b). How is fitness or, alternatively, unfitness defined under the terms of law, regulation, administrative rule, and institutional policy? What standard of practice exists for defining it? Without an understanding of the fitness criterion provided by the answers to these questions, the evaluator cannot determine his or her competence to assess the criterion, decide how to assess it, or evaluate how the particular employee/examinee measures up against it. Without a criterion, a fitness examiner is flying blind.

In an FFDE of a public safety employee, two primary sources establish the fitness criterion. The first is the collective body of statutory, regulatory, and case law pertaining to the Americans with Disabilities Act, as amended (ADA, 1991; ADAAA, 2008), and its state progeny, which may be even more restrictive. The second source is federal and state laws pertaining to the particular position. We summarize next how these laws interweave to inform both procedures and standards for conducting FFDEs of public safety employees. We also discuss several landmark cases that illustrate how courts interpret and apply these statutes in the context of litigation involving FFDEs of police officers and other public safety employees. Our discussion of the legal issues underlying an FFDE is not exhaustive and is limited primarily to U.S. federal laws and case law pertaining to them. Decisions by federal circuit courts are not precedential in other circuits, and as a result the interpretation of federal laws and regulatory guidance may differ across jurisdictions. Consequently, readers are advised to consult with local legal professionals to determine how state and federal laws apply to FFDEs in their locations.

Legal Foundations for Fitness-for-Duty Evaluations

Under the Americans with Disabilities Act of 1990 (ADA, 1991), an employer who requires an employee to submit to an evaluation of his or her physical or mental ability to perform the job must first justify that evaluation as being "job-related and consistent with business necessity" (42 U.S.C. §12112[d][4][A]; 29 C.F.R. §1630.14[c]). The Equal Employment Opportunity Commission (EEOC) regards this threshold as having been met when an employer "has a reasonable belief, based on objective evidence, that (a) an employee's ability to perform essential job functions will be impaired by a medical condition; or (b) an employee will pose a direct threat due to a medical condition" (EEOC, 2000, Question 5, p. 7).

In short, legal justification for a compulsory mental health examination of an employee generally requires objective evidence of job-related performance problems or safety threats *and* a known or reasonably suspected mental condition. One of these elements in the absence of the other represents an insufficient basis for an FFDE (Gold & Shuman, 2009, p. 244). But when an employee's essential job functions implicate public safety, this "business necessity standard" is relaxed, although not entirely ignored (Mayer & Corey, 2017).

In *Brownfield v. City of Yakima* (9th Cir. 2010), the court held that a police officer who is exhibiting troubling behavior, giving rise to reasonable concerns about his or her mental fitness, but who has not shown any impairment in his or her ability to perform the duties of a police officer, may nevertheless be ordered to submit to a "prophylactic" FFDE (that is, *before* there is objective evidence of impaired performance), "particularly when the employee is engaged in dangerous work" (slip op. at 10825; see also *Cody v. CIGNA Healthcare of St. Louis,* 1998; *Watson v. City of Miami Beach,* 1999). Thus, although the business necessity standard "is quite high and is not to be confused with mere expediency" (*Cripe v. City of San Jose,* 2001, at 890), the standard may be met even in the absence of known medical problems or observed deterioration in the employee's job performance. Although fitness-for-duty (FFD) examiners are well advised to confer with the employer or other referral source to understand the rationale for the mandated evaluation (see Corey, 2011, for a discussion of the benefits and importance of this prereferral consultation), employers who refer public safety employees for psychological FFDEs are given broad leeway and deference by the courts in light of the potential for serious harm to occur to the employees or others when their ability to perform public safety functions is impaired. Indeed, the long arc of case law in this area makes clear that when a public safety employer has an objective and reasonable basis for suspecting that an employee in a safety-sensitive position is unable to safely or effectively perform the essential functions of that position, the employer not only has a legal right but in many cases also an obligation to mandate an FFDE (see Mayer & Corey, 2017, for discussion of related case law).

The ADA's business necessity standard also has implications for determining an employee's fitness for duty (Corey, 2011; Gold & Shuman, 2009; Mayer & Corey, 2017). As just noted, the ADA requires that a medical or psychological evaluation of an employee must be predicated on business necessity. This means that the evaluation must be justified by objective evidence giving rise to reasonable concerns that the employee has a medical or mental health condition that may impair the employee's ability to perform the essential job functions or will pose a direct threat to the employee or others. Therefore, the ADA's two-pronged business necessity standard implies a similar fitness criterion: an employee is medically or psychologically unfit for duty when (a) the employee has a mental, emotional, or psychological impairment and (b) that condition limits the employee's ability to perform the essential functions of the position or poses a direct threat to him- or herself or others.

Central to an understanding of the fitness standard is whether, in order to find an employee unfit for duty, the employee's condition must satisfy either the definition of a disability under the ADA (1990 *et seq.*) or meet recognized diagnostic criteria (e.g., using current versions of the *Diagnostic and Statistical Manual for Mental Disorders* [DSM] or the International Classification of Diseases [ICD]). Several federal and state courts suggest that it is not a diagnosis per se that renders an employee unfit for duty but rather the impact of the symptom or symptoms (which may not rise to a magnitude warranting diagnosis) on the employee's ability to properly perform the duties of the position. In *Watson v. City of Miami Beach* (1999), Watson, a police officer, maintained that he did not have a mental impairment, but rather that the employer erroneously "regarded" him as having one and that this entitled him to sue under the ADA for discrimination on the basis of a perceived disability. The appeals court disagreed, noting that the FFDE mandate need not be conditioned on the employer having a reasonable belief that a *mental impairment* exists, but rather only that a *mental condition* exists that may render the employee unable to perform his or her job duties safely or effectively. The Court concluded,

> In any case where a police department reasonably perceives an officer to be even mildly paranoid, hostile, or oppositional, a fitness for duty examination is job related and consistent with business necessity. Police departments place armed officers in positions where they can do tremendous harm if they act irrationally. Contrary to Watson's contention, the ADA does not, indeed cannot, require a police department to forgo a fitness for duty examination to wait until a perceived threat becomes real or questionable behavior results in injuries. (at 935)

That a mental condition need not rise to a diagnosed mental disorder is also supported by the California Court of Appeal (2007) in *Sager v. Yuba County.* The psychologist retained by the employer to evaluate Sharon Sager, a deputy sheriff, found her unfit for duty on the basis of problematic personality traits. But in a significant clarification of the standard for judging an employee to be unfit for duty, the court ruled that "Sager's fitness for duty did not have to be shown entirely by testimony of a mental health expert" (at 4). Indeed, the court held that the sheriff, as a law enforcement expert who knew Sager well, was able to opine "that Sager was not mentally fit to work as a peace officer because she could not 'be a team player, who is able to look at things abstractly and not take everything personally, not to be upset when one is criticized, and to work in a team environment' " (at 4). Although the court observed that the employer was justified in relying on the opinion of its psychologist, it also was entitled to consider and weigh that opinion against its own experiences with the employee over the course of her employment.

It is important to note that the *Sager* court ruled that the *preemployment standards* for qualifying a peace officer candidate in California (see chapter 5 for a full discussion of these standards) apply "throughout a peace officer's career," not merely for purposes of initial hiring, and are properly used to evaluate an incumbent officer's psychological fitness for duty (see also *Brown v. Sandy City Appeal Board* [2014] in which the Utah Court of Appeals held that California's preemployment standards may also be used to assist in evaluating the psychological fitness for duty of a Utah police officer). The *Sager* court concluded, "[I]f the evidence shows she is not able to maintain *mental fitness*, that is, control her anger, work with other officers, and make sound judgments, then she is not performing the duties [of a peace officer] *in the proper manner*" (at 8; emphasis in the original).

This reliance on a broader range of personality-related traits—not just diagnosed disorders—to assess a peace officer's psychological fitness is also consistent with the guidance of the California POST Commission:

> In earlier versions of POST regulations, the stated purpose of the psychological evaluation was limited to ruling out candidates with mental or emotional disorders and/or job-relevant psychopathology (i.e., psychological *stability*). In 2009, [POST Commission] Regulation 1955 formally expanded the role of peace officer psychological screening to include the assessment of both psychological stability *and* normal-range personality traits and characteristics (i.e., psychological *suitability*). This change

> was made in recognition that personality traits encompass both normal and abnormal personality, and that personality disorders are actually extreme and inflexible manifestations of these otherwise normal traits. The peace officer psychological evaluation is, in effect, an assessment of the influence of personality traits—both normal and abnormal—on job-related behaviors. (Spilberg & Corey, 2017, p. 2)

In the federal employment environment, when evaluating employees with access to sensitive compartmented information (SCI; e.g., classified information) in which national security interests are at stake, the criteria used for evaluating eligibility for continued access to SCI include "psychological conditions." The guidelines for evaluating this criterion state,

> Certain emotional, mental, and personality conditions can impair judgment, reliability, or trustworthiness. *A formal diagnosis of a disorder is not required for there to be a concern under this guideline.* A duly qualified mental health professional (e.g., clinical psychologist or psychiatrist) employed by, or acceptable to and approved by the U.S. Government, should be consulted when evaluating potentially disqualifying and mitigating information under this guideline. (SEAD-4, 2017; emphasis added)

That a formal diagnosis is not required when identifying a disqualifying psychological condition under SEAD-4 aligns also with the text of the *DSM-5* (2013), which notes that many individuals present with symptoms that do not meet the full criteria for a diagnosis but who demonstrate a clear need for treatment or care. The OMPE Guidelines (APA, 2017b) also emphasize that "[i]t is not *per se* the diagnosis or mental health condition of an . . . employee that is occupationally relevant, but rather the impact of that diagnosis or condition on the individual's ability to perform the duties of the position in a safe, effective, and/or efficient manner" (Guideline 4).

For federal employees who are required to meet certain medical standards, or positions subject to medical evaluation programs, the proper standard for evaluating fitness for duty is, in most cases, 5 C.F.R. § 339 (cf. *Slater v. Department of Homeland Security,* 2008). Under this federal regulation, a history of a particular medical problem may be the basis of a medical disqualification "only if the condition at issue is itself disqualifying, recurrence of the condition is based on reasonable medical judgment, and the duties of the position are such that a recurrence of the condition would pose a significant risk of substantial harm to the health and safety of the applicant or employee or others that cannot be eliminated or reduced by reasonable accommodation or any other agency efforts to mitigate risk" (§ 339.206).

Thus, in both state and federal contexts, it is not necessarily the case that a currently disabling condition needs to be diagnosed for an individual to be deemed unfit for duty. Instead, what is necessary is for an individualized evaluation to document evidence of substantial impairment, as the result of a mental health condition, in that employee's ability either to perform the essential functions of the position, to perform them in the proper manner, or to perform them without posing a direct threat to him- or herself or others. Merely having a mental health diagnosis does not necessarily render an employee unfit for duty if it does not substantially limit the employee's ability to safely and effectively perform the duties of the particular position. In positions for which the consequences of failure to perform the job duties properly may be catastrophic, the magnitude of the impairment required to find the employee unfit for duty is commensurately lower (cf. *EEOC v. Amego, Inc.*, 1997; *Lassiter v. Department of Justice*, 1993).

The Use of Psychological Testing and Collateral Data in Assessing Fitness for Duty

As in all high-stakes psychological assessments, decisions about the choice and use of a test should rest on several considerations, including (a) peer-reviewed research evidence indicating that one or more scales on the test validly measure constructs pertinent to the evaluation criteria; (b) commercial availability of the test; (c) availability of a comprehensive technical manual or equivalent documentation; (d) evidence of adequate levels of reliability; (e) the test's inclusion of measures of test-taking orientation (e.g., content responsiveness, overreporting, underreporting); and (f) validity evidence that supports the test's use for the intended purpose, setting, and population (Ackerman, 2010; APA, 2017b; Melton et al., 2007; Otto et al., 2000; Spilberg & Corey, 2017). Of course, the test user must also have the qualifications necessary to use the instrument and be adequately trained in its administration, scoring, and interpretation.

As just discussed, the evaluation of a police officer's or other public safety employee's psychological fitness for duty is fundamentally an assessment of the degree to which the individual's work performance is, or is likely to be, impaired by a psychological condition. Consequently, a fitness-for-duty evaluation is concerned, in part, with dysfunction in emotion, thought, and/or behavior. Like all psychological assessments, determinations of fitness for duty depend on multiple sources of information about functioning in these domains, including employment records, collateral interviews, mental health records, clinical interview, and psychological testing. Indeed, for an FFDE to meet federal requirements as a "thorough medical assessment" that can be relied on by an employer for making employment decisions, it must be conducted by an examiner who is familiar with the relevant job duties; obtains relevant, individualized information about the employee's medical condition; has current knowledge of the employee's medical condition; examines the employee in person; and reviews the records of the employee's other treating health care provider(s) (see Mayer & Corey, 2017, for discussion of this topic).

As a validated, broadband instrument for measuring personality and psychopathology, the MMPI-2-RF is well suited to contribute to an assessment of an employee's fitness for duty. It satisfies each of the six criteria just enumerated for using a test in a high-stakes evaluation, and it provides "much individualized information" as required by federal courts (see *Michael v. City of Troy Police Department,* 2014). In particular, the instrument's hierarchical structure, which focuses on five domains of psychological dysfunction (Somatic/Cognitive, Emotional, Thought, Behavioral, and Interpersonal) and specific problems within each domain, aids the examiner in understanding how identified problems are likely to manifest on and off the job.

Owing in large part to the preselection and selection factors discussed in chapter 6, police and public safety *candidates* who complete the MMPI-2-RF constitute a fairly homogeneous group with generally good psychological adjustment. In contrast, individuals who take the test in an FFDE context—that is, *incumbent employees,* for whom there are objective concerns about psychological fitness—are comparatively heterogeneous: some have significant psychopathology, some have none, and others exhibit varying degrees of dysfunction that may be revealed on psychological testing at levels below clinical significance.

Just as with the assessment of job suitability of a candidate at the preemployment stage, the valid assessment of fitness for duty of an incumbent employee requires reliance on multiple sources of data pertinent to the individual's job performance problems and any suspected job-limiting mental condition. As described in the FFDE Guidelines (IACP-PPSS, 2014; Guideline 7.4), these collateral data sources include, but are not limited to, job class specifications and/or job description, performance evaluations, previous remediation efforts, commendations, testimonials, internal affairs investigations, formal citizen/public complaints, use-of-force incidents, reports of duty-related trauma exposure, civil claims, disciplinary actions, incident reports of any triggering events, medical and mental health treatment records, and prior psychological evaluations. These collateral sources are needed for a valid assessment of fitness for duty for the same reasons (discussed in chapter 5) as in preemployment screening; namely, to aid in validating findings from psychological testing, to protect against the possibility of an examinee's deceptive efforts, to assess how and to what degree the constructs measured by psychological testing are reflected in the examinee's behavior, and under what contexts or conditions it varies.

The OMPE Guidelines (APA, 2017b) stress the importance of selecting assessment tools that produce reliable data supporting valid inferences pertinent to the referral question(s). In the context of psychological testing, the guidelines note that reliability "implies a precise estimate of the targeted construct," whereas when applied to nontest information, reliability refers to "accuracy" (Guideline 8). Relying on multiple sources of collateral data reduces the chances that a single inaccurate item of information will have an unwarranted influence on the assessment.

Reporting FFDE Findings and Opinions

In an FFDE, the "ultimate question" is often phrased in shorthand: whether the employee is psychologically "fit for duty." However, the ADA enforcement guidance makes clear that, in the final analysis, this and all other employment decisions stemming from a medical evaluation (e.g., whether reasonable accommodation may be made to enable a qualified employee with a disability to perform the essential functions of the job) is a matter to be decided by the employer, not the FFD examiner. As stated by the EEOC, when communicating the results of a compulsory medical evaluation, "An employer is entitled only to the information necessary to determine whether the employee can do the essential functions of the job or work without posing a direct threat" (EEOC, 2000, Question 13).

In seeming opposition to this position, several state and federal courts have held that an employer who mandates an FFDE is entitled only to the examiner's "ultimate fitness determination" (*Sangirardi v. Village of Stickney,* 2003; see also *McGreal v. Ostrov,* 2004; *Pettus v. Cole,* 1996). But careful analysis of these decisions reveals that this restriction was necessitated by the examiners' failure to obtain authorization to disclose their assessment findings using a state-compliant form that is required when disclosing individually identifiable medical information. Absent specific authorization, the holder of the medical information is restricted under most state laws from disclosing "anything other than the fitness for duty determination" (*McGreal v. Ostrov,* 2004). With proper authorization, no such restrictions apply.

An adequate disclosure of medical information may also be necessary for an employer to determine whether the examination constitutes "a thorough medical assessment" (*Michael v. City of Troy Police Department,* 2014; see also *Jennings v. Dow Corning Corp.,* 2013; *Wurzel v. Whirlpool Corp.,* 2012). But on one point involving the content of an FFDE report, both the law and standards of practice are in complete agreement: "When the referral source or another party is responsible for determining the ultimate issue in a referral, psychologists strive to educate and inform rather than answer the ultimate issue" (APA, 2017b; OMPE, Guideline 13). Examiners who opine on a topic not solicited by the referral source, whether or not it is within the examiner's clinical expertise (e.g., reasonable accommodation, treatment recommendations, prognosis for recovery) "are acting outside of their contractual role and do a disservice to the referring party" (Mayer & Corey, 2017, p. 109).

As we discussed in chapter 5, the Genetic Information Nondiscrimination Act of 2008 (GINA), Title II, prohibits gathering, inquiring about, or using information about the manifestation of a disease or disorder in an individual's family members (i.e., family medical history) when making employment decisions. This applies equally to both preemployment and FFD evaluations. When requesting medical records from health care providers, it is important to include an admonishment instructing the records custodian not to disclose family medical information, using the "GINA warning" (or language similar to it) provided in chapter 5.

The importance of restricting the report of findings and opinions to those that are pertinent to the referral question(s), and not addressing an ultimate question that belongs to the employer, has particular implications for how the fitness determination is articulated. Some practitioners advocate for the inclusion of fitness determinations that reflect a fit-for-duty status conditioned on one or more contingencies, such as limited or restricted work activities (i.e., fit for light or modified duty). When doing so, care should be taken to confirm with the referring party that the proposed duty restrictions are realistic and acceptable to the employer; otherwise the recommendation can become a point of contention or cause for litigation between the parties. An even more hazardous contingency is one that conditions fitness for duty on entering or continuing in some course of remediation or treatment. Corey (2011) advised against this approach:

> When such a condition is stipulated, it typically is rationalized in one of two ways: either because the examiner believes the employee's current fitness is unlikely to be sustained without additional or ongoing treatment,

> or because the employee's current unfitness results from a minor impairment expected to respond quickly to treatment. In cases of the former, if the employee's current fitness is so fragile or unstable as to be undone in the foreseeable future without the benefit of ongoing treatment, the examiner should reconsider whether the . . . fit-for-duty conclusion [is warranted]. . . . In cases where the employee is judged currently unfit for duty due to a remediable condition, it is usually more prudent to acknowledge the current unfit status and not address recommendations designed to restore fitness unless requested by the referring party. (p. 288)

In the next chapter, we discuss the implications of contextual factors, particularly the motivation to be seen as fit or unfit, on MMPI-2-RF scores in FFDEs. We also consider the appropriateness of considering moderately elevated scales (i.e., scores below 65T) for purposes of evaluating psychological fitness of persons whose work has substantial public safety implications, and we present descriptive data for public safety employees who took the MMPI-2-RF while undergoing an FFDE. In chapter 11, we present a model for integrating data to reach a fitness determination, and we illustrate the model with a variety of actual but redacted cases.

10

Special Considerations for Using the MMPI-2-RF in Fitness-for-Duty Evaluations

As detailed in chapter 9, identification of psychological conditions that may limit public safety employees' ability to perform their essential job functions is a critical component of fitness-for-duty evaluations (FFDEs). In essence, an FFDE is a clinical evaluation triggered by specific concerns about an employee's psychological functioning. Consequently, the broad MMPI-2-RF literature on the use of the test as a measure of personality and psychopathology guides use of the inventory in FFDEs. This is fortunate because, contrary to the substantial literature on using the MMPI-2-RF in preemployment evaluations (reviewed in chapter 6), there is a surprising dearth of empirical research on using the test in FFDEs. This may be a function of some unique aspects of these evaluations, including (a) the very heterogeneous nature of the referral issues, which precludes obtaining uniform data sets; (b) legal, regulatory, and logistical constraints pertaining to the availability of collateral (i.e., non-MMPI) data for such research; and (c) a lack of information pertaining to the outcome of FFDEs other than the assessor's opinion, which is likely to be contaminated by MMPI findings. In this chapter we review two published MMPI studies that do provide some findings relevant to conducting FFDEs and then present some unpublished MMPI-2-RF FFDE data.

MMPI FFDE Research

Grossman, Haywood, Ostrov, Wasyliw, and Cavanaugh (1990) examined the sensitivity of the original MMPI Validity Scales to motivational factors in the psychological evaluations of police officers. They compared MMPI Validity Scale scores of 20 officers undergoing an FFDE who expressed a desire *not* to return to work with those of 20 officers matched for age, race, and sex also undergoing an FFDE, but who expressed a desire to return to work, and with another sample of 20 similarly matched officers who were not undergoing an FFDE and were actively working. The authors' underlying assumption was that the officers not desiring to return to work might be motivated to overreport problems, whereas the sample wishing to return to work might be motivated to underreport, and because members of the control group were told that the test results would have no bearing on their employment, members of that group would have no motivation either to over- or underreport.

Grossman et al. (1990) compared mean scores for the three groups on the original MMPI F and L scales along with several nonstandard validity scales that are not part of the MMPI-2-RF and, therefore, are not covered here. Consistent with expectations, the group presumably motivated to overreport scored higher on F than did members of the other two groups, but there were no significant differences on L. Unfortunately, data were not reported for K, which, as discussed later, appears to be more sensitive to the kind of underreporting seen in FFD evaluees. These findings highlight the need to examine MMPI-2-RF FFDE protocols for threats to protocol validity involving both overreporting and underreporting because either motivational set may be present in a given FFDE.

Also focusing on motivational factors in FFDEs, Walfish (2010) reported the results of a study on reducing MMPI underreporting in a sample of professionals undergoing an FFDE. The premise of this research was that professionals undergoing mandated psychological evaluations that could result in the loss of their license to practice would be motivated to underreport similarly to preemployment evaluees. The author sought to document the rate of underreported MMPI-2 protocols in such evaluations and to examine whether providing feedback to those who showed evidence of extreme underreporting would result in reduced underreporting if they were retested following such feedback. The 53 participants in this study included physicians (64%), dentists (11%), attorneys (9%), nurses (6%), pharmacists (4%), chiropractors (2%), optometrists (2%), and physician assistants (2%). Those with T-scores at or above 65 on L and/or 70 on K were deemed "faking good" and were provided feedback that their test results were invalid because of underreporting. They were asked to retake the MMPI-2 with a "mindset of rigorous openness and honesty on a conscious basis" (Walfish, 2010, p. 77).

Walfish (2010) reported that 31 (59%) of the FFDE participants met criteria for underreporting and were retested with the instructions just noted. All but three scored below the designated underreporting cutoffs in the second testing. A comparison of the first and second test protocols for these individuals showed marked reductions in scores on the MMPI-2 underreporting scales (e.g., L was reduced from a mean T-score of 62.26 to 47.81 following feedback), whereas F scores increased (though not to an interpretable level), as did scores on some of the MMPI-2 Clinical Scales. It is important to note that a similar pattern of increase was observed on other measures administered as part of the FFDE. For example, the initial mean Beck Depression Inventory-II (BDI-II) score for underreporting evaluees was 4.87 (SD=5.77), increasing to 11.58 (8.54) at retest. The greater dispersion of BDI-II scores in retesting is noteworthy, likely reflecting that some test takers changed their response pattern substantially, whereas others did not.

Walfish (2010) recommended on the basis of his findings that FFD evaluees who produce an underreported MMPI-2 protocol be retested. Butcher, Morfitt, Rouse, and Holden (1997) made similar recommendations for preemployment evaluations following a study of airline pilot applicants in which the authors applied a similar research design. Like Walfish (2010), Butcher et al. (1997) found that retesting following altered instructions substantially changed substantive scale findings. For example, 12% of those retested produced clinically elevated Content Scales scores.

We disagree with the practice of retesting with altered instructions and recommend against it for the following reasons. The instructions accompanying retesting necessarily require the examiner to provide some rationale for readministering the test (as Walfish did in his FFDE retesting instructions). Instructions altered in this manner deviate from the standard administration procedures used to develop, norm, and validate MMPI scales. Their use calls into question the validity and interpretability of the resulting test scores. In addition, this approach may inadvertently "coach" evaluees on how to respond not only during the current evaluation but also in possible future assessments where the examiner would not know that a test taker had been subjected previously to nonstandard instructions. Moreover, the implications of the resulting scores, particularly if demonstrating significant psychopathology (as in the Butcher et al. 1997 study), are ambiguous. Finally, Walfish's (2010) results demonstrate that underreporting can be a significant concern in FFDEs, that it serves to lower scores on substantive scales when it occurs, and that this pattern generalizes to other measures (e.g., the BDI-II) administered as part of an FFDE.

MMPI-2-RF FFDE Findings

To facilitate use of the MMPI-2-RF in FFDEs, we assembled a sample of 709 protocols (some administered originally as MMPI-2s and later converted to the MMPI-2-RF) of public safety employees referred for an FFDE. In addition to individuals from the northwestern United States and Hawaii tested by this guide's first author, data for this research were generously provided by our U.S. colleagues Matt Guller (Northeast), Michael Cuttler (Southeast), Jocelyn Roland (West), and Monica Pilarc (Northwest). The sample included 556 men and 153 women, with a mean age of 38.6 years (SD=9.1). Of these, 559 evaluees were law enforcement officers (448 men and 111 women), and 150 were employed either as corrections officers (54 men and 24 women), firefighters/paramedics (44, 6) and dispatchers (10, 12). For the purpose of the analyses reported next, the non-law enforcement cases were combined into a group labeled "public safety (PS)-other."

Table 10-1 provides means and standard deviations on the 51 MMPI-2-RF scales for the four FFDE groups (male law enforcement officers [LEO], female LEO, male public safety [PS]-other, and female PS-other). Overall, there is considerable similarity in the means and standard deviations across groups, with the female PS-other group scoring higher than the remaining groups on FBS-r, RC1, HPC, and COG and both female groups scoring higher than the male samples on MSF and lower on MEC and DISC-r—reflecting gender differences found in nearly all of the MMPI-2-RF comparison groups (Tellegen & Ben-Porath, 2008/2011). These differences notwithstanding, the overall pattern indicates that, by and large, MMPI-2-RF scores are comparable for men and women and for police officers and other public safety employees undergoing FFDEs. The small number of differences between the LEO and PS-other women need to be considered cautiously in light of the relatively small sample size for the latter.

Focusing on the overall patterns reflected in Table 10-1, FFD evaluees tend generally to score within normal limits on the MMPI-2-RF measures of non-content-based invalid responding and overreporting; on average they score about a half standard deviation above the general population mean on the underreporting indicators, with mean K-r scores somewhat higher than those found for L-r. In light of the requirement that public safety employees demonstrate some behavior suggestive either of problems in performing their duties or that they pose a direct threat to themselves or others in order to be referred for an FFDE, it is unlikely that the higher K-r scores reflect better than average adjustment. Most likely, they are an indication of underreporting. As reviewed in chapter 6, Detrick and Chibnall (2014) found that higher K-r scores are associated with underreporting of emotional dysfunction. Mean scores on the MMPI-2-RF substantive scales also fell mainly within normal limits, the exceptions being some of the measures of emotional difficulties, particularly RC7 and NFC, but also on RC9.

To complement the overall patterns reflected in these descriptive statistics, in Tables 10-2 and 10-3 we report the rates at which FFDE evaluees exceed designated MMPI-2-RF validity and substantive scale cutoffs. As seen in Table 10-2, very few test takers show any evidence of non-content-based

TABLE 10-1

Public Safety Fitness-for-Duty Evaluation Descriptive Statistics by Gender

	Male LEO (n=448)		Female LEO (n=111)		Male PS-Other (n=108)		Female PS-Other (n=42)	
	Mean	SD	Mean	SD	Mean	SD	Mean	SD
VRIN-r	45	9	45	8	45	9	49	10
TRIN-r	51F	8	50	8	51F	8	52F	8
F-r	49	11	51	11	52	15	54	11
Fp-r	46	7	48	8	48	9	48	9
Fs	48	9	49	12	51	12	52	12
FBS-r	54	11	56	14	55	12	62	11
RBS	50	11	52	11	53	13	54	12
L-r	54	11	53	11	54	11	52	10
K-r	58	11	56	11	58	11	55	11
EID	45	12	48	13	47	12	52	13
THD	47	9	45	8	48	10	49	9
BXD	48	8	46	7	48	8	44	8
RCd	47	11	49	12	48	12	54	13
RC1	47	11	50	12	49	13	56	10
RC2	48	11	50	11	50	12	55	13
RC3	44	10	48	12	43	9	45	9
RC4	48	9	46	9	49	9	48	8
RC6	53	11	51	10	52	11	54	12
RC7	42	10	45	10	43	10	46	10
RC8	45	8	44	8	47	9	47	8
RC9	44	9	43	8	43	8	42	9
MLS	51	11	52	11	51	11	57	11
GIC	51	11	53	13	52	12	56	15
HPC	49	10	53	13	49	11	55	11
NUC	49	10	50	9	51	12	54	11
COG	46	10	47	10	49	12	53	12
SUI	49	10	50	10	50	14	51	14
HLP	46	9	48	11	46	10	49	11
SFD	47	9	50	10	49	11	54	12
NFC	43	8	44	9	45	10	48	10
STW	47	10	48	11	49	11	50	10
AXY	50	12	51	12	51	12	51	10
ANP	45	10	45	10	45	9	45	8
BRF	46	7	45	7	47	8	47	8
MSF	46	8	49	9	45	8	50	9
JCP	50	9	48	9	50	9	48	10
SUB	47	8	47	7	49	10	47	7
AGG	46	8	46	8	45	8	46	8
ACT	43	9	43	9	44	10	45	12

	Male LEO (n=448)		Female LEO (n=111)		Male PS-Other (n=108)		Female PS-Other (n=42)	
	Mean	SD	Mean	SD	Mean	SD	Mean	SD
FML	44	8	47	9	45	10	49	11
IPP	48	8	48	8	49	8	52	12
SAV	52	11	52	12	52	12	53	13
SHY	44	8	45	9	45	9	47	9
DSF	47	8	48	10	49	10	50	11
AES	40	8	44	9	43	9	45	10
MEC	59	10	51	8	58	11	49	10
AGGR-r	51	8	50	8	49	8	46	9
PSYC-r	45	8	45	8	46	9	48	9
DISC-r	51	8	46	7	51	8	45	7
NEGE-r	45	10	47	11	47	11	48	10
INTR-r	52	11	54	12	53	12	56	12

invalid responding, reflecting the care with which evaluees approach this high-stakes task. Somewhat larger proportions of evaluees exceed minimal interpretive cutoffs on the MMPI-2-RF overreporting indicators. However, as discussed in chapter 3, scores on these scales are confounded with genuine psychopathology, and only if an FFD evaluee's overreporting scale T-score exceeds higher cutoffs than the ones included in Table 10-2 (e.g., 100 on F-r) would overreporting be the most likely interpretation. As expected, the most common findings are scores in excess of interpretation cutoffs on the underreporting scales. The elevation rates reflected here are comparable to the MMPI-2 findings reported by Walfish (2010), indicating that between one-third to one-half of the FFD evaluees included in these samples show some evidence of underreporting. Of note in this context is Ben-Porath's (2012) general caution that a finding of underreporting does not, in itself, indicate that the test results are invalid. Non-elevated scores on MMPI-2-RF substantive scales cannot be interpreted as reflecting the absence of problems they are used to assess; however, clinically elevated scores can be interpreted with the understanding that they may underestimate the problems assessed by those scales.

Table 10-3 provides public safety FFDE elevation rates on the substantive scales at two T-score cutoffs: 60 and 65. Generally speaking, a

TABLE 10-2
Public Safety Fitness-for-Duty Evaluations Validity Scale Elevation Rates by Gender

Criteria	Male LEO (n=448)	Female LEO (n=111)	Male PS-Other (n=108)	Female PS-Other (n=42)
VRIN-r>=70	0.7	0.0	0.0	2.4
TRIN-r>=70	1.8	0.9	2.8	2.4
F-r>=80	2.2	3.6	6.5	0.0
Fp-r>=70	1.1	0.0	2.8	2.4
Fs>=80	1.1	3.6	4.6	4.8
FBS-r>=80	2.9	7.2	4.6	7.2
RBS>=80	2.2	2.7	5.6	7.2
L-r>=65	17.2	16.2	20.4	9.5
L-r>=70	10.3	9.9	12.0	2.4
L-r>=75	5.6	7.2	6.5	2.4
L-r>=80	3.8	1.8	2.8	0.0
K-r>=60	49.3	39.6	45.4	33.3
K-r>=66	37.3	28.7	34.3	26.2
K-r>=69	22.8	17.1	25.0	19.0
K-r=72	9.4	6.3	9.3	4.8

cutoff of 65 should be used in FFDEs in light of the absence of research that presently supports using lower cutoffs and given the clinical focus of these evaluations. Elevation rates are also reported for the lower cutoff because preliminary data, presented in Table 10-4, show that mean substantive scale T-scores of individuals found unfit for duty fall generally well below 65. This likely reflects both the confound of the motivation to appear high functioning and the fact that problems measured at levels below 65T can be sufficient to render a public safety employee unfit for duty.

Examining the Higher-Order Scales first, with the exception of the relatively small female PS-other group that had a 23.8% elevation rate, roughly 10% of the overall sample produced clinically elevated EID scores, with considerably smaller proportions scoring 65T or higher on THD or BXD. The small female PS-other group is the outlier throughout these analyses, but given the small sample size, this pattern will not be interpreted here. Among the RC Scales, RCd, RC1, and RC6 were most likely to be clinically elevated. On the Specific Problems (SP) Scales, MLS, GIC, HPC, SUI, SFD, STW, AXY, SAV, and INTR-r were most likely to be

TABLE 10-3

Public Safety Fitness-for-Duty Evaluations Substantive Scale Elevation Rates by Gender

Criteria	Male LEO (n = 448)		Female LEO (n = 111)		Male PS-Other (n = 108)		Female PS-Other (n = 42)	
	<60	<65	<60	<65	<60	<65	<60	<65
EID	12.1	8.7	18	9.9	13.9	10.2	35.7	23.8
THD	9.6	2.7	10.8	1.8	13.9	3.7	14.3	2.4
BXD	10	2.7	4.5	0.9	9.3	4.6	7.1	0
RCd	13.4	8.9	19.8	14.4	18.5	11.1	35.7	21.4
RC1	12.5	7.8	18	11.7	16.7	12	38.1	23.8
RC2	13.6	10	17.1	10.8	17.6	11.1	35.7	26.2
RC3	8.7	5.6	18.9	10.8	7.4	4.6	4.8	4.8
RC4	9.2	6	4.5	2.7	11.1	10.2	4.8	2.4
RC6	27.9	17	24.3	13.5	25	15.7	38.1	28.6
RC7	6.3	4.2	8.1	6.3	8.3	5.6	11.9	9.5
RC8	4.5	2.7	3.6	1.8	7.4	5.6	4.8	0
RC9	5.4	2.5	6.3	2.7	1.9	0.9	4.8	2.4
MLS	17.6	10.5	21.6	13.5	22.2	11.1	40.5	26.2
GIC	19.9	10.7	26.1	12.6	25	14.8	35.7	26.2
HPC	11.4	11.4	19.8	19.8	13.9	13.9	23.8	23.8
NUC	9.4	9.4	6.3	6.3	18.5	18.5	28.6	28.6
COG	8.7	6.5	9.9	4.5	13.9	8.3	16.7	11.9
SUI	12.9	12.9	18	18	13.9	13.9	16.7	16.7
HLP	12.1	5.6	19.8	6.3	9.3	6.5	21.4	14.3
SFD	9.4	9.4	18	18	15.7	15.7	28.6	28.6
NFC	4	1.6	7.2	3.6	8.3	7.4	9.5	2.4
STW	10.3	10.3	15.3	15.3	13.9	13.9	19	19
AXY	11.4	11.4	16.2	16.2	18.5	18.5	9.5	9.5
ANP	9.4	9.4	8.1	8.1	5.6	5.6	4.8	4.8
BRF	4.9	1.1	2.7	1.8	8.3	2.8	7.1	4.8
MSF	3.6	3.6	9	9	2.8	2.8	7.1	7.1
JCP	15.2	5.6	9.9	3.6	14.8	3.7	14.3	7.1
SUB	7.1	4.2	6.3	1.8	11.1	5.6	9.5	2.4
AGG	7.4	3.6	7.2	3.6	7.4	1.9	2.4	2.4
ACT	2.2	2.2	4.5	4.5	4.6	4.6	11.9	11.9
FML	4.9	2	9.9	6.3	9.3	5.6	14.3	9.5
IPP	9.6	4.9	9	5.4	10.2	6.5	26.2	21.4
SAV	18.5	18.5	18	18	18.5	18.5	26.2	26.2
SHY	4.7	4.7	9	9	9.3	9.3	4.8	4.8
DSF	4.7	4.7	7.2	7.2	11.1	11.1	11.9	11.9
AGGR	17.4	9.6	17.1	6.3	12	4.6	9.5	7.1
PSYC	4	2.5	4.5	1.8	8.3	5.6	9.5	2.4
DISC	9.4	6.3	1.8	1.8	9.3	7.4	2.4	0
NEGE	8.7	5.8	11.7	8.1	11.1	7.4	7.1	4.8
INTR	23.2	12.1	27	16.2	27.8	18.5	35.7	26.2

elevated, reflecting more commonly occurring difficulties with demoralization and self-doubt, stress and anxiety, somatization, and interpersonal suspiciousness and functioning.

Clinically elevated scores on the scales just mentioned, though more common than others, occur in only 10% to 15% of the FFDE cases. However, Table 10-4 provides aggregate data showing that roughly 60% of the FFDE sample produced at least one clinically significant elevation on a substantive scale (the exception being the small female PS-other group that had a near 89% elevation rate), indicating that in most public safety FFDEs the MMPI-2-RF will likely yield at least one clinically interpretable finding. Roughly half of the FFD evaluees produced clinically elevated scores on at least one of the PSY-5 scales, which, as discussed in chapter 4, focus on personality disorder features. At least 40% of the sample produced elevated scores on at least one of the RC Scales.

Table 10-4 provides the results of a comparison of MMPI-2-RF substantive scale scores of those found fit versus unfit among the male and female police officers and the male PS-other group (as mentioned, the female group was too small to break down any further). Only those scales on which a substantial difference (at least a .50 Cohen's *d* effect size) was found across samples are included. As shown in Table 10-4, although substantial differences were found consistently for a number of scales—mainly measures of emotional dysfunction and somatization—mean T-scores for the unfit subgroups fall well below 65T, suggesting the possibility of using lower cutoffs to identify psychological conditions that render a public safety employee unfit for duty. However, these findings need to be replicated with other, larger samples before any specific recommendations can be offered along these lines. Based on the currently available data, we recommend limiting substantive scale interpretation in FFDEs to clinically elevated (65 and higher) T-scores, although slightly lower scores may be useful in identifying potential problem areas that can be assessed by extra-test data, including clinical interview, employment records, treatment records, and collateral interviews.

A significant limitation of this research is that the fitness opinions that served as the independent variable in these analyses were informed in part by MMPI results, although in the majority of these cases MMPI-2

TABLE 10-4

Public Safety Fitness-for-Duty Evaluation Fit versus Unfit Mean Score Comparisons by Gender

	Male LEO Fit (n = 170)		Male LEO Unfit (n = 150)			Female LEO Fit (n =33)		Female LEO Unfit (n = 23)			Male PS-Other Fit (n = 35)		Male PS-Other Unfit (n = 52)		
	M	SD	M	SD	*d*	M	SD	M	SD	*d*	M	SD	M	SD	*d*
EID	40	7	50	14	−.94	44	12	55	14	−.77	42	7	51	15	−.88
RCd	42	6	52	13	−1.02	46	11	56	12	−.82	43	7	53	13	−.96
RC1	43	8	51	13	−.79	46	8	58	15	−1.01	44	8	53	15	−.85
RC2	44	7	54	13	−.91	47	11	55	14	−.62	45	7	55	14	−.88
MLS	47	8	55	12	−.75	47	10	59	11	−1.15	46	6	55	13	−.98
GIC	48	7	54	14	−.62	50	10	59	15	−.70	47	7	56	15	−.84
HPC	46	7	52	12	−.61	49	10	58	16	−.68	45	8	52	12	−.67
NUC	46	7	52	12	−.61	46	7	58	12	−1.20	46	8	56	13	−.94
COG	43	5	51	13	−.90	44	10	55	11	−1.03	43	5	54	14	−1.17
HLP	44	6	49	11	−.60	46	7	54	16	−.69	43	4	49	13	−.71
SFD	44	5	51	11	−.79	48	9	55	12	−.69	45	8	51	12	−.60
ANP	42	7	48	12	−.55	44	10	50	12	−.55	41	4	47	11	−.83
AGG	43	7	48	9	−.52	45	7	51	9	−.85	42	6	47	10	−.67
NEGE-r	42	8	49	12	−.70	45	12	52	11	−.59	43	7	49	13	−.60
INTR-r	50	9	56	13	−.55	52	11	59	14	−.58	50	8	56	14	−.57

rather than MMPI-2-RF scores were available to the examiner. It is also unlikely that fitness determinations were made solely on the basis of MMPI findings, which would run counter to our recommendations. Therefore, the findings reported in Table 10-4 demonstrate that the MMPI-2-RF substantive scales are sensitive to psychological conditions that render a public safety employee unfit for duty.

Important Considerations When Using the MMPI-2-RF in Fitness-for-Duty Evaluations of Public Safety Employees

In the following chapter we note that FFDEs constitute forensic assessments because they are mandated by a third party, are often conducted in anticipation of litigation, and are not focused primarily on assessing the needs of, or providing mental health services to, the evaluee. Legal and procedural implications of this distinction are discussed there. Here, it is important to emphasize a general principle of using the MMPI-2-RF in forensic mental health evaluations: there is no empirical basis for reaching "ultimate issue" inferences based on MMPI-2-RF findings alone. Just as there is no MMPI-2-RF "profile" that differentiates defendants who are competent versus incompetent to stand trial, or disability claimants who are disabled versus not disabled as a result of a work accident, or which of two parents disputing custody of their children would better meet the children's needs, MMPI-2-RF findings alone are not dispositive on the matter of fitness for duty. As discussed and illustrated in chapter 11, they are nonetheless quite relevant and should be given due consideration in the context of an integrated assessment, but the matter of fitness is ultimately a legal/administrative question.

As detailed in the following chapter, the first step when conducting an FFDE is to determine whether a public safety employee has an emotional, cognitive, behavioral, thought, interpersonal, or other psychological condition that could render him or her unfit. Empirically supported MMPI-2-RF findings can, of course, be very informative in making this determination. The general MMPI-2-RF literature, coupled with information provided in this chapter, provides the foundation for using the test in this manner.

11

Using the MMPI-2-RF to Assess Fitness for Duty

Case Illustrations

In this chapter, we show how MMPI-2-RF score information can be integrated with information about the position (i.e., working conditions, essential job functions, and job demands), collateral information about the examinee, interview findings, and other test data to evaluate the psychological fitness for duty of employees in all four public safety job categories: police officer, corrections officer, firefighter/paramedic, and dispatcher. We include test protocols showing clinically significant elevations as well as those with moderate scale elevations, illustrating how both can be integrated with other data to inform judgments about fitness for duty in public safety positions.

An Integrative Model for Fitness-for-Duty Evaluations

Heilbrun and colleagues (2009) highlight the benefits of relying on a model to guide data gathering, data interpretation, and communication of results in forensic mental health evaluations. Fitness-for-duty evaluations (FFDEs) are forensic assessments because they are mandated by a third party, frequently address legal questions and/or are conducted in anticipation of litigation, and are not focused primarily on assessing the needs of, or providing mental health services to, the evaluee. As detailed in this chapter, FFDEs are a mental health evaluation carried out in contemplation of litigation in which an employee's property right to the position and statutory rights to nondiscrimination (on the basis of disability, perceived disability, or a record of disability) and accommodation are at issue. In chapter 8, we presented an integrative model for use in preemployment evaluations, and we demonstrated its use in a number of case examples. We now do the same for fitness evaluations.

The integrative model discussed in chapter 8 is grounded in the risk-based nature of preemployment psychological screening. Because candidates are screened out *only* when risk-related findings indicate an unacceptable risk for counterproductive behavior in the position—whether the risks derive from a mental condition, from problematic personality traits, or from behavioral propensities unrelated to either—the integrative model focuses on an evidence-based assessment of these risks. In contrast, determinations of fitness for duty derive from a different analytic framework. In chapter 9, we discussed the ADA's two-pronged "business necessity standard" for justifying any medical evaluation of an employee; namely, that there must be an objective and reasonable basis for believing (a) that the employee has a mental, emotional, or psychological condition and (b) that the condition limits the employee's ability to perform the essential functions of his or her position or poses a direct threat to the employee or others. This standard also provides fitness examiners with a model for assessing fitness. Bifurcating the second prong of the ADA business necessity standard into current and reasonably anticipated impairment, the standard can be implanted into a three-step model for integrating data across sources of assessment information. The analytic steps of this model involve three sequential questions:

Step 1. Is there evidence of an emotional, cognitive, behavioral, thought, interpersonal, or other psychological condition? If yes, proceed to Step 2. (If no condition exists, the employee does not meet the criterion necessary to be deemed psychologically unfit for duty.)
Step 2. Does the condition substantially limit the employee's **current** ability to perform the essential functions of the job, to perform them properly, or to perform them without posing a direct threat to the employee or others?
Step 3. If the employee has a mental health condition that is currently nonlimiting, is the employee's fitness sustainable?

Three-Step Model for Integrating Assessment Data

Assessing for a Psychological Condition

As with all mental health assessments, the determination of whether an employee has a psychological condition does not rely solely on psychological testing, but can be meaningfully and uniquely informed by it. Just as a test score in the clinical range (i.e., ≥65T) implicates but does not establish the presence of psychopathology, so too a score in the moderate range can reflect a comparatively high magnitude of problems that, in the context of a safety-sensitive position, may limit job functioning to a degree warranting the conclusion that the employee is psychologically unfit for duty. Nevertheless, this decision also should be informed by psychological testing but not determined by it. Other assessment data sources, such as employment records, treatment records, and clinical interview, must always be considered when carrying out all three steps of the integrative process, as discussed in chapter 9.

Evidence of an existing psychological condition may not always be apparent in psychological testing and/or in the clinical interview when an examinee is highly guarded or is determined to present him- or herself as psychologically fit for duty. In such cases, employees may understate or deny problems. Conversely, some employees who may be motivated to appear impaired for purposes of some anticipated secondary gain, such as a medical retirement, may present with feigned problems. For these reasons, forensic mental health evaluations always involve a review of multiple sources of relevant information to maximize reliability and validity (cf. Heilbrun et al., 2009), as do all occupationally mandated psychological evaluations (APA, 2017b; Guideline 10).

Some problems that lead to FFDEs are the result of interpersonal rivalries, motivational deficits, retribution, misunderstandings, or poor judgment and can occur even in the absence of an underlying psychological condition. Forensic psychologists have arrived at a variety of methods for differentiating these contextual and relationship-specific problems from disorders that are the proper focus of clinical attention, but explicating these techniques is beyond the scope of this book. Nevertheless, in the case illustrations that follow, we demonstrate for the reader how MMPI-2-RF findings can be integrated with other nontest information to make such an assessment.

Assessing for a Substantially Limiting Impairment

FFDEs can be thought of as another form of a competency evaluation—in this case, competency to perform the duties of a particular position. Grisso (2003) effectively argues that all competency evaluations necessarily involve an analysis of the *interaction* between an individual's psychological functioning and environmental demands. For example, psychologists performing a parenting competency evaluation would consider not only the parent's emotional, behavioral, cognitive, and personality functioning but also the needs of the child or children. A parent with only episodic and moderate depressive symptoms may lack the competency to provide for the needs of a young child with serious medical and/or psychological needs, or multiple children with similar needs, whereas a parent with significant and chronic depressive symptoms may still be competent to parent an independent, well-adjusted, and high-functioning teenager. In the same way, evaluating an individual's fitness (competency) for duty requires an understanding of the position's specific job demands, the working conditions in which they occur, and the consequences of an impaired ability to perform the essential functions of the position. This information can be acquired through a combination of a review of the formal job description, interviews with supervisors and incumbent employees, and on-site observations, among other methods.

Assessing the Sustainability of Fitness

Although the future course of a mental health condition can be viewed as an aspect of the second integrative step (i.e., an assessment of current *and* anticipated impairment), more contemporary thinking (cf. Mayer & Corey, 2017) regards it as a separate step in the analysis. This derives in part from how the ADA Amendments Act (ADAAA, 2008) broadens the definition of disability. The ADAAA stipulates that some disorders

> may constitute substantially limiting impairments if they are substantially limiting when active or have a high likelihood of recurrence in substantially limiting forms. For some individuals, psychiatric impairments such as bipolar disorder, major depression, and schizophrenia may remit and intensify, sometimes repeatedly, over the course of several months or several years. (EEOC, 1997/2009, at Question 8)

As such, an individual with a currently nonsymptomatic condition that is episodic or chronically relapsing may still be substantially impaired (and disabled), just as a person with a currently remitted substance use disorder may, under the law, still be regarded as engaged in "current use" if the use is recent enough to suggest the probability that it is ongoing. Various courts have interpreted the time period following symptom remission, during which a condition may be considered still active, to comprise weeks, months, or longer, depending on the nature of the condition (*Salley v. Circuit City Stores, Inc.*, 1998; *Shafer v. Preston Memorial Hospital Corp.*, 1997; *Zenor v. El Paso Healthcare Systems, Ltd.*, 1999). Thus, even when psychological test results indicate the absence of current, clinically significant dysfunction, other assessment data may nonetheless indicate otherwise or may support the conclusion that the current fitness is not sustainable. We illustrate such cases in this chapter.

About the Case Studies

The cases that follow involve employees in all four job categories: police officer, correctional officer, firefighter/paramedic, and emergency communications dispatcher. Although the facts in each case study reflect the actual material in the assessment record, details that might reveal their identities have been altered. None of these alterations meaningfully changes the record.

As with the preemployment case studies presented in chapter 8, because of space limitations we have not reproduced the full set of assessment data (e.g., complete employment and medical records, findings from other psychological assessment instruments, and the examiner's notes from the mental status examination and clinical interview). Instead, we have selected data from these various sources as appropriate to illustrate a particular case and to show how that information may be integrated with findings from the MMPI-2-RF to reach a determination of fitness for duty. And, as with the cases presented in chapter 8, some readers may arrive at different conclusions about an employee's fitness (or unfitness) for duty based on the findings presented in these case illustrations. Here, too, our goal is not to point to a single "right" conclusion in any case, but rather to enhance readers' understanding of how the integrative model can be applied to arrive at a well-reasoned fitness determination and to spur discussion of other related guidance.

Readers, particularly those who wish to delve more thoroughly into the process of data integration in public safety FFDEs, will benefit from reviewing each case, not just those from particular job categories. The material we discuss in each case is germane to all fitness evaluations, and all the cases have in common the same assessment components and integrative steps.

The MMPI-2-RF report used in all four cases is the Clinical Settings Interpretive Report. Although it was developed primarily for use in clinical assessments conducted in the context of diagnosis and treatment planning, it is appropriate and can be helpful in FFDEs because of its focus on psychological dysfunction. The report and its elements are described in detail by Ben-Porath (2012). Briefly, it consists of all of the elements of the MMPI-2-RF Score Report (discussed in chapter 8 as consisting of scale scores and item-level information) and an automated, empirically grounded interpretation of the results. The major elements of the clinical interpretive report include the Synopsis, a summary of the main findings in an MMPI-2-RF protocol; a section, Protocol Validity, identifying potential threats to protocol validity discussed in chapter 2 of this guide; and a section titled Substantive Scale Interpretation, in which findings related to Somatic/Cognitive Dysfunction, Emotional Dysfunction, Thought Dysfunction, Behavioral Dysfunction, Interpersonal Functioning, and the Interest Scales are reported. Diagnostic Considerations and Treatment Considerations sections are followed by one that provides Item-Level Information. As with the PCIR (described in chapter 7), the clinical interpretive report is fully annotated, meaning that the origin of (i.e., scale scores leading to) every statement in the report is identified and characterized as either being content based, empirically derived, or an inference of the report authors. Correlate-based statements are linked to specific publications that support them and can be accessed via hyperlinks. Primary advantages of this report are that it integrates a vast amount of information in a comprehensive, efficient, transparent, and consistent manner.

Mr. J, Firefighter/Paramedic

Assessment Issues Presented

- Integration of clinically elevated MMPI-2-RF RC and Specific Problems Scales with other relevant case information

Referral Summary

Mr. J is a 32-year-old, married, municipal firefighter/paramedic with 9 years of service in the profession, all with his current employer. He was referred for an FFDE by his employer after he lost emotional and verbal control with family members of a patient whom Mr. J and his fellow paramedic had just transported to the hospital following a heroin overdose. In this altercation (index incident), which occurred 8 weeks before the FFDE referral, Mr. J's partner had to intervene to keep him from physically assaulting one of the family members who had accused Mr. J of providing inadequate patient care. His partner reported that the provocation was nothing out of the ordinary, but Mr. J's reaction to it was "over the top" and dangerously provocative.

The referral letter from the employer stated that the purpose of the evaluation was to "determine whether, as a result of a mental health condition, Mr. J is unable to perform the essential functions of the job, perform them in a safe and effective manner, and/or pose a direct threat to his or others' safety." No other referral questions were included.

The employer reported that there had been no prior disciplinary actions or citizen complaints. During the 8 weeks between the index incident and the fitness evaluation, Mr. J was on paid administrative leave and assigned to his home.

Assessment Findings

EMPLOYMENT RECORDS

A review of Mr. J's employment records, including his complete personnel file and employee medical file, confirmed the absence of prior disciplinary actions. All the performance evaluations for the previous 6 years contained positive ratings ("meets" or "exceeds" performance standards), although a comment in the most recent evaluation noted that he had become noticeably "sarcastic" in his replies to supervisory feedback.

MENTAL STATUS EXAMINATION

Mr. J's appearance was unremarkable with regard to grooming, dress, weight, and other features. His behavior also was unremarkable. His speech was normal, as indicated by its rate, intelligibility, volume, quality, and quantity. His affective expression was normal, and his mood was dysphoric but appropriate. Mr. J displayed no abnormalities with respect to his perception, thought process, sensorium and cognition, judgment, insight, or reliability. He denied past or current suicidal and homicidal ideation. His attitude toward the examiner was cooperative, interested, and attentive.

CLINICAL INTERVIEW

Emotional control is a highly valued and acculturated trait in public safety employees. Losing that control jeopardizes a great deal: the employee's reputation and career, the safety of his or her coworkers, and community trust in the position, to name just a few of the valued assets put at risk. Mr. J's loss of emotional control was as disturbing to him as it was to his fellow firefighter/paramedic and other witnesses. He arrived at the FFDE contrite and embarrassed, but he was also worried. He knew something was wrong with him, but he could not define it. He was also afraid of what it might mean for his future.

Mr. J went to see an employee assistance counselor about 2 weeks after the index incident. According to his report, this was his first experience with any form of mental health treatment. His counselor, a psychologist, recommended that he see a psychiatrist or his primary care physician to obtain an antidepressant and, if necessary, a sleep aid. Mr. J did not follow the recommendation. He reported in the FFDE interview that he was afraid "something like that could happen again," and he wanted to understand how and why it happened. He acknowledged that the family member's provocation was not at all unusual for situations of that type and that he had previously faced many similar scenes with equanimity. Something had changed. He said, "I just remember standing there listening to the brother tell me that I had no compassion, that I had no bedside manner, and that I had no business being a paramedic. I guess I just snapped. I don't even know why."

In the course of discussing his developmental history, Mr. J disclosed that he had been the victim of horrific physical and emotional abuse by his stepfather from the age of 5 to 13, when he and a younger brother were placed in foster care. He performed poorly in school, eventually obtained a GED, and got a job working in a warehouse shortly after turning 18. His biological father, who had abandoned the family at an early age, eventually reentered his life, and he encouraged Mr. J to volunteer at the local fire department and to start taking classes at the local junior college to obtain his paramedic certificate, which he did.

Mr. J said that he had never pursued working for the fire and emergency medical service for the kinds of prosocial reasons that motivated his coworkers. He said he chose it because he wanted to have a sense of control over his own life—something he never had when growing up. He said he liked the idea of being the first person at the scene when tragedy struck.

He said he did not particularly care about people—neither the patients nor their families—and when other firefighters/paramedics showed empathy toward people, he knew he lacked that capacity. However, he considered his indifference to be a protective asset, part of his emotional armor. What surprised him about the incident at the hospital was that his lack of empathy had been transformed into outright hostility. He said he had seen a lot of "bad stuff" as a firefighter/paramedic, but he did not believe that he had posttraumatic stress disorder from these on-duty exposures to trauma.

At home, Mr. J had grown emotionally distant from his wife and children. He accompanied them on family events, but he was not engaged. He had no friends, no hobbies, and no interests. He said he had never been happy, but he thought that this was a result of the burden of being the breadwinner. For as long as he could remember, he had trouble falling and staying asleep, and he had come to view this too as normal.

One change that had begun to alarm Mr. J was his increasing reliance on alcohol to help him "come down" after work and to help him sleep on nights when he did not work the next morning. He said his wife had also expressed her concern about his drinking and had more than once suggested that he should "see somebody."

When asked if he believed that he was fit for duty, Mr. J initially replied that he believed he was fit because he felt he was the same as he had always been. However, when challenged to consider the significance of the index incident, he reconsidered and said, "I probably need some help."

MEDICAL RECORDS

Following a formal investigation of the index incident, the employer proposed suspending Mr. J for 10 shifts without pay—a significant loss of earnings considering that firefighters/paramedics may average a dozen 24-hour shifts per month. In a subsequent mitigation hearing, he presented a letter from his employee assistance program (EAP) counselor, a licensed psychologist, stating that he had voluntarily sought counseling, was dutifully attending weekly sessions, and was addressing issues that the therapist believed were causally related to the index incident. Because Mr. J had placed these records "in issue" by presenting his therapist's letter for mitigation purposes, they were no longer subject to the protections against compulsory disclosure normally afforded psychotherapy records (cf. *Flora v. Hamilton,* 1978; *Thomas v. Corwin,* 2007; *Thompson v. City of Arlington,* 1993; see also Mayer & Corey, 2017). Mr. J authorized the release of these records to the FFD examiner, after which the examiner had a brief phone consultation with the therapist.

The records received were consistent in all respects with the information provided by Mr. J during the FFDE clinical interview, except for one element: Mr. J said in the interview that he had previously never had problems managing or controlling his anger, but the therapist's notes contradicted this. In prior counseling sessions, Mr. J disclosed that he was "surprised" that he had not received a citizen's complaint in several other incidents in which he had lost control of his anger, but he suspected this was because there were no other witnesses—including his partner, who was driving the ambulance at the time of these other incidents involving hostile reactions to patients. In the phone consultation with the FFD examiner, the EAP counselor opined that Mr. J suffered from previously untreated and chronic PTSD produced by the abuse he had suffered at the hands of his stepfather.

MMPI-2-RF FINDINGS

Mr. J's MMPI-2-RF Clinical Settings Interpretive Report is reproduced in Figure 11-1. Interpretation of Mr. J's MMPI-2-RF results begins with an examination of his Validity Scale scores. He responded to all the MMPI-2-RF items, and his Validity Scale scores indicate that he did so in a relevant and consistent manner. There is no evidence of overreporting or underreporting in his protocol, although it is notable that he claimed a lower level of adjustment (K-r=31T) in comparison to the mean in the normative male sample, which, by definition, is 50T. Indeed, only 5% of the male normative sample reports this level of adjustment or lower. Nevertheless, the resulting MMPI-2-RF scores should provide an accurate assessment of Mr. J's current psychological functioning. The interpretive statements warranted by the substantive scale scores are listed in the report, and the source(s) for each statement are annotated by the endnotes linked to the superscripted numbers at the end of each statement.

MMPI 2 RF®

Minnesota Multiphasic
Personality Inventory-2
Restructured Form®

Interpretive Report: Clinical Settings

MMPI-2-RF®
Minnesota Multiphasic Personality Inventory-2-Restructured Form®
Yossef S. Ben-Porath, PhD, & Auke Tellegen, PhD

Name:	Mr. J
Age:	32
Gender:	Male
Marital Status:	Not reported
Years of Education:	Not reported
Date Assessed:	01/22/2016

PsychCorp

Copyright © 2008, 2011, 2012 by the Regents of the University of Minnesota. All rights reserved.
Distributed exclusively under license from the University of Minnesota by NCS Pearson, Inc. Portions reproduced from the MMPI-2-RF test booklet. Copyright © 2008 by the Regents of the University of Minnesota. All rights reserved. Portions excerpted from the *MMPI-2-RF Manual for Administration, Scoring, and Interpretation*. Copyright © 2008, 2011 by the Regents of the University of Minnesota. All rights reserved. Used by permission of the University of Minnesota Press.

MMPI-2-RF, the **MMPI-2-RF logo,** and **Minnesota Multiphasic Personality Inventory-2-Restructured Form** are registered trademarks of the University of Minnesota. **Pearson,** the **PSI logo,** and **PsychCorp** are trademarks in the U.S. and/or other countries of Pearson Education, Inc., or its affiliate(s).

TRADE SECRET INFORMATION
Not for release under HIPAA or other data disclosure laws that exempt trade secrets from disclosure.

[3.0 / 2 / QG]

ALWAYS LEARNING PEARSON

FIGURE 11-1 Mr. J's MMPI-2-RF Clinical Settings Interpretive Report

MMPI-2-RF Validity Scales

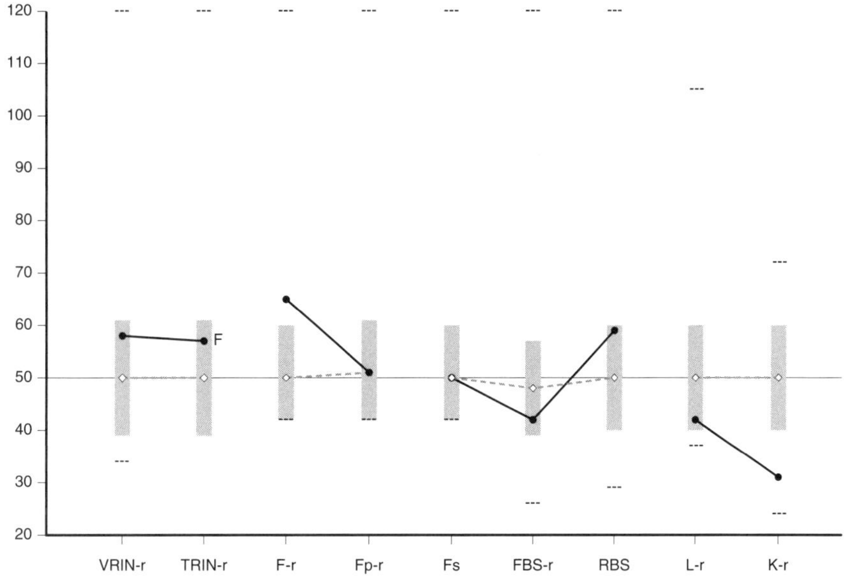

	VRIN-r	TRIN-r	F-r	Fp-r	Fs	FBS-r	RBS	L-r	K-r
Raw Score:	5	10	5	1	1	5	7	1	2
T Score:	58	57 F	65	51	50	42	59	42	31
Response %:	100	100	100	100	100	100	100	100	100

Cannot Say (Raw): 0 Percent True (of items answered): 43%

Comparison Group Data: MMPI-2-RF Normative (Men), N = 1138

Mean Score (◇--◇):	50	50	50	51	50	48	50	50	50
Standard Dev (±1 SD):	11	11	10	10	10	9	10	10	10
Percent scoring at or below test taker:	85	80	93	76	74	34	86	33	5

The highest and lowest T scores possible on each scale are indicated by a "---"; MMPI-2-RF T scores are non-gendered.

VRIN-r Variable Response Inconsistency
TRIN-r True Response Inconsistency
F-r Infrequent Responses
Fp-r Infrequent Psychopathology Responses
Fs Infrequent Somatic Responses
FBS-r Symptom Validity
RBS Response Bias Scale
L-r Uncommon Virtues
K-r Adjustment Validity

FIGURE 11-1 Mr. J's MMPI-2-RF Clinical Settings Interpretive Report, continued

MMPI-2-RF® Interpretive Report: Clinical Settings
01/22/2016, Page 3 Mr. J

MMPI-2-RF Higher-Order (H-O) and Restructured Clinical (RC) Scales

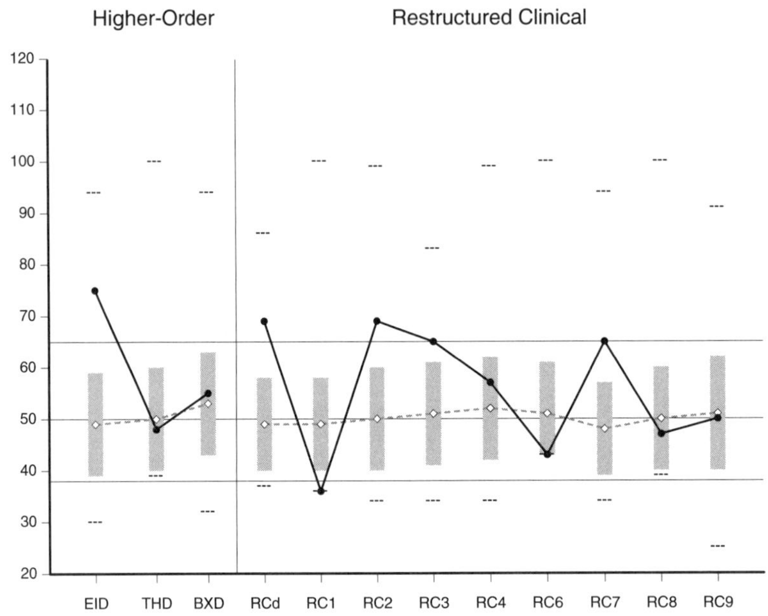

	EID	THD	BXD	RCd	RC1	RC2	RC3	RC4	RC6	RC7	RC8	RC9
Raw Score:	28	1	8	15	0	9	11	7	0	13	1	12
T Score:	75	48	55	69	36	69	65	57	43	65	47	50
Response %:	100	100	100	100	100	100	100	100	100	100	100	100

Comparison Group Data: MMPI-2-RF Normative (Men), N = 1138

	EID	THD	BXD	RCd	RC1	RC2	RC3	RC4	RC6	RC7	RC8	RC9
Mean Score (◇---◇):	49	50	53	49	49	50	51	52	51	48	50	51
Standard Dev (±1 SD):	10	10	10	9	9	10	10	10	10	9	10	11
Percent scoring at or below test taker:	99	57	65	96	17	96	92	74	54	95	53	54

The highest and lowest T scores possible on each scale are indicated by a "---"; MMPI-2-RF T scores are non-gendered.

EID Emotional/Internalizing Dysfunction
THD Thought Dysfunction
BXD Behavioral/Externalizing Dysfunction
RCd Demoralization
RC1 Somatic Complaints
RC2 Low Positive Emotions
RC3 Cynicism
RC4 Antisocial Behavior
RC6 Ideas of Persecution
RC7 Dysfunctional Negative Emotions
RC8 Aberrant Experiences
RC9 Hypomanic Activation

FIGURE 11-1 Mr. J's MMPI-2-RF Clinical Settings Interpretive Report, continued

MMPI-2-RF Somatic/Cognitive and Internalizing Scales

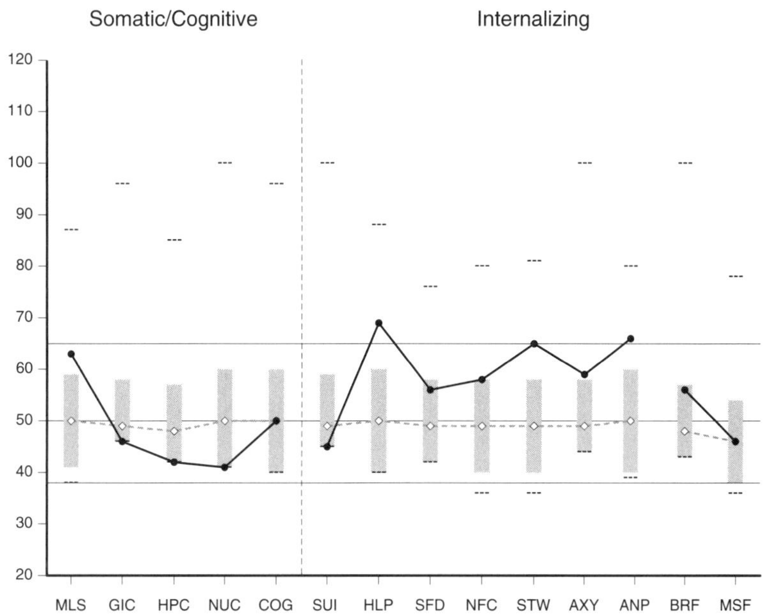

	MLS	GIC	HPC	NUC	COG	SUI	HLP	SFD	NFC	STW	AXY	ANP	BRF	MSF
Raw Score:	4	0	0	0	1	0	3	2	5	5	1	5	1	2
T Score:	63	46	42	41	50	45	69	56	58	65	59	66	56	46
Response %:	100	100	100	100	100	100	100	100	100	100	100	100	100	100

Comparison Group Data: MMPI-2-RF Normative (Men), N = 1138

	MLS	GIC	HPC	NUC	COG	SUI	HLP	SFD	NFC	STW	AXY	ANP	BRF	MSF
Mean Score (◇--◇):	50	49	48	50	50	49	50	49	49	49	49	50	48	46
Standard Dev (±1 SD):	9	9	9	10	10	10	10	9	9	9	9	10	9	8
Percent scoring at or below test taker:	95	84	57	46	63	83	99	88	90	96	93	95	89	58

The highest and lowest T scores possible on each scale are indicated by a "---"; MMPI-2-RF T scores are non-gendered.

MLS	Malaise	SUI	Suicidal/Death Ideation	AXY	Anxiety
GIC	Gastrointestinal Complaints	HLP	Helplessness/Hopelessness	ANP	Anger Proneness
HPC	Head Pain Complaints	SFD	Self-Doubt	BRF	Behavior-Restricting Fears
NUC	Neurological Complaints	NFC	Inefficacy	MSF	Multiple Specific Fears
COG	Cognitive Complaints	STW	Stress/Worry		

FIGURE 11-1 Mr. J's MMPI-2-RF Clinical Settings Interpretive Report, continued

MMPI-2-RF® Interpretive Report: Clinical Settings
01/22/2016, Page 5 Mr. J

MMPI-2-RF Externalizing, Interpersonal, and Interest Scales

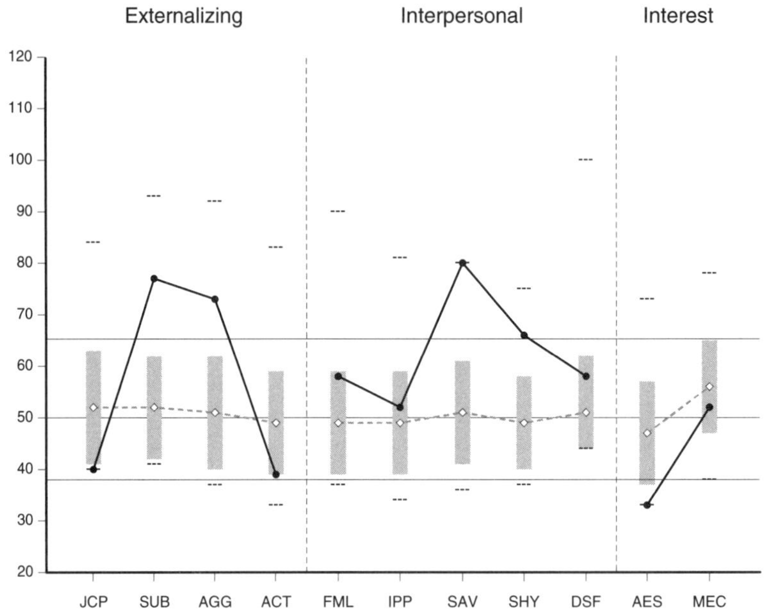

	JCP	SUB	AGG	ACT	FML	IPP	SAV	SHY	DSF	AES	MEC
Raw Score:	0	5	6	1	4	5	10	6	1	0	3
T Score:	40	77	73	39	58	52	80	66	58	33	52
Response %:	100	100	100	100	100	100	100	100	100	100	100

Comparison Group Data: MMPI-2-RF Normative (Men), N = 1138

Mean Score (◇--◇):	52	52	51	49	49	49	51	49	51	47	56
Standard Dev (±1 SD):	11	10	11	10	10	10	10	9	11	10	9
Percent scoring at or below test taker:	28	99	98	20	89	77	100	96	88	14	43

The highest and lowest T scores possible on each scale are indicated by a "---"; MMPI-2-RF T scores are non-gendered.

JCP Juvenile Conduct Problems
SUB Substance Abuse
AGG Aggression
ACT Activation

FML Family Problems
IPP Interpersonal Passivity
SAV Social Avoidance
SHY Shyness
DSF Disaffiliativeness

AES Aesthetic-Literary Interests
MEC Mechanical-Physical Interests

FIGURE 11-1 Mr. J's MMPI-2-RF Clinical Settings Interpretive Report, continued

MMPI-2-RF PSY-5 Scales

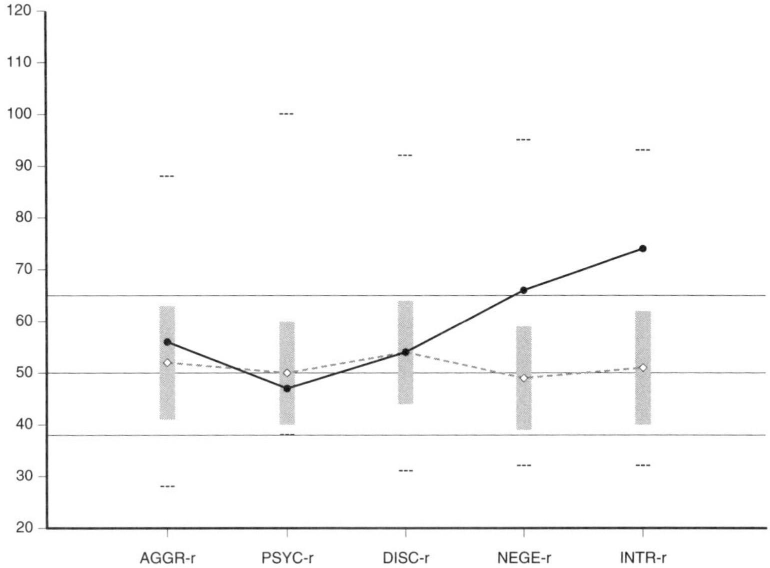

	AGGR-r	PSYC-r	DISC-r	NEGE-r	INTR-r
Raw Score:	11	1	8	12	14
T Score:	56	47	54	66	74
Response %:	100	100	100	100	100

Comparison Group Data: MMPI-2-RF Normative (Men), N = 1138

Mean Score (◇---◇):	52	50	54	49	51
Standard Dev (±1 SD):	11	10	10	10	11
Percent scoring at or below test taker:	73	53	60	95	97

The highest and lowest T scores possible on each scale are indicated by a "---"; MMPI-2-RF T scores are non-gendered.

AGGR-r Aggressiveness-Revised
PSYC-r Psychoticism-Revised
DISC-r Disconstraint-Revised
NEGE-r Negative Emotionality/Neuroticism-Revised
INTR-r Introversion/Low Positive Emotionality-Revised

FIGURE 11-1 Mr. J's MMPI-2-RF Clinical Settings Interpretive Report, continued

MMPI-2-RF® Interpretive Report: Clinical Settings
01/22/2016, Page 7 Mr. J

MMPI-2-RF T SCORES (BY DOMAIN)

PROTOCOL VALIDITY

Content Non-Responsiveness

CNS	VRIN-r	TRIN-r
0	58	57 F

Over-Reporting

F-r	Fp-r	Fs	FBS-r	RBS
65	51	50	42	59

Under-Reporting

L-r	K-r
42	31

SUBSTANTIVE SCALES

Somatic/Cognitive Dysfunction

RC1	MLS	GIC	HPC	NUC	COG
36	63	46	42	41	50

Emotional Dysfunction — EID 75

RCd	SUI	HLP	SFD	NFC
69	45	69	56	58

RC2	INTR-r
69	74

RC7	STW	AXY	ANP	BRF	MSF	NEGE-r
65	65	59	66	56	46	66

Thought Dysfunction — THD 48

RC6	RC8	PSYC-r
43	47	47

Behavioral Dysfunction — BXD 55

RC4	JCP	SUB
57	40	77

RC9	AGG	ACT	AGGR-r	DISC-r
50	73	39	56	54

Interpersonal Functioning

FML	RC3	IPP	SAV	SHY	DSF
58	65	52	80	66	58

Interests

AES	MEC
33	52

Note. This information is provided to facilitate interpretation following the recommended structure for MMPI-2-RF interpretation in Chapter 5 of the *MMPI-2-RF Manual for Administration, Scoring, and Interpretation*, which provides details in the text and an outline in Table 5-1.

FIGURE 11-1 Mr. J's MMPI-2-RF Clinical Settings Interpretive Report, continued

MMPI-2-RF® Interpretive Report: Clinical Settings
01/22/2016, Page 8 Mr. J

This interpretive report is intended for use by a professional qualified to interpret the MMPI-2-RF. The information it contains should be considered in the context of the test taker's background, the circumstances of the assessment, and other available information.

SYNOPSIS

This is a valid MMPI-2-RF protocol. Scores on the substantive scales indicate emotional, behavioral, and interpersonal dysfunction. Emotional-internalizing findings include risk for **suicidal ideation**, demoralization, depression, helplessness and hopelessness, stress and worry, and anger. Behavioral-externalizing problems include substance abuse and aggression. Interpersonal difficulties include social avoidance, social anxiety, and cynicism.

PROTOCOL VALIDITY

This is a valid MMPI-2-RF protocol. There are no problems with unscorable items. The test taker responded to the items relevantly on the basis of their content, and there are no indications of over- or under-reporting.

SUBSTANTIVE SCALE INTERPRETATION

Clinical symptoms, personality characteristics, and behavioral tendencies of the test taker are described in this section and organized according to an empirically guided framework. Statements containing the word "reports" are based on the item content of MMPI-2-RF scales, whereas statements that include the word "likely" are based on empirical correlates of scale scores. Specific sources for each statement can be accessed with the annotation features of this report.

Somatic/Cognitive Dysfunction

There are no indications of somatic or cognitive dysfunction in this protocol.

Emotional Dysfunction

The test taker's responses indicate significant and pervasive emotional distress[1]. He is at risk for suicidal ideation[2], although he did not endorse any of the MMPI-2-RF Suicidal/Death Ideation (SUI) scale items. He reports feeling sad and unhappy and being dissatisfied with his current life circumstances[3]. He is likely to complain of feeling depressed[4]. He also reports feeling hopeless[5]. He is likely to feel overwhelmed and that life is a strain[6], to believe he cannot be helped[6] and gets a raw deal from life[7], and to lack motivation for change[6]. He is also likely to be stress-reactive[8] and worry-prone[9] and to engage in obsessive rumination[10].

FIGURE 11-1 Mr. J's MMPI-2-RF Clinical Settings Interpretive Report, continued

MMPI-2-RF® Interpretive Report: Clinical Settings
01/22/2016, Page 9 Mr. J

He reports a lack of positive emotional experiences, significant anhedonia, and lack of interest[11]. He is likely to be pessimistic[12].

The test taker reports various negative emotional experiences[13] and is likely to be self-critical and guilt-prone[14]. He also reports being anger-prone[15]. He is indeed likely to have problems with anger, irritability, and low tolerance for frustration[16]; to hold grudges[17]; to have temper tantrums[17]; and to be argumentative and abusive[17].

Thought Dysfunction

There are no indications of disordered thinking in this protocol.

Behavioral Dysfunction

The test taker reports significant past and current substance abuse[18], and is indeed likely to have a history of problematic use of alcohol or drugs[19], to be sensation-seeking[20], and to have had legal problems as a result of substance abuse[20].

He reports engaging in physically aggressive, violent behavior and losing control[21], and is indeed likely to have a history of violent behavior toward others[22].

Interpersonal Functioning Scales

The test taker reports having cynical beliefs, distrust of others, and believing others look out only for their own interests[23]. He is likely to be hostile toward others[24] and feel alienated from them[25], and to have negative interpersonal experiences as a result of his cynical beliefs[26]. He also reports not enjoying social events and avoiding social situations, including parties and other events where crowds are likely to gather[27]. He is very likely to be introverted[28], to have difficulty forming close relationships[29], and to be emotionally restricted[30]. In addition, he reports being shy, easily embarrassed, and uncomfortable around others[31]. He is likely to be socially inhibited[32] and to be anxious and nervous in social situations[33].

Interest Scales

The test taker reports an average number of interests in activities or occupations of a mechanical or physical nature (e.g., fixing and building things, the outdoors, sports)[34]. He indicates little or no interest in activities or occupations of an aesthetic or literary nature (e.g., writing, music, the theater)[35].

DIAGNOSTIC CONSIDERATIONS

This section provides recommendations for psychodiagnostic assessment based on the test taker's MMPI-2-RF results. It is recommended that he be evaluated for the following:

Emotional-Internalizing Disorders

- Depression-related disorder[36]
- Disorders involving excessive stress and worry such as obsessive-compulsive disorder[37]
- Anxiety-related disorders[38]
- Anger-related disorders[39]

FIGURE 11-1 Mr. J's MMPI-2-RF Clinical Settings Interpretive Report, continued

Behavioral-Externalizing Disorders

- Substance-related disorders[40]
- Disorders associated with interpersonally aggressive behavior such as intermittent explosive disorder[41]

Interpersonal Disorders

- Personality disorders involving mistrust of and hostility toward others[42]
- Disorders associated with social avoidance such as avoidant personality disorder[43]
- Social phobia[44]

TREATMENT CONSIDERATIONS

This section provides inferential treatment-related recommendations based on the test taker's MMPI-2-RF scores.

Areas for Further Evaluation

- Need for antidepressant medication[45].

Psychotherapy Process Issues

- Emotional difficulties may motivate him for treatment[46].
- Cynicism may interfere with forming or seeking a therapeutic relationship[47].

Possible Targets for Treatment

- Loss of hope and feelings of despair as early targets for intervention[48]
- Psychological distress as an initial target[49]
- Stress management and excessive worry and rumination[50]
- Anhedonia[51]
- Dysfunctional negative emotions[52]
- Anger management[39]
- Reduction or cessation of substance abuse[53]
- Reduction in interpersonally aggressive behavior[41]
- Lack of interpersonal trust[42]
- Difficulties associated with social avoidance[54]
- Anxiety in social situations[55]

FIGURE 11-1 Mr. J's MMPI-2-RF Clinical Settings Interpretive Report, continued

ENDNOTES

This section lists for each statement in the report the MMPI-2-RF score(s) that triggered it. In addition, each statement is identified as a Test Response, if based on item content, a Correlate, if based on empirical correlates, or an Inference, if based on the report authors' judgment. (This information can also be accessed on-screen by placing the cursor on a given statement.) For correlate-based statements, research references (Ref. No.) are provided, keyed to the consecutively numbered reference list following the endnotes.

[1] Correlate: EID=75, Ref. 17, 31
[2] Correlate: RCd=69, Ref. 2, 4, 14, 30, 31
[3] Test Response: RCd=69
[4] Correlate: RCd=69, Ref. 2, 4, 5, 6, 8, 9, 11, 12, 14, 16, 19, 22, 25, 27, 29, 30, 31, 32, 33, 35, 36; RC2=69, Ref. 2, 4, 5, 6, 9, 11, 12, 14, 16, 22, 25, 27, 29, 30, 31, 32, 33, 35, 36; INTR-r=74, Ref. 31
[5] Test Response: HLP=69
[6] Correlate: HLP=69, Ref. 31
[7] Correlate: RCd=69, Ref. 31; HLP=69, Ref. 31
[8] Correlate: RC7=65, Ref. 24, 28, 31; STW=65, Ref. 6, 7, 31
[9] Correlate: STW=65, Ref. 31
[10] Correlate: RC7=65, Ref. 10, 25, 27, 31, 32; STW=65, Ref. 31
[11] Test Response: RC2=69; INTR-r=74
[12] Correlate: RC2=69, Ref. 10, 31; HLP=69, Ref. 31; INTR-r=74, Ref. 31
[13] Test Response: RC7=65; NEGE-r=66
[14] Correlate: RC7=65, Ref. 31; NEGE-r=66, Ref. 31
[15] Test Response: ANP=66
[16] Correlate: RC7=65, Ref. 9, 10, 26, 31, 32; ANP=66, Ref. 6, 13, 22, 31
[17] Correlate: ANP=66, Ref. 31
[18] Test Response: SUB=77
[19] Correlate: SUB=77, Ref. 5, 6, 31
[20] Correlate: SUB=77, Ref. 31
[21] Test Response: AGG=73
[22] Correlate: AGG=73, Ref. 31
[23] Test Response: RC3=65
[24] Correlate: RC3=65, Ref. 3, 11, 15, 26, 31
[25] Correlate: RC3=65, Ref. 7, 15, 24, 31
[26] Correlate: RC3=65, Ref. 9, 31
[27] Test Response: SAV=80
[28] Correlate: SAV=80, Ref. 3, 31; SHY=66, Ref. 3, 31
[29] Correlate: SAV=80, Ref. 13, 31
[30] Correlate: SAV=80, Ref. 31
[31] Test Response: SHY=66
[32] Correlate: SHY=66, Ref. 3, 31
[33] Correlate: SHY=66, Ref. 3, 6, 13, 31
[34] Test Response: MEC=52
[35] Test Response: AES=33

FIGURE 11-1 Mr. J's MMPI-2-RF Clinical Settings Interpretive Report, continued

[36] Correlate: RCd=69, Ref. 18, 23, 30, 31, 34; RC2=69, Ref. 18, 23, 30, 31, 34; INTR-r=74, Ref. 31
[37] Correlate: STW=65, Ref. 34
[38] Correlate: RC7=65, Ref. 25, 32, 34
[39] Inference: ANP=66
[40] Correlate: SUB=77, Ref. 5, 34
[41] Inference: AGG=73
[42] Inference: RC3=65
[43] Correlate: SAV=80, Ref. 34
[44] Correlate: RC7=65, Ref. 32; SHY=66, Ref. 31
[45] Correlate: RC2=69, Ref. 31; INTR-r=74, Ref. 31
[46] Correlate: RC7=65, Ref. 20, 21
[47] Correlate: RC3=65, Ref. 1
[48] Inference: HLP=69
[49] Inference: RCd=69
[50] Inference: STW=65
[51] Inference: RC2=69; INTR-r=74
[52] Inference: RC7=65; NEGE-r=66
[53] Inference: SUB=77
[54] Inference: SAV=80
[55] Inference: SHY=66

FIGURE 11-1 Mr. J's MMPI-2-RF Clinical Settings Interpretive Report, continued

MMPI-2-RF® Interpretive Report: Clinical Settings
01/22/2016, Page 13 Mr. J

RESEARCH REFERENCE LIST

1. Arbisi, P. A., Rusch, L., Polusny, M. A., Thuras, P. & Erbes, C. R. (2013). Does cynicism play a role in failure to obtain needed care? Mental health service utilization among returning U.S. National Guard soldiers. *Psychological Assessment, 25,* 991-996. doi: 10.1037/a0032225

2. Arbisi, P. A., Sellbom, M., & Ben-Porath, Y. S. (2008). Empirical correlates of the MMPI-2 Restructured Clinical (RC) Scales in psychiatric inpatients. *Journal of Personality Assessment, 90,* 122-128. doi: 10.1080/00223890701845146

3. Ayearst, L. E., Sellbom, M., Trobst, K. K., & Bagby, R. M. (2013). Evaluating the interpersonal content of the MMPI-2-RF Interpersonal Scales. *Journal of Personality Assessment, 95,* 187-196. doi: 10.1080/00223891.2012.730085

4. Binford, A., & Liljequist, L. (2008). Behavioral correlates of selected MMPI-2 Clinical, Content, and Restructured Clinical scales. *Journal of Personality Assessment, 90,* 608-614. doi: 10.1080/00223890802388657

5. Block, A. R., Ben-Porath, Y. S., & Marek, R. J. (2013). Psychological risk factors for poor outcome of spine surgery and spinal cord stimulator implant: A review of the literature and their assessment with the MMPI-2-RF. *The Clinical Neuropsychologist, 27,* 81-107. doi: 10.1080/13854046.2012.721007

6. Burchett, D. L., & Ben-Porath, Y. S. (2010). The impact of over-reporting on MMPI-2-RF substantive scale score validity. *Assessment, 17,* 497-516. doi: 10.1177/1073191110378972

7. Cox, A, Pant, H., Gilson, A. N., Rodriguez, J. L., Young, K. R., Kwon, S., & Weed, N. C., (2012). Effects of augmenting response options on MMPI-2 RC Scale psychometrics. *Journal of Personality Assessment, 94,* 613-619. doi: 10.1080/00223891.2012.700464

8. Erbes, C. R., Polusny, M. A., Arbisi, P. A., & Koffel, E. (2012). PTSD symptoms in a cohort of National Guard Soldiers deployed to Iraq: Evidence for nonspecific and specific components. *Journal of Affective Disorders, 142,* 269-274. doi: 10.1016/j.jad.2012.05.013

9. Forbey, J. D., Arbisi, P. A., & Ben-Porath, Y. S. (2012). The MMPI-2 computer adaptive version (MMPI-2-CA) in a VA medical outpatient facility. *Psychological Assessment, 24,* 628-639. doi: 10.1037/a0026509

10. Forbey, J. D., & Ben-Porath, Y. S. (2007). A comparison of the MMPI-2 Restructured Clinical (RC) and Clinical Scales in a substance abuse treatment sample. *Psychological Services, 4,* 46-58. doi: 10.1037/1541-1559.4.1.46

11. Forbey, J. D., & Ben-Porath, Y. S. (2008). Empirical correlates of the MMPI-2 Restructured Clinical (RC) Scales in a non-clinical setting. *Journal of Personality Assessment, 90,* 136-141. doi: 10.1080/00223890701845161

12. Forbey, J. D., Ben-Porath, Y. S., & Gartland, D. (2009). Validation of the MMPI-2 Computerized Adaptive Version (MMPI-2-CA) in a correctional intake facility. *Psychological Services, 6,* 279-292. doi: 10.1037/a0016195

FIGURE 11-1 Mr. J's MMPI-2-RF Clinical Settings Interpretive Report, continued

13. Forbey, J. D., Lee, T. T. C., & Handel, R. W. (2010). Correlates of the MMPI-2-RF in a college setting. *Psychological Assessment, 22,* 737-744. doi: 10.1037/a0020645

14. Handel, R. W., & Archer, R. P. (2008). An investigation of the psychometric properties of the MMPI-2 Restructured Clinical (RC) Scales with mental health inpatients. *Journal of Personality Assessment, 90,* 239-249. doi: 10.1080/00223890701884954

15. Ingram, P. B., Kelso, K. M., & McCord, D. M. (2011). Empirical correlates and expanded interpretation of the MMPI-2-RF Restructured Clinical Scale 3 (Cynicism). *Assessment, 18,* 95-101. doi: 10.1177/1073191110388147

16. Kamphuis, J. H., Arbisi, P. A., Ben-Porath, Y. S., & McNulty, J. L. (2008). Detecting comorbid Axis-II status among inpatients using the MMPI-2 Restructured Clinical Scales. *European Journal of Psychological Assessment, 24,* 157-164. doi: 10.1027/1015-5759.24.3.157

17. Lanyon, R. I., & Thomas, M. L. (2013). Assessment of global psychiatric categories: The PSI/PSI-2 and the MMPI-2-RF. *Psychological Assessment, 25,* 227-232. doi: 10.1037/a0030313

18. McCord, D. M., & Drerup, L. C. (2011). Relative practical utility of the Minnesota Multiphasic Personality Inventory-2 Restructured Clinical Scales versus the Clinical Scales in a chronic pain patient sample. *Journal of Clinical and Experimental Neuropsychology, 33,* 140-146. doi: 10.1080/13803395.2010.495056

19. McDevitt-Murphy, M. E., Weathers, F. W., Flood, A. M., Eakin, D. E., & Benson, T. A. (2007). The utility of the PAI and the MMPI-2 for discriminating PTSD, depression, and social phobia in trauma-exposed college students. *Assessment, 14,* 181-195. doi: 10.1177/1073191106295914

20. Scholte, W., Tiemens, B. G., Verheul, R., Meerman, A., Egger, J., & Hutschemaekers, G. (2012a). The RC Scales predict psychotherapy outcomes: The predictive validity of the MMPI-2's restructured clinical scales for psychotherapeutic outcomes. *Personality and Mental Health, 6,* 292-302. doi: 10.1002/pmh.1190

21. Scholte, W., Tiemens, B. G., Verheul, R., Meerman, A., Egger, J., & Hutschemaekers, G. (2012b). Predictive validity of the MMPI-2 Clinical, PSY-5, and RC Scales for therapy disruptive behavior. *Journal of Psychiatric Practice, 18(6),* 420-429. doi: 10.1097/01.pra.0000422740.87495.91

22. Sellbom, M., Anderson, J. L., & Bagby, R. M. (2013). Assessing DSM-5 Section III Personality Traits and Disorders with the MMPI-2-RF. *Assessment, 20,* 709-722. doi: 10.1177/1073191113508808

23. Sellbom, M., Bagby, R. M., Kushner, S., Quilty, L. C., & Ayearst, L. E. (2011). Diagnostic construct validity of the MMPI-2 Restructured Form (MMPI-2-RF) scale scores. *Assessment, 19,* 176-186. doi: 10.1177/1073191111428763

24. Sellbom, M., & Ben-Porath, Y. S. (2005). Mapping the MMPI-2 Restructured Clinical (RC) Scales onto normal personality traits: Evidence of construct validity. *Journal of Personality Assessment, 85,* 179-187. doi: 10.1207/s15327752jpa8502_10

FIGURE 11-1 Mr. J's MMPI-2-RF Clinical Settings Interpretive Report, continued

25. Sellbom, M., Ben-Porath, Y. S., & Bagby, R. M. (2008). On the hierarchical structure of mood and anxiety disorders: Confirmatory evidence and elaboration of a model of temperament markers. *Journal of Abnormal Psychology, 117,* 576-590. doi: 10.1037/a0012536

26. Sellbom, M., Ben-Porath, Y. S., & Bagby, R. M. (2008). Personality and psychopathology: Mapping the MMPI-2 Restructured Clinical (RC) Scales onto the five factor model of personality. *Journal of Personality Disorders, 22,* 291-312. doi: 10.1521/pedi.2008.22.3.291

27. Sellbom, M., Ben-Porath, Y. S., & Graham, J. R. (2006). Correlates of the MMPI-2 Restructured Clinical (RC) Scales in a college counseling setting. *Journal of Personality Assessment, 86,* 89-99. doi: 10.1207/s15327752jpa8601_10

28. Sellbom, M., Ben-Porath, Y. S., Lilienfeld, S. O., Patrick, C. J., & Graham, J. R. (2005). Assessing psychopathic personality traits with the MMPI-2. *Journal of Personality Assessment, 85,* 334-343. doi: 10.1207/s15327752jpa8503_10

29. Sellbom, M., Graham, J. R., & Schenk, P. (2006). Incremental validity of the MMPI-2 Restructured Clinical (RC) Scales in a private practice sample. *Journal of Personality Assessment, 86,* 196-205. doi: 10.1207/s15327752jpa8602_09

30. Simms, L. J., Casillas, A., Clark, L. A., Watson, D., & Doebbeling, B. I. (2005). Psychometric evaluation of the Restructured Clinical Scales of the MMPI-2. *Psychological Assessment, 17,* 345-358. doi: 10.1037/1040-3590.17.3.345

31. Tellegen, A., & Ben-Porath, Y. S. (2008/2011). *The Minnesota Multiphasic Personality Inventory-2-Restructured Form (MMPI-2-RF): Technical manual.* Minneapolis: University of Minnesota Press.

32. Tellegen, A., Ben-Porath, Y. S., Sellbom, M., Arbisi, P. A., McNulty, J. L., & Graham, J. R. (2006). Further evidence on the validity of the MMPI-2 Restructured Clinical (RC) Scales: Addressing questions raised by Rogers et al. and Nichols. *Journal of Personality Assessment, 87,* 148-171. doi: 10.1207/s15327752jpa8702_04

33. Vachon, D. D., Sellbom, M., Ryder, A. G., Miller, J. D., & Bagby, R. M. (2009). A Five-Factor Model description of depressive personality disorder. *Journal of Personality Disorders, 23,* 447-465. doi: 10.1521/pedi.2009.23.5.447

34. Van der Heijden, P. T., Egger, J. I. M., Rossi, G., Grundel, G., & Derksen, J. J. L. (2013). The MMPI-2 Restructured Form and the standard MMPI-2 Clinical Scales in relation to DSM-IV. *European Journal of Psychological Assessment, 29,* 182-188. doi: 10.1027/1015-5759/a000140

35. Wolf, E. J., Miller, M. W., Orazem, R. J., Weierich, M. R., Castillo, D. T., Milford, J., Kaloupek, D. G., & Keane, T. M. (2008). The MMPI-2 Restructured Clinical Scales in the assessment of posttraumatic stress disorder and comorbid disorders. *Psychological Assessment, 20,* 327-340. doi: 10.1037/a0012948

FIGURE 11-1 Mr. J's MMPI-2-RF Clinical Settings Interpretive Report, continued

36. Wygant, D. B., Boutacoff, L. A., Arbisi, P. A., Ben-Porath, Y. S., Kelly, P. H., & Rupp, W. M. (2007). Examination of the MMPI-2 Restructured Clinical (RC) Scales in a sample of bariatric surgery candidates. *Journal of Clinical Psychology in Medical Settings, 14,* 197-205. doi: 10.1007/s10880-007-9073-8

End of Report

This and previous pages of this report contain trade secrets and are not to be released in response to requests under HIPAA (or any other data disclosure law that exempts trade secret information from release). Further, release in response to litigation discovery demands should be made only in accordance with your profession's ethical guidelines and under an appropriate protective order.

FIGURE 11-1 Mr. J's MMPI-2-RF Clinical Settings Interpretive Report, continued

ITEM RESPONSES

1: 1	2: 1	3: 2	4: 2	5: 2	6: 2	7: 1	8: 1	9: 2	10: 1
11: 2	12: 2	13: 2	14: 2	15: 2	16: 1	17: 2	18: 2	19: 1	20: 2
21: 2	22: 1	23: 2	24: 2	25: 1	26: 1	27: 1	28: 1	29: 1	30: 1
31: 2	32: 2	33: 2	34: 2	35: 1	36: 1	37: 2	38: 1	39: 1	40: 2
41: 1	42: 2	43: 2	44: 1	45: 1	46: 2	47: 2	48: 2	49: 1	50: 2
51: 1	52: 1	53: 1	54: 2	55: 1	56: 1	57: 2	58: 1	59: 1	60: 1
61: 2	62: 2	63: 1	64: 2	65: 1	66: 2	67: 1	68: 1	69: 1	70: 1
71: 2	72: 1	73: 2	74: 2	75: 2	76: 2	77: 2	78: 1	79: 2	80: 1
81: 2	82: 1	83: 2	84: 1	85: 2	86: 2	87: 2	88: 1	89: 1	90: 2
91: 2	92: 2	93: 2	94: 2	95: 1	96: 2	97: 2	98: 1	99: 1	100: 2
101: 2	102: 1	103: 1	104: 1	105: 2	106: 2	107: 1	108: 1	109: 2	110: 2
111: 2	112: 1	113: 1	114: 1	115: 1	116: 1	117: 1	118: 1	119: 1	120: 2
121: 1	122: 2	123: 1	124: 2	125: 1	126: 2	127: 1	128: 1	129: 2	130: 1
131: 2	132: 2	133: 2	134: 2	135: 1	136: 1	137: 2	138: 1	139: 2	140: 1
141: 1	142: 2	143: 2	144: 1	145: 2	146: 2	147: 2	148: 2	149: 2	150: 2
151: 2	152: 2	153: 2	154: 1	155: 1	156: 1	157: 1	158: 2	159: 2	160: 1
161: 2	162: 1	163: 2	164: 2	165: 2	166: 2	167: 2	168: 2	169: 1	170: 2
171: 1	172: 1	173: 2	174: 1	175: 2	176: 2	177: 1	178: 2	179: 2	180: 2
181: 2	182: 2	183: 1	184: 1	185: 1	186: 1	187: 1	188: 1	189: 1	190: 1
191: 2	192: 1	193: 2	194: 2	195: 1	196: 2	197: 1	198: 2	199: 2	200: 2
201: 2	202: 2	203: 2	204: 1	205: 2	206: 1	207: 2	208: 2	209: 2	210: 2
211: 1	212: 1	213: 1	214: 2	215: 1	216: 2	217: 2	218: 2	219: 2	220: 2
221: 1	222: 2	223: 2	224: 2	225: 2	226: 2	227: 1	228: 1	229: 2	230: 2
231: 2	232: 1	233: 2	234: 2	235: 2	236: 2	237: 2	238: 2	239: 2	240: 2
241: 1	242: 2	243: 2	244: 2	245: 2	246: 1	247: 2	248: 2	249: 1	250: 1
251: 2	252: 2	253: 2	254: 1	255: 2	256: 1	257: 2	258: 2	259: 2	260: 2
261: 1	262: 2	263: 1	264: 2	265: 1	266: 2	267: 2	268: 2	269: 1	270: 2
271: 1	272: 2	273: 2	274: 2	275: 2	276: 1	277: 2	278: 1	279: 1	280: 2
281: 2	282: 1	283: 1	284: 2	285: 2	286: 1	287: 2	288: 2	289: 2	290: 1
291: 2	292: 2	293: 1	294: 2	295: 2	296: 2	297: 1	298: 2	299: 1	300: 1
301: 2	302: 2	303: 1	304: 1	305: 1	306: 2	307: 2	308: 2	309: 1	310: 2
311: 2	312: 2	313: 1	314: 2	315: 1	316: 1	317: 2	318: 1	319: 2	320: 1
321: 2	322: 1	323: 2	324: 1	325: 1	326: 1	327: 2	328: 2	329: 1	330: 2
331: 2	332: 2	333: 1	334: 2	335: 1	336: 1	337: 1	338: 1		

FIGURE 11-1 Mr. J's MMPI-2-RF Clinical Settings Interpretive Report, continued

Diagnostic considerations supported by the scale scores include depression-related disorders; disorders involving excessive stress and worry, such as obsessive-compulsive disorder, anxiety-related disorders, anger-related disorders; substance-related disorders; and disorders associated with interpersonally aggressive behavior, such as intermittent explosive disorder, personality disorders involving mistrust of and hostility toward others, disorders associated with social avoidance such as avoidant personality disorder, and social phobia.

Mr. J's MMPI-2-RF results indicate that his problems lie principally in the Emotional/Internalizing domain. Comparison group results reported on page 3 of Figure 11-1 indicate that 99% of the 1,138 men who make up the male MMPI-2-RF normative sample scored the same as or below Mr. J on the Emotional/Internalizing Dysfunction (EID) Scale. His score on the relevant RC Scales—Demoralization (RCd), Low Positive Emotions (RC2), and Dysfunctional Negative Emotions (RC7)—indicate that he is feeling sad, unhappy, and dissatisfied with his life circumstances; is anhedonic; and experiences a range of negative emotions. Also relevant is Mr. J's score on the Cynicism (RC3) scale, which is consistent with his self-reported cynical beliefs, indicating that he is distrustful of others and believes that others look out only for their own interests—all of which is consistent with Mr. J's disclosures in the clinical interview. The Internalizing Specific Problems scales further identify problems with helplessness and hopelessness, which can be associated with suicidal ideation but which Mr. J denied in responding to the test items (as indicated by a raw score of zero on the SUI scale). There are also findings indicating problems with stress and worry, and anger proneness.

In the externalizing domain, Mr. J's scores identify problems in the areas of substance abuse and physically aggressive behavior, a particularly worrisome combination. Interpersonally, his scores indicate extreme social avoidance, possibly rising to the level of an Avoidant Personality Disorder, as well as social anxiety.

Mr. J's demoralization may be a reaction to the occupational consequences he has faced as a result of the index incident, but his statements in the interview suggest that it also is a function of the duration of his despair, the broadening reach of his problems (i.e., sleep, substance use, and family, social, and work life), and the absence of any clear path to resolution.

Data Integration

STEP 1: ASSESSING FOR A MENTAL HEALTH CONDITION

In every case in which a public safety employee's MMPI-2-RF scores are clinically elevated, it is important to consider the possibility of motive, particularly the possibility of secondary gain for feigning a disability. Both Mr. J's MMPI-2-RF Validity Scale scores and his presentation in the interview indicate an absence of symptom exaggeration or feigning, or the motivation to do so.

The collective findings from test results, clinical presentation in the interview, and therapy records converge to indicate that Mr. J suffers from a clinically significant condition that impairs his functioning in the emotional/internalizing, behavioral/externalizing, and interpersonal domains. In particular, they are consistent with the treating psychologist's diagnosis of PTSD. Additionally, the FFD examiner preliminarily diagnosed "unspecified mood disorder" and "alcohol use disorder," both secondary to chronic PTSD. Of course, diagnosis requires a detailed review of evidence across multiple sources to confirm that the diagnostic criteria for a hypothesized condition have been met. In the case of Mr. J, the examiner determined that the criteria for PTSD were satisfied by the accumulation of findings in the MMPI-2-RF, the clinical interview, other assessment tools (e.g., the Detailed Assessment of Posttraumatic Stress [Briere, 2001] and the Clinician-Administered PTSD Scale for DSM-5 [Weathers et al., 2013]), and therapy records, and by ruling out alternative explanations for his symptoms. But even in cases in which a specific diagnosis cannot be ascertained to a requisite degree of medical certainty—sometimes necessitating the use of general categorical labels (e.g., the use of "other" and "unspecified" diagnoses)—the aggregate clinical evidence may still establish convincingly, as with Mr. J, the presence of a mental health condition affecting mood and behavior.[1]

STEP 2: ASSESSING FOR CURRENT WORK IMPAIRMENT

The second step in the integrative process addresses whether Mr. J's condition substantially limits his *current* ability to perform the essential functions of the job, to perform them properly, or to perform them without posing a direct threat to himself or others. We begin this analysis with the index incident. In every FFDE in which the referral was precipitated by the employer's (a) conclusion that the employee engaged in impermissible behavior and (b) belief that the behavior may be caused by a mental health condition, the most parsimonious path in this second step of analysis is to assess whether the mental health condition identified in the first step is both causally linked to the index incident and, if unresolved, likely to lead to the same or similar behavior in the foreseeable future.

Findings from the MMPI-2-RF indicate that Mr. J's anxiety, mood, and substance use symptoms are ongoing. Although he has started treatment, it has not yet resulted in symptom amelioration, much less syndromal remission. Assessing the nexus between a mental health condition and work impairment requires an understanding of both the natural course of the condition (i.e., how it typically manifests, what systems are typically affected by it, symptom intransigence, treatment effectiveness) and how it interacts with the individual's particular personality, life circumstances, and treatment engagement. Both PTSD and depression are known to manifest in irritability, and PTSD in particular is known to be associated with poor anger management, low impulse control, and alcohol use problems. For some individuals, the co-occurrence of PTSD and depression may be best conceptualized as a general traumatic stress response, rather than separate conditions and as having a shared predictive course (O'Donnell, Creamer, & Pattison, 2004).

The clinical evidence establishes a compelling nexus between Mr. J's symptoms and the index incident. Furthermore, there is no clinical basis for believing that Mr. J's condition is now sufficiently controlled as to make it more likely than not that the same or similar response to provocation would be inhibited. Said another way, the probability of recurrence remains high. The parsimony of this analysis lies in linking the employee's condition to a recurrence of the index incident, rather than speculating about what other essential job functions might be impaired by his condition.

This is not to say that such speculation is never appropriate or needed in some situations. But when, as in this case, the behavior precipitating the FFDE referral is both causally linked to the employee's mental health condition and already identified by the employer as incompatible with acceptable performance as a firefighter/paramedic, the fitness analysis does not require more.

STEP 3: ASSESSING FOR SUSTAINABILITY OF FITNESS

The third step in the integrative process is required only in cases where the employee's episodic mental health condition is currently nonlimiting. Given the fact that Mr. J's condition substantially limits his current occupational functioning, this step is moot.

Conclusion

The aggregate evidence derived from all sources indicates that Mr. J is currently experiencing substantial impairment, including occupational impairment, as a result of a current mental health condition that causes dysregulation of his mood, behavior, and interpersonal relationships. In particular, his condition substantially limits his functioning in the dimensions of Emotional Control & Stress Tolerance, Impulse Control/Attention to Safety, Social Competence, and Decision-Making and Judgment. The examiner determined that Mr. J is unfit for duty.

Mr. O, Police Officer

Assessment Issues Presented

- A police officer with a single manic episode requiring hospitalization
- Integration of clinically nonelevated substantive scores on scales measuring psychopathology with clinical evidence related to future risk

Referral Summary

Mr. O is an unmarried police officer with 7 years of experience in law enforcement, all with the same employer, a large, urban police agency. While on solo patrol duty and in uniform at about 2:30 a.m., Mr. O sent a mobile data terminal (MDT) message to a fellow patrol officer, stating that "something big is going to come down" and they needed to talk. They met in an empty parking lot, where Mr. O's fellow officer found him uncharacteristically loud, agitated, speaking rapidly about being "made" (identified) by rival neighborhood gangs, and talking unintelligibly about threats from "homegrown" domestic extremists, "media infiltrators," and an FBI sting operation. The other officer also knew Mr. O socially and knew him to be a reliably calm, humble, reserved, and professional officer. The fellow officer summoned their patrol sergeant, who on arriving at the scene and observing Mr. O, suspected that Mr. O was under the influence of a psychoactive substance and called for paramedics. The medical personnel evaluated Mr. O and found no indications of substance use or other physical explanations for his conduct. The sergeant and the fellow officer disarmed Mr. O and ordered him transported to the local hospital to be evaluated by a physician. While at the emergency department, Mr. O's bizarre conduct escalated, including overturning a medical supply tray in the examination room and shouting profanities at other patients. A psychiatrist evaluated Mr. O and ordered him admitted for involuntary examination and treatment. He was given injections of Haldol until his agitation subsided. Physical examination, including blood and urine analyses and a head CAT scan, found no physical explanation for his behavior. He was prescribed lithium, after which his symptoms progressively remitted. After 1 week, he was discharged to outpatient follow-up (medication and psychotherapy) with a diagnosis of Bipolar I Disorder (DSM-5 code 296.45, most recent episode manic, severe, with psychotic features).

Assessment Findings

EMPLOYMENT RECORDS

A review of Mr. O's employment records, including his complete personnel file and employee medical file, confirmed the absence of prior disciplinary actions. The available annual performance reviews reflected a stellar performance record and a strong reputation for reliability, work ethic, and an absence of citizen complaints. The records contained several commendations for exemplary service.

MENTAL STATUS EXAMINATION

Mr. O's appearance was unremarkable with regard to grooming, dress, weight, hair, and other features. His behavior also was unremarkable. His speech was normal, as indicated by its rate, intelligibility, volume, quality, and quantity. His affective expression was normal, and his mood was euphoric. Mr. O displayed no abnormalities with respect to his perception, thought process, sensorium and cognition, judgment, or reliability. However, his insight was poor, inasmuch as he denied having a mental health disorder. He denied past or current suicidal and homicidal ideation. His attitude toward the examiner was cooperative and friendly, but bordered on ingratiating.

CLINICAL INTERVIEW

The FFDE took place slightly more than 3 months after Mr. O's hospitalization for his manic episode (index incident). Mr. O explained that he had been "stressed out" the week before it occurred because he had failed to obtain a qualifying score on the sergeant promotional exam. He said he had not slept at all for 3 days before the exam because he was studying "every waking hour," and he also did not sleep during the 2 days after it (that is, immediately prior to the index incident) because he was "amped up" when he learned he had not earned a qualifying score. Mr. O lives alone.

Concerning his behavior during the index incident, Mr. O said he has only a vague memory of it. He said that whatever his sergeant and patrol partner reported, it "must be true because they wouldn't lie." He said that he does not use alcohol or other substances except for lithium, which he has taken daily as prescribed since he was discharged from the hospital. Mr. O reported that he is seeing his primary care physician for medication management and refills, but has not yet seen a therapist for outpatient counseling. He explained that he is "certain" that he will not have another episode like the index incident because he has decided not to pursue promotion, is no longer dating a "troubled" woman he had been seeing for 7 months but who broke up with him 2 weeks before the index incident (he said this also contributed to his difficulty sleeping and his "distractibility" during the exam), and he is starting to get his finances back together after paying off several credit cards that he had "maxed out." (Information gathered from collateral references and in a follow-up interview with Mr. O revealed that he had been making large purchases of luxury items on the Home Shopping Network, including expensive jewelry for his girlfriend.)

In response to the examiner's question concerning his diagnosis, Mr. O said that he "was never given a diagnosis" and believes that he had "some kind of breakdown" owing to the accumulation of stress but was "now okay." He said it was a "once-in-a-lifetime thing" resulting from sleep deprivation, financial worries, a relationship breakup, and work stress. He said he intends to see a counselor, but "it hasn't been a priority because I'm fine now, but I'll do whatever I need to do to get back to work."

MEDICAL RECORDS

A review of the records from Mr. O's involuntary hospitalization confirms reports of his psychotic behavior on admission and his gradual recovery over the course of his weeklong treatment. Clinical staff reported nonbizarre delusions, flight of ideas, thought derailment, and tangentiality; irritable mood, with negativism; garrulous and pressured speech; distractibility; and psychomotor agitation. During the 3 days following admission, he awoke seemingly rested after 3 hours of sleep, in spite of Haldol administration.

Records from Mr. O's primary care physician confirmed that he was continuing to receive an ongoing prescription for lithium. His physician reported that this was his first known manic episode, and he appears to have achieved full recovery. The examiner also spoke to Mr. O's treating physician and conducted a comprehensive review of the empirical literature on the long-term effectiveness of mood stabilizers.

MMPI-2-RF FINDINGS

Mr. O's MMPI-2-RF Clinical Settings Interpretive Report is reproduced in Figure 11-2. The report indicates that there are no unscorable items, and Mr. O responded to the MMPI-2-RF in a remarkably consistent manner, as indicated by his VRIN-r and TRIN-r scale scores (34T and 50T, respectively). There are no indications of overreporting in the protocol, and he claimed no uncommon virtues (i.e., his raw score on L-r was 0). However, consistent with his self-report in the clinical interview, he presented himself as well adjusted (K-r=62T). For a test taker with Mr. O's referral questions and documented evidence of a recent manic episode, this score indicates significant underreporting that renders nonelevated substantive scale scores uninterpretable. Indeed all of his scores on these scales were clinically nonelevated except for Social Avoidance (SAV=75T) and Introversion/Low Positive Emotionality-Revised (INTR-r=67T). These latter scale scores indicate that he reports not enjoying social events, avoids social situations, and has a lack of positive emotional experiences. The absence of elevation on MMPI-2-RF indicators of possible manic experiences reflects either an unwillingness to acknowledge these documented problems or a lack of insight.

Data Integration

STEP 1: ASSESSING FOR A MENTAL HEALTH CONDITION

Mr. O's contention is that he has no mental health condition because he has recovered from his recent "breakdown." This is a common but erroneous belief among laypersons and professionals alike—that the resolution of symptoms equates to resolution of the underlying disorder. The clinical evidence establishes convincingly that Mr. O meets the diagnostic criteria for Bipolar I Disorder, including a distinct period of abnormally and persistently elevated and irritable mood with psychotic features (the

MMPI 2 RF®

Minnesota Multiphasic
Personality Inventory-2
Restructured Form®

Interpretive Report: Clinical Settings

MMPI-2-RF®

Minnesota Multiphasic Personality Inventory-2-Restructured Form®

Yossef S. Ben-Porath, PhD, & Auke Tellegen, PhD

Name:	Mr. O
Age:	34
Gender:	Male
Marital Status:	Single
Years of Education:	16
Date Assessed:	10/30/2015

PsychCorp

Copyright © 2008, 2011, 2012 by the Regents of the University of Minnesota. All rights reserved. Distributed exclusively under license from the University of Minnesota by NCS Pearson, Inc. Portions reproduced from the MMPI-2-RF test booklet. Copyright © 2008 by the Regents of the University of Minnesota. All rights reserved. Portions excerpted from the *MMPI-2-RF Manual for Administration, Scoring, and Interpretation.* Copyright © 2008, 2011 by the Regents of the University of Minnesota. All rights reserved. Used by permission of the University of Minnesota Press.

MMPI-2-RF, the **MMPI-2-RF logo,** and **Minnesota Multiphasic Personality Inventory-2-Restructured Form** are registered trademarks of the University of Minnesota. **Pearson,** the **PSI logo,** and **PsychCorp** are trademarks in the U.S. and/or other countries of Pearson Education, Inc., or its affiliate(s).

TRADE SECRET INFORMATION
Not for release under HIPAA or other data disclosure laws that exempt trade secrets from disclosure.

[3.0 / 2 / QG]

ALWAYS LEARNING PEARSON

FIGURE 11-2 Mr. O's MMPI-2-RF Clinical Settings Interpretive Report

MMPI-2-RF® Interpretive Report: Clinical Settings
10/30/2015, Page 2 Mr. O

MMPI-2-RF Validity Scales

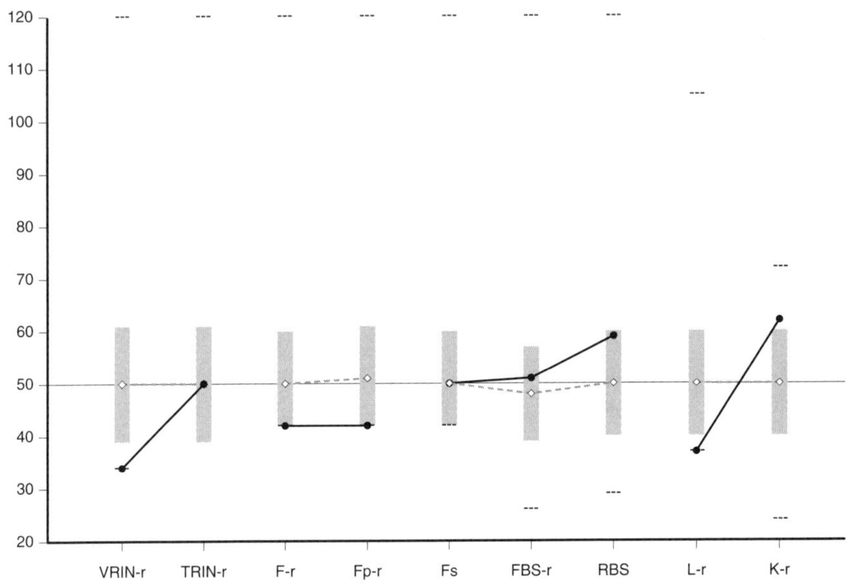

	VRIN-r	TRIN-r	F-r	Fp-r	Fs	FBS-r	RBS	L-r	K-r
Raw Score:	0	11	0	0	1	8	7	0	11
T Score:	34	50	42	42	50	51	59	37	62
Response %:	100	100	100	100	100	100	100	100	100

Cannot Say (Raw): 0 Percent True (of items answered): 32%

Comparison Group Data: MMPI-2-RF Normative (Men), N = 1138

	VRIN-r	TRIN-r	F-r	Fp-r	Fs	FBS-r	RBS	L-r	K-r
Mean Score (◇--◇):	50	50	50	51	50	48	50	50	50
Standard Dev (±1 SD):	11	11	10	10	10	9	10	10	10
Percent scoring at or below test taker:	6	40	35	47	74	76	86	13	91

The highest and lowest T scores possible on each scale are indicated by a "---"; MMPI-2-RF T scores are non-gendered.

VRIN-r	Variable Response Inconsistency	Fs	Infrequent Somatic Responses	L-r	Uncommon Virtues
TRIN-r	True Response Inconsistency	FBS-r	Symptom Validity	K-r	Adjustment Validity
F-r	Infrequent Responses	RBS	Response Bias Scale		
Fp-r	Infrequent Psychopathology Responses				

FIGURE 11-2 Mr. O's MMPI-2-RF Clinical Settings Interpretive Report, continued

MMPI-2-RF® Interpretive Report: Clinical Settings
10/30/2015, Page 3

Mr. O

MMPI-2-RF Higher-Order (H-O) and Restructured Clinical (RC) Scales

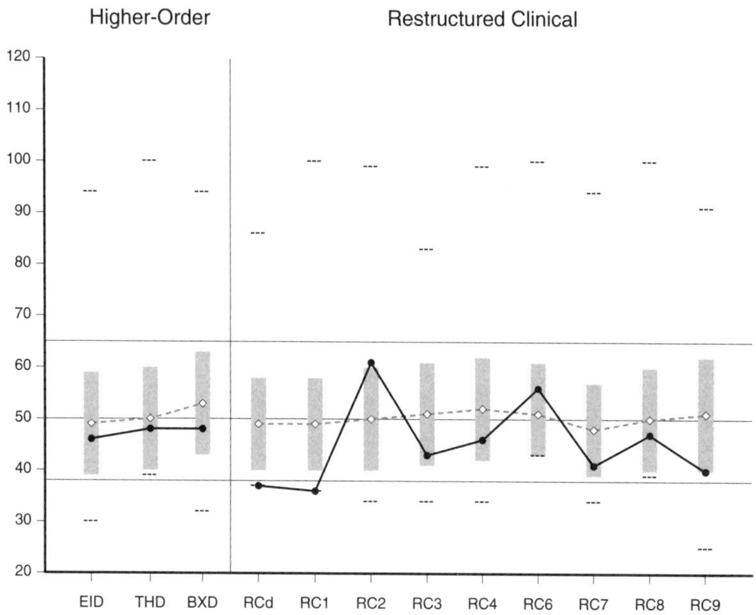

	EID	THD	BXD	RCd	RC1	RC2	RC3	RC4	RC6	RC7	RC8	RC9
Raw Score:	7	1	5	0	0	7	3	3	1	2	1	6
T Score:	46	48	48	37	36	61	43	46	56	41	47	40
Response %:	100	100	100	100	100	100	100	100	100	100	100	100

Comparison Group Data: MMPI-2-RF Normative (Men), N = 1138

	EID	THD	BXD	RCd	RC1	RC2	RC3	RC4	RC6	RC7	RC8	RC9
Mean Score (◇--◇):	49	50	53	49	49	50	51	52	51	48	50	51
Standard Dev (±1 SD):	10	10	10	9	9	10	10	10	10	9	10	11
Percent scoring at or below test taker:	45	57	40	17	17	89	26	35	79	26	53	13

The highest and lowest T scores possible on each scale are indicated by a "---"; MMPI-2-RF T scores are non-gendered.

EID Emotional/Internalizing Dysfunction
THD Thought Dysfunction
BXD Behavioral/Externalizing Dysfunction

RCd Demoralization
RC1 Somatic Complaints
RC2 Low Positive Emotions
RC3 Cynicism
RC4 Antisocial Behavior

RC6 Ideas of Persecution
RC7 Dysfunctional Negative Emotions
RC8 Aberrant Experiences
RC9 Hypomanic Activation

FIGURE 11-2 Mr. O's MMPI-2-RF Clinical Settings Interpretive Report, continued

MMPI-2-RF Somatic/Cognitive and Internalizing Scales

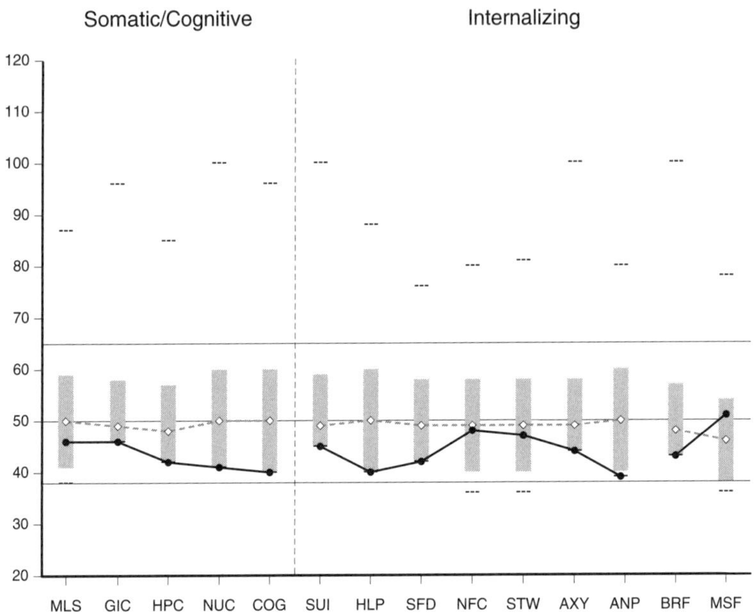

	MLS	GIC	HPC	NUC	COG	SUI	HLP	SFD	NFC	STW	AXY	ANP	BRF	MSF
Raw Score:	1	0	0	0	0	0	0	0	2	2	0	0	0	4
T Score:	46	46	42	41	40	45	40	42	48	47	44	39	43	51
Response %:	100	100	100	100	100	100	100	100	100	100	100	100	100	100

Comparison Group Data: MMPI-2-RF Normative (Men), N = 1138

	MLS	GIC	HPC	NUC	COG	SUI	HLP	SFD	NFC	STW	AXY	ANP	BRF	MSF
Mean Score (◇--◇):	50	49	48	50	50	49	50	49	49	49	49	50	48	46
Standard Dev (±1 SD):	9	9	9	10	10	10	10	9	9	9	9	10	9	8
Percent scoring at or below test taker:	54	84	57	46	37	83	43	53	59	58	75	30	67	82

The highest and lowest T scores possible on each scale are indicated by a "---"; MMPI-2-RF T scores are non-gendered.

MLS Malaise
GIC Gastrointestinal Complaints
HPC Head Pain Complaints
NUC Neurological Complaints
COG Cognitive Complaints
SUI Suicidal/Death Ideation
HLP Helplessness/Hopelessness
SFD Self-Doubt
NFC Inefficacy
STW Stress/Worry
AXY Anxiety
ANP Anger Proneness
BRF Behavior-Restricting Fears
MSF Multiple Specific Fears

FIGURE 11-2 Mr. O's MMPI-2-RF Clinical Settings Interpretive Report, continued

MMPI-2-RF Externalizing, Interpersonal, and Interest Scales

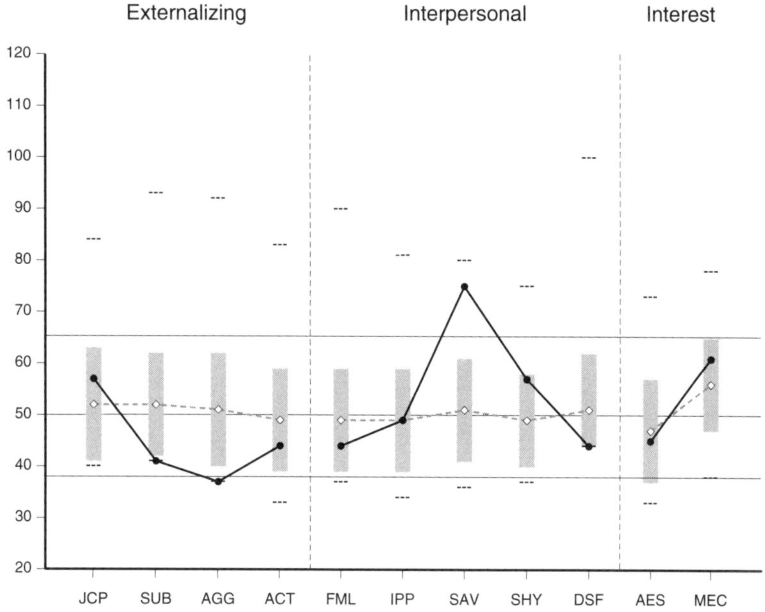

	JCP	SUB	AGG	ACT	FML	IPP	SAV	SHY	DSF	AES	MEC
Raw Score:	2	0	0	2	1	4	9	5	0	2	5
T Score:	57	41	37	44	44	49	75	57	44	45	61
Response %:	100	100	100	100	100	100	100	100	100	100	100

Comparison Group Data: MMPI-2-RF Normative (Men), N = 1138

	JCP	SUB	AGG	ACT	FML	IPP	SAV	SHY	DSF	AES	MEC
Mean Score (◇---◇):	52	52	51	49	49	49	51	49	51	47	56
Standard Dev (±1 SD):	11	10	11	10	10	10	10	9	11	10	9
Percent scoring at or below test taker:	79	33	20	41	46	67	99.0	88	67	55	77

The highest and lowest T scores possible on each scale are indicated by a "---"; MMPI-2-RF T scores are non-gendered.

JCP Juvenile Conduct Problems
SUB Substance Abuse
AGG Aggression
ACT Activation

FML Family Problems
IPP Interpersonal Passivity
SAV Social Avoidance
SHY Shyness
DSF Disaffiliativeness

AES Aesthetic-Literary Interests
MEC Mechanical-Physical Interests

FIGURE 11-2 Mr. O's MMPI-2-RF Clinical Settings Interpretive Report, continued

MMPI-2-RF® Interpretive Report: Clinical Settings
10/30/2015, Page 6

Mr. O

MMPI-2-RF PSY-5 Scales

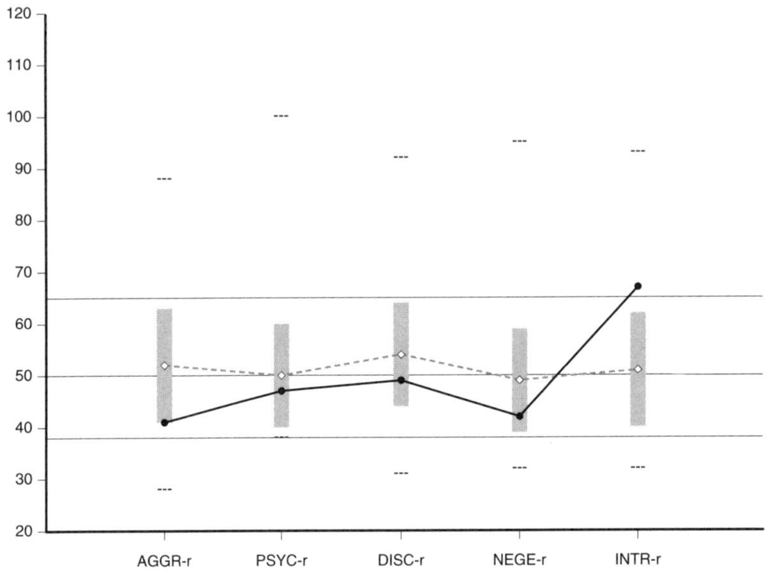

	AGGR-r	PSYC-r	DISC-r	NEGE-r	INTR-r
Raw Score:	5	1	6	3	12
T Score:	41	47	49	42	67
Response %:	100	100	100	100	100

Comparison Group Data: MMPI-2-RF Normative (Men), N = 1138

Mean Score (◇--◇):	52	50	54	49	51
Standard Dev (±1 SD):	11	10	10	10	11
Percent scoring at or below test taker:	15	53	40	31	93

The highest and lowest T scores possible on each scale are indicated by a "---"; MMPI-2-RF T scores are non-gendered.

AGGR-r Aggressiveness-Revised
PSYC-r Psychoticism-Revised
DISC-r Disconstraint-Revised
NEGE-r Negative Emotionality/Neuroticism-Revised
INTR-r Introversion/Low Positive Emotionality-Revised

FIGURE 11-2 Mr. O's MMPI-2-RF Clinical Settings Interpretive Report, continued

MMPI-2-RF T SCORES (BY DOMAIN)

PROTOCOL VALIDITY

Domain						
Content Non-Responsiveness	0 CNS	34 VRIN-r	50 TRIN-r			
Over-Reporting	42 F-r	42 Fp-r		50 Fs	51 FBS-r	59 RBS
Under-Reporting	37 L-r	62 K-r				

SUBSTANTIVE SCALES

Domain	Higher-order							
Somatic/Cognitive Dysfunction		36 RC1	46 MLS	46 GIC	42 HPC	41 NUC	40 COG	
Emotional Dysfunction	46 EID	37 RCd	45 SUI	40 HLP	42 SFD	48 NFC		
		61 RC2	67 INTR-r					
		41 RC7	47 STW	44 AXY	39 ANP	43 BRF	51 MSF	42 NEGE-r
Thought Dysfunction	48 THD	56 RC6						
		47 RC8						
		47 PSYC-r						
Behavioral Dysfunction	48 BXD	46 RC4	57 JCP	41 SUB				
		40 RC9	37 AGG	44 ACT	41 AGGR-r	49 DISC-r		
Interpersonal Functioning		44 FML	43 RC3	49 IPP	75 SAV	57 SHY	44 DSF	
Interests		45 AES	61 MEC					

Note. This information is provided to facilitate interpretation following the recommended structure for MMPI-2-RF interpretation in Chapter 5 of the *MMPI-2-RF Manual for Administration, Scoring, and Interpretation*, which provides details in the text and an outline in Table 5-1.

FIGURE 11-2 Mr. O's MMPI-2-RF Clinical Settings Interpretive Report, continued

MMPI-2-RF® Interpretive Report: Clinical Settings
10/30/2015, Page 8 Mr. O

This interpretive report is intended for use by a professional qualified to interpret the MMPI-2-RF. The information it contains should be considered in the context of the test taker's background, the circumstances of the assessment, and other available information.

SYNOPSIS

Scores on the MMPI-2-RF validity scales raise concerns about the possible impact of under-reporting on the validity of this protocol. With that caution noted, scores on the substantive scales indicate interpersonal dysfunction. Interpersonal difficulties relate to social avoidance.

PROTOCOL VALIDITY

Content Non-Responsiveness

There are no problems with unscorable items in this protocol. The test taker responded to the MMPI-2-RF in a remarkably consistent manner. He was deliberate in his approach to the assessment.

Over-Reporting

There are no indications of over-reporting in this protocol.

Under-Reporting

The test taker presented himself as well-adjusted. If there is evidence that this individual is not well adjusted, any absence of elevation on the substantive scales should be interpreted with caution[1]. Elevated scores on the substantive scales may underestimate the problems assessed by those scales[2].

SUBSTANTIVE SCALE INTERPRETATION

Clinical symptoms, personality characteristics, and behavioral tendencies of the test taker are described in this section and organized according to an empirically guided framework. Statements containing the word "reports" are based on the item content of MMPI-2-RF scales, whereas statements that include the word "likely" are based on empirical correlates of scale scores. Specific sources for each statement can be accessed with the annotation features of this report.

The following interpretation needs to be considered in light of cautions noted about the possible impact of under-reporting on the validity of this protocol.

FIGURE 11-2 Mr. O's MMPI-2-RF Clinical Settings Interpretive Report, continued

Somatic/Cognitive, Emotional, Thought, and Behavioral Dysfunction

There are no indications of somatic, cognitive, emotional, thought, or behavioral dysfunction in this protocol. However, because of indications of under-reporting described earlier, such problems cannot be ruled out.

Interpersonal Functioning Scales

The test taker reports not enjoying social events and avoiding social situations[3]. He is likely to be introverted[4], to have difficulty forming close relationships[5], and to be emotionally restricted[6].

Interest Scales

The test taker reports an average number of interests in activities or occupations of an aesthetic or literary nature (e.g., writing, music, the theater)[7]. He also reports an average number of interests in activities or occupations of a mechanical or physical nature (e.g., fixing and building things, the outdoors, sports)[8].

DIAGNOSTIC CONSIDERATIONS

This section provides recommendations for psychodiagnostic assessment based on the test taker's MMPI-2-RF results. It is recommended that he be evaluated for the following:

Interpersonal Disorders

- Disorders associated with social avoidance such as avoidant personality disorder[9]

TREATMENT CONSIDERATIONS

This section provides inferential treatment-related recommendations based on the test taker's MMPI-2-RF scores.

Possible Targets for Treatment

- Difficulties associated with social avoidance[10]

ITEM-LEVEL INFORMATION

Unscorable Responses

The test taker produced scorable responses to all the MMPI-2-RF items.

Critical Responses

Seven MMPI-2-RF scales--Suicidal/Death Ideation (SUI), Helplessness/Hopelessness (HLP), Anxiety (AXY), Ideas of Persecution (RC6), Aberrant Experiences (RC8), Substance Abuse (SUB), and Aggression (AGG)--have been designated by the test authors as having critical item content that may

FIGURE 11-2 Mr. O's MMPI-2-RF Clinical Settings Interpretive Report, continued

require immediate attention and follow-up. Items answered by the individual in the keyed direction (True or False) on a critical scale are listed below if his T score on that scale is 65 or higher.

The test taker has not produced an elevated T score (≥ 65) on any of these scales.

FIGURE 11-2 Mr. O's MMPI-2-RF Clinical Settings Interpretive Report, continued

ENDNOTES

This section lists for each statement in the report the MMPI-2-RF score(s) that triggered it. In addition, each statement is identified as a Test Response, if based on item content, a Correlate, if based on empirical correlates, or an Inference, if based on the report authors' judgment. (This information can also be accessed on-screen by placing the cursor on a given statement.) For correlate-based statements, research references (Ref. No.) are provided, keyed to the consecutively numbered reference list following the endnotes.

[1] Correlate: K-r=62, Ref. 4, 5
[2] Correlate: K-r=62, Ref. 2, 5, 6
[3] Test Response: SAV=75
[4] Correlate: SAV=75, Ref. 1, 6
[5] Correlate: SAV=75, Ref. 3, 6
[6] Correlate: SAV=75, Ref. 6
[7] Test Response: AES=45
[8] Test Response: MEC=61
[9] Correlate: SAV=75, Ref. 7
[10] Inference: SAV=75

FIGURE 11-2 Mr. O's MMPI-2-RF Clinical Settings Interpretive Report, continued

RESEARCH REFERENCE LIST

1. Ayearst, L. E., Sellbom, M., Trobst, K. K., & Bagby, R. M. (2013). Evaluating the interpersonal content of the MMPI-2-RF Interpersonal Scales. *Journal of Personality Assessment, 95,* 187-196. doi: 10.1080/00223891.2012.730085

2. Forbey, J. D., Lee, T. T. C., Ben-Porath, Y. S., Arbisi, P. A., & Gartland, D. (2013). Associations between MMPI-2-RF validity scale scores and extra-test measures of personality and psychopathology. *Assessment, 20,* 448-461. doi: 10.1177/1073191113478154

3. Forbey, J. D., Lee, T. T. C., & Handel, R. W. (2010). Correlates of the MMPI-2-RF in a college setting. *Psychological Assessment, 22,* 737-744. doi: 10.1037/a0020645

4. Marion, B. E., Sellbom, M., Salekin, R. T., Toomey, J. A., Kucharski, T., & Duncan, S. (2013). An examination of the association between psychopathy and dissimulation using the MMPI-2-RF Validity Scales. *Law and Human Behavior, 37,* 219-230. doi: 10.1037/lhb0000008

5. Sellbom, M., & Bagby, R. M. (2008). The validity of the MMPI-2-RF (Restructured Form) L-r and K-r scales in detecting under-reporting in clinical and non-clinical samples. *Psychological Assessment, 20,* 370-376. doi: 10.1037/a0012952

6. Tellegen, A., & Ben-Porath, Y. S. (2008/2011). *The Minnesota Multiphasic Personality Inventory-2-Restructured Form (MMPI-2-RF): Technical manual.* Minneapolis: University of Minnesota Press.

7. Van der Heijden, P. T., Egger, J. I. M., Rossi, G., Grundel, G., & Derksen, J. J. L. (2013). The MMPI-2 Restructured Form and the standard MMPI-2 Clinical Scales in relation to DSM-IV. *European Journal of Psychological Assessment, 29,* 182-188. doi: 10.1027/1015-5759/a000140

End of Report

This and previous pages of this report contain trade secrets and are not to be released in response to requests under HIPAA (or any other data disclosure law that exempts trade secret information from release). Further, release in response to litigation discovery demands should be made only in accordance with your profession's ethical guidelines and under an appropriate protective order.

FIGURE 11-2 Mr. O's MMPI-2-RF Clinical Settings Interpretive Report, continued

ITEM RESPONSES

1: 1	2: 1	3: 2	4: 1	5: 2	6: 2	7: 1	8: 1	9: 2	10: 2
11: 2	12: 2	13: 2	14: 2	15: 2	16: 1	17: 2	18: 2	19: 1	20: 2
21: 2	22: 2	23: 2	24: 2	25: 1	26: 2	27: 2	28: 1	29: 2	30: 2
31: 2	32: 2	33: 2	34: 2	35: 2	36: 2	37: 1	38: 1	39: 2	40: 2
41: 2	42: 2	43: 2	44: 1	45: 1	46: 2	47: 2	48: 2	49: 2	50: 2
51: 1	52: 1	53: 2	54: 2	55: 2	56: 2	57: 2	58: 1	59: 1	60: 1
61: 2	62: 2	63: 2	64: 1	65: 1	66: 1	67: 2	68: 1	69: 1	70: 1
71: 2	72: 1	73: 1	74: 2	75: 1	76: 2	77: 2	78: 1	79: 2	80: 1
81: 2	82: 2	83: 1	84: 2	85: 1	86: 2	87: 2	88: 1	89: 2	90: 2
91: 1	92: 2	93: 2	94: 1	95: 1	96: 2	97: 1	98: 1	99: 2	100: 2
101: 2	102: 1	103: 2	104: 1	105: 1	106: 2	107: 2	108: 2	109: 2	110: 2
111: 1	112: 2	113: 1	114: 1	115: 2	116: 1	117: 2	118: 2	119: 2	120: 2
121: 2	122: 2	123: 2	124: 2	125: 1	126: 1	127: 1	128: 1	129: 2	130: 2
131: 2	132: 2	133: 2	134: 1	135: 2	136: 2	137: 2	138: 2	139: 2	140: 1
141: 2	142: 1	143: 2	144: 2	145: 2	146: 2	147: 1	148: 2	149: 2	150: 2
151: 2	152: 2	153: 2	154: 1	155: 2	156: 2	157: 1	158: 2	159: 2	160: 2
161: 2	162: 1	163: 1	164: 2	165: 2	166: 2	167: 2	168: 2	169: 2	170: 2
171: 2	172: 2	173: 2	174: 1	175: 2	176: 2	177: 1	178: 2	179: 2	180: 2
181: 2	182: 2	183: 1	184: 1	185: 2	186: 1	187: 2	188: 2	189: 1	190: 2
191: 2	192: 2	193: 2	194: 1	195: 1	196: 1	197: 1	198: 2	199: 1	200: 2
201: 2	202: 2	203: 2	204: 2	205: 2	206: 2	207: 1	208: 2	209: 2	210: 2
211: 1	212: 1	213: 1	214: 2	215: 2	216: 2	217: 1	218: 2	219: 2	220: 2
221: 1	222: 2	223: 1	224: 2	225: 2	226: 1	227: 1	228: 2	229: 2	230: 2
231: 2	232: 2	233: 2	234: 2	235: 2	236: 2	237: 1	238: 2	239: 2	240: 2
241: 1	242: 2	243: 2	244: 1	245: 2	246: 1	247: 2	248: 2	249: 1	250: 2
251: 2	252: 2	253: 2	254: 1	255: 2	256: 2	257: 2	258: 2	259: 1	260: 2
261: 2	262: 1	263: 2	264: 2	265: 1	266: 2	267: 2	268: 2	269: 1	270: 2
271: 2	272: 1	273: 2	274: 2	275: 2	276: 2	277: 2	278: 1	279: 1	280: 2
281: 2	282: 1	283: 1	284: 2	285: 2	286: 1	287: 2	288: 2	289: 2	290: 1
291: 2	292: 2	293: 1	294: 2	295: 1	296: 1	297: 2	298: 1	299: 2	300: 2
301: 2	302: 2	303: 2	304: 2	305: 1	306: 2	307: 2	308: 2	309: 1	310: 2
311: 2	312: 2	313: 1	314: 2	315: 2	316: 2	317: 2	318: 2	319: 1	320: 1
321: 1	322: 2	323: 1	324: 1	325: 1	326: 2	327: 2	328: 2	329: 2	330: 2
331: 2	332: 2	333: 1	334: 2	335: 2	336: 2	337: 2	338: 2		

FIGURE 11-2 Mr. O's MMPI-2-RF Clinical Settings Interpretive Report, continued

duration is irrelevant if hospitalization is necessary), in which the following symptoms were present: decreased need for sleep, more talkative than usual or pressure to keep talking, flight of ideas, distractibility, psychomotor agitation, and excessive involvement in activities that have a high potential for painful consequences (e.g., engaging in unrestrained buying sprees). An individual hospitalized for a single manic episode continues to have Bipolar I Disorder, regardless of his or her postrecovery status.

STEP 2: ASSESSING FOR CURRENT WORK IMPAIRMENT

The clinical evidence suggests that Mr. O has recovered normal functioning following his index manic episode with psychotic features. But the duration of risk does not end with recovery from a chronic, episodic disorder that is substantially limiting when active and has a high likelihood of recurrence in substantially limiting forms, as discussed next.

STEP 3: ASSESSING FOR SUSTAINABILITY OF FITNESS

The third step in the integrative process is reserved for cases in which the employee's episodic mental health condition is currently nonimpairing. Although Bipolar I Disorder characteristically involves complete interepisode recovery (that is, a full remission of symptoms between manic episodes), it also has high rates of relapse chronicity (Angst & Sellaro, 2000). In a large longitudinal study (Coryell et al., 1995), for example, it was found that, 7 years after recovery, the cumulative likelihood of recurrence was 4 in 5 for all bipolar patients and 2 in 3 for those whose index episode had been followed by at least 3 years without symptoms. Bipolar disorder follows a relapsing course with, on average, approximately eight episodes over the 10 years following diagnosis in hospitalized samples (Goodwin, 2009). The lifetime risk of suicide in individuals with bipolar disorder is estimated to be at least 15 times that of the general population and may account for one-quarter of all completed suicides (*DSM-5*, p. 131); 25% to 50% of patients with bipolar disorder attempt suicide at least once in their lifetime; and 10% to 19% die as a result of suicide (Chen & Dilsaver, 1996; Jamison, 2000). Research shows that persons with bipolar disorder experience some degree of disability during the majority of time in long-term follow-up (54% to 59% of months), including 19% to 23%

of months with moderate and 7% to 9% of months with severe overall impairment (Judd et al., 2008).

Despite the development of new medications for treating bipolar disorder that have fewer side effects and greater effectiveness, treatment remains suboptimal, even among patients who adhere consistently to their treatment regimens (Batista, Baes, & Juruena, 2011). Longitudinal studies indicate that even when patients are protected by state-of-the-art pharmacotherapy, about 40% relapse in 1 year, 60% in 2 years, and 73% over 5 years. Thus, the duration of Mr. O's risk for Bipolar I Disorder relapse continues throughout his life, and the risk for harm resulting from his actions as a police officer when impaired by his condition endures for the remaining term of his career as a police officer. This risk is exacerbated by Mr. O's lack of insight into his condition (documented by the MMPI-2-RF results and in his clinical interview), which can result in discontinuation of medication that presently assists with its stabilization.

Conclusion

The aggregate clinical evidence derived from all sources indicates that Mr. O has recovered from a recent manic episode with psychotic features requiring hospitalization. However, Mr. O requires long-term treatment for Bipolar I Disorder, which is an episodic and recurrent mental health condition with a high risk of relapse. When symptomatic, his condition can lead to behavior with catastrophic consequences to him, his fellow officers, and the public in the context of his duties as a police officer. In particular, his condition impairs his functioning in the dimensions of Emotional Control & Stress Tolerance, Impulse Control/Attention to Safety, and Decision-Making and Judgment. These risks are aggravated by the fact that Mr. O is not receiving treatment consistent with best practices, which combines medication management with relapse prevention counseling (Goodwin, 2009), in part because he believes he does not have a mental condition requiring treatment. In consideration of all these facts, the examiner determined that Mr. O is unfit for duty.

Mr. H, Correctional Officer

Assessment Issues Presented

- Clinically nonelevated RC Scale scores and of most substantive scale scores, but a recent history of suicidal ideation and problems with emotional control and work performance

Referral Summary

Mr. H is a 41-year-old married, male correctional officer with 17 years of service in this position, 12 years of which were with his current employer, a large state maximum security correctional facility. Two years before the FFDE referral, Mr. H was assigned to a tower post overlooking an exercise yard when an inmate viciously attacked a correctional officer. Mr. H sounded the warning alarm (in response, all inmates in the yard are to drop immediately to the ground or risk being shot), but the inmate ignored it and continued his attack. Mr. H then shot and killed the inmate, but his fellow correctional officer was disabled from the injuries he sustained. Mr. H was placed on paid administrative leave and assigned to home duty during a 7-month postshooting investigation. During this time on leave, he was seen once by a psychologist for debriefing 2 days after the shooting, but he received no other treatment. He returned to duty, but in a control module, where he was responsible for opening and closing access points in the prison (prison officials and Mr. H agreed that he should no longer interact with the inmate population for fear of a revenge attack). During the first month back at work, he called in sick for 10 of the 16 shifts he was assigned, and during the shifts he worked he was observed to be inattentive, easily distracted, and unfocused. Mr. H's supervisor called him in to discuss his concerns. Mr. H acknowledged that he had not been himself lately, but he would try to do better. His supervisor commented about his frequent sick leave use since returning to work, and Mr. H tearfully replied, "I just don't know if I want to do this anymore." Concerned that Mr. H may pose a risk to public safety in his position, prison officials referred him for an FFDE.

Assessment Findings

EMPLOYMENT RECORDS

A review of Mr. H's employment records, including his complete personnel file and employee medical file, confirmed the absence of prior disciplinary actions. The available annual performance reviews indicated that he met or exceeded performance standards. The records contained a factual recitation of the shooting incident and Mr. H's exemplary performance in it. The file also included a citation for life-saving heroism issued by the governor.

MENTAL STATUS EXAMINATION

Mr. H's appearance was remarkable for his uncombed hair, rumpled clothing, unshaven face, and slow gait. He explained that he had trouble sleeping the night before and that after he finally fell asleep he failed to hear his alarm. He displayed poor eye contact, and his speech reflected a taciturn quality as indicated by its low volume and quantity. His affective expression was dysphoric, but he reported feeling "fine, just a little nervous." During the clinical interview, he became tearful when discussing his wish to die, but he quickly regained composure. Mr. H displayed no abnormalities with respect to his perception, thought process, sensorium and cognition, judgment, insight, or reliability. He denied past or current homicidal ideation. He reported a desire to be dead but not to kill himself, and said he had no plan to end his life. His attitude toward the examiner was cooperative and frank.

CLINICAL INTERVIEW

Mr. H's recitation of the story of the exercise yard shooting was consistent with the investigative report found in his employment records. Most notable about his story was the degree of personal responsibility he felt for the injuries to his fellow correctional officer, who was permanently disabled from the incident. Mr. H said that he feels sorry for the inmate's family, but he feels no guilt for having shot and killed the prisoner when he continued to assault the correctional officer even after the warning alarm was sounded. "Every inmate in the yard dropped to the ground and knew what would happen next. I don't blame myself for having to shoot him." On the other hand, he said he feels enormous guilt for not having taken more effective action sooner, action that might have spared the correctional officer from his disabling injuries but that, according to the investigation report, could not realistically have been done. Mr. H was of two minds on this subject: he understood rationally that he did his best, but he knew his best was not good enough.

Mr. H said that he has had difficulty falling asleep since the incident, and when he finally does sleep, he does not want to wake up. He said his wife and teenage children have come home and found him still in bed hours after he called in sick. He said he has had no specific plans to kill himself, but he does have thoughts that he would prefer to not wake up or to die in an accident. He complains of gastrointestinal problems, but has not gone to see a physician. He had one meeting with a prison psychologist to debrief after the incident, but he had not followed up with recommended counseling. He said he drinks one or two shots of hard alcohol—unusual for him, he said—to help him sleep, but he does not feel he has an alcohol use problem. He said his wife and children are worried about him.

Mr. H said that he has spontaneous memories of the exercise yard attack on his fellow correctional officer, with a frequency of recurrent dreams related to the attack of about 4 nights a week, and he experiences intense and prolonged distress when he has these thoughts and awakens from the dreams. He has difficulty falling asleep every night, but he eventually sleeps within about 3 hours of going to bed. He denied efforts to avoid persons, places, or topics that remind him of the attack.

Asked whether he considers himself to be psychologically fit for duty, Mr. H said that he believes he is fit because he is "hanging in there" and calls in sick when he feels he cannot focus. When reminded that his supervisor and coworkers reported that he has not been sufficiently focused and attentive when working in the control module, he said he would not let that happen again. He acknowledged that he told his supervisor that he is not sure he wants to continue to be a correctional officer, but he said that was just a feeling he had in the moment. He said he would quit if he won the lottery, but he has no other viable employment options.

MEDICAL RECORDS

No medical records were available for review, and none were deemed relevant in light of Mr. H's report that he had not sought medical or mental health care other than the employer-mandated debriefing session immediately following the shooting incident.

MMPI-2-RF FINDINGS

Mr. H's MMPI-2-RF Clinical Settings Interpretive Report is reproduced in Figure 11-3. It is a valid protocol with no unscorable items. Although he provided more variable inconsistent responses than is typically found in the male normative sample (VRIN-r=68T), the level of inconsistent responding reflected in this score is not cause for concern about the validity of the test results, particularly in light of his consistent responding to true-true and false-false item pairs measured by TRIN-r (50T). There are no indications of overreporting or underreporting in this protocol.

There are no indications of substantial internalizing, thought, or externalizing dysfunction in Mr. H's MMPI-2-RF protocol. There are, however, a number of anomalous and problematic findings, particularly in light of the employer's report concerning recent safety-jeopardizing performance problems and his disclosure concerning recent suicidal ideation.

Mr. H reports having had recent thoughts of killing himself (Figure 11-3, p. 4; SUI=66T), which puts him at risk for current suicidal ideation and attempts. Additionally, he reports self-doubt (SFD=65T), which is associated with rumination, feelings of insecurity and inferiority, and self-disparaging and intropunitive tendencies.

Although the findings from the MMPI-2-RF provide no indications of pervasive, clinically significant internalizing dysfunction, they do alert the user to areas of potential concern warranting further clinical assessment. Mr. H's score on the Malaise (MLS) scale may reflect evolving problems involving poor health and physical debilitation (MLS=63T), particularly gastrointestinal complaints (GIC=64T), that are an appropriate target of medical monitoring. In addition, his score on the Demoralization scale (RCd=62T) may reveal early indications of sadness, unhappiness, and dissatisfaction with his current life circumstances that, left unchecked, may contribute to his already established risk for suicide. In consideration

MMPI 2 RF®

Minnesota Multiphasic
Personality Inventory-2
Restructured Form®

Interpretive Report: Clinical Settings

MMPI-2-RF®
Minnesota Multiphasic Personality Inventory-2-Restructured Form®
Yossef S. Ben-Porath, PhD, & Auke Tellegen, PhD

Name:	Mr. H
Age:	41
Gender:	Male
Marital Status:	Not reported
Years of Education:	Not reported
Date Assessed:	01/24/2016

PsychCorp

Copyright © 2008, 2011, 2012 by the Regents of the University of Minnesota. All rights reserved.
Distributed exclusively under license from the University of Minnesota by NCS Pearson, Inc. Portions reproduced from the MMPI-2-RF test booklet. Copyright © 2008 by the Regents of the University of Minnesota. All rights reserved. Portions excerpted from the *MMPI-2-RF Manual for Administration, Scoring, and Interpretation.* Copyright © 2008, 2011 by the Regents of the University of Minnesota. All rights reserved. Used by permission of the University of Minnesota Press.

MMPI-2-RF, the **MMPI-2-RF logo,** and **Minnesota Multiphasic Personality Inventory-2-Restructured Form** are registered trademarks of the University of Minnesota. **Pearson,** the **PSI logo,** and **PsychCorp** are trademarks in the U.S. and/or other countries of Pearson Education, Inc., or its affiliate(s).

TRADE SECRET INFORMATION
Not for release under HIPAA or other data disclosure laws that exempt trade secrets from disclosure.

[3.0 / 2 / QG]

ALWAYS LEARNING PEARSON

FIGURE 11-3 Mr. H's MMPI-2-RF Clinical Settings Interpretive Report

MMPI-2-RF® Interpretive Report: Clinical Settings
01/24/2016, Page 2 Mr. H

MMPI-2-RF Validity Scales

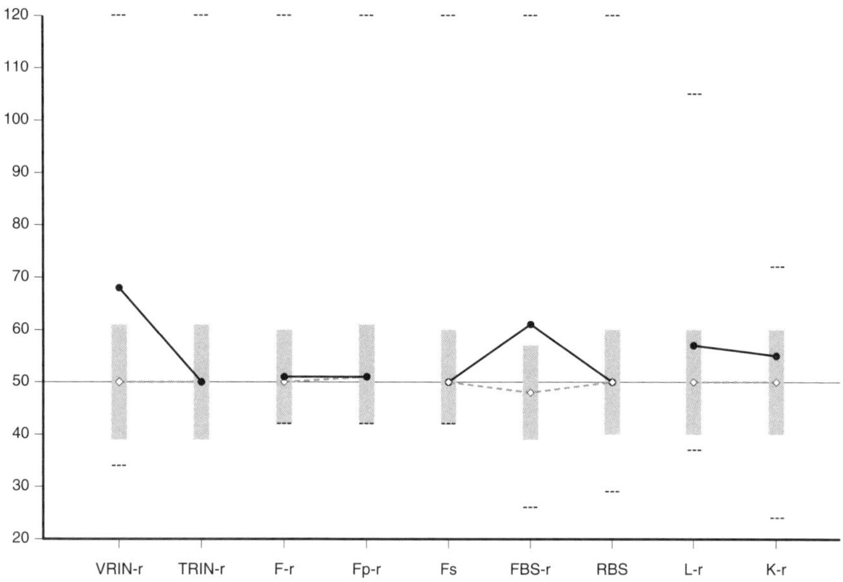

	VRIN-r	TRIN-r	F-r	Fp-r	Fs	FBS-r	RBS	L-r	K-r
Raw Score:	7	11	2	1	1	11	5	4	9
T Score:	68	50	51	51	50	61	50	57	55
Response %:	100	100	100	100	100	100	100	100	100

Cannot Say (Raw): 0 Percent True (of items answered): 35%

Comparison Group Data: MMPI-2-RF Normative (Men), N = 1138

	VRIN-r	TRIN-r	F-r	Fp-r	Fs	FBS-r	RBS	L-r	K-r
Mean Score (◇- - -◇):	50	50	50	51	50	48	50	50	50
Standard Dev (±1 SD):	11	11	10	10	10	9	10	10	10
Percent scoring at or below test taker:	96	40	76	76	74	93	63	83	74

The highest and lowest T scores possible on each scale are indicated by a "---"; MMPI-2-RF T scores are non-gendered.

VRIN-r Variable Response Inconsistency
TRIN-r True Response Inconsistency
F-r Infrequent Responses
Fp-r Infrequent Psychopathology Responses
Fs Infrequent Somatic Responses
FBS-r Symptom Validity
RBS Response Bias Scale
L-r Uncommon Virtues
K-r Adjustment Validity

FIGURE 11-3 Mr. H's MMPI-2-RF Clinical Settings Interpretive Report, continued

MMPI-2-RF Higher-Order (H-O) and Restructured Clinical (RC) Scales

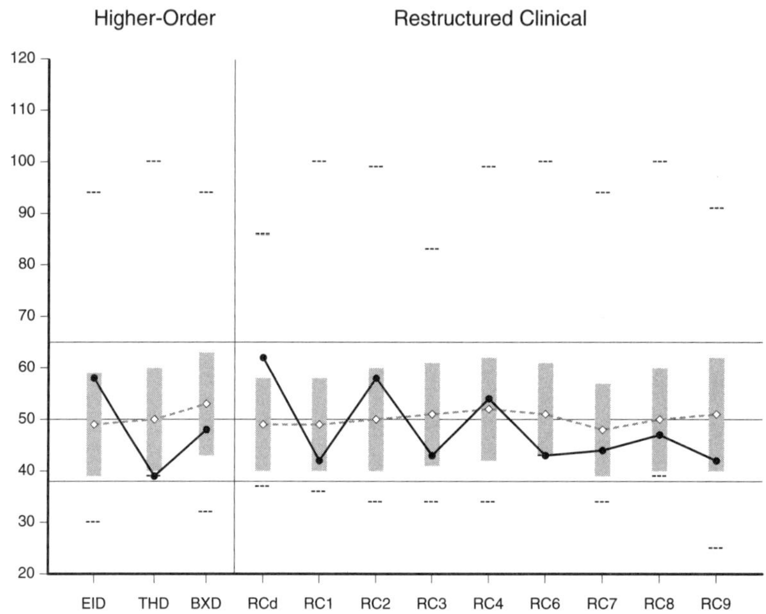

	EID	THD	BXD	RCd	RC1	RC2	RC3	RC4	RC6	RC7	RC8	RC9
Raw Score:	16	0	5	11	1	6	3	6	0	3	1	7
T Score:	58	39	48	62	42	58	43	54	43	44	47	42
Response %:	100	100	100	100	100	100	100	100	100	100	100	100

Comparison Group Data: MMPI-2-RF Normative (Men), N = 1138

	EID	THD	BXD	RCd	RC1	RC2	RC3	RC4	RC6	RC7	RC8	RC9
Mean Score (◇- - -◇):	49	50	53	49	49	50	51	52	51	48	50	51
Standard Dev (±1 SD):	10	10	10	9	9	10	10	10	10	9	10	11
Percent scoring at or below test taker:	86	31	40	92	37	82	26	67	54	36	53	19

The highest and lowest T scores possible on each scale are indicated by a "---"; MMPI-2-RF T scores are non-gendered.

EID Emotional/Internalizing Dysfunction
THD Thought Dysfunction
BXD Behavioral/Externalizing Dysfunction

RCd Demoralization
RC1 Somatic Complaints
RC2 Low Positive Emotions
RC3 Cynicism
RC4 Antisocial Behavior

RC6 Ideas of Persecution
RC7 Dysfunctional Negative Emotions
RC8 Aberrant Experiences
RC9 Hypomanic Activation

FIGURE 11-3 Mr. H's MMPI-2-RF Clinical Settings Interpretive Report, continued

MMPI-2-RF® Interpretive Report: Clinical Settings
01/24/2016, Page 4 Mr. H

MMPI-2-RF Somatic/Cognitive and Internalizing Scales

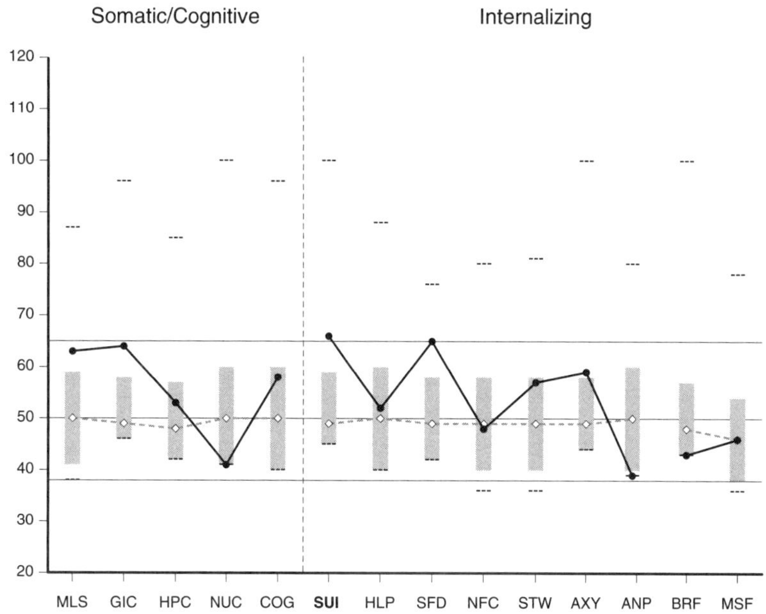

	MLS	GIC	HPC	NUC	COG	**SUI**	HLP	SFD	NFC	STW	AXY	ANP	BRF	MSF
Raw Score:	4	1	1	0	3	1	1	3	2	4	1	0	0	2
T Score:	63	64	53	41	58	**66**	52	65	48	57	59	39	43	46
Response %:	100	100	100	100	100	100	100	100	100	100	100	100	100	100

Comparison Group Data: MMPI-2-RF Normative (Men), N = 1138

	MLS	GIC	HPC	NUC	COG	SUI	HLP	SFD	NFC	STW	AXY	ANP	BRF	MSF
Mean Score (◇--◇):	50	49	48	50	50	49	50	49	49	49	49	50	48	46
Standard Dev (±1 SD):	9	9	9	10	10	10	10	9	9	9	9	10	9	8
Percent scoring at or below test taker:	95	94	80	46	87	97	76	96	59	88	93	30	67	58

The highest and lowest T scores possible on each scale are indicated by a "---"; MMPI-2-RF T scores are non-gendered.

MLS Malaise
GIC Gastrointestinal Complaints
HPC Head Pain Complaints
NUC Neurological Complaints
COG Cognitive Complaints
SUI Suicidal/Death Ideation
HLP Helplessness/Hopelessness
SFD Self-Doubt
NFC Inefficacy
STW Stress/Worry
AXY Anxiety
ANP Anger Proneness
BRF Behavior-Restricting Fears
MSF Multiple Specific Fears

FIGURE 11-3 Mr. H's MMPI-2-RF Clinical Settings Interpretive Report, continued

MMPI-2-RF Externalizing, Interpersonal, and Interest Scales

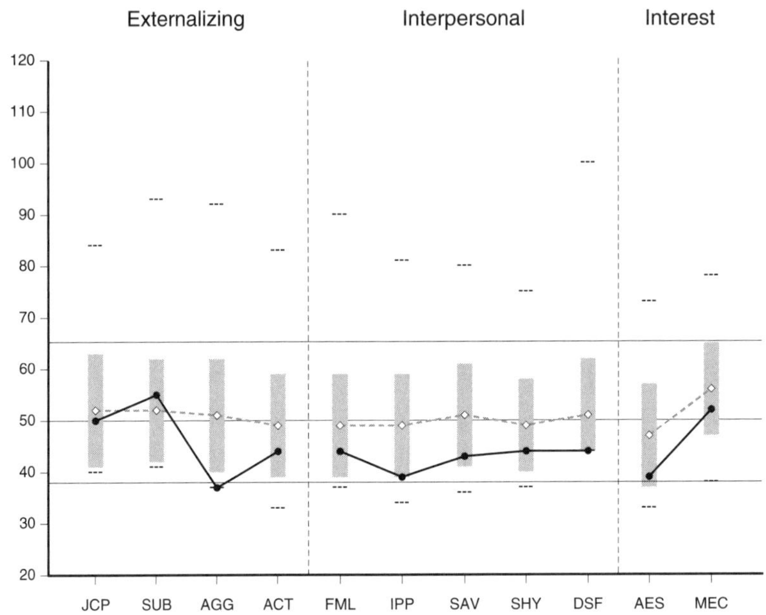

	JCP	SUB	AGG	ACT	FML	IPP	SAV	SHY	DSF	AES	MEC
Raw Score:	1	2	0	2	1	1	1	1	0	1	3
T Score:	50	55	37	44	44	39	43	44	44	39	52
Response %:	100	100	100	100	100	100	100	100	100	100	100

Comparison Group Data: MMPI-2-RF Normative (Men), N = 1138

	JCP	SUB	AGG	ACT	FML	IPP	SAV	SHY	DSF	AES	MEC
Mean Score (◇--◇):	52	52	51	49	49	49	51	49	51	47	56
Standard Dev (±1 SD):	11	10	11	10	10	10	10	9	11	10	9
Percent scoring at or below test taker:	62	75	20	41	46	22	30	39	67	34	43

The highest and lowest T scores possible on each scale are indicated by a "---"; MMPI-2-RF T scores are non-gendered.

JCP	Juvenile Conduct Problems	FML	Family Problems	AES	Aesthetic-Literary Interests
SUB	Substance Abuse	IPP	Interpersonal Passivity	MEC	Mechanical-Physical Interests
AGG	Aggression	SAV	Social Avoidance		
ACT	Activation	SHY	Shyness		
		DSF	Disaffiliativeness		

FIGURE 11-3 Mr. H's MMPI-2-RF Clinical Settings Interpretive Report, continued

MMPI-2-RF PSY-5 Scales

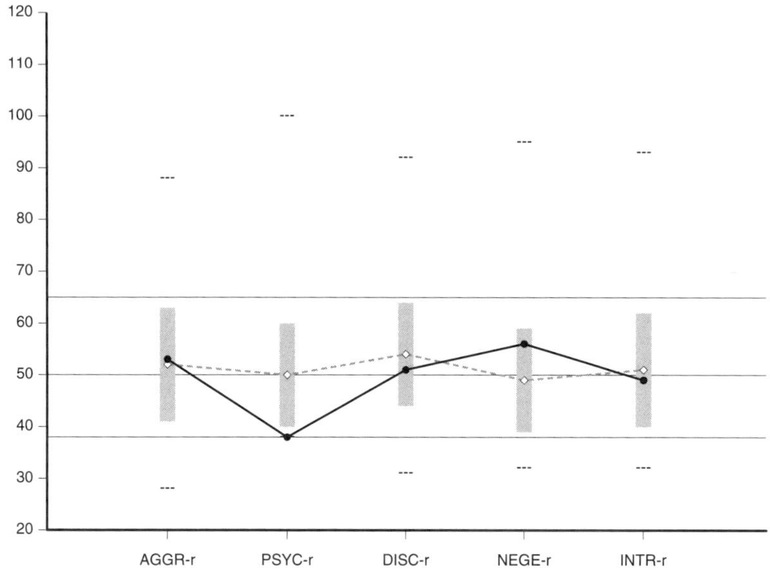

	AGGR-r	PSYC-r	DISC-r	NEGE-r	INTR-r
Raw Score:	10	0	7	9	6
T Score:	53	38	51	56	49
Response %:	100	100	100	100	100

Comparison Group Data: MMPI-2-RF Normative (Men), N = 1138

Mean Score (◇--◇):	52	50	54	49	51
Standard Dev (±1 SD):	11	10	10	10	11
Percent scoring at or below test taker:	63	27	49	84	53

The highest and lowest T scores possible on each scale are indicated by a "---"; MMPI-2-RF T scores are non-gendered.

AGGR-r Aggressiveness-Revised
PSYC-r Psychoticism-Revised
DISC-r Disconstraint-Revised
NEGE-r Negative Emotionality/Neuroticism-Revised
INTR-r Introversion/Low Positive Emotionality-Revised

FIGURE 11-3 Mr. H's MMPI-2-RF Clinical Settings Interpretive Report, continued

MMPI-2-RF T SCORES (BY DOMAIN)

PROTOCOL VALIDITY

Content Non-Responsiveness

0	68	50
CNS	VRIN-r	TRIN-r

Over-Reporting

51	51		50	61	50
F-r	Fp-r		Fs	FBS-r	RBS

Under-Reporting

57	55
L-r	K-r

SUBSTANTIVE SCALES

Somatic/Cognitive Dysfunction

42	63	64	53	41	58
RC1	MLS	GIC	HPC	NUC	COG

Emotional Dysfunction

58
EID

62	66	52	65	48
RCd	SUI	HLP	SFD	NFC

58	49
RC2	INTR-r

44	57	59	39	43	46	56
RC7	STW	AXY	ANP	BRF	MSF	NEGE-r

Thought Dysfunction

39
THD

43
RC6

47
RC8

38
PSYC-r

Behavioral Dysfunction

48
BXD

54	50	55
RC4	JCP	SUB

42	37	44	53	51
RC9	AGG	ACT	AGGR-r	DISC-r

Interpersonal Functioning

44	43	39	43	44	44
FML	RC3	IPP	SAV	SHY	DSF

Interests

39	52
AES	MEC

Note. This information is provided to facilitate interpretation following the recommended structure for MMPI-2-RF interpretation in Chapter 5 of the *MMPI-2-RF Manual for Administration, Scoring, and Interpretation*, which provides details in the text and an outline in Table 5-1.

FIGURE 11-3 Mr. H's MMPI-2-RF Clinical Settings Interpretive Report, continued

This interpretive report is intended for use by a professional qualified to interpret the MMPI-2-RF. The information it contains should be considered in the context of the test taker's background, the circumstances of the assessment, and other available information.

SYNOPSIS

This is a valid MMPI-2-RF protocol. Scores on the substantive scales indicate emotional dysfunction. Emotional-internalizing findings include **suicidal ideation** and self-doubt.

PROTOCOL VALIDITY

This is a valid MMPI-2-RF protocol. There are no problems with unscorable items. The test taker responded to the items relevantly on the basis of their content, and there are no indications of over- or under-reporting.

SUBSTANTIVE SCALE INTERPRETATION

Clinical symptoms, personality characteristics, and behavioral tendencies of the test taker are described in this section and organized according to an empirically guided framework. Statements containing the word "reports" are based on the item content of MMPI-2-RF scales, whereas statements that include the word "likely" are based on empirical correlates of scale scores. Specific sources for each statement can be accessed with the annotation features of this report.

Somatic/Cognitive Dysfunction

There are no indications of somatic or cognitive dysfunction in this protocol.

Emotional Dysfunction

The test taker reports a history of suicidal ideation and/or attempts[1]. He is likely to be preoccupied with suicide and death[2] and to be at risk for current suicidal ideation and attempts[2].

He reports self-doubt[3] and is likely to be prone to rumination, to feel insecure and inferior, and to be self-disparaging and intropunitive[4].

Thought Dysfunction

There are no indications of disordered thinking in this protocol.

FIGURE 11-3 Mr. H's MMPI-2-RF Clinical Settings Interpretive Report, continued

MMPI-2-RF® Interpretive Report: Clinical Settings
01/24/2016, Page 9 Mr. H

Behavioral Dysfunction

There are no indications of maladaptive externalizing behavior in this protocol. The test taker reports a below average level of aggressive behavior[5].

Interpersonal Functioning Scales

These scales provide no further evidence of dysfunction.

Interest Scales

The test taker reports an average number of interests in activities or occupations of an aesthetic or literary nature (e.g., writing, music, the theater)[6]. He also reports an average number of interests in activities or occupations of a mechanical or physical nature (e.g., fixing and building things, the outdoors, sports)[7].

DIAGNOSTIC CONSIDERATIONS

No specific psychodiagnostic recommendations are indicated by this MMPI-2-RF protocol.

TREATMENT CONSIDERATIONS

This section provides inferential treatment-related recommendations based on the test taker's MMPI-2-RF scores.

Areas for Further Evaluation

- **Risk for suicide should be assessed immediately**[8].

Possible Targets for Treatment

- Low self-esteem and other manifestations of self-doubt[9]

ITEM-LEVEL INFORMATION

Unscorable Responses

The test taker produced scorable responses to all the MMPI-2-RF items.

Critical Responses

Seven MMPI-2-RF scales--Suicidal/Death Ideation (SUI), Helplessness/Hopelessness (HLP), Anxiety (AXY), Ideas of Persecution (RC6), Aberrant Experiences (RC8), Substance Abuse (SUB), and Aggression (AGG)--have been designated by the test authors as having critical item content that may require immediate attention and follow-up. Items answered by the individual in the keyed direction (True or False) on a critical scale are listed below if his T score on that scale is 65 or higher. The percentage of the MMPI-2-RF normative sample (NS) and of the MMPI-2-RF Normative (Men)

FIGURE 11-3 Mr. H's MMPI-2-RF Clinical Settings Interpretive Report, continued

comparison group (CG) that answered each item in the keyed direction are provided in parentheses following the item content.

Suicidal/Death Ideation (SUI, T Score = 66)

93. Item Content Omitted. (True; NS 3.7%, CG 4.2%)

FIGURE 11-3 Mr. H's MMPI-2-RF Clinical Settings Interpretive Report, continued

ENDNOTES

This section lists for each statement in the report the MMPI-2-RF score(s) that triggered it. In addition, each statement is identified as a Test Response, if based on item content, a Correlate, if based on empirical correlates, or an Inference, if based on the report authors' judgment. (This information can also be accessed on-screen by placing the cursor on a given statement.) For correlate-based statements, research references (Ref. No.) are provided, keyed to the consecutively numbered reference list following the endnotes.

[1] Test Response: SUI=66
[2] Correlate: SUI=66, Ref. 1
[3] Test Response: SFD=65
[4] Correlate: SFD=65, Ref. 1
[5] Test Response: AGG=37
[6] Test Response: AES=39
[7] Test Response: MEC=52
[8] Inference: SUI=66
[9] Inference: SFD=65

FIGURE 11-3 Mr. H's MMPI-2-RF Clinical Settings Interpretive Report, continued

RESEARCH REFERENCE LIST

1. Tellegen, A., & Ben-Porath, Y. S. (2008/2011). *The Minnesota Multiphasic Personality Inventory-2-Restructured Form (MMPI-2-RF): Technical manual.* Minneapolis: University of Minnesota Press.

End of Report

This and previous pages of this report contain trade secrets and are not to be released in response to requests under HIPAA (or any other data disclosure law that exempts trade secret information from release). Further, release in response to litigation discovery demands should be made only in accordance with your profession's ethical guidelines and under an appropriate protective order.

FIGURE 11-3 Mr. H's MMPI-2-RF Clinical Settings Interpretive Report, continued

ITEM RESPONSES

1: 2	2: 1	3: 2	4: 2	5: 2	6: 2	7: 1	8: 1	9: 2	10: 2
11: 1	12: 2	13: 2	14: 2	15: 2	16: 2	17: 1	18: 2	19: 1	20: 2
21: 1	22: 1	23: 2	24: 2	25: 2	26: 2	27: 1	28: 1	29: 1	30: 1
31: 2	32: 1	33: 2	34: 2	35: 2	36: 1	37: 2	38: 2	39: 1	40: 2
41: 2	42: 2	43: 2	44: 2	45: 2	46: 2	47: 2	48: 1	49: 2	50: 2
51: 2	52: 1	53: 2	54: 2	55: 2	56: 2	57: 1	58: 2	59: 2	60: 1
61: 1	62: 2	63: 2	64: 2	65: 1	66: 2	67: 2	68: 2	69: 1	70: 1
71: 2	72: 1	73: 1	74: 2	75: 1	76: 2	77: 2	78: 2	79: 2	80: 1
81: 2	82: 2	83: 1	84: 2	85: 1	86: 2	87: 2	88: 2	89: 2	90: 2
91: 2	92: 2	93: 1	94: 1	95: 1	96: 2	97: 2	98: 1	99: 2	100: 1
101: 2	102: 1	103: 2	104: 2	105: 2	106: 2	107: 1	108: 2	109: 1	110: 2
111: 2	112: 2	113: 1	114: 2	115: 1	116: 1	117: 2	118: 1	119: 2	120: 2
121: 2	122: 2	123: 1	124: 2	125: 1	126: 1	127: 1	128: 1	129: 2	130: 2
131: 2	132: 2	133: 2	134: 1	135: 1	136: 1	137: 2	138: 2	139: 2	140: 1
141: 1	142: 2	143: 2	144: 1	145: 2	146: 2	147: 1	148: 2	149: 2	150: 2
151: 2	152: 1	153: 1	154: 2	155: 2	156: 1	157: 1	158: 2	159: 2	160: 1
161: 2	162: 1	163: 2	164: 2	165: 2	166: 2	167: 2	168: 2	169: 2	170: 2
171: 2	172: 2	173: 2	174: 1	175: 2	176: 2	177: 2	178: 2	179: 2	180: 2
181: 2	182: 2	183: 1	184: 1	185: 2	186: 1	187: 1	188: 1	189: 1	190: 2
191: 1	192: 2	193: 2	194: 2	195: 1	196: 2	197: 1	198: 2	199: 2	200: 2
201: 1	202: 2	203: 2	204: 1	205: 2	206: 1	207: 1	208: 2	209: 1	210: 1
211: 1	212: 1	213: 2	214: 2	215: 2	216: 2	217: 2	218: 2	219: 2	220: 2
221: 1	222: 1	223: 2	224: 2	225: 2	226: 2	227: 1	228: 1	229: 2	230: 2
231: 2	232: 1	233: 2	234: 2	235: 2	236: 2	237: 1	238: 2	239: 1	240: 2
241: 1	242: 2	243: 2	244: 1	245: 2	246: 1	247: 1	248: 2	249: 1	250: 2
251: 2	252: 2	253: 2	254: 1	255: 2	256: 2	257: 2	258: 2	259: 2	260: 1
261: 2	262: 1	263: 1	264: 2	265: 1	266: 1	267: 2	268: 2	269: 1	270: 2
271: 2	272: 1	273: 2	274: 2	275: 2	276: 1	277: 2	278: 2	279: 2	280: 2
281: 2	282: 1	283: 1	284: 2	285: 2	286: 1	287: 2	288: 1	289: 2	290: 1
291: 2	292: 2	293: 1	294: 2	295: 1	296: 2	297: 2	298: 1	299: 2	300: 1
301: 2	302: 1	303: 2	304: 2	305: 2	306: 1	307: 1	308: 2	309: 1	310: 2
311: 2	312: 2	313: 1	314: 2	315: 2	316: 2	317: 2	318: 2	319: 2	320: 2
321: 1	322: 2	323: 1	324: 2	325: 1	326: 1	327: 1	328: 2	329: 2	330: 2
331: 2	332: 2	333: 1	334: 2	335: 2	336: 2	337: 2	338: 1		

FIGURE 11-3 Mr. H's MMPI-2-RF Clinical Settings Interpretive Report, continued

of these scores and Mr. H's disclosures during the clinical interview, the FFD examiner also administered the Detailed Assessment of Posttraumatic Stress (DAPS; Briere, 2001), which produced valid results, and the Clinician-Administered PTSD Scale for DSM-5 (CAPS-5; Weathers et al., 2013), both of which indicated some symptoms associated with PTSD, as well as low-magnitude emotional distress, but neither at a level strongly supporting a PTSD diagnosis.

Data Integration

STEP 1: ASSESSING FOR A MENTAL HEALTH CONDITION

As we have noted throughout this guide, the diagnosis of a mental health condition is made on the basis of a thorough, comprehensive assessment, not merely on the basis of the MMPI-2-RF or any other assessment tool alone. These data together provide the diagnosis with convergent and discriminant validity that no single instrument can give. Collectively, the data persuaded the examiner that Mr. H suffers from PTSD and is in need of mental health treatment. This need is particularly noteworthy in light of Mr. H's failure to report his PTSD symptoms in response to the MMPI-2-RF items, which is consistent with his failure to follow up on the recommendation that he obtain counseling following the critical incident.

STEP 2: ASSESSING FOR CURRENT WORK IMPAIRMENT

Mr. H has good days and bad days. On bad days, he calls in sick; on good days, he goes to work. But as is so often the case with these decisions, the traumatized individual can be a poor judge of his or her own level of functioning. Many of Mr. H's MMPI-2-RF scores on the substantive scales are just below 65T, indicating a magnitude of problems falling just short of clinical significance. His now heightened awareness of his impaired work performance may, in the short run, be sufficient to enable him to perform his duties effectively and safely, but in the absence of effective treatment, there is good reason to be pessimistic about the long-term prospects for improvement.

STEP 3: ASSESSING FOR SUSTAINABILITY OF FITNESS

It is arguable that the examiner has sufficient clinical data to support finding Mr. H unfit for duty simply on the basis of his current performance, but the reasonably anticipated trajectory of his functioning, given his diagnosis, his recent and current symptoms, and the absence of follow-up treatment, led the examiner to conduct the third step in the data integration analysis. Left untreated, the course of PTSD is well known, particularly in a suicidal individual who is experiencing marked distress from the reexperiencing and hyperarousal symptom clusters. In addition, at the rate that Mr. H had been using his sick leave, he would deplete his leave benefits in only a few months, making it impossible to rely on his usual strategy of staying home on his bad days without going on protected, unpaid medical leave. For this reason, the examiner concluded that even if Mr. H were able to improve his attention and focus in the short term through heightened motivation and self-monitoring, that improvement is unlikely to be sustainable without effective treatment for PTSD.

Conclusion

The aggregate clinical evidence derived from all sources indicates that Mr. H is currently experiencing moderate impairment, including occupational impairment, as a result of PTSD. In particular, his condition substantially limits his functioning in the dimensions of Emotional Control & Stress Tolerance, and Decision-Making and Judgment. The examiner determined that Mr. H is unfit for duty.

Ms. W, Dispatcher

Assessment Issues Presented

- Integration of findings from the MMPI-2-RF Clinical Settings Interpretive Report with assessment data from the clinical interview, employment records, and medical records to assess the fitness for duty of an incumbent dispatcher with a recent history of DUI arrest

Referral Summary

Ms. W, a 52-year-old dispatcher with 26 years of service with the same municipal employer, was arrested for drunk driving 12 weeks prior to this FFDE. She faced termination because this was her third DUI arrest in 15 years (the second occurred 7 years ago). At her mitigation hearing, Ms. W said that she began drinking at home after her husband died about a year before. On the day of her most recent arrest, she was the lead dispatcher on a difficult 18-minute 911 call involving failed efforts to resuscitate a man as she instructed his wife on the administration of CPR. She left work early to attend a brief, scheduled medical appointment for treatment of a nondebilitating neurological condition. Afterward, she said she stopped at a bar to "wind down" before her long commute home, and she had three mixed drinks over about a 90-minute period.

Assessment Findings

EMPLOYMENT RECORDS

The records provided by the employer included a copy of the police report from Ms. W's most recent DUI arrest, which showed her blood alcohol level (.08) to be consistent with her self-reported consumption. The records also confirmed the failed resuscitation call, which her supervisor said Ms. W handled well, although she was "clearly distraught" once it ended. She left for her medical appointment shortly afterward, and the supervisor said that she regretted not having time to debrief with her or assess her status before she left for the day. Ms. W was regarded as a reliable and competent dispatcher. The only history of discipline pertained to the most recent DUI arrest and the two prior ones. Employment records pertaining to the most recent incident include a detailed last-chance agreement with requirements for weekly monitoring of Ms. W's compliance with all requirements of the recommended treatment program (which included total abstinence from alcohol use) and random screening.

MENTAL STATUS EXAMINATION

Ms. W's appearance was unremarkable with respect to her grooming and dress. Her speech was normal as indicated by its rate, volume, quality, and quantity. Her affective expression was euthymic, and she reported her mood similarly. She evidenced no abnormalities in perception, thought process, sensorium and cognition, judgment, or insight. Her attitude toward the examiner was cooperative.

CLINICAL INTERVIEW

Ms. W reported that she was a casual and periodic user of alcohol before her first DUI arrest. Since that incident, she has had only a court-ordered substance use evaluation, but no treatment. She said she stopped drinking alcohol entirely for 6 years and remained abstinent from the use of all intoxicants until about a year before her second DUI arrest. Ms. W said she had convinced herself that she could go out with friends and drink responsibly, but before long she was drinking increasing amounts with greater frequency. Following her second DUI arrest she was ordered by the court to participate in outpatient treatment, which she then continued voluntarily for a period of 1 year, in addition to AA meetings that she attended for more than 3 years.

Ms. W said she remained sober for another 6 years until after her husband died. She said she never drank more than three drinks, always in the company of others, and never more than once a week. She said she had convinced herself that this pattern was something she could manage. It is important to note that she said when she went into the bar to "wind down" following the difficult 911 call and her visit to her doctor for a progressive but nondisabling neurological condition affecting her coordination, she intended to have only one drink, but wound up having three.

MEDICAL RECORDS

The examiner received the records of the most recent court-ordered substance use assessment, including recommendations for relapse prevention and management. The counselor reported that Ms. W is compliant with all treatment recommendations, including total abstinence from alcohol (with random screening), group counseling 3 days per week, weekly individual counseling, and AA meetings daily for 90 days and a minimum of 3 days a week thereafter. Records from Ms. W's treating physician confirmed the self-reported neurological disorder, which is in its early stages and is treated with medication (not a drug of abuse) that slows the progressive course and manages but does not eliminate her symptoms, which mostly affect gait coordination and occasional hand dexterity.

MMPI-2-RF FINDINGS

Ms. W's MMPI-2-RF Clinical Settings Interpretive Report is reproduced in Figure 11-4. A review of her Validity Scale scores indicates that there are no unscorable items, that she responded to the items relevantly on the basis of their content, and there are no indications of over- or underreporting. There are no indications of emotional-internalizing dysfunction or thought dysfunction.

In the Somatic/Cognitive Dysfunction domain, Ms. W reports vague neurological complaints (NUC=70T). As a general rule, it is useful to look for consonance between what a test taker reports on the MMPI-2-RF and what is otherwise known through collateral sources. In Ms. W's case, we would expect to see elevation on the NUC scale, just as we also would expect to see elevation on the Substance Abuse (SUB) scale, which we do find in her protocol (69T). No other scales are clinically elevated.

Data Integration

STEP 1: ASSESSING FOR A MENTAL HEALTH CONDITION

Ms. W has an alcohol use disorder, in early remission, as indicated by her consumption of larger amounts of alcohol than was intended, continued alcohol use despite having recurrent social and occupational problems

MMPI 2 RF®

Minnesota Multiphasic
Personality Inventory-2
Restructured Form®

Interpretive Report: Clinical Settings

MMPI-2-RF®
Minnesota Multiphasic Personality Inventory-2-Restructured Form®
Yossef S. Ben-Porath, PhD, & Auke Tellegen, PhD

Name:	Ms. W
Age:	52
Gender:	Female
Marital Status:	Widowed
Years of Education:	13
Date Assessed:	01/15/2016

PsychCorp

Copyright © 2008, 2011, 2012 by the Regents of the University of Minnesota. All rights reserved.
Distributed exclusively under license from the University of Minnesota by NCS Pearson, Inc. Portions reproduced from the MMPI-2-RF test booklet. Copyright © 2008 by the Regents of the University of Minnesota. All rights reserved. Portions excerpted from the *MMPI-2-RF Manual for Administration, Scoring, and Interpretation.* Copyright © 2008, 2011 by the Regents of the University of Minnesota. All rights reserved. Used by permission of the University of Minnesota Press.

MMPI-2-RF, the **MMPI-2-RF logo,** and **Minnesota Multiphasic Personality Inventory-2-Restructured Form** are registered trademarks of the University of Minnesota. **Pearson,** the **PSI logo,** and **PsychCorp** are trademarks in the U.S. and/or other countries of Pearson Education, Inc., or its affiliate(s).

TRADE SECRET INFORMATION
Not for release under HIPAA or other data disclosure laws that exempt trade secrets from disclosure.

[3.0 / 1 / 3.1.13]

ALWAYS LEARNING PEARSON

FIGURE 11-4 Ms. W's MMPI-2-RF Clinical Settings Interpretive Report

MMPI-2-RF® Interpretive Report: Clinical Settings
01/15/2016, Page 2

Ms. W

MMPI-2-RF Validity Scales

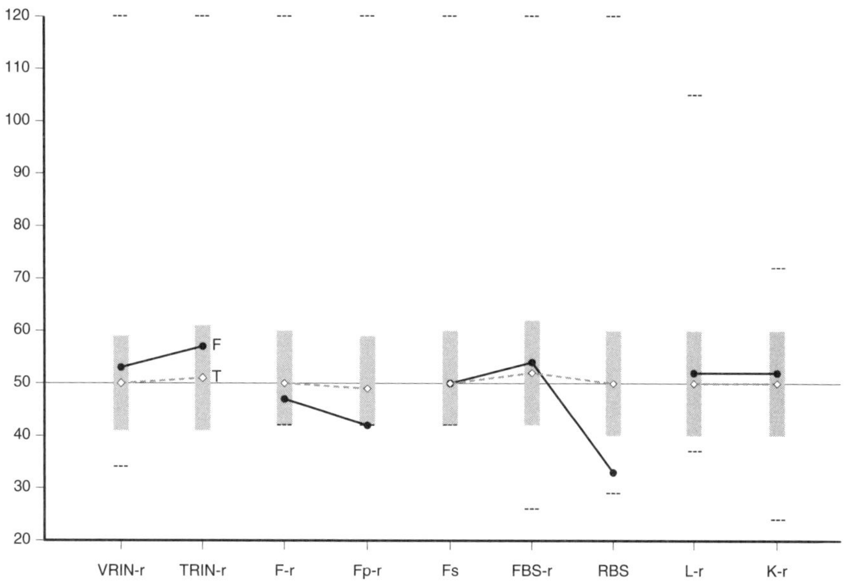

	VRIN-r	TRIN-r	F-r	Fp-r	Fs	FBS-r	RBS	L-r	K-r
Raw Score:	4	10	1	0	1	9	1	3	8
T Score:	53	57 F	47	42	50	54	33	52	52
Response %:	100	100	100	100	100	100	100	100	100

Cannot Say (Raw): 0 Percent True (of items answered): 27%

Comparison Group Data: MMPI-2-RF Normative (Women), N = 1138

	VRIN-r	TRIN-r	F-r	Fp-r	Fs	FBS-r	RBS	L-r	K-r
Mean Score (◇--◇):	50	51 T	50	49	50	52	50	50	50
Standard Dev (±1 SD):	9	10	10	10	10	10	10	10	10
Percent scoring at or below test taker:	74	81	65	51	75	69	5	75	65

The highest and lowest T scores possible on each scale are indicated by a "---"; MMPI-2-RF T scores are non-gendered.

VRIN-r Variable Response Inconsistency
TRIN-r True Response Inconsistency
F-r Infrequent Responses
Fp-r Infrequent Psychopathology Responses
Fs Infrequent Somatic Responses
FBS-r Symptom Validity
RBS Response Bias Scale
L-r Uncommon Virtues
K-r Adjustment Validity

FIGURE 11-4 Ms. W's MMPI-2-RF Clinical Settings Interpretive Report, continued

MMPI-2-RF Higher-Order (H-O) and Restructured Clinical (RC) Scales

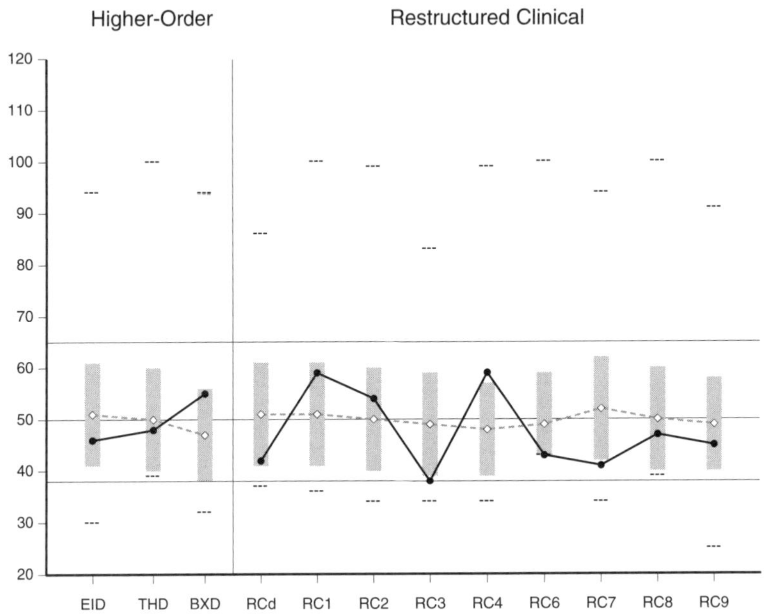

	EID	THD	BXD	RCd	RC1	RC2	RC3	RC4	RC6	RC7	RC8	RC9
Raw Score:	7	1	8	1	6	5	1	8	0	2	1	9
T Score:	46	48	55	42	59	54	38	59	43	41	47	45
Response %:	100	100	100	100	100	100	100	100	100	100	100	100

Comparison Group Data: MMPI-2-RF Normative (Women), N = 1138

	EID	THD	BXD	RCd	RC1	RC2	RC3	RC4	RC6	RC7	RC8	RC9
Mean Score (◇---◇):	51	50	47	51	51	50	49	48	49	52	50	49
Standard Dev (±1 SD):	10	10	9	10	10	10	10	9	10	10	10	9
Percent scoring at or below test taker:	38	56	87	28	80	78	12	92	65	19	54	40

The highest and lowest T scores possible on each scale are indicated by a "---"; MMPI-2-RF T scores are non-gendered.

EID Emotional/Internalizing Dysfunction
THD Thought Dysfunction
BXD Behavioral/Externalizing Dysfunction
RCd Demoralization
RC1 Somatic Complaints
RC2 Low Positive Emotions
RC3 Cynicism
RC4 Antisocial Behavior
RC6 Ideas of Persecution
RC7 Dysfunctional Negative Emotions
RC8 Aberrant Experiences
RC9 Hypomanic Activation

FIGURE 11-4 Ms. W's MMPI-2-RF Clinical Settings Interpretive Report, continued

MMPI-2-RF Somatic/Cognitive and Internalizing Scales

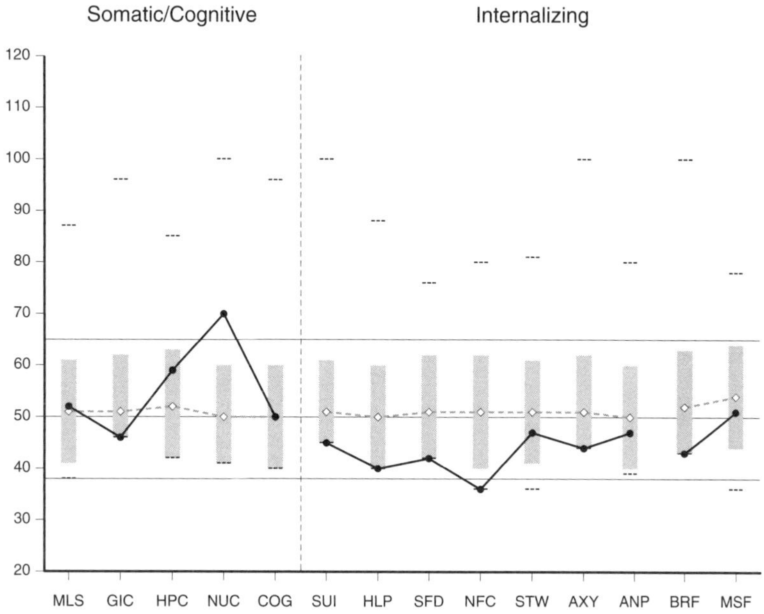

	MLS	GIC	HPC	NUC	COG	SUI	HLP	SFD	NFC	STW	AXY	ANP	BRF	MSF
Raw Score:	2	0	2	4	1	0	0	0	0	2	0	1	0	4
T Score:	52	46	59	70	50	45	40	42	36	47	44	47	43	51
Response %:	100	100	100	100	100	100	100	100	100	100	100	100	100	100

Comparison Group Data: MMPI-2-RF Normative (Women), N = 1138

	MLS	GIC	HPC	NUC	COG	SUI	HLP	SFD	NFC	STW	AXY	ANP	BRF	MSF
Mean Score (◇--◇):	51	51	52	50	50	51	50	51	51	51	51	50	52	54
Standard Dev (±1 SD):	10	11	11	10	10	10	10	11	11	10	11	10	11	10
Percent scoring at or below test taker:	69	79	85	97	66	78	41	46	13	53	64	48	52	53

The highest and lowest T scores possible on each scale are indicated by a "---"; MMPI-2-RF T scores are non-gendered.

MLS Malaise
GIC Gastrointestinal Complaints
HPC Head Pain Complaints
NUC Neurological Complaints
COG Cognitive Complaints

SUI Suicidal/Death Ideation
HLP Helplessness/Hopelessness
SFD Self-Doubt
NFC Inefficacy
STW Stress/Worry

AXY Anxiety
ANP Anger Proneness
BRF Behavior-Restricting Fears
MSF Multiple Specific Fears

FIGURE 11-4 Ms. W's MMPI-2-RF Clinical Settings Interpretive Report, continued

MMPI-2-RF Externalizing, Interpersonal, and Interest Scales

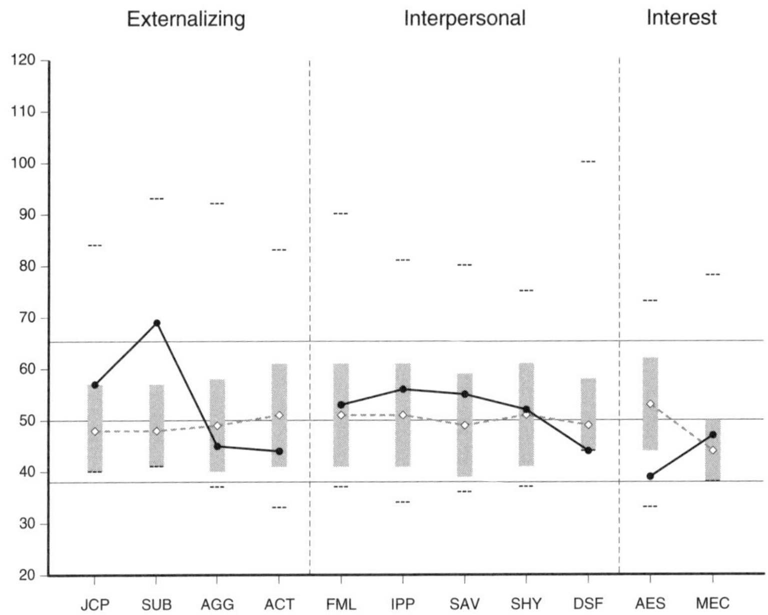

	JCP	SUB	AGG	ACT	FML	IPP	SAV	SHY	DSF	AES	MEC
Raw Score:	2	4	1	2	3	6	5	4	0	1	2
T Score:	57	69	45	44	53	56	55	52	44	39	47
Response %:	100	100	100	100	100	100	100	100	100	100	100

Comparison Group Data: MMPI-2-RF Normative (Women), N = 1138

	JCP	SUB	AGG	ACT	FML	IPP	SAV	SHY	DSF	AES	MEC
Mean Score (◇--◇):	48	48	49	51	51	51	49	51	49	53	44
Standard Dev (±1 SD):	9	9	9	10	10	10	10	10	9	9	6
Percent scoring at or below test taker:	92	98	48	33	71	80	84	70	72	13	81

The highest and lowest T scores possible on each scale are indicated by a "---"; MMPI-2-RF T scores are non-gendered.

JCP Juvenile Conduct Problems
SUB Substance Abuse
AGG Aggression
ACT Activation

FML Family Problems
IPP Interpersonal Passivity
SAV Social Avoidance
SHY Shyness
DSF Disaffiliativeness

AES Aesthetic-Literary Interests
MEC Mechanical-Physical Interests

FIGURE 11-4 Ms. W's MMPI-2-RF Clinical Settings Interpretive Report, continued

MMPI-2-RF® Interpretive Report: Clinical Settings
01/15/2016, Page 6

Ms. W

MMPI-2-RF PSY-5 Scales

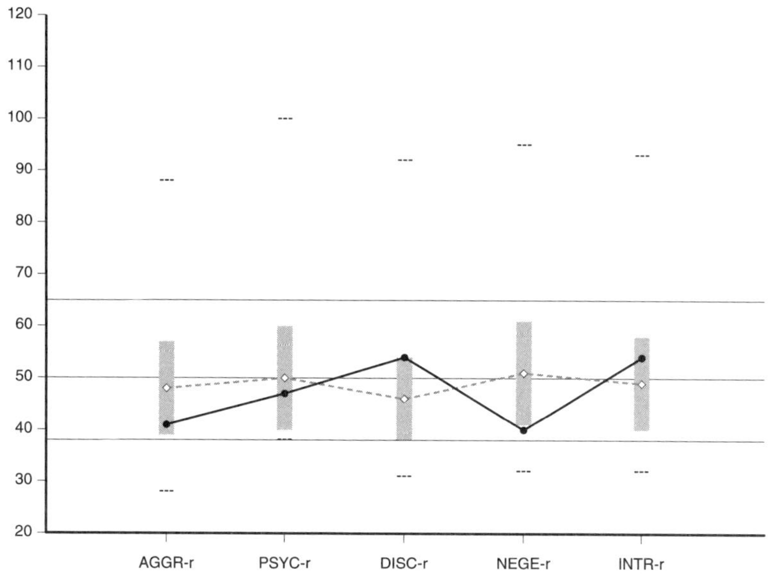

	AGGR-r	PSYC-r	DISC-r	NEGE-r	INTR-r
Raw Score:	5	1	8	2	8
T Score:	41	47	54	40	54
Response %:	100	100	100	100	100

Comparison Group Data: MMPI-2-RF Normative (Women), N = 1138

	AGGR-r	PSYC-r	DISC-r	NEGE-r	INTR-r
Mean Score (◇--◇):	48	50	46	51	49
Standard Dev (±1 SD):	9	10	8	10	9
Percent scoring at or below test taker:	27	53	88	14	80

The highest and lowest T scores possible on each scale are indicated by a "---"; MMPI-2-RF T scores are non-gendered.

AGGR-r Aggressiveness-Revised
PSYC-r Psychoticism-Revised
DISC-r Disconstraint-Revised
NEGE-r Negative Emotionality/Neuroticism-Revised
INTR-r Introversion/Low Positive Emotionality-Revised

FIGURE 11-4 Ms. W's MMPI-2-RF Clinical Settings Interpretive Report, continued

MMPI-2-RF® Interpretive Report: Clinical Settings
01/15/2016, Page 7

Ms. W

MMPI-2-RF T SCORES (BY DOMAIN)

PROTOCOL VALIDITY

Content Non-Responsiveness

0	53	57 F
CNS	VRIN-r	TRIN-r

Over-Reporting

47	42	50	54	33
F-r	Fp-r	Fs	FBS-r	RBS

Under-Reporting

52	52
L-r	K-r

SUBSTANTIVE SCALES

Somatic/Cognitive Dysfunction

59	52	46	59	70	50
RC1	MLS	GIC	HPC	NUC	COG

Emotional Dysfunction

46	42	45	40	42	36		
EID	RCd	SUI	HLP	SFD	NFC		
	54	54					
	RC2	INTR-r					
	41	47	44	47	43	51	40
	RC7	STW	AXY	ANP	BRF	MSF	NEGE-r

Thought Dysfunction

48	43
THD	RC6
	47
	RC8
	47
	PSYC-r

Behavioral Dysfunction

55	59	57	69		
BXD	RC4	JCP	SUB		
	45	45	44	41	54
	RC9	AGG	ACT	AGGR-r	DISC-r

Interpersonal Functioning

53	38	56	55	52	44
FML	RC3	IPP	SAV	SHY	DSF

Interests

39	47
AES	MEC

Note. This information is provided to facilitate interpretation following the recommended structure for MMPI-2-RF interpretation in Chapter 5 of the *MMPI-2-RF Manual for Administration, Scoring, and Interpretation*, which provides details in the text and an outline in Table 5-1.

FIGURE 11-4 Ms. W's MMPI-2-RF Clinical Settings Interpretive Report, continued

This interpretive report is intended for use by a professional qualified to interpret the MMPI-2-RF. The information it contains should be considered in the context of the test taker's background, the circumstances of the assessment, and other available information.

SYNOPSIS

This is a valid MMPI-2-RF protocol. Scores on the substantive scales indicate somatic complaints and behavioral dysfunction. Somatic complaints relate to neurological symptoms. Behavioral-externalizing problems relate to substance abuse.

PROTOCOL VALIDITY

This is a valid MMPI-2-RF protocol. There are no problems with unscorable items. The test taker responded to the items relevantly on the basis of their content, and there are no indications of over- or under-reporting.

SUBSTANTIVE SCALE INTERPRETATION

Clinical symptoms, personality characteristics, and behavioral tendencies of the test taker are described in this section and organized according to an empirically guided framework. Statements containing the word "reports" are based on the item content of MMPI-2-RF scales, whereas statements that include the word "likely" are based on empirical correlates of scale scores. Specific sources for each statement can be accessed with the annotation features of this report.

Somatic/Cognitive Dysfunction

The test taker reports vague neurological complaints[1] and is likely to present with multiple somatic complaints[2], to be preoccupied with physical health concerns[2], and to be prone to developing physical symptoms in response to stress[3].

Emotional Dysfunction

There are no indications of emotional-internalizing dysfunction in this protocol. The test taker is likely to be self-reliant and power-oriented[4].

Thought Dysfunction

There are no indications of disordered thinking in this protocol.

FIGURE 11-4 Ms. W's MMPI-2-RF Clinical Settings Interpretive Report, continued

Behavioral Dysfunction

The test taker reports significant past and current substance abuse[5], and is indeed likely to have a history of problematic use of alcohol or drugs[6], to be sensation-seeking[7], and to have had legal problems as a result of substance abuse[7].

Interpersonal Functioning Scales

The test taker describes others as well-intentioned and trustworthy and disavows cynical beliefs about them[8]. She is possibly overly trusting[9].

Interest Scales

The test taker reports an average number of interests in activities or occupations of an aesthetic or literary nature (e.g., writing, music, the theater)[10]. She also reports an average number of interests in activities or occupations of a mechanical or physical nature (e.g., fixing and building things, the outdoors, sports)[11].

DIAGNOSTIC CONSIDERATIONS

This section provides recommendations for psychodiagnostic assessment based on the test taker's MMPI-2-RF results. It is recommended that she be evaluated for the following:

Emotional-Internalizing Disorders

- Somatoform disorder, if physical origins for neurological complaints have been ruled out[12]

Behavioral-Externalizing Disorders

- Substance-related disorders[13]

TREATMENT CONSIDERATIONS

This section provides inferential treatment-related recommendations based on the test taker's MMPI-2-RF scores.

Areas for Further Evaluation

- Extent to which genuine physical health problems contribute to the score on the Neurological Complaints (NUC) scale[12].

Psychotherapy Process Issues

- Likely to reject psychological interpretations of somatic complaints[12].

Possible Targets for Treatment

- Reduction or cessation of substance abuse[14]

FIGURE 11-4 Ms. W's MMPI-2-RF Clinical Settings Interpretive Report, continued

ITEM-LEVEL INFORMATION

Unscorable Responses

The test taker produced scorable responses to all the MMPI-2-RF items.

Critical Responses

Seven MMPI-2-RF scales--Suicidal/Death Ideation (SUI), Helplessness/Hopelessness (HLP), Anxiety (AXY), Ideas of Persecution (RC6), Aberrant Experiences (RC8), Substance Abuse (SUB), and Aggression (AGG)--have been designated by the test authors as having critical item content that may require immediate attention and follow-up. Items answered by the individual in the keyed direction (True or False) on a critical scale are listed below if her T score on that scale is 65 or higher. The percentage of the MMPI-2-RF normative sample (NS) and of the MMPI-2-RF Normative (Women) comparison group (CG) that answered each item in the keyed direction are provided in parentheses following the item content.

Substance Abuse (SUB, T Score = 69)

141. Item Content Omitted. (True; NS 34.2%, CG 23.9%)
192. Item Content Omitted. (True; NS 11.2%, CG 8.2%)
237. Item Content Omitted. (False; NS 27.4%, CG 25.1%)
266. Item Content Omitted. (True; NS 5.0%, CG 3.3%)

FIGURE 11-4 Ms. W's MMPI-2-RF Clinical Settings Interpretive Report, continued

ENDNOTES

This section lists for each statement in the report the MMPI-2-RF score(s) that triggered it. In addition, each statement is identified as a Test Response, if based on item content, a Correlate, if based on empirical correlates, or an Inference, if based on the report authors' judgment. (This information can also be accessed on-screen by placing the cursor on a given statement.) For correlate-based statements, research references (Ref. No.) are provided, keyed to the consecutively numbered reference list following the endnotes.

[1] Test Response: NUC=70
[2] Correlate: NUC=70, Ref. 2, 5
[3] Correlate: NUC=70, Ref. 5
[4] Correlate: NFC=36, Ref. 5
[5] Test Response: SUB=69
[6] Correlate: SUB=69, Ref. 1, 2, 5
[7] Correlate: SUB=69, Ref. 5
[8] Test Response: RC3=38
[9] Correlate: RC3=38, Ref. 3, 4, 5
[10] Test Response: AES=39
[11] Test Response: MEC=47
[12] Inference: NUC=70
[13] Correlate: SUB=69, Ref. 1, 6
[14] Inference: SUB=69

FIGURE 11-4 Ms. W's MMPI-2-RF Clinical Settings Interpretive Report, continued

RESEARCH REFERENCE LIST

1. Block, A. R., Ben-Porath, Y. S., & Marek, R. J. (2013). Psychological risk factors for poor outcome of spine surgery and spinal cord stimulator implant: A review of the literature and their assessment with the MMPI-2-RF. *The Clinical Neuropsychologist, 27,* 81-107. doi: 10.1080/13854046.2012.721007

2. Burchett, D. L., & Ben-Porath, Y. S. (2010). The impact of over-reporting on MMPI-2-RF substantive scale score validity. *Assessment, 17,* 497-516. doi: 10.1177/1073191110378972

3. Sellbom, M., Ben-Porath, Y. S., & Bagby, R. M. (2008). Personality and psychopathology: Mapping the MMPI-2 Restructured Clinical (RC) Scales onto the five factor model of personality. *Journal of Personality Disorders, 22,* 291-312. doi: 10.1521/pedi.2008.22.3.291

4. Simms, L. J., Casillas, A., Clark, L. A., Watson, D., & Doebbeling, B. I. (2005). Psychometric evaluation of the Restructured Clinical Scales of the MMPI-2. *Psychological Assessment, 17,* 345-358. doi: 10.1037/1040-3590.17.3.345

5. Tellegen, A., & Ben-Porath, Y. S. (2008/2011). *The Minnesota Multiphasic Personality Inventory-2-Restructured Form (MMPI-2-RF): Technical manual.* Minneapolis: University of Minnesota Press.

6. Van der Heijden, P. T., Egger, J. I. M., Rossi, G., Grundel, G., & Derksen, J. J. L. (2013). The MMPI-2 Restructured Form and the standard MMPI-2 Clinical Scales in relation to DSM-IV. *European Journal of Psychological Assessment, 29,* 182-188. doi: 10.1027/1015-5759/a000140

End of Report

This and previous pages of this report contain trade secrets and are not to be released in response to requests under HIPAA (or any other data disclosure law that exempts trade secret information from release). Further, release in response to litigation discovery demands should be made only in accordance with your profession's ethical guidelines and under an appropriate protective order.

FIGURE 11-4 Ms. W's MMPI-2-RF Clinical Settings Interpretive Report, continued

caused by the effects of alcohol, and recurrent use of alcohol in situations in which it is physically hazardous.

STEP 2: ASSESSING FOR CURRENT WORK IMPAIRMENT

Ms. W is receiving appropriate treatment and demonstrates reasonably good insight and accountability. In addition, she currently exhibits no symptoms at a magnitude that would be expected to substantially limit her ability to safely and effectively perform the essential functions of her position. Employment records indicate that Ms. W's performance as a dispatcher has been good even during periods when she was engaged in off-duty alcohol use, and it is noted that her work is constantly monitored by at least one supervisor or coworker who could intervene in the event of any observed impairment. However, because alcohol use disorder tends to be episodic and chronically reoccurring—both for people generally and for Ms. W by history—the third step in the fitness analysis is important as well.

STEP 3: ASSESSING FOR SUSTAINABILITY OF FITNESS

The sustainability of Ms. W's fitness for duty depends entirely on her ability to remain sober. In light of her failed efforts to remain sober after attempting controlled drinking, this requires that she abstain from the use of alcohol in any amount. Her substance use counselor identified no specific threats to sustained remission, except for the fact that she has a history of relapse and her condition is one that is prone to relapse. If enforced, the last-chance agreement governing her return to work can play an important role in motivating and enforcing her continued commitment to sobriety and mental health treatment. The latter is especially important for maintaining her abstinence from alcohol use because of the various nonwork stressors she is experiencing (primarily grief and a progressive neurological condition) and because her stress coping abilities are poorly developed. In particular, the provision in the last-chance agreement for weekly monitoring of Ms. W's compliance with all requirements of the recommended treatment program is especially imperative, inasmuch as relapse is likely to be accompanied or preceded by lapses in treatment compliance.

Conclusion

The aggregate clinical evidence derived from all sources indicates that Ms. W has an alcohol use disorder that is currently in early remission and poses no current, substantial limitations in her ability to perform the essential functions of her position as a dispatcher. Although the prognosis for sustained remission is guarded, the examiner determined that Ms. W was psychologically fit for duty under the condition of the enforced last-chance agreement.

Ms. E, Correctional Officer

Assessment Issues Presented

- Integration of findings from the MMPI-2-RF Clinical Settings Interpretive Report with assessment data from the clinical interview, employment records, and medical records to assess fitness for duty of an incumbent correctional officer who became upset after an argument at work and cut her wrists

Referral Summary

Ms. E, a 40-year-old correctional officer with 5 years of service with the same county sheriff's office, was observed by a fellow deputy to have lacerations on both arms. The coworker asked her about the cause of these injuries, assuming she had received them from a physical altercation with an inmate. In a calm and nonchalant manner, she replied, "I did it myself with an Exacto knife. It's what I do when I get upset." The deputy reported the incident to a superior officer. Jail administrators interviewed Ms. E, who said that just before the end of her shift the day before, she had a conversation with another deputy who became "critical and demeaning." She said she became increasingly upset, and as she said she often did when she could not console herself, she deliberately inflicted superficial cuts on her arms. The jail administrators were concerned that Ms. E, as a result of a mental health condition, may be unable to safely and effectively perform the duties of her position and ordered her to submit to a fitness-for-duty evaluation.

Assessment Findings

EMPLOYMENT RECORDS

Ms. E's employment records, which included information from her separate employment medical file, showed that she had exhausted her available bank of sick leave hours and that she had sought reasonable accommodation a year prior, requesting not to work mandatory overtime. This accommodation was supported by a letter from her treating psychiatrist, who wrote that "sleep regulation is integral in managing her disability—overtime is not an option." However, the accommodation request was denied because it was deemed to pose an undue hardship for the employer and its around-the-clock operational requirements. Ms. E's personnel records also contained two "counseling memos" and a performance evaluation in the previous year, documenting complaints from coworkers about excessive irritability, moodiness, and argumentativeness.

MENTAL STATUS EXAMINATION

Ms. E's affect was remarkably euthymic given the circumstances and the high stakes associated with the evaluation. Her attitude toward the examiner was cooperative. She was well groomed and appropriately dressed. Her speech was normal for rate, volume, quality, and quantity, and she exhibited no abnormalities in perception, thought process, sensorium, or cognition. However, Ms. E's insight and judgment were poor, as evidenced by her insistence that what she did "on [her] own time" is of no relevance to the employer. She described a causal connection between her coworker's "demeaning" treatment of her at work and her self-inflicted injury, but she considered the self-injury to be "no one's business" but her own. She denied past or current homicidal ideation.

CLINICAL INTERVIEW

Ms. E disclosed a history of self-cutting since at least her teens. She said she does not cut deep enough to leave scars, stating that the cuts are "more of a scratch." She said that her self-cutting acts are typically triggered by anger: "I get mad about something I have no control over and I need to release the anger, release the pain, whatever." She estimated that her self-cutting the evening after her argument with the deputy at work was the first time she had done so in more than a year.

Ms. E said that she was diagnosed with Borderline Personality Disorder at the age of 20, shortly after she enlisted in the military. She said that she had a major depressive episode while in the service, attempted suicide by overdosing on over-the-counter medication (but ultimately regurgitated the drugs and did not report it to anyone), and was eventually hospitalized for depression. She was then involuntarily separated from the military. She attempted suicide again 3 years later by overdosing on prescribed antidepressant medication and was hospitalized again. Over the next 17 years, Ms. E was hospitalized no fewer than six times, each subsequent to a suicide attempt. Her most recent hospitalization was a year prior to the FFDE referral. Ms. E said that she has "improved immensely since I started taking my treatment seriously," which she said began after her last hospitalization. She reported a long history of episodic alcohol abuse, but denied abuse in the past year. Finally, she reported that she suffers from early-morning awakening nearly every day, resulting in less than 5 hours of sleep, and she has no interest in socializing with friends or doing much of anything outside of work.

MEDICAL RECORDS

The examiner requested and received medical records pertaining to Ms. E's most recent hospitalization and her subsequent mental health treatment.[2] These records showed that Ms. E was diagnosed with Borderline Personality Disorder (primary diagnosis) and Major Depressive Disorder during the latest hospital admission. Her medical records also reveal a history of treatment for migraine headaches. It is important to note that, contradicting Ms. E's self-reported treatment progress, the clinical notes document a refractory period of depression, repeated self-injurious behavior, and recent suicidal ideation with a lethal plan.

MMPI-2-RF FINDINGS

Ms. E's MMPI-2-RF Clinical Settings Interpretive Report is reproduced in Figure 11-5. A review of her Validity Scale scores indicates no unscorable items and that she responded to the items relevantly on the basis of their content. As reflected in her scores on FBS-r (80T) and RBS (84T), she provided an unusual combination of responses that is associated with noncredible reporting of somatic and/or cognitive symptoms; although these response combinations could reflect exaggeration, they also may occur in individuals with significant medical problems (FBS-r) and emotional dysfunction (RBS). The protocol also shows no indications of underreporting; indeed, among the items on the Adjustment Validity (K-r) scale, Ms. E answered only one in the keyed direction, resulting in a T-score of 28 and indicating a very poor self-assessment of her current psychological adjustment.

As shown on page 3 of Figure 11-5, Ms. E's score on the Higher-Order (H-O) scale EID (Emotional/Internalizing Dysfunction; 79T) indicates significant and pervasive emotional distress. More specifically, her clinically elevated scores on RCd (Demoralization; 77T), RC1 (Somatic Complaints; 68T); RC2 (Low Positive Emotions; 73T), RC6 (Ideas of Persecution; 66T), and RC7 (Dysfunctional Negative Emotions; 70T) indicate, respectively, marked feelings of sadness and unhappiness, and dissatisfaction with her current life circumstances; multiple somatic complaints; a lack of positive emotional experiences, significant anhedonia, and a lack of interest; significant persecutory ideation, such as believing that others seek to harm her; and various negative emotional experiences.

Ms. E's scores on the Specific Problems scales (Figure 11-5, pp. 4–5) further elucidate the problems indicated in her elevated H-O and RC scales. Ben-Porath (2012) provides a detailed framework for organizing MMPI-2-RF findings and for identifying the scale scores relevant to each of the domains assessed with the test. This framework is reflected in the organization of scales on page 7 of every MMPI-2-RF report (Score Report, PCIR, and Clinical Settings Interpretive Report). In Figure 11-5 (p. 7),

MMPI 2 RF®

Minnesota Multiphasic
Personality Inventory-2
Restructured Form®

Interpretive Report: Clinical Settings

MMPI-2-RF®

Minnesota Multiphasic Personality Inventory-2-Restructured Form®

Yossef S. Ben-Porath, PhD, & Auke Tellegen, PhD

Name:	Ms. E
Age:	40
Gender:	Female
Marital Status:	Never Married
Years of Education:	14
Date Assessed:	04/28/2016

PsychCorp

Copyright © 2008, 2011, 2012 by the Regents of the University of Minnesota. All rights reserved.
Distributed exclusively under license from the University of Minnesota by NCS Pearson, Inc. Portions reproduced from the MMPI-2-RF test booklet. Copyright © 2008 by the Regents of the University of Minnesota. All rights reserved. Portions excerpted from the *MMPI-2-RF Manual for Administration, Scoring, and Interpretation.* Copyright © 2008, 2011 by the Regents of the University of Minnesota. All rights reserved. Used by permission of the University of Minnesota Press.

MMPI-2-RF, the **MMPI-2-RF logo,** and **Minnesota Multiphasic Personality Inventory-2-Restructured Form** are registered trademarks of the University of Minnesota. **Pearson,** the **PSI logo,** and **PsychCorp** are trademarks in the U.S. and/or other countries of Pearson Education, Inc., or its affiliate(s).

TRADE SECRET INFORMATION
Not for release under HIPAA or other data disclosure laws that exempt trade secrets from disclosure.

[3.1 / 57 / 3.3.10]

ALWAYS LEARNING PEARSON

FIGURE 11-5 Ms. E's MMPI-2-RF Clinical Settings Interpretive Report

MMPI-2-RF Validity Scales

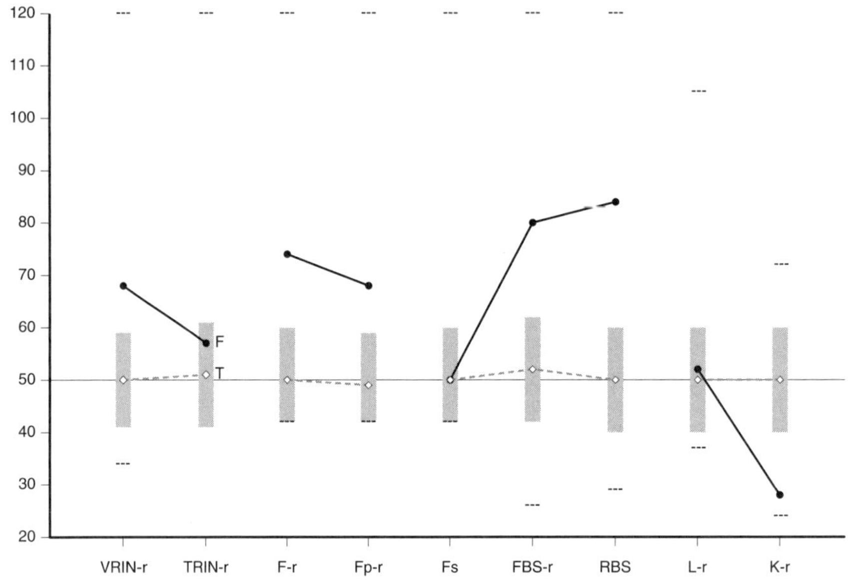

	VRIN-r	TRIN-r	F-r	Fp-r	Fs	FBS-r	RBS	L-r	K-r
Raw Score:	7	10	7	3	1	17	13	3	1
T Score:	68	57 F	74	68	50	80	84	52	28
Response %:	100	100	100	100	100	100	100	100	100

Cannot Say (Raw): 0 Percent True (of items answered): 44%

Comparison Group Data: MMPI-2-RF Normative (Women), N = 1138

	VRIN-r	TRIN-r	F-r	Fp-r	Fs	FBS-r	RBS	L-r	K-r
Mean Score (◇--◇):	50	51 T	50	49	50	52	50	50	50
Standard Dev (±1 SD):	9	10	10	10	10	10	10	10	10
Percent scoring at or below test taker:	97	81	97	96	75	99	99.9	75	1

The highest and lowest T scores possible on each scale are indicated by a "---"; MMPI-2-RF T scores are non-gendered.

VRIN-r Variable Response Inconsistency
TRIN-r True Response Inconsistency
F-r Infrequent Responses
Fp-r Infrequent Psychopathology Responses
Fs Infrequent Somatic Responses
FBS-r Symptom Validity
RBS Response Bias Scale
L-r Uncommon Virtues
K-r Adjustment Validity

FIGURE 11-5 Ms. E's MMPI-2-RF Clinical Settings Interpretive Report, continued

MMPI-2-RF Higher-Order (H-O) and Restructured Clinical (RC) Scales

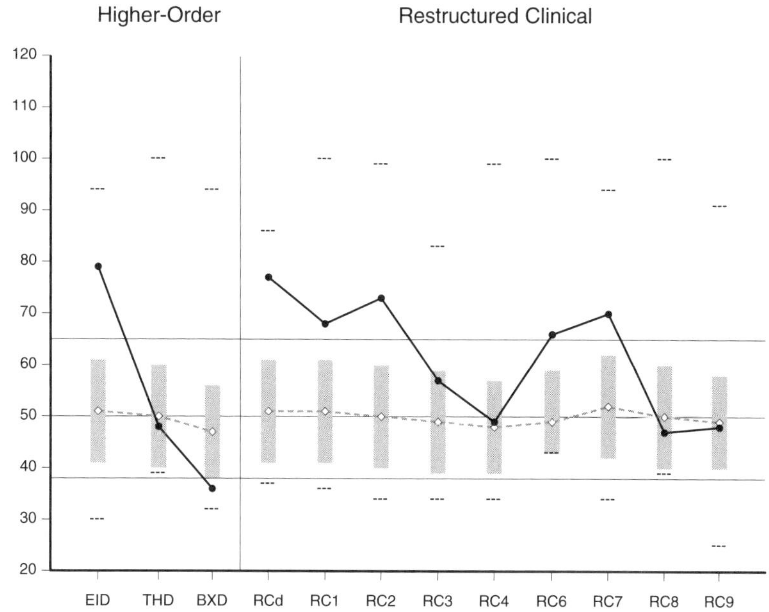

	EID	THD	BXD	RCd	RC1	RC2	RC3	RC4	RC6	RC7	RC8	RC9
Raw Score:	31	1	1	19	10	10	9	4	3	15	1	11
T Score:	79	48	36	77	68	73	57	49	66	70	47	48
Response %:	100	100	100	100	100	100	100	100	100	100	100	100

Comparison Group Data: MMPI-2-RF Normative (Women), N = 1138

	EID	THD	BXD	RCd	RC1	RC2	RC3	RC4	RC6	RC7	RC8	RC9
Mean Score (◇---◇):	51	50	47	51	51	50	49	48	49	52	50	49
Standard Dev (±1 SD):	10	10	9	10	10	10	10	9	10	10	10	9
Percent scoring at or below test taker:	99.3	56	14	98	94	99	85	66	95	95	54	57

The highest and lowest T scores possible on each scale are indicated by a "---"; MMPI-2-RF T scores are non-gendered.

EID Emotional/Internalizing Dysfunction
THD Thought Dysfunction
BXD Behavioral/Externalizing Dysfunction
RCd Demoralization
RC1 Somatic Complaints
RC2 Low Positive Emotions
RC3 Cynicism
RC4 Antisocial Behavior
RC6 Ideas of Persecution
RC7 Dysfunctional Negative Emotions
RC8 Aberrant Experiences
RC9 Hypomanic Activation

FIGURE 11-5 Ms. E's MMPI-2-RF Clinical Settings Interpretive Report, continued

MMPI-2-RF Somatic/Cognitive and Internalizing Scales

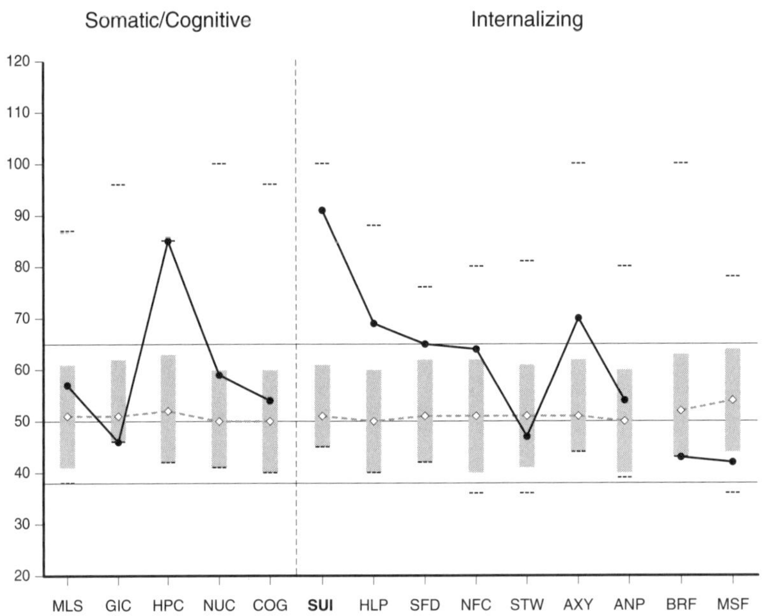

	MLS	GIC	HPC	NUC	COG	SUI	HLP	SFD	NFC	STW	AXY	ANP	BRF	MSF
Raw Score:	3	0	6	2	2	3	3	3	6	2	2	3	0	1
T Score:	57	46	85	59	54	**91**	69	65	64	47	70	54	43	42
Response %:	100	100	100	100	100	100	100	100	100	100	100	100	100	100

Comparison Group Data: MMPI-2-RF Normative (Women), N = 1138

	MLS	GIC	HPC	NUC	COG	SUI	HLP	SFD	NFC	STW	AXY	ANP	BRF	MSF
Mean Score (◇--◇):	51	51	52	50	50	51	50	51	51	51	51	50	52	54
Standard Dev (±1 SD):	10	11	11	10	10	10	10	11	11	10	11	10	11	10
Percent scoring at or below test taker:	84	79	100	88	80	99.7	96	91	89	53	96	77	52	14

The highest and lowest T scores possible on each scale are indicated by a "---"; MMPI-2-RF T scores are non-gendered.

MLS Malaise
GIC Gastrointestinal Complaints
HPC Head Pain Complaints
NUC Neurological Complaints
COG Cognitive Complaints
SUI Suicidal/Death Ideation
HLP Helplessness/Hopelessness
SFD Self-Doubt
NFC Inefficacy
STW Stress/Worry
AXY Anxiety
ANP Anger Proneness
BRF Behavior-Restricting Fears
MSF Multiple Specific Fears

FIGURE 11-5 Ms. E's MMPI-2-RF Clinical Settings Interpretive Report, continued

MMPI-2-RF® Interpretive Report: Clinical Settings
04/28/2016, Page 5 Ms. E

MMPI-2-RF Externalizing, Interpersonal, and Interest Scales

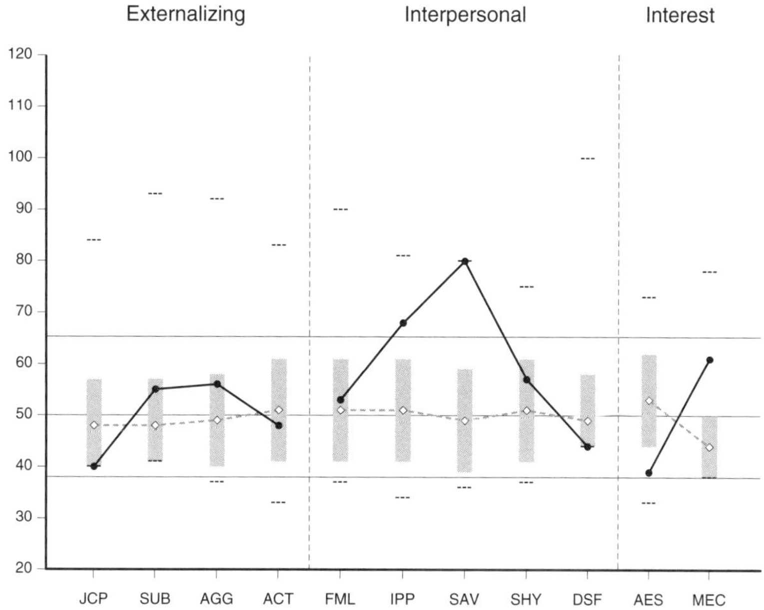

	JCP	SUB	AGG	ACT	FML	IPP	SAV	SHY	DSF	AES	MEC
Raw Score:	0	2	3	3	3	8	10	5	0	1	5
T Score:	40	55	56	48	53	68	80	57	44	39	61
Response %:	100	100	100	100	100	100	100	100	100	100	100

Comparison Group Data: MMPI-2-RF Normative (Women), N = 1138

	JCP	SUB	AGG	ACT	FML	IPP	SAV	SHY	DSF	AES	MEC
Mean Score (◇---◇):	48	48	49	51	51	51	49	51	49	53	44
Standard Dev (±1 SD):	9	9	9	10	10	10	10	10	9	9	6
Percent scoring at or below test taker:	49	87	88	55	71	95	100	83	72	13	99

The highest and lowest T scores possible on each scale are indicated by a "---"; MMPI-2-RF T scores are non-gendered.

JCP Juvenile Conduct Problems
SUB Substance Abuse
AGG Aggression
ACT Activation

FML Family Problems
IPP Interpersonal Passivity
SAV Social Avoidance
SHY Shyness
DSF Disaffiliativeness

AES Aesthetic-Literary Interests
MEC Mechanical-Physical Interests

FIGURE 11-5 Ms. E's MMPI-2-RF Clinical Settings Interpretive Report, continued

MMPI-2-RF PSY-5 Scales

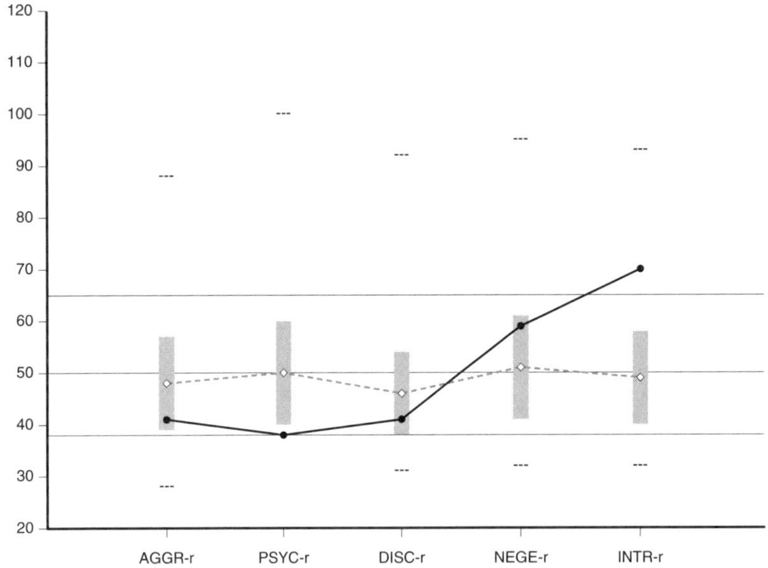

	AGGR-r	PSYC-r	DISC-r	NEGE-r	INTR-r
Raw Score:	5	0	3	10	13
T Score:	41	38	41	59	70
Response %:	100	100	100	100	100

Comparison Group Data: MMPI-2-RF Normative (Women), N = 1138

Mean Score (◇--◇):	48	50	46	51	49
Standard Dev (±1 SD):	9	10	8	10	9
Percent scoring at or below test taker:	27	28	37	81	98

The highest and lowest T scores possible on each scale are indicated by a "---"; MMPI-2-RF T scores are non-gendered.

AGGR-r Aggressiveness-Revised
PSYC-r Psychoticism-Revised
DISC-r Disconstraint-Revised
NEGE-r Negative Emotionality/Neuroticism-Revised
INTR-r Introversion/Low Positive Emotionality-Revised

FIGURE 11-5 Ms. E's MMPI-2-RF Clinical Settings Interpretive Report, continued

MMPI-2-RF T SCORES (BY DOMAIN)

PROTOCOL VALIDITY

Content Non-Responsiveness	CNS 0; VRIN-r 68; TRIN-r 57 F
Over-Reporting	F-r 74; Fp-r 68; Fs 50; FBS-r 80; RBS 84
Under-Reporting	L-r 52; K-r 28

SUBSTANTIVE SCALES

Domain	Higher-Order	Scores
Somatic/Cognitive Dysfunction		RC1 68; MLS 57; GIC 46; HPC 85; NUC 59; COG 54
Emotional Dysfunction	EID 79	RCd 77; SUI 91; HLP 69; SFD 65; NFC 64
		RC2 73; INTR-r 70
		RC7 70; STW 47; AXY 70; ANP 54; BRF 43; MSF 42; NEGE-r 59
Thought Dysfunction	THD 48	RC6 66
		RC8 47
		PSYC-r 38
Behavioral Dysfunction	BXD 36	RC4 49; JCP 40; SUB 55
		RC9 48; AGG 56; ACT 48; AGGR-r 41; DISC-r 41
Interpersonal Functioning		FML 53; RC3 57; IPP 68; SAV 80; SHY 57; DSF 44
Interests		AES 39; MEC 61

Note. This information is provided to facilitate interpretation following the recommended structure for MMPI-2-RF interpretation in Chapter 5 of the *MMPI-2-RF Manual for Administration, Scoring, and Interpretation*, which provides details in the text and an outline in Table 5-1.

FIGURE 11-5 Ms. E's MMPI-2-RF Clinical Settings Interpretive Report, continued

This interpretive report is intended for use by a professional qualified to interpret the MMPI-2-RF. The information it contains should be considered in the context of the test taker's background, the circumstances of the assessment, and other available information.

SYNOPSIS

Scores on the MMPI-2-RF validity scales raise concerns about the possible impact of over-reporting (specifically, of somatic and/or cognitive symptoms) on the validity of this protocol. With that caution noted, scores on the substantive scales indicate somatic complaints and emotional, thought, and interpersonal dysfunction. Somatic complaints include preoccupation with poor health and head pain. Emotional-internalizing findings include **suicidal ideation**, demoralization, depression, helplessness and hopelessness, self-doubt, and anxiety. Dysfunctional thinking relates to ideas of persecution. Interpersonal difficulties include passivity and social avoidance.

PROTOCOL VALIDITY

Content Non-Responsiveness

There are no problems with unscorable items in this protocol. The test taker responded relevantly to the items on the basis of their content.

Over-Reporting

The test taker provided an unusual combination of responses that is associated with non-credible reporting of somatic and/or cognitive symptoms. This combination of responses may occur in individuals with substantial medical problems who report credible symptoms, but it could also reflect exaggeration[1]. She also provided an unusual combination of responses that is associated with non-credible memory complaints. This combination of responses may occur in individuals with significant emotional dysfunction, but it could also reflect exaggeration[2]. Scores on the somatic scales--Somatic Complaints (RC1), Malaise (MLS), Gastrointestinal Complaints (GIC), Head Pain Complaints (HPC), and Neurological Complaints (NUC)--and the Cognitive Complaints (COG) scale should be interpreted in light of this caution[3].

Under-Reporting

There are no indications of under-reporting in this protocol.

FIGURE 11-5 Ms. E's MMPI-2-RF Clinical Settings Interpretive Report, continued

MMPI-2-RF® Interpretive Report: Clinical Settings
04/28/2016, Page 9 Ms. E

SUBSTANTIVE SCALE INTERPRETATION

Clinical symptoms, personality characteristics, and behavioral tendencies of the test taker are described in this section and organized according to an empirically guided framework. Statements containing the word "reports" are based on the item content of MMPI-2-RF scales, whereas statements that include the word "likely" are based on empirical correlates of scale scores. Specific sources for each statement can be accessed with the annotation features of this report.

The following interpretation needs to be considered in light of cautions noted about the possible impact of over-reporting on the validity of this protocol.

Somatic/Cognitive Dysfunction

The test taker reports multiple somatic complaints[4] including diffuse head and neck pain, recurring headaches, and developing head pain when upset[5]. She is likely to be preoccupied with physical health concerns[6], to be prone to developing physical symptoms in response to stress[7], and to complain of fatigue[8].

Emotional Dysfunction

The test taker reports a history of suicidal ideation and/or attempts[9]. She is likely to be preoccupied with suicide and death[10] and to be at risk for current suicidal ideation and attempts[10].

Her responses indicate significant and pervasive emotional distress[11]. More specifically, she reports feeling sad and unhappy and being dissatisfied with her current life circumstances[12]. She is likely to complain of feeling depressed[13]. She also reports feeling hopeless[14]. She is likely to feel overwhelmed and that life is a strain[15], to believe she cannot be helped[15] and gets a raw deal from life[16], and to lack motivation for change[15]. In addition, she reports self-doubt[17] and is likely to be prone to rumination, to feel insecure and inferior, and to be self-disparaging and intropunitive[18].

The test taker reports a lack of positive emotional experiences, significant anhedonia, and lack of interest[19]. She is likely to be pessimistic[20].

She reports various negative emotional experiences[21] and is likely to be self-critical and guilt-prone[22]. She also reports feeling anxious[23] and is likely to experience significant anxiety and anxiety-related problems[24], intrusive ideation, and nightmares[25].

Thought Dysfunction

The test taker reports significant persecutory ideation such as believing that others seek to harm her[26]. She is likely to be suspicious of and alienated from others[27], to experience interpersonal difficulties as a result of suspiciousness[28], and to lack insight[28].

Behavioral Dysfunction

There are no indications of maladaptive externalizing behavior in this protocol. The test taker's responses indicate a higher than average level of behavioral constraint[29]. She is unlikely to engage in externalizing, acting-out behavior[29].

FIGURE 11-5 Ms. E's MMPI-2-RF Clinical Settings Interpretive Report, continued

Interpersonal Functioning Scales

The test taker reports being unassertive[30] and is indeed likely to be passive and submissive in interpersonal relationships[31]. She also reports not enjoying social events and avoiding social situations, including parties and other events where crowds are likely to gather[32]. She is very likely to be introverted[33], to have difficulty forming close relationships[34], and to be emotionally restricted[35].

Interest Scales

The test taker reports an average number of interests in activities or occupations of an aesthetic or literary nature (e.g., writing, music, the theater)[36]. She also reports an average number of interests in activities or occupations of a mechanical or physical nature (e.g., fixing and building things, the outdoors, sports)[37].

DIAGNOSTIC CONSIDERATIONS

This section provides recommendations for psychodiagnostic assessment based on the test taker's MMPI-2-RF results. It is recommended that she be evaluated for the following:

Emotional-Internalizing Disorders

- Somatoform disorder[38], if physical origins for head pain complaints have been ruled out[39]
- Depression-related disorder[40]
- Anxiety-related disorders including PTSD[41]

Thought Disorders

- Disorders involving persecutory ideation[42]

Interpersonal Disorders

- Disorders characterized by passive-submissive behavior such as dependent personality disorder[43]
- Disorders associated with social avoidance such as avoidant personality disorder[44]

TREATMENT CONSIDERATIONS

This section provides inferential treatment-related recommendations based on the test taker's MMPI-2-RF scores.

Areas for Further Evaluation

- **<u>Risk for suicide</u> should be assessed immediately**[45].
- Need for antidepressant medication[46].
- Extent to which genuine physical health problems contribute to the score on the Somatic Complaints (RC1) scale[47].
- Origin of head pain complaints[39].

FIGURE 11-5 Ms. E's MMPI-2-RF Clinical Settings Interpretive Report, continued

Psychotherapy Process Issues

- Likely to reject psychological interpretations of somatic complaints[47].
- Serious emotional difficulties may motivate her for treatment[48].
- Persecutory ideation may interfere with forming a therapeutic relationship and treatment compliance[49].

Possible Targets for Treatment

- Psychological distress as an initial target[48]
- Loss of hope and feelings of despair as early targets for intervention[50]
- Pain management for head pain complaints[39]
- Low self-esteem and other manifestations of self-doubt[51]
- Anhedonia[52]
- Dysfunctional negative emotions[53]
- Anxiety[54]
- Persecutory ideation[49]
- Reducing passive, submissive behavior[43]
- Difficulties associated with social avoidance[55]

ITEM-LEVEL INFORMATION

Unscorable Responses

The test taker produced scorable responses to all the MMPI-2-RF items.

Critical Responses

Seven MMPI-2-RF scales--Suicidal/Death Ideation (SUI), Helplessness/Hopelessness (HLP), Anxiety (AXY), Ideas of Persecution (RC6), Aberrant Experiences (RC8), Substance Abuse (SUB), and Aggression (AGG)--have been designated by the test authors as having critical item content that may require immediate attention and follow-up. Items answered by the individual in the keyed direction (True or False) on a critical scale are listed below if her T score on that scale is 65 or higher. The percentage of the MMPI-2-RF normative sample (NS) and of the MMPI-2-RF Normative (Women) comparison group (CG) that answered each item in the keyed direction are provided in parentheses following the item content.

Suicidal/Death Ideation (SUI, T Score = 91)

93. Item Content Omitted. (True; NS 3.7%, CG 3.2%)
120. Item Content Omitted. (True; NS 2.4%, CG 3.3%)
251. Item Content Omitted. (True; NS 3.0%, CG 4.6%)

Helplessness/Hopelessness (HLP, T Score = 69)

135. Item Content Omitted. (True; NS 24.2%, CG 27.0%)
282. Item Content Omitted. (False; NS 17.3%, CG 16.7%)
336. Item Content Omitted. (True; NS 38.0%, CG 38.2%)

FIGURE 11-5 Ms. E's MMPI-2-RF Clinical Settings Interpretive Report, continued

Anxiety (AXY, T Score = 70)

79. Item Content Omitted. (True; NS 6.2%, CG 6.3%)
289. Item Content Omitted. (True; NS 12.7%, CG 18.2%)

Ideas of Persecution (RC6, T Score = 66)

110. Item Content Omitted. (True; NS 9.9%, CG 10.8%)
194. Item Content Omitted. (True; NS 17.1%, CG 15.9%)
310. Item Content Omitted. (True; NS 3.0%, CG 2.3%)

User-Designated Item-Level Information

The following item-level information is based on the report user's selection of additional scales, and/or of lower cutoffs for the critical scales from the previous section. Items answered by the test taker in the keyed direction (True or False) on a selected scale are listed below if her T score on that scale is at the user-designated cutoff score or higher. The percentage of the MMPI-2-RF normative sample (NS) and of the MMPI-2-RF Normative (Women) comparison group (CG) that answered each item in the keyed direction are provided in parentheses following the item content.

Emotional/Internalizing Dysfunction (EID, T Score = 79)

17. Item Content Omitted. (False; NS 28.8%, CG 24.4%)
22. Item Content Omitted. (True; NS 32.5%, CG 33.7%)
30. Item Content Omitted. (True; NS 7.4%, CG 9.0%)
35. Item Content Omitted. (True; NS 36.6%, CG 41.3%)
37. Item Content Omitted. (False; NS 56.3%, CG 66.9%)
48. Item Content Omitted. (True; NS 22.1%, CG 27.1%)
57. Item Content Omitted. (False; NS 22.1%, CG 17.0%)
64. Item Content Omitted. (False; NS 26.0%, CG 22.1%)
83. Item Content Omitted. (False; NS 5.1%, CG 5.1%)
89. Item Content Omitted. (True; NS 35.9%, CG 37.4%)
91. Item Content Omitted. (True; NS 37.7%, CG 46.6%)
105. Item Content Omitted. (False; NS 10.6%, CG 10.6%)
119. Item Content Omitted. (True; NS 39.5%, CG 39.1%)
120. Item Content Omitted. (True; NS 2.4%, CG 3.3%)
158. Item Content Omitted. (True; NS 17.0%, CG 17.9%)
172. Item Content Omitted. (True; NS 16.9%, CG 17.4%)
187. Item Content Omitted. (True; NS 40.4%, CG 43.5%)
202. Item Content Omitted. (False; NS 53.4%, CG 51.6%)
204. Item Content Omitted. (True; NS 18.2%, CG 19.0%)
217. Item Content Omitted. (False; NS 30.1%, CG 35.3%)
222. Item Content Omitted. (False; NS 19.6%, CG 19.0%)
232. Item Content Omitted. (True; NS 21.9%, CG 24.3%)
234. Item Content Omitted. (False; NS 53.9%, CG 56.9%)
246. Item Content Omitted. (False; NS 5.9%, CG 6.4%)

FIGURE 11-5 Ms. E's MMPI-2-RF Clinical Settings Interpretive Report, continued

250. Item Content Omitted. (True; NS 42.4%, CG 47.3%)
261. Item Content Omitted. (True; NS 22.4%, CG 30.1%)
282. Item Content Omitted. (False; NS 17.3%, CG 16.7%)
293. Item Content Omitted. (False; NS 18.5%, CG 23.8%)
322. Item Content Omitted. (True; NS 46.8%, CG 57.5%)
331. Item Content Omitted. (True; NS 11.5%, CG 14.3%)
335. Item Content Omitted. (True; NS 30.1%, CG 34.5%)

Demoralization (RCd, T Score = 77)

6. Item Content Omitted. (True; NS 12.7%, CG 12.1%)
22. Item Content Omitted. (True; NS 32.5%, CG 33.7%)
30. Item Content Omitted. (True; NS 7.4%, CG 9.0%)
48. Item Content Omitted. (True; NS 22.1%, CG 27.1%)
74. Item Content Omitted. (True; NS 5.1%, CG 5.4%)
89. Item Content Omitted. (True; NS 35.9%, CG 37.4%)
105. Item Content Omitted. (False; NS 10.6%, CG 10.6%)
117. Item Content Omitted. (True; NS 4.0%, CG 3.4%)
130. Item Content Omitted. (True; NS 15.8%, CG 17.0%)
158. Item Content Omitted. (True; NS 17.0%, CG 17.9%)
172. Item Content Omitted. (True; NS 16.9%, CG 17.4%)
187. Item Content Omitted. (True; NS 40.4%, CG 43.5%)
204. Item Content Omitted. (True; NS 18.2%, CG 19.0%)
217. Item Content Omitted. (False; NS 30.1%, CG 35.3%)
232. Item Content Omitted. (True; NS 21.9%, CG 24.3%)
247. Item Content Omitted. (True; NS 28.8%, CG 33.1%)
261. Item Content Omitted. (True; NS 22.4%, CG 30.1%)
274. Item Content Omitted. (True; NS 17.7%, CG 20.4%)
331. Item Content Omitted. (True; NS 11.5%, CG 14.3%)

Somatic Complaints (RC1, T Score = 68)

88. Item Content Omitted. (False; NS 29.2%, CG 31.8%)
101. Item Content Omitted. (True; NS 5.2%, CG 7.1%)
113. Item Content Omitted. (False; NS 11.0%, CG 11.2%)
162. Item Content Omitted. (False; NS 12.8%, CG 16.3%)
176. Item Content Omitted. (True; NS 5.2%, CG 7.0%)
189. Item Content Omitted. (False; NS 20.3%, CG 26.0%)
242. Item Content Omitted. (True; NS 9.9%, CG 11.8%)
254. Item Content Omitted. (False; NS 28.6%, CG 27.2%)
265. Item Content Omitted. (False; NS 18.7%, CG 19.2%)
328. Item Content Omitted. (True; NS 16.8%, CG 24.3%)

FIGURE 11-5 Ms. E's MMPI-2-RF Clinical Settings Interpretive Report, continued

MMPI-2-RF® Interpretive Report: Clinical Settings
04/28/2016, Page 14 Ms. E

Low Positive Emotions (RC2, T Score = 73)

17. Item Content Omitted. (False; NS 28.8%, CG 24.4%)
64. Item Content Omitted. (False; NS 26.0%, CG 22.1%)
83. Item Content Omitted. (False; NS 5.1%, CG 5.1%)
182. Item Content Omitted. (False; NS 66.3%, CG 74.7%)
195. Item Content Omitted. (False; NS 28.0%, CG 23.1%)
202. Item Content Omitted. (False; NS 53.4%, CG 51.6%)
222. Item Content Omitted. (False; NS 19.6%, CG 19.0%)
246. Item Content Omitted. (False; NS 5.9%, CG 6.4%)
282. Item Content Omitted. (False; NS 17.3%, CG 16.7%)
302. Item Content Omitted. (False; NS 32.1%, CG 36.7%)

Dysfunctional Negative Emotions (RC7, T Score = 70)

23. Item Content Omitted. (True; NS 39.0%, CG 38.6%)
35. Item Content Omitted. (True; NS 36.6%, CG 41.3%)
51. Item Content Omitted. (True; NS 15.4%, CG 17.0%)
77. Item Content Omitted. (True; NS 24.8%, CG 28.3%)
91. Item Content Omitted. (True; NS 37.7%, CG 46.6%)
119. Item Content Omitted. (True; NS 39.5%, CG 39.1%)
149. Item Content Omitted. (True; NS 26.2%, CG 29.1%)
161. Item Content Omitted. (True; NS 8.8%, CG 8.2%)
206. Item Content Omitted. (True; NS 41.6%, CG 47.0%)
250. Item Content Omitted. (True; NS 42.4%, CG 47.3%)
263. Item Content Omitted. (True; NS 64.0%, CG 67.4%)
289. Item Content Omitted. (True; NS 12.7%, CG 18.2%)
318. Item Content Omitted. (True; NS 19.9%, CG 22.5%)
322. Item Content Omitted. (True; NS 46.8%, CG 57.5%)
335. Item Content Omitted. (True; NS 30.1%, CG 34.5%)

Head Pain Complaints (HPC, T Score = 85)

88. Item Content Omitted. (False; NS 29.2%, CG 31.8%)
101. Item Content Omitted. (True; NS 5.2%, CG 7.1%)
176. Item Content Omitted. (True; NS 5.2%, CG 7.0%)
189. Item Content Omitted. (False; NS 20.3%, CG 26.0%)
265. Item Content Omitted. (False; NS 18.7%, CG 19.2%)
328. Item Content Omitted. (True; NS 16.8%, CG 24.3%)

FIGURE 11-5 Ms. E's MMPI-2-RF Clinical Settings Interpretive Report, continued

Self-Doubt (SFD, T Score = 65)

48. Item Content Omitted. (True; NS 22.1%, CG 27.1%)
89. Item Content Omitted. (True; NS 35.9%, CG 37.4%)
232. Item Content Omitted. (True; NS 21.9%, CG 24.3%)

Interpersonal Passivity (IPP, T Score = 68)

24. Item Content Omitted. (True; NS 25.1%, CG 31.6%)
104. Item Content Omitted. (False; NS 32.8%, CG 34.2%)
147. Item Content Omitted. (False; NS 24.8%, CG 25.6%)
197. Item Content Omitted. (False; NS 37.3%, CG 37.8%)
239. Item Content Omitted. (False; NS 38.9%, CG 46.7%)
302. Item Content Omitted. (False; NS 32.1%, CG 36.7%)
321. Item Content Omitted. (False; NS 68.6%, CG 76.4%)
327. Item Content Omitted. (False; NS 58.0%, CG 61.7%)

Introversion/Low Positive Emotionality-Revised (INTR-r, T Score = 70)

11. Item Content Omitted. (False; NS 50.2%, CG 38.6%)
17. Item Content Omitted. (False; NS 28.8%, CG 24.4%)
47. Item Content Omitted. (False; NS 57.1%, CG 59.5%)
57. Item Content Omitted. (False; NS 22.1%, CG 17.0%)
64. Item Content Omitted. (False; NS 26.0%, CG 22.1%)
109. Item Content Omitted. (False; NS 40.0%, CG 40.2%)
153. Item Content Omitted. (False; NS 25.9%, CG 23.6%)
181. Item Content Omitted. (False; NS 64.6%, CG 64.0%)
195. Item Content Omitted. (False; NS 28.0%, CG 23.1%)
201. Item Content Omitted. (False; NS 24.8%, CG 20.5%)
207. Item Content Omitted. (False; NS 33.1%, CG 30.1%)
222. Item Content Omitted. (False; NS 19.6%, CG 19.0%)
246. Item Content Omitted. (False; NS 5.9%, CG 6.4%)

FIGURE 11-5 Ms. E's MMPI-2-RF Clinical Settings Interpretive Report, continued

ENDNOTES

This section lists for each statement in the report the MMPI-2-RF score(s) that triggered it. In addition, each statement is identified as a Test Response, if based on item content, a Correlate, if based on empirical correlates, or an Inference, if based on the report authors' judgment. (This information can also be accessed on-screen by placing the cursor on a given statement.) For correlate-based statements, research references (Ref. No.) are provided, keyed to the consecutively numbered reference list following the endnotes.

[1] Correlate: FBS-r=80, Ref. 7, 20, 21, 22, 23, 25, 26, 30, 32, 35, 38, 39, 48, 49, 54, 66, 67, 69, 72
[2] Correlate: RBS=84, Ref. 9, 18, 19, 22, 23, 25, 26, 28, 32, 35, 36, 37, 38, 39, 51, 52, 53, 54, 58, 59, 62, 63, 64, 66, 69, 70, 71
[3] Correlate: FBS-r=80, Ref. 7, 10, 55; RBS=84, Ref. 55
[4] Test Response: RC1=68
[5] Test Response: HPC=85
[6] Correlate: RC1=68, Ref. 6, 7, 13, 15, 16, 24, 45, 46, 55, 57
[7] Correlate: RC1=68, Ref. 16, 55; HPC=85, Ref. 55
[8] Correlate: RC1=68, Ref. 4, 55
[9] Test Response: SUI=91
[10] Correlate: SUI=91, Ref. 55
[11] Correlate: EID=79, Ref. 29, 55
[12] Test Response: RCd=77
[13] Correlate: RCd=77, Ref. 2, 5, 6, 7, 11, 13, 15, 16, 24, 27, 34, 40, 44, 45, 46, 50, 55, 56, 60, 65, 68; RC2=73, Ref. 2, 5, 6, 7, 13, 15, 16, 24, 27, 40, 44, 45, 46, 50, 55, 56, 60, 65, 68; INTR-r=70, Ref. 55
[14] Test Response: HLP=69
[15] Correlate: HLP=69, Ref. 55
[16] Correlate: RCd=77, Ref. 55; HLP=69, Ref. 55
[17] Test Response: SFD=65
[18] Correlate: SFD=65, Ref. 55
[19] Test Response: RC2=73; INTR-r=70
[20] Correlate: RC2=73, Ref. 14, 55; HLP=69, Ref. 55; INTR-r=70, Ref. 55
[21] Test Response: RC7=70
[22] Correlate: RC7=70, Ref. 55
[23] Test Response: AXY=70
[24] Correlate: RC7=70, Ref. 12, 13, 14, 44, 45, 46, 55, 56; AXY=70, Ref. 6, 47
[25] Correlate: RC7=70, Ref. 6, 12, 34, 55, 65; AXY=70, Ref. 55
[26] Test Response: RC6=66
[27] Correlate: RC6=66, Ref. 2, 7, 8, 24, 40, 43, 46, 55
[28] Correlate: RC6=66, Ref. 55
[29] Correlate: BXD=36, Ref. 29, 55
[30] Test Response: IPP=68
[31] Correlate: IPP=68, Ref. 3, 7, 55
[32] Test Response: SAV=80
[33] Correlate: SAV=80, Ref. 3, 55
[34] Correlate: SAV=80, Ref. 17, 55

FIGURE 11-5 Ms. E's MMPI-2-RF Clinical Settings Interpretive Report, continued

[35] Correlate: SAV=80, Ref. 55
[36] Test Response: AES=39
[37] Test Response: MEC=61
[38] Correlate: RC1=68, Ref. 30, 31, 61
[39] Inference: HPC=85
[40] Correlate: RCd=77, Ref. 33, 42, 50, 55, 61; RC2=73, Ref. 33, 42, 50, 55, 61; INTR-r=70, Ref. 55
[41] Correlate: RC7=70, Ref. 12, 34, 41, 44, 56, 65; AXY=70, Ref. 1, 47, 55
[42] Correlate: RC6=66, Ref. 42, 61
[43] Inference: IPP=68
[44] Correlate: SAV=80, Ref. 61
[45] Inference: SUI=91
[46] Correlate: RC2=73, Ref. 55; INTR-r=70, Ref. 55
[47] Inference: RC1=68
[48] Inference: RCd=77
[49] Inference: RC6=66
[50] Inference: HLP=69
[51] Inference: SFD=65
[52] Inference: RC2=73; INTR-r=70
[53] Inference: RC7=70
[54] Inference: AXY=70
[55] Inference: SAV=80

FIGURE 11-5 Ms. E's MMPI-2-RF Clinical Settings Interpretive Report, continued

RESEARCH REFERENCE LIST

1. Anderson, J. L., Sellbom, M., Ayearst, L., Quilty, L. C., Chmielewski, M., & Bagby, R. M. (2015). Associations between DSM-5 Section III personality traits and the Minnesota Multiphasic Personality Inventory 2-Restructured Form (MMPI-2-RF) scales in a psychiatric patient sample. *Psychological Assessment, 27,* 801-815. doi: 10.1037/pas0000096

2. Anderson, J. L., Sellbom, M., Pymont, C., Smid, W., De Saeger, H. & Kamphuis, J. H. (2015). Measurement of DSM-5 Section II personality disorder constructs using the MMPI-2-RF in clinical and forensic samples. *Psychological Assessment, 27,* 786-800. doi: 10.1037/pas0000103

3. Arbisi, P. A., Polusny, M. A., Erbes, C. R., Thuras, P., & Reddy, M. K. (2011). The Minnesota Multiphasic Personality Inventory-2 Restructured Form in National Guard soldiers screening positive for posttraumatic stress disorder and mild traumatic brain injury. *Psychological Assessment, 23,* 203-214. doi: 10.1037/a0021339

4. Arbisi, P. A., Sellbom, M., & Ben-Porath, Y. S. (2008). Empirical correlates of the MMPI-2 Restructured Clinical (RC) Scales in psychiatric inpatients. *Journal of Personality Assessment, 90,* 122-128. doi: 10.1080/00223890701845146

5. Ayearst, L. E., Sellbom, M., Trobst, K. K., & Bagby, R. M. (2013). Evaluating the interpersonal content of the MMPI-2-RF Interpersonal Scales. *Journal of Personality Assessment, 95,* 187-196. doi: 10.1080/00223891.2012.730085

6. Benitez, A., & Gunstad, J. (2012). Poor sleep quality diminishes cognitive functioning independent of depression and anxiety in healthy young adults. *The Clinical Neuropsychologist, 26,* 214-223. doi: 10.1080/13854046.2012.658439

7. Binford, A., & Liljequist, L. (2008). Behavioral correlates of selected MMPI-2 Clinical, Content, and Restructured Clinical scales. *Journal of Personality Assessment, 90,* 608-614. doi: 10.1080/00223890802388657

8. Block, A. R., Ben-Porath, Y. S., & Marek, R. J. (2013). Psychological risk factors for poor outcome of spine surgery and spinal cord stimulator implant: A review of the literature and their assessment with the MMPI-2-RF. *The Clinical Neuropsychologist, 27,* 81-107. doi: 10.1080/13854046.2012.721007

9. Bolinger, E., Reese, C., Suhr, J., & Larrabee, G. J. (2014). Susceptibility of the MMPI-2-RF Neurological Complaints and Cognitive Complaints Scales to over-reporting in simulated head injury. *Archives of Clinical Neuropsychology, 29,* 7-15. doi: 10.1093/arclin/act082

10. Burchett, D. L., & Ben-Porath, Y. S. (2010). The impact of over-reporting on MMPI-2-RF substantive scale score validity. *Assessment, 17,* 497-516. doi: 10.1177/1073191110378972

11. Cox, A, Pant, H., Gilson, A. N., Rodriguez, J. L., Young, K. R., Kwon, S., & Weed, N. C., (2012). Effects of augmenting response options on MMPI-2 RC Scale psychometrics. *Journal of Personality Assessment, 94,* 613-619. doi: 10.1080/00223891.2012.700464

FIGURE 11-5 Ms. E's MMPI-2-RF Clinical Settings Interpretive Report, continued

12. Dionysus, K. E., Denney, R. L., & Halfaker, D. A. (2011). Detecting negative response bias with the Fake Bad Scale, Response Bias Scale, Henry-Heilbronner Index of the Minnesota Multiphasic Personality Inventory-2. *Archives of Clinical Neuropsychology, 26,* 81-88. doi: 10.1093/arclin/acq

13. Downing, S. K., Denney, R. L., Spray, B. J., Houston, C. M., & Halfaker, D. H. (2008). Examining the relationship between the Restructured Scales and the Fake Bad Scale of the MMPI-2. *The Clinical Neuropsychologist, 22,* 680-688. doi: 10.1080/13854040701562825

14. Erbes, C. R., Polusny, M. A., Arbisi, P. A., & Koffel, E. (2012). PTSD symptoms in a cohort of National Guard Soldiers deployed to Iraq: Evidence for nonspecific and specific components. *Journal of Affective Disorders, 142,* 269-274. doi: 10.1016/j.jad.2012.05.013

15. Finn, J. A., Ben-Porath, Y. S., & Tellegen, A. (2015). Dichotomous versus polytomous response options in psychopathology assessment: Method or meaningful variance? *Psychological Assessment, 27,* 184-193. doi: 10.1037/pas0000044

16. Forbes, D., Elhai, J. D., Miller, M. W., & Creamer, M. (2010). Internalizing and externalizing classes in posttraumatic stress disorder: A latent class analysis. *Journal of Traumatic Stress, 23,* 340-349. doi: 10.1002/jts.20526

17. Forbey, J. D., Arbisi, P. A., & Ben-Porath, Y. S. (2012). The MMPI-2 computer adaptive version (MMPI-2-CA) in a VA medical outpatient facility. *Psychological Assessment, 24,* 628-639. doi: 10.1037/a0026509

18. Forbey, J. D., & Ben-Porath, Y. S. (2007). A comparison of the MMPI-2 Restructured Clinical (RC) and Clinical Scales in a substance abuse treatment sample. *Psychological Services, 4,* 46-58. doi: 10.1037/1541-1559.4.1.46

19. Forbey, J. D., & Ben-Porath, Y. S. (2008). Empirical correlates of the MMPI-2 Restructured Clinical (RC) Scales in a non-clinical setting. *Journal of Personality Assessment, 90,* 136-141. doi: 10.1080/00223890701845161

20. Forbey, J. D., Ben-Porath, Y. S., & Gartland, D. (2009). Validation of the MMPI-2 Computerized Adaptive Version (MMPI-2-CA) in a correctional intake facility. *Psychological Services, 6,* 279-292. doi: 10.1037/a0016195

21. Forbey, J. D., Lee, T. T. C., & Handel, R. W. (2010). Correlates of the MMPI-2-RF in a college setting. *Psychological Assessment, 22,* 737-744. doi: 10.1037/a0020645

22. Gervais, R. O., Ben-Porath, Y. S., Wygant, D. B., & Green, P. (2007). Development and validation of a Response Bias Scale (RBS) for the MMPI-2. *Assessment, 14,* 196-208. doi: 10.1177/1073191106295861

23. Gervais, R. O., Ben-Porath, Y. S., Wygant, D. B., & Green, P. (2008). Differential sensitivity of the Response Bias Scale (RBS) and MMPI-2 validity scales to memory complaints. *The Clinical Neuropsychologist, 22,* 1061-1079. doi: 10.1080/13854040701756930

FIGURE 11-5 Ms. E's MMPI-2-RF Clinical Settings Interpretive Report, continued

24. Gervais, R. O., Ben-Porath, Y. S., Wygant, D. B., & Sellbom, M. (2010). Incremental validity of the MMPI-2-RF over-reporting scales and RBS in assessing the veracity of memory complaints. *Archives of Clinical Neuropsychology, 25,* 274-284. doi: 10.1093/arclin/acq018

25. Gervais, R. O., Wygant, D. B., Sellbom, M., & Ben-Porath, Y. S. (2011). Associations between Symptom Validity Test failure and scores on the MMPI-2-RF validity and substantive scales. *Journal of Personality Assessment, 93,* 508-517. doi: 10.1080/00223891.2011.594132

26. Goodwin, B. E., Sellbom, M., & Arbisi, P. A. (2013). Post-Traumatic Stress Disorder in veterans: The utility of the MMPI-2-RF validity scales in detecting over-reported symptoms. *Psychological Assessment, 25,* 671-678. doi: 10.1037/a0032214

27. Gottfried, E., Bodell, L. M., Carbonell, J., & Joiner, T. (2014). The clinical utility of the MMPI-2-RF Suicidal/Death Ideation Scale. *Psychological Assessment, 26,* 1205-1211. doi: 10.1037/pas0000017

28. Greiffenstein, M., Gervais, R. O., Baker, W. J., Artiola, L., & Smith, H. (2013). Symptom validity testing in medically unexplained pain: A Chronic Regional Pain Syndrome Type 1 case series. *The Clinical Neuropsychologist, 27,* 138-147. doi: 10.1080/13854046.2012.722686

29. Haber, J. C., & Baum, L. J. (2014). Minnesota Multiphasic Personality Inventory-2 Restructured Form (MMPI-2-RF) Scales as predictors of psychiatric diagnoses. *South African Journal of Psychology, 44,* 439-453. doi: 10.1177/0081246314532788

30. Handel, R. W., & Archer, R. P. (2008). An investigation of the psychometric properties of the MMPI-2 Restructured Clinical (RC) Scales with mental health inpatients. *Journal of Personality Assessment, 90,* 239-249. doi: 10.1080/00223890701884954

31. Jones, A., & Ingram, M. V. (2011). A comparison of selected MMPI-2 and MMPI-2-RF Validity Scales in assessing effort on cognitive tests in a military sample. *The Clinical Neuropsychologist, 25,* 1207-1227. doi: 10.1080/13854046.2011.600726

32. Jones, A., Ingram, M. V., & Ben-Porath, Y. S. (2012). Scores on the MMPI-2-RF scales as a function of increasing levels of failure on cognitive symptom validity tests in a military sample. *The Clinical Neuropsychologist, 26,* 790-815. doi: 10.1080/13854046.2012.693202

33. Kamphuis, J. H., Arbisi, P. A., Ben-Porath, Y. S., & McNulty, J. L. (2008). Detecting comorbid Axis-II status among inpatients using the MMPI-2 Restructured Clinical Scales. *European Journal of Psychological Assessment, 24,* 157-164. doi: 10.1027/1015-5759.24.3.157

34. Lange, R. T., Sullivan, K. A., & Scott, C. (2010). Comparison of MMPI-2 and PAI validity indicators to detect feigned depression and PTSD symptom reporting. *Psychiatry Research, 176,* 229-235. doi: 10.1016/j.psychres.2009.03.004

35. Lanyon, R. I., & Thomas, M. L. (2013). Assessment of global psychiatric categories: The PSI/PSI-2 and the MMPI-2-RF. *Psychological Assessment, 25,* 227-232. doi: 10.1037/a0030313

FIGURE 11-5 Ms. E's MMPI-2-RF Clinical Settings Interpretive Report, continued

36. Locke, D. E. C., Kirlin, K. A., Thomas, M. L., Osborne, D., Hurst, D. F., Drazkowsi, J. F., Sirven, J. I., & Noe, K. H. (2010). The Minnesota Multiphasic Personality Inventory-2-Restructured Form in the epilepsy monitoring unit. *Epilepsy & Behavior, 17,* 252-258. doi: 10.1016/j.yebeh.2009.12.004

37. Locke, D. E. C., Kirlin, K. A., Wershba, R., Osborne, D., Drazkowski, J. F., Sirven, J. I., & Noe, K. H. (2011). Randomized comparison of the Personality Assessment Inventory and the Minnesota Multiphasic Personality Inventory-2 in the epilepsy monitoring unit. *Epilepsy & Behavior, 21,* 397-401. doi: 10.1016/j.yebeh.2011.05.023

38. Martin, P. K., Schroeder, R. W., Heinrichs, R. J., Baade, L. E. (2015). Does true neurocognitive dysfunction contribute to Minnesota Multiphasic Personality Inventory-2nd Edition-Restructured Form cognitive validity scores? *Archives of Clinical Neuropsychology, 30,* 377-386. doi: 10.1093/arclin/acv032

39. Mason, L. H., Shandera-Ochsner, A. L., Williamson, K. D., Harp, J. P., Edmundson, M., Berry, D. T. R., & High, W. M. (2013). Accuracy of MMPI-2-RF Validity Scales for identifying feigned PTSD symptoms, random responding, and genuine PTSD. *Journal of Personality Assessment, 95,* 585-593. doi: 10.1080/00223891.2013.819512

40. McCord, D. M., & Drerup, L. C. (2011). Relative practical utility of the Minnesota Multiphasic Personality Inventory-2 Restructured Clinical Scales versus the Clinical Scales in a chronic pain patient sample. *Journal of Clinical and Experimental Neuropsychology, 33,* 140-146. doi: 10.1080/13803395.2010.495056

41. McDevitt-Murphy, M. E., Weathers, F. W., Flood, A. M., Eakin, D. E., & Benson, T. A. (2007). The utility of the PAI and the MMPI-2 for discriminating PTSD, depression, and social phobia in trauma-exposed college students. *Assessment, 14,* 181-195. doi: 10.1177/1073191106295914

42. Nelson, N. W., Hoelzle, J. B., McGuire, K. A., Sim, A. H., Goldman, D. J., Ferrier-Auerbach, A. G., Charlesworth, M. J., Arbisi, P. A., & Sponheim, S. R. (2011). Self-report of psychological function among OEF/OIF personnel who also report combat-related concussion. *The Clinical Neuropsychologist, 25,* 716-740. doi: 10.1080/13854046.2011.579174

43. Nelson, N. W., Sweet, J. J., & Heilbronner, R. L. (2007). Examination of the new MMPI-2 Response Bias Scale (Gervais): Relationship with MMPI-2 validity scales. *Journal of Clinical and Experimental Neuropsychology, 29,* 67-72. doi: 10.1080/13803390500488546

44. Nguyen, C. T., Green, D., & Barr, W. B. (2015). Evaluation of the MMPI-2-RF for detecting over-reported symptoms in civil forensic and disability setting. *The Clinical Neuropsychologist, 29,* 255-271. doi: 1080/13854046.2015.1033020

45. Patrick, R. E., & Horner, M. D. (2014). Psychological characteristics of individuals who put forth inadequate effort in a secondary gain context. *Archives of Clinical Neuropsychology, 29,* 754-766. doi: 10.1093/arclin/acu054

FIGURE 11-5 Ms. E's MMPI-2-RF Clinical Settings Interpretive Report, continued

MMPI-2-RF® Interpretive Report: Clinical Settings
04/28/2016, Page 22 Ms. E

46. Peck, C. P., Schroeder, R. W., Heinrichs, R. J., VonDran, E. J., Brockman, C. J., Webster, B. K., & Baade, L. E. (2013). Differences in MMPI-2 FBS and RBS scores in brain injury, probable malingering, and conversion disorder groups: A preliminary study. *The Clinical Neuropsychologist, 27,* 693-707. doi: 10.1080/13854046.2013.779032

47. Rogers, R., Gillard, N. D., Berry, D. T. R., & Granacher, R. P. (2011). Effectiveness of the MMPI-2-RF Validity Scales for feigned mental disorders and cognitive impairment: A known-groups study. *Journal of Psychopathology and Behavioral Assessment, 33,* 355-367. doi: 10.1007/s10862-011-9222-0

48. Schroeder, R. W., Baade, L. E., Peck, C. P., VonDran, E. J., Brockman, C. J., Webster, B. K., & Heinrichs, R. J. (2012). Validation of the MMPI-2-RF Validity Scales in criterion group neuropsychological samples. *The Clinical Neuropsychologist, 26,* 129-146. doi: 10.1080/13854046.2011.639314

49. Sellbom, M., Anderson, J. L., & Bagby, R. M. (2013). Assessing DSM-5 Section III Personality Traits and Disorders with the MMPI-2-RF. *Assessment, 20,* 709-722. doi: 10.1177/1073191113508808

50. Sellbom, M., & Bagby, R. M. (2009). Identifying PTSD personality subtypes in a workplace trauma sample. *Journal of Traumatic Stress, 22,* 471-475. doi: 10.1002/jts.20452

51. Sellbom, M., Bagby, R. M., Kushner, S., Quilty, L. C., & Ayearst, L. E. (2011). Diagnostic construct validity of the MMPI-2 Restructured Form (MMPI-2-RF) scale scores. *Assessment, 19,* 176-186. doi: 10.1177/1073191111428763

52. Sellbom, M., & Ben-Porath, Y. S. (2005). Mapping the MMPI-2 Restructured Clinical (RC) Scales onto normal personality traits: Evidence of construct validity. *Journal of Personality Assessment, 85,* 179-187. doi: 10.1207/s15327752jpa8502_10

53. Sellbom, M., Ben-Porath, Y. S., & Bagby, R. M. (2008). On the hierarchical structure of mood and anxiety disorders: Confirmatory evidence and elaboration of a model of temperament markers. *Journal of Abnormal Psychology, 117,* 576-590. doi: 10.1037/a0012536

54. Sellbom, M., Ben-Porath, Y. S., & Graham, J. R. (2006). Correlates of the MMPI-2 Restructured Clinical (RC) Scales in a college counseling setting. *Journal of Personality Assessment, 86,* 89-99. doi: 10.1207/s15327752jpa8601_10

55. Sellbom, M., Graham, J. R., & Schenk, P. (2006). Incremental validity of the MMPI-2 Restructured Clinical (RC) Scales in a private practice sample. *Journal of Personality Assessment, 86,* 196-205. doi: 10.1207/s15327752jpa8602_09

56. Sellbom, M., Lee, T. T. C., Ben-Porath, Y. S., Arbisi, P. A., & Gervais, R. O. (2012). Differentiating PTSD Symptomatology with the MMPI-2-RF (Restructured Form) in a Forensic Disability Sample. *Psychiatry Research, 197,* 172-179. doi: 10.1016/j.psychres.2012.02.003

FIGURE 11-5 Ms. E's MMPI-2-RF Clinical Settings Interpretive Report, continued

57. Sellbom, M., Toomey, J. A., Wygant, D. B., Kucharski, L. T., & Duncan, S. A. (2010). Utility of the MMPI-2-RF (Restructured Form) validity scales in detecting malingering in a criminal forensic setting: A known-groups design. *Psychological Assessment, 22,* 22-31. doi: 10.1037/a0018222

58. Sellbom, M., Wygant, D. B., & Bagby, R. M. (2012). Utility of the MMPI-2-RF in detecting non-credible somatic complaints. *Psychiatry Research, 197,* 295-301. doi: 10.1016/j.psychres.2011.12.043

59. Shkalim, E. (2015). Psychometric evaluation of the MMPI-2/MMPI-2-RF Restructured Clinical Scales in an Israeli sample. *Assessment.* doi: 10.1177/1073191114555884

60. Simms, L. J., Casillas, A., Clark, L. A., Watson, D., & Doebbeling, B. I. (2005). Psychometric evaluation of the Restructured Clinical Scales of the MMPI-2. *Psychological Assessment, 17,* 345-358. doi: 10.1037/1040-3590.17.3.345

61. Smart, C. M., Nelson, N. W., Sweet, J. J., Bryant, F. B., Berry, D. T., Granacher, R. P., & Heilbronner, R. L. (2008). Use of MMPI-2 to predict cognitive effort: A hierarchically optimal classification tree analysis. *Journal of the International Neuropsychological Society, 14,* 842-852. doi: 10.1017/S1355617708081034

62. Sullivan, K. A., & Elliott, C. (2012). An investigation of the validity of the MMPI-2 Response Bias Scale using an analog simulation design. *The Clinical Neuropsychologist, 26,* 160-176. doi: 10.1080/13854046.2011.647084

63. Sullivan, K. A., Elliott, C. D., Lange, R. T., & Anderson, D. S. (2013). A known groups evaluation of the Response Bias Scale in a neuropsychological setting. *Applied Neuropsychology: Adult, 20,* 20-32. doi: 10.1080/09084282.2012.670149

64. Tarescavage, A. M., Scheman, J., & Ben-Porath, Y. S. (2015). Reliability and validity of the Minnesota Multiphasic Personality Inventory-2-Restructured Form (MMPI-2-RF) in evaluations of chronic low back pain patients. *Psychological Assessment, 27,* 433-446. doi: 10.1037/pas0000056

65. Tarescavage, A., Wygant, D. B., Gervais, R. O., & Ben-Porath, Y. S. (2013). Association between the MMPI-2 Restructured Form (MMPI-2-RF) and malingered neurocognitive dysfunction among non-head injury disability claimants. *The Clinical Neuropsychologist, 27,* 313-335. doi: 10.1080/13854046.2012.744099

66. Tellegen, A., & Ben-Porath, Y. S. (2008/2011). *The Minnesota Multiphasic Personality Inventory-2-Restructured Form (MMPI-2-RF): Technical manual.* Minneapolis: University of Minnesota Press.

67. Tellegen, A., Ben-Porath, Y. S., Sellbom, M., Arbisi, P. A., McNulty, J. L., & Graham, J. R. (2006). Further evidence on the validity of the MMPI-2 Restructured Clinical (RC) Scales: Addressing questions raised by Rogers et al. and Nichols. *Journal of Personality Assessment, 87,* 148-171. doi: 10.1207/s15327752jpa8702_04

68. Thomas, M. L., & Locke, D. E. C. (2010). Psychometric properties of the MMPI-2-RF Somatic Complaints (RC1) Scale. *Psychological Assessment, 22,* 492-503. doi: 10.1037/a0019229

FIGURE 11-5 Ms. E's MMPI-2-RF Clinical Settings Interpretive Report, continued

69. Tolin, D. F., Steenkamp, M. M, Marx, B. P., & Litz, B. T. (2010). Detecting symptom exaggeration in combat veterans using the MMPI-2 symptom validity scales: A mixed group validation. *Psychological Assessment, 22,* 729-736. doi: 10.1037/a0020973

70. Tsushima, W. T., Geling, O., & Fabrigas, J. (2001). Comparison of MMPI-2 Validity Scale scores of personal injury litigants and disability claimants. *The Clinical Neuropsychologist, 25,* 1403-1414. doi: 10.1080/13854046.2011.613854

71. Vachon, D. D., Sellbom, M., Ryder, A. G., Miller, J. D., & Bagby, R. M. (2009). A Five-Factor Model description of depressive personality disorder. *Journal of Personality Disorders, 23,* 447-465. doi: 10.1521/pedi.2009.23.5.447

72. Van der Heijden, P. T., Egger, J. I. M., Rossi, G., Grundel, G., & Derksen, J. J. L. (2013). The MMPI-2 Restructured Form and the standard MMPI-2 Clinical Scales in relation to DSM-IV. *European Journal of Psychological Assessment, 29,* 182-188. doi: 10.1027/1015-5759/a000140

73. Van Dyke, S. A., Axelrod, B. N., & Schutte, C. (2010). The utility of the Post-concussive Syndrome Questionnaire. *Archives of Clinical Neuropsychology, 25,* 634-639. doi: 10.1093/arclin/acq063

74. Whitney, K. A. (2013). Predicting Test of Memory Malingering and Medical Symptom Validity Test Failure within a Veterans Affairs Medical Center: Use of the Response Bias Scale and the Henry-Heilbronner Index. *Archives of Clinical Neuropsychology, 28,* 222-235. doi: 10.1093/arclin/act012

75. Whitney, K. A., Davis, J. J., Shephard, P. H., & Herman, S. M. (2008). Utility of the Response Bias Scale and other MMPI-2 validity scales in predicting TOMM performance. *Archives of Clinical Neuropsychology, 23,* 777-786. doi: 10.1016/j.acn.2008.09.001

76. Wolf, E. J., Miller, M. W., Orazem, R. J., Weierich, M. R., Castillo, D. T., Milford, J., Kaloupek, D. G., & Keane, T. M. (2008). The MMPI-2 Restructured Clinical Scales in the assessment of posttraumatic stress disorder and comorbid disorders. *Psychological Assessment, 20,* 327-340. doi: 10.1037/a0012948

77. Wygant, D. B., Anderson, J. L., Sellbom, M., Rapier, J. L., Allgeier, L. M., & Granacher, R. P. (2011). Association of MMPI-2 Restructured Form (MMPI-2-RF) validity scales with structured malingering criteria. *Psychological Injury and Law, 4,* 13-23. doi: 10.1007/s12207-011-9098-z

78. Wygant, D. B., Ben-Porath, Y. S., Arbisi, P. A., Berry, D. T. R., Freeman, D. B., & Heilbronner, R. L. (2009). Examination of the MMPI-2 Restructured Form (MMPI-2-RF) validity scales in civil forensic settings: Findings from simulation and known group samples. *Archives of Clinical Neuropsychology, 24,* 671-680. doi: 10.1093/arclin/acp073

79. Wygant, D. B., Boutacoff, L. A., Arbisi, P. A., Ben-Porath, Y. S., Kelly, P. H., & Rupp, W. M. (2007). Examination of the MMPI-2 Restructured Clinical (RC) Scales in a sample of bariatric surgery candidates. *Journal of Clinical Psychology in Medical Settings, 14,* 197-205. doi: 10.1007/s10880-007-9073-8

FIGURE 11-5 Ms. E's MMPI-2-RF Clinical Settings Interpretive Report, continued

80. Wygant, D. B., Sellbom, M., Gervais, R. O., Ben-Porath, Y. S., Stafford, K. P., Freeman, D. B., & Heilbronner, R. L. (2010). Further validation of the MMPI-2 and MMPI-2-RF Response Bias Scale: Findings from disability and criminal forensic settings. *Psychological Assessment, 22,* 745-756. doi: 10.1037/a0020042

81. Young, J. C., & Gross, A. M. (2011). Detection of response bias and noncredible performance in adult Attention-Deficit/Hyperactivity Disorder. *Archives of Clinical Neuropsychology, 26,* 165-175. doi: 10.1093/arclin/acr013

82. Young, J. C., Kearns, L. A., & Roper, B. L. (2011). Validation of the MMPI-2 Response Bias Scale and Henry-Heilbronner Index in a U.S. veteran population. *Archives of Clinical Neuropsychology, 26,* 194-204. doi: 10.1093/arclin/acr015

83. Youngjohn, J. R., Wershba, R., Stevenson, M., Sturgeon, J., & Thomas, M. L. (2011). Independent validation of the MMPI-2-RF Somatic/Cognitive and Validity Scales in TBI litigants tested for effort. *The Clinical Neuropsychologist, 25,* 463-476. doi: 10.1080/13854046.2011.554444

End of Report

This and previous pages of this report contain trade secrets and are not to be released in response to requests under HIPAA (or any other data disclosure law that exempts trade secret information from release). Further, release in response to litigation discovery demands should be made only in accordance with your profession's ethical guidelines and under an appropriate protective order.

FIGURE 11-5 Ms. E's MMPI-2-RF Clinical Settings Interpretive Report, continued

a review of Ms. E's scores in the Somatic/Cognitive Dysfunction domain indicates that the HPC (Head Pain Complaints; 85T) score is the most prominent manifestation of the somatization reflected in her RC1 elevation. Also, this page shows that clinically elevated scores on SUI (Suicidal/Death Ideation; 91T), HLP (Helplessness/Hopelessness; 69T), and SFD (Self-Doubt; 65T) are the principal concerns related to the demoralization reflected in Ms. E's RCd score; that the PSY-5 scale INTR-r (Introversion/Low Positive Emotionality-Revised; 70T) score reflects the likely chronic problems associated with her RC2 score; and that Ms. E's problems in the Interpersonal Functioning domain can be understood as primarily related to difficulties associated with interpersonal passivity (IPP; 68T) and social avoidance (SAV; 80T). Pages 9–10 (Figure 11-5) of the Clinical Settings Interpretive Report provide the test user with interpretive statements for each clinically elevated scale (≥65T); all of these statements can also be found in the *MMPI-2-RF Manual for Administration, Scoring and Interpretation* (Ben-Porath & Tellegen, 2008/2011), but are also organized in the interpretive report by the same problem domains listed on page 7. Particularly noteworthy is Ms. E's score on the SUI (91T) scale, indicating a self-reported history of suicidal ideation and/or attempts, a possible preoccupation with suicide and death, and a risk for current suicidal ideation and attempts.

Data Integration

STEP 1: ASSESSING FOR A MENTAL HEALTH CONDITION

The clinical symptoms, personality characteristics, and behavior tendencies identified by Ms. E's MMPI-2-RF scale scores comprise an important source of evidence of ongoing mental health problems. Although, as with all tests of personality and psychopathology, these scores are insufficient to diagnose Ms. E, they did direct the clinician's focus to an array of emotional/internalizing and interpersonal problems that comport with her recent diagnosis of Borderline Personality Disorder (BPD) and Major Depressive Disorder (MDD). When integrated with Ms. E's interview statements and treatment records, the examiner found evidence supporting the diagnosis of BPD as indicated by (a) a pattern of unstable and intense interpersonal relationships characterized by alternating between extremes of idealization and devaluation; (b) markedly and persistently unstable self-image or sense of self; (c) recurrent suicidal behavior, gestures, threats, and self-mutilating behavior; (d) affective instability owing to a marked reactivity of mood; (e) chronic feelings of emptiness; and (f) inappropriate, intense anger or difficulty controlling anger. The examiner found diagnostic support for MDD in the form of daily or nearly daily (a) anhedonia, (b) insomnia, (c) excessive or inappropriate guilt, (d) indecisiveness, and (e) recurrent thoughts of death. It is important to note that, as seen in Ms. E's MMPI-2-RF scores, these symptoms cause clinically significant distress and, as seen in her employment records, impairment in occupational functioning.

STEP 2: ASSESSING FOR CURRENT WORK IMPAIRMENT

In assessing impairment in Ms. E's role as a correctional officer, the examiner initially focused on evidence indicating that she posed a direct threat of substantial harm to herself or others that could not be eliminated or reduced by reasonable accommodation. The examiner reasoned that her most recent self-cutting behavior was triggered by her anxiety and distress over what amounted to an innocuous interaction with a coworker that, by her own admission, was not unusual within the context of the jail environment. Employment and treatment records documented that she was prone to being hypersensitive to perceived slights, particularly in response to any kind of criticism or corrective feedback. Treatment records indicated that her past suicidal ideation and attempts resulted from an accumulation of normal stresses occurring in the context of impaired psychological adaptation, rather than from unusual or dramatic events. The examiner concluded that Ms. E's risk for suicide was high in light of her chronic 20-year history of repeated attempts, contemporary suicidal ideation and self-mutilation, ongoing emotional instability, and the history of relatively benign workplace interactions stimulating her acts of self-injury. Although the examiner cited evidence of impaired work functioning, as indicated by her repeated admonishments for emotional overreactions at work, the impairment analysis centered on the direct-threat prong of the fitness determination, rather than on work impairment per se.

STEP 3: ASSESSING FOR SUSTAINABILITY OF FITNESS

As noted in earlier case studies, the third step in the integrative process is indicated only in cases in which the employee has an episodic mental health condition that is currently nonimpairing. Ms. E's chronic, ongoing condition is active and poses a direct threat; therefore, this step is moot.

Conclusion

The collective evidence from all sources indicates that Ms. E has personality and mood disorders that pose a significant risk of substantial harm to the safety of herself (and potentially others) in her position as a correctional officer. Consequently, the examiner determined that Ms. E was unfit for duty. [Note: As a result of this finding, the employer terminated Ms. E's employment in this public safety position, but in the course of accommodation negotiations through her labor representative she was given a nonsafety position elsewhere in the county. Ten years later, Ms. E committed suicide at work.]

APPENDIX

Interpretive guidelines for each of the MMPI-2-RF scales, incorporating the research and comparison group findings reviewed in this practical guide, are presented in Tables A-1 through A-50. Tables A-1 through A-10 provide detailed guidelines for interpreting scores on Cannot Say and the nine MMPI-2-RF Validity Scales. Tables A-11 through A-50 include guidelines for interpreting candidates' scores on the substantive scales. Importantly, these guidelines are intended to supplement the ones included in the *MMPI-2-RF Manual for Administration, Scoring and Interpretation* (Ben-Porath & Tellegen, 2008/2011), not replace them. However, if a different cutoff for the same interpretation is listed in an Appendix A table, it should be used rather than the one listed in the test manual. For example, Table A-9 provides substantially different cutoffs for interpreting L-r than does Table 5-10 of the test manual. When using the MMPI-2-RF as part of a preemployment assessment, the guidelines included in Table A-9 should be applied.

The substantive scale Tables A-11 through A-50 include police candidate–focused interpretive guidelines that incorporate research findings and comparison group data reviewed in chapter 6. These guidelines supplement those found in the parallel test manual tables, which need to be consulted whenever a T-score reaches or exceeds 65, for clinically focused statements that apply in all settings. The tables in this appendix list police candidate–specific implications of clinically elevated scores, in addition to providing interpretive guidelines for lower cutoffs associated with adverse outcomes in police candidates, as discussed in chapter 6.

Importantly, the correlates listed in Tables A-11 through A-50 are based on literature available through the end of 2016. These correlates are amended or expanded based on newly published research. Changes and updates will be reflected in the MMPI-2-RF Police Candidate Interpretive Report (PCIR, discussed in detail in chapter 7), which is periodically updated to incorporate the most recent research findings. The PCIR also includes a list of research citations in support of each correlate-based statement; these citations are a valuable source of information for the test user both for understanding the validity evidence and for justifying suitability determinations in the event of a legal or administrative challenge.

TABLE A-1
Cannot Say (CNS)

Raw Score	
≥ 5	The test taker provided unscorable responses to MMPI-2-RF items at a much higher rate than usual. This level of nonresponding is extremely rare among police officer candidates. Less than 1% of the Police Officer Candidate comparison group members provided this number of unscorable responses.

TABLE A-2
Variable Response Inconsistency (VRIN-r)

T-Score Level	
70–79	There is some evidence of inconsistency because of variable responding to the MMPI-2-RF items. This may result from reading or language comprehension problems, cognitive impairment, errors in recording responses, or carelessness. This level of inconsistency does not invalidate the test protocol; however, it is extremely rare for a police officer candidate. Less than 1% of the Police Officer Candidate comparison group produced this level of inconsistent responding. Scores on the MMPI-2-RF should be interpreted with some caution.
≥ 80	There is evidence of excessive inconsistency because of variable responding to the MMPI-2-RF items. Therefore, this protocol is invalid and uninterpretable. This may result from reading or language comprehension problems, cognitive impairment, or a noncooperative test-taking approach. Erroneously recorded item responses can also produce this level of inconsistency. No member of the Police Officer Candidate comparison group produced this level of inconsistent responding.

TABLE A-3
True Response Inconsistency (TRIN-r)

T-Score Level	
70T–79T	There is some evidence of inconsistency because of fixed true responding to the MMPI-2-RF items. This level of inconsistency does not invalidate the test protocol; however, it is extremely rare for a police officer candidate. Less than 1% of the Police Officer Candidate comparison group produced this level of inconsistent responding. Scores on the MMPI-2-RF scales should be interpreted with some caution.
≥ 80T	There is evidence of excessive inconsistency because of fixed true responding to the MMPI-2-RF items. Therefore, this protocol is invalid and uninterpretable. This level of inconsistency most likely reflects a noncooperative test-taking approach. No member of the Police Officer Candidate comparison group produced this level of inconsistent responding.
70F–79F	There is some evidence of inconsistency because of fixed false responding to the MMPI-2-RF items. This level of inconsistency does not invalidate the test protocol; however, it is extremely rare for a police officer candidate. Less than 1% of the Police Officer Candidate comparison group produced this level of inconsistent responding. Scores on the MMPI-2-RF scales should be interpreted with some caution.
≥ 80F	There is evidence of excessive inconsistency because of fixed false responding to the MMPI-2-RF items. Therefore, this protocol is invalid and uninterpretable. This level of inconsistency most likely reflects a noncooperative test-taking approach. No member of the Police Officer Candidate comparison group produced this level of inconsistent responding.

TABLE A-4
Infrequent Responses (F-r)

T-Score Level	
79–89	The test taker generated a considerably larger than average number of infrequent responses to the MMPI-2-RF items in comparison with police officer candidates. This level of infrequent responding, which is found in less than 0.1% of members of the Police Officer Candidate comparison group, may occur in individuals with genuine psychological difficulties who report credible symptoms. However, for individuals with no history or current corroborating evidence of dysfunction it likely indicates overreporting.
90–99	The test taker generated a considerably larger than average number of infrequent responses to the MMPI-2-RF items in comparison with police officer candidates. This level of infrequent responding, which is not found in any members of the Police Officer Candidate comparison group, may occur in individuals with genuine, substantial psychological difficulties who report credible symptoms. However, for individuals with no history or current corroborating evidence of substantial dysfunction it very likely indicates overreporting.
100–119	The test taker generated a considerably larger than average number of infrequent responses to the MMPI-2-RF items. This level of infrequent responding, which is not found in any members of the Police Officer Candidate comparison group, may occur in individuals with genuine, severe psychological difficulties who report credible symptoms. However, for individuals with no history or current corroborating evidence of severe dysfunction it most likely indicates overreporting.
≥ 120	This protocol is invalid because the test taker generated an excessive number of infrequent responses to the MMPI-2-RF items. This level of infrequent responding, which is not found in any members of the Police Officer Candidate comparison group, is uncommon even in individuals with genuine, severe psychopathology. Scores on the substantive scales of the MMPI-2-RF should not be interpreted.

TABLE A-5
Infrequent Psychopathology Responses (Fp-r)

T-Score Level	
70–79	The test taker reported a considerably larger than average number of symptoms rarely described by individuals with genuine, severe psychopathology in comparison with police officer candidates. This level of infrequent responding, which is found in less than 0.1% of members of the Police Officer Candidate comparison group, may occur in individuals with genuine, severe psychopathology who report credible symptoms. However, for individuals with no history or current corroborating evidence of psychopathology it likely indicates overreporting.
80–99	The test taker reported a considerably larger than average number of symptoms rarely described by individuals with genuine, severe psychopathology in comparison with police officer candidates. This level of infrequent responding, which is found in less than 0.1% of members of the Police Officer Candidate comparison group, may occur in individuals with genuine, severe psychopathology who report credible symptoms, but could also reflect exaggeration. For individuals with no history or current corroborating evidence of psychopathology it very likely indicates overreporting.
≥ 100	This protocol is invalid because the test taker reported a considerably larger than average number of symptoms rarely described by individuals with genuine, severe psychopathology. This level of infrequent responding is uncommon even in individuals with genuine, severe psychopathology who report credible symptoms. Scores on the substantive scales of the MMPI-2-RF should not be interpreted.

TABLE A-6
Infrequent Somatic Responses (Fs)

T-Score Level	
80–99	The test taker reported a considerably larger than average number of somatic symptoms rarely described by individuals with genuine medical conditions in comparison with police officer candidates. This level and type of infrequent responding, which is found in less than 1% of members of the Police Officer Candidate comparison group, may occur in individuals with substantial medical problems who report credible symptoms, but could also reflect exaggeration. In individuals with no history or other corroborating evidence of physical health problems this likely indicates noncredible reporting of somatic symptoms.
≥ 100	The test taker reported a considerably larger than average number of somatic symptoms rarely described by individuals with genuine medical conditions. No members of the Police Officer Candidate comparison group produced this level of infrequent responding, which is uncommon even in individuals with substantial medical problems who report credible symptoms. It very likely indicates noncredible reporting of somatic symptoms.

TABLE A-7
Symptom Validity (FBS-r)

T-Score Level	
80–99	The test taker provided a very unusual combination of responses that is associated with noncredible reporting of somatic and/or cognitive symptoms in comparison with police officer candidates. This combination of responses, which is found in less than 0.1% of members of the Police Officer Candidate comparison group, may occur in individuals with substantial medical problems who report credible symptoms, but could also reflect exaggeration.
≥ 100	The test taker provided a very unusual combination of responses that is associated with noncredible reporting of somatic and/or cognitive symptoms. No member of the Police Officer Candidate comparison group produced this combination of responses, which is uncommon even in individuals with substantial medical problems who report credible symptoms.

TABLE A-8
Response Bias (RBS)

T-Score Level	
80–99	The test taker provided a very unusual combination of responses that is associated with noncredible memory complaints in comparison with police officer candidates. No member of the Police Officer Candidate comparison group produced this combination of responses, which may occur in individuals with substantial emotional dysfunction who report credible symptoms, but could also reflect exaggeration.
≥ 100	The test taker provided a very unusual combination of responses that is strongly associated with noncredible memory complaints. No member of the Police Officer Candidate comparison group produced this combination of responses, which is uncommon even in individuals with significant emotional dysfunction who report credible symptoms.

TABLE A-9
Uncommon Virtues (L-r)

T-Score Level	
37	The test taker claimed no uncommon virtues. This very rare pattern of responding is found in only 4.0% of the Police Officer Candidate comparison group members.
66–76	The test taker presented her/himself in a positive light by denying minor faults and shortcomings that most people acknowledge. This level of virtuous self-presentation may reflect a background stressing traditional values. It is also common among police officer candidates.
81	The test taker presented her/himself in a very positive light by denying many minor faults and shortcomings that most people acknowledge. This level of virtuous self-presentation is uncommon even among individuals with a background stressing traditional values. It is also uncommon among police officer candidates. Only 10.1% of the comparison group members claimed this many or more uncommon virtues. Any absence of elevation on the substantive scales should be interpreted with caution. Elevated scores on the substantive scales may underestimate the problems assessed by those scales.
86	The test taker presented her/himself in an extremely positive light by denying many minor faults and shortcomings that most people acknowledge. This level of virtuous self-presentation is very uncommon even among individuals with a background stressing traditional values. It is also uncommon among police officer candidates. Only 5.8% of the comparison group members claimed this many or more uncommon virtues. Any absence of elevation on the substantive scales is uninterpretable. Elevated scores on the substantive scales may underestimate the problems assessed by those scales.
91	The test taker presented her/himself in an extremely positive light by denying a very large number of minor faults and shortcomings that most people acknowledge. This level of virtuous self-presentation is very uncommon even among individuals with a background stressing traditional values. It is also quite uncommon among police officer candidates. Only 2.6% of the comparison group members claimed this many or more uncommon virtues. Any absence of elevation on the substantive scales is uninterpretable. Elevated scores on the substantive scales may underestimate the problems assessed by those scales.
95	The test taker presented her/himself in an extremely positive light by denying an extraordinarily large number of minor faults and shortcomings that most people acknowledge. This level of virtuous self-presentation is very uncommon even among individuals with a background stressing traditional values. It is also very uncommon among police officer candidates. Only 1.1% of the comparison group members claimed this many or more uncommon virtues. Any absence of elevation on the substantive scales is uninterpretable. Elevated scores on the substantive scales may underestimate the problems assessed by those scales.
100	The test taker presented her/himself in an extremely positive light by denying an extraordinarily large number of minor faults and shortcomings that most people acknowledge. This level of virtuous self-presentation is implausible, even for individuals with a background stressing traditional values. It is also very rare among police officer candidates. Only 0.1% of the comparison group members claimed this many uncommon virtues. Any absence of elevation on the substantive scales is uninterpretable. Elevated scores on the substantive scales may underestimate the problems assessed by those scales.
105	The test taker presented her/himself in an extremely positive light by responding to all statements reflecting minor faults and shortcomings that most people acknowledge in the keyed direction. This level of virtuous self-presentation is implausible, even for individuals with a background stressing traditional values. No member of the Police Officer Candidate comparison group responded this extremely. Any absence of elevation on the substantive scales is uninterpretable. Elevated scores on the substantive scales may underestimate the problems assessed by those scales.

TABLE A-10
Adjustment Validity (K-r)

T-Score Level	
≤31	The test taker reported being considerably less well adjusted than members of the general population. Less than 0.1% of the Police Officer Candidate comparison group reported this low level of psychological adjustment.
35–38	The test taker reported being much less well adjusted than members of the general population. Less than 1% of the Police Officer Candidate comparison group reported this low level of psychological adjustment.
42–45	The test taker reported being much less well adjusted than a typical police officer candidate. Less than 4% of members of the Police Officer Candidate comparison group reported this low level of psychological adjustment.
69	The test taker presented her/himself as very well adjusted. This reported level of psychological adjustment is relatively rare in the general population, but is more common among police officer candidates.
72	The test taker presented her/himself as remarkably well adjusted. This reported level of psychological adjustment is rare in the general population and relatively uncommon among police officer candidates. Only 17.6% of comparison group members reported this level of good psychological adjustment. Any absence of elevation on the substantive scales should be interpreted with caution. Elevated scores on the substantive scales may underestimate the problems assessed by those scales.

TABLE A-11
Emotional/Internalizing Dysfunction (EID)

Comparison Group Findings

T-Score Level

T-Score Level	
54–64	The test taker reports a comparatively large number of emotional problems for a police officer candidate.
≥65	The test taker's responses indicate a level of emotional distress that may be incompatible with public safety requirements for good emotional adjustment. This level of emotional distress is very uncommon among police officer candidates.

Job-Relevant Correlates

≥56

Compared with other police officer candidates, the test taker is more likely to:

- Become easily discouraged
- Have difficulty coping with stress
- Worry about problems and be uncertain how to deal with them
- Behave in a self-defeating fashion
- Become impatient with others over minor infractions
- Be lacking in confidence in his/her own abilities
- Avoid seemingly complex challenges
- Have a difficult time making use of his/her talents
- Be made anxious by change and uncertainty
- Avoid situations that others generally view as benign and nonintimidating
- Be ill at ease in dealing with others
- Give up easily and not persevere in the face of challenges

The test taker is more likely than most police officers or trainees to exhibit difficulties:

- Applying instructions appropriately under stressful conditions
- Performing under stressful conditions
- Carrying out tasks under nonstressful conditions
- Multitasking
- Accepting and responding to constructive performance feedback
- Cooperating with peers and/or supervisors
- Reacting to situations with the proper degree of emotional and behavioral restraint and control, and avoiding impulsive and/or unnecessarily risky behavior

TABLE A-12
Thought Dysfunction (THD)

Comparison Group Findings	
T-Score Level	
57–63	The test taker reports a comparatively high level of unusual thinking for a police officer candidate.
≥ 65	The test taker's responses indicate significant thought dysfunction that may be incompatible with public safety requirements for sound judgment. This level of disordered thinking is very uncommon among police officer candidates.
Job-Relevant Correlates	
≥ 60	**Compared with other police officer candidates, the test taker is more likely to:** • Have thoughts, perceptions, and/or experiences that are rarely reported **The test taker is more likely than most police officers or trainees to exhibit difficulties:** • Reliably attending court

TABLE A-13
Behavioral/Externalizing Dysfunction (BXD)

Comparison Group Findings

T-Score Level	
57–63	The test taker reports a comparatively large number of behavioral problems for a police officer candidate.
≥65	The test taker's responses indicate significant externalizing behavior that may be incompatible with public safety requirements for behavioral control. This level of acting-out behavior is very uncommon among police officer candidates.

Job-Relevant Correlates

≥60 **Compared with other police officer candidates, the test taker is more likely to:**

- Easily become irritated and annoyed by others
- Become impatient with others over minor infractions
- Have a history of motor vehicle violations or difficulties
- Have a history of job performance problems
- Be self-centered
- Engage in conflicts with authority
- Have a history of problems getting along with others
- Be opinionated and outspoken
- Fail to consider others' needs and feelings
- Have difficulty creating and sustaining mutually satisfying relationships
- Fail to integrate ethical considerations into his/her decision making
- Have a history of conflicts with the law and other violations of social norms
- Have skeptical and/or antisocial views of the world
- Lack a commitment to societal rules
- Be self-indulgent
- Have a history of absenteeism or tardiness
- Have a history of substance use problems
- Behave impulsively or without adequate consideration of the consequences or implications of his/her actions

The test taker is more likely than most police officers or trainees to exhibit difficulties leading to:

- Integrity violations
- Sustained internal affairs investigations
- Investigations about conduct unbecoming a police officer
- Anger management problems

TABLE A-14
Demoralization (RCd)

Comparison Group Findings

T-Score Level

T-Score Level	
54–64	The test taker reports a comparatively high level of unhappiness and dissatisfaction for a police officer candidate.
≥65	The test taker's responses indicate a level of general unhappiness and dissatisfaction that may be incompatible with public safety requirements for good morale. This level of unhappiness is very uncommon among police officer candidates.

Job-Relevant Correlates

≥55 **Compared with other police officer candidates, the test taker is more likely to:**

- Become easily discouraged
- Have skeptical and/or antisocial views of the world
- Believe that life is unfair and that exploiting opportunities for personal gain is justified
- Have a history of absenteeism or tardiness

The test taker is more likely than most police officers or trainees to exhibit difficulties leading to:

- Integrity violations
- Sustained internal affairs investigations

TABLE A-15
Somatic Complaints (RC1)

Comparison Group Findings

T-Score Level	
54–63	The test taker reports a comparatively high level of somatic complaints for a police officer candidate.
≥65	The test taker's responses indicate a level of somatic complaints that may be incompatible with public safety requirements for good psychological adjustment. This level of diffuse health complaints is very uncommon among police officer candidates.

Job-Relevant Correlates

NONE

TABLE A-16
Low Positive Emotions (RC2)

Comparison Group Findings

T -Score Level	
54–61	The test taker reports a comparatively low level of positive emotional experiences for a police officer candidate.
≥65	The test taker's responses indicate a lack of positive emotional experiences that may be incompatible with public safety requirements for good emotional adjustment. This lack of positive emotional responsiveness is very uncommon among police officer candidates.

Job-Relevant Correlates

≥58	**Compared with other police officer candidates, the test taker is more likely to:** • Become easily discouraged • Have difficulty coping with stress • Worry about problems and be uncertain about how to deal with them • Be ill at ease in dealing with others **The test taker is more likely than most police officers or trainees to exhibit difficulties:** • Applying instructions appropriately under stressful conditions • Performing under stressful conditions • Carrying out tasks under nonstressful conditions • Engaging or confronting subjects in circumstances in which an officer would normally approach or intervene • Cooperating with peers and/or supervisors • Reliably attending court • In his/her dedication to improvement of knowledge and skills • With punctuality and attendance

TABLE A-17
Cynicism (RC3)

Comparison Group Findings

T-Score Level

T-Score	
61	The test taker reports a comparatively high level of distrust and low opinion of others for a police officer candidate.
≥65	The test taker's responses indicate a level of cynicism that may be incompatible with public safety requirements for good interpersonal functioning. This level of distrust and low opinion of others is very uncommon among police officer candidates.

Job-Relevant Correlates

≥61 **Compared with other police officer candidates, the test taker is more likely to:**

- Become impatient with others over minor infractions
- Be demanding
- Have a limited social support network
- Hold overly suspicious views about the motives and actions of others
- Have difficulty trusting others
- Have a history of problems getting along with others
- Have skeptical and/or antisocial views of the world
- Believe that life is unfair and that exploiting opportunities for personal gain is justified

The test taker is more likely than most police officers or trainees to exhibit difficulties:

- Accepting and responding to constructive performance feedback
- Stemming from rude and/or overbearing behavior that results in complaints from the public
- Leading to complaints from the public
- Leading to investigations about conduct unbecoming of a police officer
- Leading to integrity violations

TABLE A-18
Antisocial Behavior (RC4)

Comparison Group Findings

T-Score Level

57–62	The test taker reports a comparatively high level of irresponsible behavior for a police officer candidate.
≥65	The test taker's responses indicate a level of antisocial behavior that may be incompatible with public safety requirements for behavioral control. This level of rule-breaking behavior is very uncommon among police officer candidates.

Job-Relevant Correlates

≥59	**Compared with other police officer candidates, the test taker is more likely to:** • Become easily discouraged • Have a history of motor vehicle violations or difficulties • Have a history of job performance problems • Engage in conflicts with authority • Fail to integrate ethical considerations into his/her decision making • Have a history of conflicts with the law and other violations of social norms • Lack a commitment to societal rules • Be self-indulgent • Have a history of substance use problems • A history of absenteeism or tardiness **The test taker is more likely than most police officers or trainees to exhibit difficulties leading to:** • Integrity violations • Sustained internal affairs investigations

TABLE A-19
Ideas of Persecution (RC6)

Comparison Group Findings

T-Score Level	
61	The test taker reports a comparatively high level of persecutory beliefs for a police officer candidate.
≥65	The test taker's responses indicate a level of persecutory ideation that may be incompatible with public safety requirements for sound judgment. This level of belief that others pose a threat is very uncommon among police officer candidates.

Job-Relevant Correlates

≥61	**The test taker is more likely than most police officers or trainees to exhibit difficulties leading to:** • Complaints from the public • Investigations about conduct unbecoming a police officer

TABLE A-20
Dysfunctional Negative Emotions (RC7)

Comparison Group Findings

T-Score Level	
55–62	The test taker reports a comparatively high level of negative emotions for a police officer candidate.
≥65	The test taker's responses indicate a level of negative emotionality that may be incompatible with public safety requirements for good emotional adjustment. This level of dysfunctional negative emotions is very uncommon among police officer candidates.

Job-Relevant Correlates

≥55	**Compared with other police officer candidates, the test taker is more likely to:** • Have difficulty coping with stress • Have trouble tolerating ambiguous, confusing, and unstructured environments • Avoid making decisions, fail to take action, or do anything that may prompt scrutiny from others • Feel inadequate • Have a history of problems getting along with others • Be demanding • Hold overly suspicious views about the motives and actions of others • Have difficulty trusting others • Have a history of substance use problems

TABLE A-21
Aberrant Experiences (RC8)

Comparison Group Findings

T-Score Level

59–63	The test taker reports a comparatively high level of odd perceptions and thoughts for a police officer candidate.
≥65	The test taker's responses indicate a level of aberrant experiences that may be incompatible with public safety requirements for sound thinking. This level of odd perceptions and thoughts is very uncommon among police officer candidates.

Job-Relevant Correlates

≥59	**Compared with other police officer candidates, the test taker is more likely to:** • Have thoughts, perceptions, and/or experiences that are rarely reported **The test taker is more likely than most police officers or trainees to exhibit difficulties:** • Carrying out tasks under nonstressful conditions • Leading to integrity violations • Leading to sustained internal affairs investigations • Reliably attending court

TABLE A-22
Hypomanic Activation (RC9)

Comparison Group Findings

T -Score Level	
≤31	The test taker's responses indicate a very low level of energy that may be incompatible with public safety requirements to remain actively engaged with one's environment. This level of low energy and low activation is very uncommon among police officer candidates.
56–63	The test taker reports a comparatively high level of excitability for a police officer candidate.
≥65	The test taker's responses indicate a level of energy, aggression, and impulsivity that may be incompatible with public safety requirements for behavioral control. This level of excitability is very uncommon among police officer candidates.

Job-Relevant Correlates

≤28 **The test taker is more likely than most police officers or trainees to exhibit difficulties:**

- Engaging or confronting subjects in circumstances in which an officer would normally approach or intervene
- In demonstrating a command presence and controlling situations requiring order or resolution

≥58 **Compared with other police officer candidates, the test taker is more likely to:**

- Become impatient with others over minor infractions
- Have a history of problems getting along with others
- Be opinionated and outspoken
- Be demanding
- Have difficulty trusting others
- Have skeptical and/or antisocial views of the world
- Believe that life is unfair and that exploiting opportunities for personal gain is justified
- Have a history of substance use problems
- Behave impulsively or without adequate consideration of the consequences or implications of his/her actions

The test taker is more likely than most police officers or trainees to exhibit difficulties:

- Stemming from rude and/or overbearing behavior that results in complaints from the public
- Reacting to situations with the proper degree of emotional and behavioral restraint and control, and avoiding impulsive and/or unnecessarily risky behavior

TABLE A-23
Malaise (MLS)

Comparison Group Findings

T-Score Level

57–63	The test taker reports a comparatively high level of concern about his/her health for a police officer candidate.
≥65	The test taker's responses indicate a level of malaise that may be incompatible with public safety requirements for good psychological adjustment. This level of self-perceived physical debilitation and poor health is very uncommon among police officer candidates.

Job-Relevant Correlates

≥57	**Compared with other police officer candidates, the test taker is more likely to:** • Develop physical symptoms in response to stress and worry about his/her health • Exhibit difficulties with initiative and drive, such as obtaining information and evidence needed to solve crimes and explain incidents

TABLE A-24
Gastrointestinal Complaints (GIC)

Comparison Group Findings

T-Score Level

≥65	The test taker reports a comparatively high level of gastrointestinal complaints for a police officer candidate.

Job-Relevant Correlates

NONE

TABLE A-25
Head Pain Complaints (HPC)

Comparison Group Findings

T-Score Level

≥65	The test taker reports a comparatively high level of head pain complaints for a police officer candidate.

Job-Relevant Correlates

NONE

TABLE A-26
Neurological Complaints (NUC)

Comparison Group Findings

T-Score Level	
> 65	The test taker reports a comparatively high level of neurological complaints for a police officer candidate.

Job-Relevant Correlates

NONE

TABLE A-27
Cognitive Complaints (COG)

Comparison Group Findings

T-Score Level	
58–64	The test taker reports a comparatively high level of cognitive complaints for a police officer candidate.
≥ 65	The test taker's responses indicate a level of cognitive complaints that may be incompatible with public safety requirements for sound thinking. This level of concern about cognitive functioning is very uncommon among police officer candidates.

Job-Relevant Correlates

NONE

TABLE A-28
Suicidal/Death Ideation (SUI)

Comparison Group Findings

T-Score Level	
≥ 65	The test taker reported suicidal thoughts. These are very uncommon responses that require immediate follow-up.

Job-Relevant Correlates

NONE

TABLE A-29
Helplessness/Hopelessness (HLP)

Comparison Group Findings

T-Score Level

60	The test taker reports a high level of beliefs that he/she cannot solve problems and reach important goals compared to other police officer candidates.
≥65	The test taker's responses indicate a level of helplessness and hopelessness that may be incompatible with public safety requirements for good emotional adjustment. This level of beliefs that he/she cannot solve problems and reach important goals is very uncommon among police officer candidates.

Job-Relevant Correlates

≥60 **Compared with other police officer candidates, the test taker is more likely to:**

- Cooperating with peers and/or supervisors

The test taker is more likely than most police officers or trainees to exhibit difficulties:

- Using tactical thinking, legal knowledge, and awareness of ethics to reach decisions quickly
- Engaging or confronting subjects in circumstances in which an officer would normally approach or intervene
- In demonstrating a command presence and controlling situations requiring order or resolution
- Cooperating with peers and/or supervisors

TABLE A-30
Self-Doubt (SFD)

Comparison Group Findings

T-Score Level

56	The test taker reports a comparatively high level of self-doubt for a police officer candidate
≥65	The test taker's responses indicate a level of self-doubt that may be incompatible with public safety requirements for good emotional adjustment. This lack of confidence is very uncommon among police officer candidates.

Job-Relevant Correlates

NONE

TABLE A-31
Inefficacy (NFC)

Comparison Group Findings

T -Score Level

54–58	The test taker reports a comparatively high level of inefficacious decision making for a police officer candidate.
≥64	The test taker's responses indicate a level of inefficacy that may be incompatible with public safety requirements for good emotional adjustment and resilience. This level of beliefs that he/she cannot make effective decisions is very uncommon among police officer candidates.

Job-Relevant Correlates

≥58	**Compared with other police officer candidates, the test taker is more likely to:** • Have a difficult time making use of his/her talents • Avoid making decisions, fail to take action, or do anything that may prompt scrutiny from others • Feel inadequate

TABLE A-32
Stress/Worry (STW)

Comparison Group Findings

T -Score Level

57	The test taker reports a comparatively high level of problems with stress and worries for a police officer candidate.
≥65	The test taker's responses indicate a level of stress and worry that may be incompatible with public safety requirements for good emotional adjustment. This level of stress reactivity is very uncommon among police officer candidates.

Job-Relevant Correlates

≥57	**Compared with other police officer candidates, the test taker is more likely to:** • Have difficulty coping with stress • Worry about problems and be uncertain about how to deal with them • Easily become irritated and annoyed by others • Have a history of absenteeism or tardiness **The test taker is more likely than most police officers or trainees to exhibit difficulties:** • Applying instructions appropriately under stressful conditions

TABLE A-33
Anxiety (AXY)

Comparison Group Findings

T-Score Level

T-Score Level	
≥ 65	The test taker's responses indicate a level of anxiety that may be incompatible with public safety requirements for good emotional adjustment. This level of pervasive anxiety is very uncommon among police officer candidates.

Job-Relevant Correlates

NONE

TABLE A-34
Anger Proneness (ANP)

Comparison Group Findings

T-Score Level

T-Score Level	
≥ 65	The test taker's responses indicate a level of anger proneness that may be incompatible with public safety requirements for emotional adjustment. This level of anger is very uncommon among police officer candidates.

Job-Relevant Correlates

NONE

TABLE A-35
Behavior-Restricting Fears (BRF)

Comparison Group Findings

T-Score Level

T-Score Level	
63	The test taker reports a comparatively high level of behavior-restricting fears for a police officer candidate
≥ 65	The test taker's responses indicate a level of behavior-restricting fears that may be incompatible with public safety requirements for good emotional adjustment. This level of fears that restrict normal behavior is very uncommon among police officer candidates.

Job-Relevant Correlates

≥ 63 **Compared with other police officer candidates, the test taker is more likely to:**

- Have trouble tolerating ambiguous, confusing, and unstructured environments

TABLE A-36
Multiple Specific Fears (MSF)

Comparison Group Findings

T-Score Level

≥65	The test taker's responses indicate a level of multiple specific fears that may be incompatible with public safety requirements for good emotional adjustment. This level of fearfulness is very uncommon among police officer candidates.

Job-Relevant Correlates

NONE

TABLE A-37
Juvenile Conduct Problems (JCP)

Comparison Group Findings

T-Score Level

≥65	The test taker's responses indicate a history of juvenile conduct problems that may be incompatible with public safety requirements for behavioral control and adherence to rules. This level of juvenile misconduct is very uncommon among police officer candidates.

Job-Relevant Correlates

≥70 **The test taker is more likely than most police officers or trainees to exhibit difficulties:**

- Leading to integrity violations
- Leading to investigations about conduct unbecoming a police officer
- With punctuality and attendance
- Reacting to situations with the proper degree of emotional and behavioral restraint and control, and avoiding impulsive and/or unnecessarily risky behavior

TABLE A-38
Substance Abuse (SUB)

Comparison Group Findings	
T-Score Level	
55–61	The test taker reports a comparatively large number of problems with substance use for a police officer candidate.
≥65	The test taker's responses indicate past and/or current substance use that may be incompatible with public safety requirements for refraining from substance misuse. This level of alcohol and possible drug use is very uncommon among police officer candidates.
Job-Relevant Correlates	
≥61	**Compared with other police officer candidates, the test taker is more likely to:** • Have a history of substance use problems **The test taker is more likely than most police officers or trainees to exhibit difficulties leading to:** • Integrity violations • Sustained internal affairs investigations

TABLE A-39
Aggression (AGG)

Comparison Group Findings	
T-Score Level	
56–61	The test taker reports a comparatively high level of physically aggressive behavior for a police officer candidate.
≥65	The test taker's responses indicate a level of physically violent behavior that may be incompatible with public safety requirements for behavioral control. This level of aggression is very uncommon among police officer candidates.
Job-Relevant Correlates	
≥56	**The test taker is more likely than most police officers or trainees to exhibit difficulties:** • Accepting and responding to constructive performance feedback • Stemming from rude and/or overbearing behavior that results in complaints from the public • Cooperating with peers and/or supervisors

TABLE A-40
Activation (ACT)

Comparison Group Findings

T-Score Level

T-Score Level	
≥ 65	The test taker's responses indicate a level of over-activation that may be incompatible with public safety requirements for behavioral control and sound judgment. This level of excitability is very uncommon among police officer candidates.

Job-Relevant Correlates

NONE

TABLE A-41
Family Problems (FML)

Comparison Group Findings

T-Score Level

T-Score Level	
58–63	The test taker reports a comparatively high level of family conflict for a police officer candidate.
≥ 65	The test taker's responses indicate a level of family problems that may be incompatible with public safety requirements for good interpersonal functioning. This level of family conflict is very uncommon among police officer candidates.

Job-Relevant Correlates

≥ 58

Compared with other police officer candidates, the test taker is more likely to:

- Worry about problems and be uncertain about how to deal with them

The test taker is more likely than most police officers or trainees to exhibit difficulties:

- Carrying out tasks under nonstressful conditions

TABLE A-42
Interpersonal Passivity (IPP)

Comparison Group Findings

T-Score Level

34	The test taker's responses indicate a level of overly assertive behavior that may be incompatible with public safety requirements for behavioral control. This level of domineering behavior is very uncommon among police officer candidates.
56–62	The test taker reports a comparatively high level of interpersonal passivity for a police officer candidate
≥65	The test taker's responses indicate a level of interpersonal passivity that may be incompatible with public safety requirements for assertiveness. This level of passive behavior is very uncommon among police officer candidates.

Job-Relevant Correlates

≥62 **Compared with other police officer candidates, the test taker is more likely to:**

- Be made anxious by change and uncertainty
- Be ill at ease in dealing with others

TABLE A-43
Social Avoidance (SAV)

Comparison Group Findings

T-Score Level

59	The test taker reports a comparatively high level of social avoidance for a police officer candidate.
≥65	The test taker's responses indicate a level of social avoidance that may be incompatible with public safety requirements for good interpersonal functioning. This level of socially avoidant behavior is very uncommon among police officer candidates.

Job-Relevant Correlates

≥65 **Compared with other police officer candidates, the test taker is more likely to:**

- Avoid situations that others generally view as benign and nonintimidating
- Be ill at ease in dealing with others
- Have a limited social support network

The test taker is more likely than most police officers or trainees to exhibit difficulties:

- Performing under stressful conditions
- In demonstrating a command presence and controlling situations requiring order or resolution
- Reading people, listening to others, and adapting his/her language and approach to the requirements of the situation
- With punctuality and attendance
- With reliable work behavior and dependable follow-through

TABLE A-44
Shyness (SHY)

Comparison Group Findings

T-Score Level

57	The test taker reports a comparatively high level of social anxiety for a police officer candidate.
≥ 65	The test taker's responses indicate a level of shyness that may be incompatible with public safety requirements for good interpersonal functioning. This level of social anxiety is very uncommon among police officer candidates.

Job-Relevant Correlates

≥ 57 **Compared with other police officer candidates, the test taker is more likely to:**

- Avoid making decisions, fail to take action, or do anything that may prompt scrutiny from others
- Be ill at ease in dealing with others
- Feel inadequate
- Be unsure and act hesitantly
- Give up easily and not persevere in the face of challenges

The test taker is more likely than most police officers or trainees to exhibit difficulties:

- With punctuality and attendance

TABLE A-45
Disaffiliativeness (DSF)

Comparison Group Findings

T -Score Level

≥ 65	The test taker's responses indicate a level of disaffiliativeness that may be incompatible with public safety requirements for good interpersonal functioning. This level of disinterest in interacting with others is very uncommon among police officer candidates.

Job-Relevant Correlates

≥ 68 **Compared with other police officer candidates, the test taker is more likely to:**

- Become impatient with others over minor infractions
- Have a history of problems getting along with others
- Be demanding
- Have a limited social support network

The test taker is more likely than most police officers or trainees to exhibit difficulties:

- Engaging or confronting subjects in circumstances in which an officer would normally approach or intervene
- In demonstrating a command presence and controlling situations requiring order or resolution
- With reliable work behavior and dependable follow-through

TABLE A-46
Aggressiveness (AGGR-r)

Comparison Group Findings

T-Score Level

≤ 39 The test taker's responses indicate a level of interpersonal passivity that may be incompatible with public safety requirements for assertiveness. This level of passive behavior is very uncommon in police officer candidates.

≥ 65 The test taker's responses indicate a level of overassertiveness that may be incompatible with public safety requirements for behavioral control. This level of domineering behavior is very uncommon in police officer candidates.

Job-Relevant Correlates

≤ 39 **Compared with other police officer candidates, the test taker is more likely to:**

- Be made anxious by change and uncertainty
- Be ill at ease in dealing with others

The test taker is more likely than most police officers or trainees to exhibit difficulties:

- In demonstrating a command presence and controlling situations requiring order or resolution

≥ 69 **Compared with other police officer candidates, the test taker is more likely to:**

- Become impatient with others over minor infractions
- Cooperating with peers and/or supervisors

TABLE A-47
Psychoticism (PSYC-r)

Comparison Group Findings

T-Score Level

59–63 The test taker reports a comparatively high level of eccentric beliefs for a police officer candidate.

≥ 65 The test taker's responses indicate a level of disconnection from reality that may be incompatible with public safety requirements for sound judgment. This level of eccentric thinking is very uncommon in police officer candidates.

Job-Relevant Correlates

≥ 63 **Compared with other police officer candidates, the test taker is more likely to:**

- Easily become irritated and annoyed by others
- Become impatient with others over minor infractions
- Develop physical symptoms in response to stress and worry about his/her health
- Have thoughts, perceptions, and/or experiences that are rarely reported
- Avoid situations that others generally view as benign and nonintimidating
- Have a history of problems getting along with others
- Be demanding
- Hold overly suspicious views about the motives and actions of others
- Have difficulty trusting others
- Have skeptical and/or antisocial views of the world

The test taker is more likely than most police officers or trainees to exhibit difficulties:

- Leading to integrity violations
- Leading to sustained internal affairs investigations
- With initiative and drive, such as obtaining information and evidence needed to solve crimes and explain incidents
- Reliably attending court

TABLE A-48
Disconstraint (DISC-r)

Comparison Group Findings

T-Score Level

T-Score Level	
≤35	The test taker's responses indicate a level of behavioral constraint that may be incompatible with public safety requirements for adaptability. This level of overly controlled behavior is very uncommon among police officer candidates.
≥65	The test taker's responses indicate a level of disconstraint that may be incompatible with public safety requirements for good behavioral control. This level of poor impulse control is very uncommon among police officer candidates.

Job-Relevant Correlates

≤35 **Compared with other police officer candidates, the test taker is more likely to:**

- Be unprepared to take decisive action in times of stress or emergency

The test taker is more likely than most police officers or trainees to exhibit difficulties:

- Performing under stressful condition
- Engaging or confronting subjects in circumstances in which an officer would normally approach or intervene

≥66 **Compared with other police officer candidates, the test taker is more likely to:**

- Not reflect on his/her behavior
- Brush off criticism and other negative feedback
- Have a history of substance abuse problems

The test taker is more likely than most police officers or trainees to exhibit difficulties:

- Leading to integrity violations
- Leading to sustained internal affairs complaints
- Behaving impulsively or without adequate consideration of the consequences or implications of his/her actions
- Reacting to situations with the proper degree of emotional and behavioral restraint and control, and avoiding impulsive and/or unnecessarily risky behavior

TABLE A-49
Negative Emotionality/Neuroticism (NEGE-r)

Comparison Group Findings

T-Score Level

56–62	The test taker reports a comparatively high level of negative emotions for a police officer candidate.
≥ 65	The test taker's responses indicate a level of negative emotionality that may be incompatible with public safety requirements for good emotional adjustment. This level of dysfunctional negative emotions is very uncommon in police officer candidates.

Job-Relevant Correlates

≥ 56 **Compared with other police officer candidates, the test taker is more likely to:**

- Become easily discouraged
- Have difficulty coping with stress
- Worry about problems and be uncertain about how to deal with them
- Behave in a self-defeating fashion
- Have trouble tolerating ambiguous, confusing, and unstructured environments
- Develop physical symptoms in response to stress and worry about his/her health
- Behave impulsively or without adequate consideration of the consequences or implications of his/her actions

The test taker is more likely than most police officers or trainees to exhibit difficulties:

- Accepting and responding to constructive performance feedback

TABLE A-50
Introversion/Low Positive Emotionality (INTR-r)

Comparison Group Findings

T-Score Level

≥ 64	The test taker's responses indicate a level of introversion and low positive emotions that may be incompatible with public safety requirements for good interpersonal skills and emotional adjustment. This level of introversion is very uncommon in police officer candidates.

Job-Relevant Correlates

≥ 64 **Compared with other police officer candidates, the test taker is more likely to:**

- Be made anxious by change and uncertainty
- Be ill at ease in dealing with others
- Have a limited social support network

The test taker is more likely than most police officers or trainees to exhibit difficulties:

- Applying instructions appropriately under stressful conditions
- Carrying out tasks under nonstressful conditions
- Accepting and responding to constructive performance feedback
- Engaging or confronting subjects in circumstances in which an officer would normally approach or intervene
- Cooperating with peers and/or supervisors
- With reliable work behavior and dependable follow-through

NOTES

Chapter 1

1. We use the labels *law enforcement officer, peace officer,* and *police officer* interchangeably throughout this book. These terms are intended to refer to armed (or armable) public sector employees vested by the legislating jurisdiction with law enforcement authority and who are authorized to arrest or refer an arrest for criminal prosecution. Examples include city police officers; reserve police officers; deputy sheriffs; parole and probation officers; sworn personnel of law enforcement subunits of port, transit, and housing authorities; campus police officers employed by universities and colleges; and federal law enforcement officers.
2. Correctional officers consist of public sector employees responsible for the supervision, safety, and security of inmates (adult or juvenile) in a prison, jail, or similar form of secure custody.
3. Throughout this book, we refer to *a candidate* to mean an individual who has received an offer of employment conditioned on the findings of the post-offer psychological evaluation. We refer to an *applicant* as an individual who is still at the pre-offer stage of the application process.
4 In some jurisdictions, 911 dispatchers perform many other functions that may also involve processing and storing evidence and seized assets, including money. Additionally, some firefighters, such as those who also perform services as arson investigators, have use-of-force and enforcement powers.
5. The *hiring agency* is the agency or department in which the candidate has applied to work. The *hiring authority* is responsible for processing the candidate through the application and selection process. These entities are often the same, but will differ when, for example, the application process for a police department is administered by a separate human resources department.

Chapter 5

1. Throughout Part II, we interchangeably use "qualified" and "suitable" to indicate a judgment that a candidate meets the selection criteria, and we use both "unqualified" and "unsuitable" to refer to a determination that a candidate does not meet the selection criteria.
2. The prohibition against communicating the findings from a psychological evaluation conducted for one employer derives from federal law under the ADA [(29 C.F.R. §1630.10[a]) and (2)]. Some state jurisdictions may have laws that run counter to this prohibition. For example, in the state of Washington, administrative code 139-07-030 permits findings from one psychological evaluation of a police officer candidate to be shared with more than one law enforcement agency under the following circumstances:

   (a) the agency that initiated the psychological examination and the qualified professional conducting the examination agreed to share the psychological examination report and recommendations with the other law enforcement agency;
   (b) the applicant signed a release permitting the other agency to have the psychological examination report;
   (c) the psychological examination was completed within 6 months of the request by the other law enforcement agency; and
   (d) the job analyses of the initiating and other law enforcement agencies must be substantially similar.

   Screening professionals who agree to share an examination report and recommendations with more than one law enforcement agency may wish to consult first with legal counsel to determine how to proceed when state and federal regulations appear to be in opposition to that sharing.
3. This is commonly referred to as the "business necessity standard" and is discussed in greater detail in chapter 9 in the context of fitness-for-duty evaluations. In pre-employment evaluations, however, when a person with a disability is not hired because of that disability (and an adverse hiring decision will presumptively result in that conclusion), the business necessity standard requires generally that the exclusionary criterion reasonably achieves the employer's legitimate business interests and that another less exclusionary alternative would not satisfy those interests. For this reason, criteria used to disqualify police and other public safety candidates in any medical evaluation should be assiduously linked to safety and other essential performance requirements of the particular position.
4. The Age Discrimination in Employment Act of 1967 provides similar protections for persons 40 years of age or older.
5. MMPI-2-RF standard T-scores are based on nongendered norms derived from an equal number of male and female subjects in the normative sample. When a test publisher calculates nongendered norms for a police officer candidate sample using the naturally occurring distribution of male and female candidates in a candidate

pool, the normative sample will, in most cases, be composed of predominantly male subjects, since 88% of local law enforcement officers in the United States are male (Bureau of Justice Statistics, 2015).

6. Reference to "clinical evaluations" versus "nonclinical evaluations" is intended to reflect the legal distinction between "medical" examinations or inquiries and procedures or tests that generally are not considered medical examinations. This use of "clinical evaluations" is consistent with the concept of "medical examinations" under the Americans with Disabilities Act (ADA, 1991) in that both terms denote any procedure or test that seeks information about an individual's physical or mental impairments or health and includes, but is not limited to, psychological tests that are designed to identify a mental disorder or impairment. In contrast, psychological tests that measure only personality traits such as honesty, preferences, and habits would not be considered a medical examination (Equal Employment Opportunity Commission [EEOC], 2000, at Question 2).
7. In California, this determination is made by evaluating the condition's impact on the 10 POST Psychological Screening Dimensions.
8. The President's Commission on Law Enforcement and Administration of Justice (1967), whose call for the increased use of psychological testing and interviews of police officer candidates is widely credited for the nearly universal use of psychological screening today (Trompetter, 2017), also made a plea for higher-quality background investigations. The Commission noted,

> If properly conducted a background investigation can provide invaluable information on the character of applicants. . . . In many cities, however, character investigations are extremely limited in scope and investigators seldom probe deeply enough to uncover the information needed for professional evaluation. Few municipal forces have yet devoted enough attention to the character investigation of applicants. Civil Service routines often merely require that the applicant provide character vouchers or "references" which are accepted without further question. . . . No department should admit any person into the police service until his background has been comprehensively investigated. Trained investigators should examine school, credit, and criminal records; interview persons used as references and other persons in the applicant's neighborhood; and interview past and present employers. The investigative process should extend to other communities as well, if the applicant has lived elsewhere. . . . Prior convictions, work habits, prejudices, emotional stability, among other characteristics, should be determined to ascertain whether the applicant is fit to perform police work. Since background investigations are expensive, if properly conducted, they should be restricted to those who otherwise have qualified. (p. 129)

Fifty years later, the Commission's admonishment is no less fitting. Background investigations vary considerably in quality from agency to agency, and the information provided about a candidate's character and other characteristics from a high-quality investigation contributes immeasurably to the validity of the psychological evaluation.

9. Some states require evaluation of a police officer candidate's positive traits and characteristics (i.e., assets or strengths). However, this assessment alone does not comprise an adequate preemployment psychological evaluation that, in most jurisdictions, includes the minimum requirement that an "applicant be free from any emotional or mental condition that might adversely affect the performance of safety-based duties and responsibilities and be capable of withstanding the psychological demands inherent in the prospective position" (IACP-PPSS, 2015; Guideline 3.2).

Chapter 7

1. The base rates reflect the percent of individuals who score at or above the test taker on a given scale. If added to the percent scoring at or above the test taker (listed on the profile page below the scale score) the result will exceed 100% because the percent of comparison group test takers who score the same as the test taker is included in both figures.

Chapter 8

1. Reserve police officers in this agency perform a more restricted range of police duties—and are conducted under a higher level of supervision—than those performed by regular police officers. In addition, they function as volunteers with no property rights to the position; therefore, they are easily dismissed in the face of conduct or performance problems.
2. For purposes of brevity, the Firefighter/Paramedic Candidate comparison group is titled "Firefighter Candidate comparison group."

Chapter 11

1. Diagnostic specificity is not a prerequisite for a fitness-for-duty determination. Precision in diagnosis is often impeded in occupationally mandated psychological evaluations because of a wide range of factors, including defensiveness on the part of the examinee, limited access to collateral sources outside of the work setting, legal disputes that result in relevant records being held until compelled by the discovery process, and health care professionals failing to cooperate with records acquisition. In *Sager v. Yuba County* (Cal.App. 2007), the court ruled that a fitness

examiner's failure to provide a precise diagnosis was not grounds for discrediting a finding of unfitness for duty when the psychologist was able to describe the nature of the employee's impairment (i.e., uncharacterized personality disorder leading to marked deficits in emotional regulation, interpersonal functioning, and adaptability). Furthermore, diagnostic specificity is often impeded by the overlapping contours of many mental disorders—a fact acknowledged by the authors of the *DSM-5* (American Psychiatric Association, 2013): "Although some mental disorders may have well-defined boundaries around symptom clusters, scientific evidence now places many, if not most, disorders on a spectrum with closely related disorders that have shared symptoms, shared genetic and environmental risk factors, and possibly shared neural substrates. . . . In short, we have come to recognize that the boundaries between disorders are more porous than originally perceived" (p. 6).

2. The ADA permits an employer to obtain only that medical information necessary to determine whether the employee can perform the essential functions of the job or work without posing a direct threat (EEOC, 2000, Question 13, p. 12). "This means that, in most situations, an employer cannot request an employee's complete medical records because they are likely to contain information unrelated to whether the employee can perform his/her essential functions or work without posing a direct threat" (p. 12). However, when an employer has a reasonable belief that an employee's present ability to perform essential job functions will be limited by a medical condition or that he or she will pose a direct threat due to a medical condition, the employer may ask the employee for additional documentation regarding his or her medications or treatment (EEOC, 2000, Question 17, p. 13).

REFERENCES

Aamodt, A. (2004). *Research in law enforcement selection.* Boca Raton, Fla.: Brown Walker Press.

Achenbach, T. M., & Edelbrock, C. S. (1978). The classification of child psychopathology: A review and analysis of empirical efforts. *Psychological Bulletin, 85*(6), 1275–1301.

Ackerman, M. J. (2010). *Essentials of psychological assessment* (2nd ed.). Hoboken, N.J.: John Wiley & Sons.

ADA Amendments Act, Pub. L. 110-325 (2008).

Age Discrimination in Employment Act of 1967, Pub. L. No. 90-202, 29 U.S.C. § 621 through § 634.

Aldrup v. Caldera, #01-50369, 2001 U.S. App. Lexis 26347 (5th Cir. 2001).

Allard, G., & Faust, D. (2000). Errors in scoring objective personality tests. *Assessment, 7*(2), 119–131.

American Board of Police & Public Safety Psychology (2016). Chapel Hill, N.C.: Author.

American Educational Research Association (AERA), American Psychological Association (APA), & National Council on Measurement in Education (NCME). (2014). Standards for educational and psychological testing. Washington, DC: American Educational Research Association.

American Psychiatric Association. (2013). *Diagnostic and statistical manual of mental disorders* (5th ed.). Washington: Author.

American Psychological Association. (2017a). Ethical principles of psychologists and code of conduct. Retrieved from www.apa.org/ethics/code/ethics-code-2017.pdf

American Psychological Association. (2017b). Professional practice guidelines for occupationally mandated psychological evaluations. *American Psychologist.* Retrieved from www.apa.org/practice/guidelines/occupationally-mandated-psychological-evaluations.pdf

Americans with Disabilities Act of 1990, Pub. L. No. 101-336, §2, 104 Stat. 328 (1991).

Angst, J., & Sellaro, R. (2000). Historical perspectives and natural history of bipolar disorder. *Biological Psychiatry, 48,* 445–447.

Appelbaum, K. L. (2010). Commentary: The art of forensic report writing. *Journal of the American Academy of Psychiatry and Law, 38*(1), 43–45.

Azen, S. P., Snibbe, H. M., & Montgomery, H. R. (1973). A longitudinal predictive study of success and performance of law enforcement officers. *Journal of Applied Psychology, 57*(2), 190–192.

Bandura, A. (1994). Social cognitive theory of mass communication. In J. Bryant & D. Zillmann (Eds.), *Media effects: Advances in theory and research* (pp. 61–90). Hillsdale, N.J.: Erlbaum.

Bandura, A. (2001). Social cognitive theory: An agentic perspective. *Annual Review of Psychology, 52,* 1–26.

Batista, T. A., Baes, C. V. W., & Juruena, M. F. (2011). Efficacy of psychoeducation in bipolar patients: Systematic review of randomized trials. *Psychology & Neuroscience, 4*(3), 409–416.

Ben-Porath, Y. S. (2012). *Interpreting the MMPI-2-RF.* Minneapolis: University of Minnesota Press.

Ben-Porath, Y. S. (2016). Inaugural editorial for *Psychological Assessment. Psychological Assessment, 28,* 1–2.

Ben-Porath, Y. S., & Butcher, J. N. (1989a). The psychometric stability of rewritten MMPI items. *Journal of Personality Assessment, 53,* 645–653.

Ben-Porath, Y. S., & Butcher, J. N. (1989b). The comparability of MMPI and MMPI-2 scales and profiles. *Psychological Assessment, 1,* 345–347.

Ben-Porath, Y. S., Corey, D. M., & Tarescavage, A. M. (2017). Using the MMPI-2-RF in preemployment evaluations of police officer candidates. In C. L. Mitchell & E. Dorian (Eds.), *Police psychology and its growing impact on modern law enforcement* (pp. 51–78). Hershey, Pa.: IGI Global.

Ben-Porath, Y. S., & Forbey, J. D. (2003). *Non-gendered norms for the MMPI-2.* Minneapolis: University of Minnesota Press.

Ben-Porath, Y. S., & Tellegen, A. (2008/2011). *MMPI-2-RF: Manual for administration, scoring and interpretation.* Minneapolis: University of Minnesota Press.

Ben-Porath, Y. S., & Tellegen, A. (2008). *Minnesota Multiphasic Personality Inventory-2-Restructured Form: User's guide for reports.* Minneapolis: University of Minnesota Press.

Ben-Porath, Y. S., & Tellegen, A. (2011). *MMPI-2-RF (Minnesota Multiphasic Personality Inventory-2-Restructured Form): User's guide for reports* (2nd ed.). Minneapolis: University of Minnesota Press.

Beutler, L. E., Storm, A., Kirkish, P., Scogin, F., & Gaines, J. A. (1985). Parameters in the prediction of police officer performance. *Professional Psychology: Research and Practice, 16*(2), 324–335.

Bhar, S. S., Ghahramanlou-Holloway, M., Brown, G. K., & Beck, A. T. (2008). Self-esteem and suicide ideation in psychiatric outpatients. *Suicide and Life Threatening Behavior, 38*(5), 511–516.

Blonigen, D. M., Hicks, B. M., Krueger, R. F., Patrick, C. J., & Iacono, W. G. (2005). Psychopathic personality traits: Heritability and genetic overlap with internalizing and externalizing psychopathology. *Psychological Medicine, 35*(5), 637–648.

Blum, R. H. (1964). *Police selection.* Springfield, Ill.: Charles C. Thomas.

Blumstein, A., & Nakamura, K. (2009). Redemption in the presence of widespread criminal background checks. *Criminology, 47*(2), 327–359.

Boes, J. O., Chandler, C. J., & Timm, H. W. (1997). *Police integrity: Use of personality measures to identify corruption-prone officers.* Monterey, Calif.: Defense Personnel Security Research Center, Publication No. PERSTR-97-003.

Bornstein, R. F. (2005). Context-specific deficits and strengths. *The Dependent Patient,* 57–72.

Briere, J. (2001). *Detailed Assessment of Posttraumatic Stress (DAPS).* Odessa, Fla.: Psychological Assessment Resources.

Brown v. Sandy City Appeal Board, No. 20130433-CA, 2014 UT App 158.

Brownfield v. City of Yakima, 612 F.3d 1140 (9th Cir. 2010).

Bureau of Justice Statistics. (2015). *Local police departments, 2013: Personnel, policies, and practices.* Washington: Author.

Buss, A. H., & Perry, M. (1992). The Aggression Questionnaire. *Journal of Personality and Social Psychology, 63,* 452–459.

Butcher, J. N. (1972). *Objective personality assessment: Changing perspectives.* Oxford: Academic Press.

Butcher, J. N., Dahlstrom, W. G., Graham, J. R., Tellegen, A., & Kaemmer, B. (1989). *Manual for the restandardized Minnesota Multiphasic Personality Inventory: MMPI-2.* Minneapolis: University of Minnesota Press.

Butcher, J. N., Graham, J. R., Ben-Porath, Y. S., Tellegen, A., Dahlstrom, W. G., & Kaemmer, B. (2001). *MMPI-2: Manual for administration and scoring* (revised ed.). Minneapolis: University of Minnesota Press.

Butcher, J. N., Graham, J. R., Williams, C. L., & Ben-Porath, Y. S. (1990). *Development and use of the MMPI-2 Content Scales.* Minneapolis: University of Minnesota Press.

Butcher, J. N., Morfitt, R. C., Rouse, S. V., & Holden, R. R. (1997). Reducing MMPI-2 defensiveness: The effect of specialized instructions on retest validity in a job applicant sample. *Journal of Personality Assessment, 68*(2), 385–401.

Butcher, J. N., Williams, C. L., Graham, J. R., Archer, R., Tellegen, A., Ben-Porath, Y. S., & Kaemmer, B. (1992). *MMPI-A manual for administration, scoring, and interpretation.* Minneapolis: University of Minnesota Press.

Castaneda, L. W., & Ridgeway, G. (2010). *Today's police and sheriff recruits: Insights from the newest members of America's law enforcement community.* Santa Monica, Calif.: RAND.

Chen, Y. W., & Dilsaver, S. C. (1996). Lifetime rates of suicide attempts among subjects with bipolar and unipolar disorders relative to subjects with other Axis I disorders. *Biological Psychiatry, 30,* 896–899.

Civil Rights Act of 1964, Title VII, Pub. L. 88-352 (78 Stat. 241) (1964).

Civil Rights Act of 1991, Pub. L. 102-166 (1991).

Cleckley, H. (1941). *The mask of sanity; An attempt to reinterpret the so-called psychopathic personality.* Oxford: Mosby.

Cody v. CIGNA Healthcare of St. Louis, Inc., 139 F.3d 595 (8th Cir. 1998).

Coffman v. Indianapolis Fire Dept., 2009 U.S. App. Lexis 18717 (7th Cir. 2009).

Colon v. City of Newark, #A-3260-03T23260-03T2, 2006 WL 1194230 (N.J.A.D. 2006).

Conte v. Horcher, 365 N.E.2d 567 (Ill. App. Ct. 1977).

Corey, D. M. (2011). Principles of fitness-for-duty evaluations for police psychologists. In J. Kitaeff (Ed.), *Handbook of police psychology* (pp. 263–293). New York: Routledge Psychology Press.

Corey, D. M. (2016, October). Assessment protocols, procedures and pass rates for psychological evaluations of police candidates: A contemporary national survey. Paper presented at the annual meeting of the International Association of Chiefs of Police, Police Psychological Services Section, San Diego.

Corey, D. M., & Ben-Porath, Y. S. (2014). *User's guide for the MMPI-2-RF Police Candidate Interpretive Report.* Minneapolis: University of Minnesota Press.

Corey, D. M., & Borum, R. (2013). Forensic assessment for high-risk occupations. In R. K. Otto & I. B. Weiner (Eds.), *Forensic psychology* (Vol. 11, 2nd ed., pp. 246–270). Hoboken, N.J.: John Wiley & Sons, Inc.

Corey, D. M., & Stewart, C. O. (2014). Under the color of authority: Police officers as violent offenders. In C. A. Pietz & C. Mattson (Eds.), *Violent offenders: Understanding and assessment* (pp. 249–268). New York: Oxford University Press.

Coryell, W., Endicott, J., Mastger, J. D., Mueller, T., Lavori, P., & Keller, M. (1995). The likelihood of recurrence in bipolar affective disorder. *Journal of Affective Disorders, 33*(3), 201–206.

Cripe v. City of San Jose, 261 F.3d 877 (9th Cir. 2001).

Cuttler, M. J., & Muchinsky, P. M. (2006). Prediction of law enforcement training performance and dysfunctional job performance with general mental ability, personality and life history variables. *Criminal Justice and Behavior, 33*(1), 3–25.

Detrick, P., Ben-Porath, Y. S., & Sellbom, M. (2016). Associations between MMPI-2-RF (Restructured Form) and Inwald Personality Inventory (IPI) scale scores in a law enforcement preemployment screening sample. *Journal of Police and Criminal Psychology, 31*(2), 81–95. doi: 10.1007/s11896-015-9172-7

Detrick, P., & Chibnall, J. T. (2013). Revised NEO Personality Inventory normative data for police officer selection. *Psychological Services, 10*, 372–373.

Detrick, P., & Chibnall, J. T. (2014). Underreporting on the MMPI-2-RF in a high-demand police officer selection context: An illustration. *Psychological Assessment, 26*(3), 1044–1049. doi: 10.1037/pas0000013

Detrick, P., Chibnall, J. T., & Rosso, M. (2001). Minnesota Multiphasic Personality Inventory-2 in police officer selection: Normative data and relation to the Inwald Personality Inventory. *Professional Psychology: Research and Practice, 32*, 484–490.

Dick, D. M. (2007). Identification of genes influencing a spectrum of externalizing psychopathology. *Current Directions in Psychological Science, 16*(6), 331–335.

Dohrenwend, B. P., Shrout, P. E., Egri, G., & Mendelsohn, F. S. (1980). Nonspecific psychological distress and other dimensions of psychopathology. *Archives of General Psychiatry, 37*(11), 1229–1236.

Dunkley, D. M., & Grilo, C. M. (2007). Self-criticism, low self-esteem, depressive symptoms, and over-evaluation of shape and weight in binge eating disorder patients. *Behaviour Research and Therapy, 45,* 139–149.

Duran v. City of Douglas, 904 F.2d 1372 (9th Cir. 1990).

Eckblad, M., & Chapman, L. J. (1986). Development and validation of a scale for hypomanic personality. *Journal of Abnormal Psychology, 95*(3), 214–222.

Eckhardt, C. I., Norlander, B., & Deffenbacher, J. L. (2004). The assessment of anger and hostility: A critical review. *Aggression and Violent Behavior, 9,* 17–43.

EEOC. (1979). Adoption of questions and answers to clarify and provide a common interpretation of the Uniform Guidelines on Employee Selection Procedures. *Federal Register, 44,* 11996–12009.

EEOC. (1995). *ADA enforcement guidance: Preemployment disability-related questions and medical examinations: Compliance manual* (Vol. II, Sect. 902, No. 915.002). Washington: Equal Employment Opportunity Commission. Retrieved on August 16, 2015, from www.eeoc.gov/policy/docs/guidance-inquiries.html

EEOC. (1997/2009). *Enforcement guidance on the Americans with Disabilities Act and Psychiatric Disabilities* (No. 915.002, March 25, 2997; modified March 5, 2009). Washington: Equal Employment Opportunity Commission. Retrieved on January 22, 2016, from www.eeoc.gov/policy/docs/psych.html

EEOC. (2000). *Enforcement guidance on disability-related inquiries and medical examinations of employees under the Americans with Disabilities Act: Compliance manual* (Vol. II, Sect. 902, No. 915.002). Washington: Author.

EEOC. (2008). *Questions and answers for small businesses: EEOC final rule on Title II of the Genetic Information Nondiscrimination Act of 2008.* Washington: Equal Employment Opportunity Commission.

EEOC v. Amego, Inc. (1997). No. 96-1837, U.S. Court of Appeals, First Circuit.

Elliot, T. R., & Gramling, S. E. (1990). Personal assertiveness and the effects of social support among college students. *Journal of Counseling Psychology, 37,* 427–436.

Fernández-Ballesteros, R., Godoy, A., Hornke, L. F., Ter Laak, J., Vizcarro, C., Westhoff, K., Westmeyer, H., & Zaccagnini, J. L. (2001). Guidelines for the Assessment Process (GAP): A proposal for discussion. *European Journal of Psychological Assessment, 17*(3), 187–200.

Flora v. Hamilton, 81 F.R.D. 576 (M.D.N.C. 1978).

Flynn v. Sandahl, 58 F.3d 383 (7th Cir. 1995).

Forbey, J. D., Lee, T. C., Ben-Porath, Y. S., Arbisi, P. A., & Gartland, D. M. (2013). Associations between MMPI-2-RF validity scale scores and extra-test measures of personality and psychopathology. *Assessment, 20*(4), 448–461.

Frances, A. J., Widiger, T. A., & Sabshin, M. (1991). Psychiatric diagnosis and normality. In D. Offer & M. Sabshin (Eds.), *The diversity of normal behavior: Further contributions to normatology* (pp. 3–38). New York: Basic Books.

Frank, J. D. (1974). Psychotherapy: The restoration of morale. *American Journal of Psychiatry, 131,* 271–274.

Frank, J. D. (1985). Further thoughts on the anti-demoralization hypothesis of psychotherapeutic effectiveness. *Integrative Psychiatry, 3,* 17–20.

Gallo, F. J., & Halgin, R. P. (2011). A guide for establishing a practice in police pre-employment postoffer psychological evaluations. *Professional Psychology: Research and Practice, 42*(3), 269–275.

Gaspar, J. P., Seabright, M. A., Reynolds, S. J., & Yam, K. C. (2015). Counterfactual and factual reflection: The influence of past misdeeds on future immoral behavior. *Journal of Social Psychology, 155*(4), 370–380. doi: http://dx.doi.org/10.1080/00224545.2015.1015477

Genetic Information Nondiscrimination Act of 2008 (GINA). Pub. L. 110-233, 122 Stat. 881, 42 U.S.C. 2000 (2008).

Gilberstadt, H., & Duker, J. (1965). *A handbook for clinical and actuarial MMPI interpretation.* Philadelphia: Saunders.

Glassmire, D. M., Stolberg, R. A., Greene, R. L., & Bongar, B. (2001). The utility of MMPI-2 suicide items for assessing suicidal potential: Development of a suicidal potential scale. *Assessment, 8*(3), 281–290.

Gold, L. H., & Shuman, D. W. (2009). *Evaluating mental health disability in the workplace.* New York: Springer Science.

Golder, S., Hall, M. T., Engstrom, M., Higgins, G. E., & Logan, T. K. (2014). Correlates of recent drug use among victimized women on probation and parole. *Psychology of Addictive Behaviors, 28*(4), 1105–1116. doi: http://dx.doi.org/10.1037/a0038351

Goodwin, G. M. (2009). Evidence-based guidelines for treating bipolar disorder: Revised second edition—Recommendations from the British Association for Psychopharmacology. *Journal of Psychopharmacology, 23*(4), 346–388.

Gough, H. G. (1946). Diagnostic patterns on the MMPI. *Journal of Clinical Psychology, 2,* 23–37.

Gough, H. G. (1956). *California Psychological Inventory.* Palo Alto, Calif.: Consulting Psychologists Press.

Gough, H. G., & Bradley, P. (1996). *California Psychological Inventory manual* (3rd ed.). Palo Alto, Calif.: CPP, Inc.

Graham, J. R. (2012). *MMPI-2: Assessing personality and psychopathology.* New York: Oxford University Press.

Gray, J. A. (1970). The psychophysiological basis of introversion-extraversion. *Behaviour Research and Therapy, 8*(3), 249–266.

Green, P., Lees-Haley, P. R., & Allen, L. M. (2002). The Word Memory Test and the validity of neuropsychological test scores. *Journal of Forensic Neuropsychology, 2,* 97–124.

Greene, R. L. (2011). *The MMPI-2/MMPI-2-RF: An interpretive manual* (3rd ed.). New York: Pearson.

Grisso, T. (2003). *Evaluating competencies: Forensic assessments and instruments.* New York: Kluwer Academic/Plenum.

Grisso, T. (2008, May 17). *Writing forensic reports.* Workshop for the American Academy of Forensic Psychology, San Francisco, Calif.

Grossman, L. S., Haywood, T. W., Ostrov, E., Wasyliw, O., & Cavanaugh, J. (1990). Sensitivity of MMPI validity scales to motivational factors in psychological evaluations of police officers. *Journal of Personality Assessment, 55*(3–4), 549–561. doi: 10.1080/00223891.1990.9674090

Hargrave, G. E., Hiatt, D., Ogard, E. M., & Carr, C. (1994). Comparison of the MMPI and the MMPI-2 for a sample of peace officers. *Psychological Assessment, 6*(1), 27–32.

Harkness, A. R. (1992). Fundamental topics in the personality disorders: Candidate trait dimensions from lower regions of the hierarchy. *Psychological Assessment, 4,* 251–259.

Harkness, A. R., Finn, J. A., McNulty, J. L., & Shields, S. M. (2012). The Personality Psychopathology Five (PSY–5): Recent constructive replication and assessment literature review. *Psychological Assessment, 24,* 432–443.

Harkness, A. R., & McNulty, J. L. (1994). The Personality Psychopathology Five (PSY-5): Issues from the pages of a diagnostic manual instead of a dictionary. In S. Strack & M. Lorr (Eds.), *Differentiating normal and abnormal personality* (pp. 291–315). New York: Springer.

Harkness, A. R., McNulty, J. L., & Ben-Porath, Y. S. (1995). The Personality Psychopathology Five (PSY-5): Constructs and MMPI-2 scales. *Psychological Assessment, 7,* 104–114.

Harris, R., & Lingoes, J. (1955). *Subscales for the Minnesota Multiphasic Personality Inventory.* Mimeographed materials. Langley Porter Clinic, San Francisco.

Hathaway, S. R. (1960). Forward. In W. G. Dahlstrom & G. S. Welsh (Eds.), *An MMPI handbook: A guide to use in clinical practice and research* (vii–xi). Minneapolis: University of Minnesota Press.

Hathaway, S. R. (1972). Forward. In W. G. Dahlstrom, G. S. Welsh, and L. E. Dahlstrom (Eds.), *An MMPI handbook: Vol. 1. Clinical interpretation* (pp. xiii–xiv). Minneapolis: University of Minnesota Press.

Hathaway, S. R., & McKinley, J. C. (1940). A multiphasic personality schedule (Minnesota): I. Construction of the schedule. *Journal of Psychology, 10,* 249–254.

Hathaway, S. R., & McKinley, J. C. (1943). *The Minnesota Multiphasic Personality Inventory.* Minneapolis: University of Minnesota Press.

Heilbrun, K., DeMatteo, D., Marczyk, G., & Goldstein, A. M. (2008). Standards of practice and care in forensic mental health assessment: Legal, professional, and principles-based consideration. *Psychology, Public Policy, and Law, 14*(1), 1.

Heilbrun, K., Grisso, T., & Goldstein, A. M. (2009). *Foundations of forensic mental health assessment.* New York: Oxford University Press.

Herbig, K. L. (2011). *The evolution of adjudicative guidelines in the Department of Defense.* Technical Report 11-04, September. Monterey, Calif.: PERSEREC.

Hicks, B. M., DiRago, A. C., Iacono, W. G., & McGue, M. (2009). Gene-environment interplay in internalizing disorders: Consistent findings across six environmental risk factors. *Journal of Child Psychology and Psychiatry, 50*(10), 1309–1317.

Hoelzle, J. B., & Meyer, G. J. (2009). The invariant component structure of the Personality Assessment Inventory (PAI) full scales. *Journal of Personality Assessment, 91*(2), 175–186.

Hough, L. M. (2016). Community-oriented policing: Hiring in the spirit of service. *Industrial and Organizational Psychology, 9*(3), 573–582.

Hunter, J. E., & Schmidt, F. L. (1990). *Methods of meta-analysis: Correcting error and bias in research findings.* Newbury, Calif.: Sage Publications.

IACP-PPSS. (2014). *Psychological fitness-for-duty evaluation guidelines.* Retrieved August 29, 2017, from www.theiacp.org/portals/0/documents/pdfs/Psych-FitnessforDutyEvaluation.pdf

IACP-PPSS. (2015). *Preemployment psychological evaluation guidelines.* Retrieved August 29, 2017, from www.theiacp.org/portals/0/documents/pdfs/Psych-PreemploymentPsychEval.pdf

Inwald, R. (1992). *Inwald Personality Inventory technical manual (revised).* New York: Hilson Research.

Inwald, R., Knatz, H., & Shusman, E. (1982). *Inwald Personality Inventory manual.* Kew Gardens, N.Y.: Hilson Research.

Jager, J., Keyes, K. M., & Schulenberg, J. E. (2015). Historical variation in young adult binge drinking trajectories and its link to historical variation in social roles and minimum legal drinking age. *Developmental Psychology, 51*(7), 962–974. doi: http://dx.doi.org/10.1037/dev0000022

James, L., & Taylor, J. (2008). Revisiting the structure of mental disorder: Borderline personality disorder and the internalizing/externalizing spectra. *British Journal of Clinical Psychology, 47,* 361–380.

Jamison, K. R. (2000). Suicide and bipolar disorder. *Journal of Clinical Psychiatry, 61*(Suppl. 9), 47–51.

Jenkins v. City of Sandusky, #E-07-067, 2008 Ohio App. Lexis 3966 (6th App. Dist.).

Jennings v. Dow Corning Corp., No. 12-12227, 2013 WL 1962333, 10 (E.D. Mich. 2013).

Judd, L. L., Schettler, P. J., Solomon, D. A., Maser, J. D., Coryell, W., Endicott, J., & Akiskal, H.S. (2008). Psychosocial disability and work role function compared across the long-term course of bipolar I, bipolar II and unipolar major depressive disorders. *Journal of Affective Disorders, 73,* 123–131.

Karraker v. Rent-A-Center, Inc., 411 F.3d 831 (7th Cir. 2005).

Kashdan, T. B., Uswatte, G., Steger, M. F., & Julian, T. (2006). Fragile self-esteem and affective instability in posttraumatic stress disorder. *Behaviour Research and Therapy, 44,* 1609–1619.

Klein, D. F. (1974). Endogenomorphic depression: A conceptual and terminological revision. *Archives of General Psychiatry, 31,* 447–454.

Kraemer, H. C., Kazdin, A. E., Offord, D. R., Kessler, R. C., Jensen, P. S., & Kupfer, D. J. (1997). Coming to terms with the terms of risk. *Archives of General Psychiatry, 54*(4), 337–343. doi:10.1001/archpsyc.1997.01830160065009

Kraepelin, E. (1921). Ueber Entwurtzelung. *Zeitschrift fur die Gesamte Neurologie und Psychiatrie, 63,* 1–8.

Kramer, M. D., Krueger, R. F., & Hicks, B. M. (2008). The role of internalizing and externalizing liability factors in accounting for gender differences in the prevalence of common psychopathological syndromes. *Psychological Medicine, 38*(1), 51–61.

Kring, A. M., & Germans, M. K. (2000). Anhedonia. In A. E. Kazdin (Ed.), *Encyclopedia of psychology* (Vol. 1, pp. 174–175). Washington: American Psychological Association.

Krocka v. City of Chicago, 203 F.3d 507 (7th Cir. 2000).

Kropp, P. R., Hart, S. D., Webster, C. D., & Eaves, D. (1995). *Manual for the Spousal Assault Risk Assessment Guide* (2nd ed.). Vancouver, BC: British Columbia Institute Against Family Violence.

Krueger, R. F., Chentsova-Dutton, Y. E., Markon, K. E., Goldberg, D., & Ormel, J. (2003). A cross-cultural study of the structure of comorbidity among common psychopathological syndromes in the general health care setting. *Journal of Abnormal Psychology, 112*, 437–447.

Krueger, R. F., Hicks, B. M., Patrick, C. J., Carlson, S. R., Iacono, W. G., & McGue, M. (2002). Etiologic connections among substance dependence, antisocial behavior and personality: Modeling the externalizing spectrum. *Journal of Abnormal Psychology, 111*(3), 411–424.

Krueger, R. F., & Markon, K. E. (2006). Reinterpreting comorbidity: A model-based approach to understanding and classifying psychopathology. *Annual Review of Clinical Psychology, 2*, 111–133.

Krueger, R. F., Markon, K. E., Patrick, C. J., & Iacono, W. G. (2005). Externalizing psychopathology in adulthood: A dimensional-spectrum conceptualization and its implications for DSM-V. *Journal of Abnormal Psychology, 114*, 537–550.

Kwapil, T. R., Miller, M. B., Zinser, M. C., Chapman, L. J., Chapman, J., & Eckblad, M. (2000). A longitudinal study of high scorers on the Hypomanic Personality Scale. *Journal of Abnormal Psychology, 109*, 222–226.

Lamberty, G. (2008). *Understanding somatization in the practice of clinical neuropsychology*. New York: Oxford University Press.

Lassiter v. Department of Justice, 60 M.S.P.R. 138 (December 21, 1993).

Lee, S., & Swanson-Crockett, M. (1994). Effect of assertiveness training on levels of stress and assertiveness experienced by nurses in Taiwan, Republic of China. *Issues in Mental Health Nursing, 15*, 419–432.

Leonel v. American Airlines, Inc., 400 F.3d 702 (9th Cir. 2005).

Lowmaster, S. E., & Morey, L. C. (2012). Predicting law enforcement officer job performance with the Personality Assessment Inventory. *Journal of Police Science and Administration, 94*(3), 254–261.

Lynum, L. I., Wilberg, T., & Karterud, S. (2008). Self-esteem in patients with borderline and avoidant personality disorders. *Scandinavian Journal of Psychology, 49*(5), 469–477.

MacAndrew, C. (1965). The differentiation of male alcoholic out-patients from nonalcoholic psychiatric patients by means of the MMPI. *Quarterly Journal of the Studies on Alcohol, 26*, 238–246.

Marek, R. J., Ben-Porath, Y. S., Sellbom, M., McNulty, J. L., & Heinberg, L. J. (2015). Validity of Minnesota Multiphasic Personality Inventory-2-Restructured Form (MMPI-2-RF) scores as a function of gender, ethnicity, and age of bariatric surgery candidates. *Surgery for Obesity and Related Diseases, 11*, 627–636.

Marks, P. A., & Seeman, W. (1963). *The actuarial description of abnormal personality: An atlas for use with the MMPI*. Baltimore: Williams & Wilkins.

Marsh, S. H. (1962). Validating the selection of deputy sheriffs. *Public Personnel Review, 23,* 41–44.

Marshall, G. N., Miles, J. N. V., & Stewart, S. H. (2010). Anxiety sensitivity and PTSD symptom severity are reciprocally related: Evidence from a longitudinal study of physical trauma survivors. *Journal of Abnormal Psychology 119,* 143–150.

Mayer, M. J., & Corey, D. M. (2017). Current issues in psychological fitness-for-duty evaluations for law enforcement officers: Legal and practice implications. In C. L. Mitchell & E. H. Dorian (Eds.), *Police psychology and its growing impact on modern law enforcement* (pp. 93–117). Hershey, Pa.: IGI Global.

McGreal v. Ostrov, #98-CV-3958, Docket entry No. 177 (N.D. Ill. Oct. 1, 2004); interim ruling on a motion at 2004 U.S. Dist. Lexis 18420, on remand from 368 F.3d 657, #02-3405, 2004 U.S. App. Lexis 9059 (7th Cir. 2004).

McLellan, A. T., Luborsky, L., O'Brien, C. P., & Woody, G. E. (1980). An improved diagnostic instrument for substance abuse patients: The Addiction Severity Index. *Journal of Nervous and Mental Diseases, 168,* 26–33.

Meehl, P. E. (1946). Profile analysis of the MMPI in differential diagnosis. *Journal of Applied Psychology, 30,* 517–524.

Meehl, P. E. (1954). *Clinical versus statistical prediction: A theoretical analysis and a review of the evidence.* Minneapolis: University of Minnesota Press.

Meehl, P. E. (1956). Wanted—A good cookbook. *American Psychologist, 11,* 263–272.

Meehl, P. E. (1962). Schizotaxia, schizotypy, schizophrenia. *American Psychologist, 17*(12), 827–838.

Melton, G. B., Petrila, J., Poythress, N. G., & Slobogin, C. (2007). *Psychological evaluations for the courts: A handbook for mental health professionals and lawyers* (3rd ed.). New York: Guilford.

Meyer, G. J., Finn, S. E., Eyde, L. D., Kay, G. G., Moreland, K. L., Dies, R. R., . . . Reed, G. M. (2001). Psychological testing and psychological assessment. *American Psychologist, 56*(2), 128–165.

Michael v. City of Troy Police Department, 2014 U.S. District Lexis 149367 (E.D. Mich. 2014).

Miller, M. W., Fogler, J. M., Wolf, E. J., Kaloupek, D. G., & Keane, T. M. (2008). The internalizing and externalizing structure of psychiatric comorbidity in combat veterans. *Journal of Traumatic Stress, 21*(1), 58–65.

Miranda, R., Fontes, M., & Marroquin, B. (2008). Cognitive content-specificity in future expectancies: Role of hopelessness and intolerance of uncertainty in depression and GAD symptoms. *Behaviour Research and Therapy, 46,* 1151–1159.

Mitchell, C. L. (2017). Preemployment psychological screening of police officer applicants: Basic considerations and recent advances. In C. L. Mitchell & E. H. Dorian (Eds.), *Police psychology and its growing impact on modern law enforcement* (pp. 28–50). Hershey, Pa.: IGI Global.

Novaco, R. W. (1994). *Novaco Anger Scale and Provocation Inventory (NAS-PI).* Los Angeles: Western Psychological Services.

O'Donnell, M. L., Creamer, M., & Pattison, P. (2004). Posttraumatic stress disorder and depression following trauma: Understanding comorbidity. *American Journal of Psychiatry, 161*(8), 1390–1396.

Orth, U., Robins, R. W., Trzesniewski, K. H., Maes, J., & Schmitt, M. (2009). Low self-esteem is a risk factor for depressive symptoms from young adulthood to old age. *Journal of Abnormal Psychology, 118,* 472–478.

Otto, R. K., DeMier, R., & Boccaccini, M. (2014). *Forensic reports and testimony: A guide to effective communication for psychologists and psychiatrists.* Hoboken, N.J.: John Wiley & Sons.

Otto, R. K., Edens, J. F., & Barcus, E. H. (2000). The use of psychological testing in child custody evaluations. *Family & Conciliation Courts Review, 38*(3), 312–340.

Peck, J. A., & Levashina, J. (2017). Impression management and interview and job performance ratings: A meta-analysis of research design with tactics in mind. *Frontiers in Psychology, 8,* 201.

Pedersen, S. S., Denollet, J., Erdman, R. A. M., Serruys, P. W., & van Domburg, R. T. (2009). Co-occurrence of diabetes and hopelessness predicts adverse prognosis following percutaneous coronary intervention. *Journal of Behavioral Medicine, 32*(3), 294–301.

Pettus v. Cole, 57 Cal.Rptr. 2d 46, 49 Cal.App. 4th 402 (Cal.App. 1st Dist. 1996).

President's Commission on Law Enforcement and Administration of Justice. (1967). *Task force report: The police.* Washington: U.S. Government Printing Office.

President's Task Force on 21st Century Policing. (2015). *Final report of the President's Task Force on 21st Century Policing.* Washington: Office of Community Oriented Policing Services.

Rado, S. (1956). *Psychoanalysis of behavior; collected papers.* Oxford: Grune & Stratton.

Reiss, S., & McNally, R. (1985). Expectancy model of fear. In S. Reiss & R. R. Bootzin (Eds.), *Theoretical issues in behavior therapy* (pp. 107–121). New York: Academic Press.

Rice v. City of Oakland, No. 97-1897, 1999 U.S. Dist. LEXIS 8330 (N.D. Cal. May 24, 1999).

Roberts, M. D., & Johnson, M. (2001). *CPI police and public safety selection report: Technical manual.* Los Gatos, Calif.: Law Enforcement Psychological Services, Inc.

Rosen, G. M., Baldwin, S. A., & Smith, R. E. (2016). Reassessing the "traditional background hypothesis" for elevated MMPI and MMPI-2 Lie-scale scores. *Psychological Assessment, 28,* 1136–1343.

Rostow, C. D., & Davis, R. D. (2004). *A handbook for psychological fitness-for-duty evaluations in law enforcement.* Binghamton, N.Y.: Haworth Press.

Sager v. Yuba County, 68 Cal.Rptr.3d 1, 156 Cal.App.4th 1049 (Cal.App. 2007).

Salley v. Circuit City Stores, Inc., 160 F.3d 977 (3d Cir. 1998).

Sangirardi v. Village of Stickney, 342 Ill.App.3d 1, 276 Ill.Dec. 28, 793 N.E.2d 787 (2003).

Saxe, S. J., & Reiser, M. (1976). A comparison of three police applicant groups using the MMPI. *Journal of Police Science & Administration, 4*(4), 419–425.

Scarpa, A., & Raine, A. (1997). Psychophysiology of anger and violent behavior. *Psychiatric Clinics of North America, 20,* 375–394.

Schinka, J. A., & LaLone, L. (1997). MMPI-2 norms: Comparisons with a census-matched subsample. *Psychological Assessment, 9,* 307–311.

Schmidt, H. O. (1945). Test profiles as a diagnostic aid: the Minnesota Multiphasic Inventory. *Journal of Applied Psychology, 29,* 115–131.

Security Executive Agent Directive (SEAD) 4. (2017, June). *National security adjudicative guidelines.* Washington: Office of the Director of National Intelligence.

Sellbom, M., Ben-Porath, Y. S., & Bagby, R. M. (2008). On the hierarchical structure of mood and anxiety disorders: Confirmatory evidence and elaboration of a model of temperament markers. *Journal of Abnormal Psychology, 117,* 576–590.

Sellbom, M., Fischler, G. L., & Ben-Porath, Y. S. (2007). Identifying MMPI-2 predictors of police officer integrity and misconduct. *Criminal Justice and Behavior, 34*(8), 985–1004. doi: 10.1177/0093854807301224

Selzer, M. L. (1971). The Michigan Alcoholism Screening Test: The quest for a new diagnostic instrument. *American Journal of Psychiatry, 127,* 1653–1658.

Serafino, G. F. (2010). Fundamental issues in police psychological assessment. In P. A. Weiss (Ed.), *Personality assessment in police psychology: A 21st century perspective* (pp. 29–55). Springfield, Ill.: Charles C. Thomas.

Shafer v. Preston Memorial Hospital Corp., 107 F.3d 274 (4th Cir. 1997).

Simons, R., Goddard, R., & Patton, W. (2002). Hand-scoring error rates in psychological testing. *Assessment, 9,* 292–300.

Skinner, B. F. (1983). *A matter of consequences.* New York: Knopf.

Skinner, H. A., & Jackson, D. N. (1978). A model of psychopathology based on an integration of MMPI actuarial systems. *Journal of Consulting and Clinical Psychology, 46,* 231–238.

Slater v. Department of Homeland Security, 2008 MSPB 73, Docket No. SF-0752-06-0805-I-2.

Spielberger, C. D., Jacobs, G., Russell, S., & Crane, R. S. (1983). Assessment of anger: The state-trait anger scale. *Advances in Personality Assessment, 2,* 161–189.

Spilberg, S. W., & Corey, D. M. (2017). *Peace officer psychological screening manual* (revised edition). Sacramento: California Commission on Peace Officer Standards and Training.

Stein, L. A. R., Graham, J. R., Ben-Porath, Y. S., & McNulty, J. L. (1999). Using the MMPI-2 to detect substance abuse in an outpatient mental health setting. *Psychological Assessment, 11,* 94–100.

Stern, S. L., Dhanda, R., & Hazuda, H. P. (2009). Helplessness predicts the development of hypertension in older Mexican and European Americans. *Journal of Psychosomatic Research, 67,* 333–337.

Stone, A. V. (2000). *Fitness for duty: Principles, methods and legal issues.* New York: CRC Press.

Sundberg, N. D. (1961). The practice of psychological testing in clinical services in the United States. *American Psychologist, 16*(2), 79–83.

Swanson, S. C., Templer, D. I., Thomas-Dobson, S., Cannon, W. G., Streiner, D. L., Reynolds, R. M., & Miller, H. R. (1995). Development of a three-scale MMPI: The MMPI-TRI. *Journal of Clinical Psychology, 51*(3), 361–374.

Tackett, J. L., Herzhoff, K., Kushner, S. C., & Rule, N. (2015). Thin slices of child personality: Perceptual, situational, and behavioral contributions. *Journal of Personality and Social Psychology.* Advance online publication. http://dx.doi.org/10.1037/pspp0000044

Tarescavage, A. M., Alosco, M. L., Ben-Porath, Y. S., Wood, A., & Luna-Jones, L. (2015). MMPI-2-RF scores generated from the MMPI-2 and MMPI-2-RF test booklets: Comparability in a sample of criminal defendants. *Assessment, 22*(2), 188–197.

Tarescavage, A. M., Brewster, J. A., Corey, D. M., & Ben-Porath, Y. S. (2015). Use of prehire MMPI-2-RF police candidate scores to predict supervisor ratings of post-hire performance. *Assessment, 22*(4), 411–428. doi: 10.1177/1073191114548445

Tarescavage, A. M., Corey, D. M., & Ben-Porath, Y. S. (2015). Minnesota Multiphasic Personality Inventory-2-Restructured Form (MMPI-2-RF) predictors of police officer problem behavior. *Assessment, 22*(1), 116–132. doi: 10.1177/1073191114534885

Tarescavage, A. M., Corey, D. M., & Ben-Porath, Y. S. (2016). A prorating method for estimating MMPI-2-RF scores from MMPI responses: Examination of score fidelity and illustration of empirical utility in the PERSEREC Police Integrity Study sample. *Assessment, 23,* 173–190.

Tarescavage, A. M., Corey, D. M., Gupton, H. M., & Ben-Porath, Y. S. (2015). Criterion validity and practical utility of the Minnesota Multiphasic Personality Inventory-2-Restructured Form (MMPI-2-RF) in assessments of police officer candidates. *Journal of Personality Assessment, 97*(4), 382–394. doi: 10.1080/00223891.2014.995800

Tarescavage, A. M., Fischler, G., Cappo, B., Hill, D., Corey, D. M., & Ben-Porath, Y. S. (2015). Minnesota Multiphasic Personality Inventory-2-Restructured Form (MMPI-2-RF) predictors of police officer problem behavior and collateral self-report test scores. *Psychological Assessment, 27*(1), 125–137. doi: 10.1037/pas0000041

Tellegen, A. (1985). Structures of mood and personality and their relevance to assessing anxiety, with an emphasis on self-report. In A. H. Tuma & J. D. Master (Eds.), *Anxiety and the anxiety disorders* (pp. 681–706). Hillsdale, N.J.: Erlbaum.

Tellegen, A. (1995/2003). *Multidimensional Personality Questionnaire-276 (MPQ-276) test booklet.* Minneapolis: University of Minnesota Press.

Tellegen, A., & Ben-Porath, Y. S. (1992). The new uniform T-scores for the MMPI-2: Rationale, derivation, and appraisal. *Psychological Assessment, 4,* 145–155.

Tellegen, A., & Ben-Porath, Y. S. (2008/2011). *The Minnesota Multiphasic Personality Inventory-2 Restructured Form: Technical manual.* Minneapolis: University of Minnesota Press.

Tellegen, A., Ben-Porath, Y. S., McNulty, J. L., Arbisi, P. A., Graham, J. R., & Kaemmer, B. (2003). *The MMPI-2 Restructured Clinical Scales: Development, validation, and interpretation.* Minneapolis: University of Minnesota Press.

Tellegen, A., & Waller, N. G. (2008). Exploring personality through test construction: Development of the Multidimensional Personality Questionnaire. In

S. R. Briggs & J. M. Cheek (Eds.), *Personality measures: Development and evaluation* (pp. 261–292). Greenwich, Conn.: JAI Press.

Thomas v. Corwin, 483 F.3d 516 (8th Cir. 2007), U.S. App. Lexis 7601, 100 FEP Cases (BNA) 297.

Thompson v. City of Arlington, 838 F.Supp. 1137; 1993 U.S. Dist. LEXIS 17093; 2 Am.Disabilities Cas. (BNA) 1756.

Trimble, M. (2004). *Somatoform disorders: A medicolegal guide.* New York: Cambridge University Press.

Trompetter, P. S. (2017). A history of police psychology. In C. Mitchell & E. Dorian (Eds.), *Police psychology and its growing impact on modern law enforcement* (pp. 1–26). Hershey, Pa.: IGI Global.

Vaidyanathan, U., Patrick, C., & Cuthbert, B. (2009). Linking dimensional models of internalizing psychopathology to neurobiological systems: Affect-modulated startle as an indicator of fear and distress disorders and affiliated traits. *Psychological Bulletin, 135,* 909–942.

Valtonen, H. M., Suominen, K., Haukka, J., Mantere, O., Arvilommi, P., Leppämäki, S., & Isometsä, E. (2009). Hopelessness across phases of bipolar I or II disorder: A prospective study. *Journal of Affective Disorders, 115* (1–2), 11–17.

Valtonen, H. M., Suominen, K., Haukka, J., Mantere, O., Leppämäki, S., Arvilommi, P., & Isometsä, E. (2008). Differences in incidence of suicide attempts during phases of bipolar I and II disorders. *Bipolar Disorders, 10,* 588–596.

van der Heijden, P. T., Egger, J. I. M., & Derksen, J. J. L (2010). Comparability of scores on the MMPI-2-RF scales generated with the MMPI-2 and MMPI-2-RF booklets. *Journal of Personality Assessment, 92,* 254–259.

Walfish, S. (2010). Reducing MMPI-defensiveness in professionals presenting for evaluation. *Journal of Addictive Diseases, 30*(1), 75–80.

Washington Administrative Code, § 139-07-030 (2013).

Watson, D., & Clark, L. A. (1984). Negative affectivity: The disposition to experience aversive emotional states. *Psychological Bulletin, 96,* 465–490.

Watson, L. C., Quilty, L. C., & Bagby, R. M. (2010). Differentiating bipolar disorder from major depressive disorder using the MMPI-2-RF: A receiver operating characteristics (roc) analysis. *Journal of Psychopathology and Behavioral Assessment, 33*(3), 368–374.

Watson v. City of Miami Beach, 177 F.3d 932 (11th Cir. 1999).

Weathers, F. W., Blake, D. D., Schnurr, P. P., Kaloupek, D. G., Marx, B. P., & Keane, T. M. (2013). *The Clinician-Administered PTSD Scale for DSM-5 (CAPS-5).* Charlottesville, Va.: National Center for PTSD.

Webb, J. T., Levitt, E. E., & Rojdev, R. (1993). After three years: A comparison of the clinical use of the MMPI and MMPI-2. Paper presented at the 53rd Annual Meeting of the Society for Personality Assessment, San Francisco.

Weed, N. C., Butcher, J. N., McKenna, T., & Ben-Porath, Y. S. (1992). New measures for assessing alcohol and drug abuse with the MMPI-2: The APS and AAS. *Journal of Personality Assessment, 58,* 389–404.

Weiss, P. A., & Weiss, W. U. (2010). Using the MMPI-2 in police psychological assessment. In P. A. Weiss (Ed.), *Personality assessment in police psychology* (pp. 59–61). Springfield, Ill.: Charles C. Thomas.

Welsh, G. S., & Dahlstrom, W. G. (Eds.). (1956). *Basic readings on the MMPI in psychology and medicine.* Minneapolis: University of Minnesota Press.

Widiger, T. A., & Costa, P. T. (2002). Five factor model personality disorder research. In P. T. Costa & T. A. Widiger (Eds.), *Personality disorders and the five factor model of personality* (2nd ed., pp. 59–87). Washington: American Psychological Association.

Wiener, D. N., & Harmon, L. R. (1946). *Subtle and obvious keys for the MMPI: Their development.* Minneapolis VA, Advisement Bulletin, No. 16.

Wiggins, J. S. (1966). Substantive dimensions of self-report in the MMPI item pool. *Psychological Monographs, 80* (22, Whole No. 630).

Williams, C. B., Galanter, M., Dermatis, H., & Schwartz, V. (2008). The importance of hopelessness among university students seeking psychiatric counseling. *Psychiatric Quarterly, 79*(4), 311–319.

Wilson, C. M., Desmarais, S. L., Nicholls, T. L., Hart, S. D., & Brink, J. (2013). Predictive validity of dynamic factors: Assessing violence risk in forensic psychiatric inpatients. *Law and Human Behavior, 37*(6), 377–388. doi: http://dx.doi.org/10.1037/lhb0000025

Wingate, L., Joiner, T., Walker, R., Rudd, M. D., & Jobes, D. (2004). Empirically informed approaches to topics in suicide risk assessment. *Behavioral Sciences & the Law, 22,* 1–15.

Wisbey v. City of Lincoln, #4:08-CV-3093, 2009 U.S. Dist. Lexis 30819, 21 AD Cases (BNA) 1377 (D. Neb.).

Woodhams, J., & Toye, K. (2007). An empirical test of the assumptions of case linkage and offender profiling with serial commercial robberies. *Psychology, Public Policy, and Law, 13*(1), 59–85. doi: http://dx.doi.org/10.1037/1076-8971.13.1.59

Wu, C. (2009). Factor analysis of the general self-efficacy scale and its relationship with individualism/collectivism among twenty-five countries: Application of multilevel confirmatory factor analysis. *Personality and Individual Differences, 46,* 699–703.

Wurzel v. Whirlpool Corp., 482 F. App'x 1 (6th Cir. 2012).

Zenor v. El Paso Healthcare Systems, Ltd., 76 F.3d 847 (5th Cir. 1999).

INDEX

David M. Corey, PhD

David M. Corey is in private practice in Portland, Oregon, and is board certified in forensic psychology and police and public safety psychology. Dr. Corey is the founding president of the American Board of Police & Public Safety Psychology. He is coauthor of the MMPI-2-RF *Police Candidate Interpretive Report* (Corey & Ben-Porath, 2014), the *California POST Peace Officer Psychological Screening Manual* (Spilberg & Corey, 2017), and *Evaluations of Police Suitability and Fitness for Duty* (Corey & Zelig, in preparation). He is the author or coauthor of more than 20 peer-reviewed research manuscripts and book chapters pertaining to pre-employment and fitness-for-duty evaluations of police and public safety personnel.

Yossef S. Ben-Porath, PhD

Yossef S. Ben-Porath is professor of psychological sciences at Kent State University. He received his doctoral training at the University of Minnesota and has been involved extensively in MMPI research for more than 30 years. He is a codeveloper of the MMPI-2-RF and coauthor of test manuals, books, book chapters, and articles on the MMPI instruments. He is editor-in-chief of the journal *Psychological Assessment.* His clinical practice involves supervision of assessments at Kent State's Psychological Clinic, consultation to agencies that screen candidates for public safety positions, and provision of consultation and expert witness services in forensic cases.

Drs. Corey and Ben-Porath are both paid consultants for the University of Minnesota Press, publisher of the MMPI-2-RF. They receive royalties on sales of the *MMPI-2-RF Police Candidate Interpretive Report.* Dr. Ben-Porath receives royalties on MMPI-2-RF sales.